AF321561

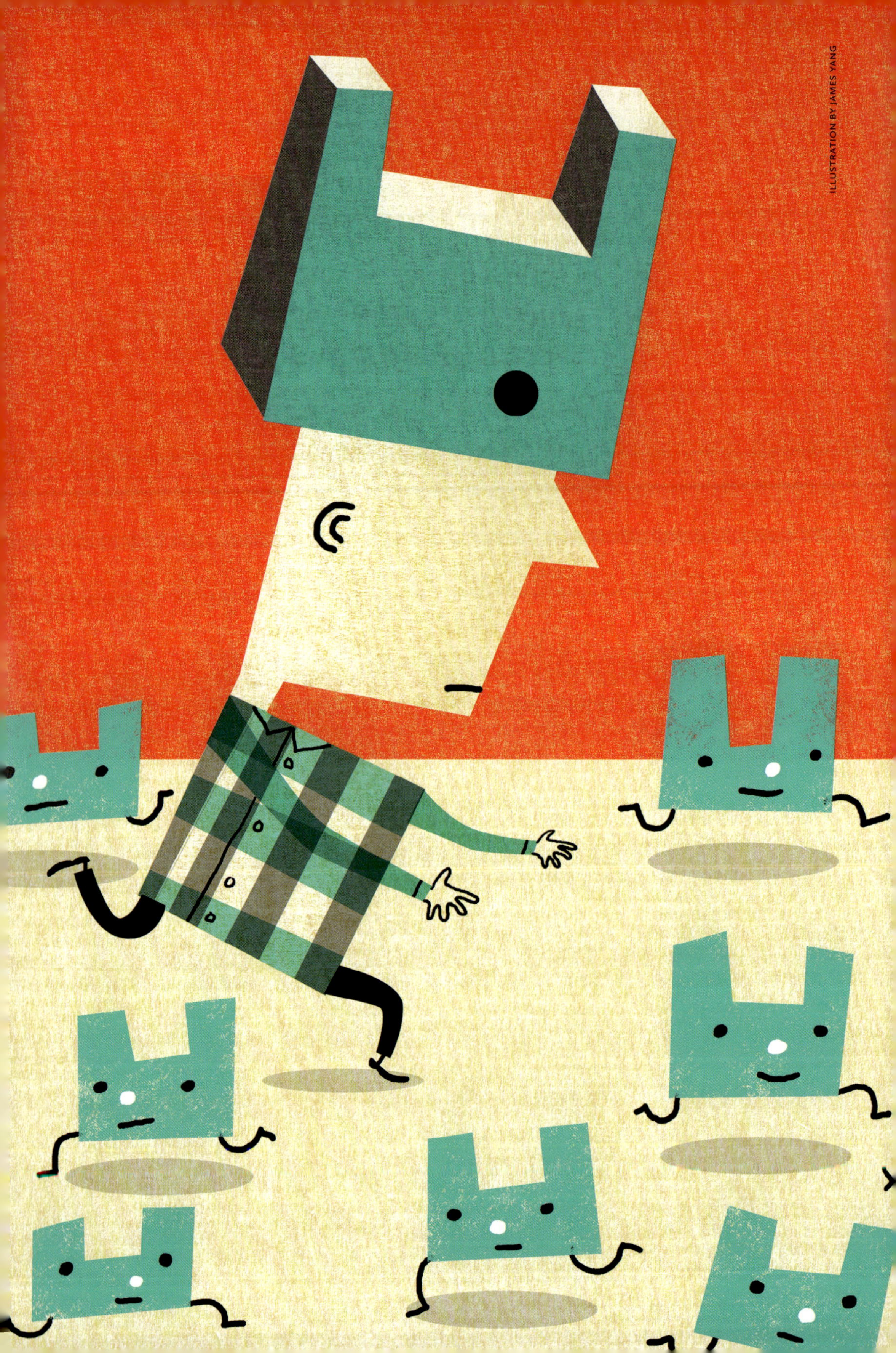
ILLUSTRATION BY JAMES YANG

# 3x3 Annual 12

THREE BY THREE ILLUSTRATION ANNUAL
SPONSORED BY 3X3 THE MAGAZINE OF CONTEMPORARY ILLUSTRATION

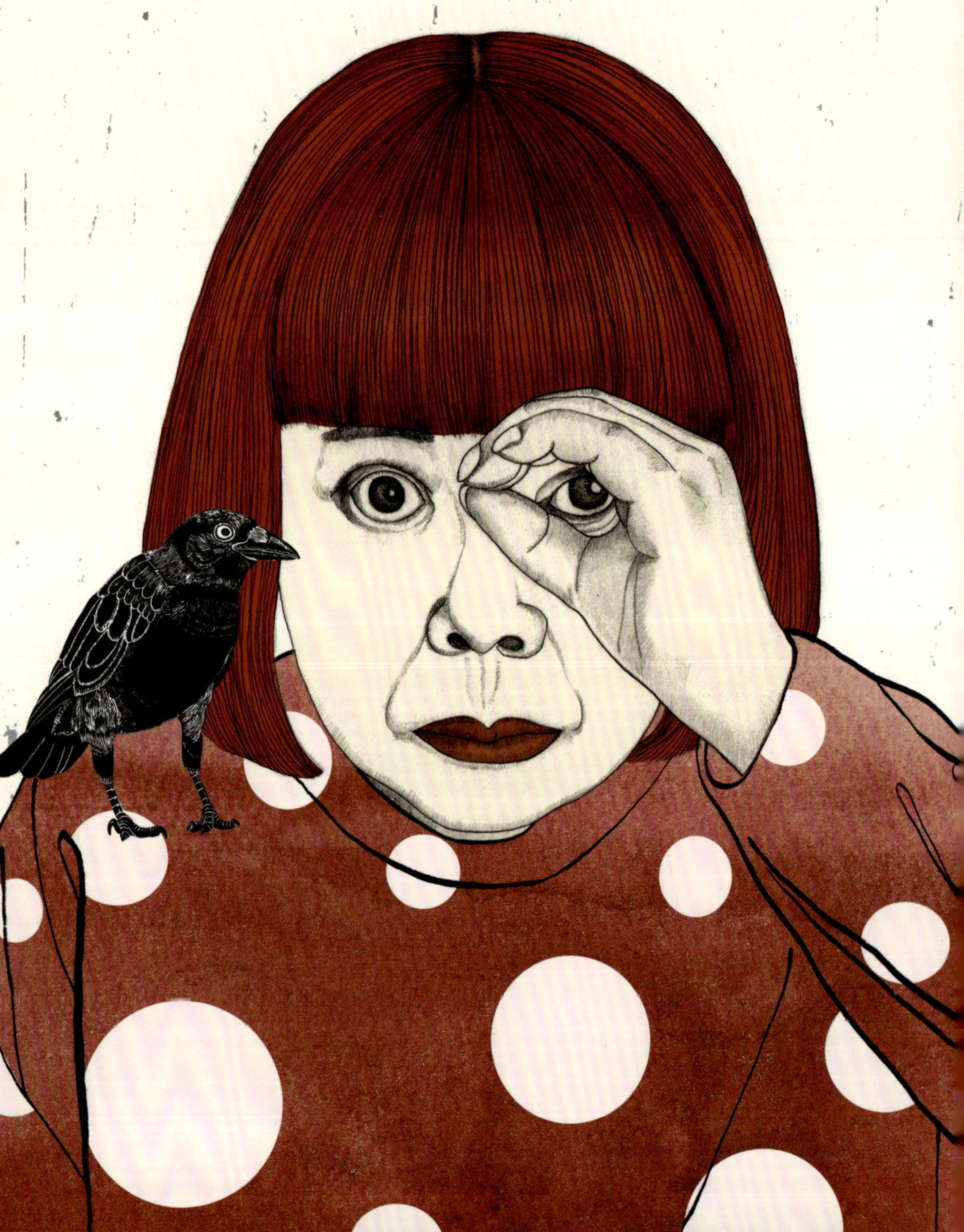

# CONTENTS

6 JUDGES

8 INTRODUCTION

9 ILLUSTRATOR : EDUCATOR
OF THE YEAR

13 PROFESSIONAL SHOW

217 PICTURE BOOK SHOW

295 STUDENT SHOW

407 INDEX

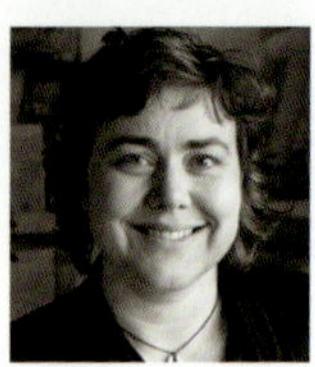

### Janette Bornmarker
PICTURE BOOK SHOW

Janette is an illustrator from Stockholm. She lives and works from the island of Gotland in the Baltic Sea.

Janette graduated from the Beckmans School of Design in Stockholm, in addition she has studied screenwriting at the University of Gotland and picture book manuscripts at the School of Design and Crafts in Gothenburg. She has also worked as an art school teacher and was one of the founders of a showroom/exhibition space for profesionals. Since many years Janette served as a board member of the Illustrators' Centre in Sweden.

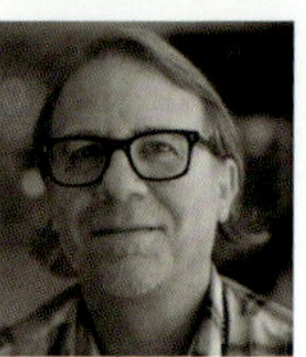

### Calef Brown
PICTURE BOOK SHOW

Calef has been working as a freelance illustrator for over 20 years. His work has appeared in *Time, Newsweek, Rolling Stone, The New Yorker, Entertainment Weekly, The New York Times* and other magazines and newspapers.

He has created CD and book covers, posters, billboards, murals, packaging and character development for clients including Coca Cola, Levi Strauss, Adidas, Laika Studios, Disney/Pixar and Nickelodeon. Calef has also authored and illustrate more than a dozen award-winning picture books, including the bestseller *Flamingos on the Roof*.

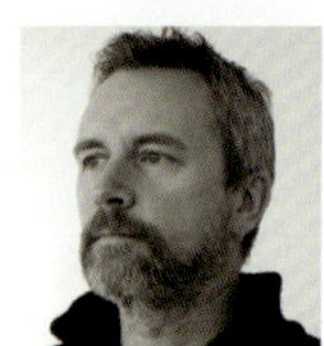

### Paul Burgess
STUDENT SHOW

Paul is senior lecturer on the illustration course at the University of Brighton. He also works as an illustrator, designer, author and photographer.

Paul completed his studys at Camberwell School of Art and the Royal College of Art, London. He has exhibited in numerous solo and group exhibitions in both the UK and abroad. He spent a six-year period making photographic studies of Jarvis Cocker and Pulp and has worked with the Sex Pistols on numerous occasions as graphic designer and photographer.

Paul has spoken at conferences in the US and Europe.

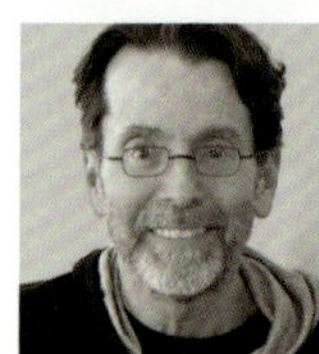

### Ronn Campisi
PROFESSIONAL SHOW

Ronn specializes in publication design. Ronn has won many awards for his work. In 1983, he was the designer and part of the team that won a Pulitzer Prize for a special *Boston Globe* magazine section.

His work has appeared in the *Graphis Annual* as well as *Graphis, The Type Directors Club Annual, Print* magazine and *Communication Arts* magazine.

His Boston-based studio, Ronn Campisi Design, currently art directs and designs publications on a regular basis for Amherst Colege, Boston University and Harvard Law School.

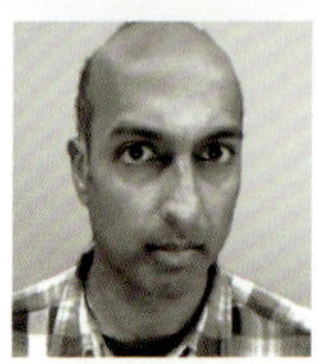

### Nishant Choksi
PROFESSIONAL SHOW

Nishant is an illustrator based in the UK. He regularly contributes to many publications including *The New Yorker, The Wall Street Journal* and *The Guardian* as well as working with advertising agencies and publishers. Drawing with brush and ink, Nishant creates character-based ideas with a humorous graphic style.

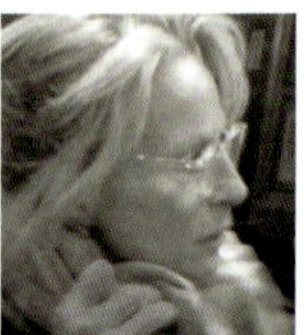

### Christian Potter Drury
PROFESSIONAL SHOW

Christian designs book jackets, magazines, paints and designs and prints fabrics. She has most recently been senior art director for *The Wall Street Journal* for the past 4 years. Previously she was the Features design director for *The Los Angeles Times*, winning numerous awards. She redesigned the entire *Hartford Courant* and twice won the honor of best designed newspaper in the world from The Society of News Design.

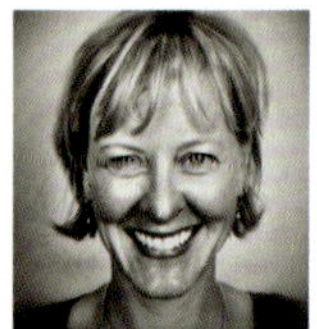

### Pamela Fogg
STUDENT SHOW

Pamela received a BFA from the New York's School of Visual Arts. She is the design director at Middlebury College where she oversees the creation of everything from admissions recruitment materials to fundraising and video. Her real passion is the award-winning *Middlebury Magazine* and cultivating relationships with illustrators to bring its content to life. Pam has been involved with organizations such as UCDA, AIGA and CASE. She works tirelessly to explain to designers and editors (or anyone who will listen) the value of illustration.

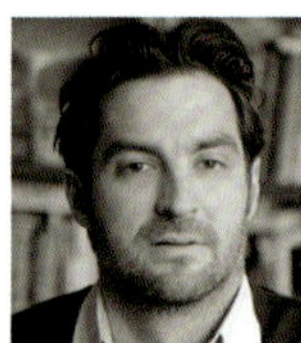

### Christian Gralingen
PROFESSIONAL SHOW

Christian is an illustrator based in Berlin. His client list includes design agencies, publishing houses and magazines such as *The New Yorker*.

Additionally he works for Anna B. Design Berlin and supports clients from the media industry and the financial sector. Their projects also include art books and university publications.

Christian's work has been recognized by *3x3, Creative Quarterly, Freistil* and Society of Illustrators.

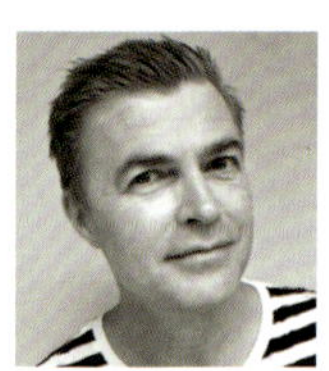

### Martin Haake
STUDENT SHOW

After studying at the University of Arts, Berlin, Martin moved to Hamburg and London to work as a freelance illustrator. Since 2000 he has lived in Berlin with his wife and two sons.

Martin has worked for clients such as Bacardi, *The New York Times*, Penguin Books and Yahoo.

His work has been showcased in American Illustration, *Communication Arts, 3x3*, Taschen's *Illustration Now* and *Illusive*. He has received numerous awards, including the D&AD yellow pencil from the British Art Director's Club.

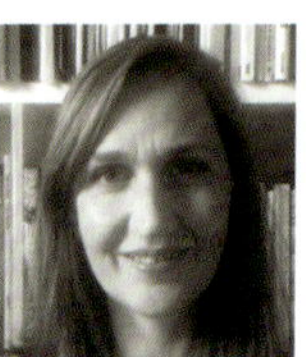

### Samantha Johnson
PROFESSIONAL SHOW

Samantha has been picture editor at Penguin Press in London since 2004. She researches and commissions photography, illustration and fine art.

Sam studied history, art history and literature at university. She has subsequently worked with the historical collections of the Royal Photographic Society and the University of London.

In 2001 she co-founded a design partnership, Bickford Smith & Johnson with Coralie Bickford-Smith working on pattern design beyond the book publishing world.

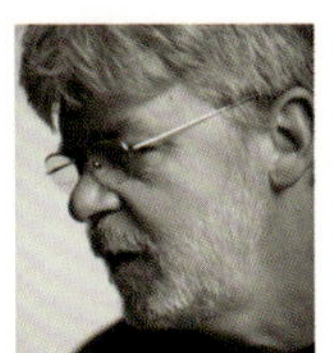

## Cedomir Kostovic
STUDENT SHOW

Born in Sarajevo, Cedomir earned his BFA and MFA degrees from the Sarajevo Academy of Fine Arts, where he taught graphic design until 1991. Since 1992 he has been teaching graphic design and illustration classes in the Department of Art and Design at Missouri State University.

He has been active on the international poster scene since 1980 and has exhibited at most major poster events around the world. His work has been awarded with over hundred national and international prizes and featured in many books, catalogs and periodicals.

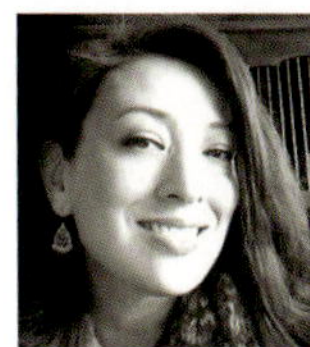

## April Montgomery
PROFESSIONAL SHOW

April is a New York-born, New England-based designer hooked on the arts, storytelling and technology. She is currently an art director for IDG Enterprise, meeting the editorial design needs of technology-focused media brands such as *Computerworld*.

Her work has been recognized by the Society of Publication Designers, *Folio: Magazine* and the American Society of Business Publication Editors (ASBPE), with select projects featured on visual forums by Robert Newman and CoverJunkie.

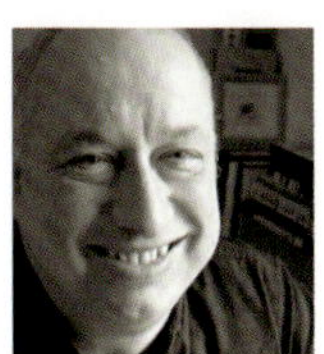

## Ben Norland
PICTURE BOOK SHOW

Ben is executive art director at Walker Books Ltd—the leading independent publisher for children's books in the United Kingdom. Ben began work there as a intern, "making tea, emptying bins." He has worked on all kind of books from board books to Young Adult novels with all kinds of illustrators and writers. He loves his job.

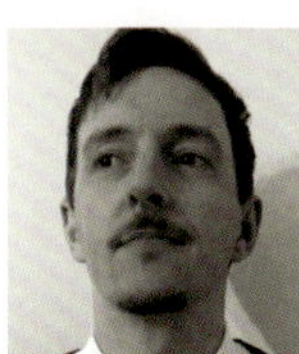

## Simon Peplow
STUDENT SHOW

Simon is a freelance illustrator based in Birmingham, UK, working primarily in advertising, editorial and publishing.

Selected clients include: *Anorak Magazine*, Carhartt WIP, NikeSB, *The New York Times, The Washington Post* and Passion Pictures.

He has exhibited extensively both in Europe and internationally, and has been featured in numerous acclaimed creative magazines and books.

Simon is also co-founder of independent arts co-operative Outcrowd Collective.

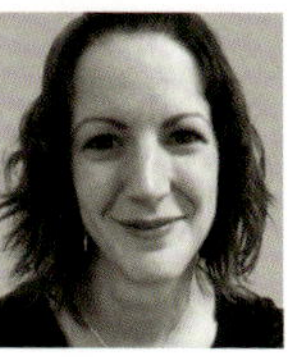

## Hannah Ray
PICTURE BOOK SHOW

Hannah is editorial manager at Macmillan Children's Books in London. With a degree in English, she has worked in children's publishing for the last 12 years and has been editing picture and gift books at Macmillan for the last 7 years.

Hannah works with established authors and illustrators as well as exciting new talent, as part of a lively and creative publishing team. She has commissioned and edited a number of award-winning books, and also worked on the official picture-book edition of Nelson Mandela's *Long Walk to Freedom*.

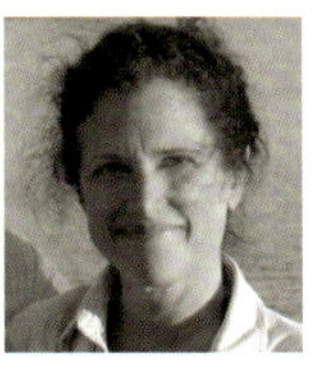

## Debra Sfetsios
PICTURE BOOK SHOW

Since 2000, Debra has been an art director in the children's division of Simon and Schuster. She works on picture books, middle-grade and young adult books. She has worked with many illustrators, including Barry Blitt, Joost Swarte, and Chris Raschka. She is always on the look out for fresh new talent.

Prior to joining Simon and Schuster, Debra worked at Smallwood and Stewart and Rodale Press.

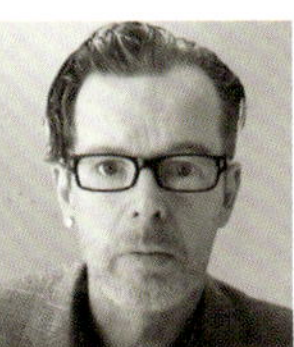

## Steve Simpson
PICTURE BOOK SHOW

For 30 years Steve has applied his multi-disciplinary skills to creative projects for a diverse range of clients across the globe. Steve's innovative approach combining graphic design, typography and illustration is built on fresh thinking, traditional skills and a dose of fun. Steve lives on the east coast of Ireland where a good sense of humor is essential.

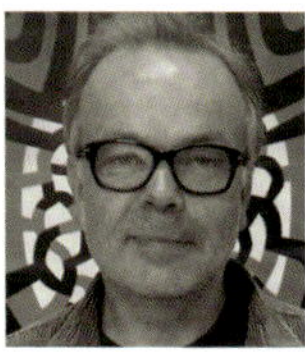

## Lasse Skarbövik
PROFESSIONAL SHOW

Born in Norway, Lasse has been living in Stockholm since he graduated from Berghs School of Communication. A founder of Stockholm Illustration, he now works as a freelance artist for clients all around the world. Apart from his illustration work he has produced murals for interiors and exhibitions. Recently he designed several patterns for textile collections.

He work has been featured in many international design magazines.

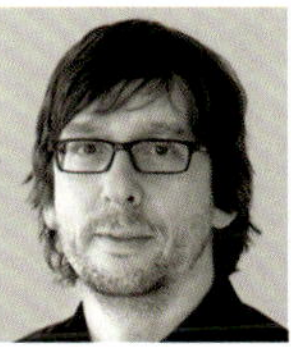

## Svein Størksen
PICTURE BOOK SHOW

Svein is the founder and editor-in-chief at Magikon Publishing, producing picture books and art books in Norway.

Since it began in 2007, Magikon's books have received numerous awards and have been translated into many languages. Størksen has more than 15 years of experience as a freelance illustrator, photographer and graphic designer. His work has been varied, from commercial work to free artistic imagery. He has a MA in illustration and graphic design from Oslo's National College of Art and Design.

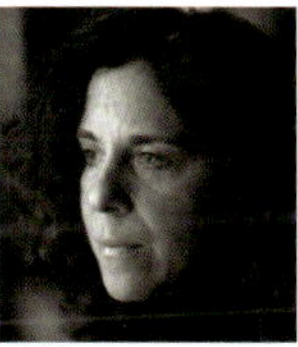

## Ellen Weinstein
PROFESSIONAL SHOW

Ellen was born and raised in New York City. She is a graduate of Pratt Institute. Awards include American Illustration, Society of Illustrators, *Communication Arts and Print's Regional Design Annual*.

In addition to her commercial work she exhibits in galleries in the US and Italy. She also lectures and conducts workshops internationally and is an instructor at the Rhode Island School of Design.

Ellen served as the president of ICON8 and is a member of the Society of Illustrators board of directors.

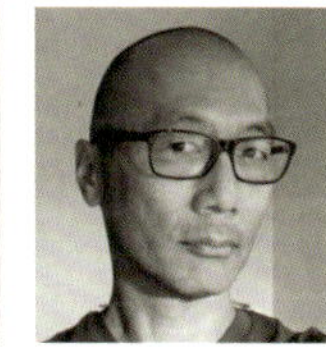

## James Yang
STUDENT SHOW

James was born and raised in Oklahoma. He graduated with a BFA from Virginia Commonwealth University.

He has worked with many clients including *Bloomberg Magazine*, IBM, Herman Miller, *L.A. Times*, Microsoft, *The New York Times*, and *The Wall Street Journal*. He has also authored/illustrated 3 children's books.

James has won over 200 awards for design and illustration.

He is in-demand as a guest lecturer and is currently on the executive board for ICON, The Illustration Conference.

WELCOME TO THE TWELFTH YEARLY COMPILATION OF WHAT HAS BECOME ONE OF THE FEW, IF ONLY, ILLUSTRATION ANNUALS WITH A DISTINCT INTERNATIONAL FLAVOR. AND ONE WITH A LOT OF FRESH FACES. OUR TWENTY-FOUR MEDALISTS REPRESENT THIRTEEN COUNTRIES INCLUDING AUSTRIA, BRAZIL, CANADA, FRANCE, GERMANY, ISRAEL, ITALY, POLAND, PORTUGAL, SWEDEN, TAIWAN, UNITED KINGDOM AND THE UNITED STATES. OUR REMAINING WINNERS ADD AN ADDITIONAL TWENTY COUNTRIES, WITH A TOTAL OF FORTY-FIVE COUNTRIES REPRESENTED IN OUR SHOW—AND FOR THE FIRST TIME, CHINA. WE ALSO ENLIST JUDGES FROM OUTSIDE THE UNITED STATES, ART DIRECTORS, EDITORS AND DESIGNERS WHO COMMISSION ILLUSTRATION FOR NEWSPAPERS, MAGAZINES, BOOKS, CHILDREN'S BOOKS, ADVERTISING AND A WIDE VARIETY OF ASSIGNMENTS. WE ROUND OUT THE PANEL WITH EQUALLY DISTINGUISHED ILLUSTRATORS. THIS YEAR OUR JUDGES VIEWED NEARLY 4,500 IMAGES TO SELECT 396 MEDAL AND MERIT WINNERS WITH HONORABLE MENTIONS ADDING ANOTHER 283 WINNERS WHO ARE SHOWCASED IN OUR ONLINE GALLERY. OUR JUDGES WORKED INDEPENDENTLY WITHOUT CONSULTATION OVER A TWO-WEEK PERIOD. THEY HAD NO QUOTA, NO MAGIC NUMBER THEY TRIED TO REACH. THEY WERE ONLY CHARGED WITH SELECTING THE VERY BEST WORK. WE ARE PROUD TO SHARE THE RESULTS OF THEIR WISDOM, WORK THAT HAS MET THE STANDARD OF EXCELLENCE WE STRIVE TO REPRESENT HERE AT 3X3. *ENJOY!*

—THE PUBLISHER

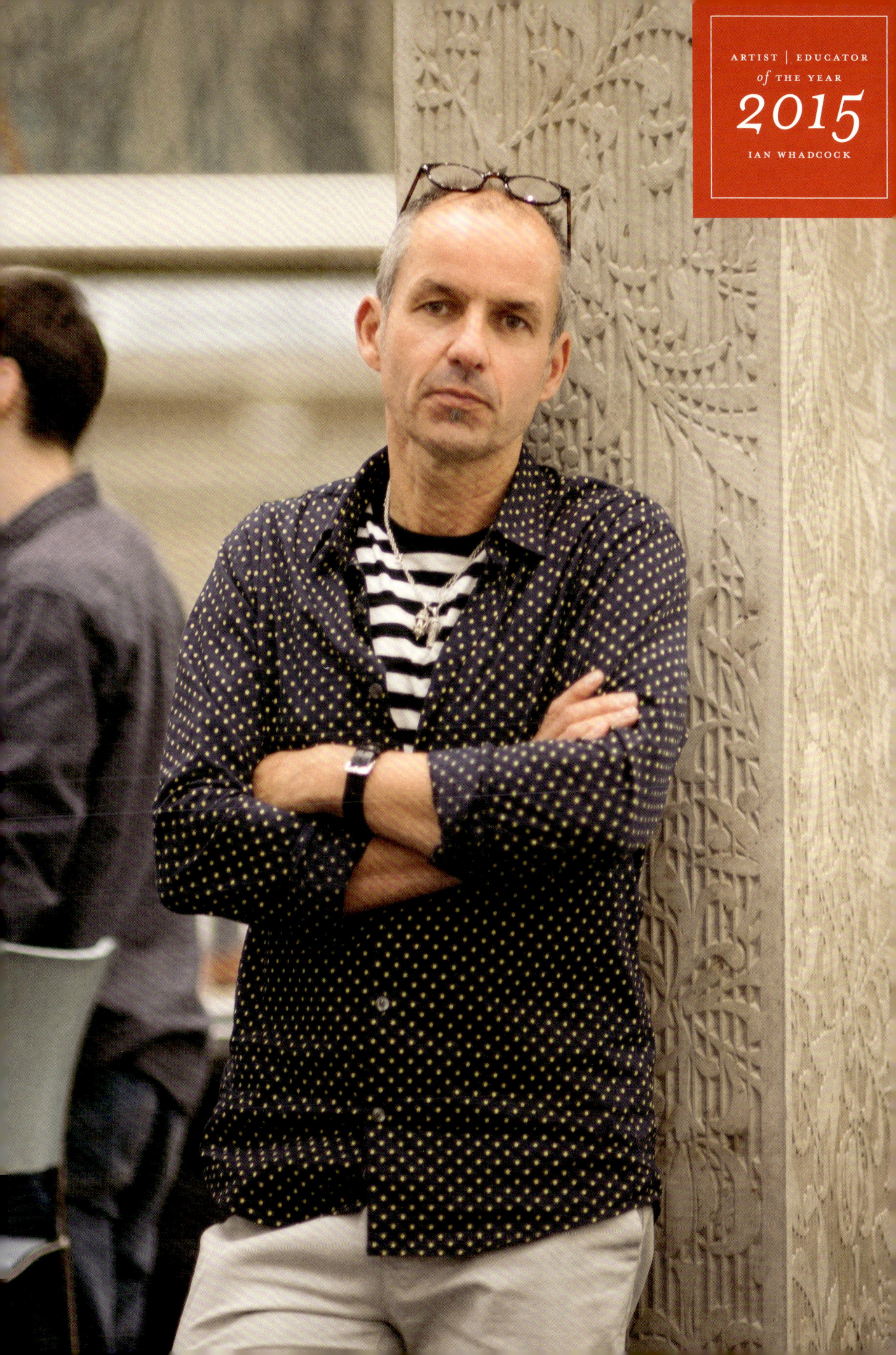

ARTIST | EDUCATOR
of THE YEAR
2015
IAN WHADCOCK

*Speak with* **IAN WHADCOCK** *and you'll discover his intense interest in all things visual. Watch him with students and you'll see the patience he exudes as the critique progresses. Listen to his encouragement and desire to have all young illustrators succeed. Realizing the difficulty of the task ahead he spares no pretense when evaluating a creative idea. Weakness is never tolerated, the idea is paramount. Style is never a cover-up. Students gain invaluable insights from this accomplished illustrator. His own practice runs the gamut of editorial assignments to publishing to short animations. His engagement with local theater provides an added avenue for his talents. To honor his ongoing devotion to the field of illustration we are pleased to name Ian as our 3x3 Illustrator/Educator of the Year, 2015.*

**Q** Tell us about your early schooling, did you always want to be an artist?

**A** My memories of school are of always gaining attention through drawing. I remember being told by a teacher that people didn't have green hair and feeling for the first time any concept of rightness or wrongness in drawing.

**Q** What were some of your early influences?

**A** Early influences were Storm Thorgerson and Hipgnosis artwork and although I wouldn't know it at the time, work by George Hardie.

Q What were your early impressions of illustration?

**Q** What were your early impressions of illustration?

**A** I remember looking at an early AOI annual and forming a connection with things I could own, like record covers, posters and T-shirts. And things that I could imitate. I didn't know it as illustration as such.

**Q** How did university change you?

**A** I was never terribly comfortable with being an illustrator, it felt far less exciting than what I saw in the print room and fine art studios. And yet was painfully aware that I was not a fine artist nor had the confidence to move towards graphic design.

Thankfully an exchange program at the Philadelphia College of Art was hugely influential in knocking a sense of risk and rigor back into my practice.

I still had no idea if I could be an illustrator so I enrolled in a post-grad printmaking course in London as a way of extending any attempt at deciding.

**Q** How did you get your first big break?

**A** I struggled at first like most illustrators. Debi Angel from *Elle* gave me my first few jobs and it was genuinely exciting to be part of that world. But really it was after spending time in the studio dealing with the figure in my work that I arrived at a more mannered approach which caught the eye of both my agents Sharp Practice and Caz Hilderbrand at Penguin Books. The resulting commission, a series of titles for Edward De Bono on the subject of lateral thinking, launched me into a decade or so of full-time work.

**Q** Your work is mostly editorial, have you had any opportunity to work in advertising?

**A** I had worked intermittently for advertising and design groups, up until around 1999 when I was contacted by a London agency to work on a series of animated television spots for an energy company in the UK, Powergen PLC. This grew into an enormous project covering all aspects of printed and screen-based materials including large site-specific works for airports and rail stations. This project lasted for just over two years, in truth it nearly killed me, the whole project was so fast paced and at times prescriptive that despite some good work coming out of it I rarely show it in lectures.

The problem with such high-profile work is that for a long time no one else will touch you for advertising as you are so closely associated with one brand I think in many ways it held me back rather than opened new doors.

**Q** How is today's work different than when you were first starting out?

**A** My early work was based on my interest in printmaking, I worked with colored papers, tracing paper and acetates to physically layer and collage drawings together, I would then re-copy these assemblages by playing around with settings on a color copier to effectively 'print' the final artwork. Later, I made the painfully slow and expensive move to computers which allowed me to combine the two previous ways of working into a kind of merged 2½-D space. Fundamentally it liberated the drawn line from a fixed surface much like a print process, yet still enabled me to work with color as if I was painting.

Q Talk with us a bit about your process?

A I have become less cautious with ideas over time, I used to invest more 'craft' skill in the execution of roughs before showing the client. I remember taking an A1 roll of charcoal roughs to *The Times* in the early 90s—it's about time I did that again. However these days I tend to think faster, working in pen in the margins of the brief. I take these thoughts onto layout paper and work my way through sheets of ideas often refining and remixing thoughts, re-reading the text, changing the emphasis and looking for multiple ways in. I know that I work best when I loosen up and let the drawing lead the drawing. At a certain point, I reach a stage where I have a few workable anchor ideas or elements and start to play around with these ideas, making and breaking connections at will and allowing absurdity and despair into the mix. I love/hate the process, more often than not a late night leaves heaps of drawings on the floor and a sense of tired frustration but in the morning there often emerges a clearer direction. It never ever gets easier, learning that uncertainty and doubt was the place my best ideas came from took time to accept.

Q What do you think about the current state of illustration?

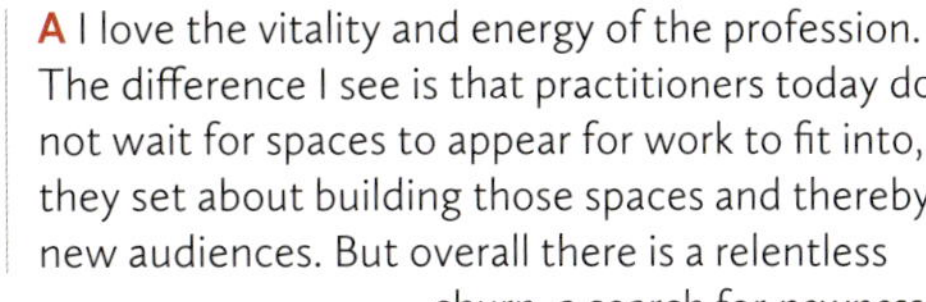


A I love the vitality and energy of the profession. The difference I see is that practitioners today do not wait for spaces to appear for work to fit into, they set about building those spaces and thereby new audiences. But overall there is a relentless churn, a search for *newness* that means nothing/nobody seems to stay around for very long.

Q Where do you see it headed?

A There is an abundance of talent emerging from art schools across the world—or maybe there always was but new media makes it more visible—and I think the growing international awareness and reach of Illustration is the most noticeable change I can see.

The strength it seems to me is the willingness of illustration to embrace many diverse forms of practice under this umbrella term. I see more site-specific and mixed-media works emerging that rely on collaborative practice and a move away from the printed page. I see movement and sound merging fields of animation, moving image and illustration. I see definitions of practice being blurred and stretched in ways that defy categorization.

Q Have you ever had an artist representative?

A I have had three agents so far and I am at present talking to a fourth. In each case they were appropriate at the time, initially as a way of attracting a wider range of clients and raising my profile, by association with other artists on the book you were taken more seriously perhaps?

Later I needed an agent to deal with complex advertising contracts and licenses and simply administering the workflow when it became really busy. Now with an increased role in academia I have once again sought out representation. It is certainly easier today to promote your own work, but I still believe a good agent is a huge asset and undoubtedly attracts work that on your own you would struggle to obtain.

Q Let's talk about your experiences as a teacher, how long have you been teaching?

A I have been working in education on and off for over around 15 years, initially working as a visiting speaker and then as a sessional lecturer at a range of courses across the UK and now as a

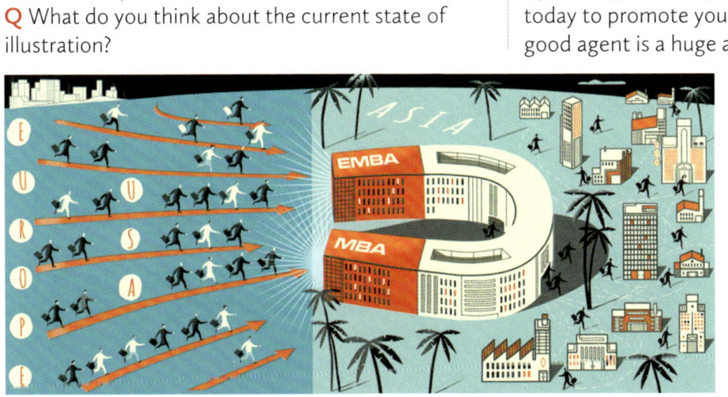

permanent Senior Lecturer at Manchester School of Art. In every role I have found that the experience changes my practice, reengages me with experimentation and makes me re-evaluate my ideas and revisit earlier influences. But more importantly teaching has given me back the diverse peer group influence I enjoyed as a student.

I am still in touch with my high school teacher Steve Arrandale and I owe a lot of my not wanting to conform to expectations to his approach to teaching.

**Q** What do you feel the role of an instructor is?

**A** I see my role as one of giving permission, space to the students to be the artist or designer they wish to be. To provide provocations and interventions that question assumptions, challenge preconceptions and hopefully allow the emergence of diverse practice in appropriate and sustainable forms. A lot of the time I feel my role is to absorb uncertainty, but not provide answers.

**Q** How are you able to juggle teaching and commissions?

**A** This can be challenging, I have always been careful to only take on work where I know time is available, never short-changing either side. Often time is tight I will do an hour or two private work before I start lecturing in order to meet deadlines if necessary.

I find students are interested in the minutiae of commissions as much as the outcome, and it is a level of insight that only comes through proximity to practice.

**Q** Do you feel there is anything missing in today's education of an illustrator?

**A** There is a demand for skills teaching and yet a reluctance to engage with real content, this creates technical stylists raised on YouTube tutorials made by enthusiasts looking for hits and followers. I think we have to be careful to engage students with real-world problems and the ability to see that illustration has a role in society beyond the Print Fair and Etsy—although both have their place—and be engaged in real social movements for change. At times illustration talks to itself and ignores its potential to communicate beyond this.

**Q** What is your advice to graduates entering the field today?

**A** Be open to what illustration, art and design can be, not what you think it is. There are diverse and varied opportunities for illustrators out there, but you need to be open, prepared and receptive to the call when it comes, passionate and professional in equal balance and above all remain curious about the world.

**Q** Final words to teachers?

**A** I hesitate to offer any words to staff. The best lecturers I had always enabled me to seek out *why* rather than *how*. Provide questions not answers. Also maintain an active practice, but not to be defined by the area you lecture in or been successful in or gained recognition in previously. In a sense retain a part of you that is always a student.

**Q** Final words to practicing illustrators?

**A** Be curious about the world, engage with the society you live in and use your creativity to give voice to untold stories, be you the author or the interpreter. Use your voice with integrity, wit and imagination and in time an audience will find you.

**Q** And finally, what's in your future, personally and professionally?

**A** At present I am enjoying my return to education. Manchester School of Art is much more outward facing and engaged in collaboration with the city, its archives, venues and events than it was when I last taught here in the late 90s. This is generating new opportunities for site-specific work, one-off installations and performative outputs for practice. This is where my head is focused at present.

In terms of my own output over the past three years I have worked with theater and performing arts groups and I can see the potential for this to develop further in terms of crossover with writers and venues in the city.

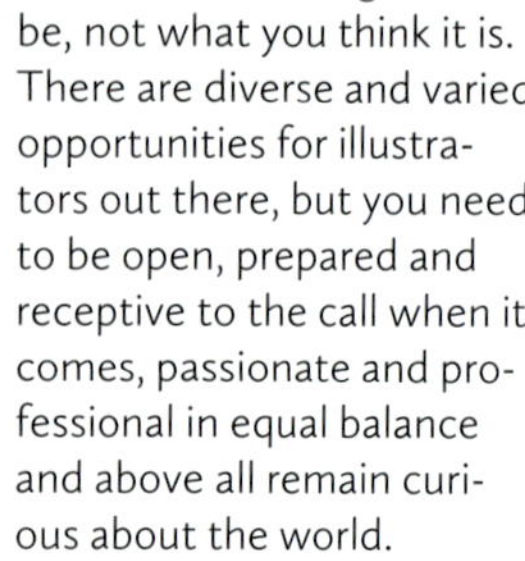
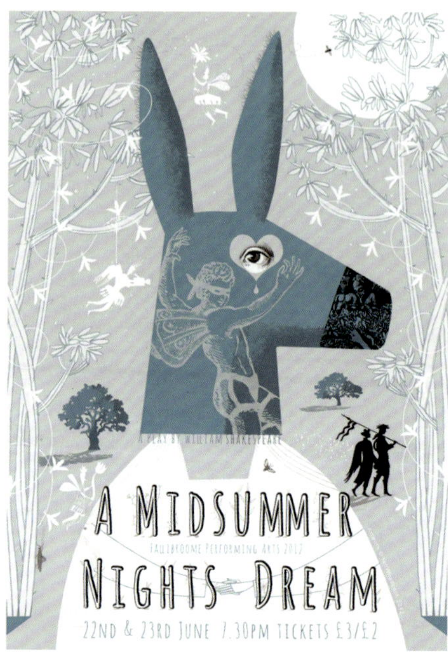


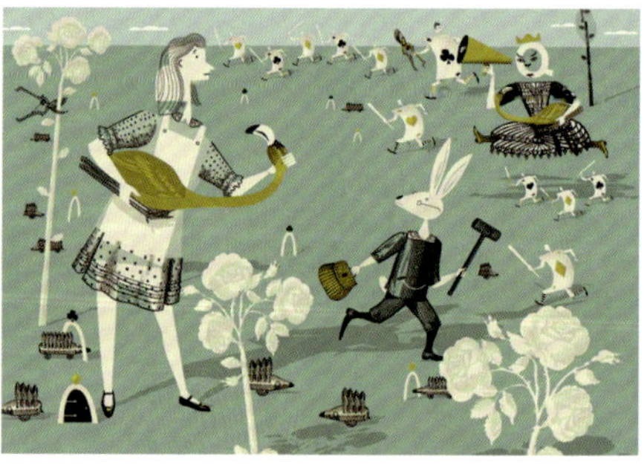

**PROFESSIONAL SHOW**

14     ADVERTISING

32     BOOKS

50     CALENDARS

54     COMICS

57     CORPORATE COMMUNICATIONS

64     COVERS

76     EDITORIAL

147     FASHION

148     GALLERY

156     GREETING CARDS

157     PACKAGING

158     POSTERS

174     SCI-FI

176     SELF-PROMOTION

194     TEXTILES + PATTERNS

198     UNPUBLISHED

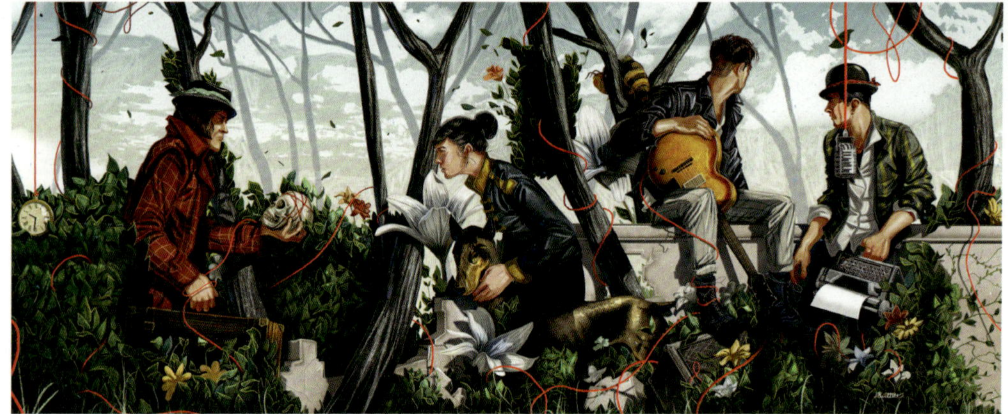

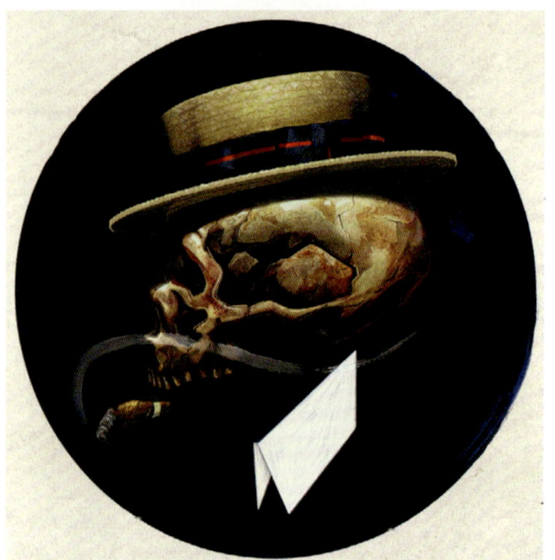

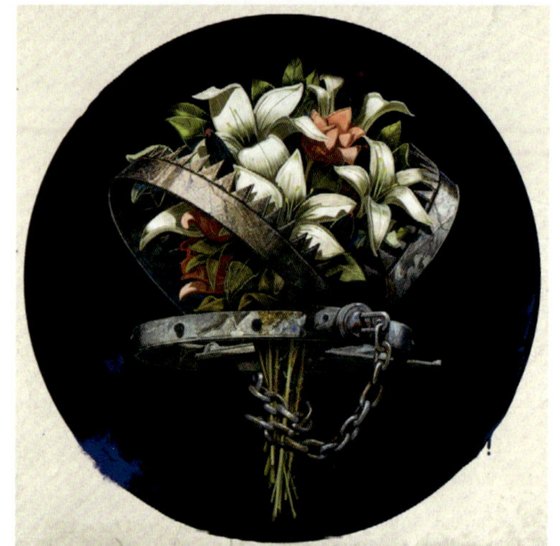

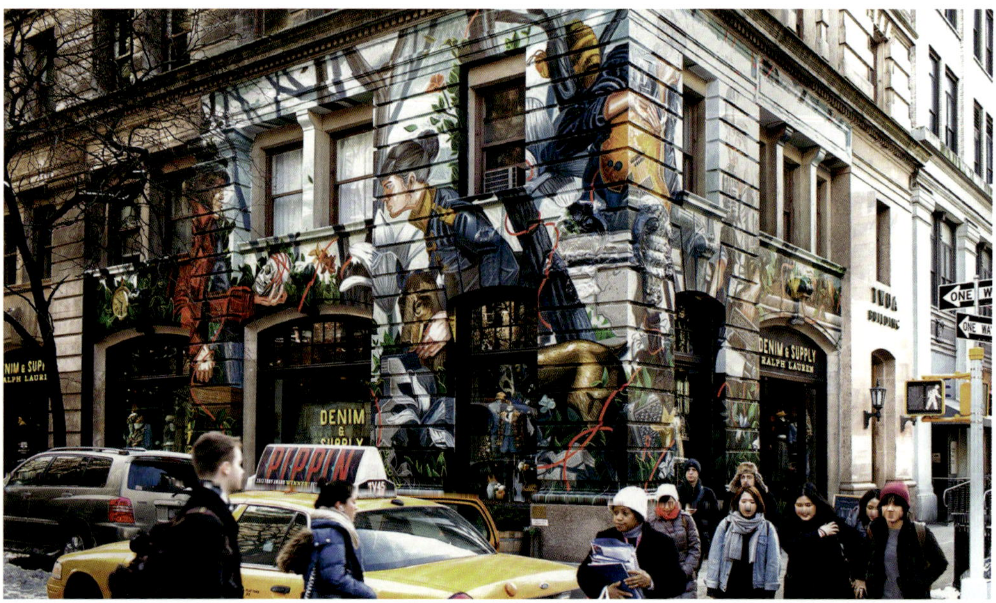

MERIT *Jonathan Bartlett*

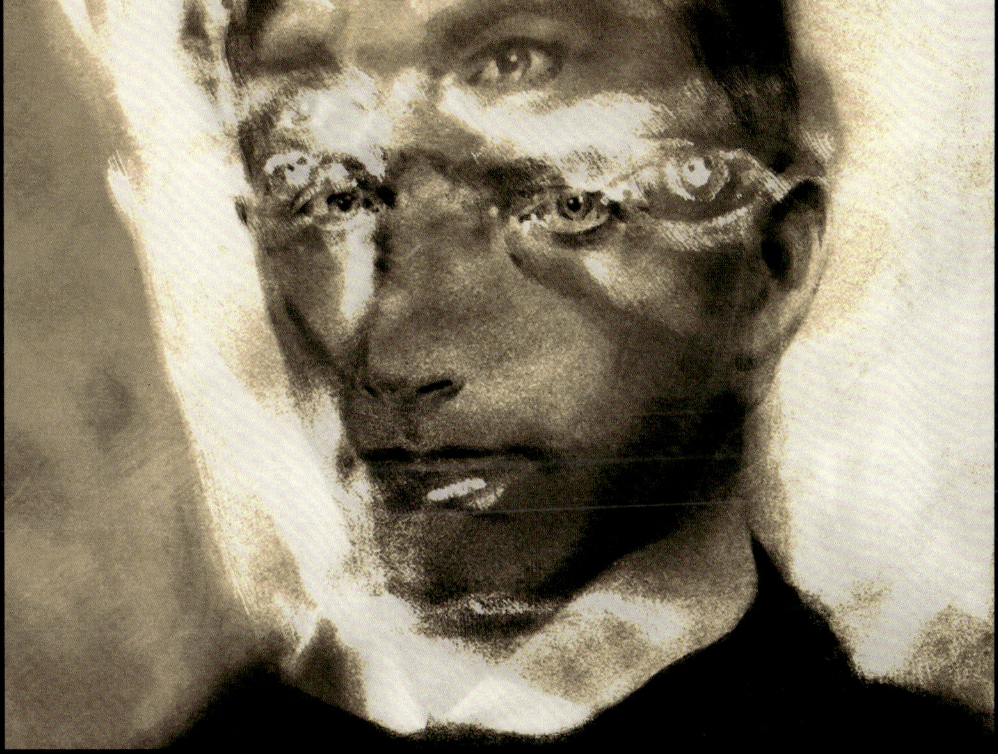

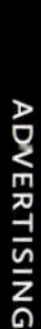

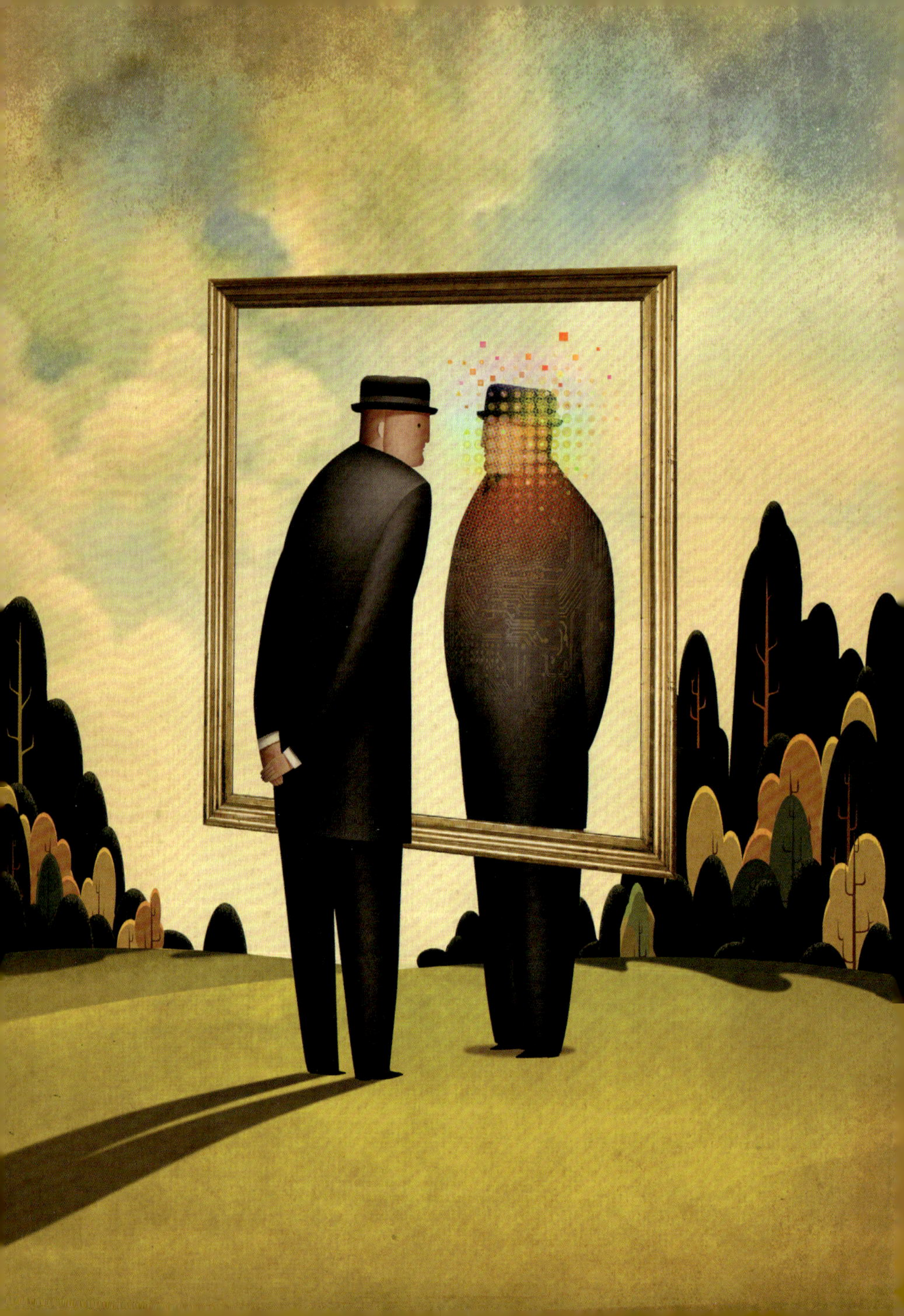

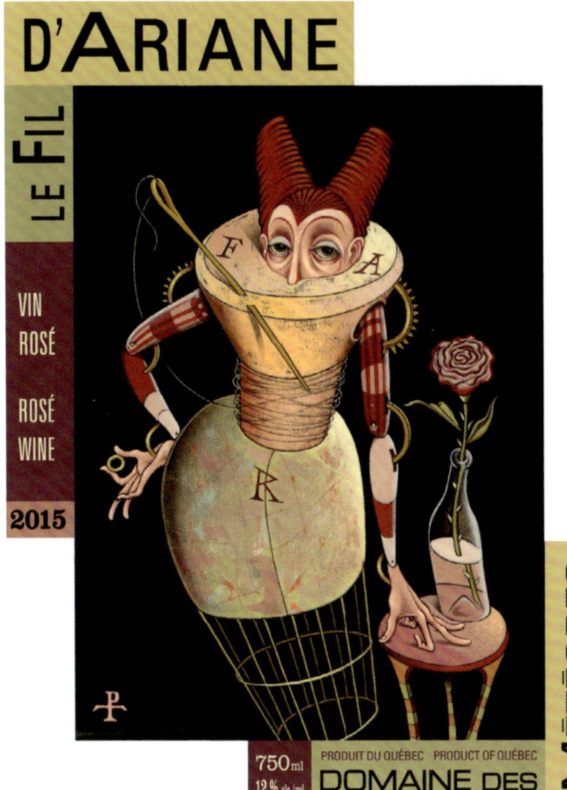


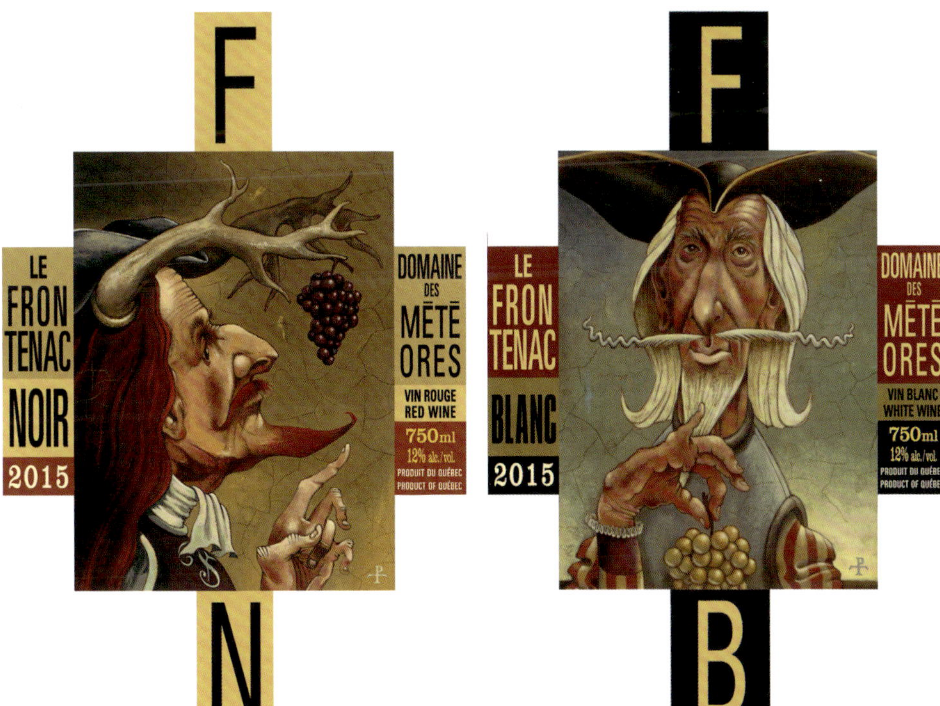


MERIT *Pol Turgeon*

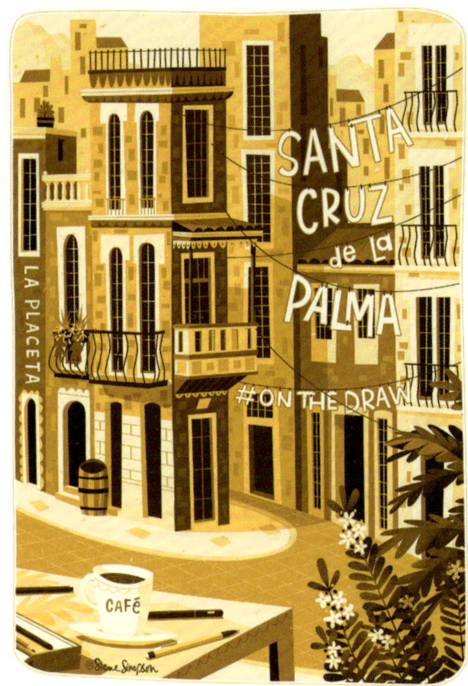


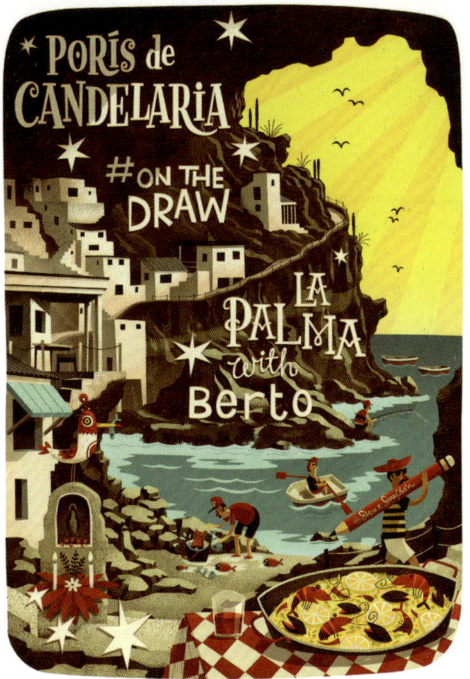


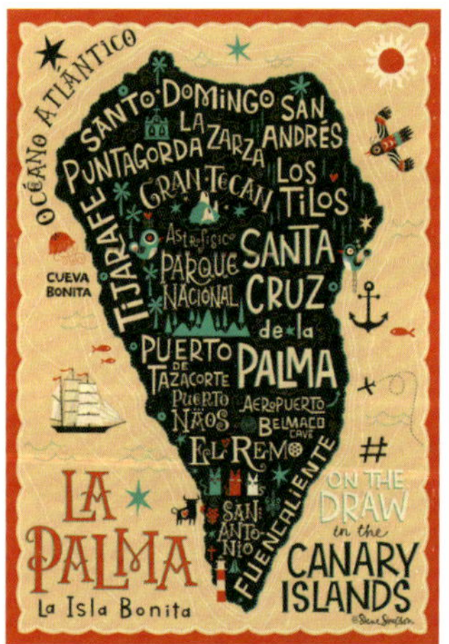


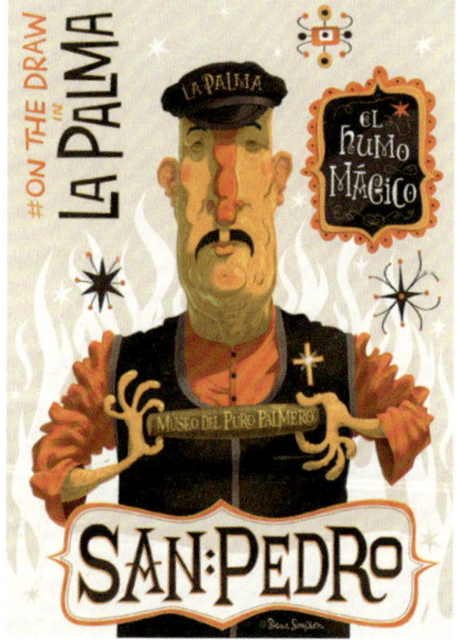


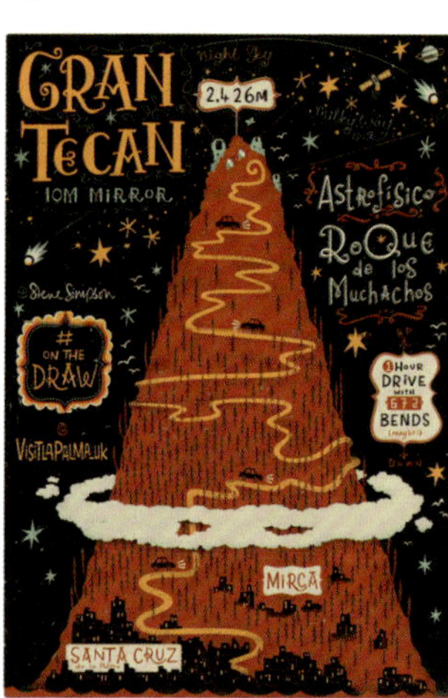


MERIT *Steve Simpson*

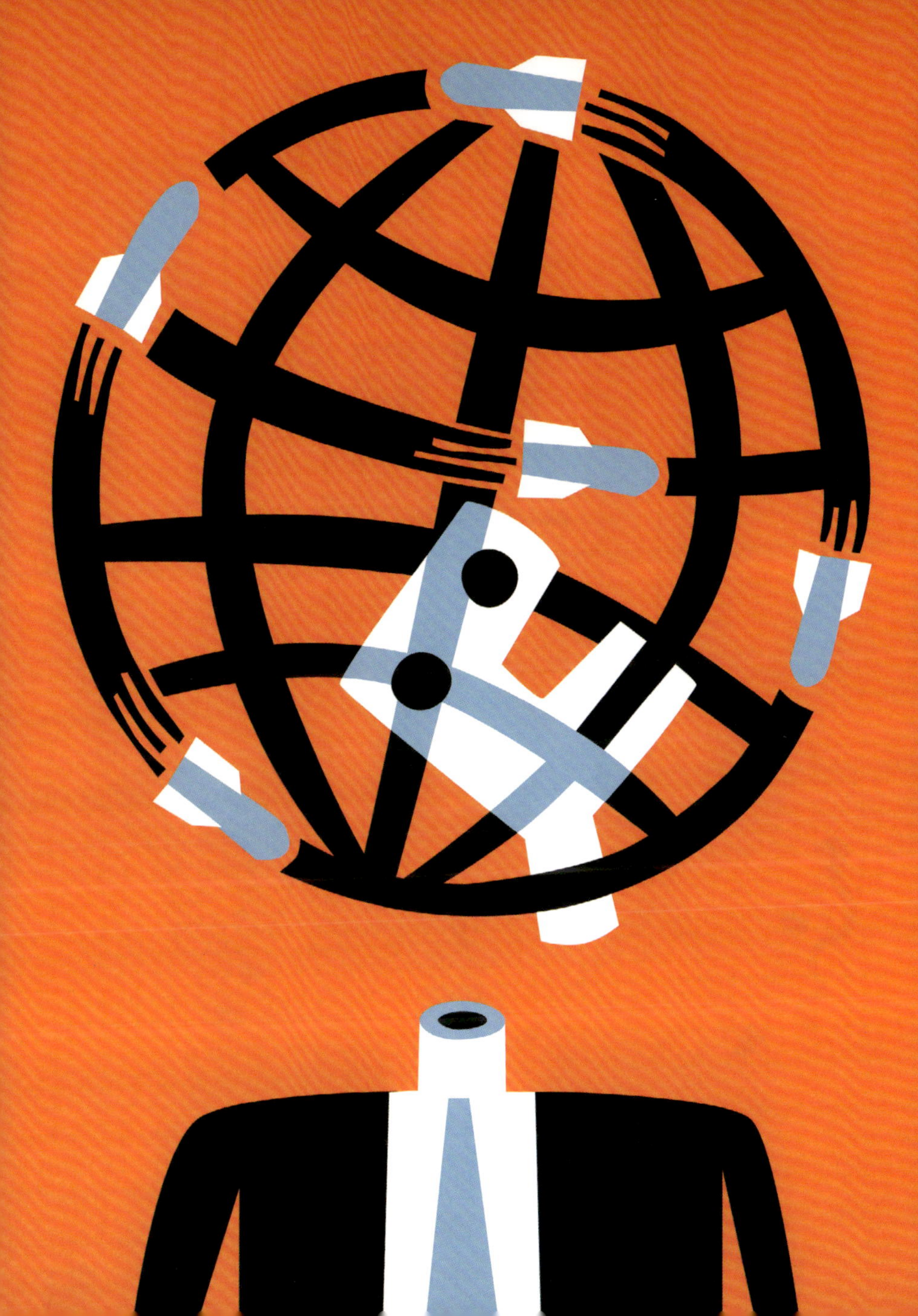

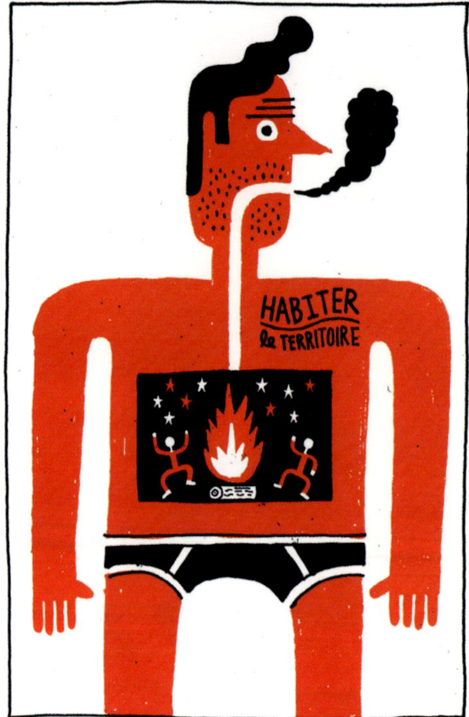


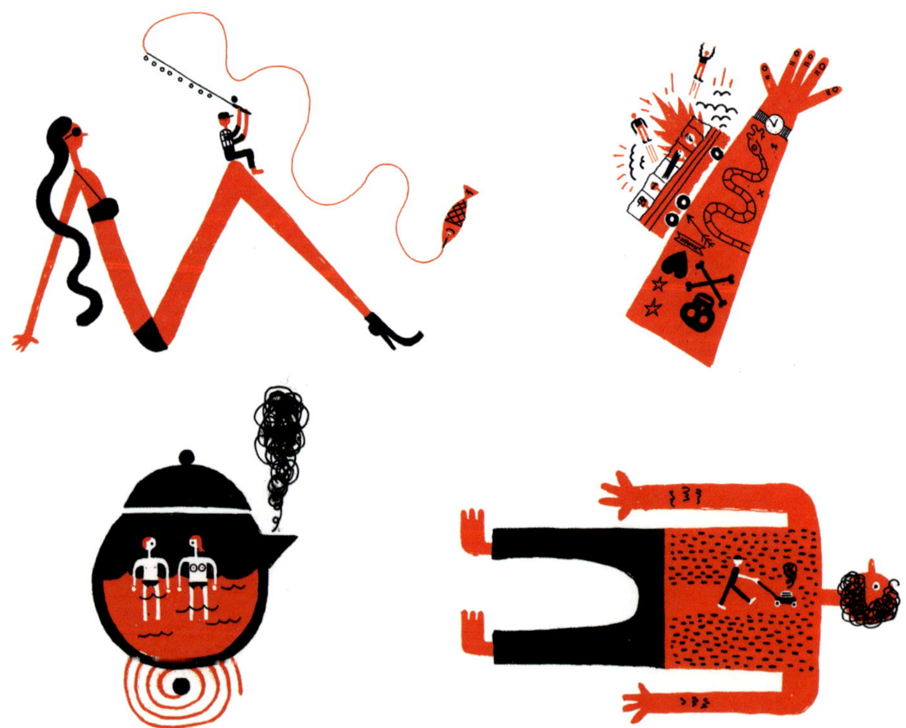

MERIT *Benoit Tardif*

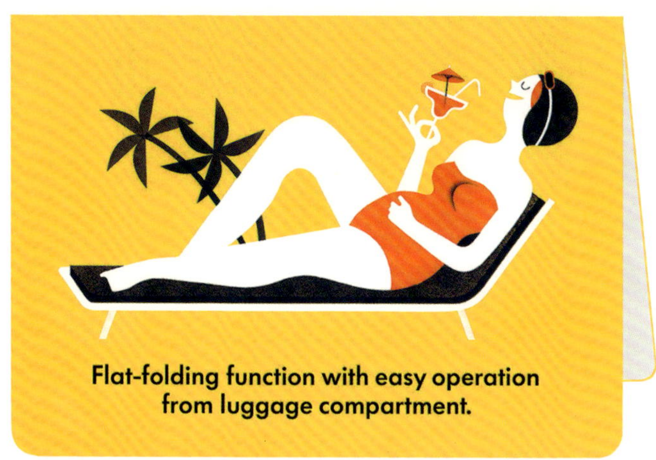


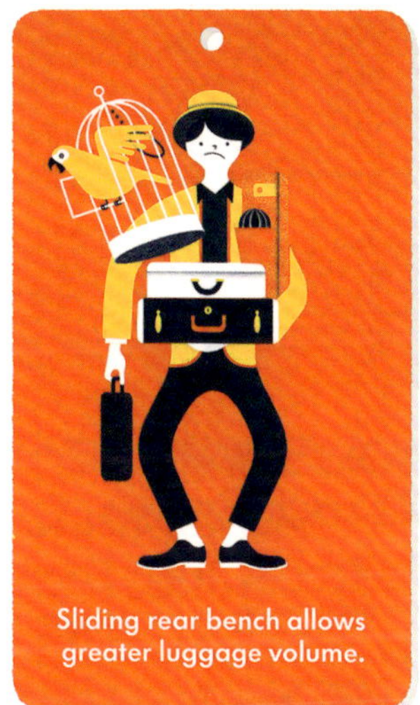


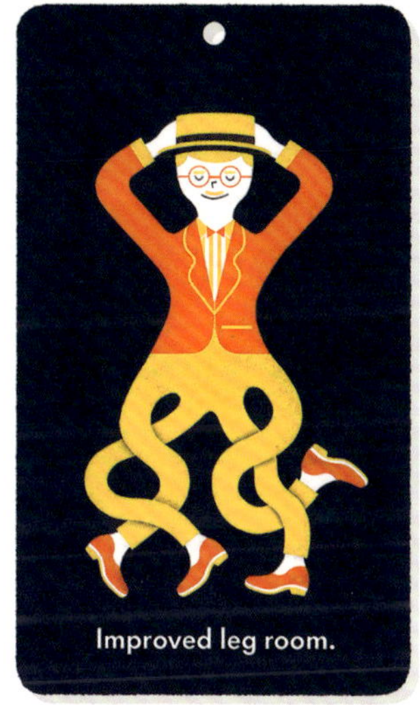


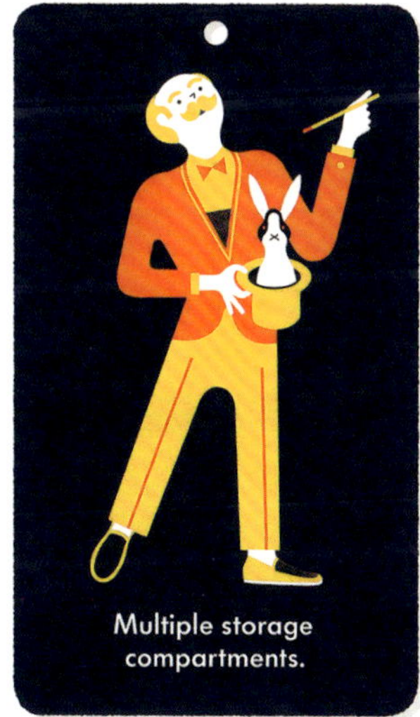


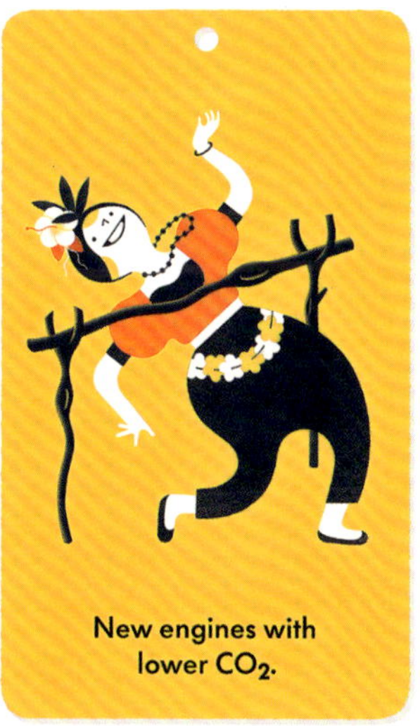


MERIT *Ella Cohen*

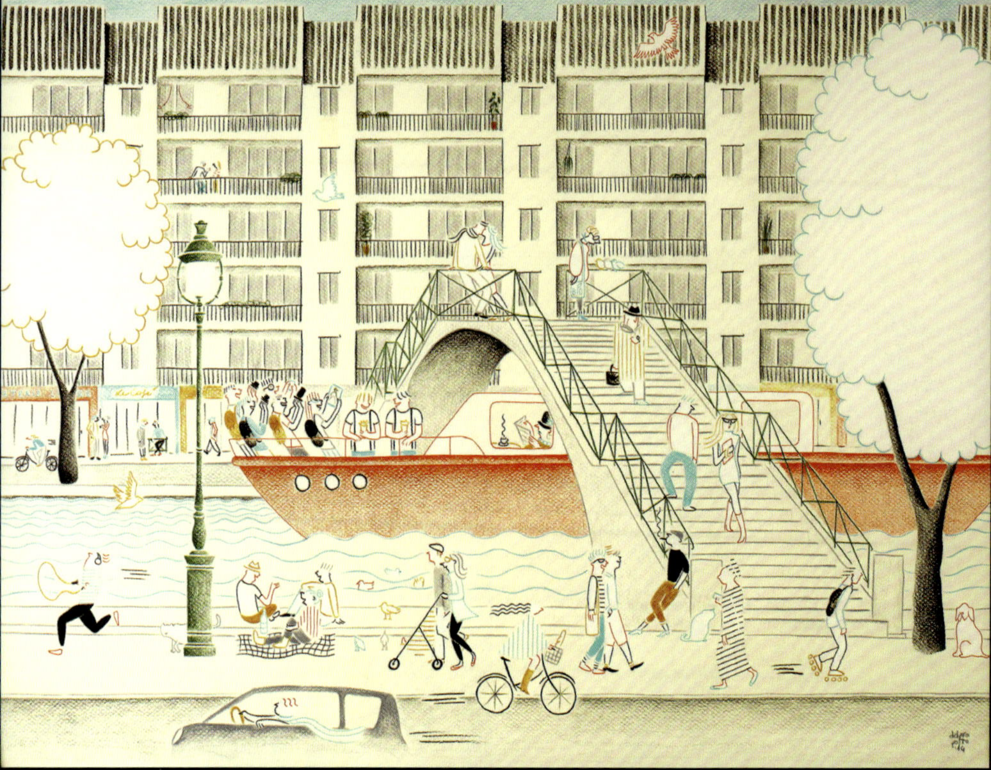

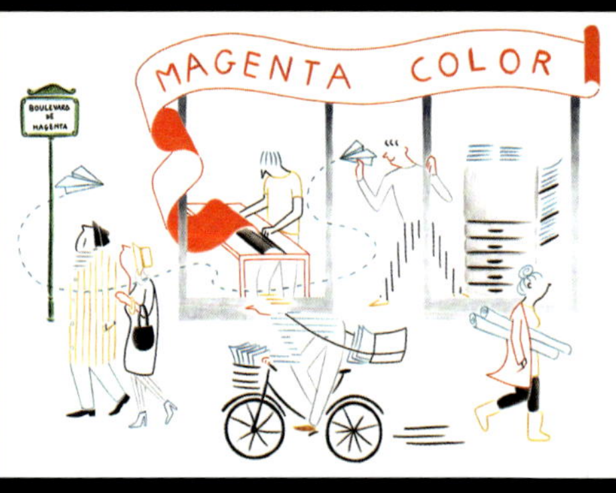

MAGENTA COLOR
BOULEVARD DE MAGENTA


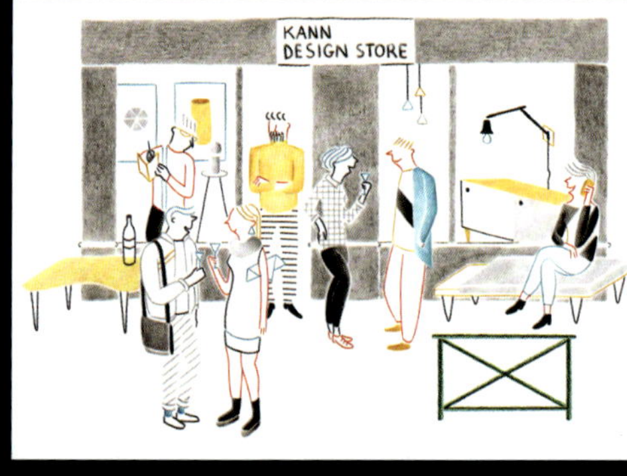

KANN DESIGN STORE


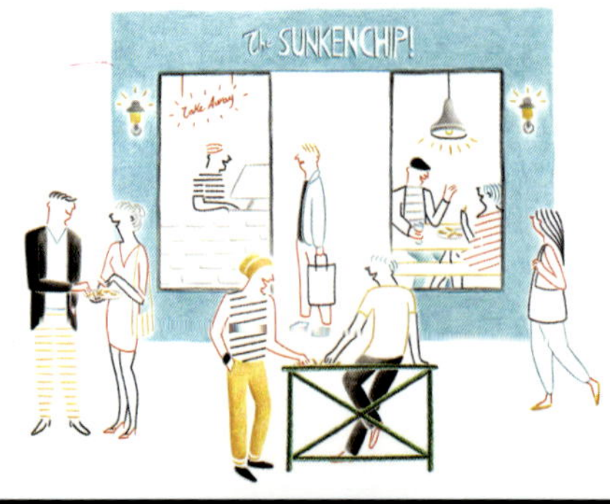

The SUNKENCHIP!
Take Away


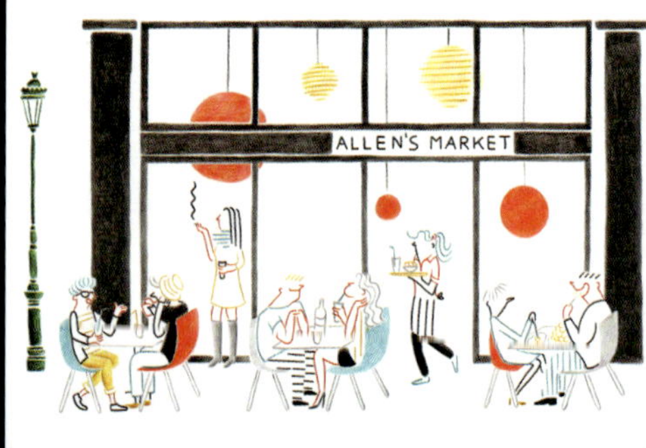

ALLEN'S MARKET

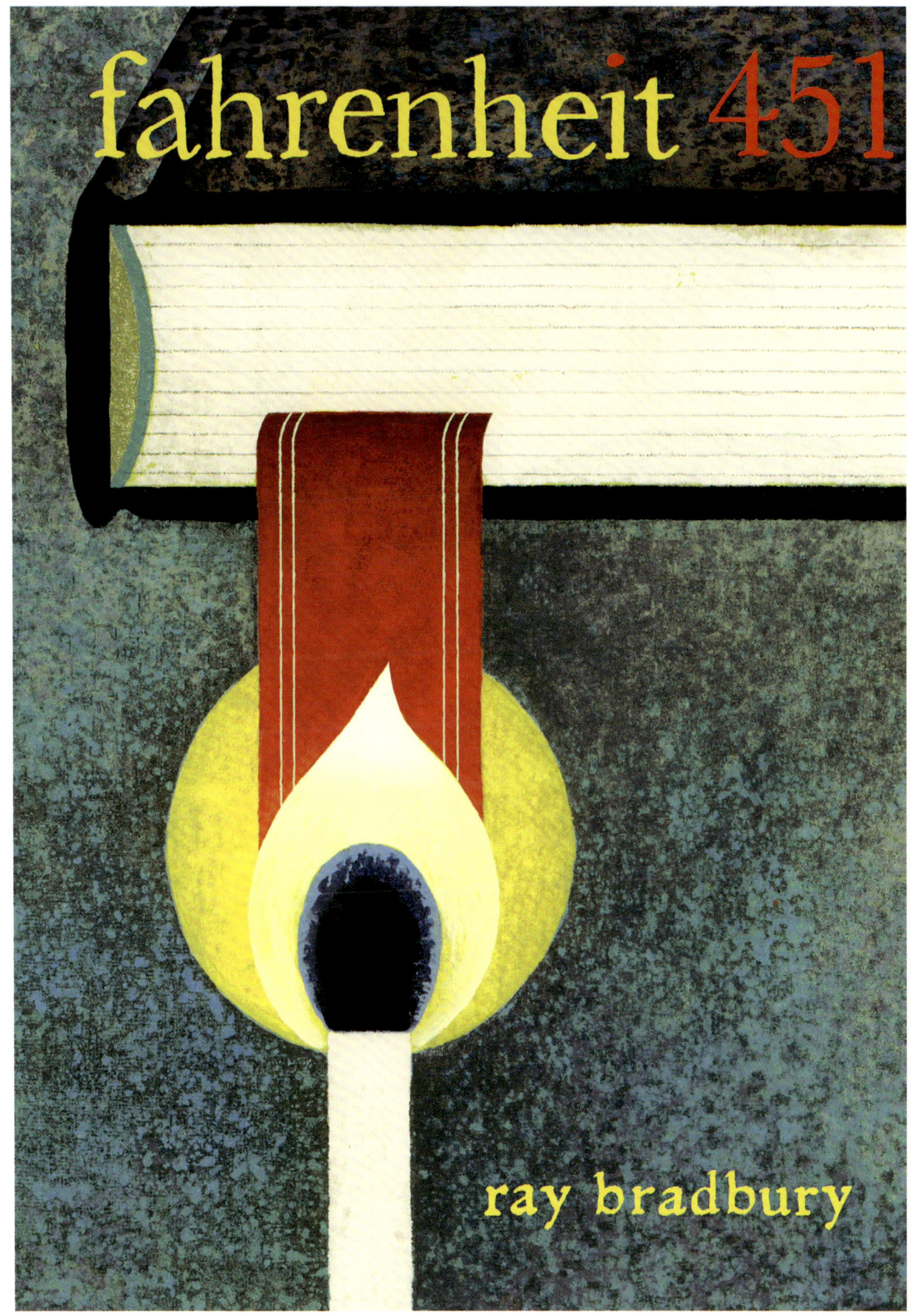

fahrenheit 451
ray bradbury

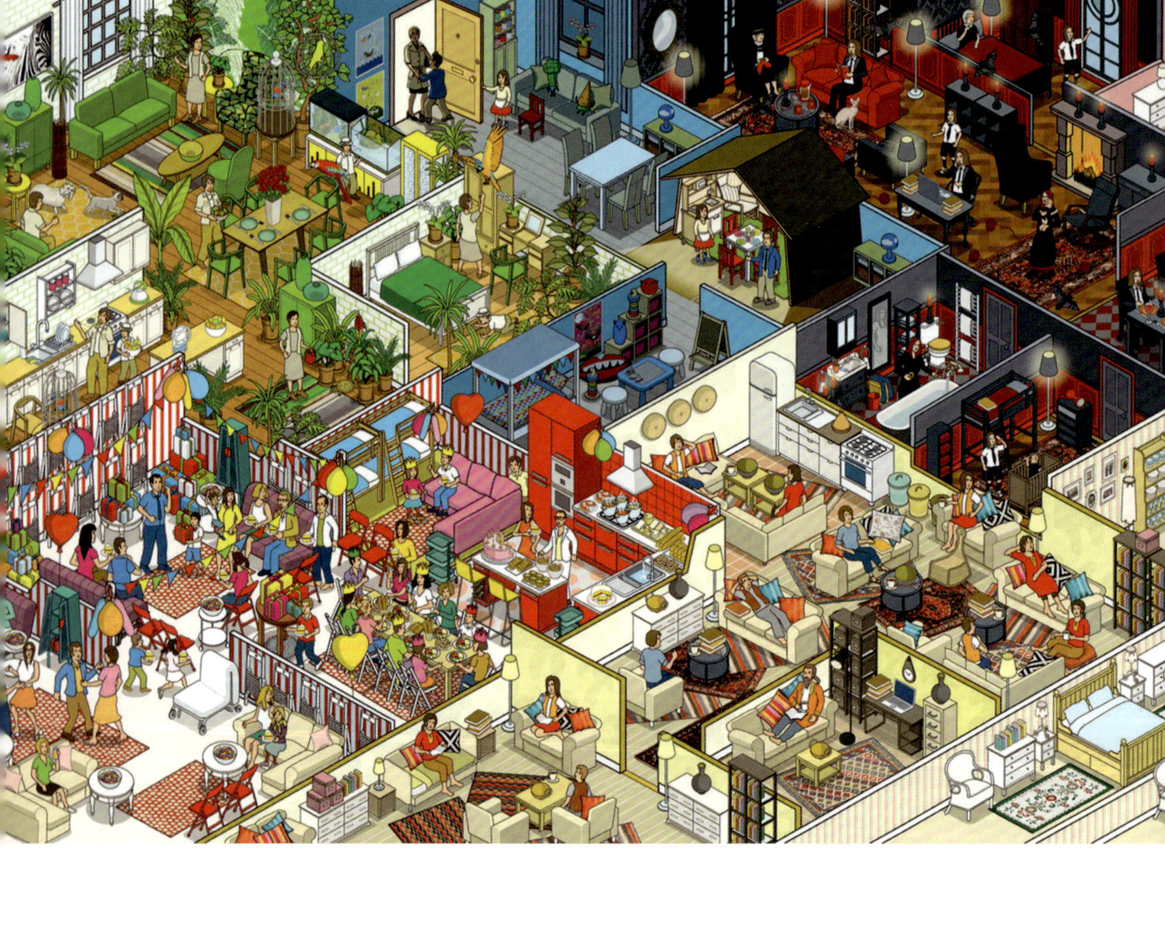



MERIT *Rod Hunt*

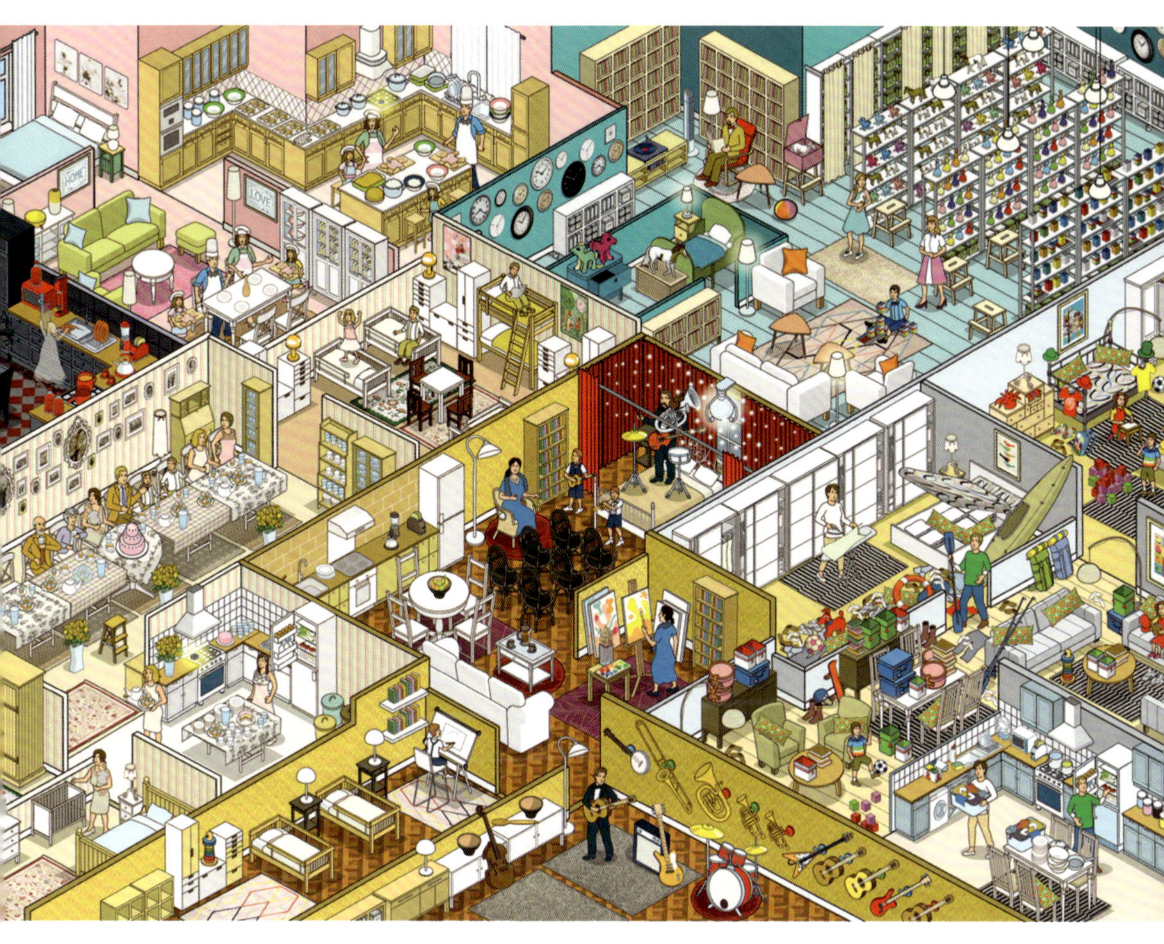

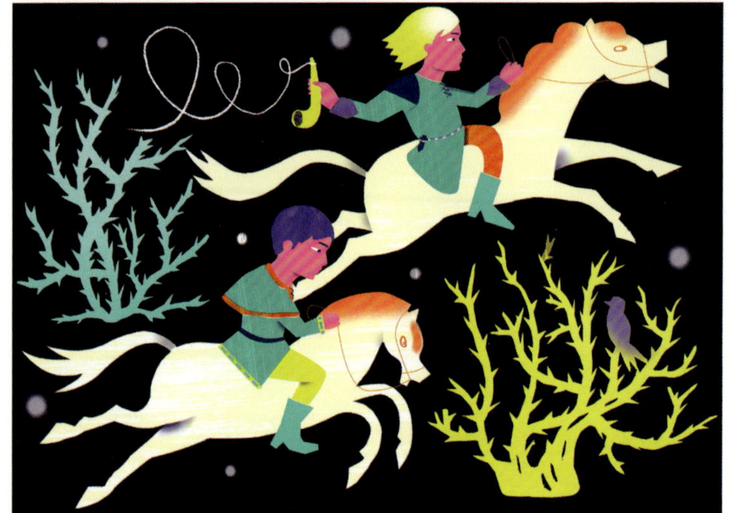

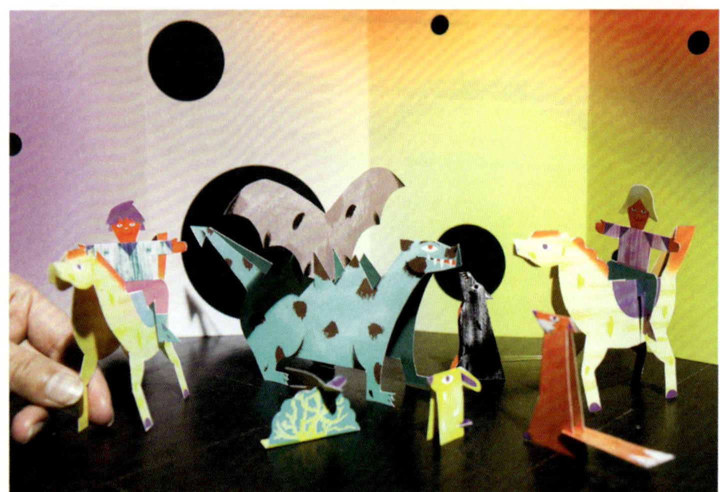

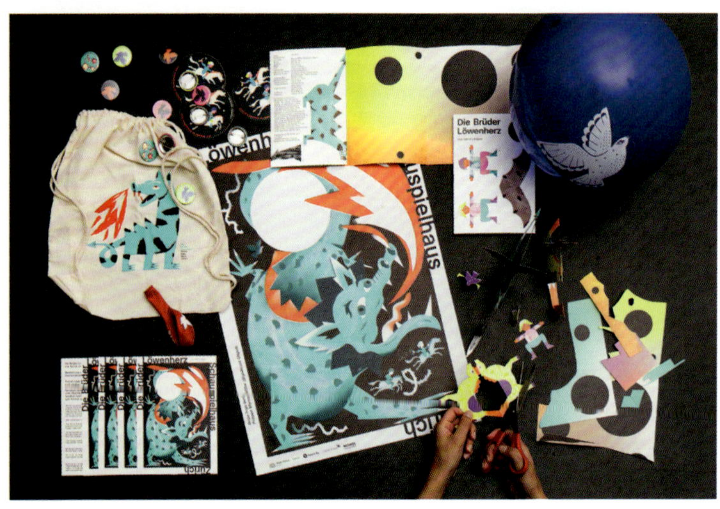

MERIT *Alice Kolb*

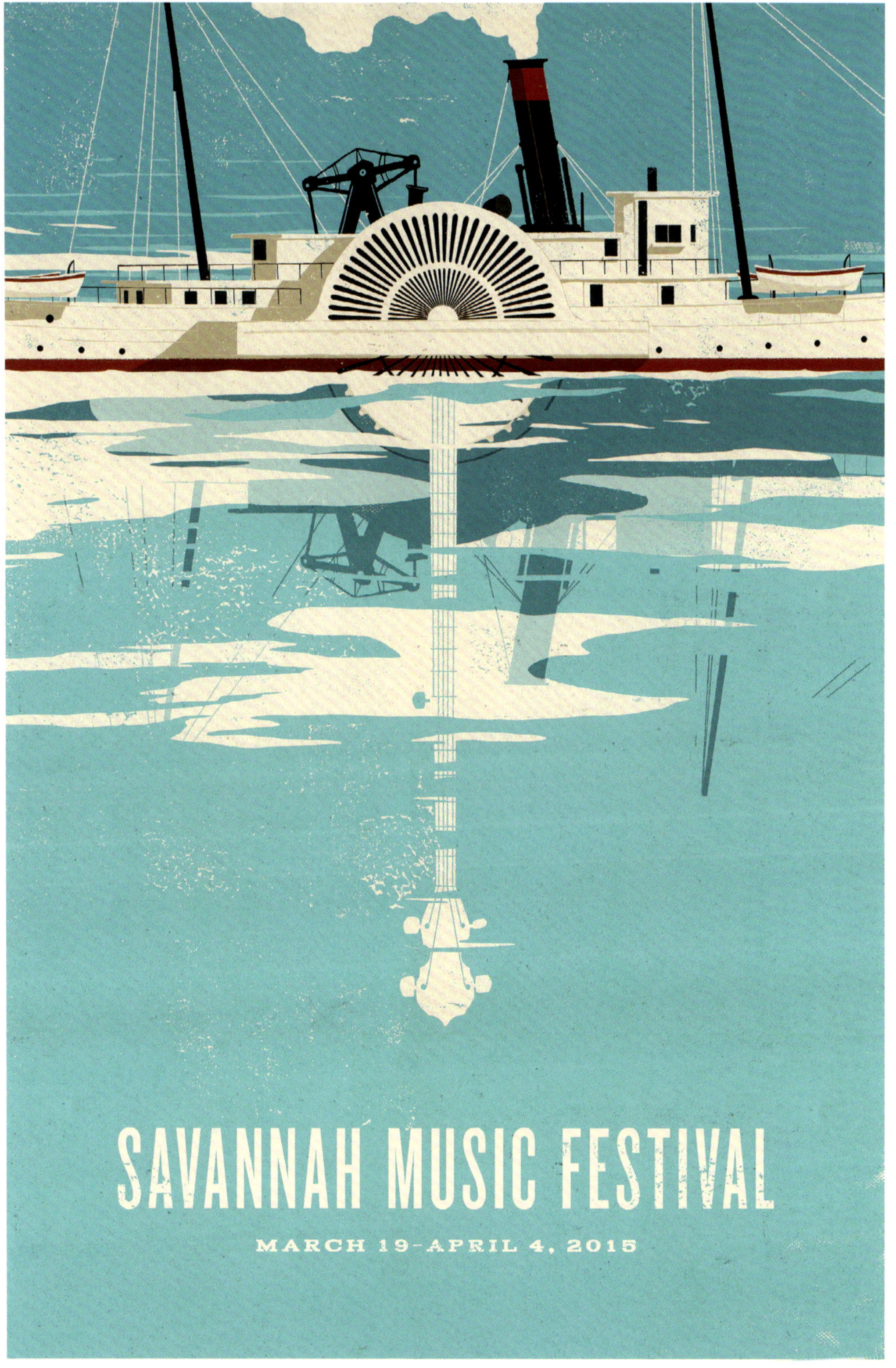


MERIT *Mark Smith*

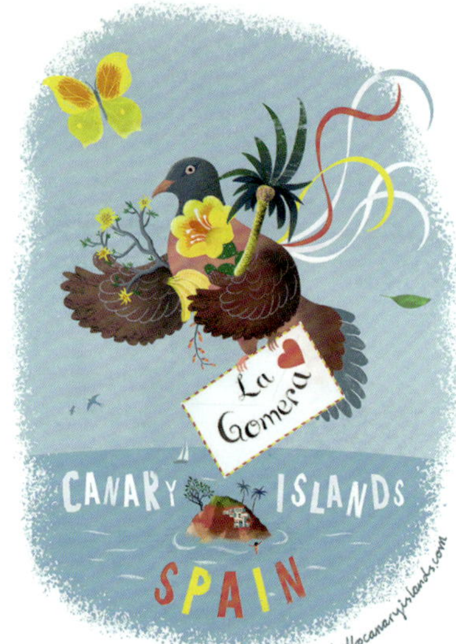



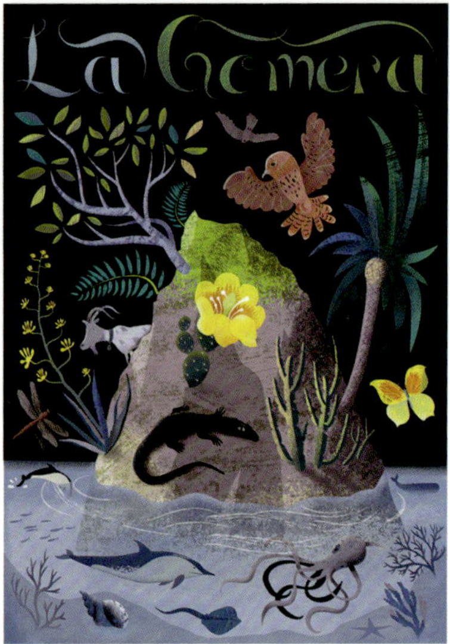



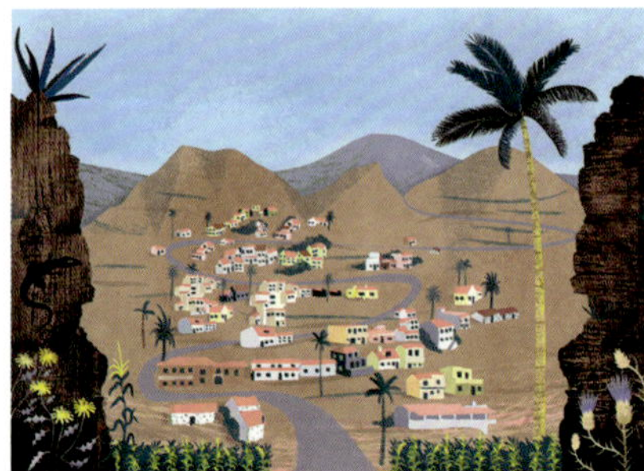

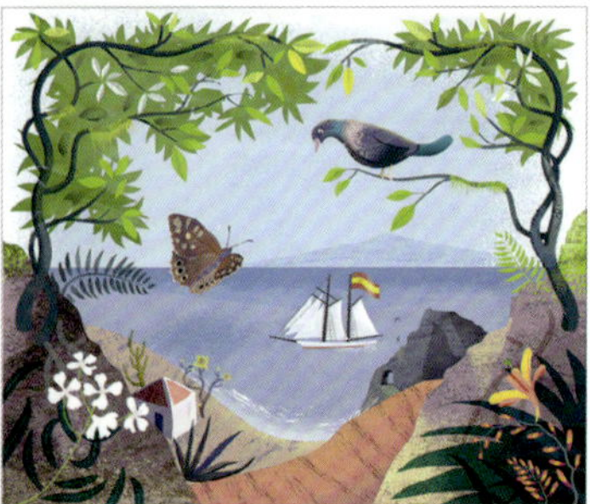

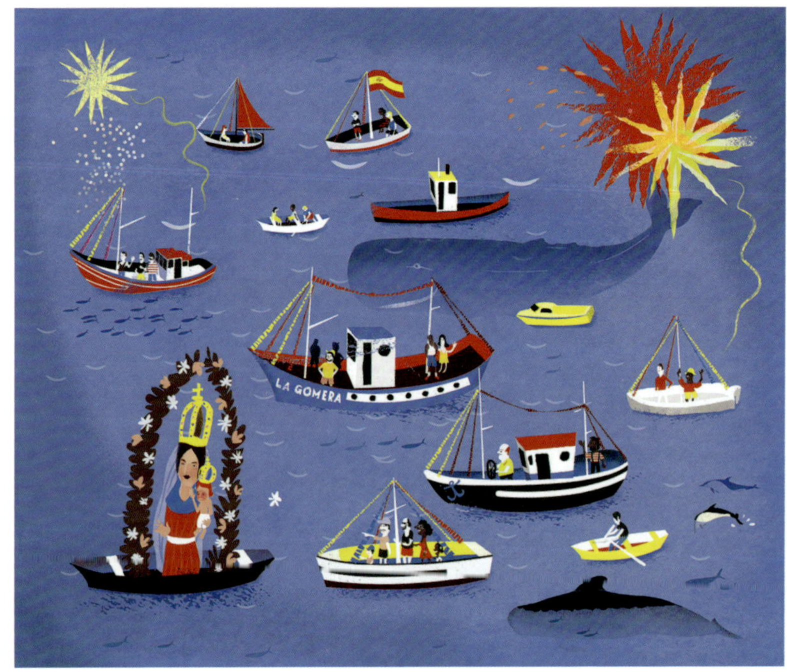



MERIT *Jens Magnusson*

28

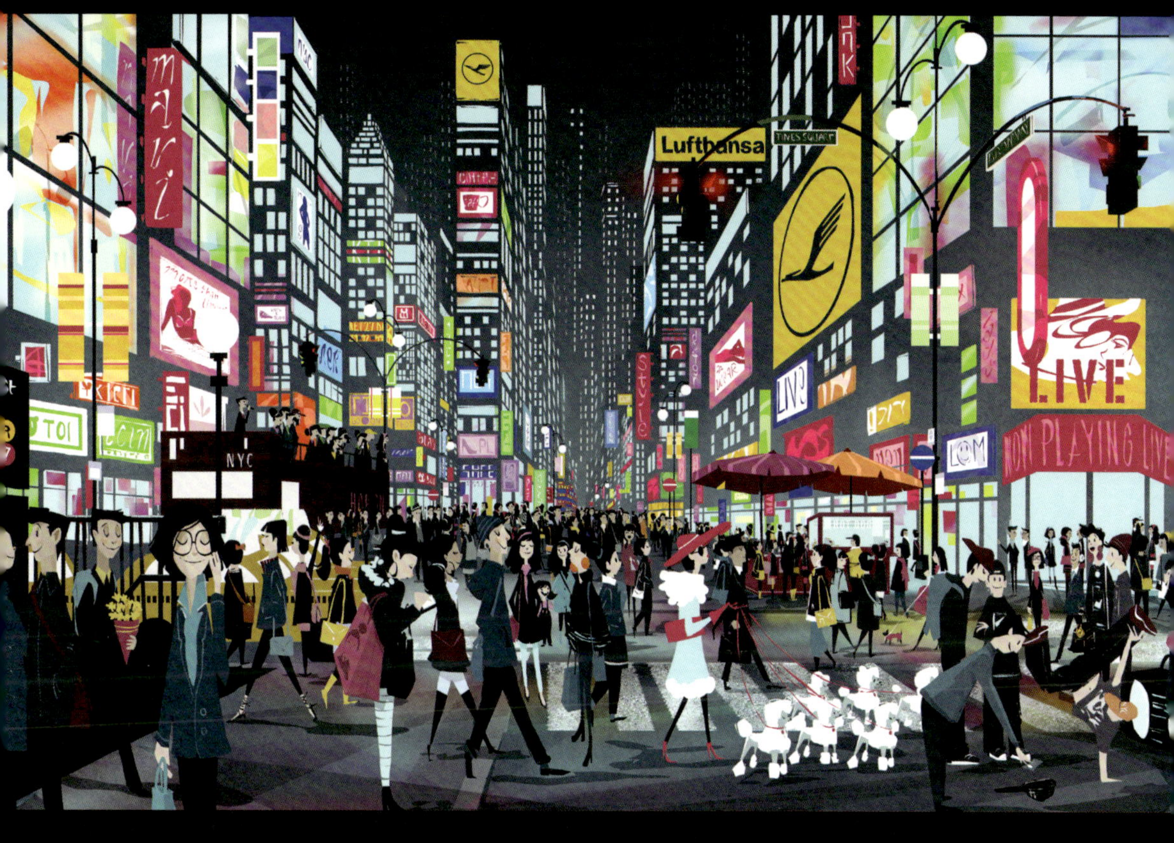



MERIT *Eda Kaban*

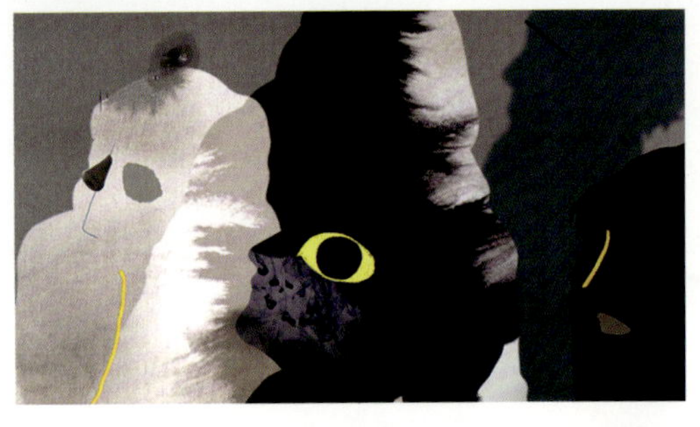
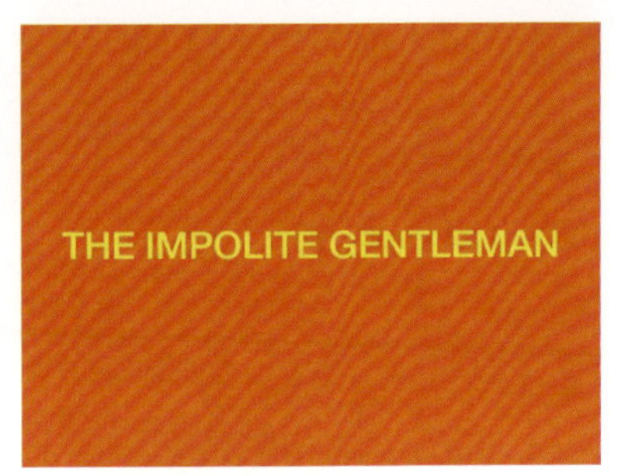



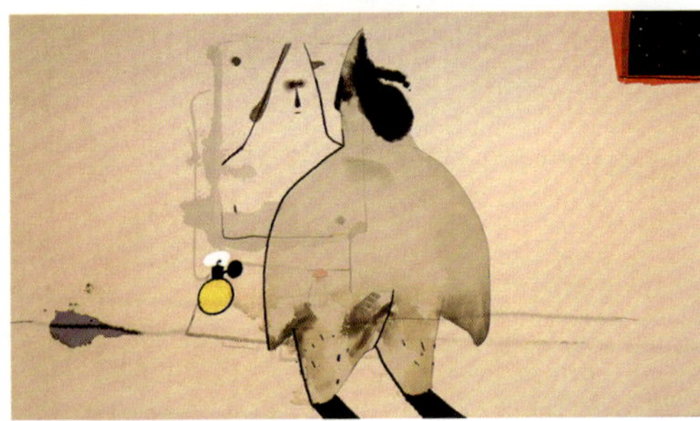
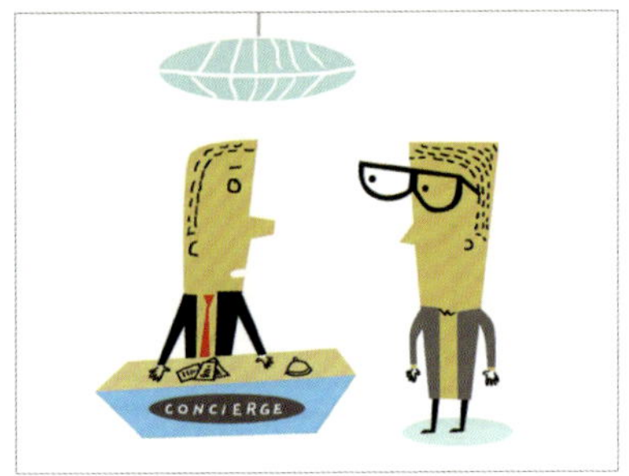



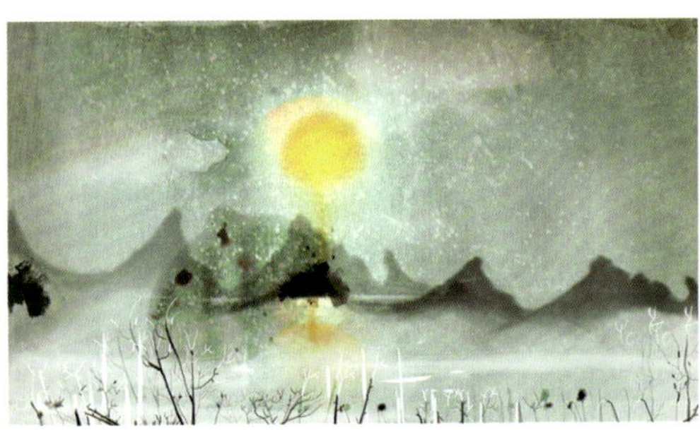
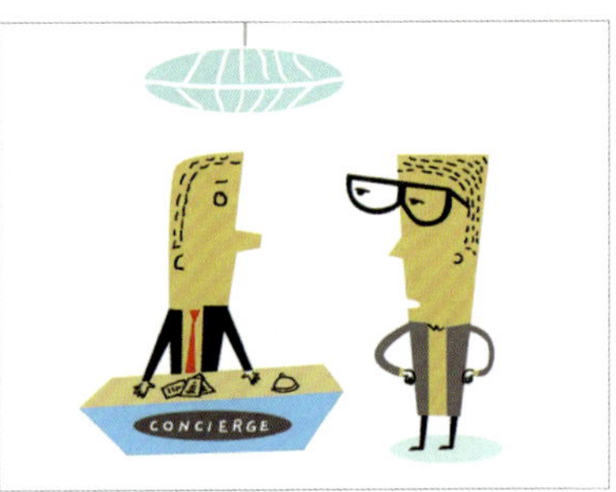



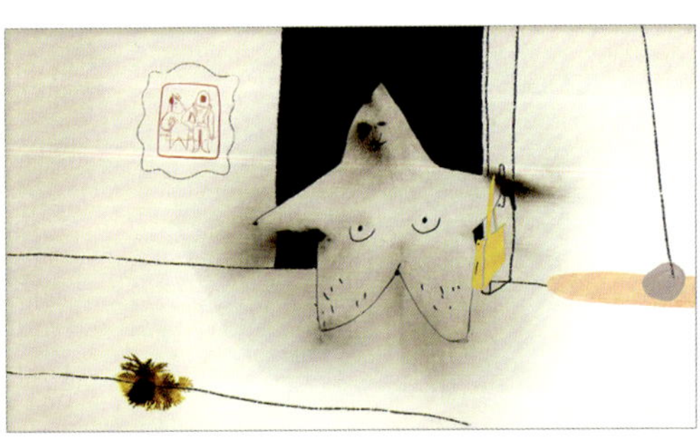
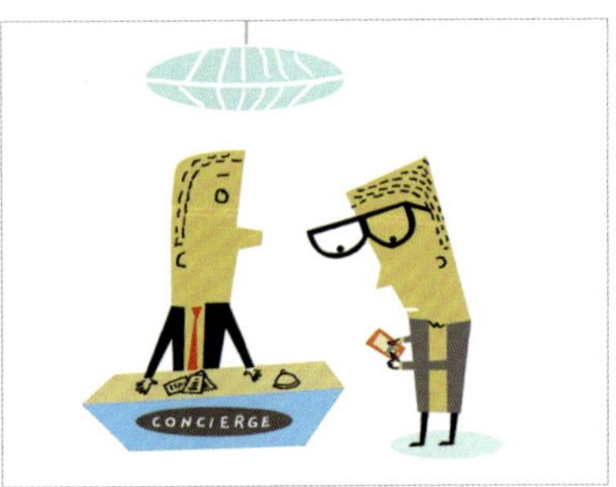



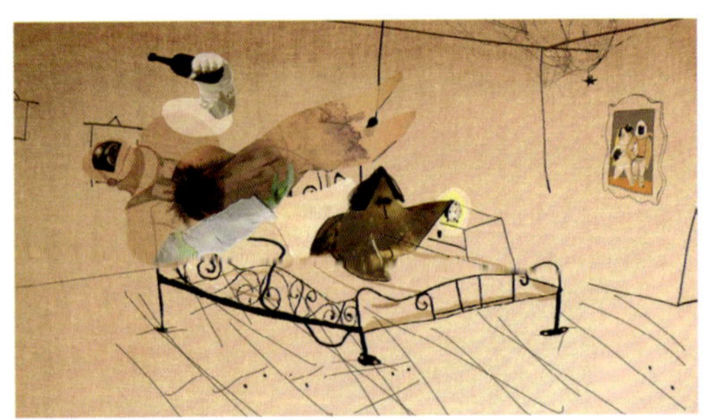
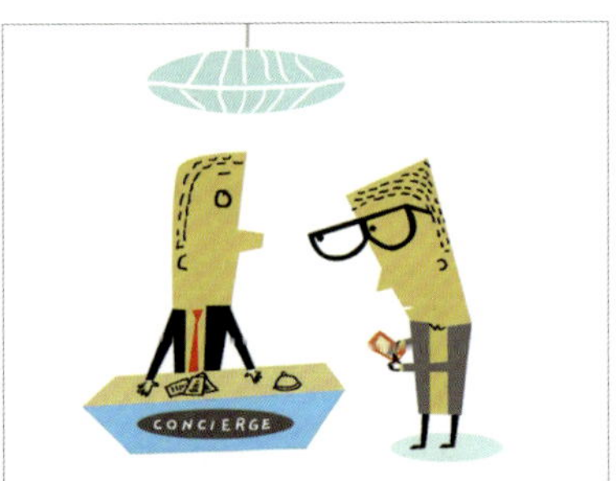



(L) GOLD *Emma Vakarelova*   (R) MERIT *James Yang*

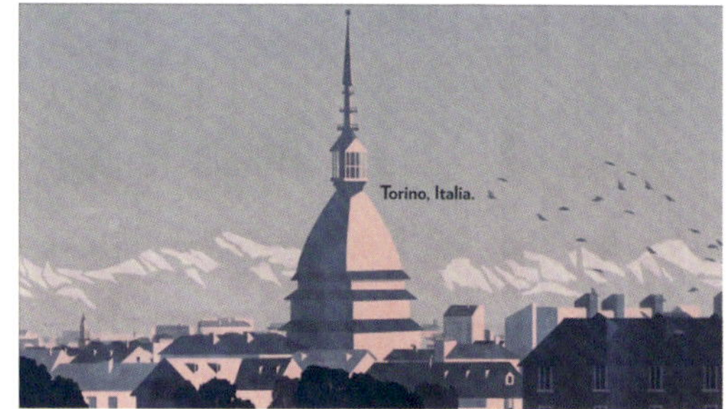


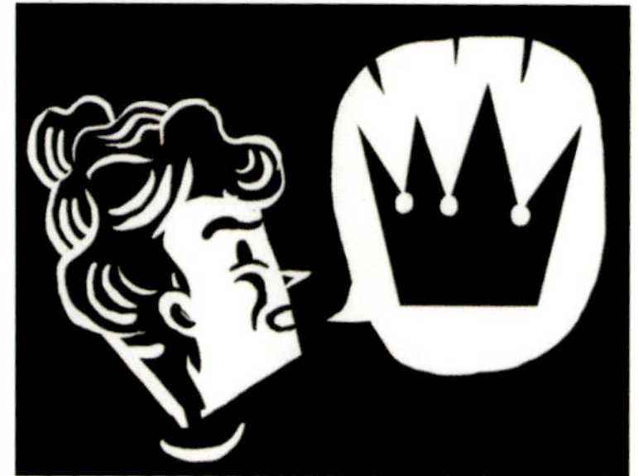

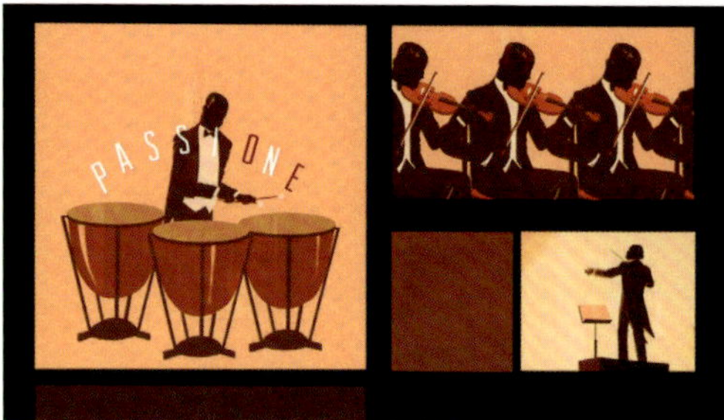


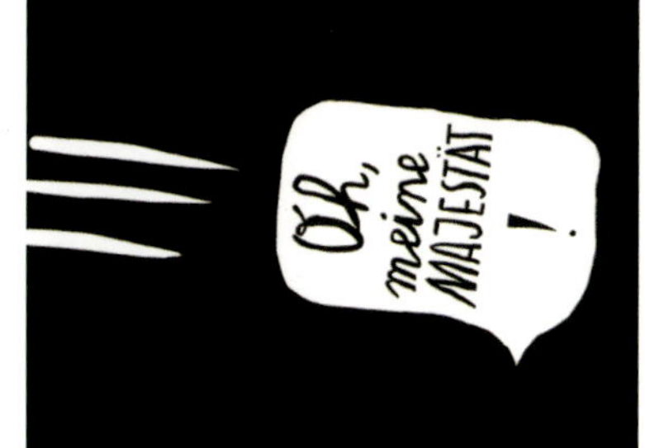


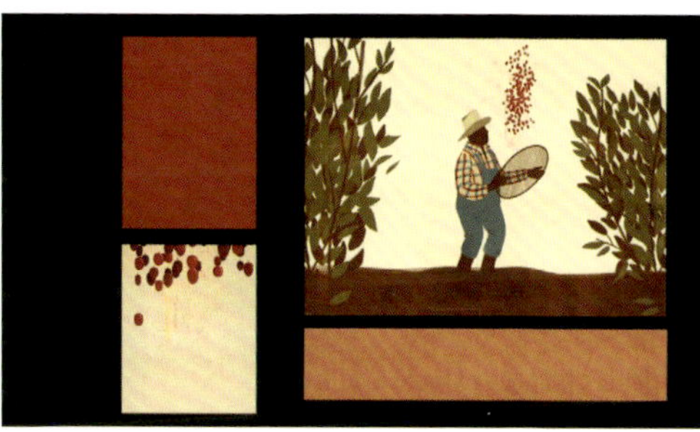

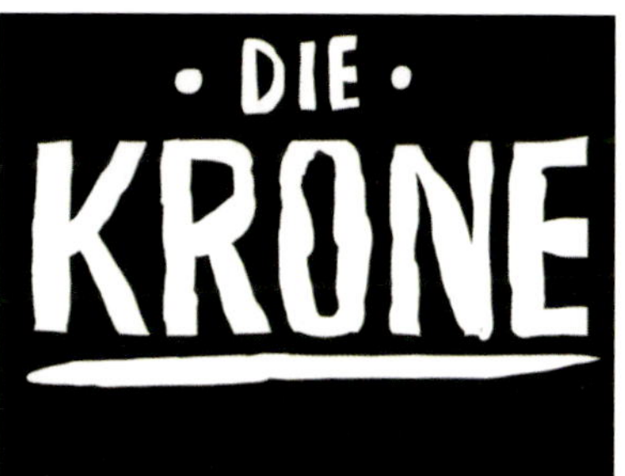


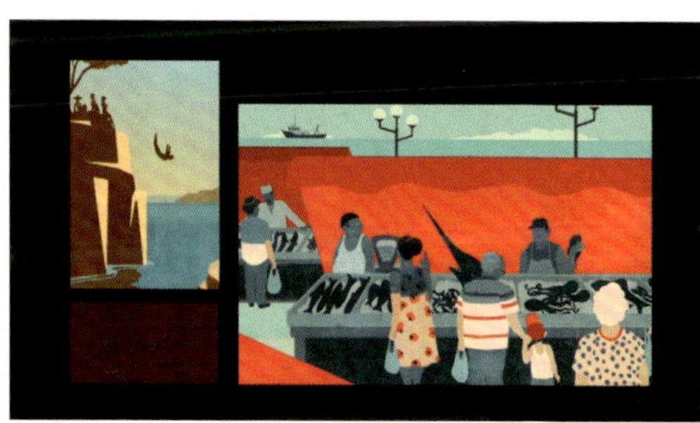

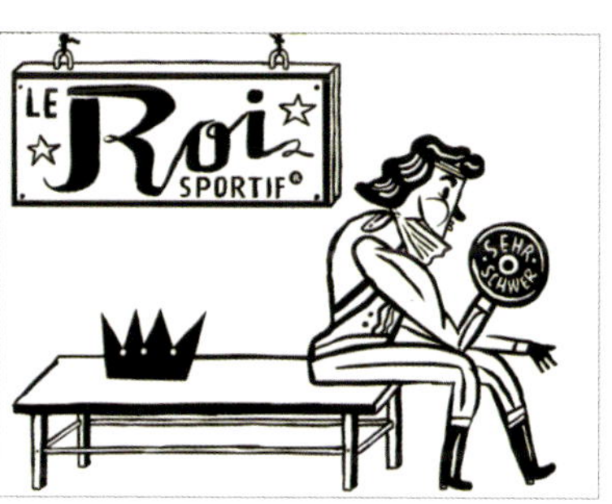


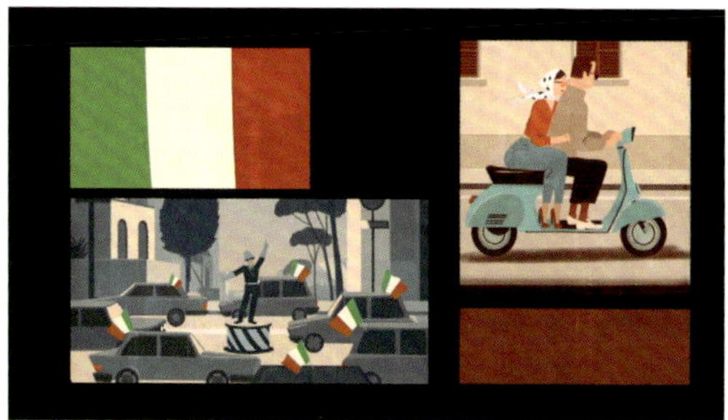

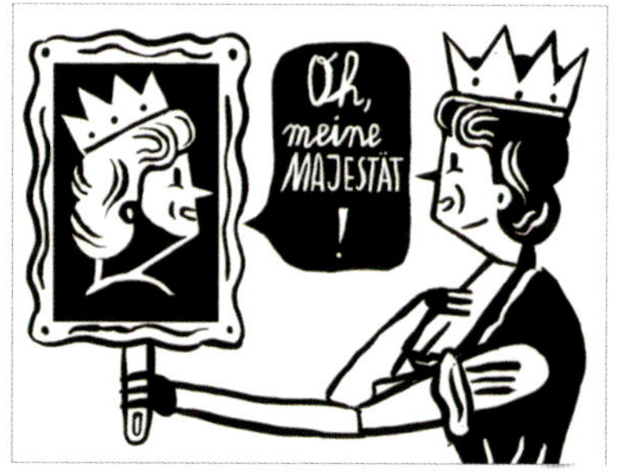


(L) MERIT *Emiliano Ponzi*  (R) MERIT *Jakob Hinrichs*

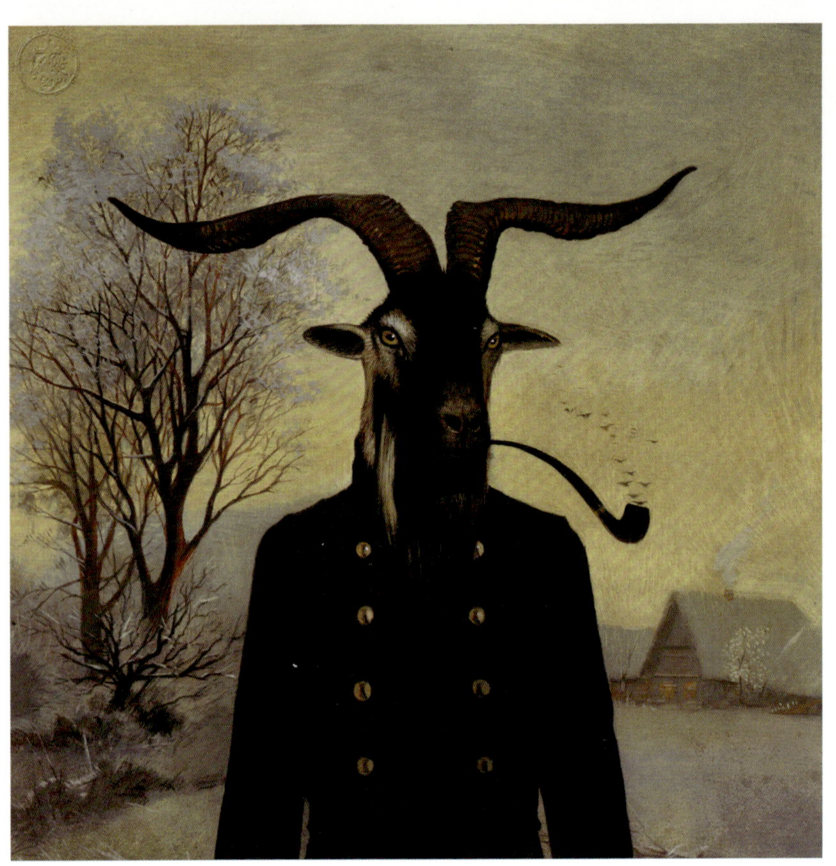

MERIT *Bill Mayer*

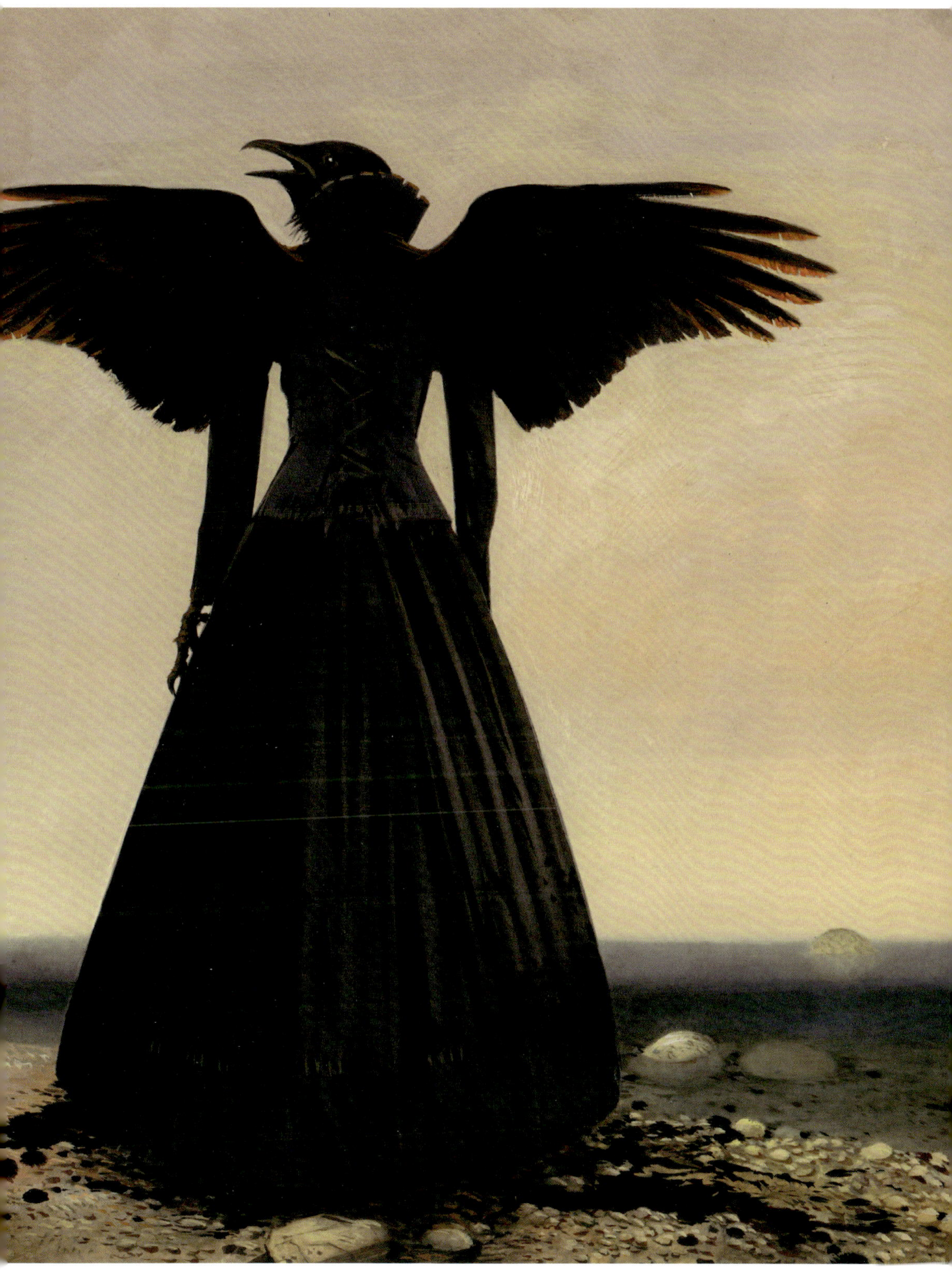





BOOKS

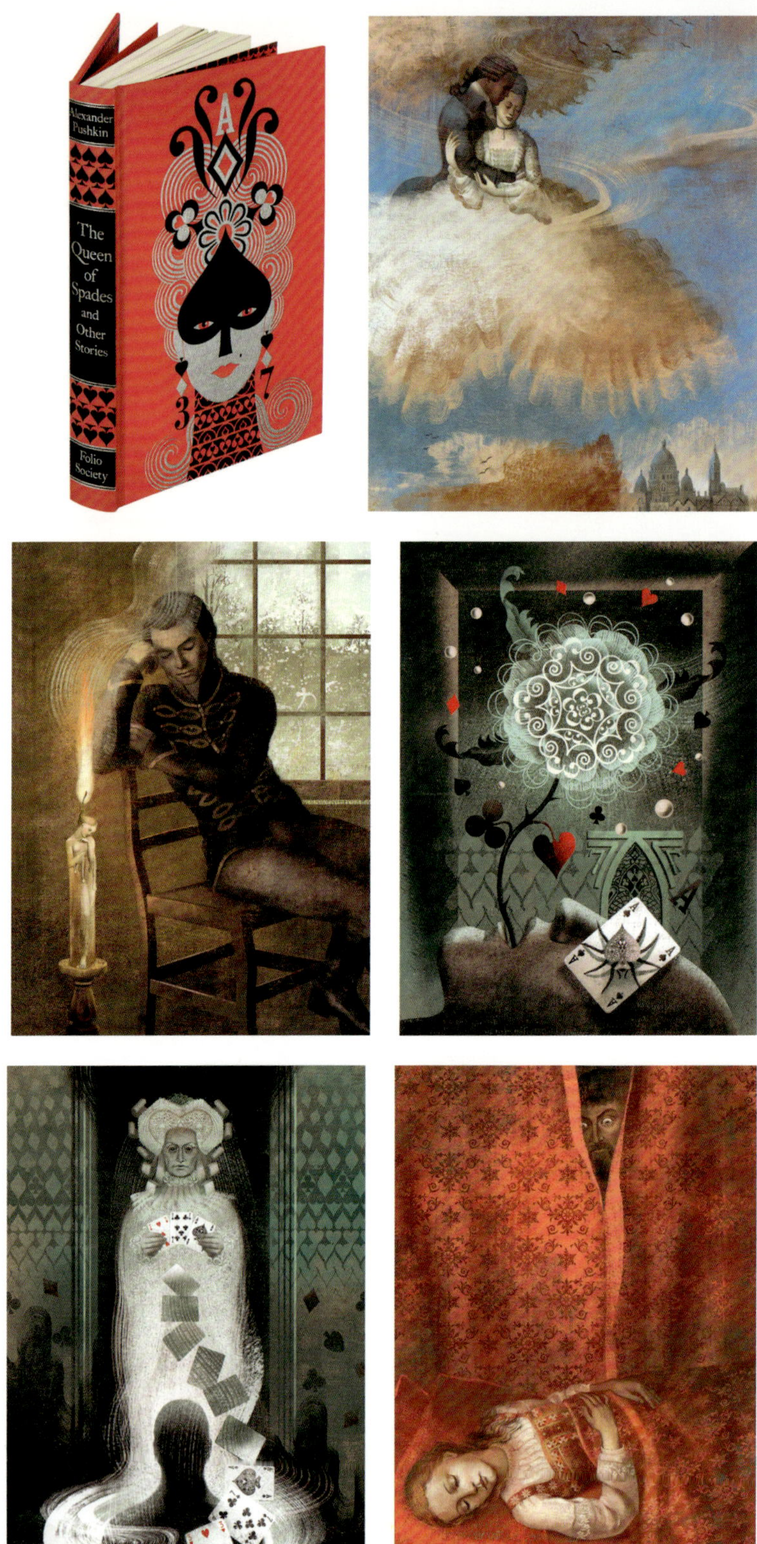



MERIT *Anna and Elena Balbusso*

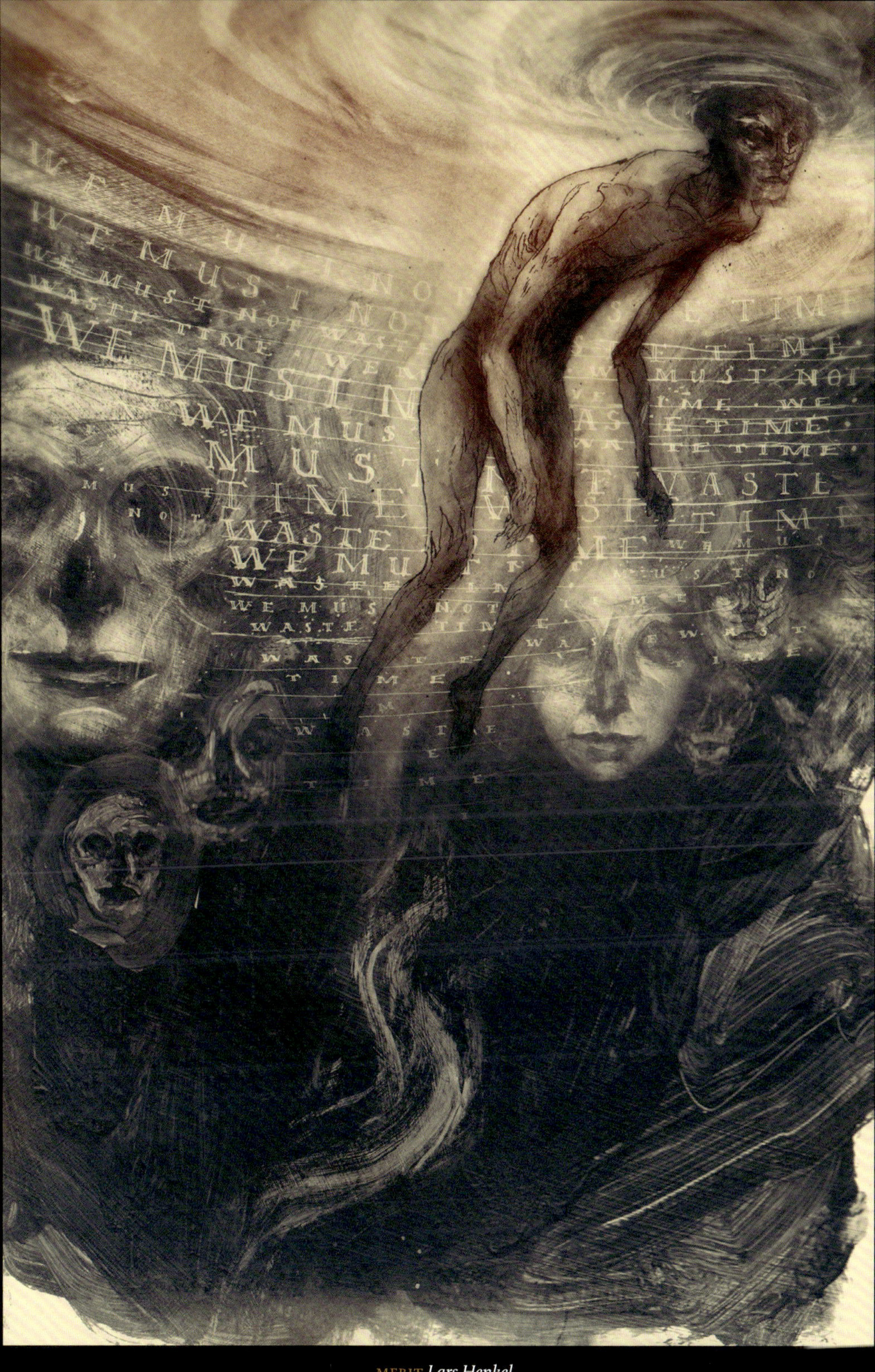

WE MUST NOT WASTE TIME
WE MUST NOT WASTE TIME
WE MUST NOT WASTE TIME
WE MUST NOT WASTE TIME
WE MUST NOT WASTE TIME

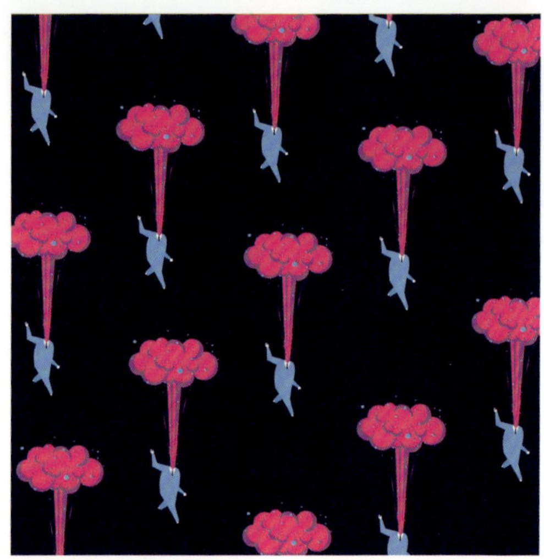

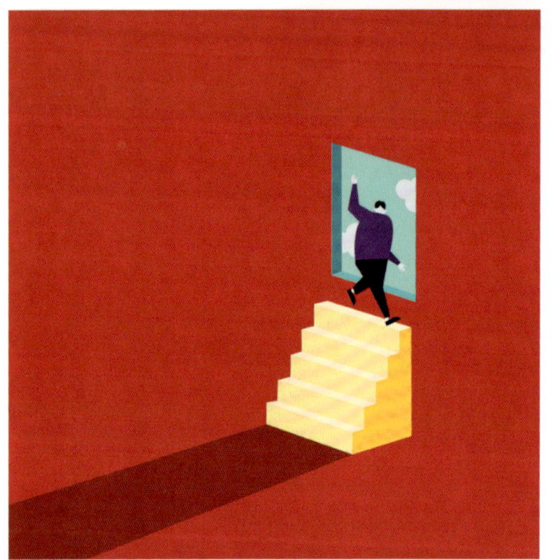

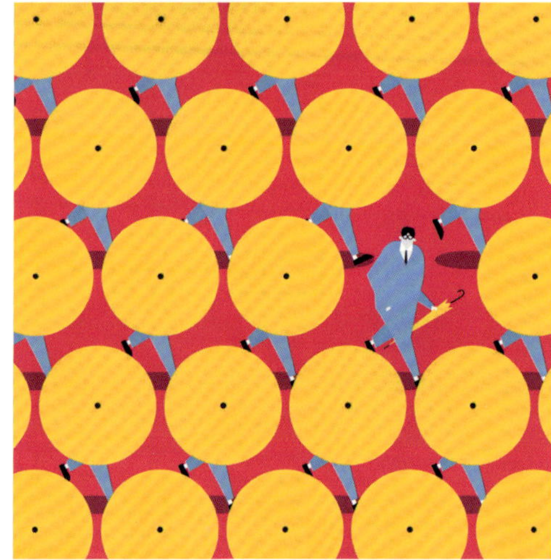

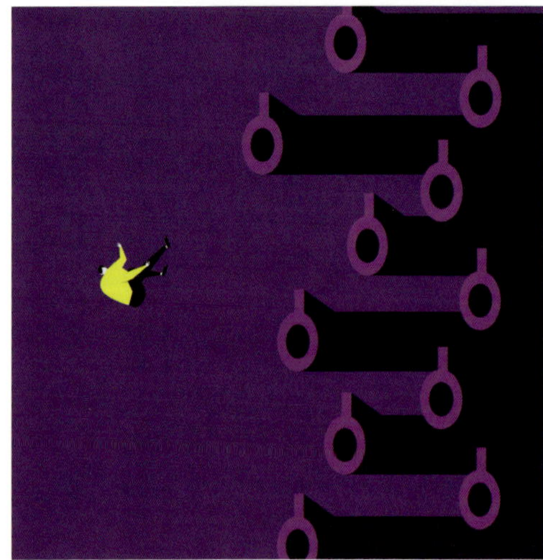

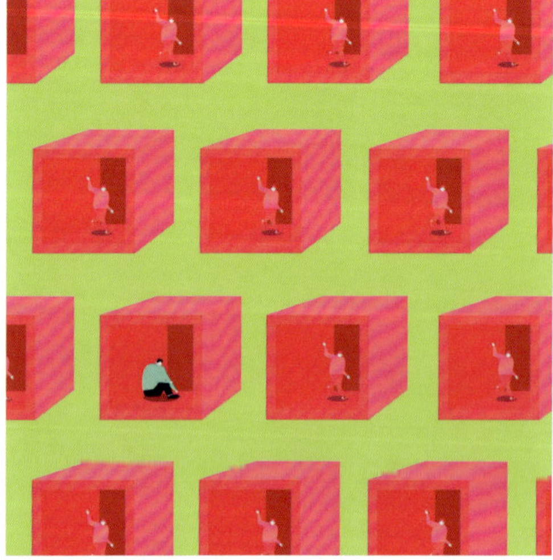

MERIT *Jongik Park*

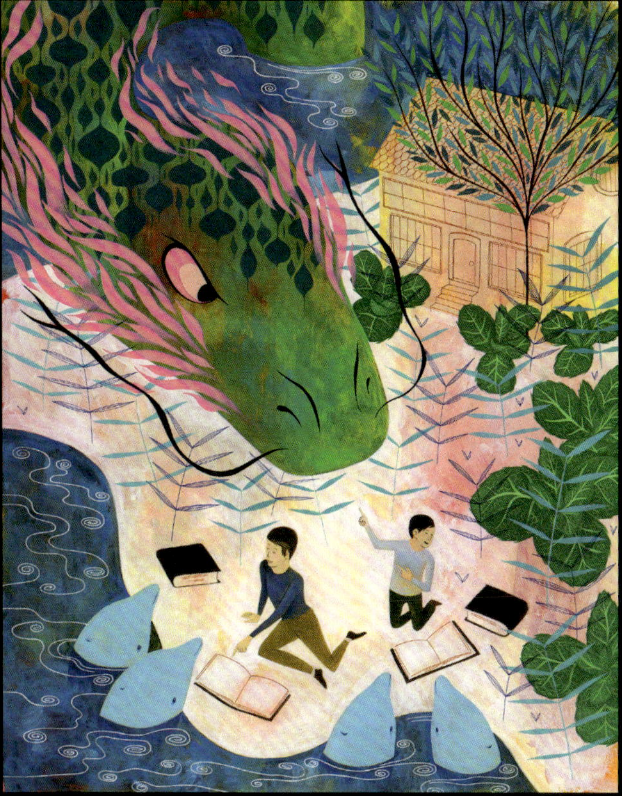

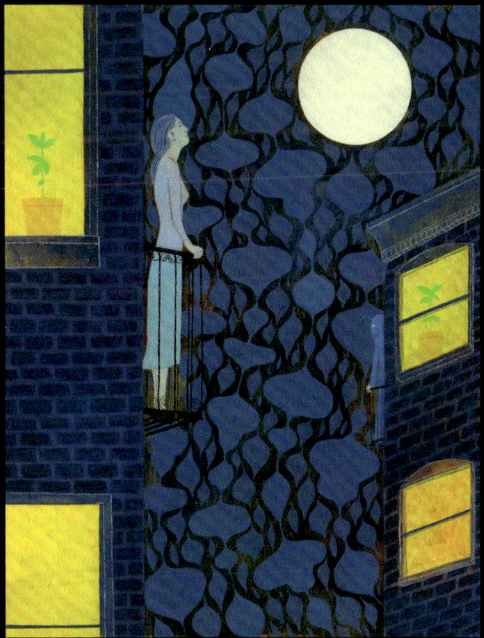

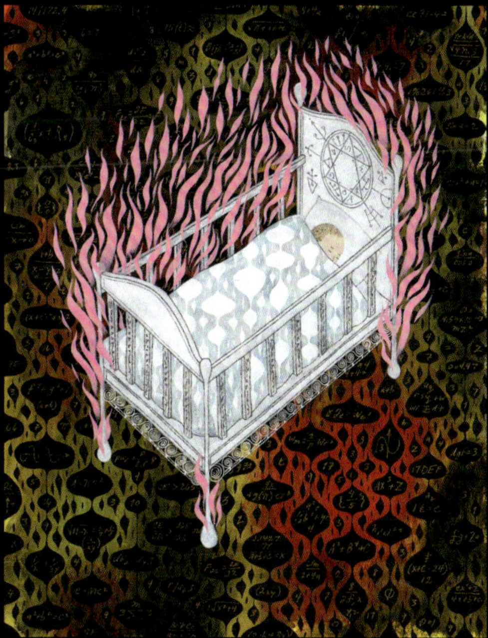

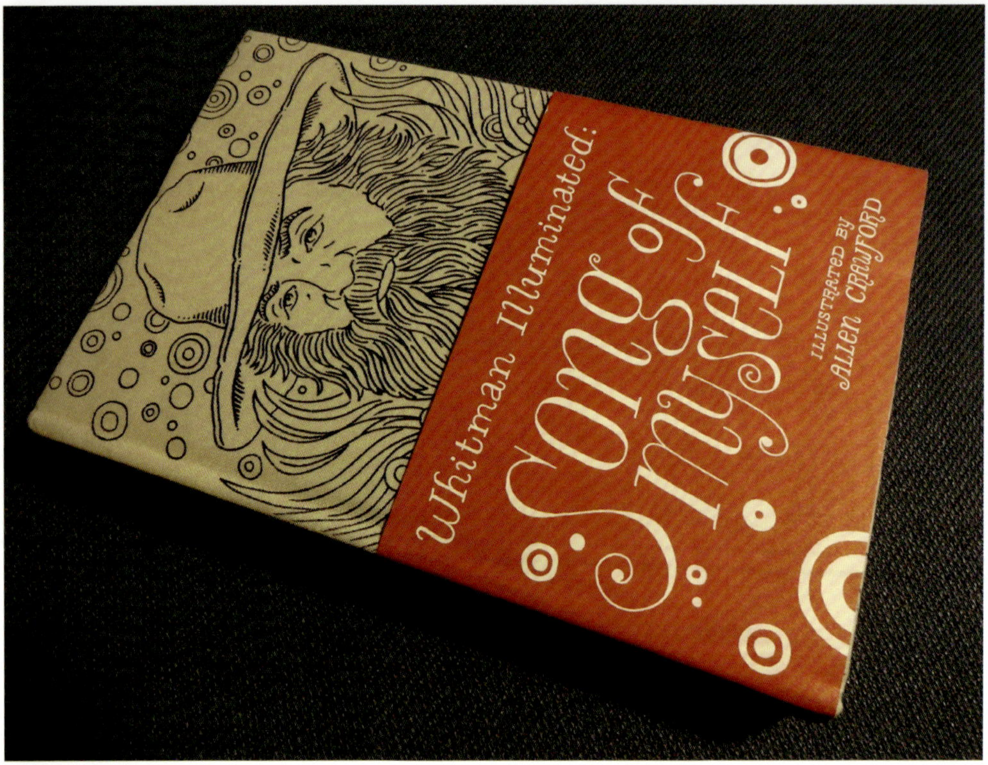

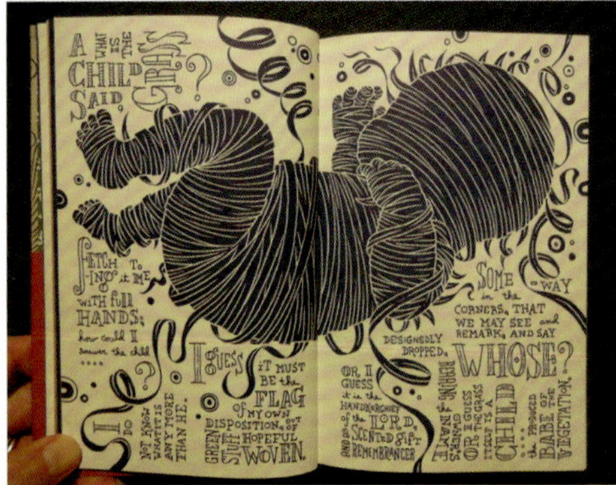

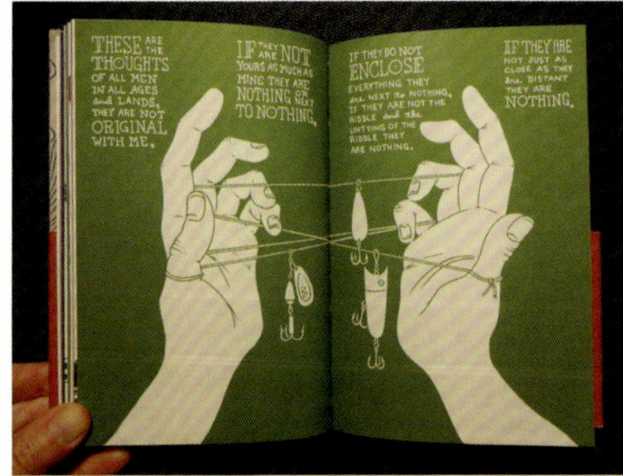

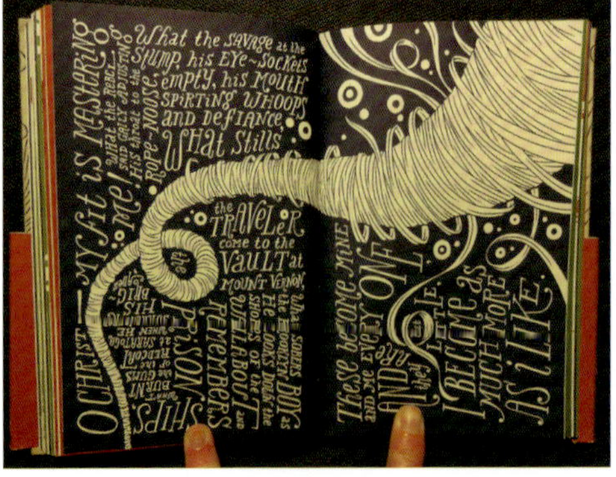

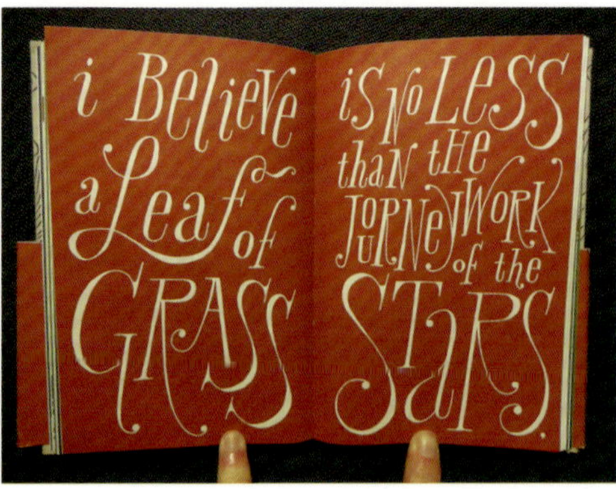



BEST OF SHOW *Allen Crawford*

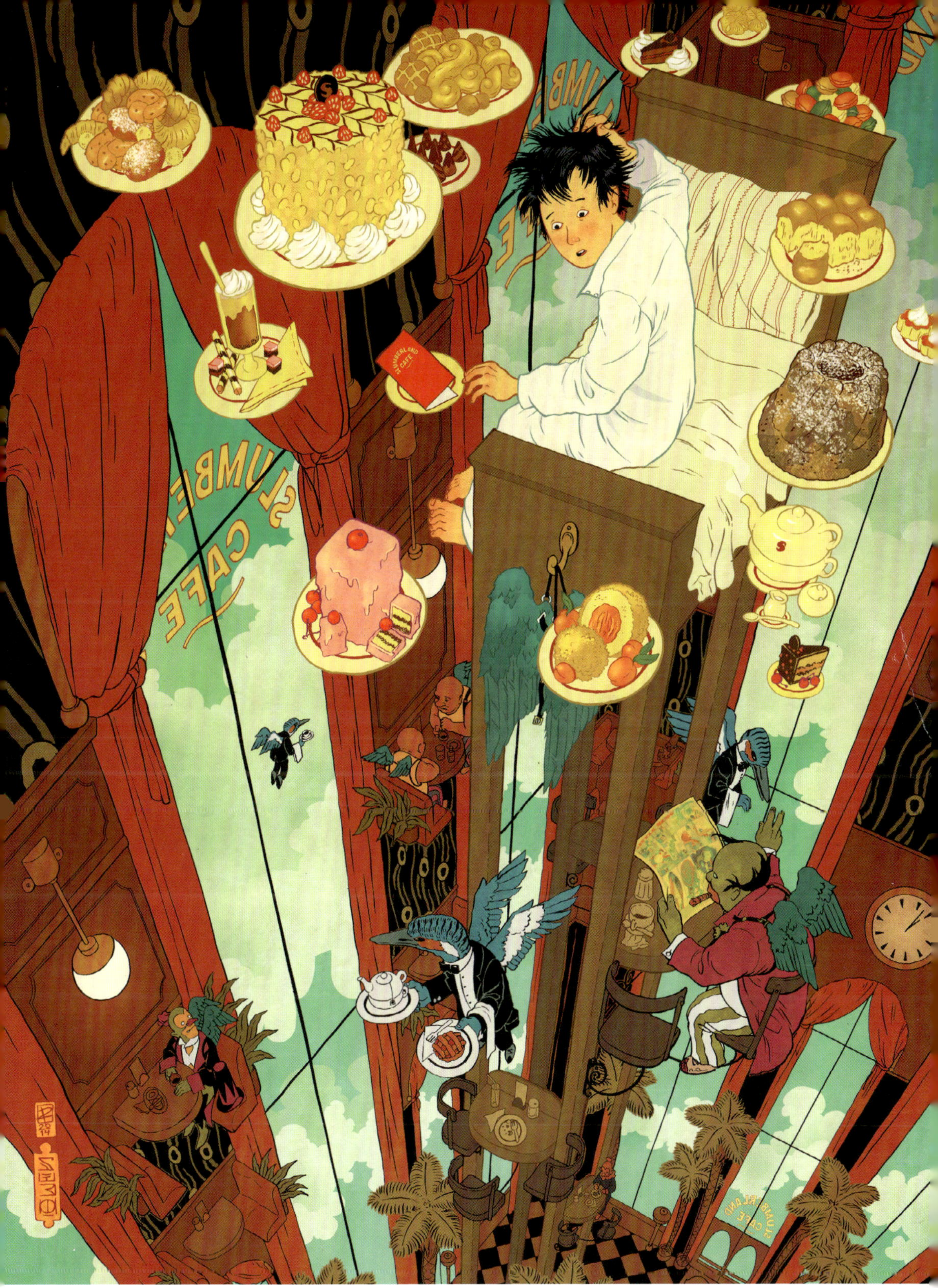

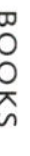

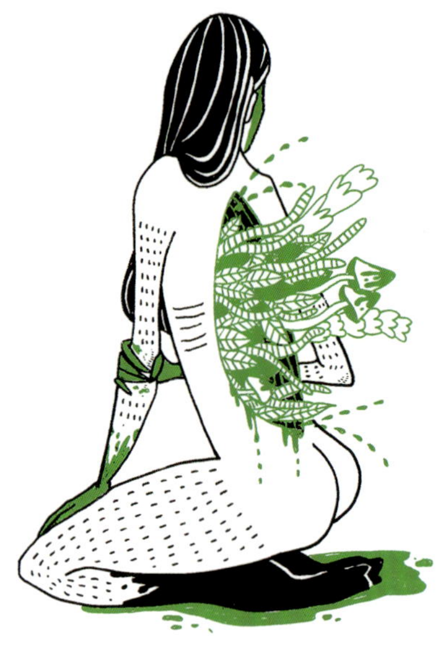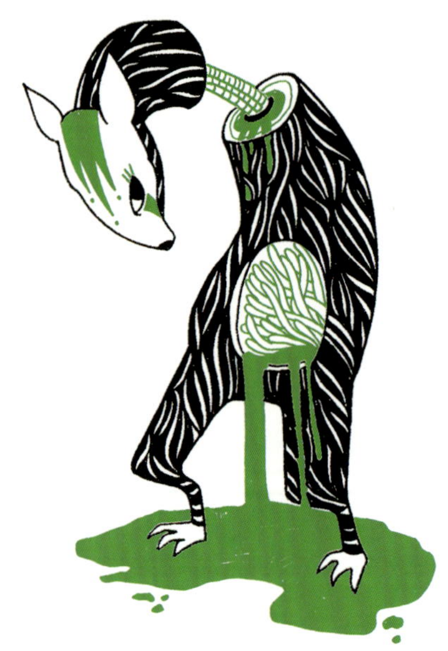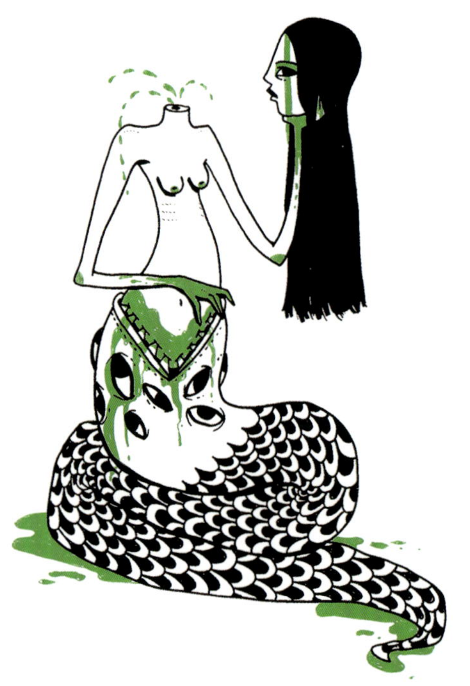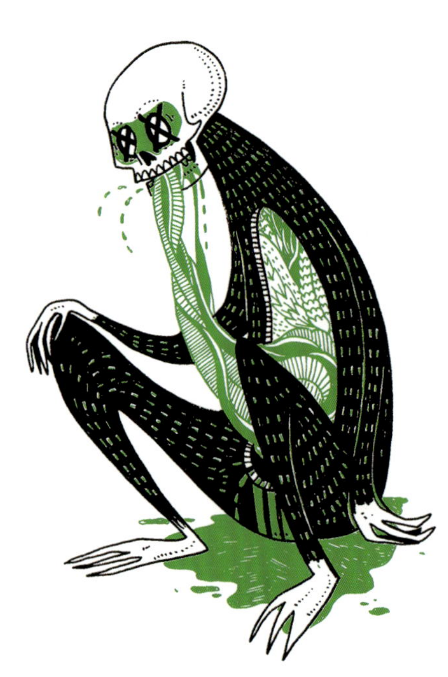



MERIT *Cassie Hart Kelly*

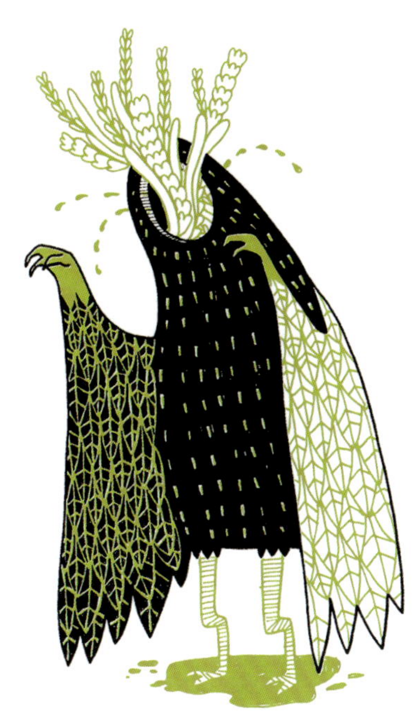

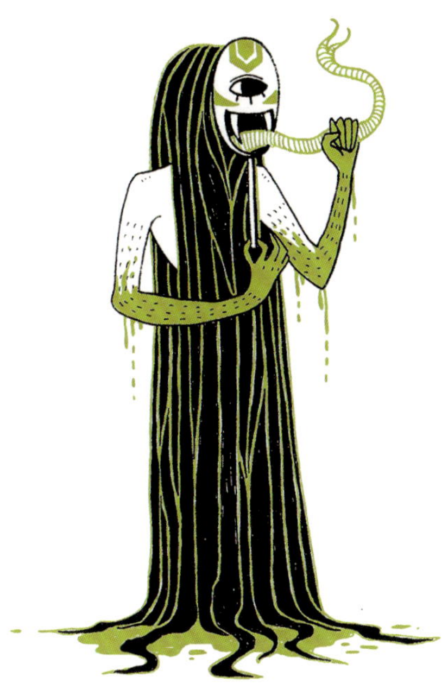

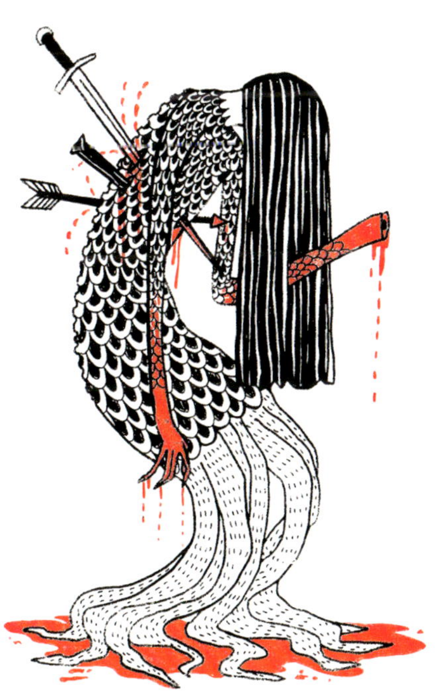

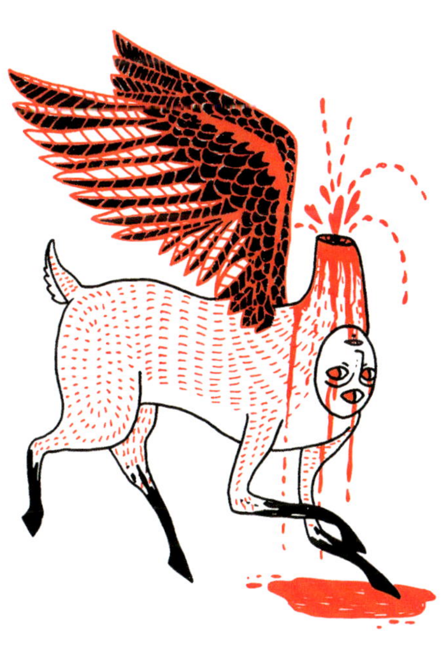

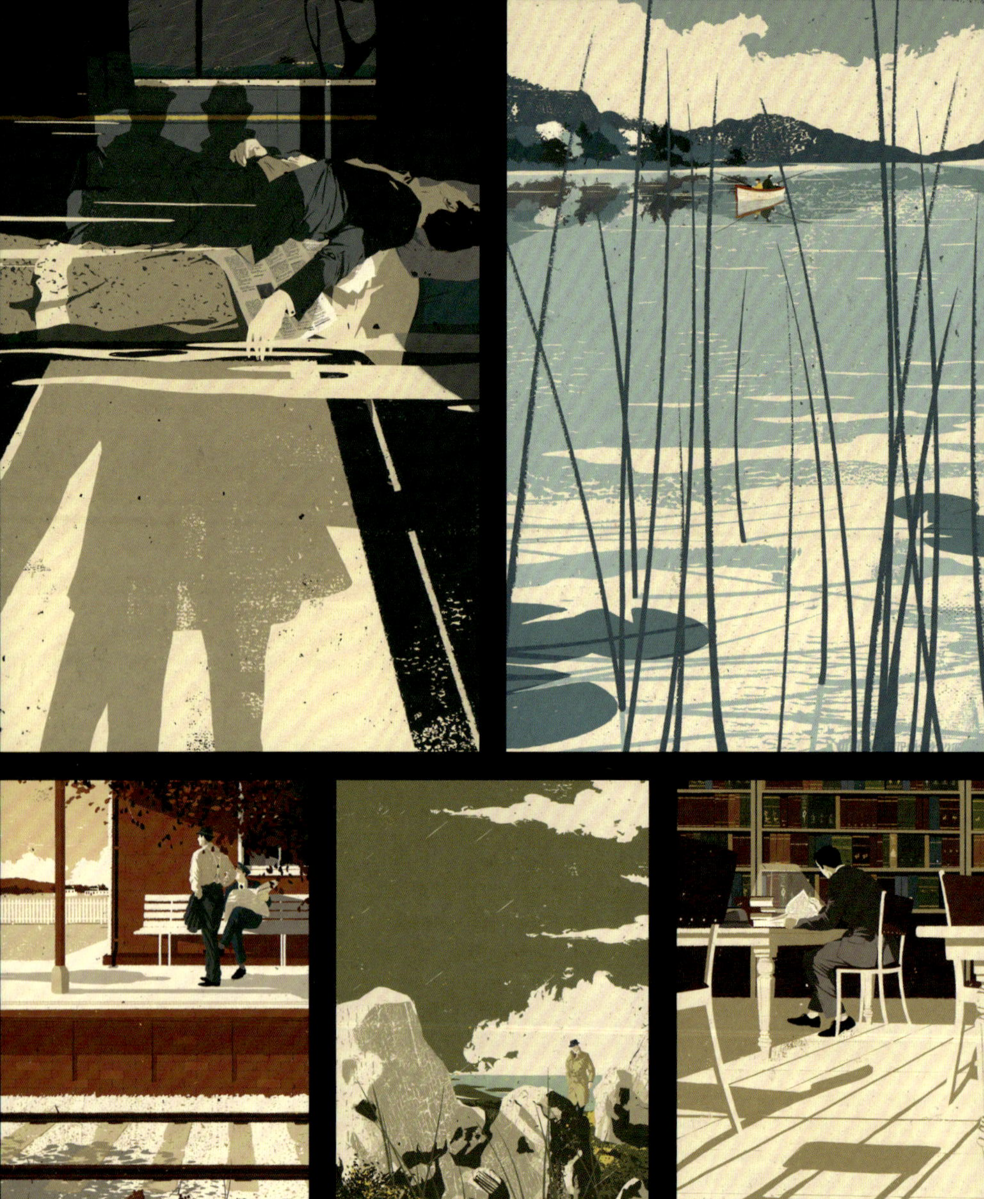

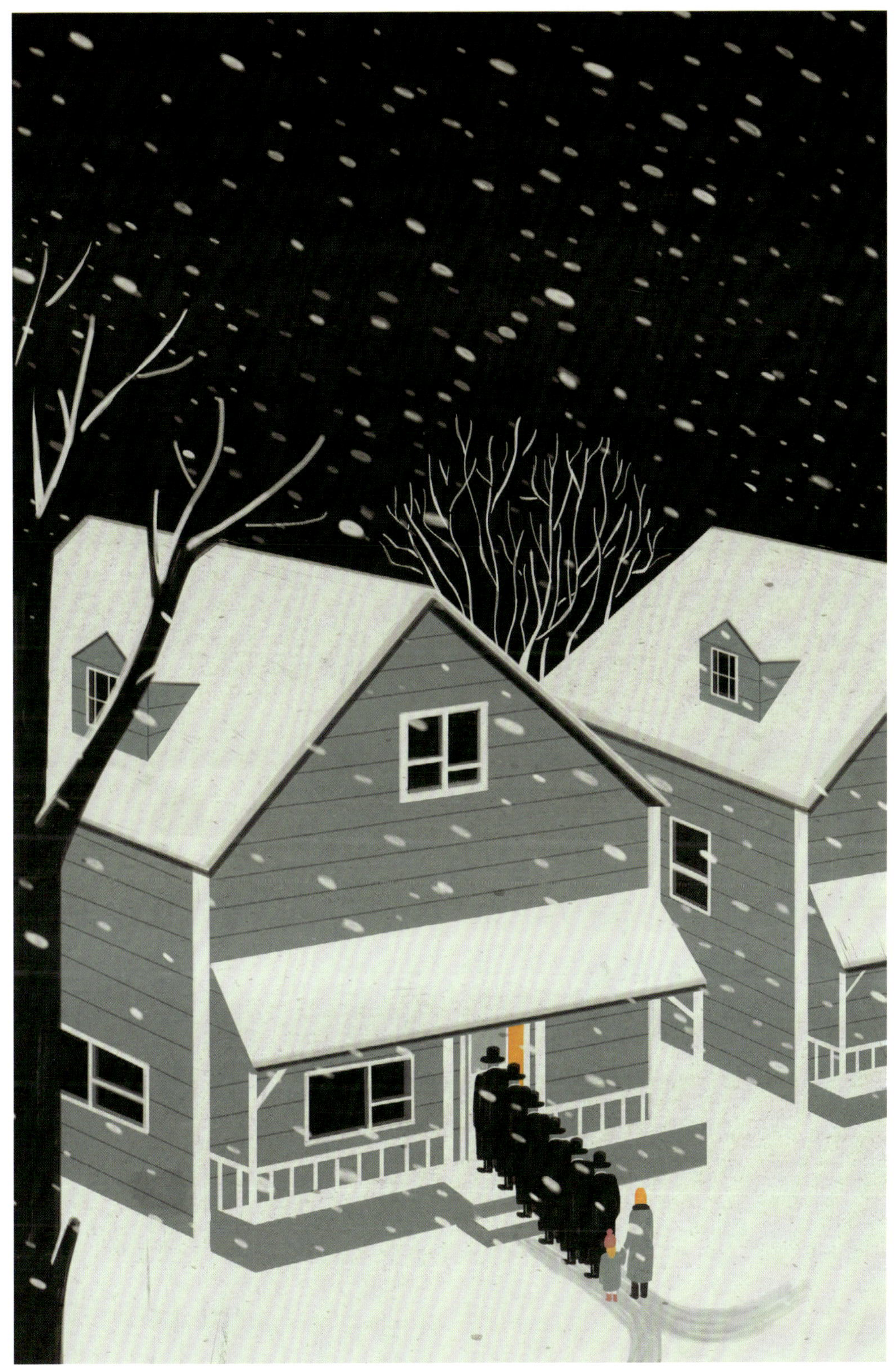



MERIT Emiliano Ponzi

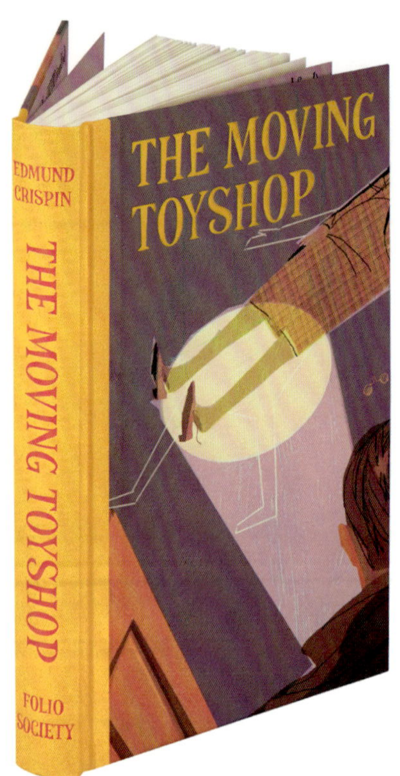
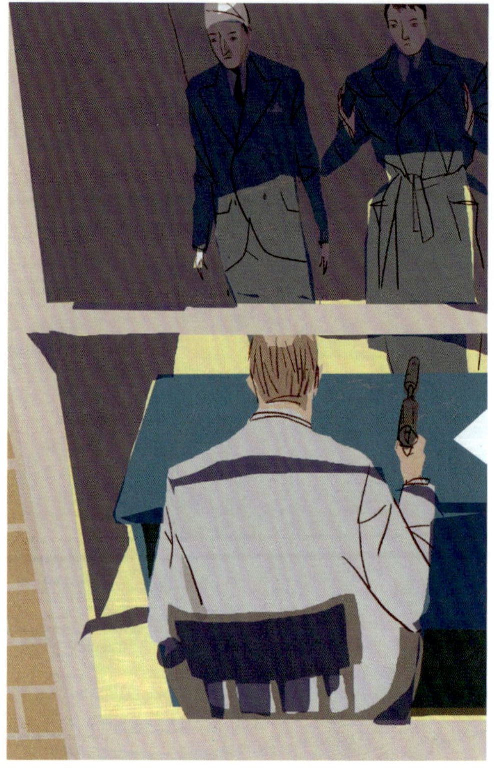
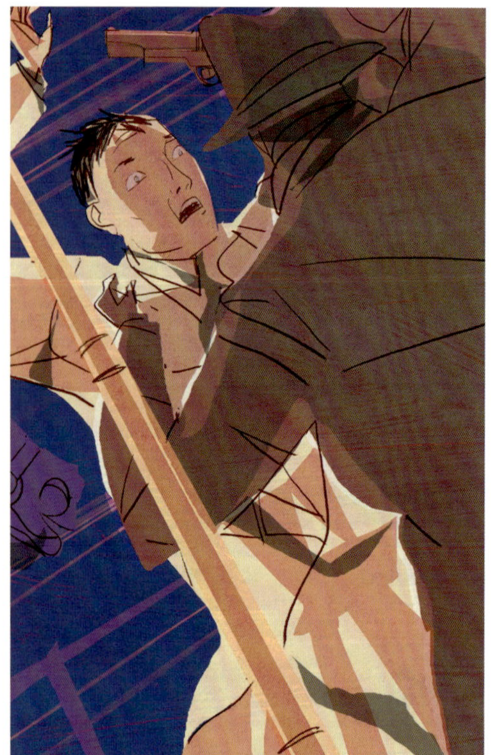
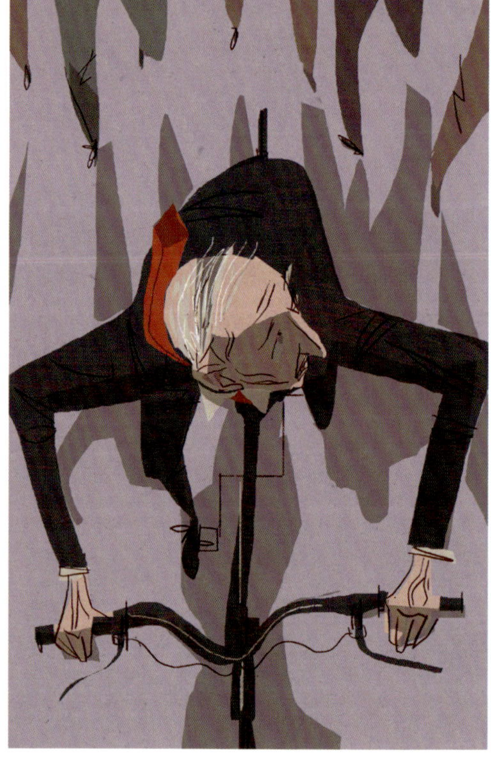



MERIT *A. Richard Allen*

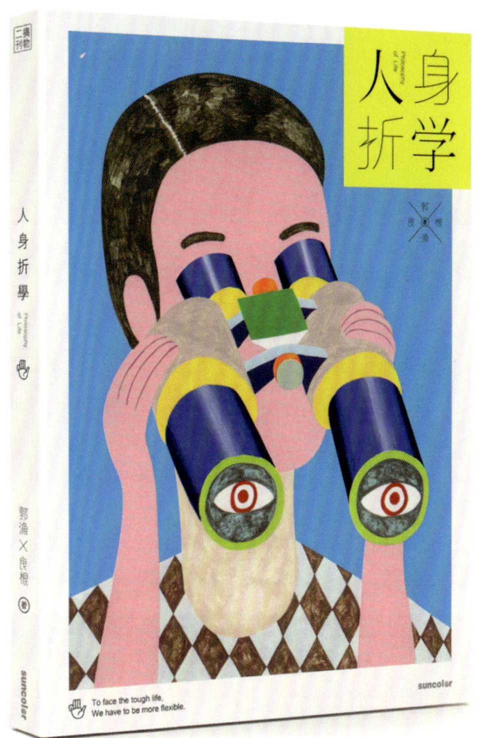

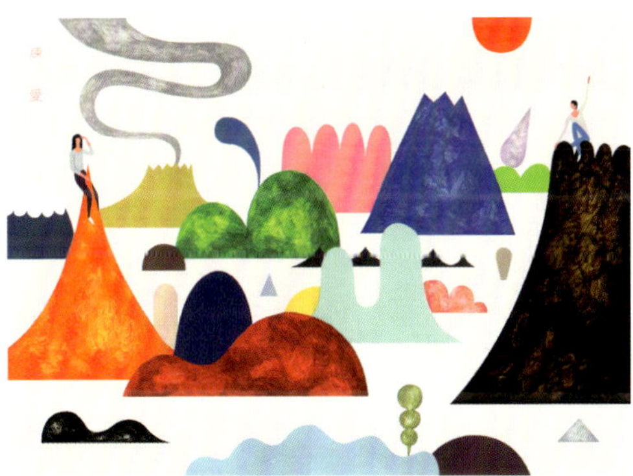

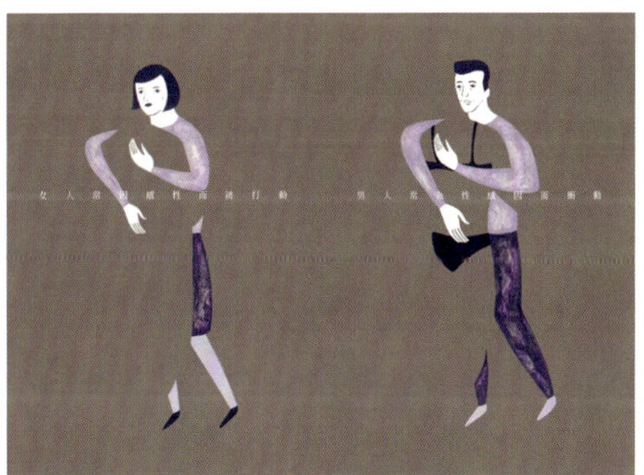

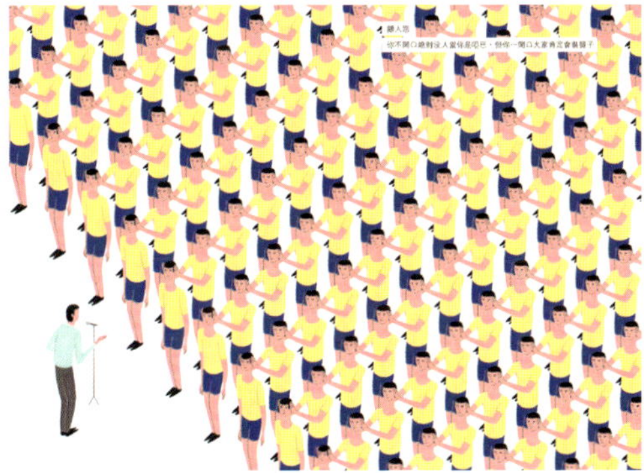

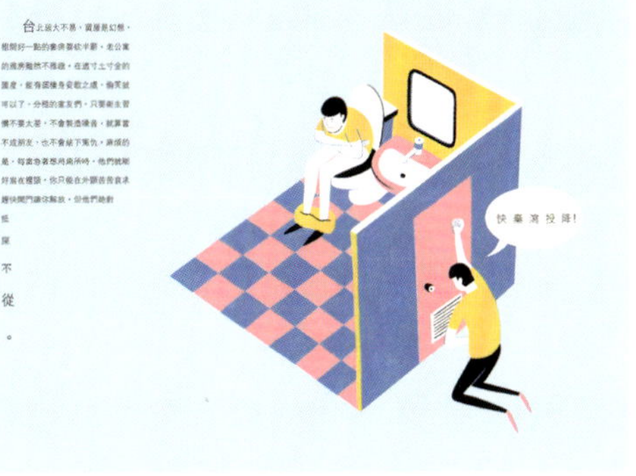



MERIT *Yenting Kuo, Yufeng Kuo*

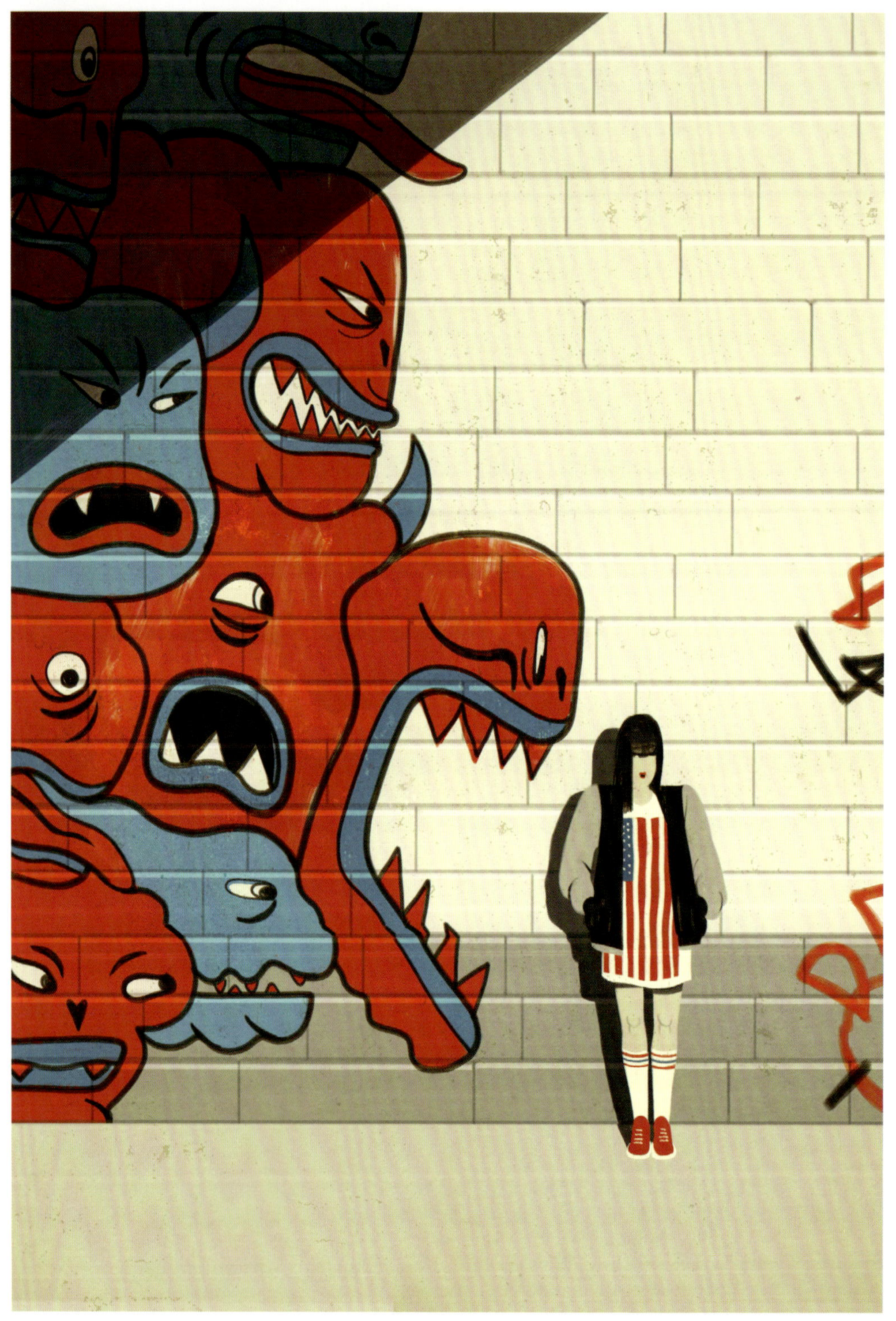



MERIT *Emiliano Ponzi*

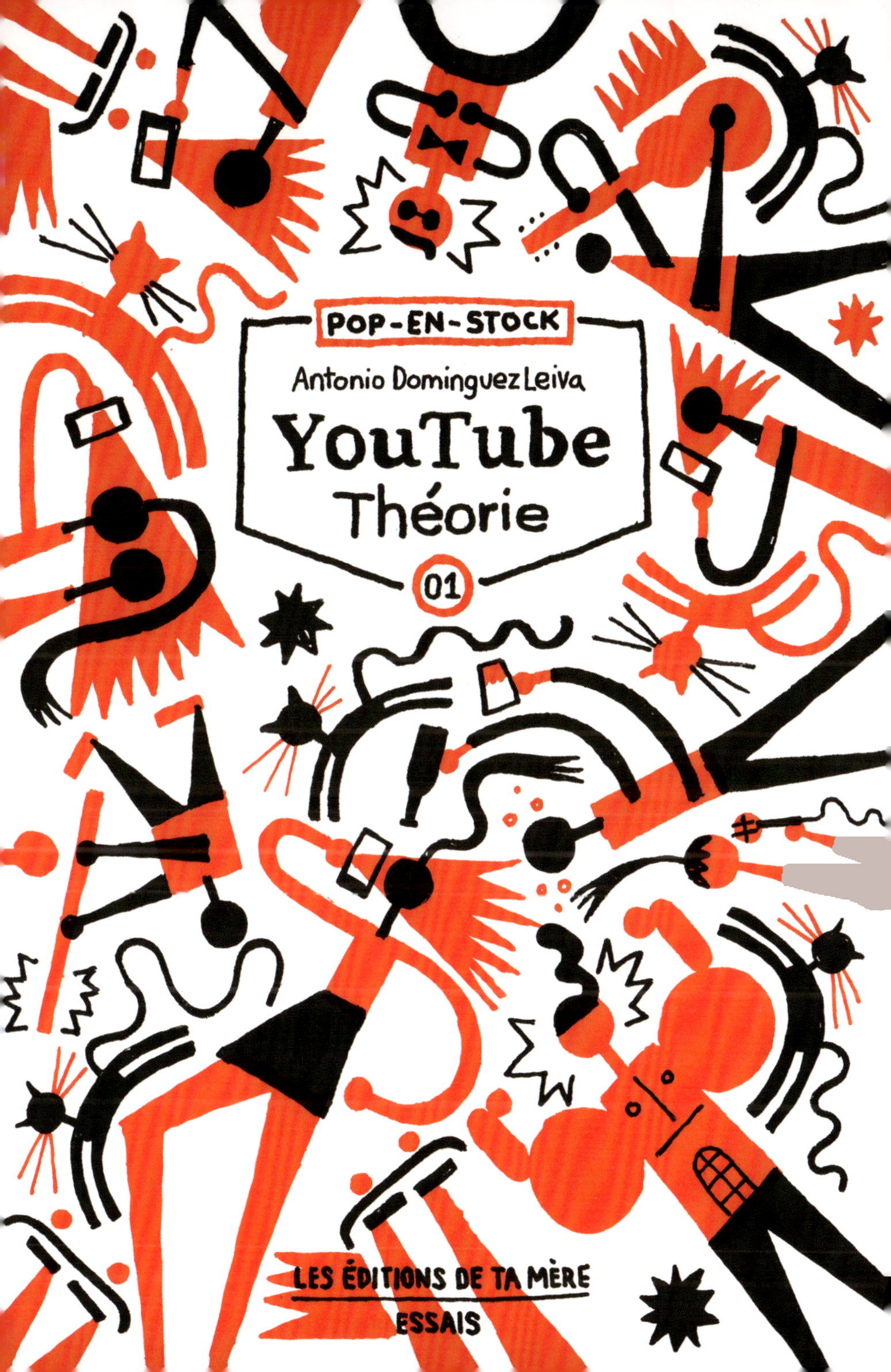

POP-EN-STOCK
Antonio Dominguez Leiva
YouTube
Théorie
01
LES ÉDITIONS DE TA MÈRE
ESSAIS

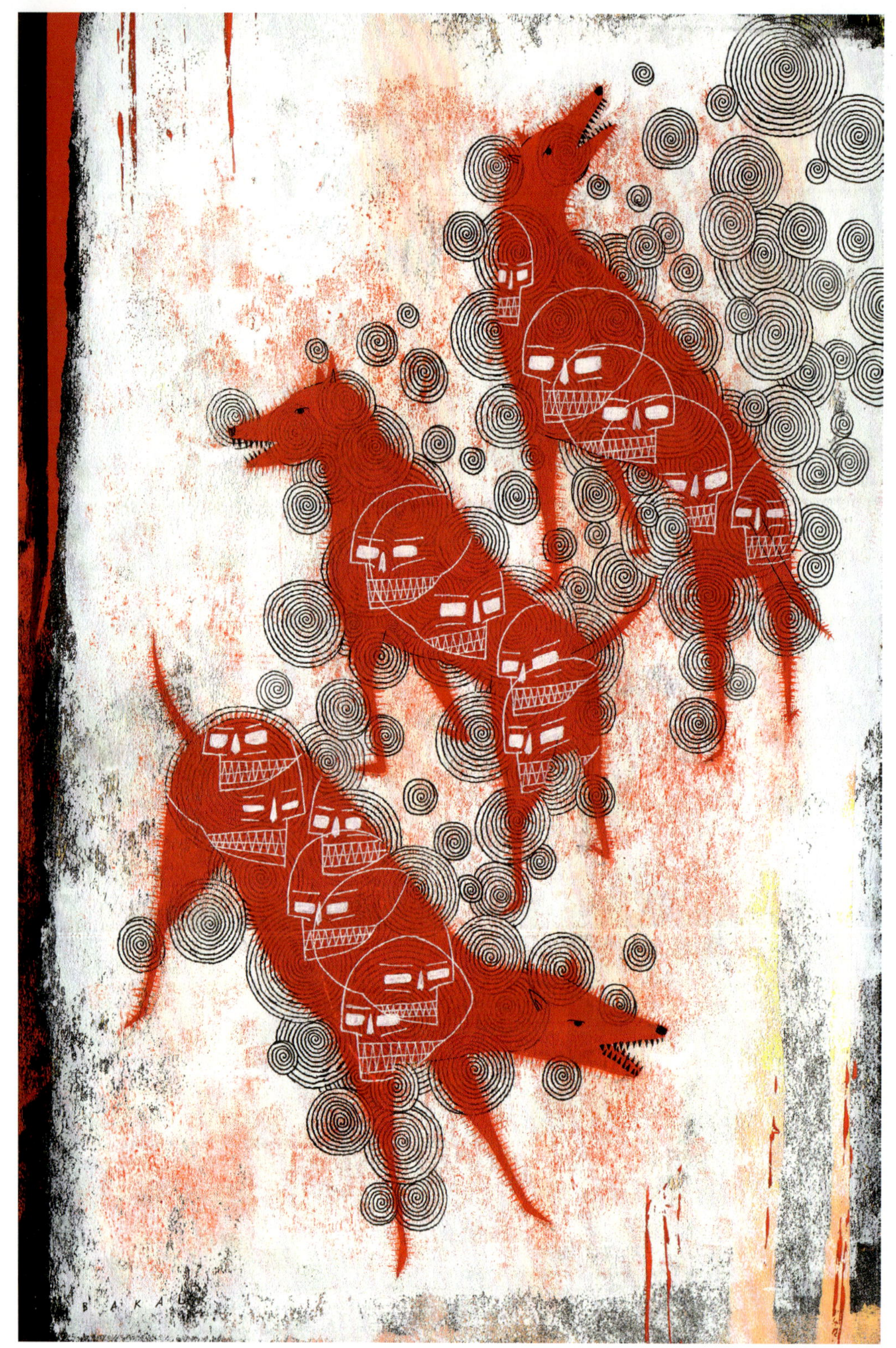



DISTINGUISHED MERIT *Scott Bakal*

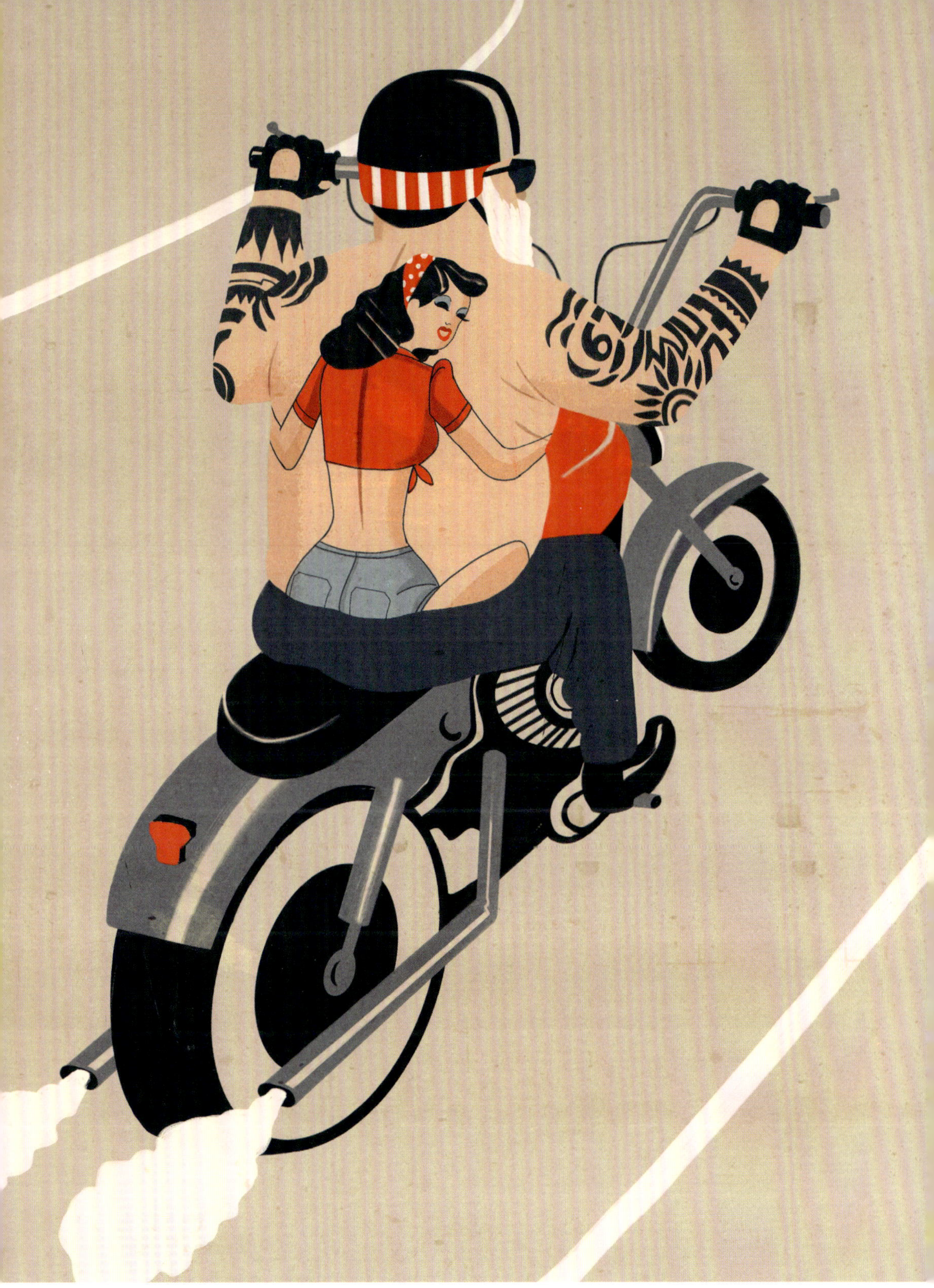



MERIT *Emiliano Ponzi*

49

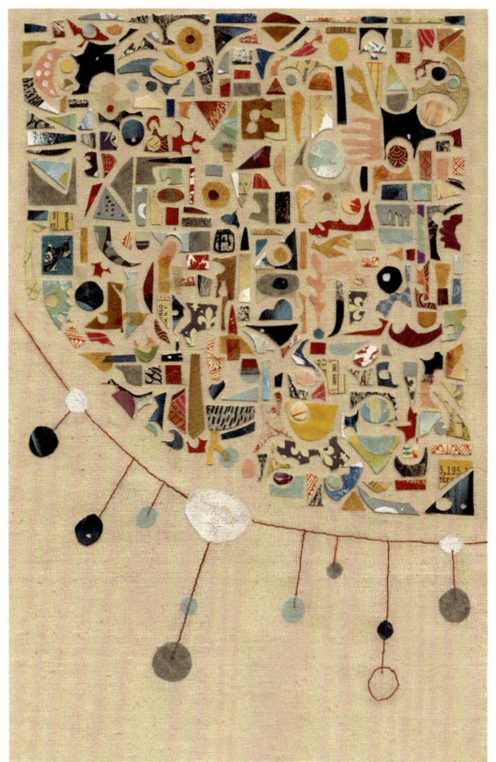
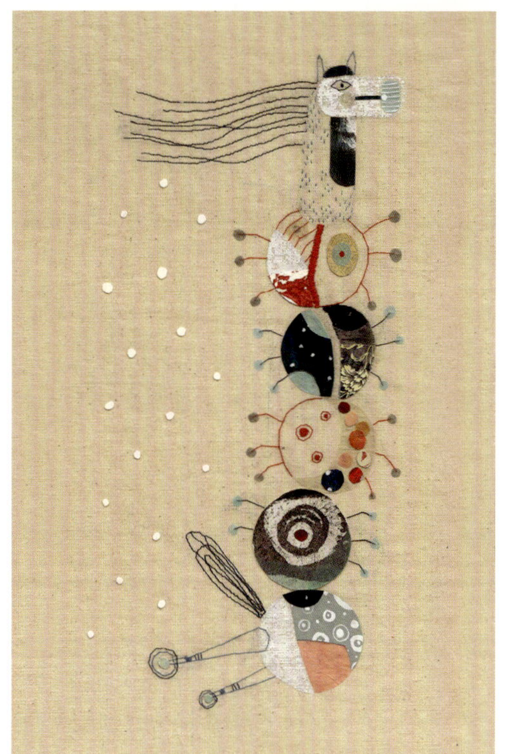
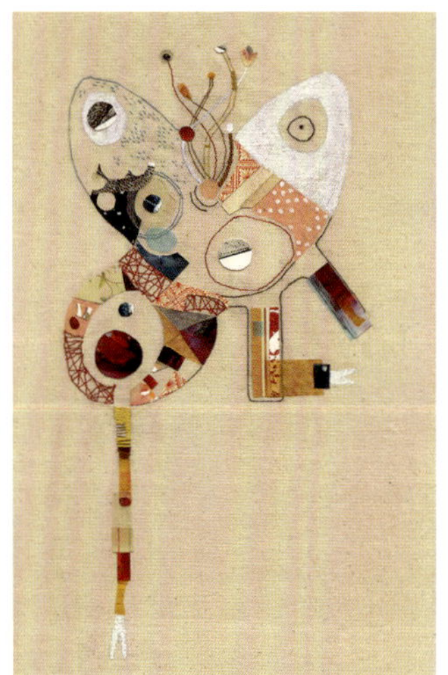
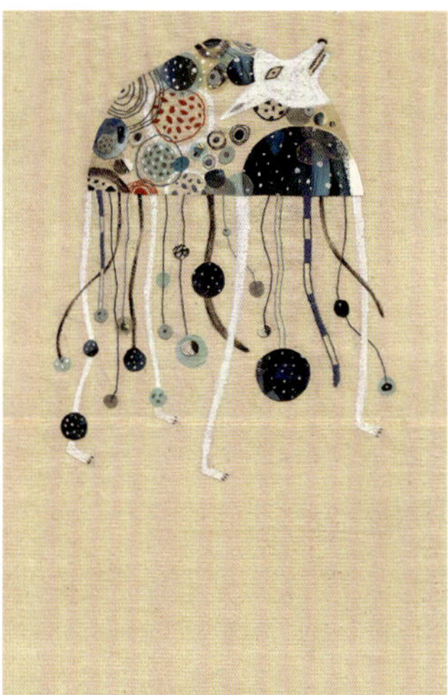
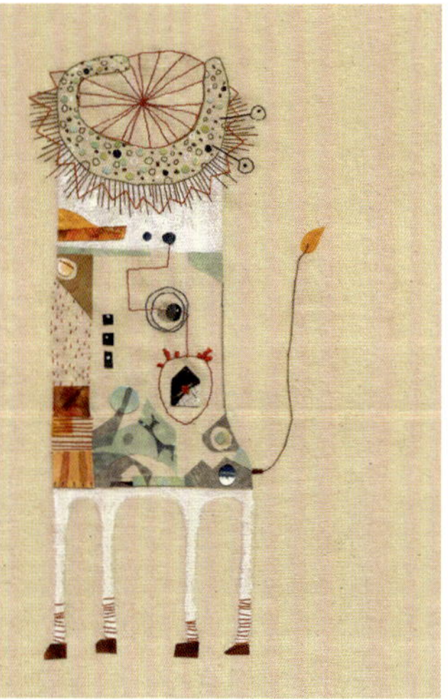

MERIT *Annalisa Bollini*

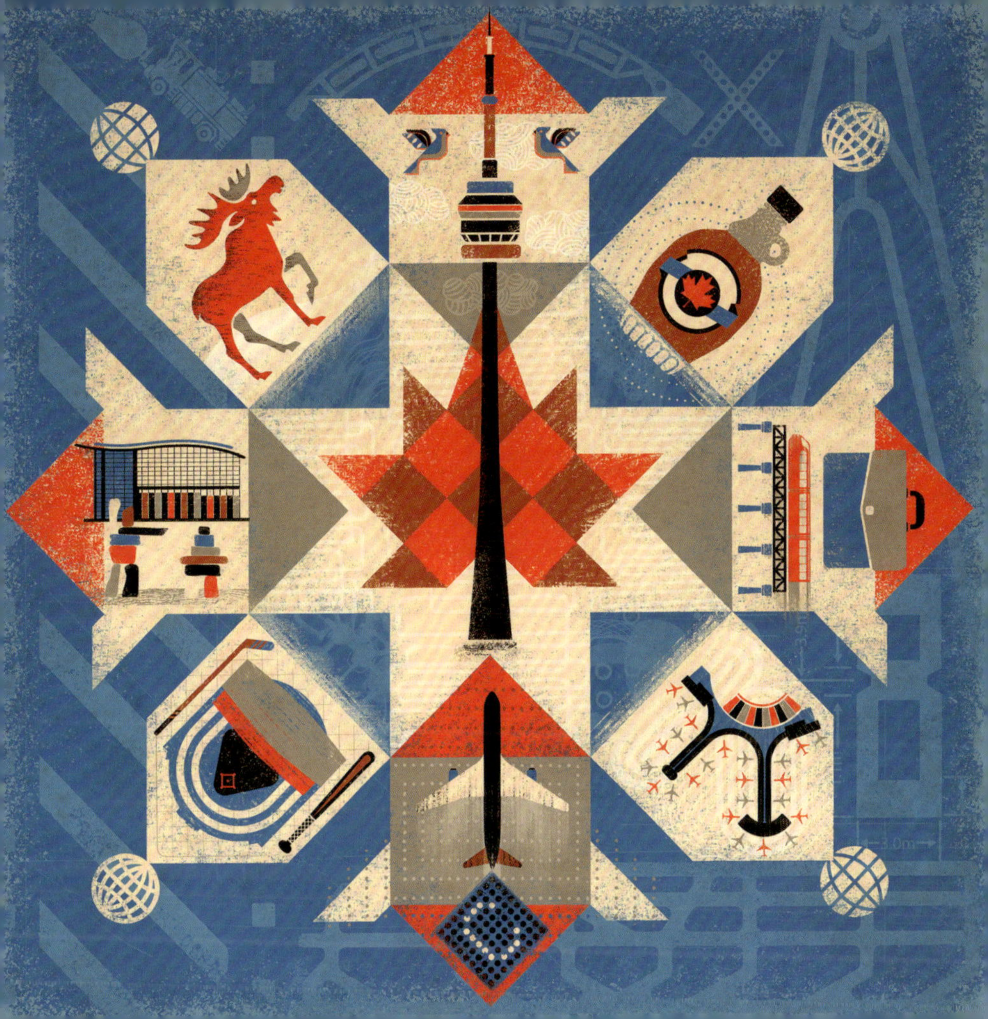

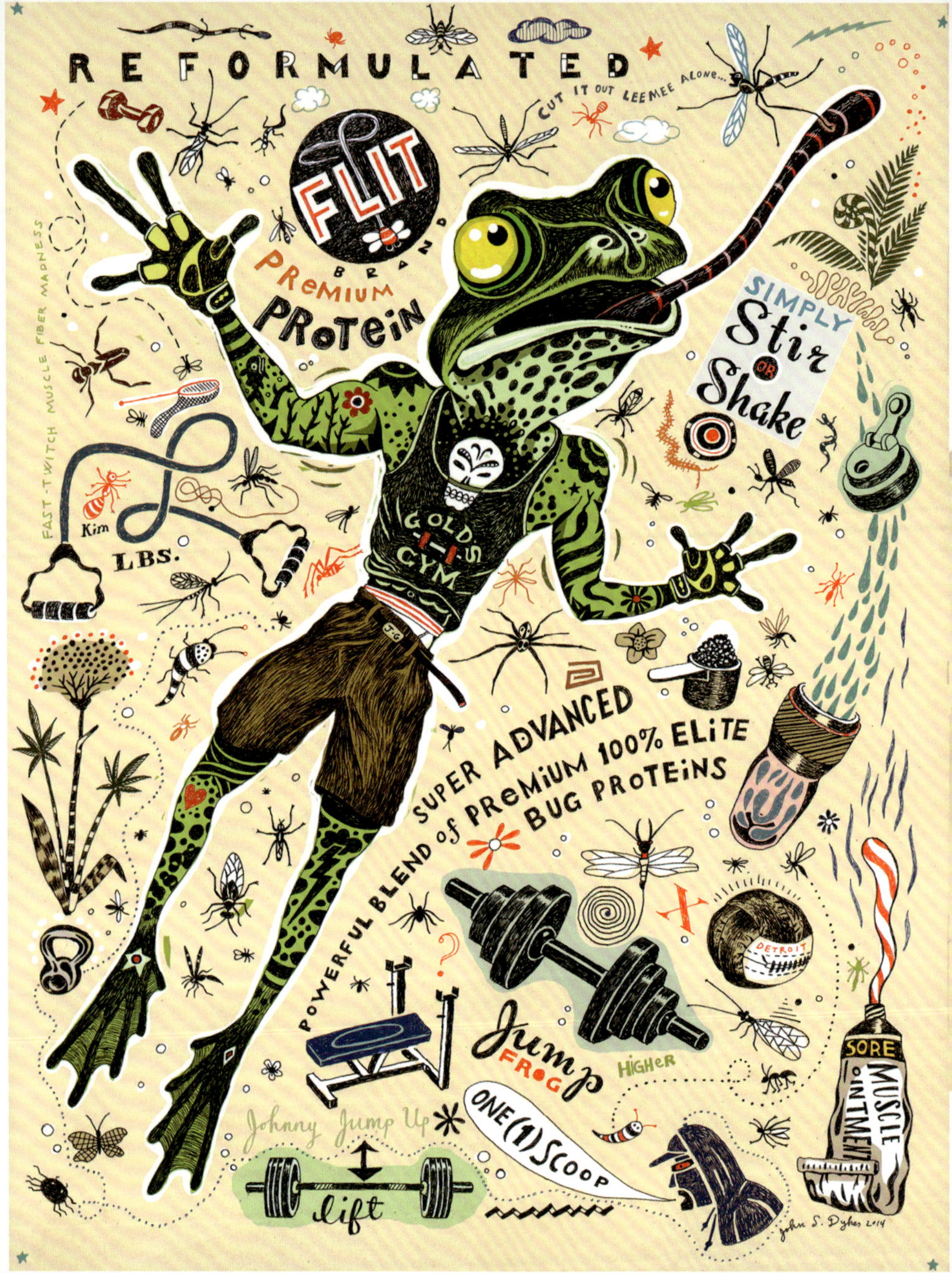

REFORMULATED
FLIT BRAND
PREMIUM PROTEIN
CUT IT OUT LEEMEE ALONE...
SIMPLY Stir or Shake
FAST-TWITCH MUSCLE FIBER MADNESS
Kim
LBS.
GOLD'S GYM
SUPER ADVANCED BLEND of PREMIUM 100% ELITE BUG PROTEINS
POWERFUL BLEND of PREMIUM 100% ELITE BUG PROTEINS
DETROIT
Jump FROG HIGHER
Johnny Jump Up
ONE (1) SCOOP
lift
SORE MUSCLE OINTMENT
John S. Dykes 2014

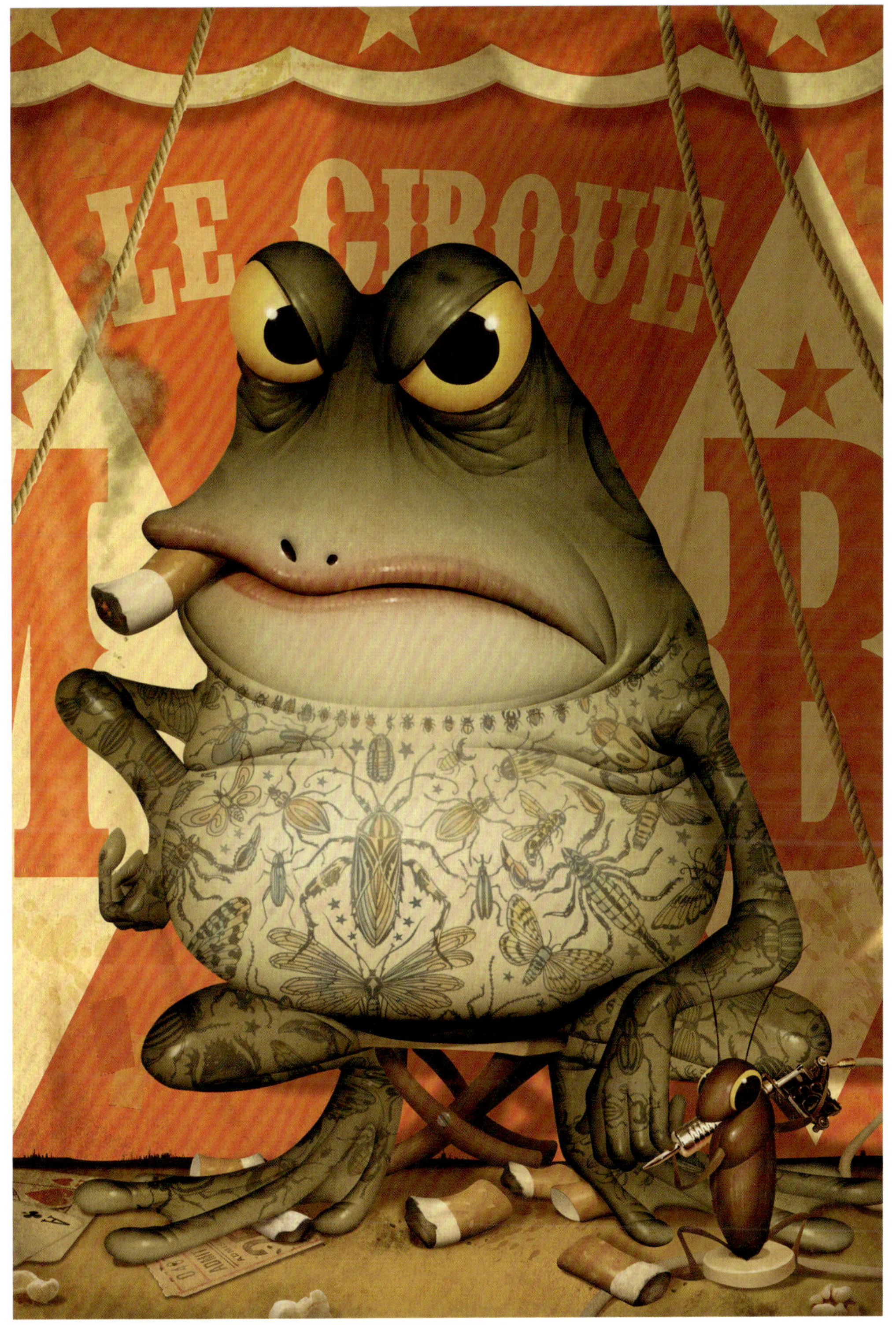



MERIT *Bill Mayer*

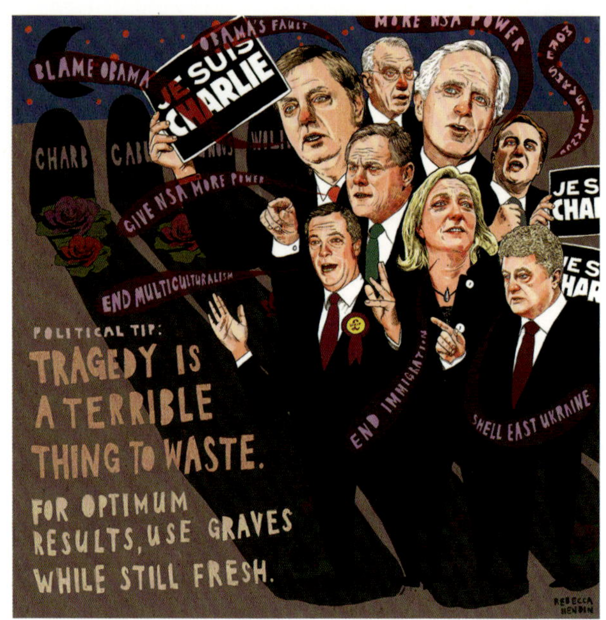


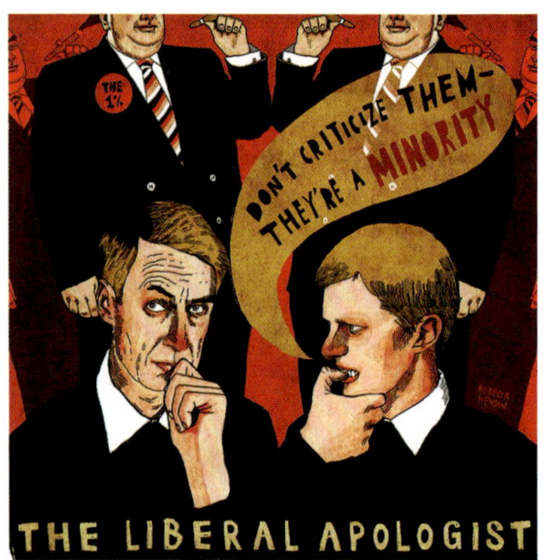


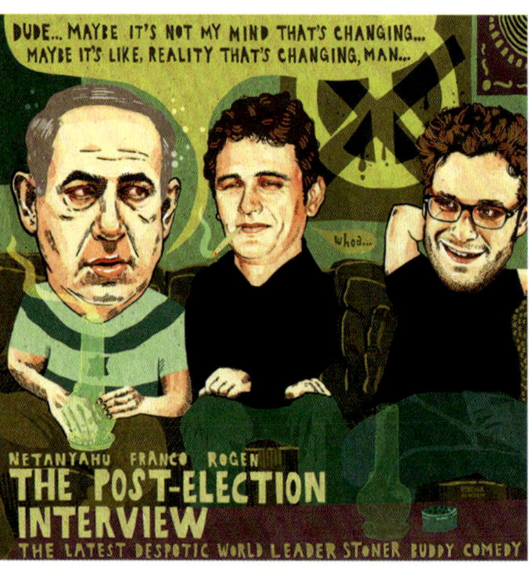


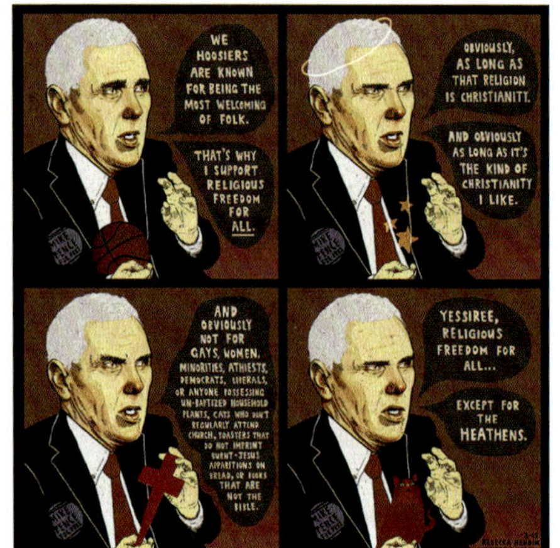


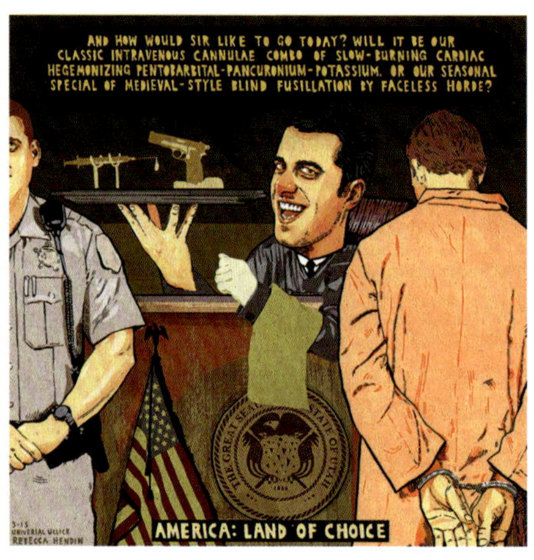


MERIT *Rebecca Hendin*

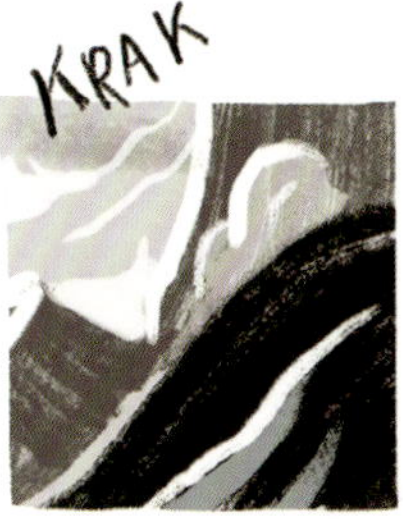


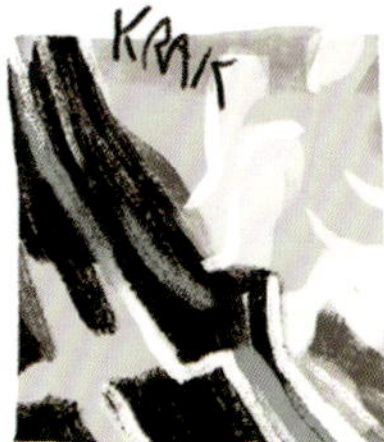


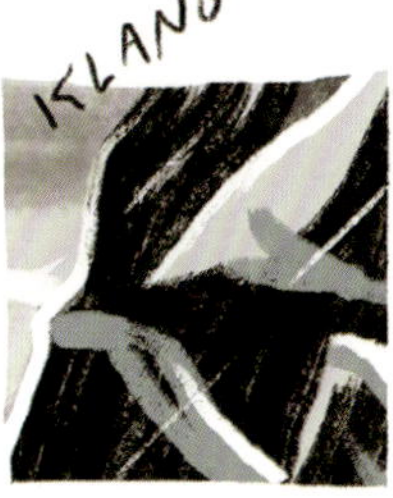


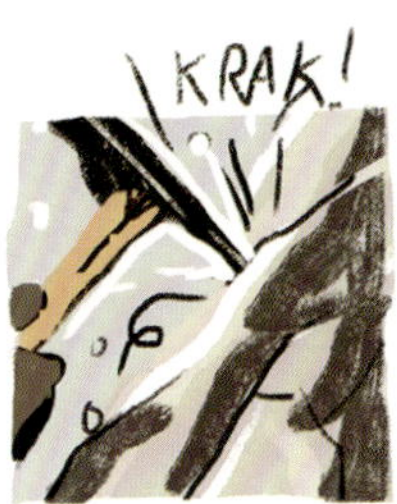


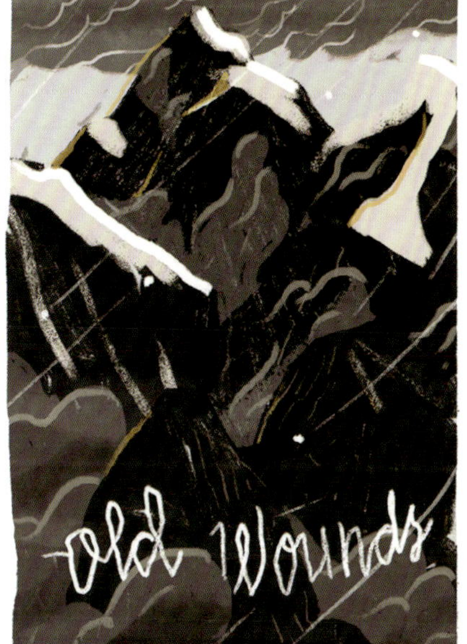


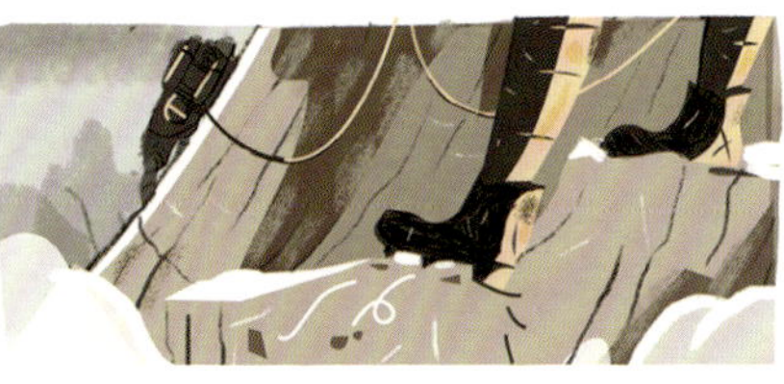

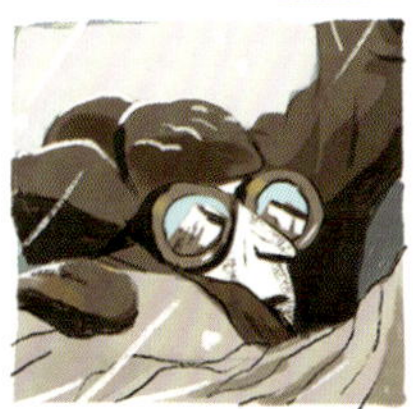

On June 8TH 1924, George Mallory and Andrew Irvine crossed the northeast ridge of Mount Everest before disappearing into the mist forever.

This was their third attempt to scale Everest.

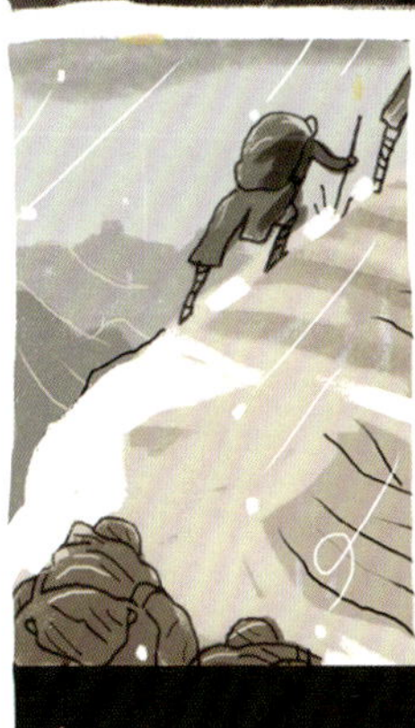


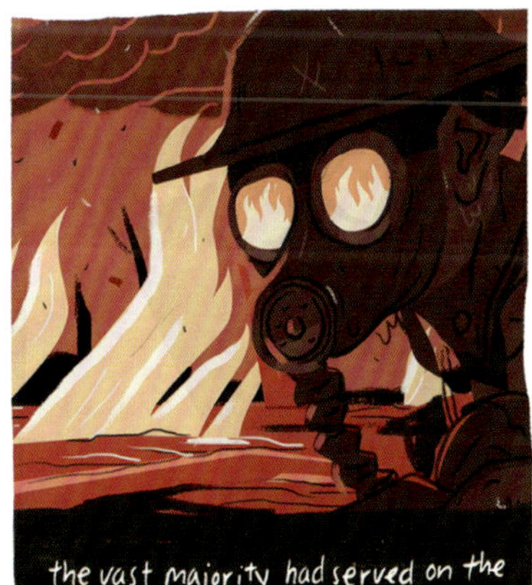


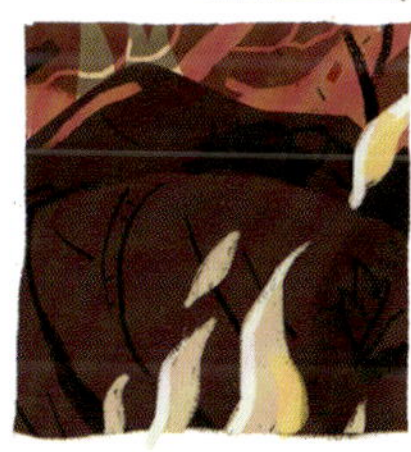

There is little doubt this experience informed their post war quest for glory at Everest.

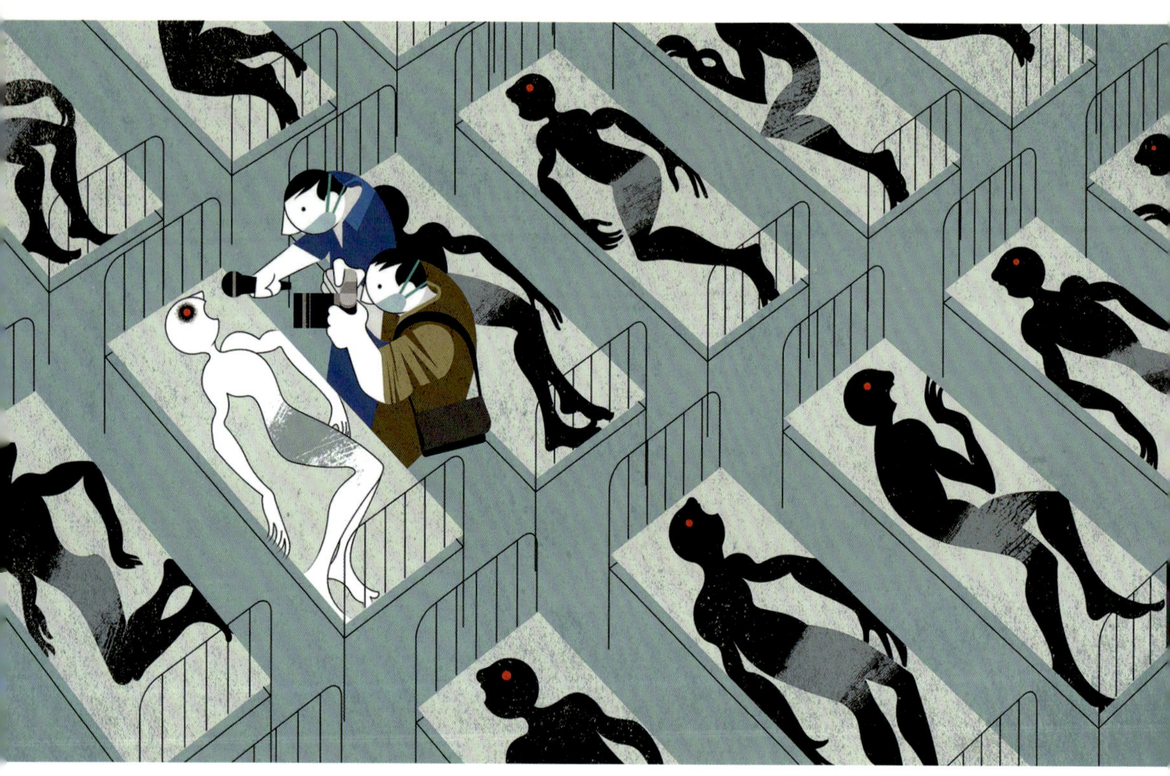

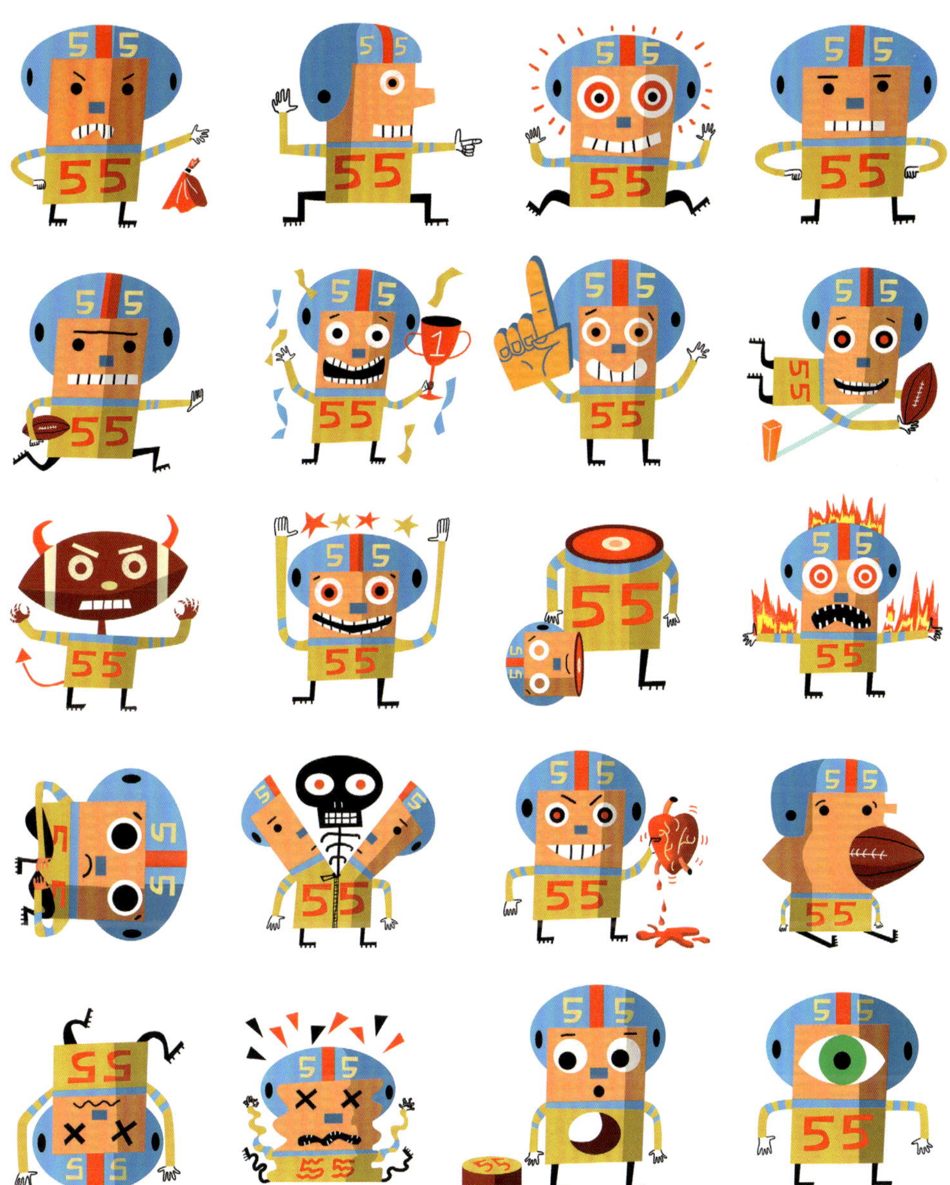

MERIT *James Yang*

57

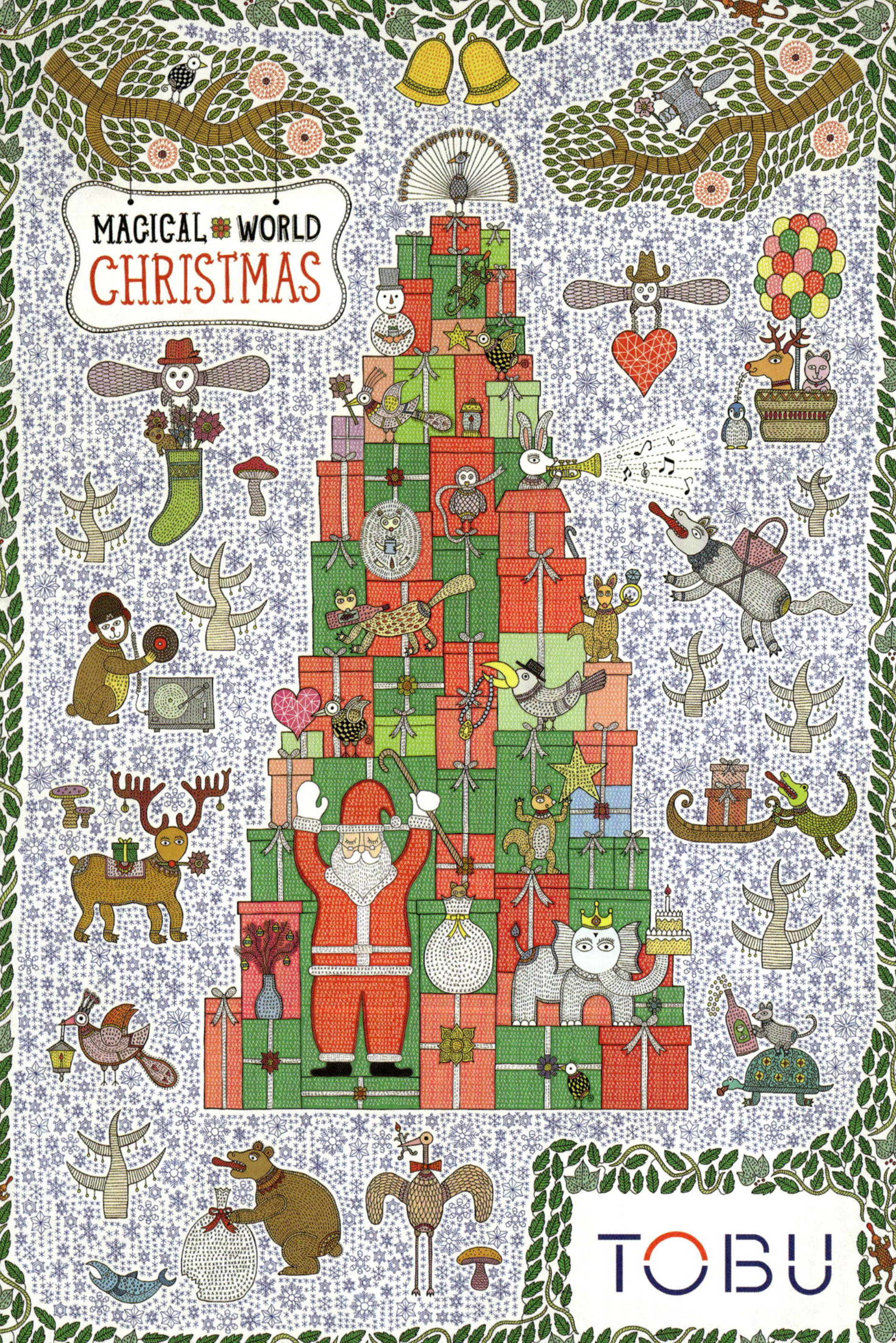
MAGICAL WORLD
CHRISTMAS
TOBU

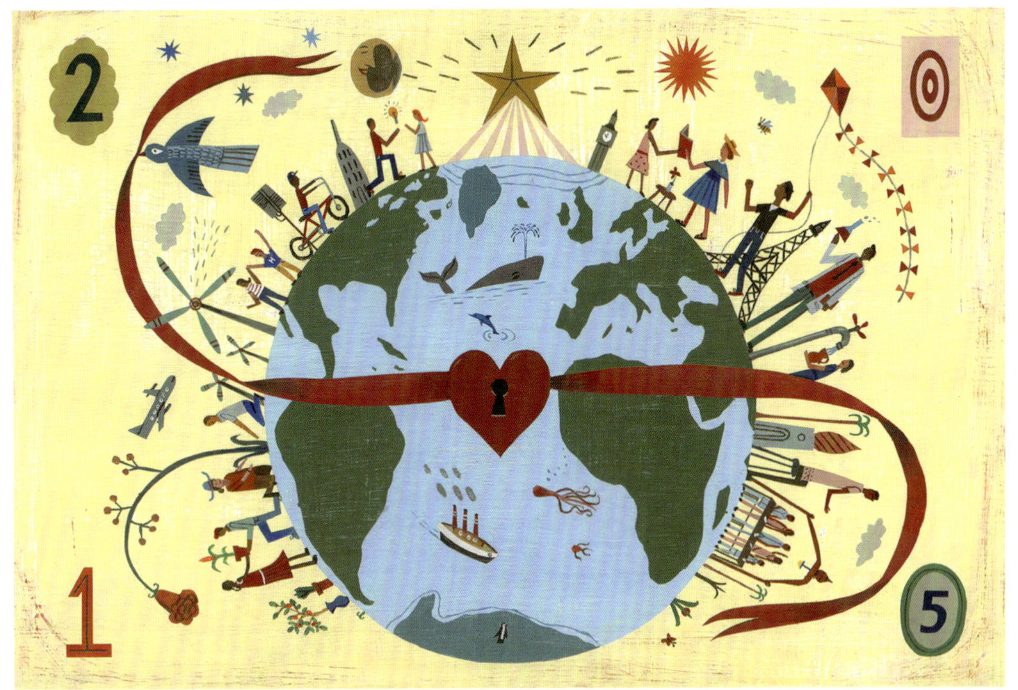

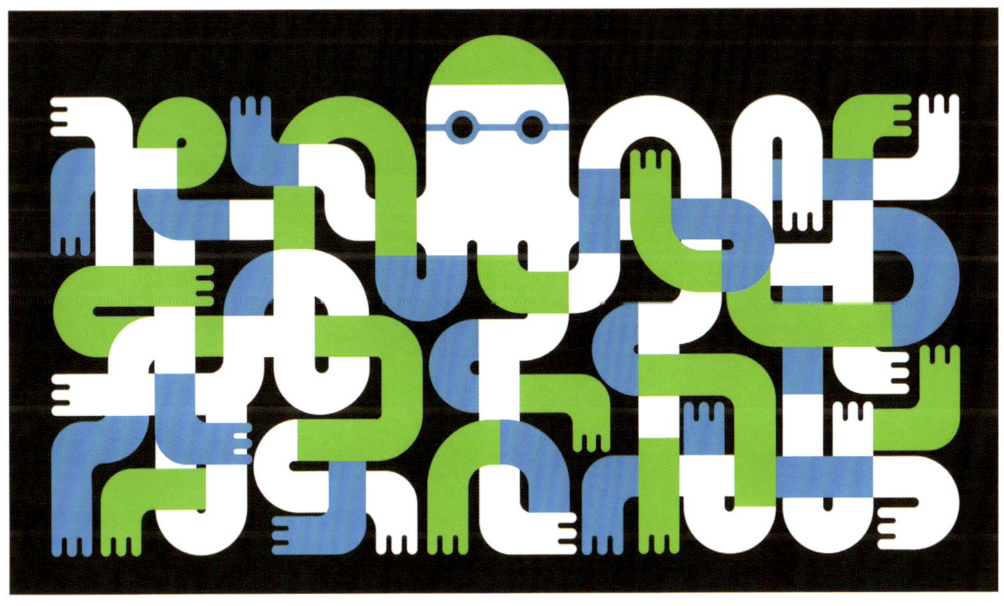

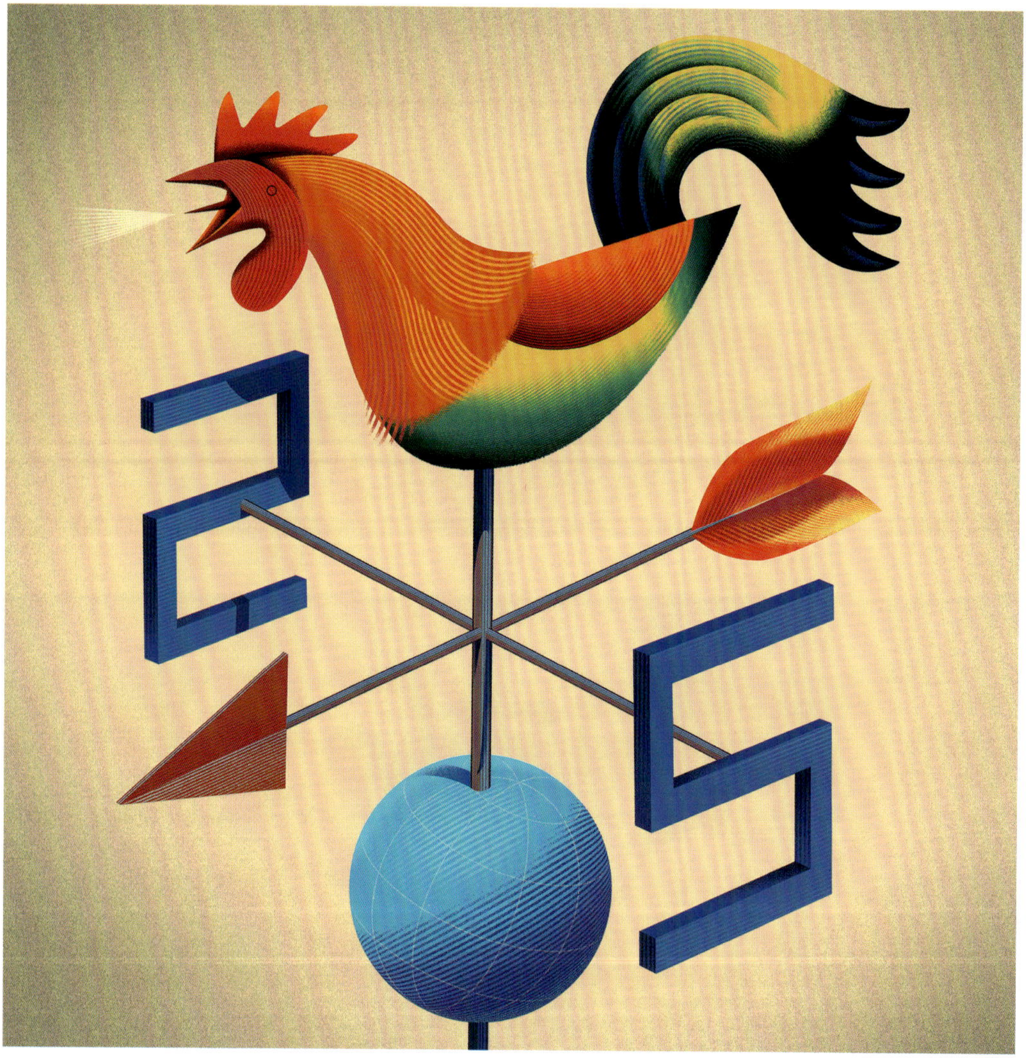

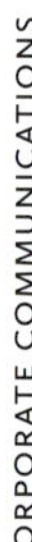



60

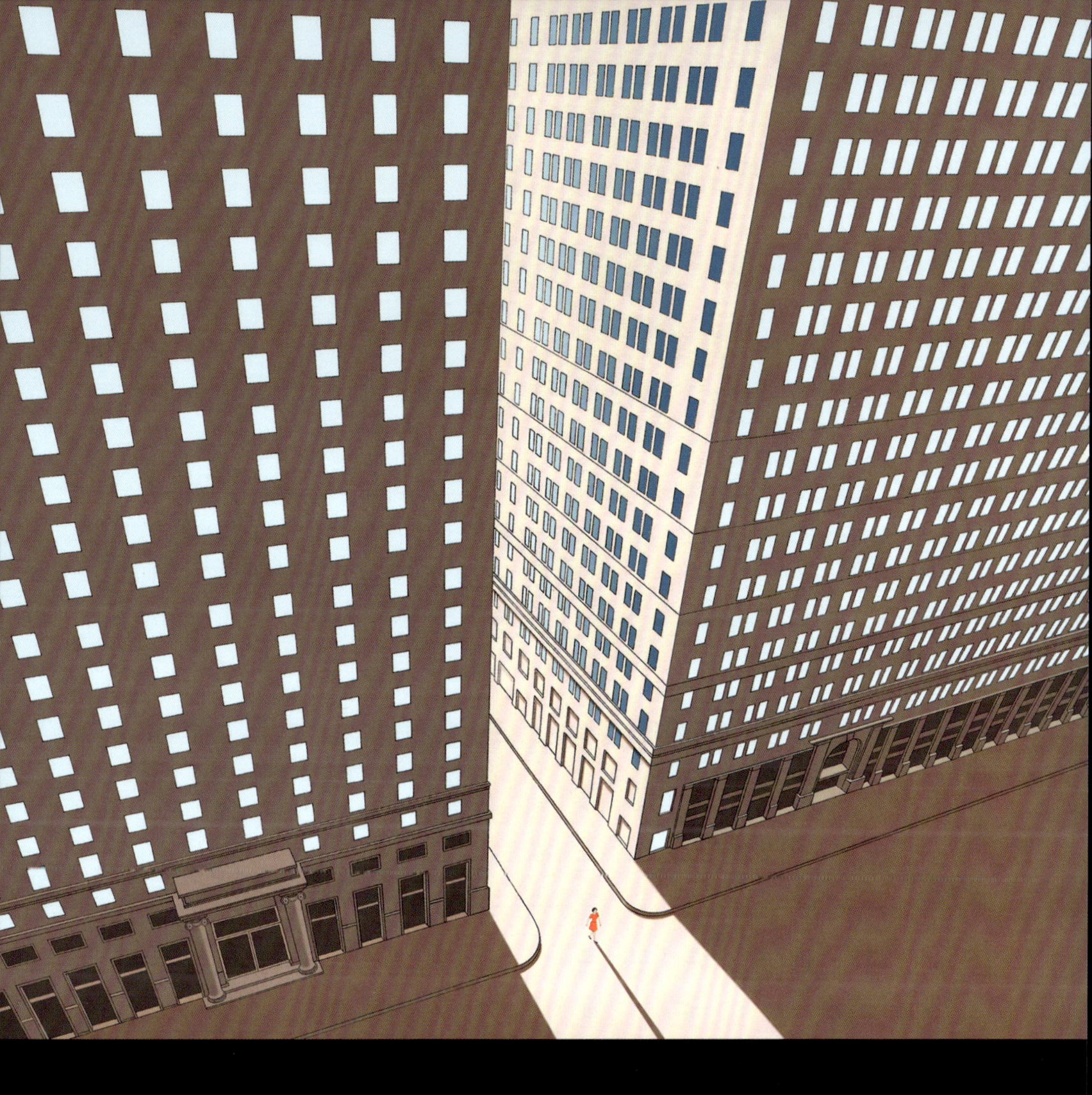

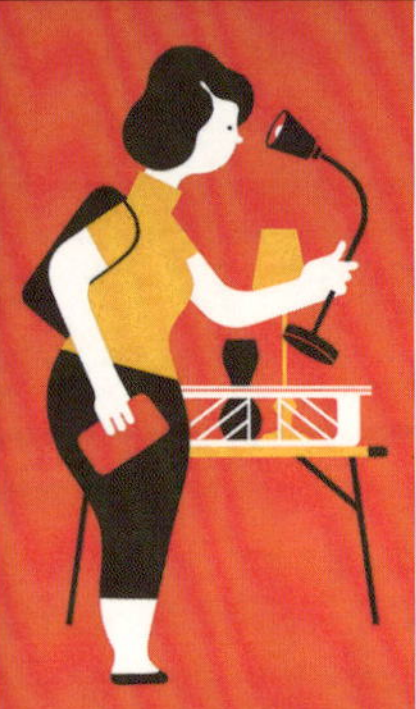

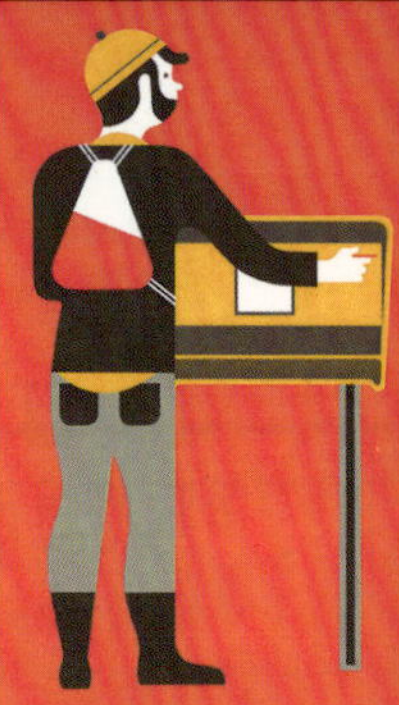

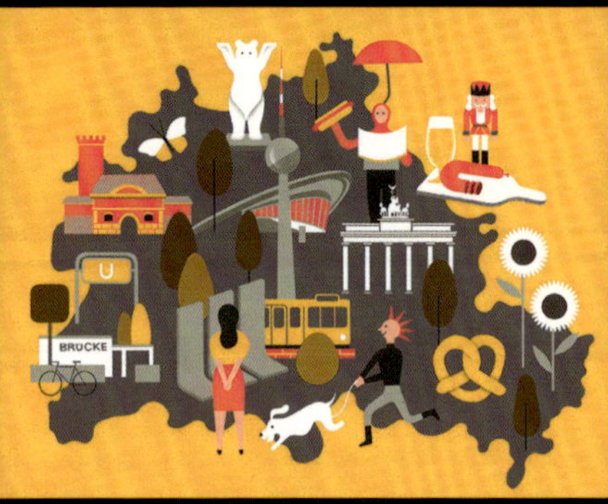
BRÜCKE

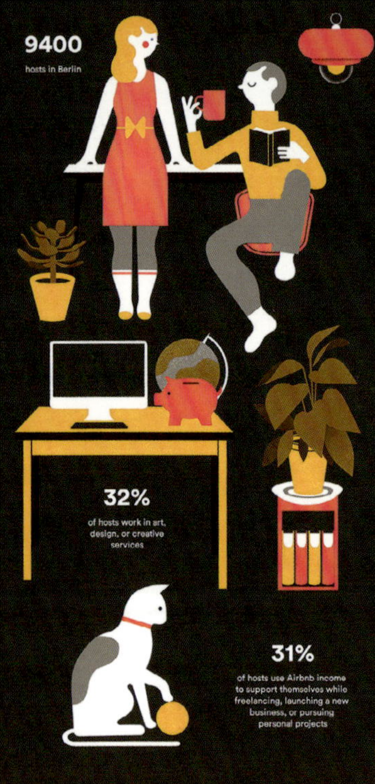
9400
hosts in Berlin

32%
of hosts work in art,
design, or creative
services

31%
of hosts use Airbnb income
to support themselves while
freelancing, launching a new
business, or pursuing
personal projects

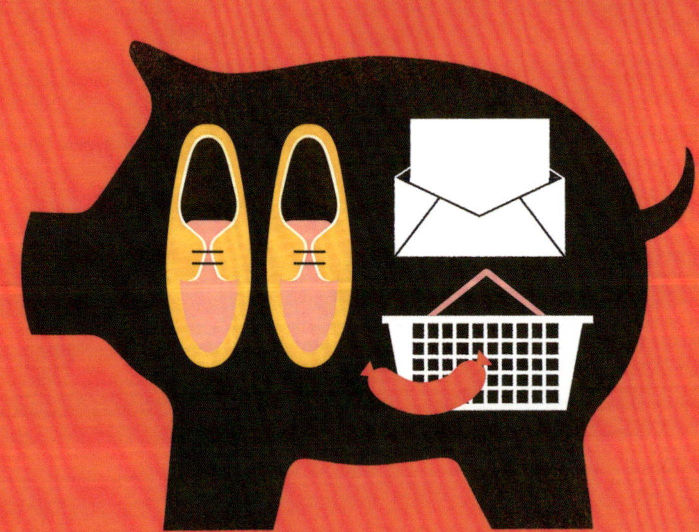
31,5m €
Total host earnings in
the past year

210 €
Typical host monthly
earnings, hosting
4 days/month

48%
of host earnings are
spent on living and
household expenses

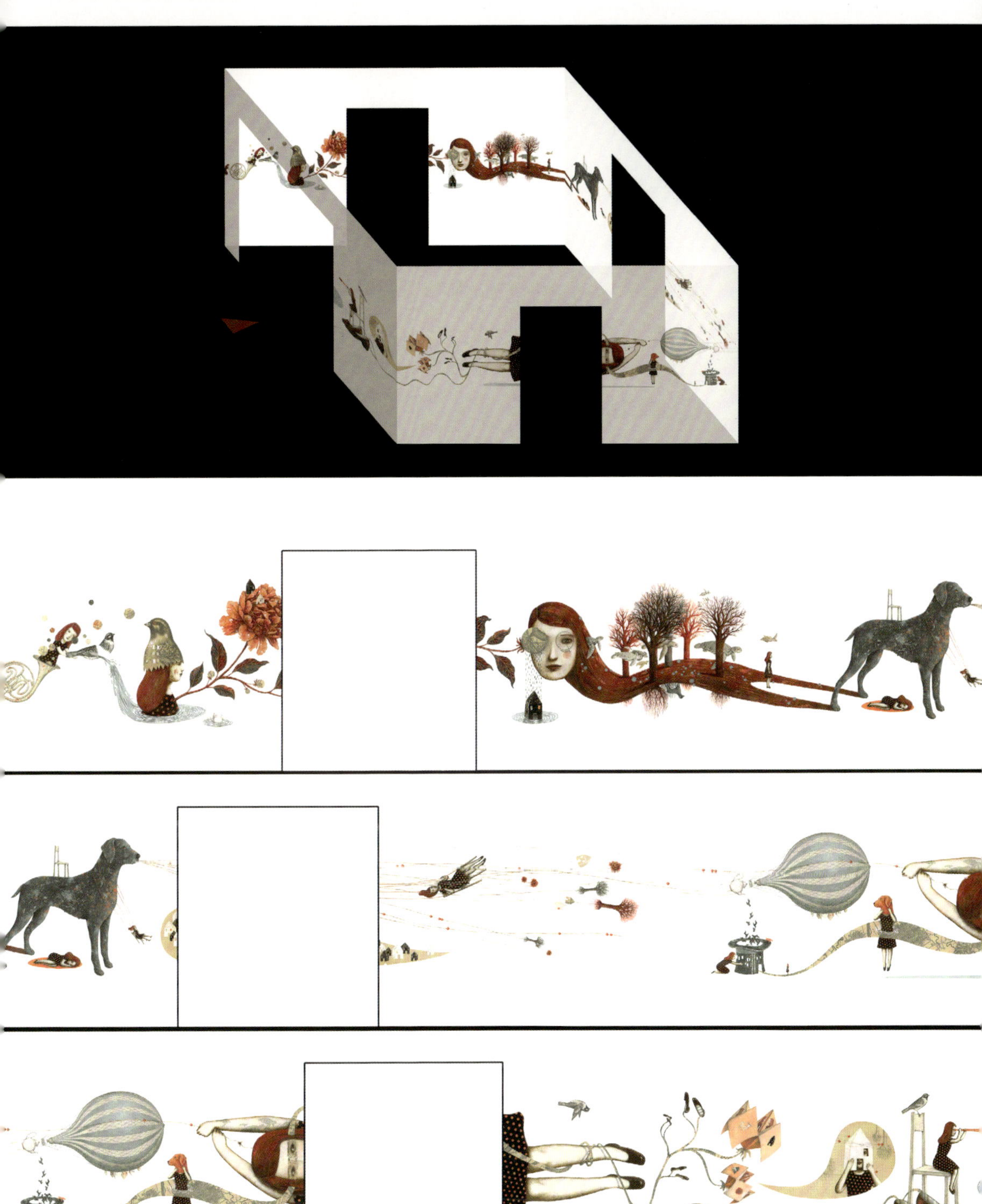

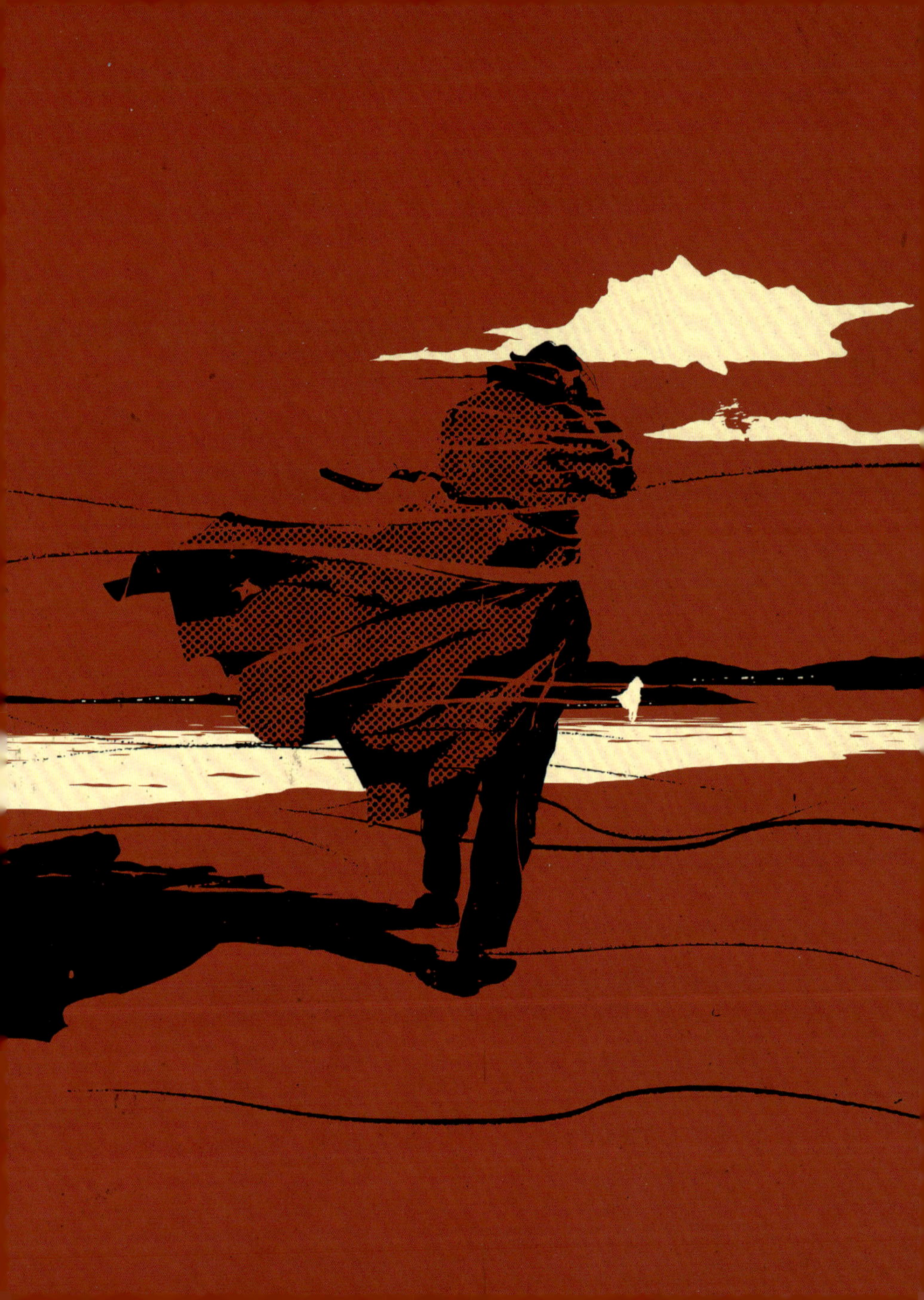

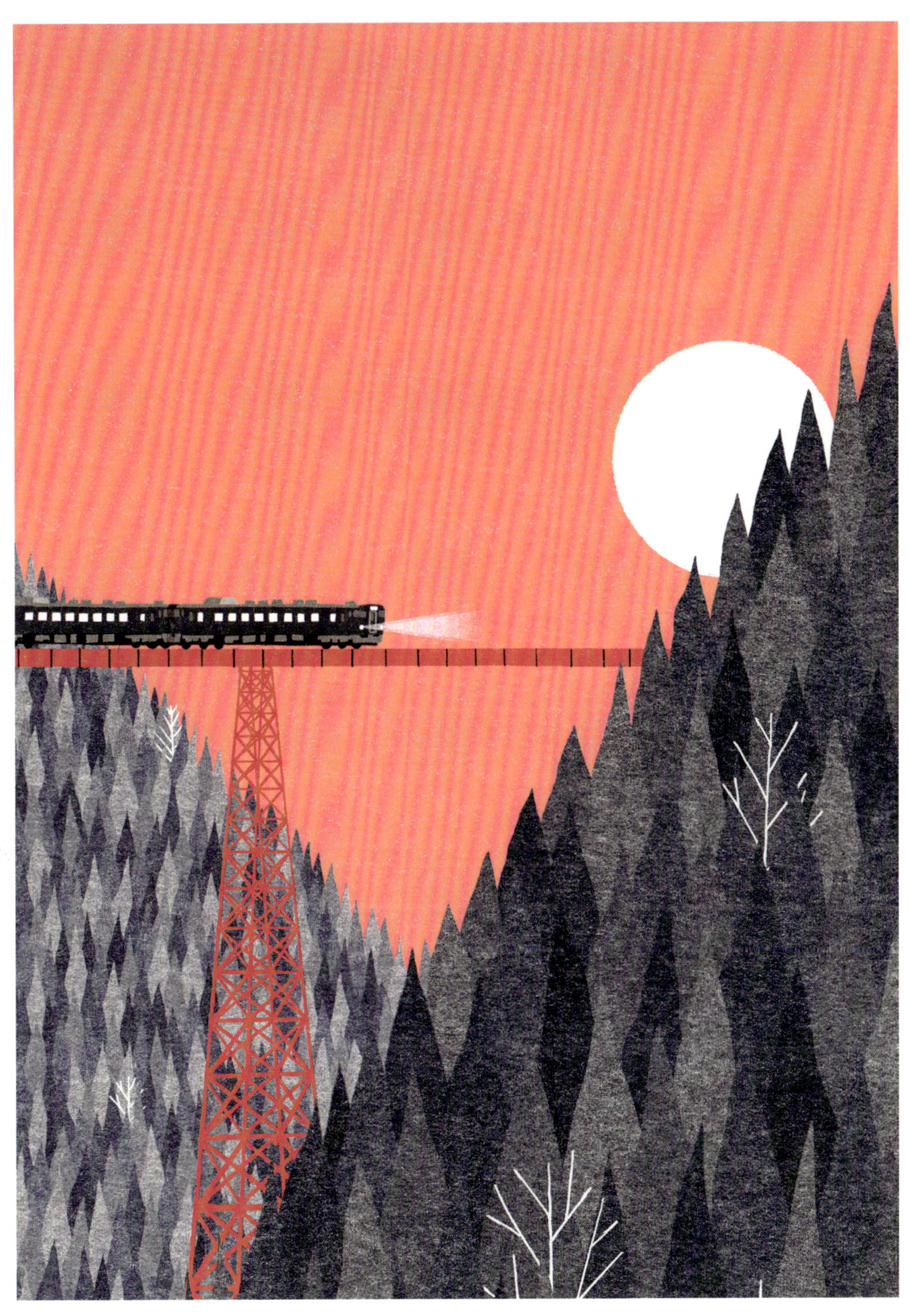



65

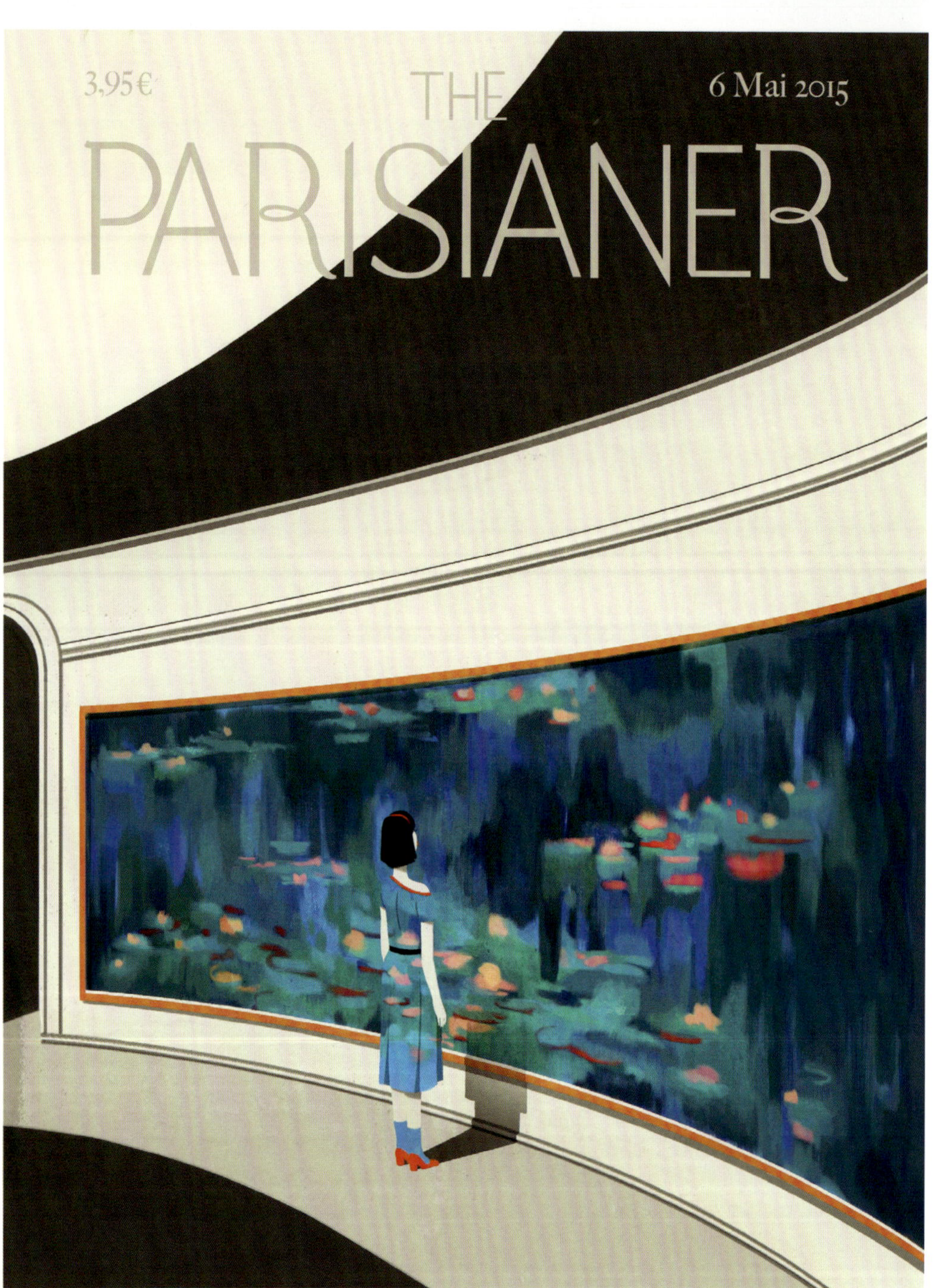


3,95€
6 Mai 2015
THE
PARISIANER

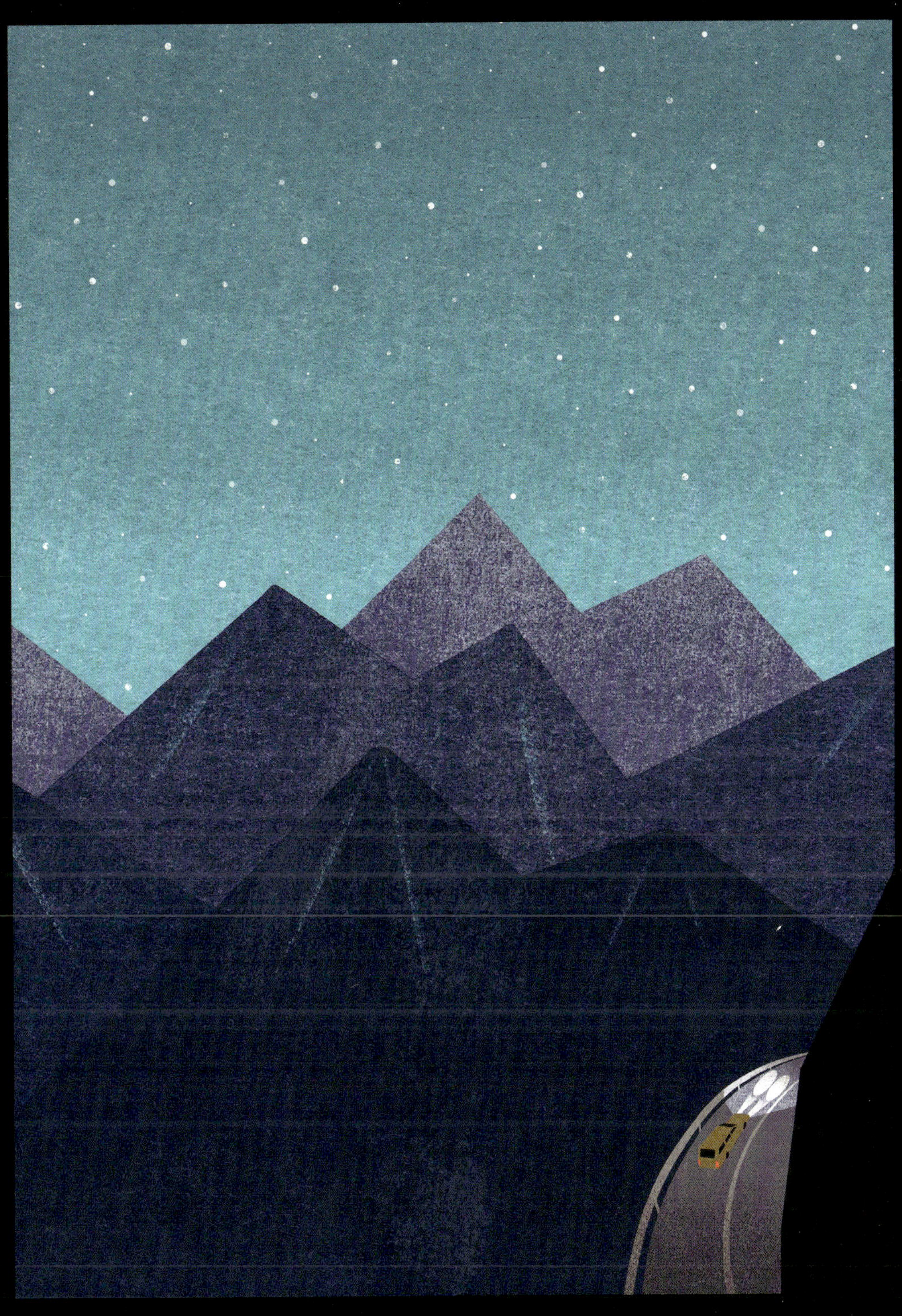

MERIT *Ryo Takemasa*

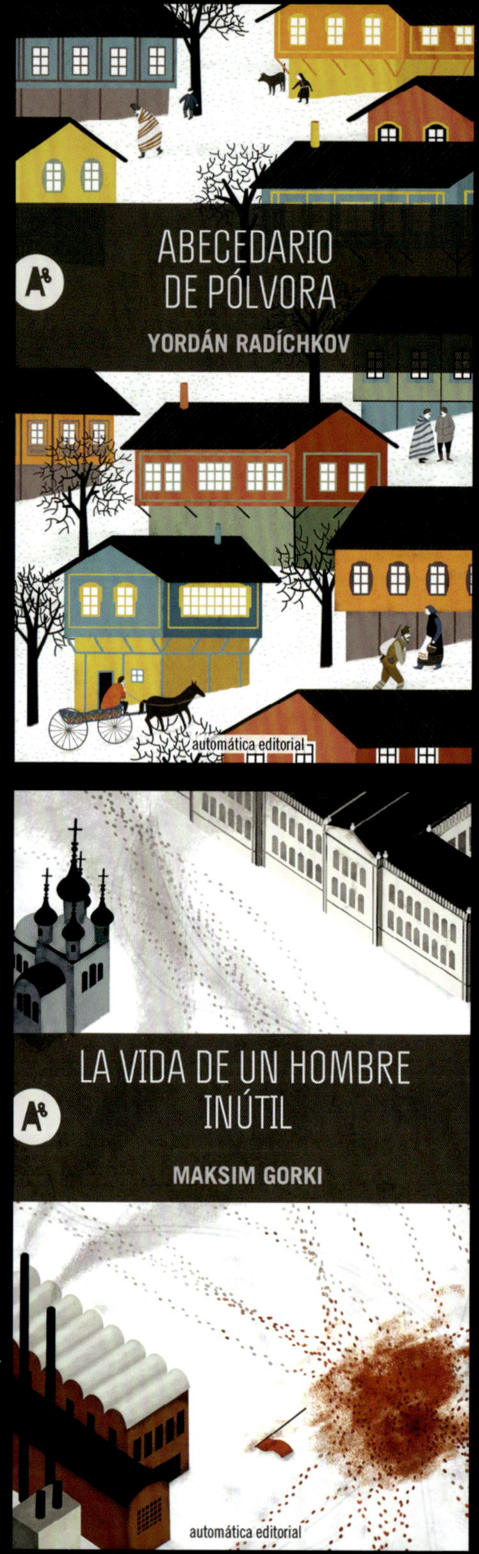
ABECEDARIO DE PÓLVORA
YORDÁN RADÍCHKOV
automática editorial
LA VIDA DE UN HOMBRE INÚTIL
MAKSIM GORKI
automática editorial

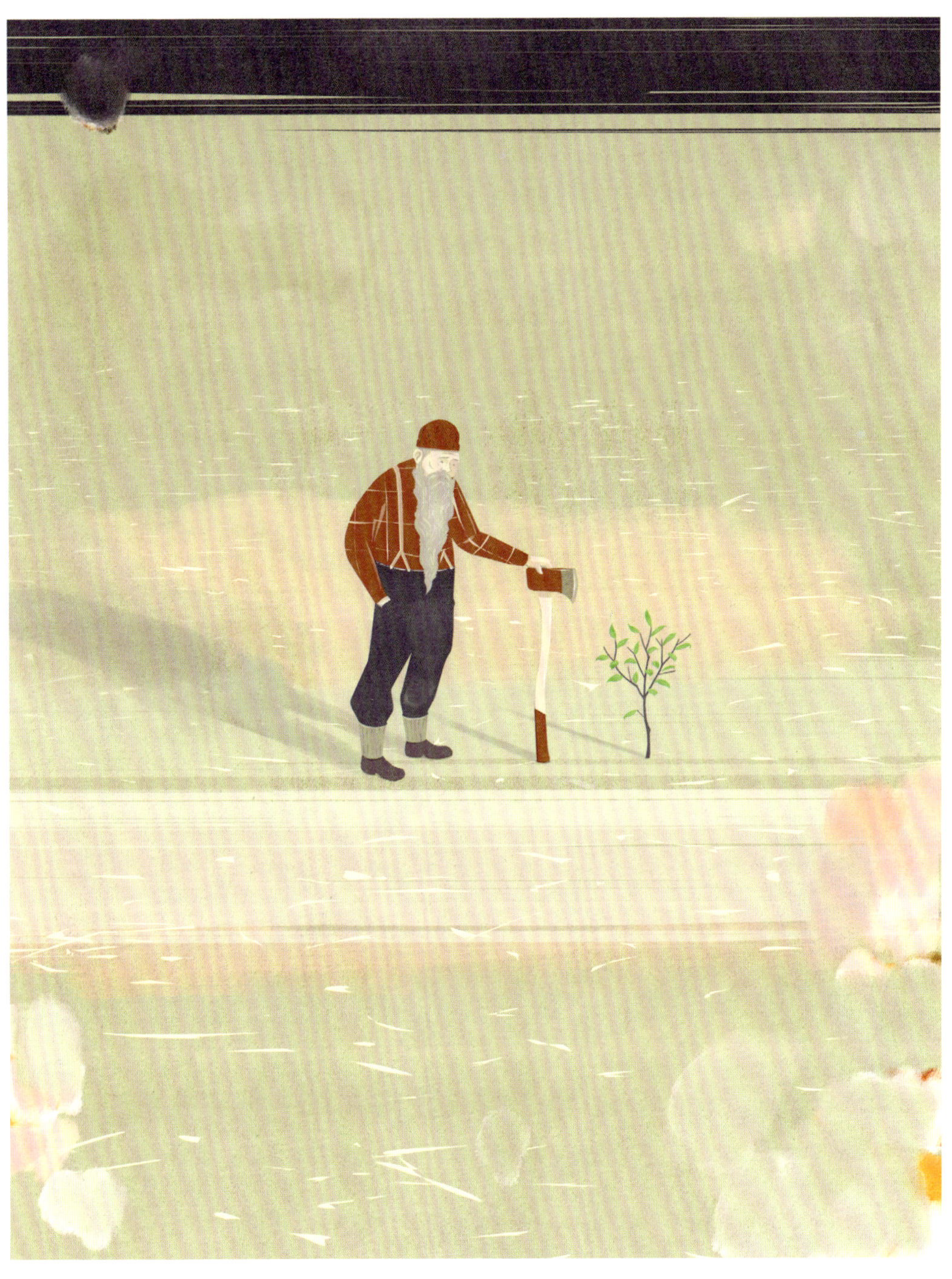



MERIT *Francesco Bongiorni*

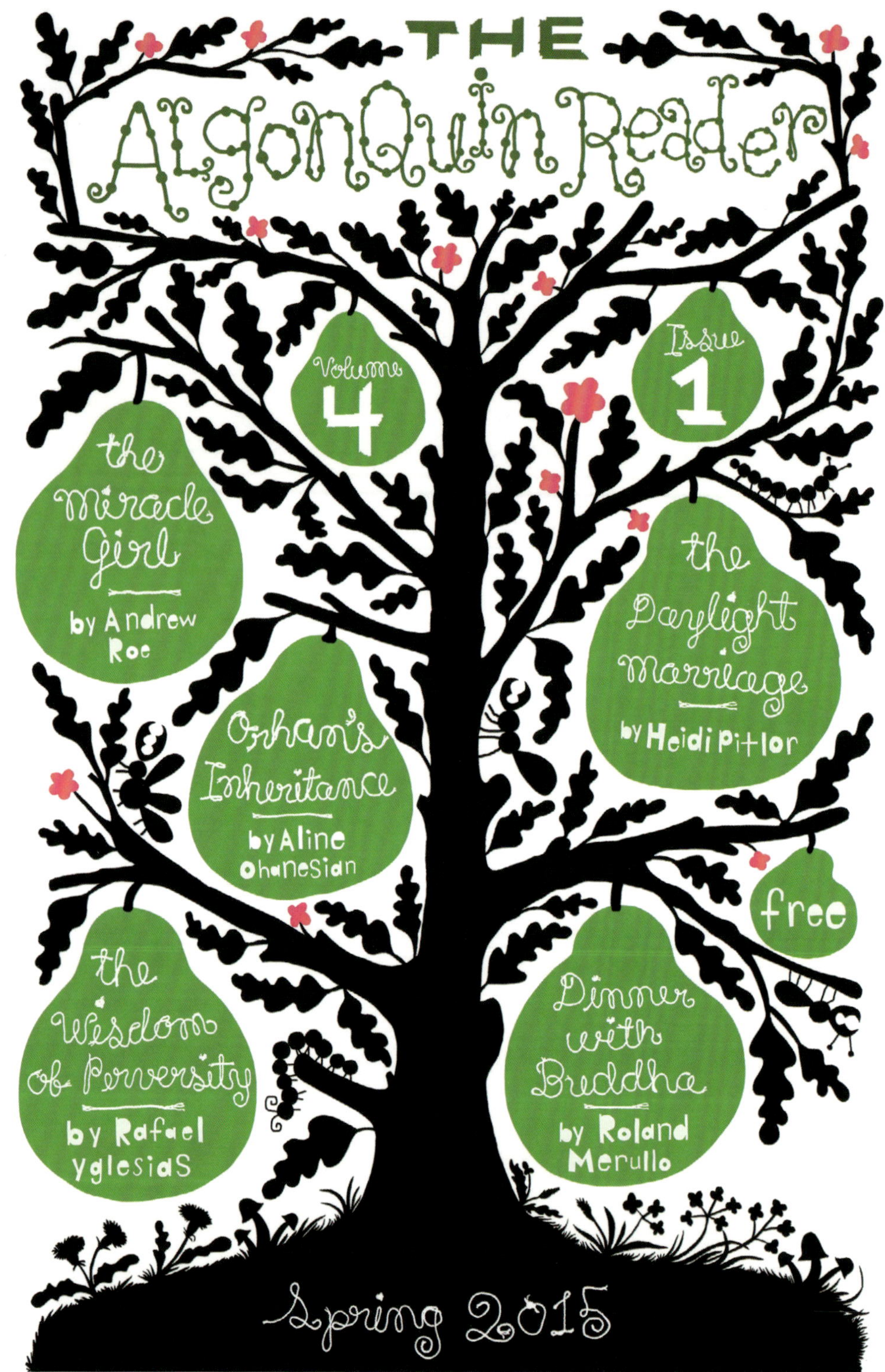


MERIT *Melinda Beck*

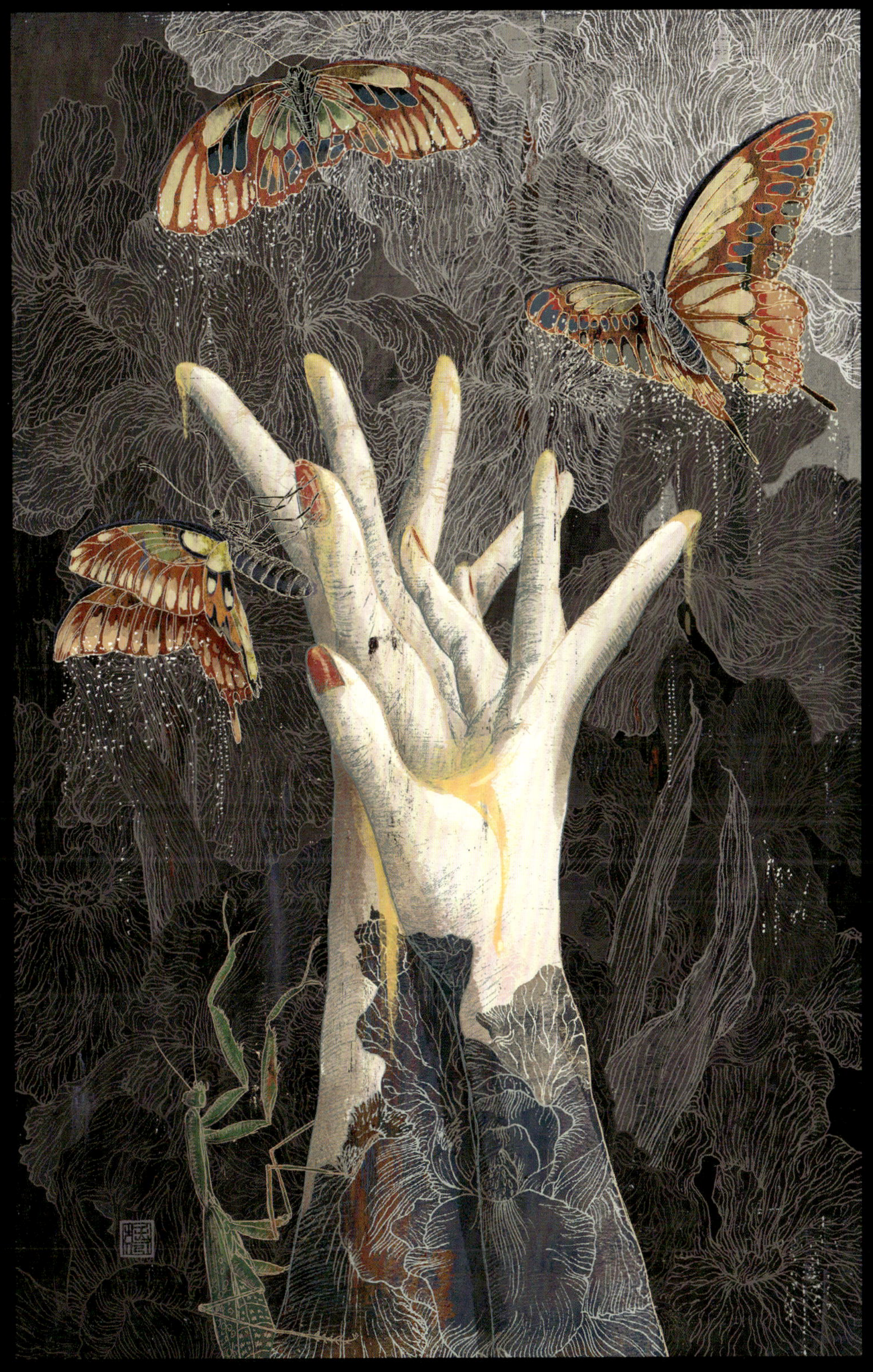


MERIT *Yohey Horishita*

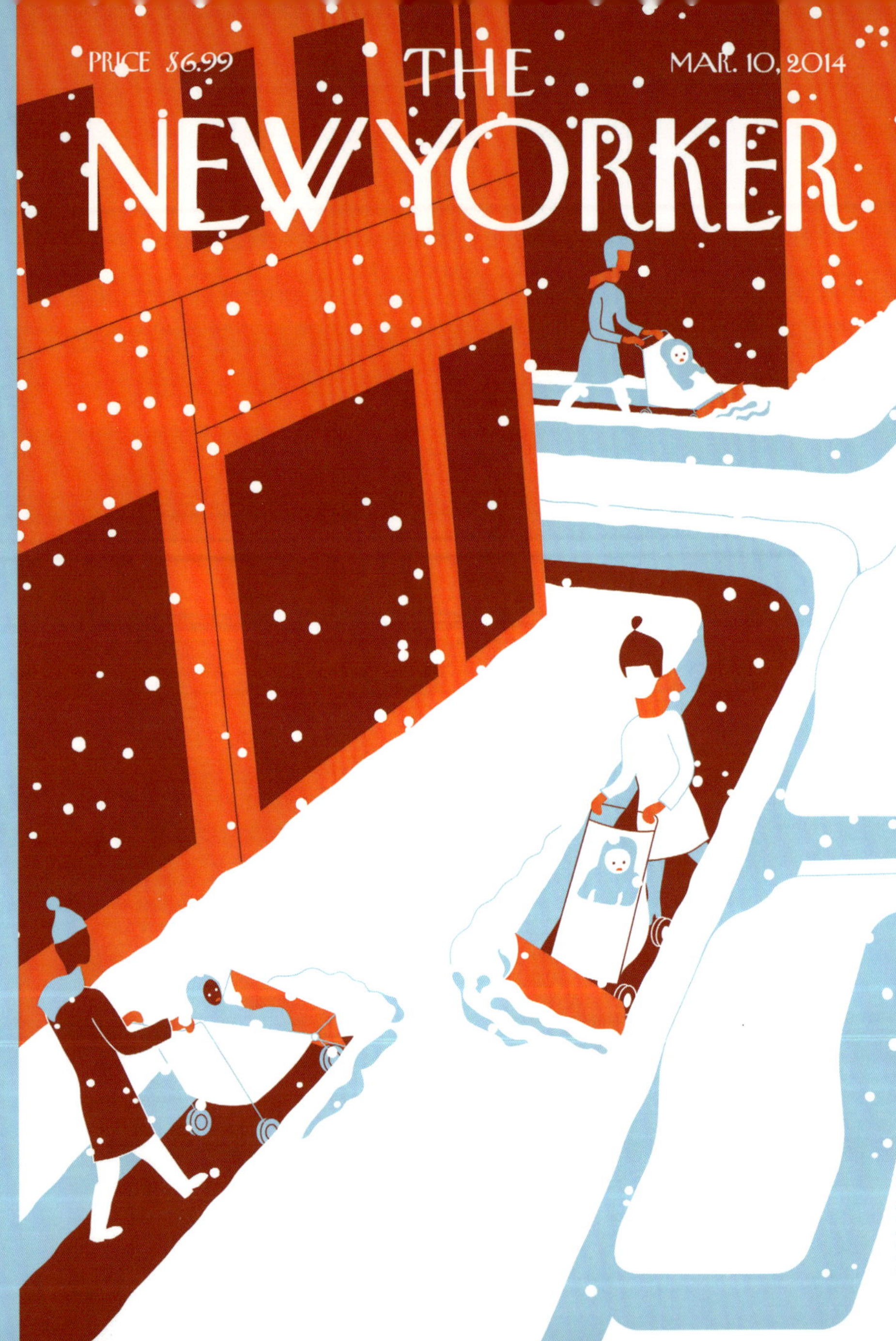

PRICE $6.99
THE
NEW YORKER
MAR. 10, 2014

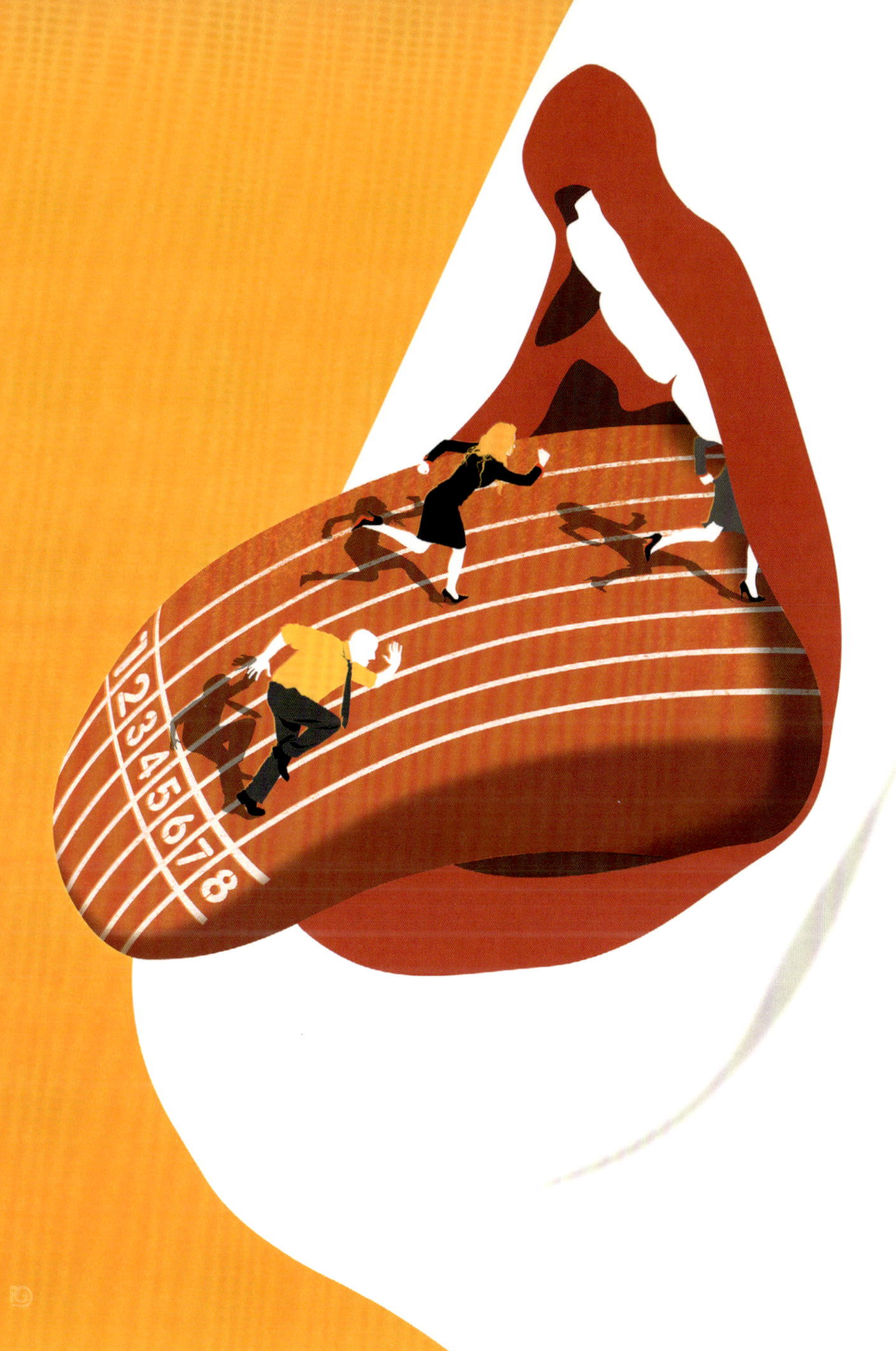

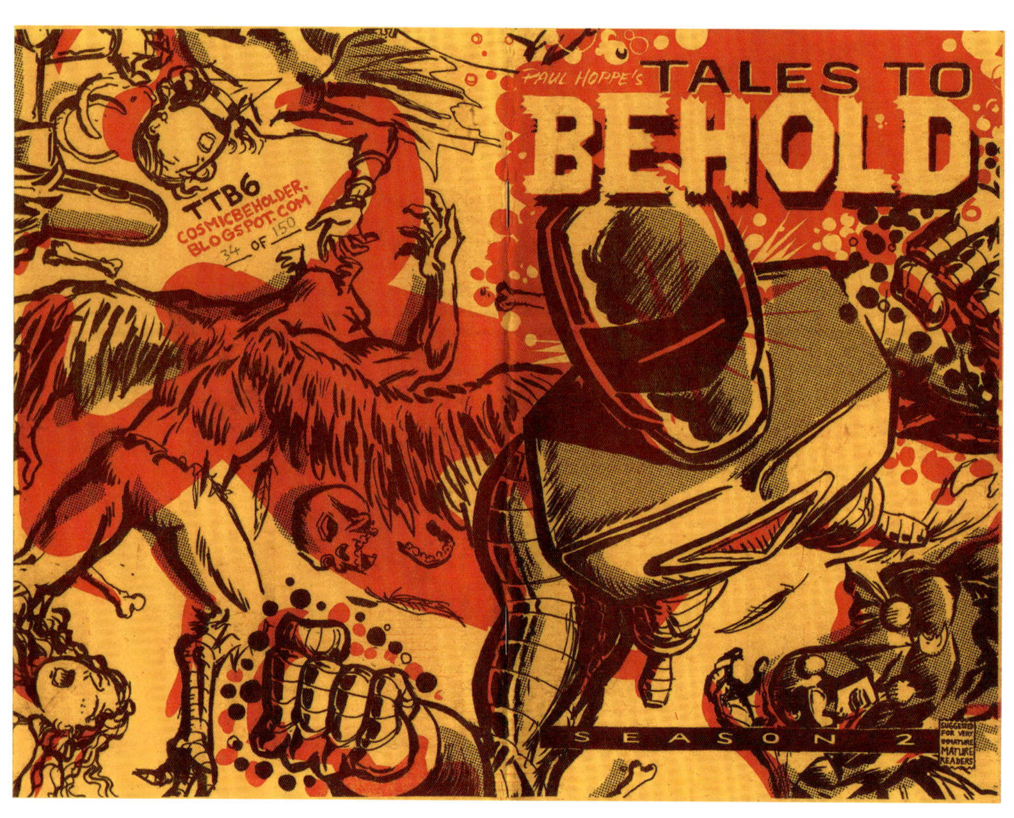


DISTINGUISHED MERIT *Paul Hoppe*

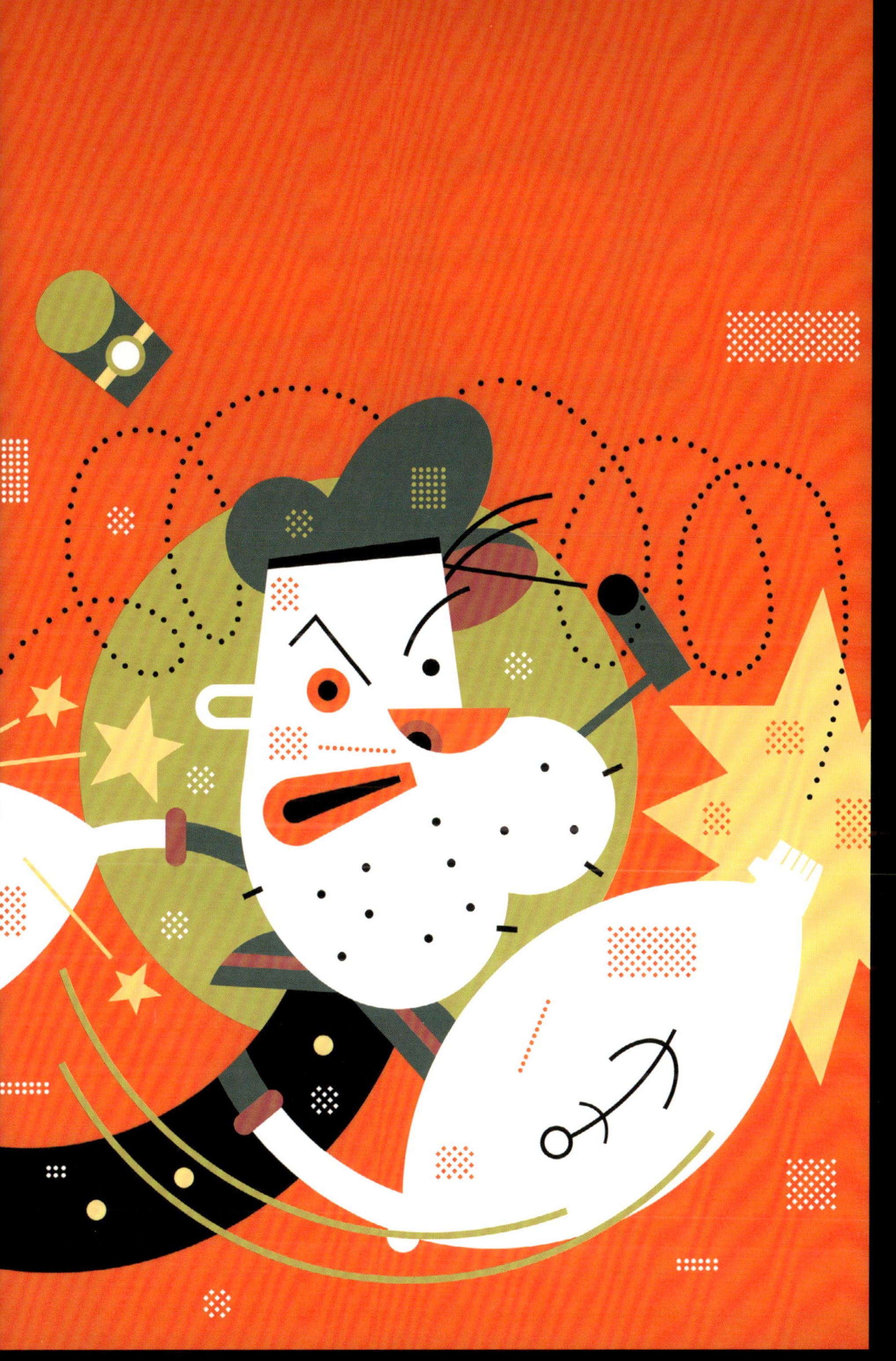

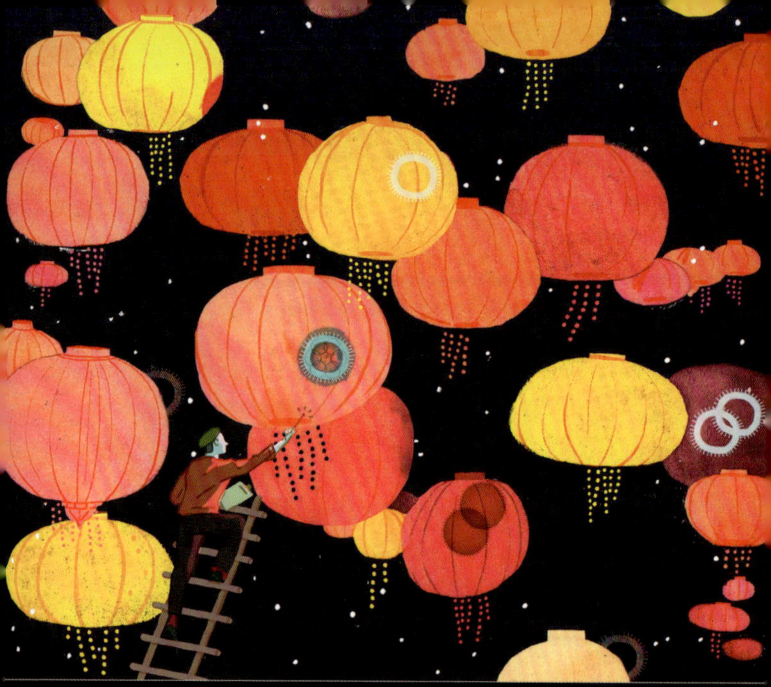

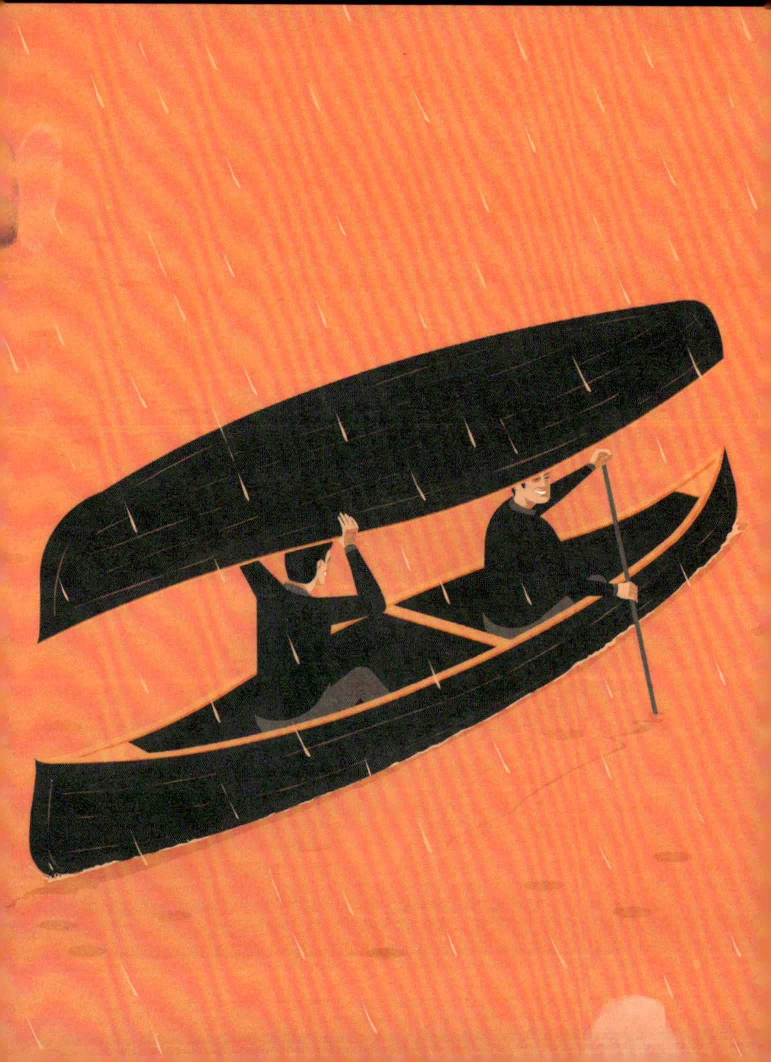

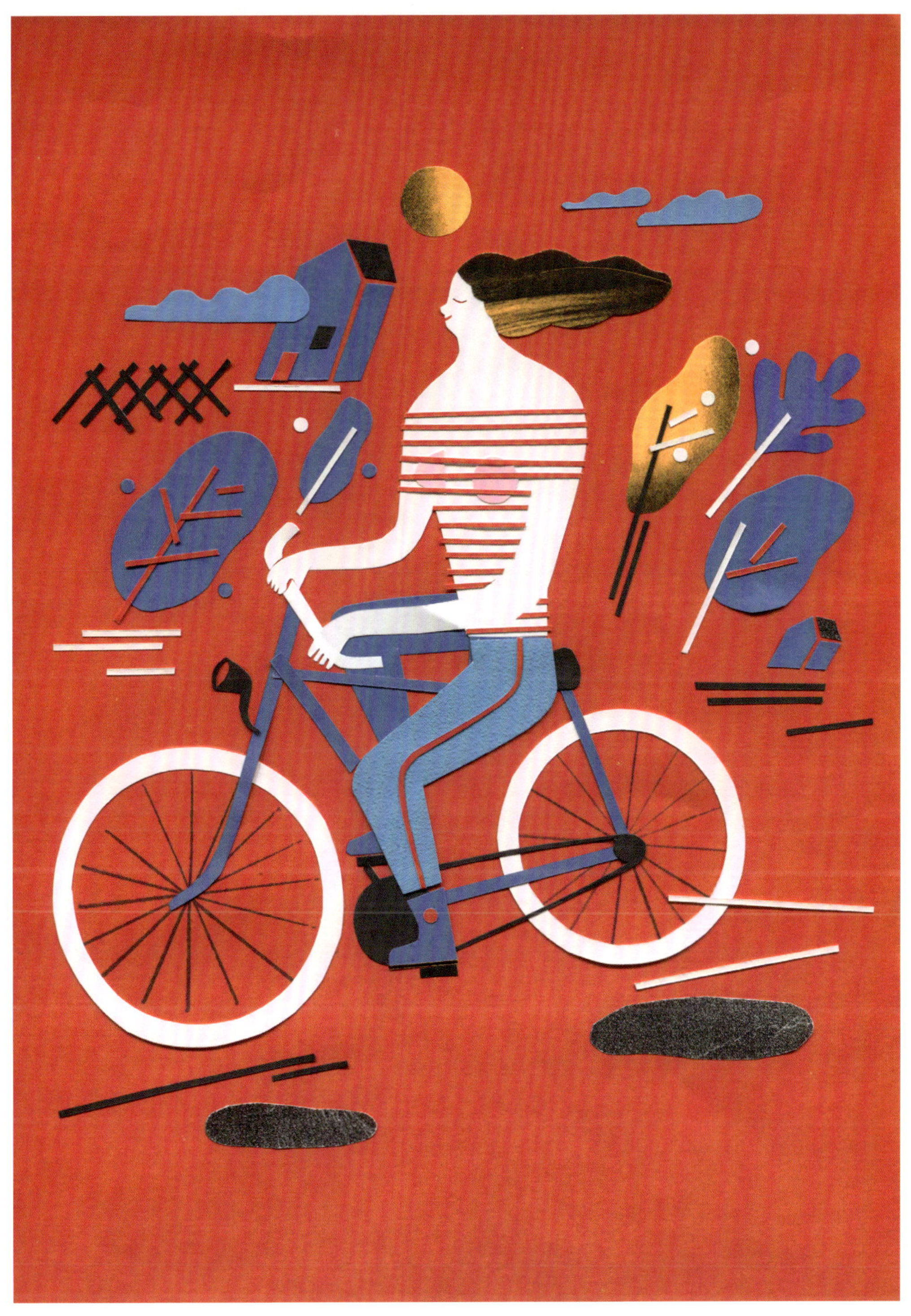

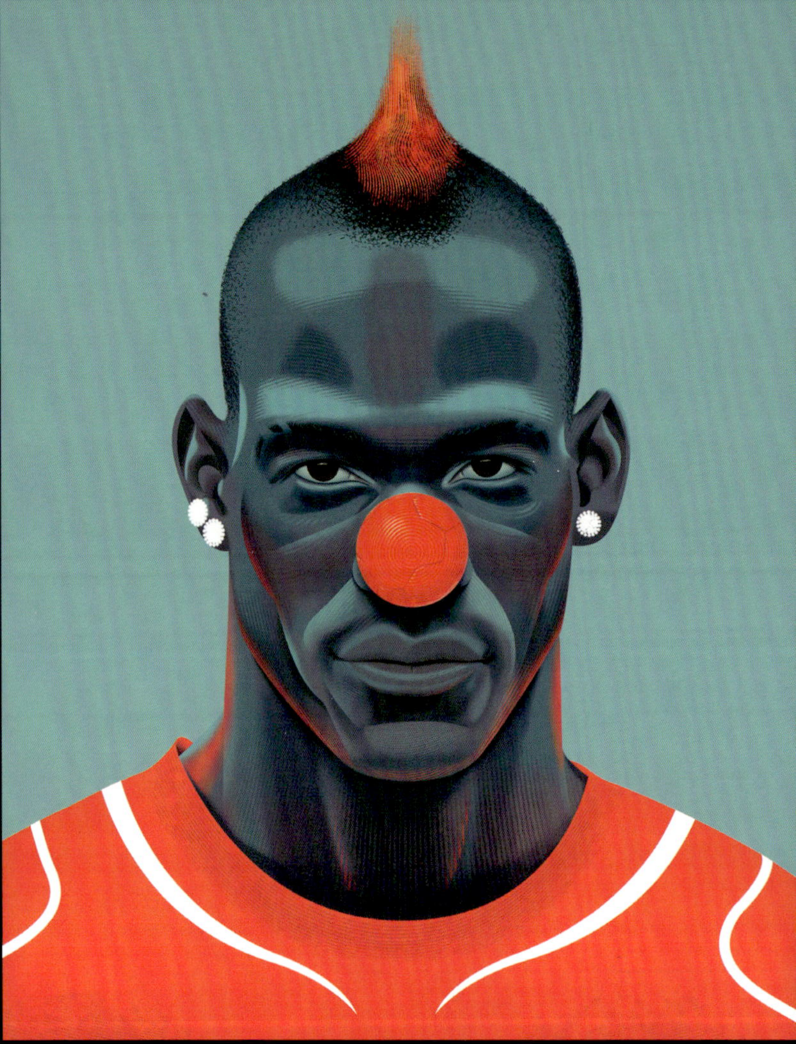

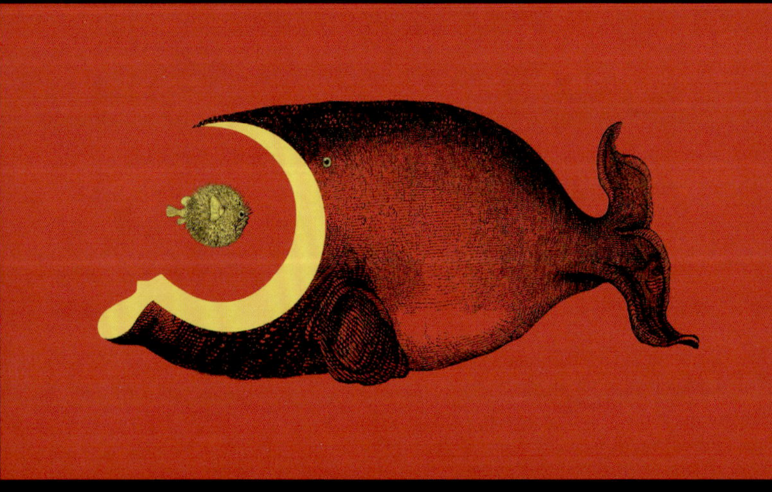

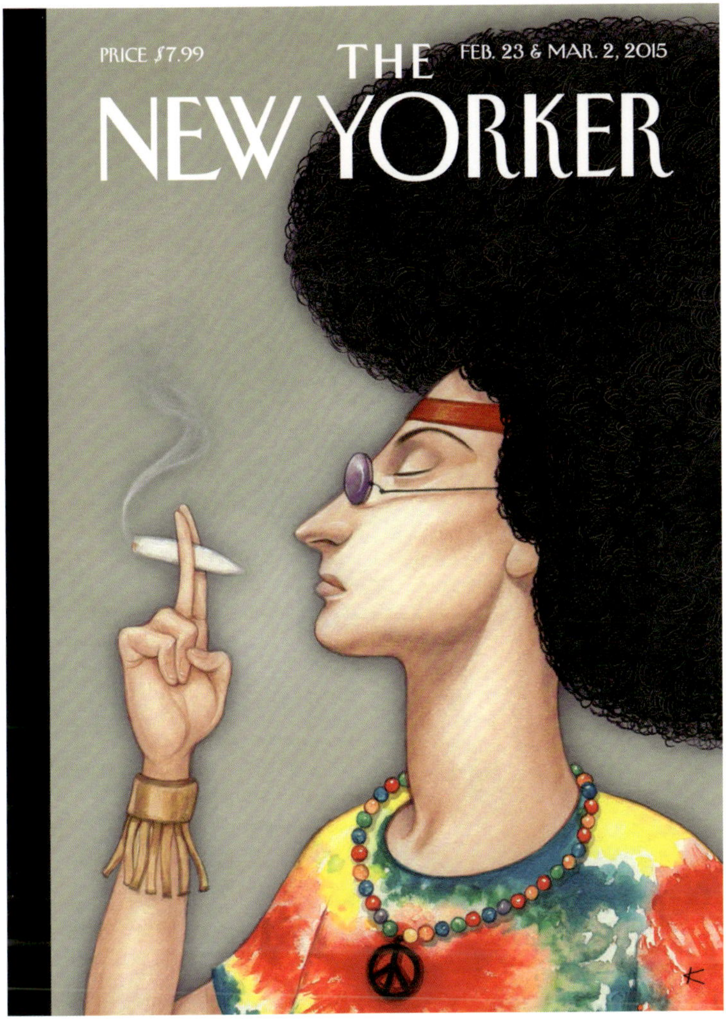

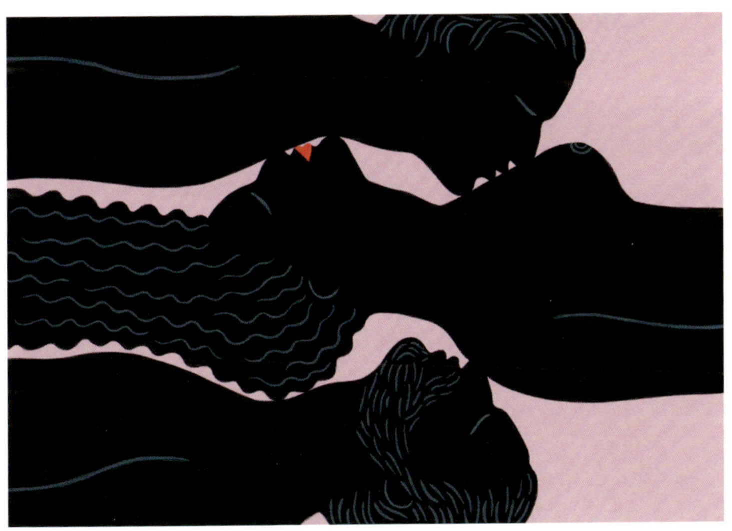


(T) MERIT *Anita Kunz*　　(B) MERIT *Valeria Petrone*

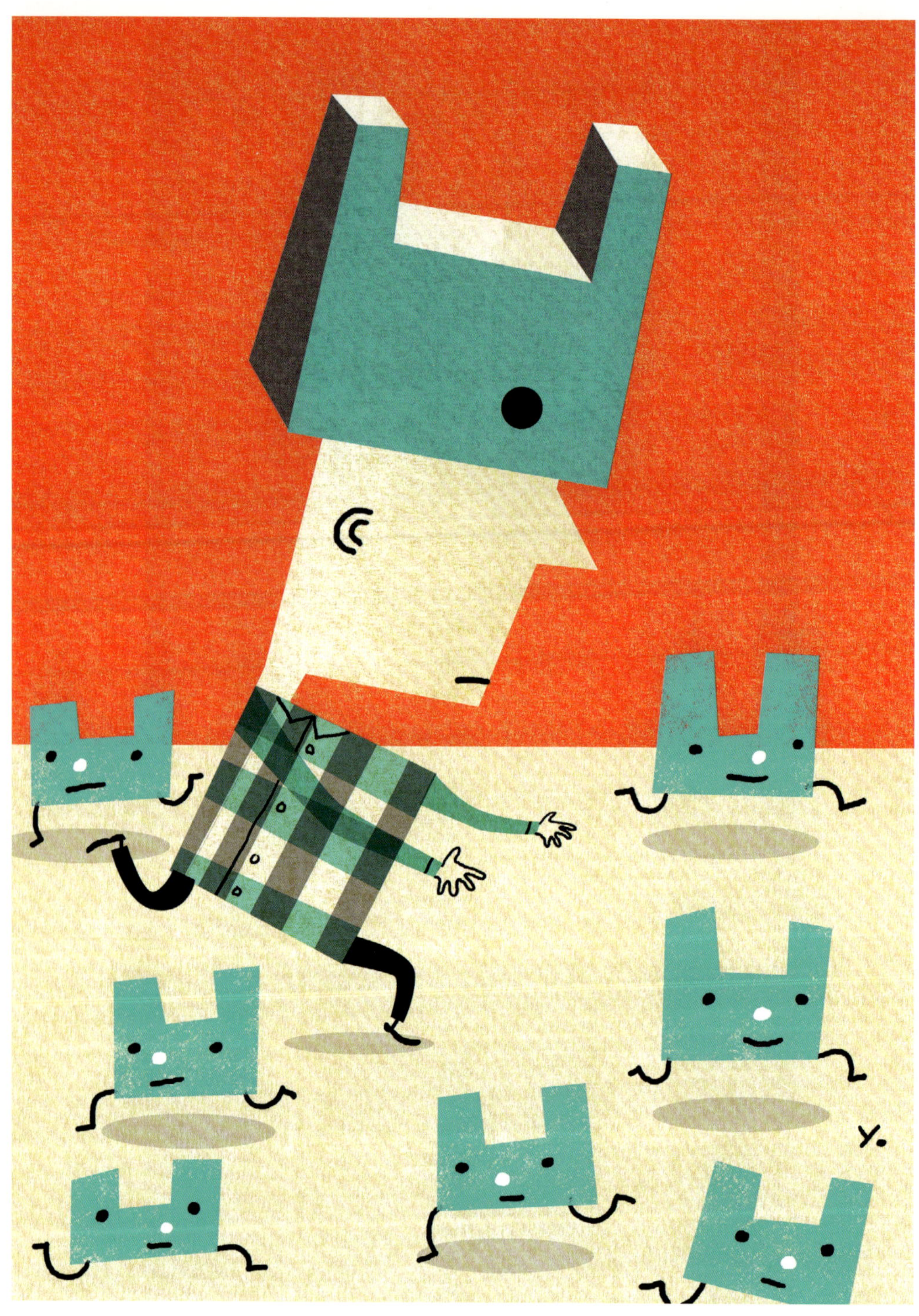





(L) MERIT *James Yang*    (R) MERIT *Anna and Elena Balbusso*

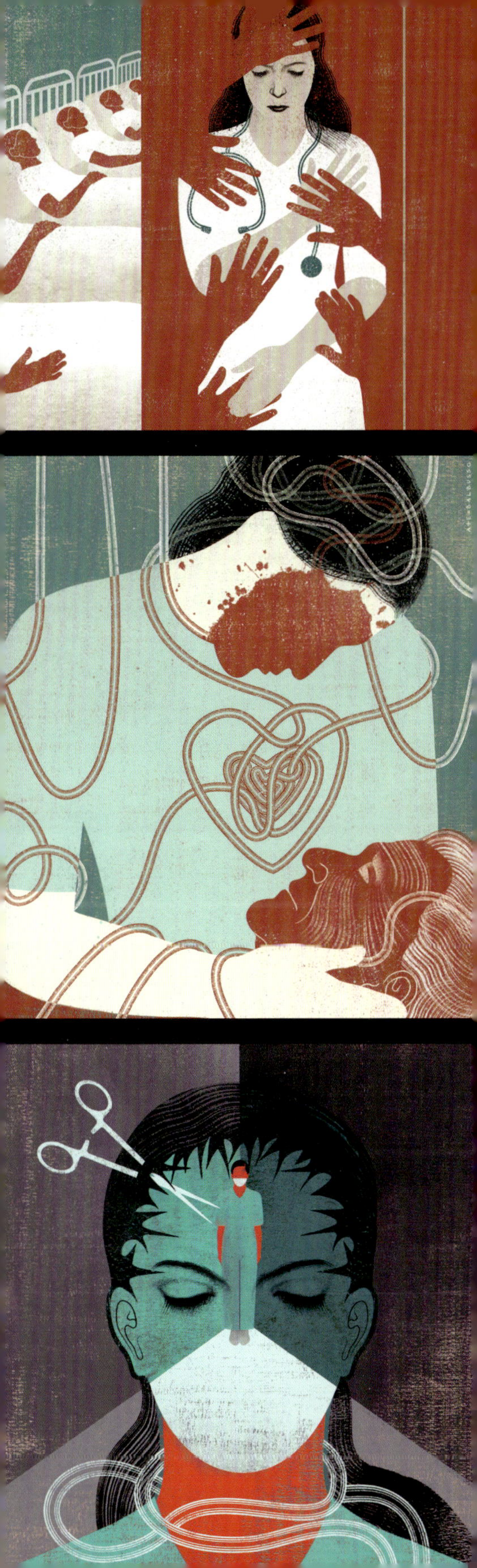

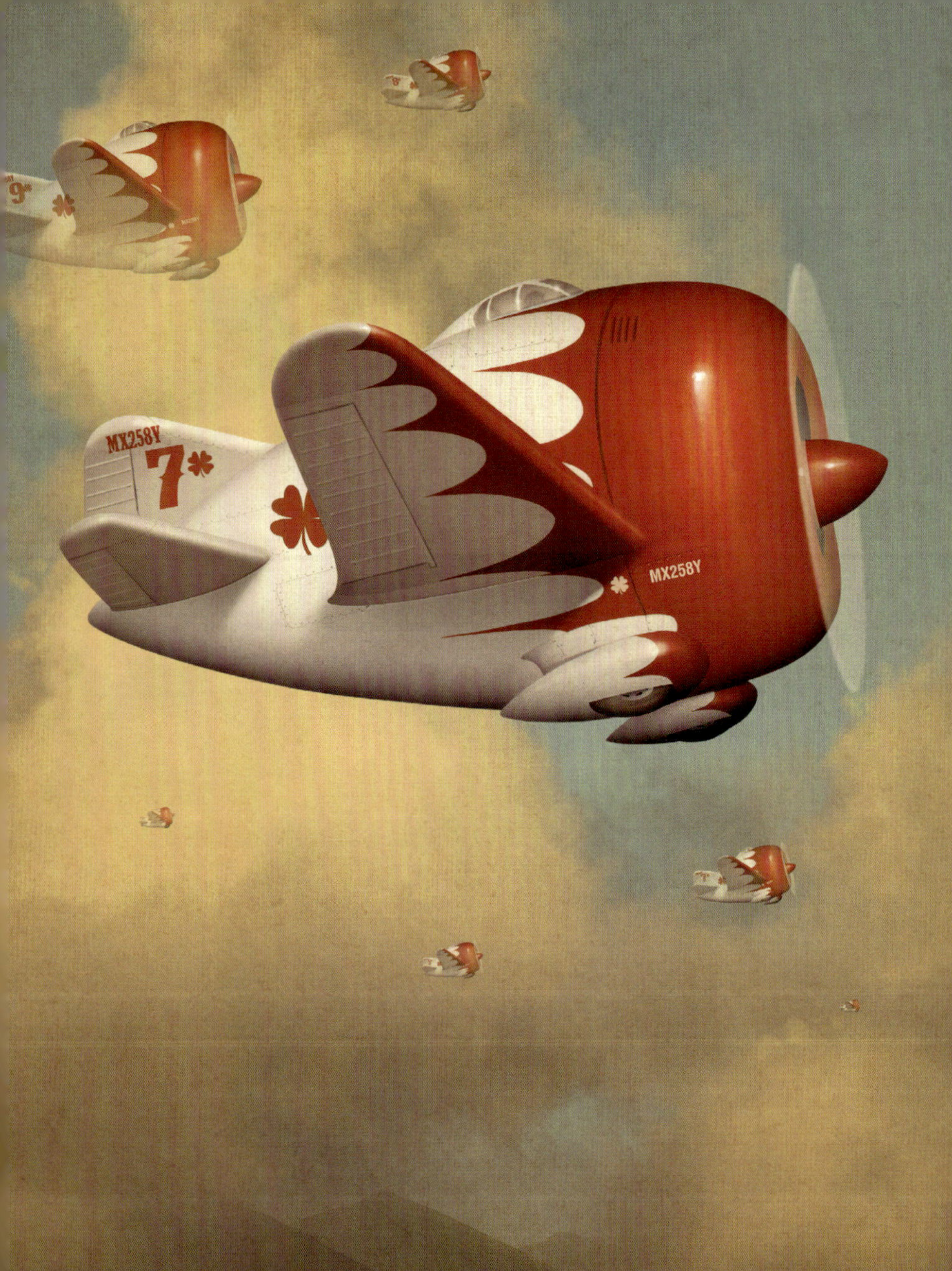
9*
MX258Y
7*
MX258Y

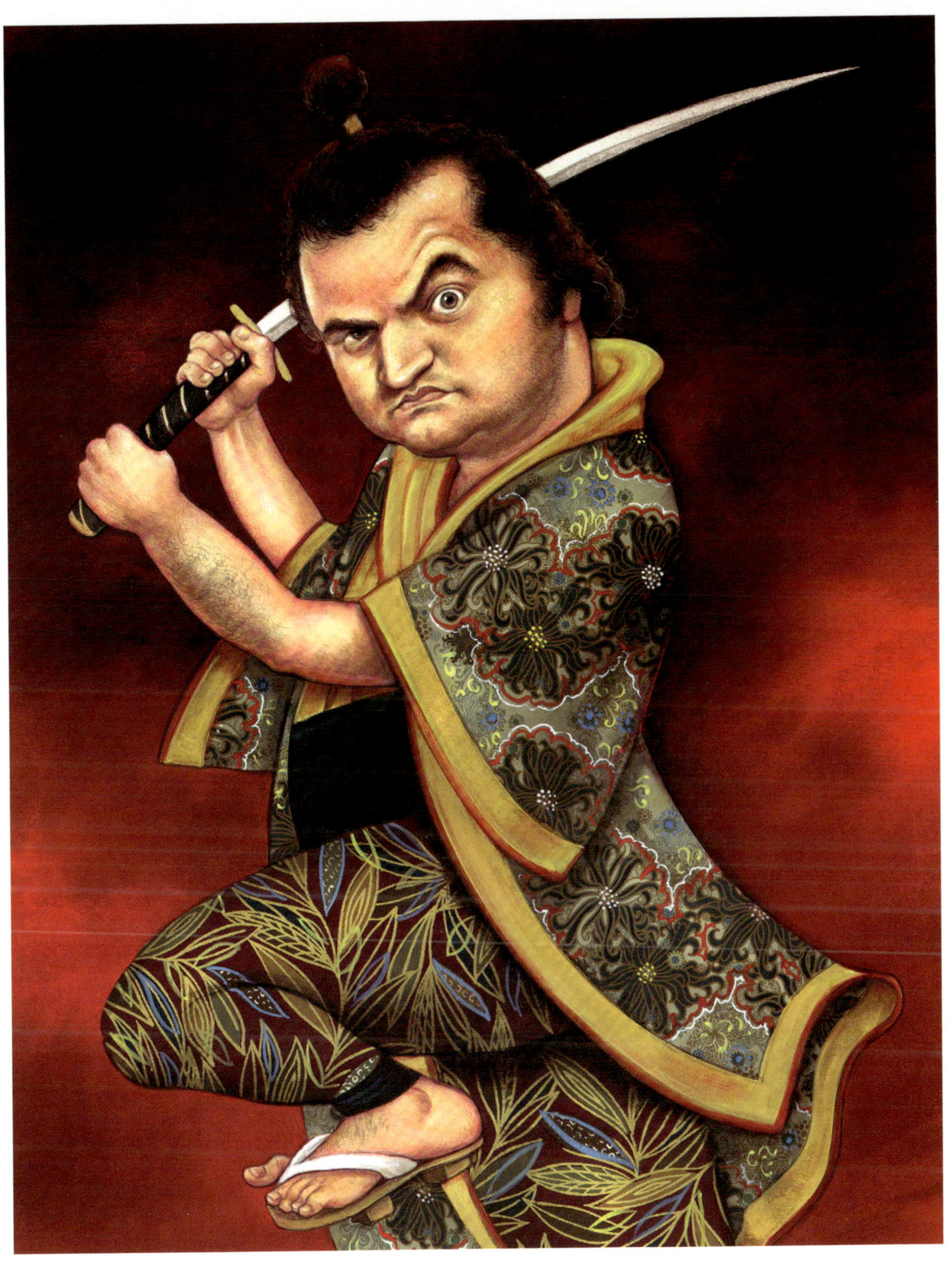



83

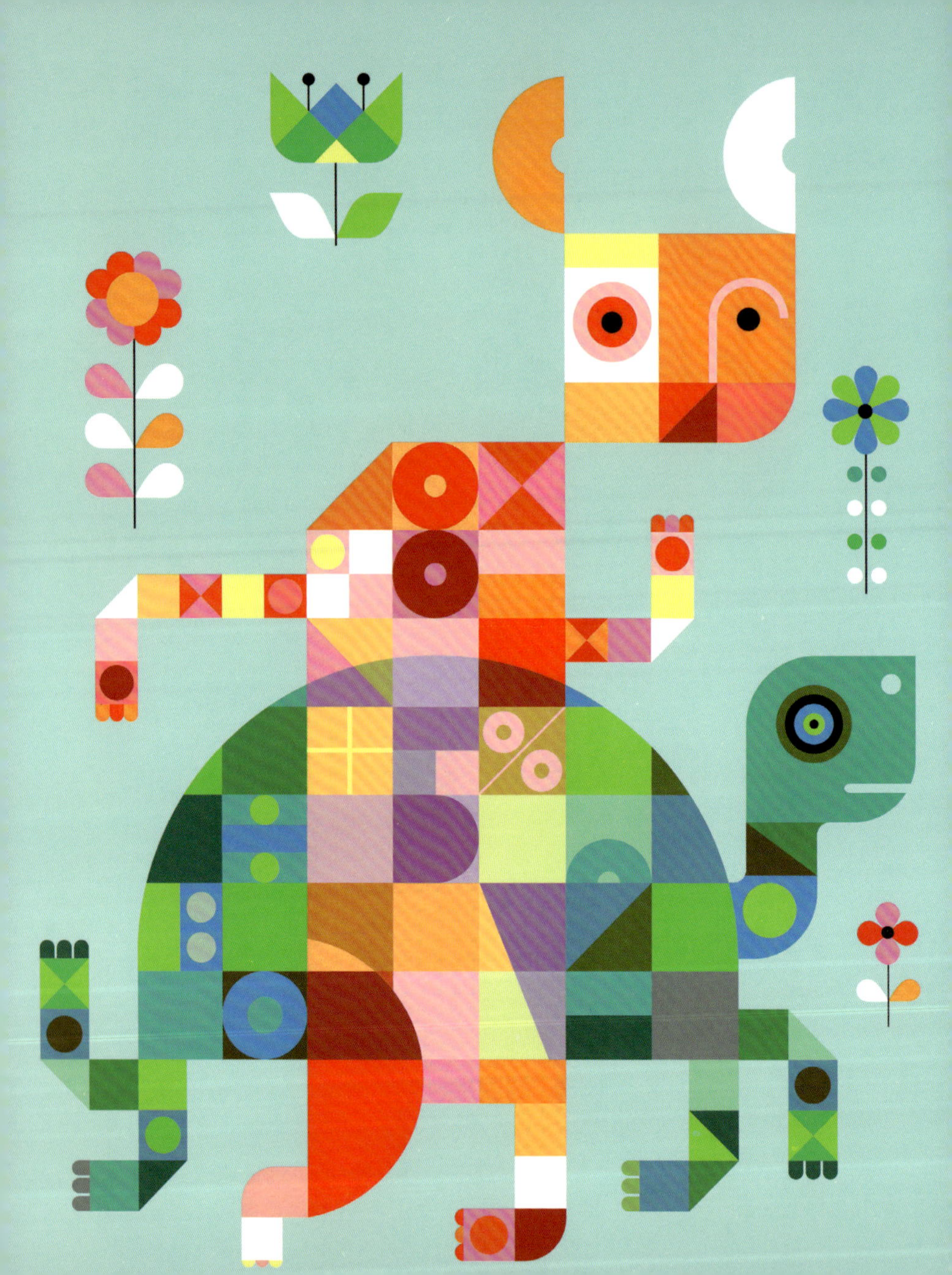

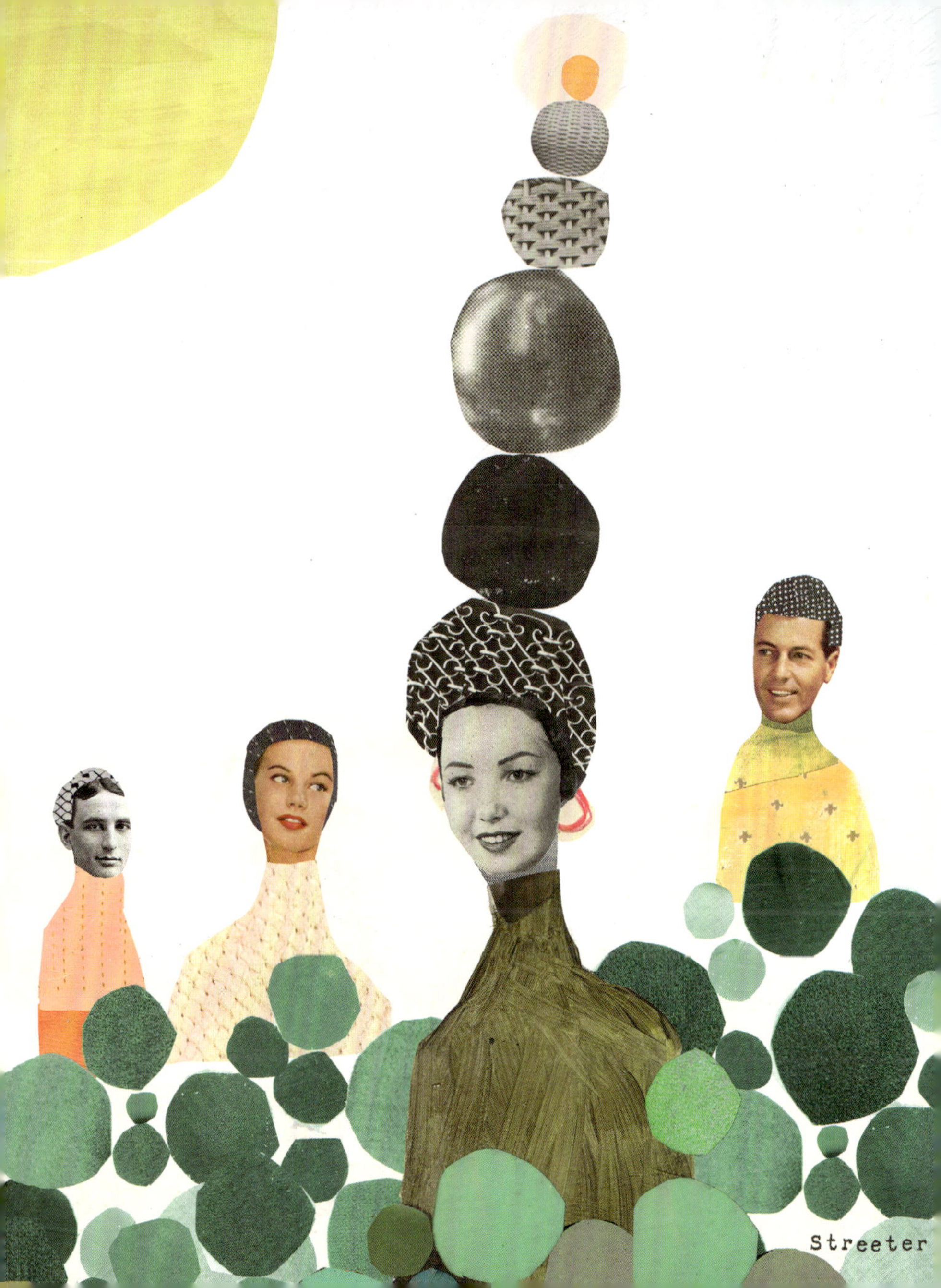

Streeter

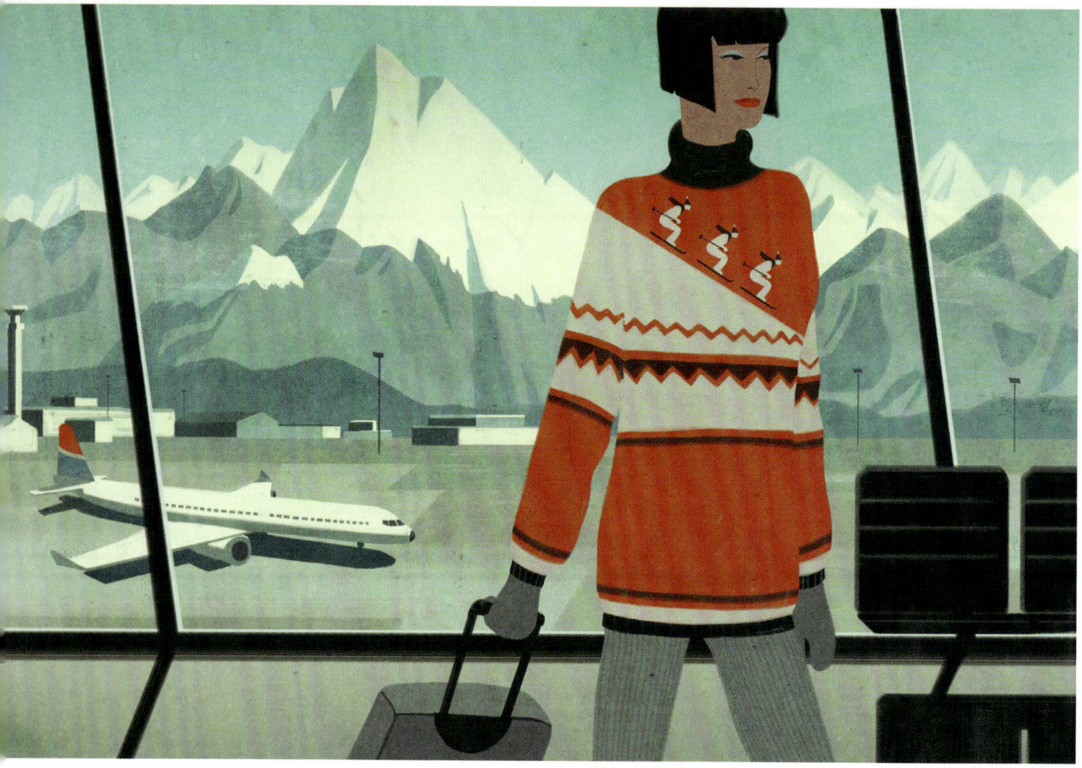

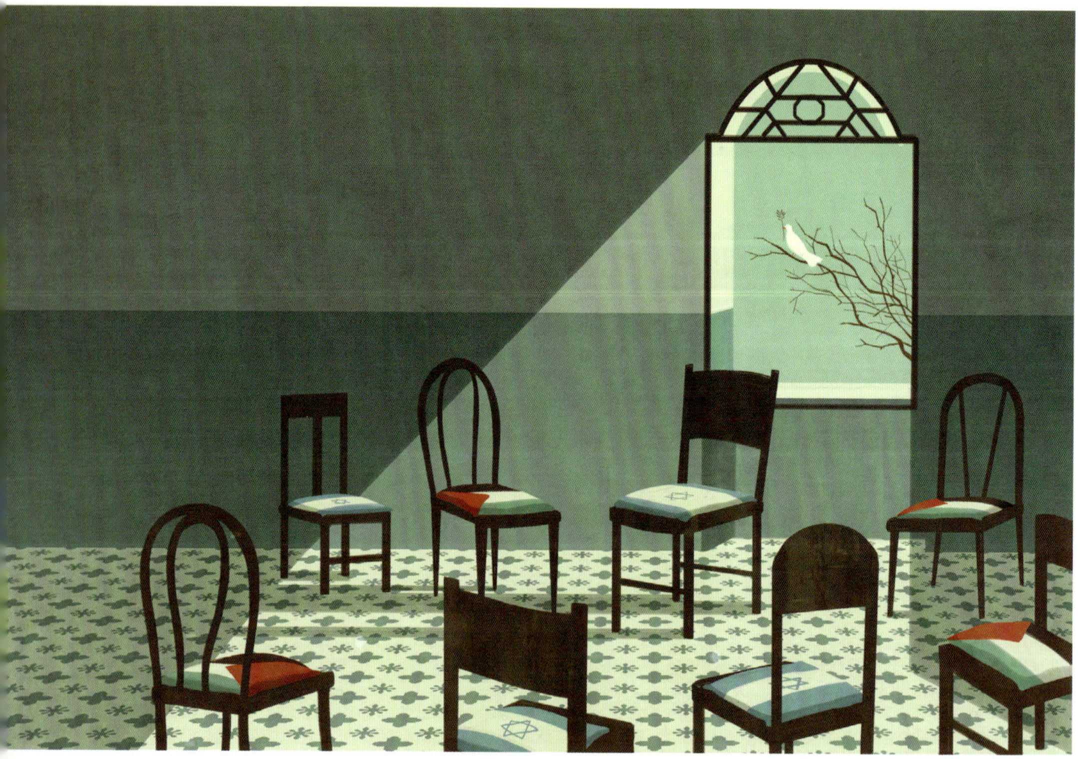

(T) MERIT *Emiliano Ponzi*    (B) MERIT *Emiliano Ponzi*

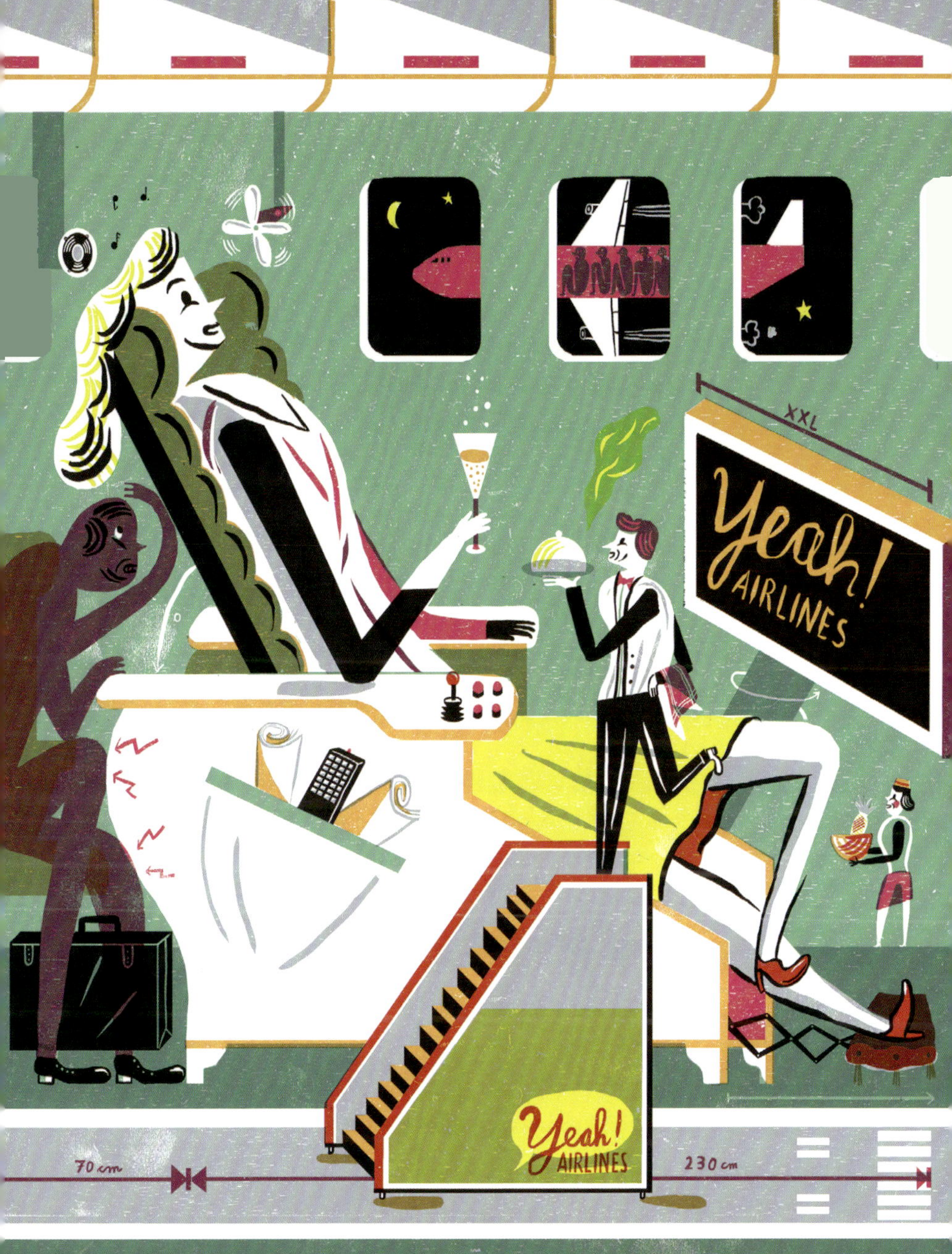
XXL
Yeah!
AIRLINES
Yeah!
AIRLINES
70 cm
230 cm

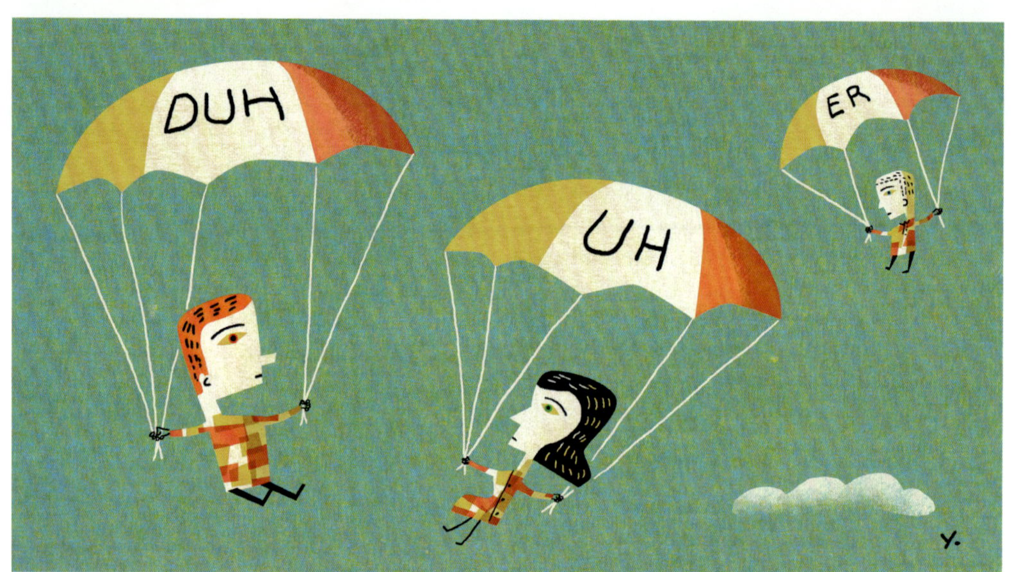

DUH
UH
ER


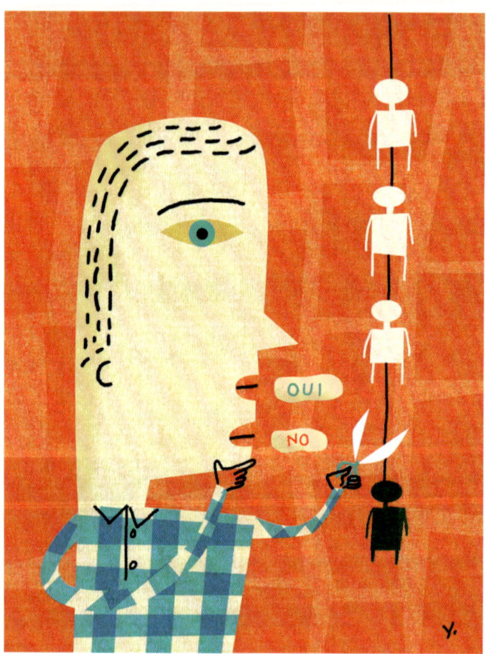

OUI
NO


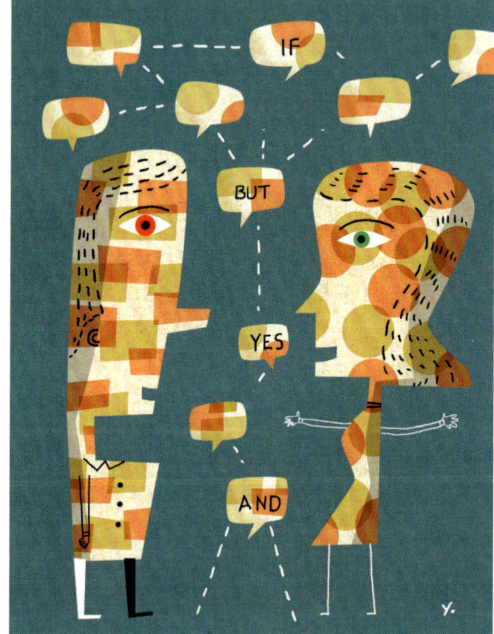

IF
BUT
YES
AND

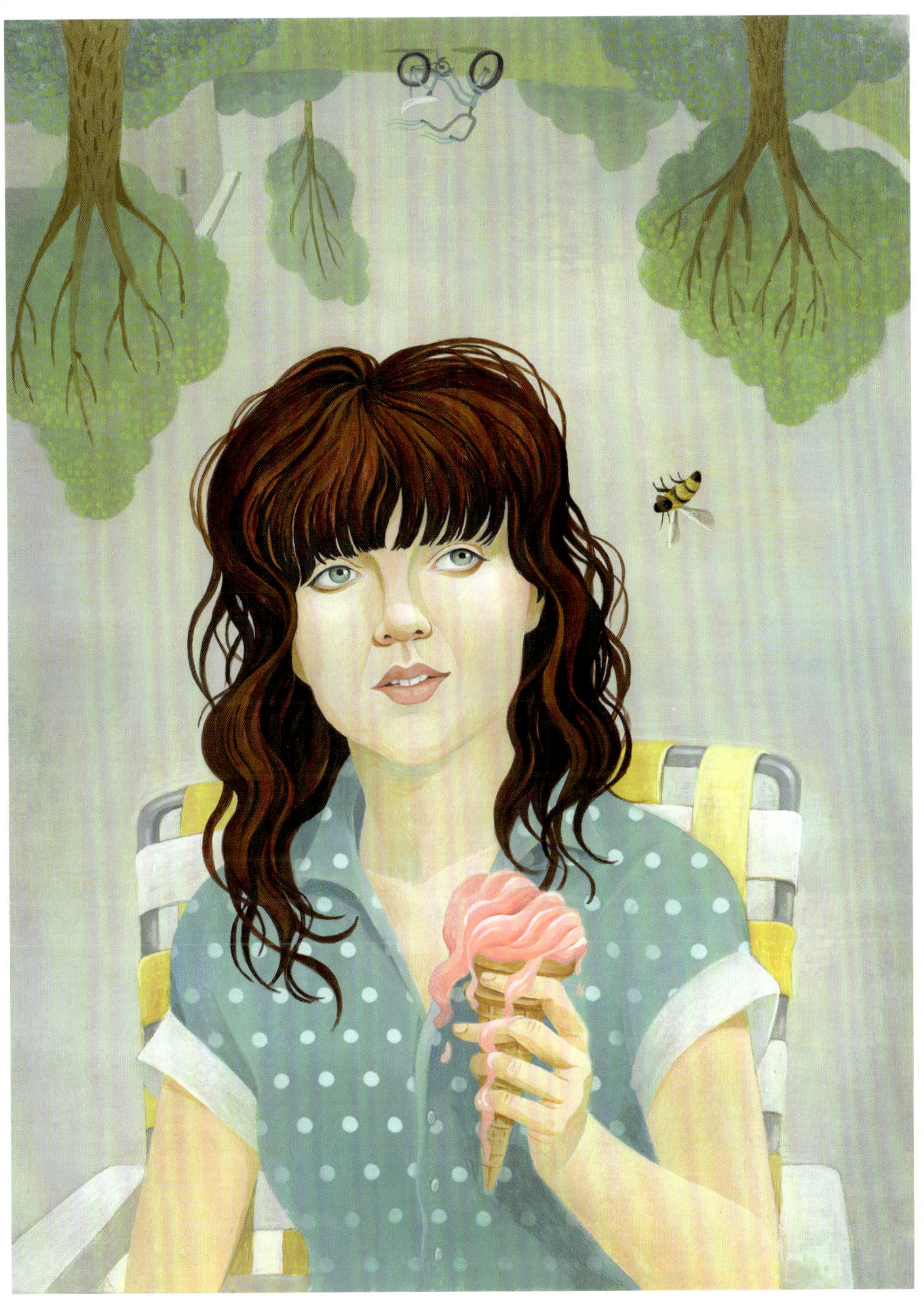

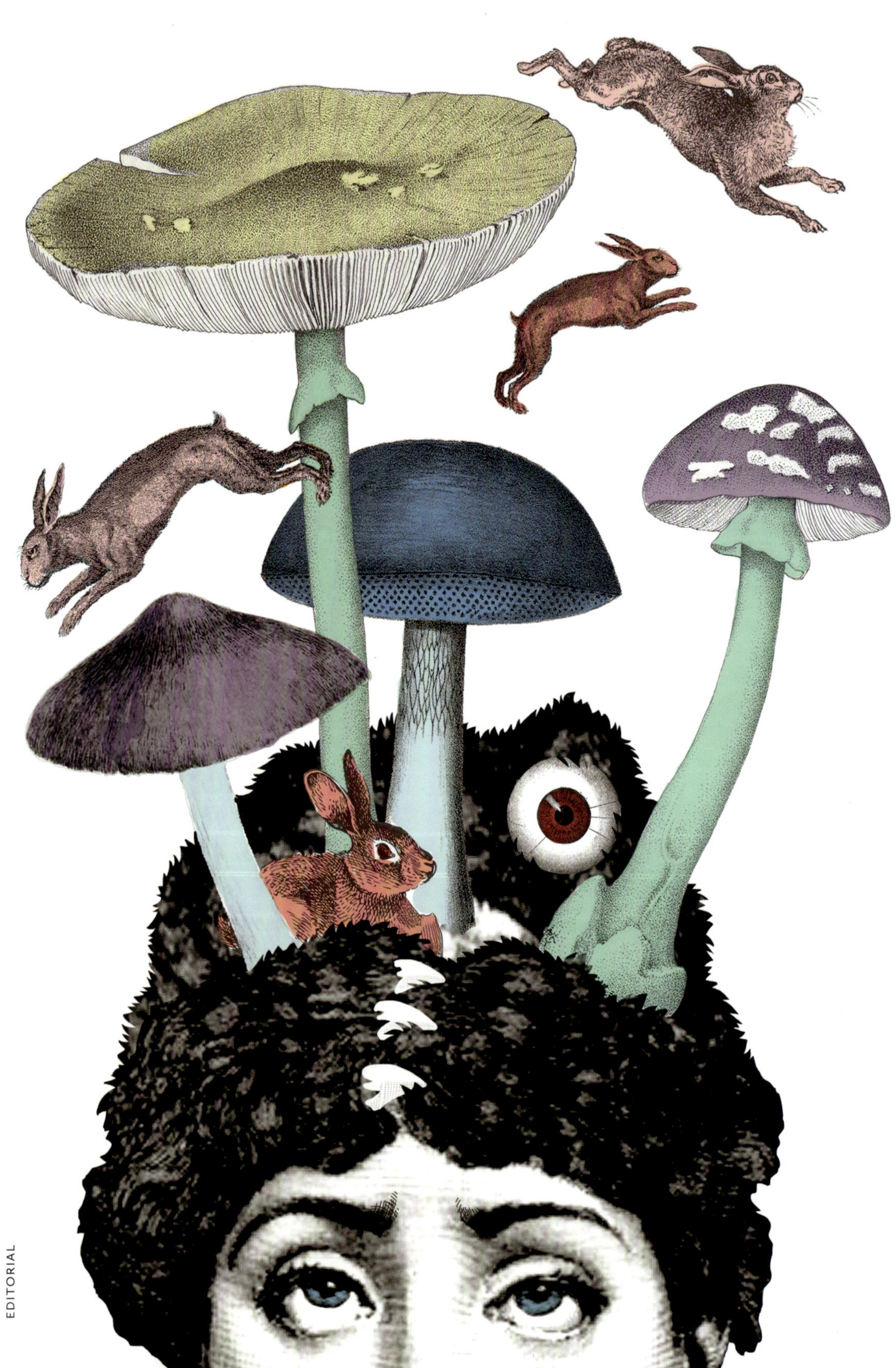
EDITORIAL

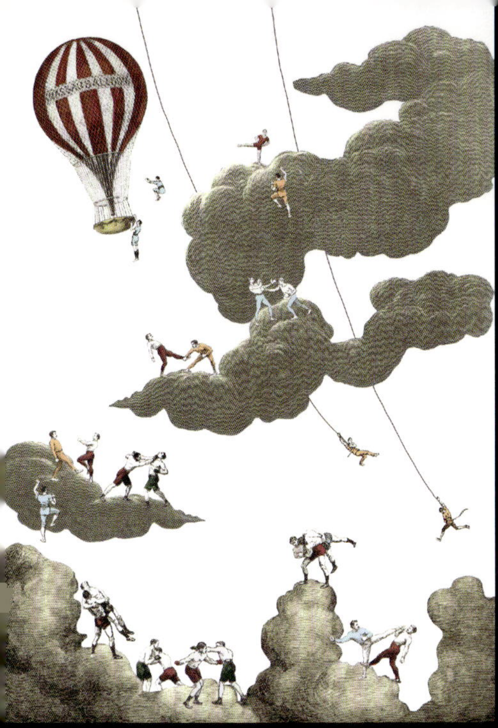

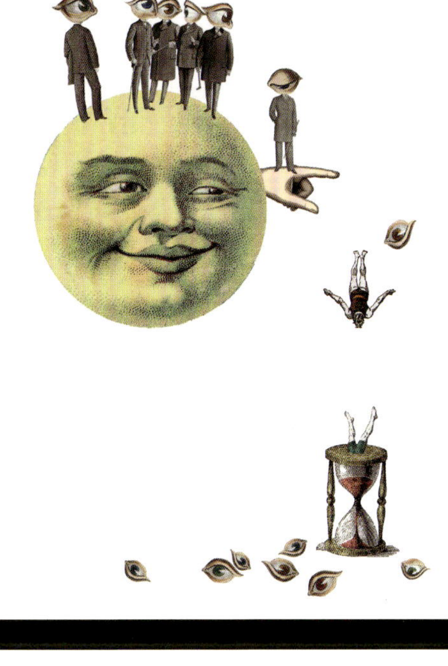

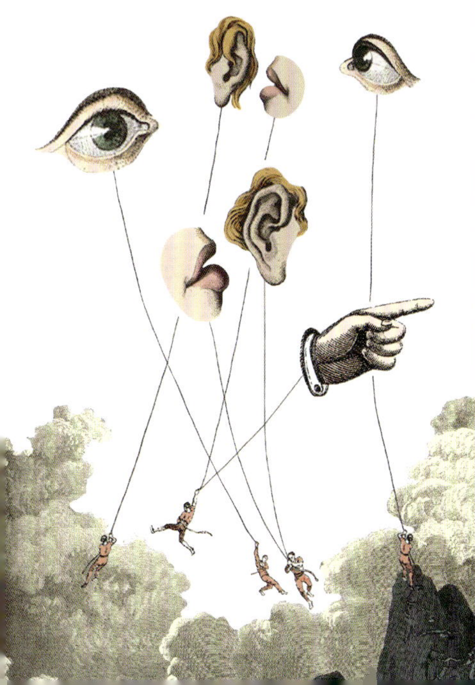

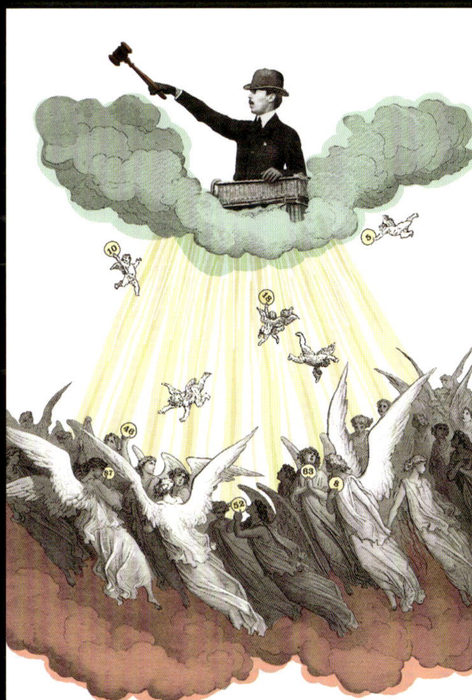

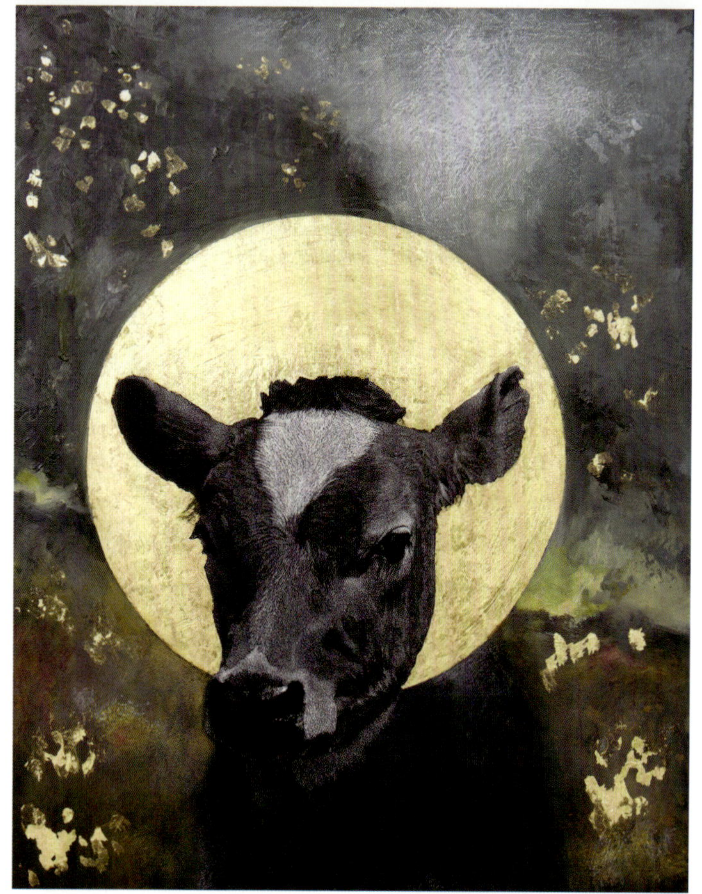

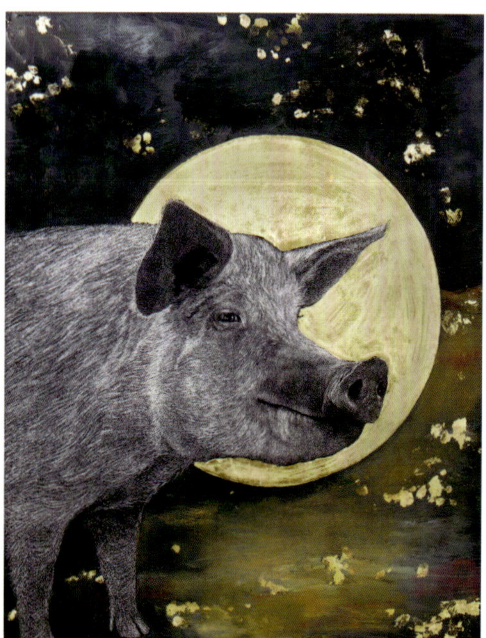

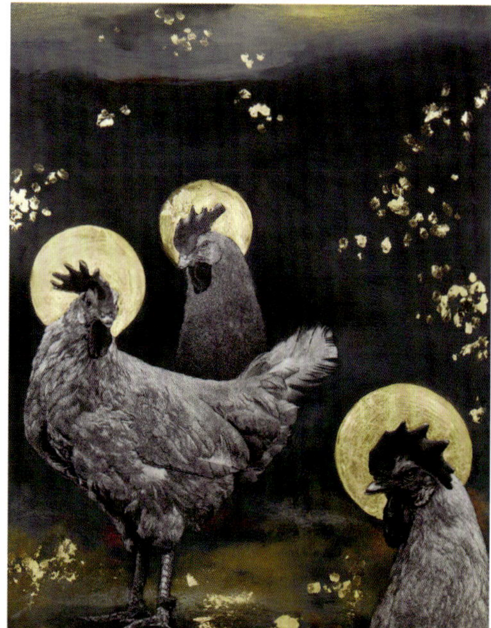

MERIT *Heather Heckel*

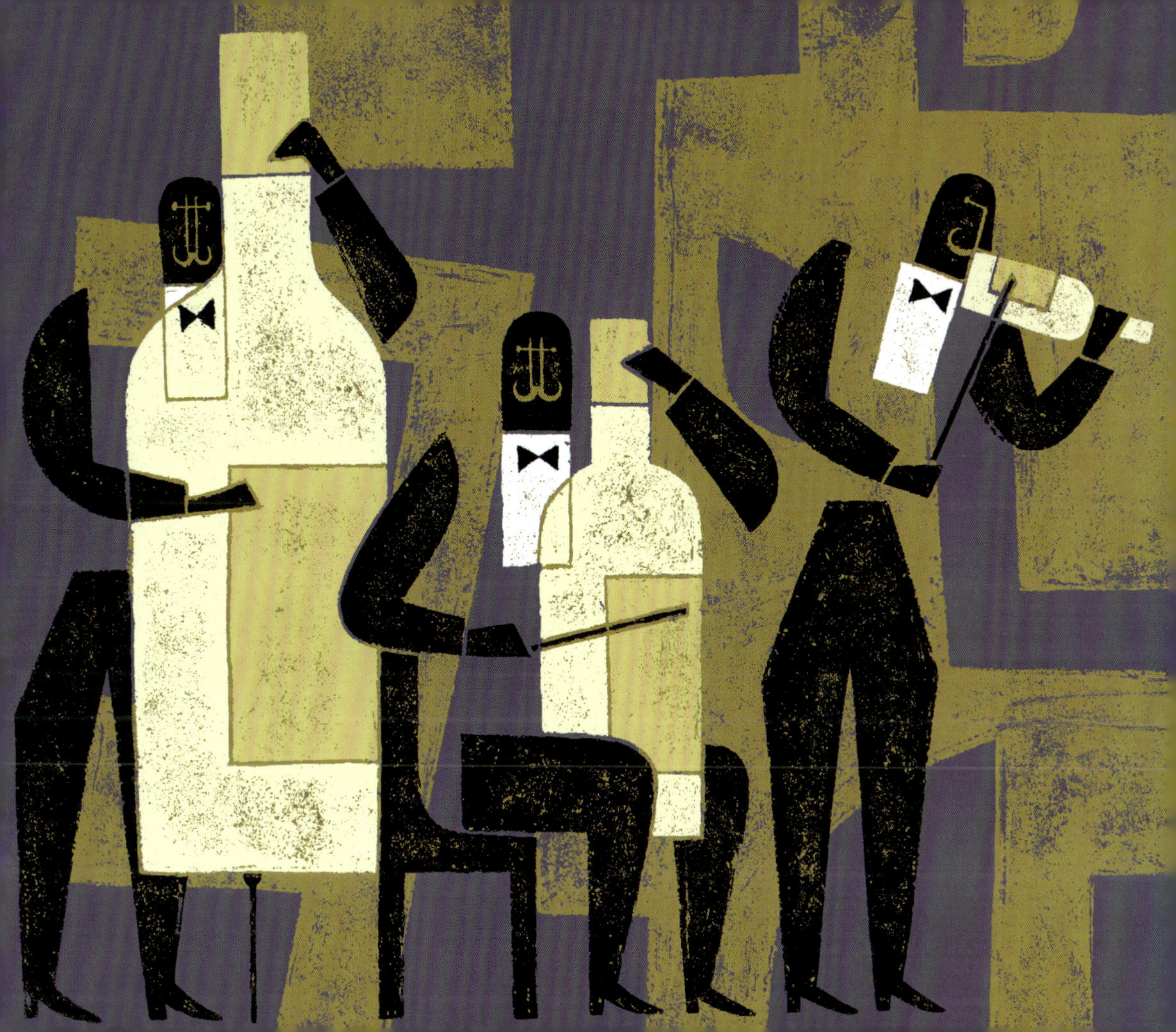

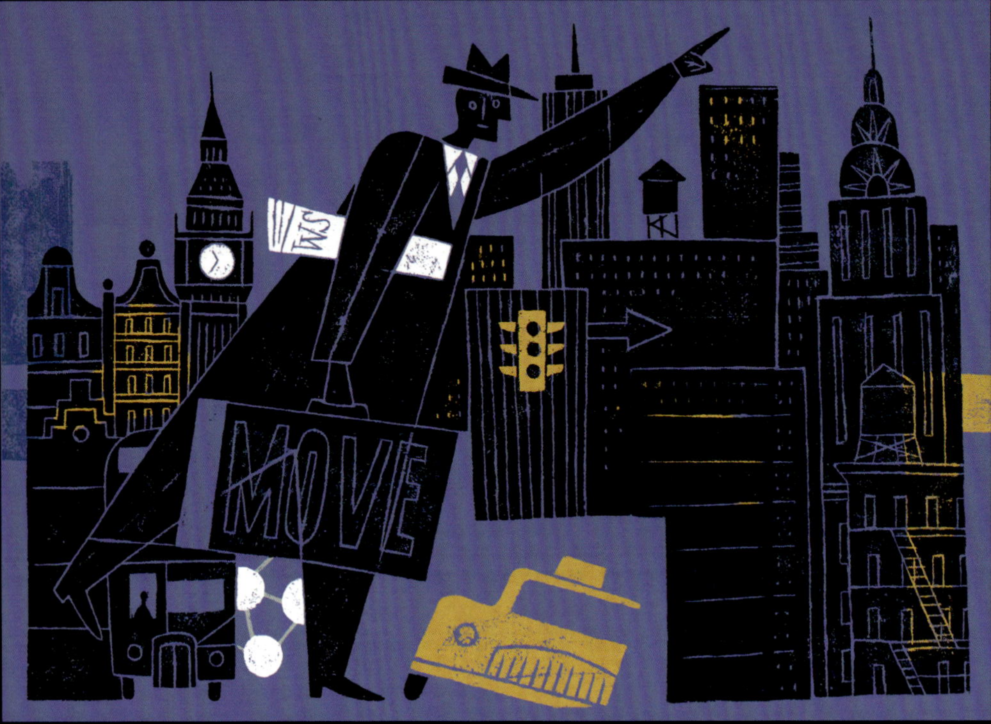

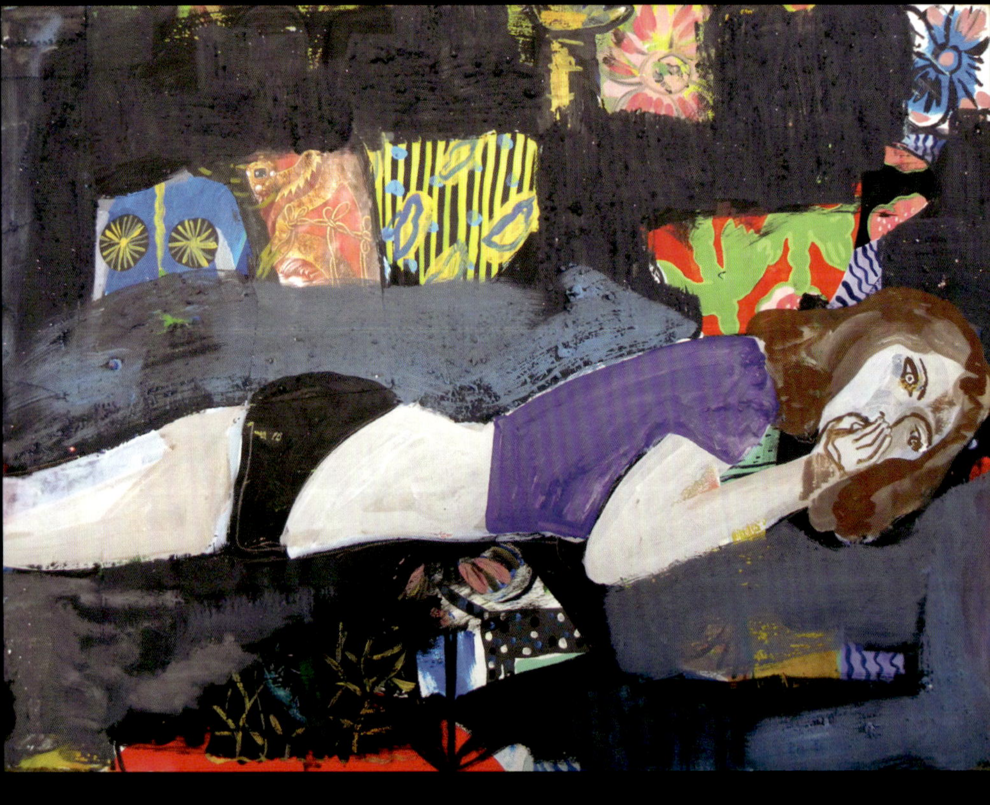

(T) MERIT *Jean-Manuel Duvivier*    (B) MERIT *Karen Barbour*

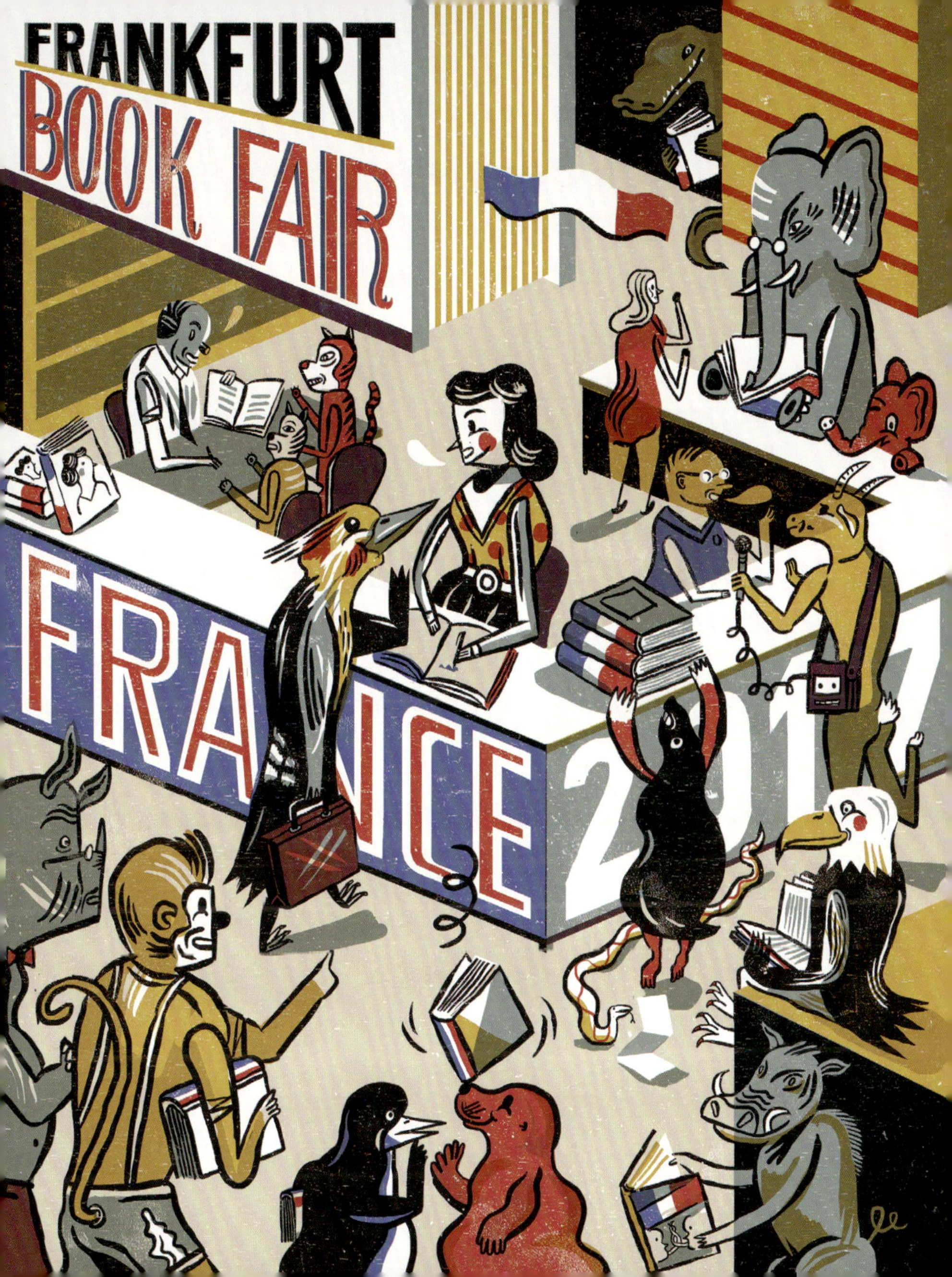
FRANKFURT
BOOK FAIR
FRANCE
2017

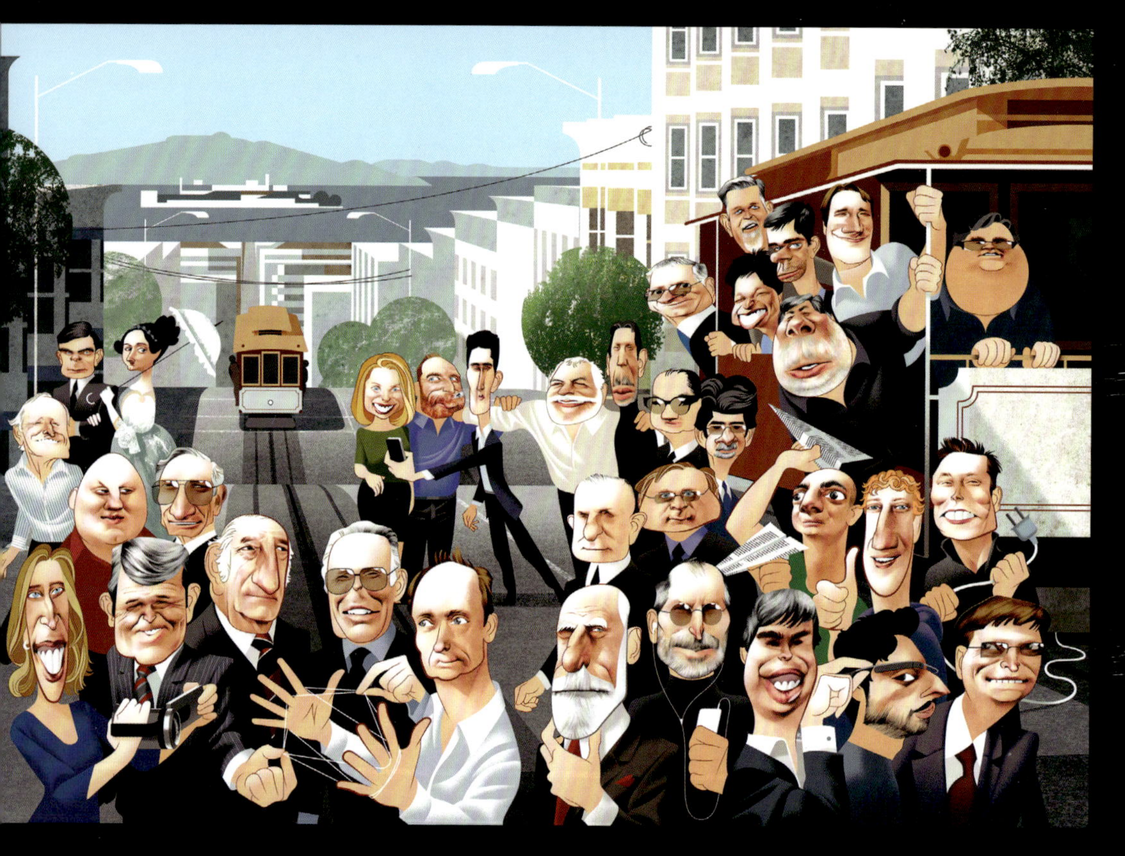

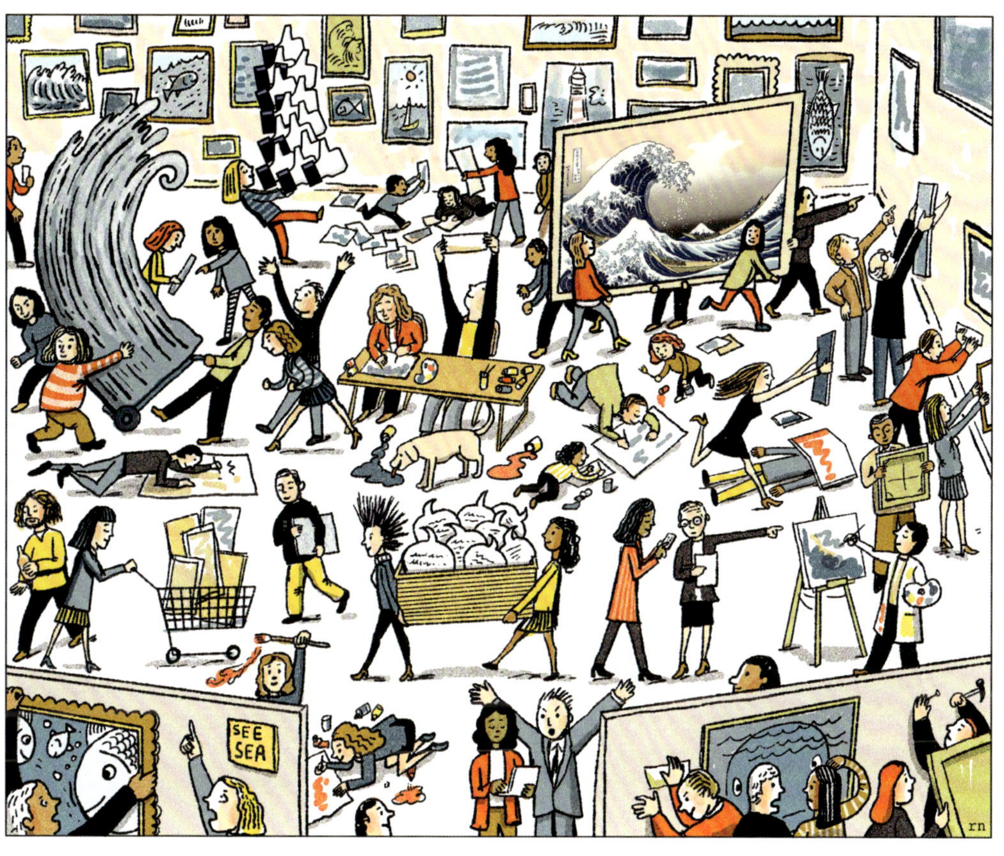





MERIT *Robert Neubecker*

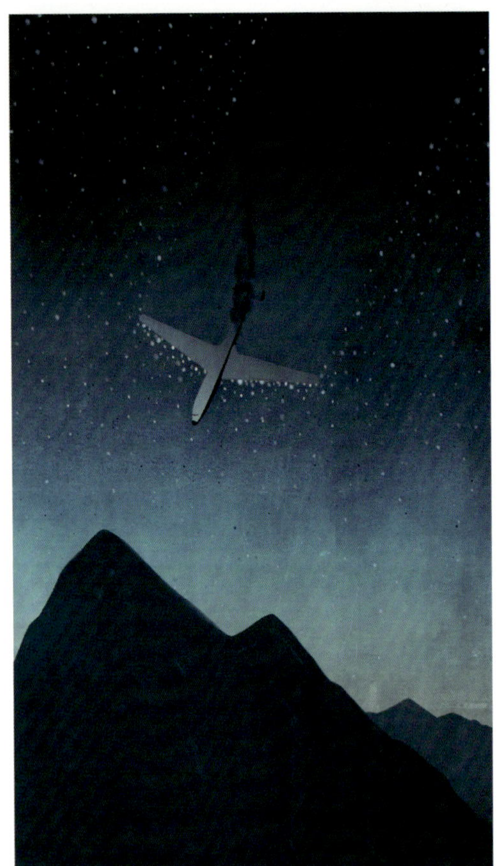
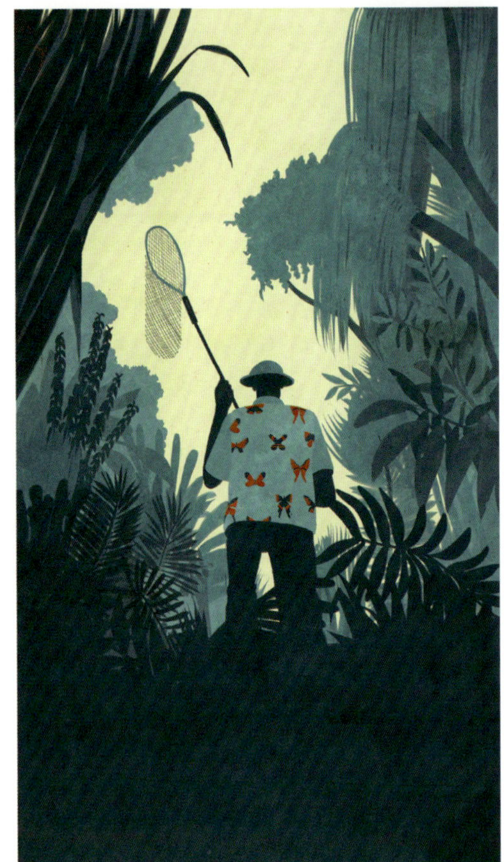
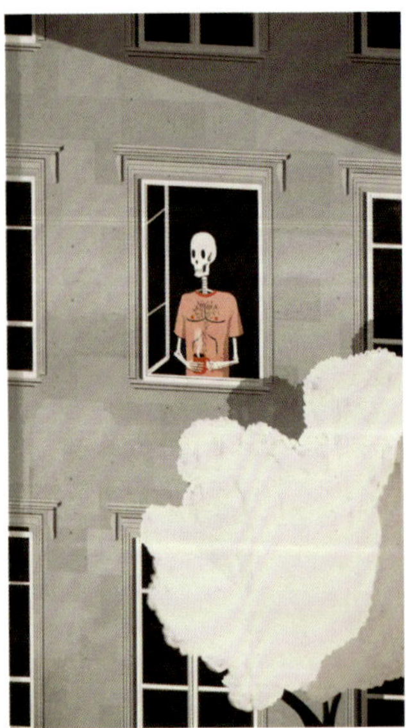
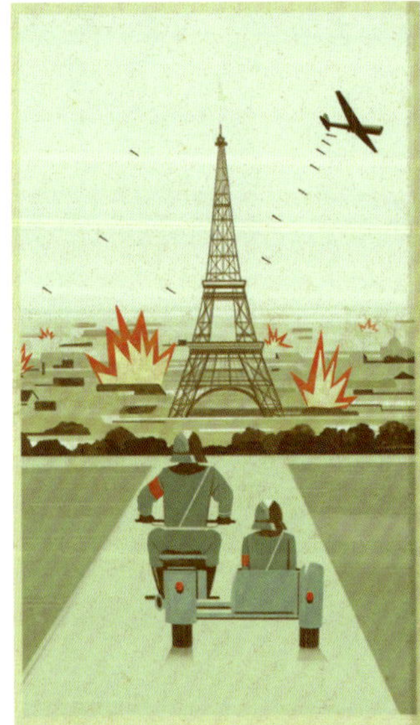
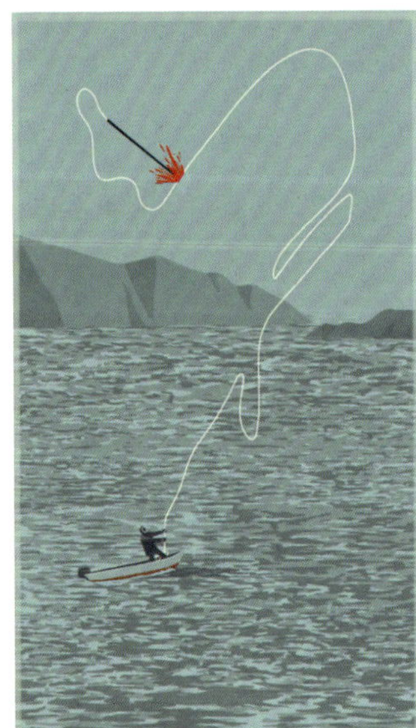



(L) MERIT *Emiliano Ponzi*    (R) MERIT *Aart-Jan Venema*

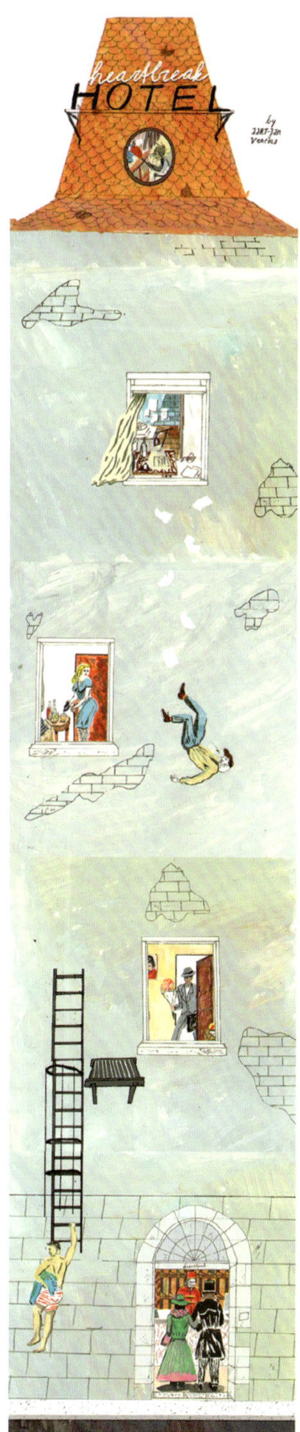

heartbreak
HOTEL
by
Jart-Jan
Venema


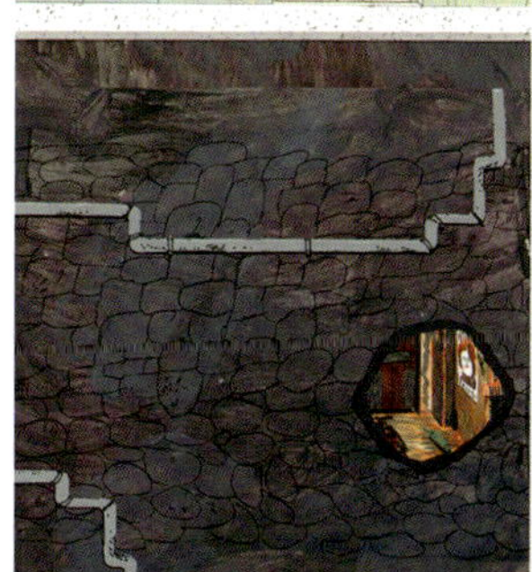

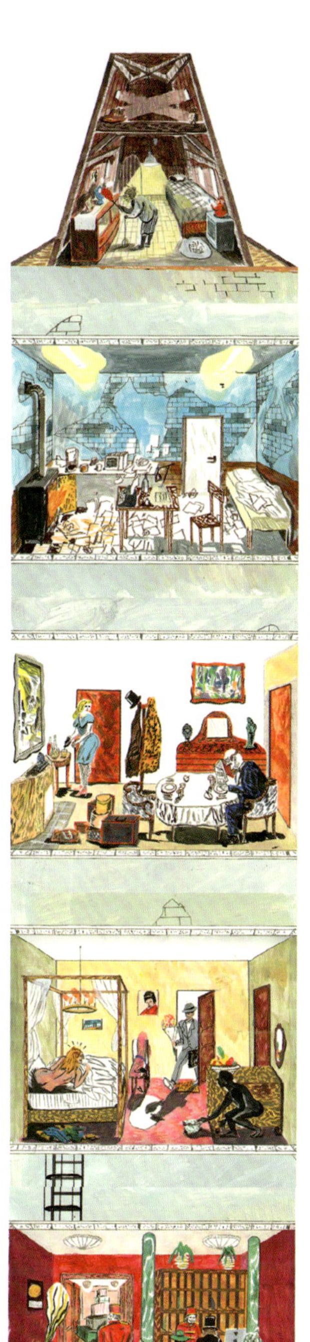

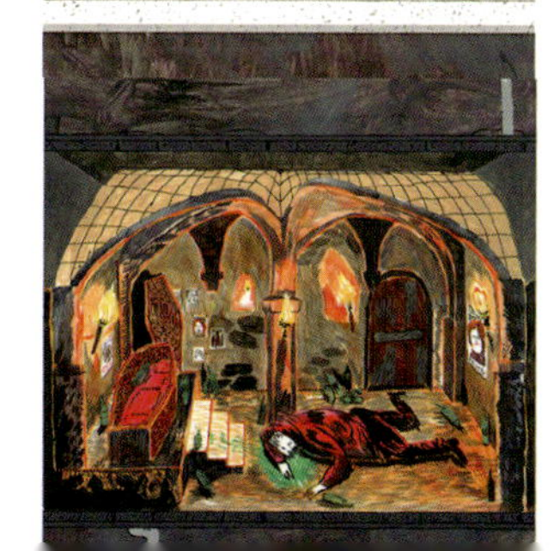

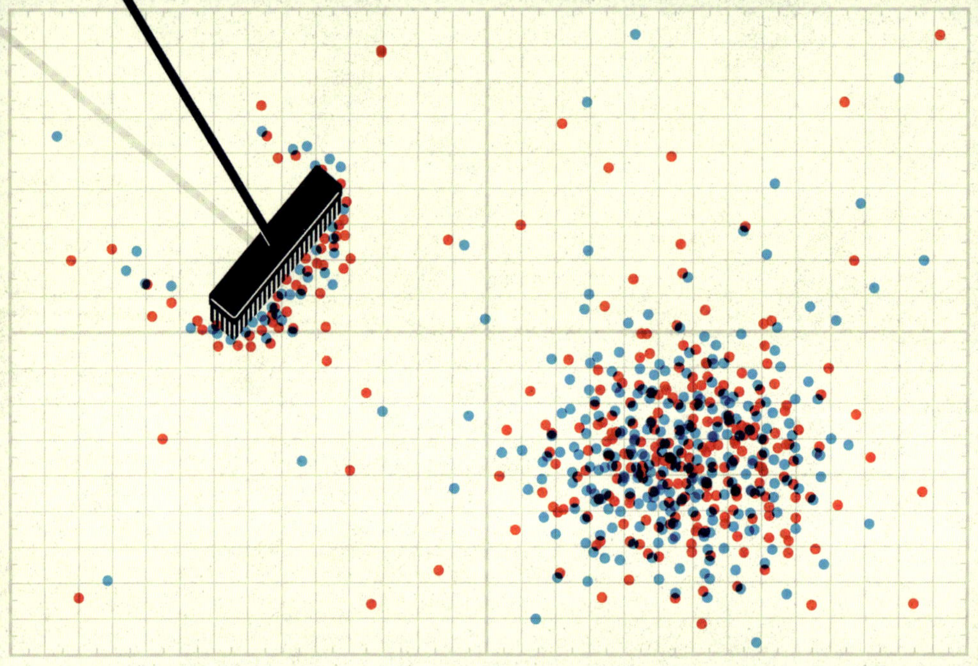

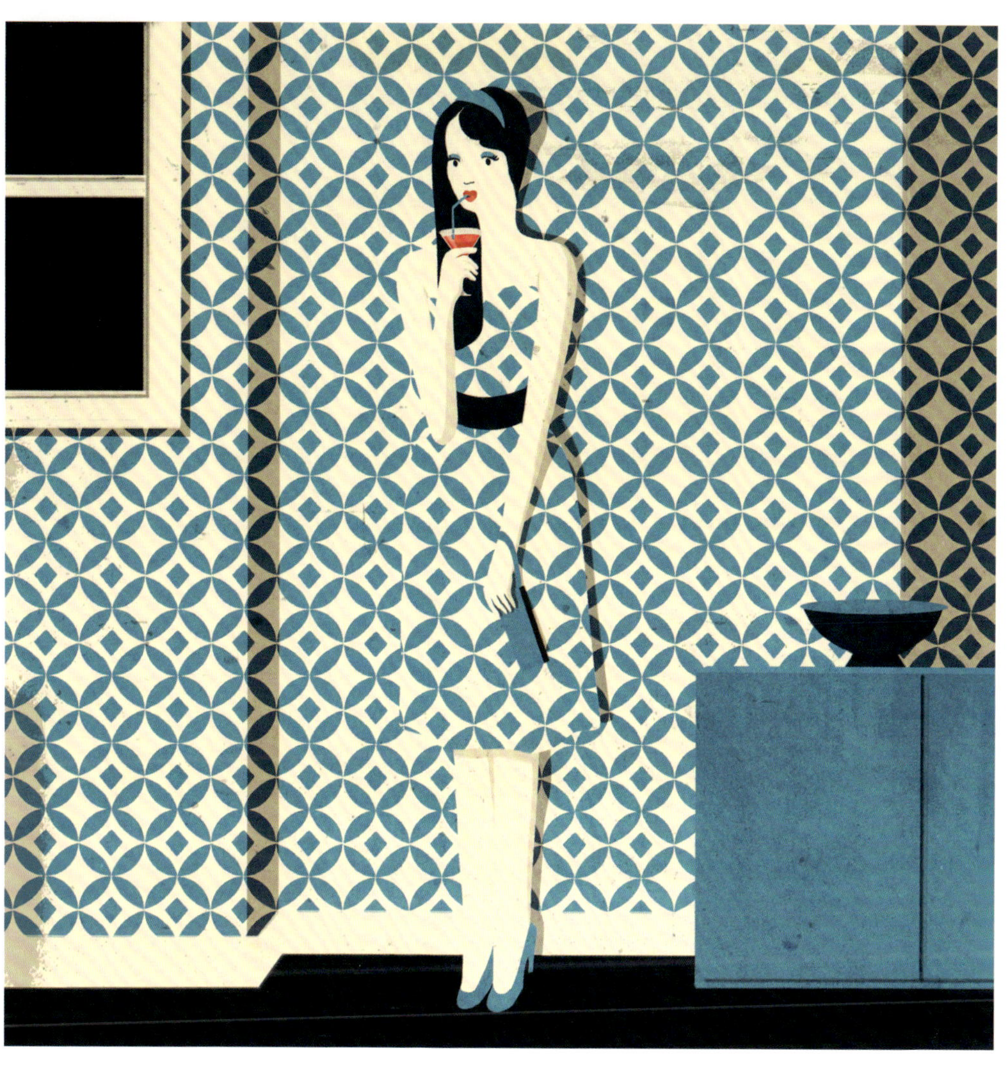

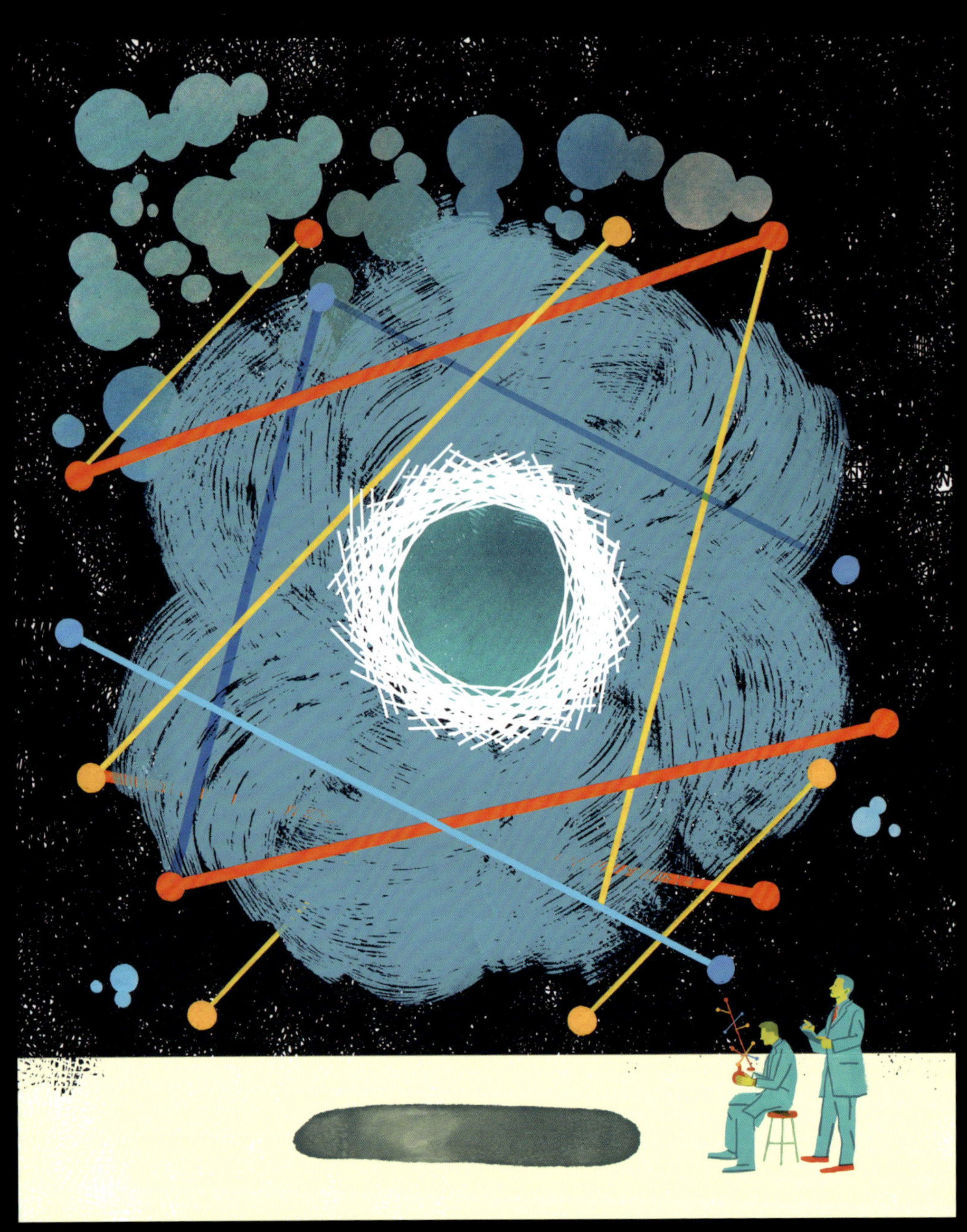

MERIT *Justin Gabbard*

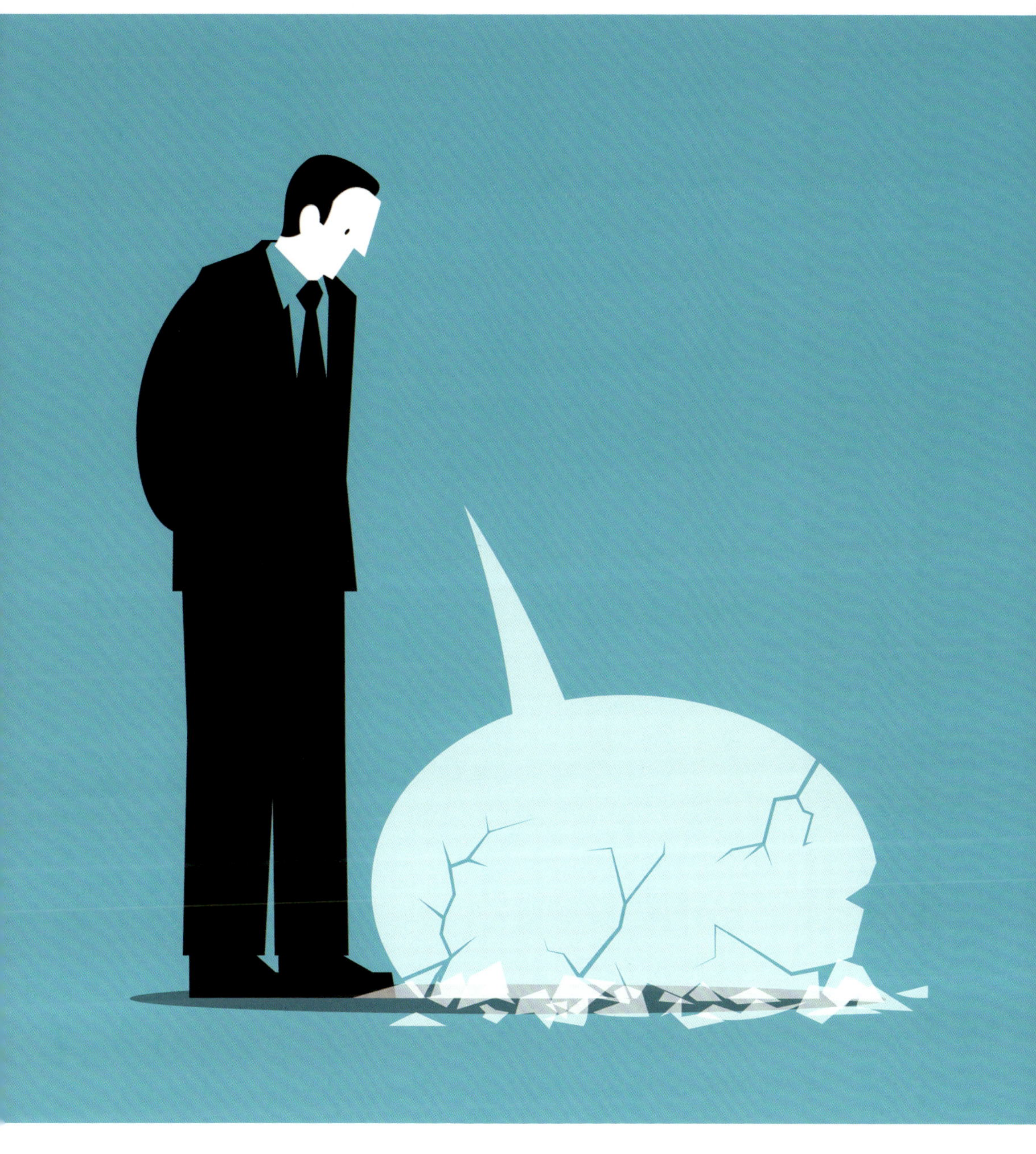



MERIT *Aad Goudappel*

103

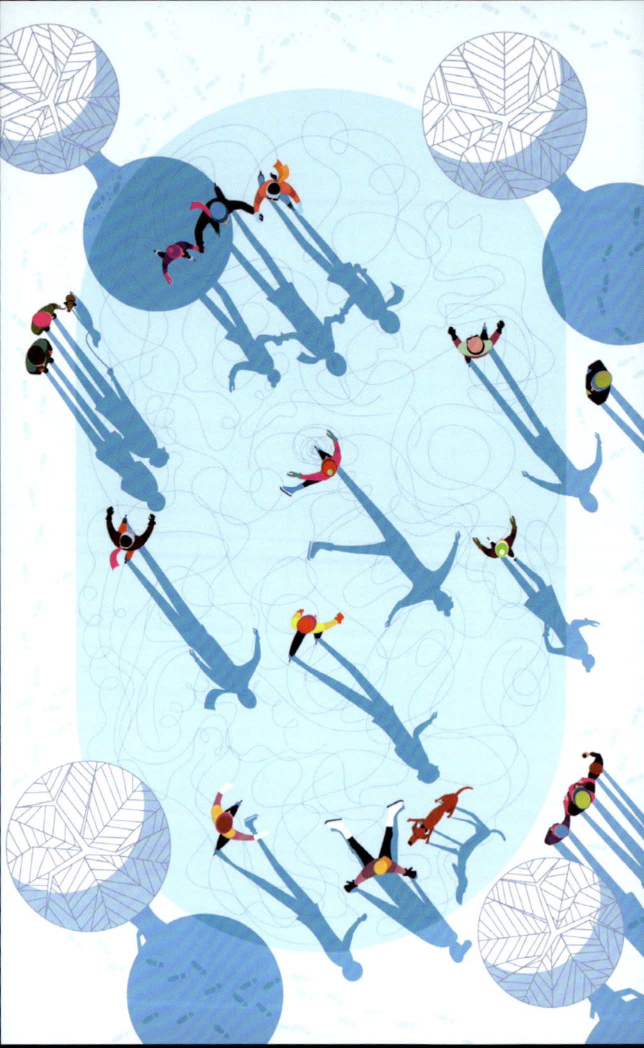

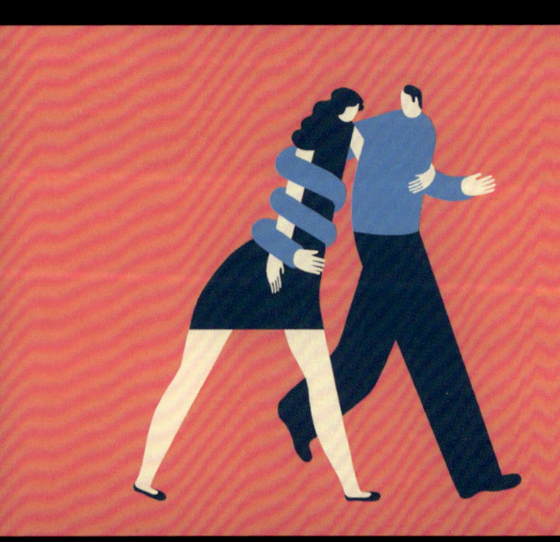

(T) MERIT Peter Greenwood    (B) MERIT Magoz

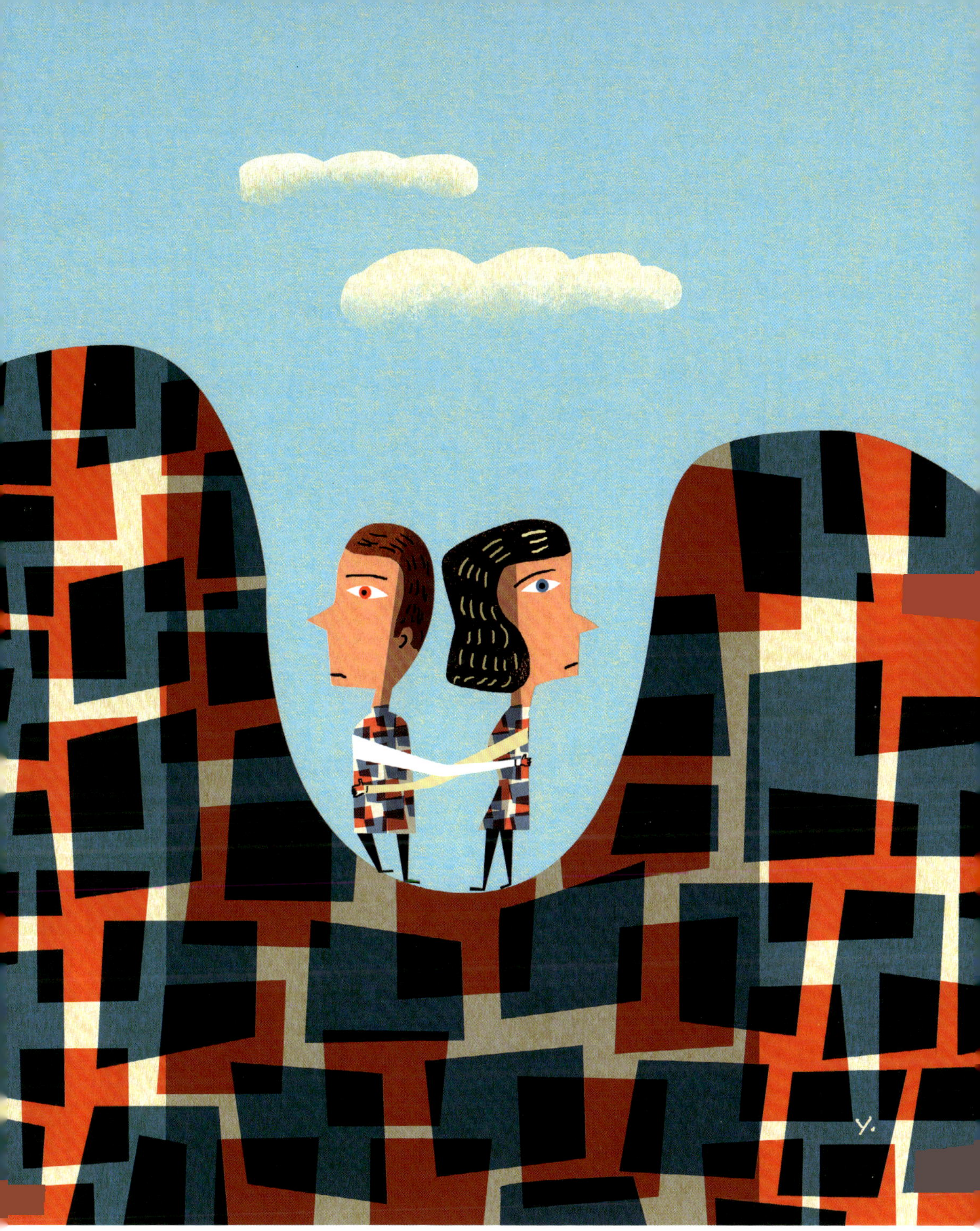

MERIT *James Yang*

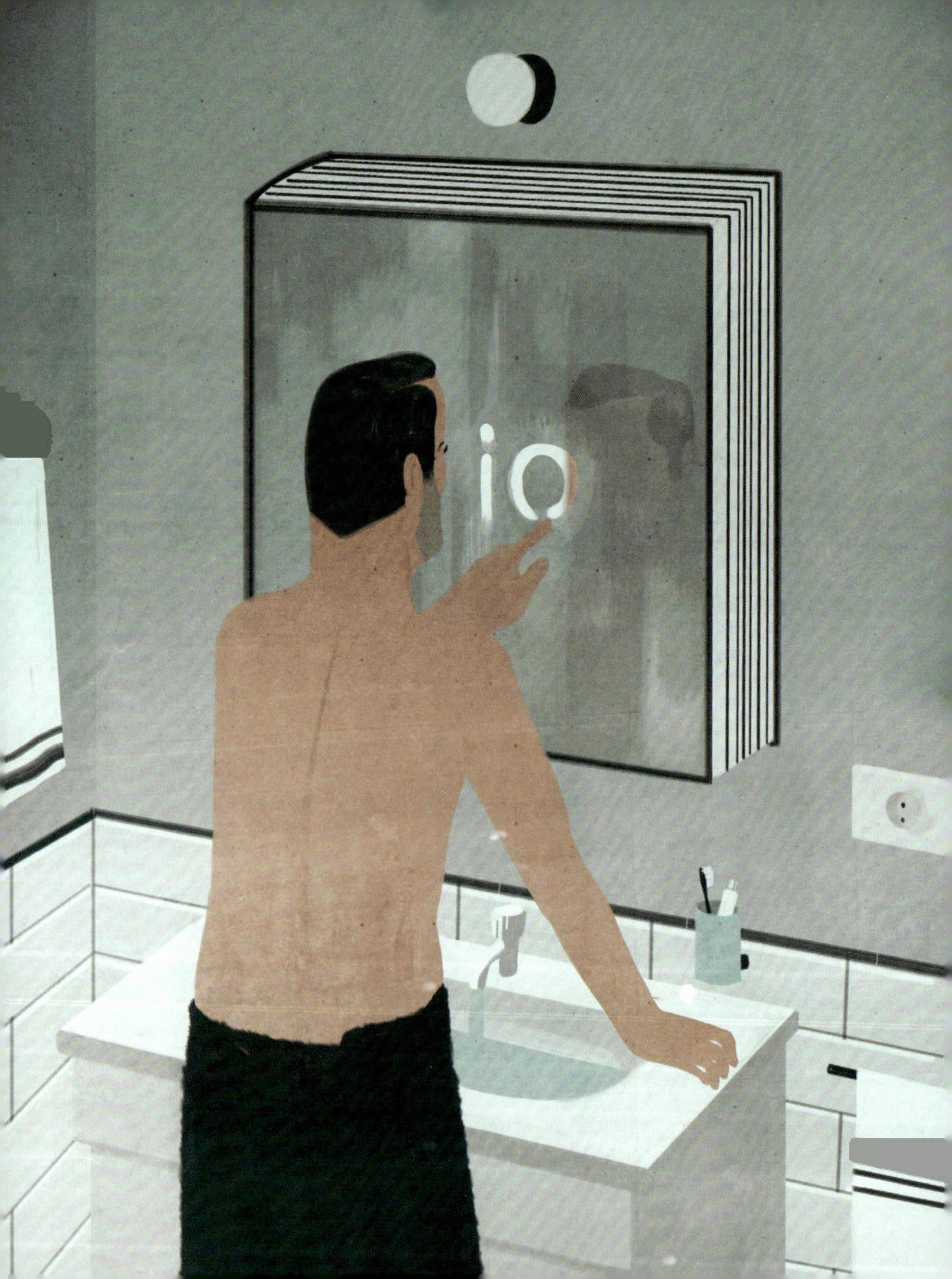
io

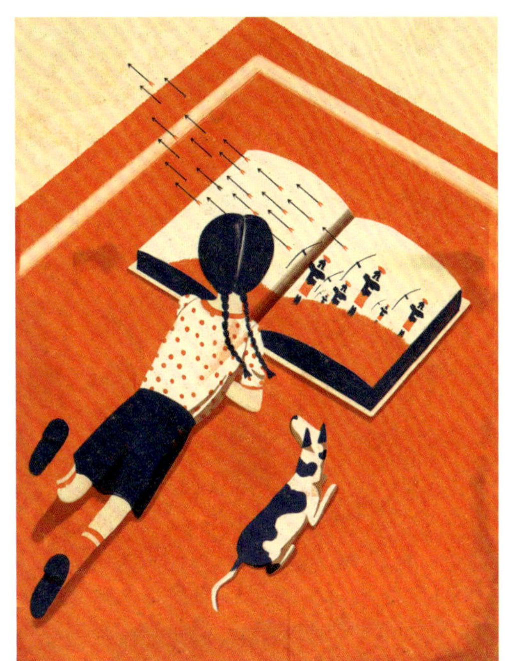

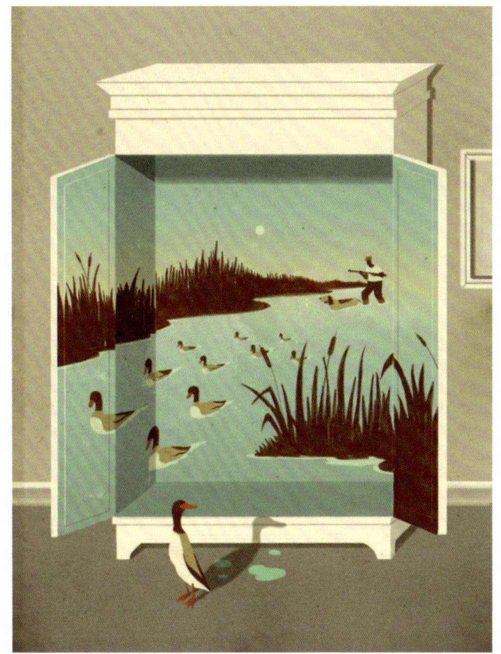

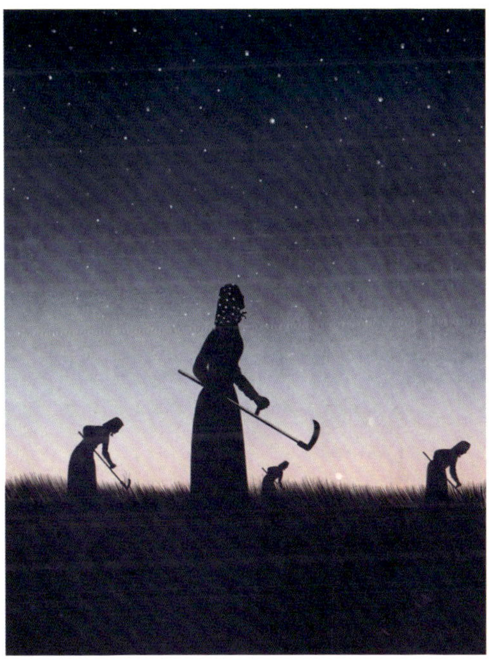

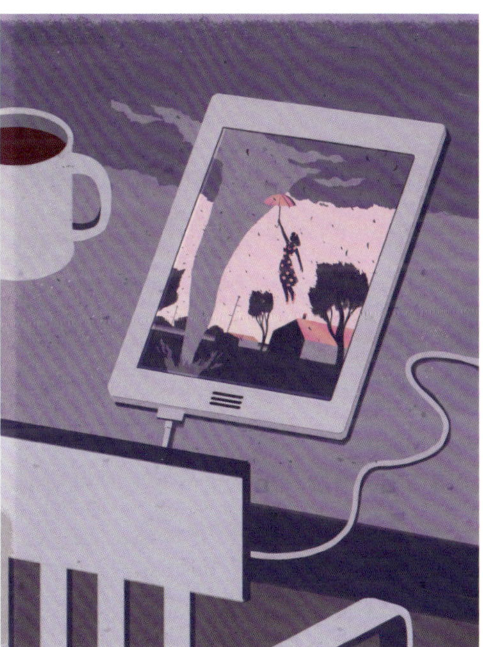

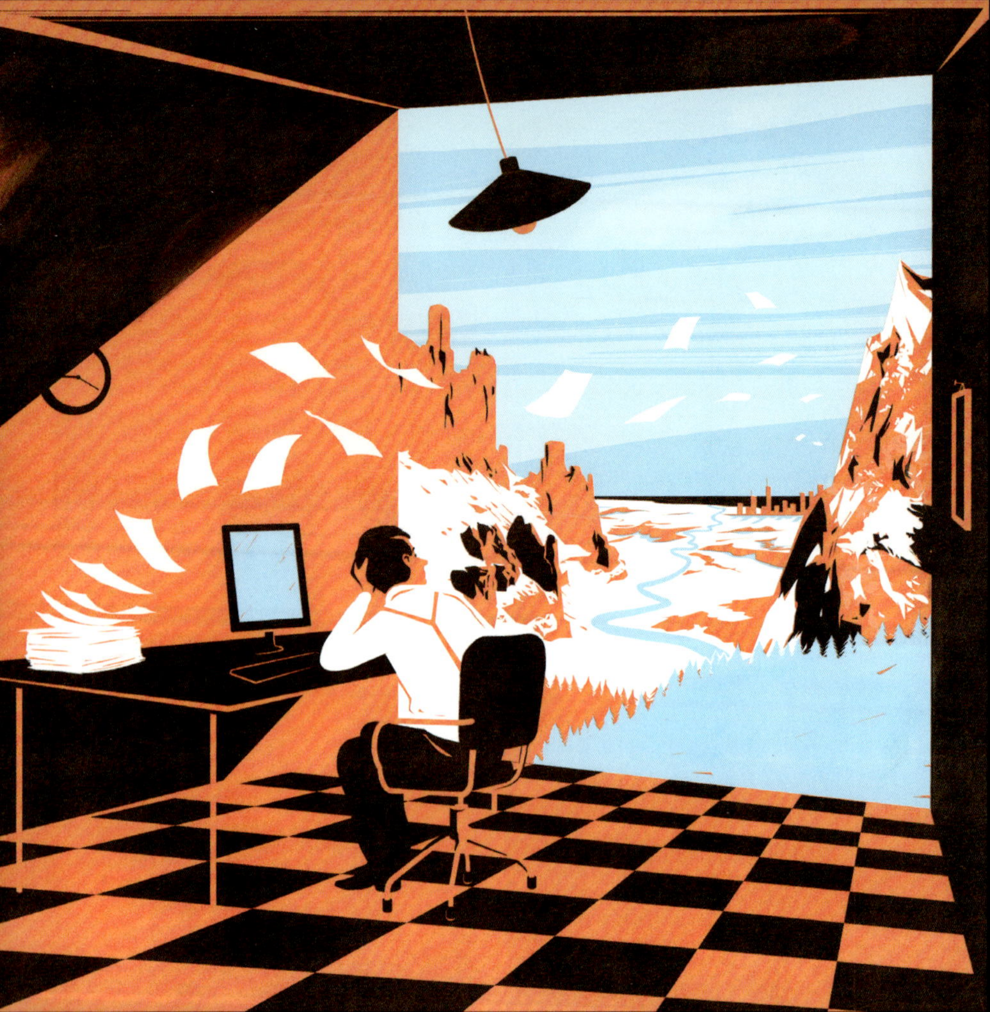

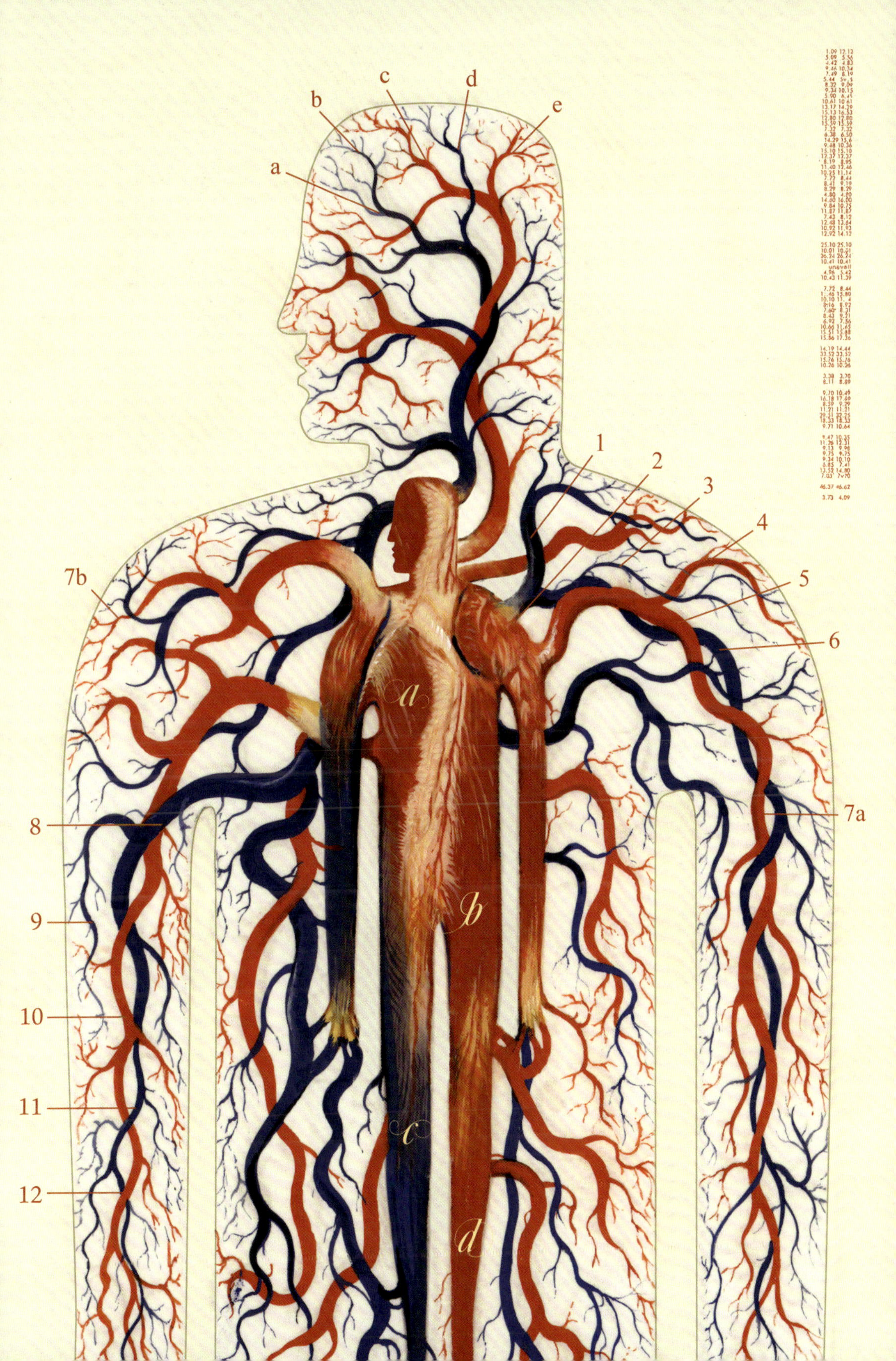

a
b
c
d
e
1
2
3
4
5
6
7a
7b
8
9
10
11
12
a
b
c
d

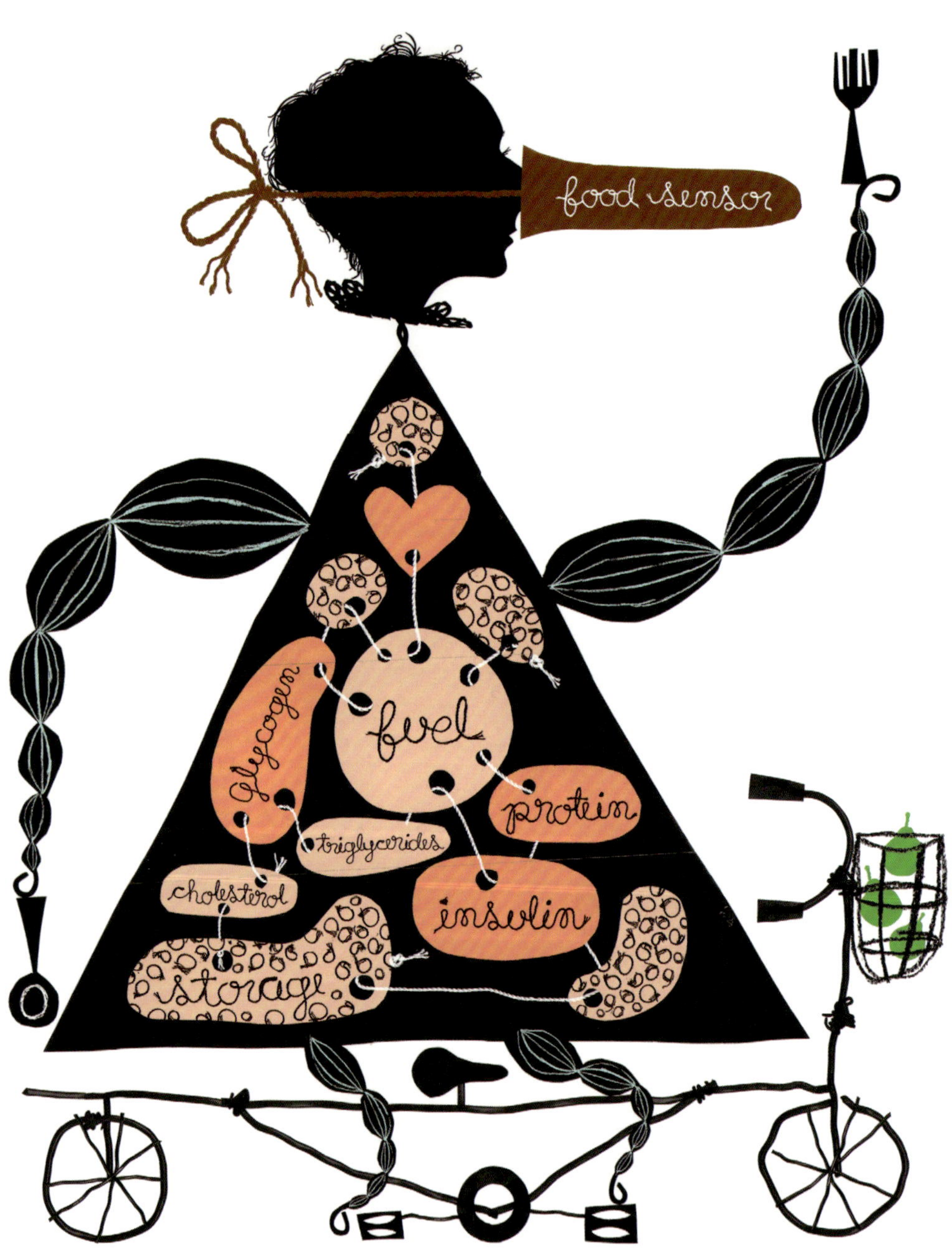

food sensor
glycogen
fuel
protein
triglycerides
cholesterol
insulin
storage

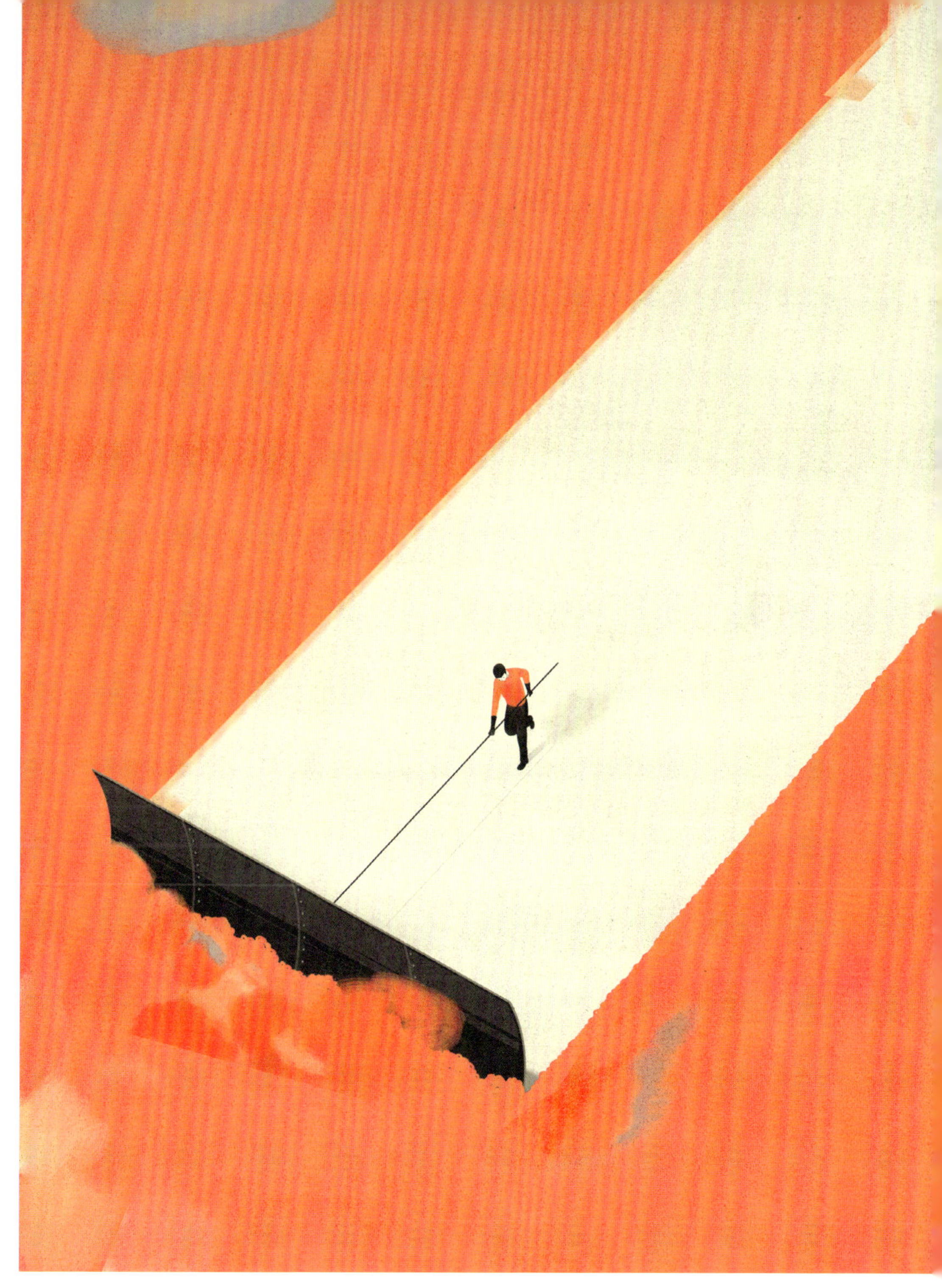



III

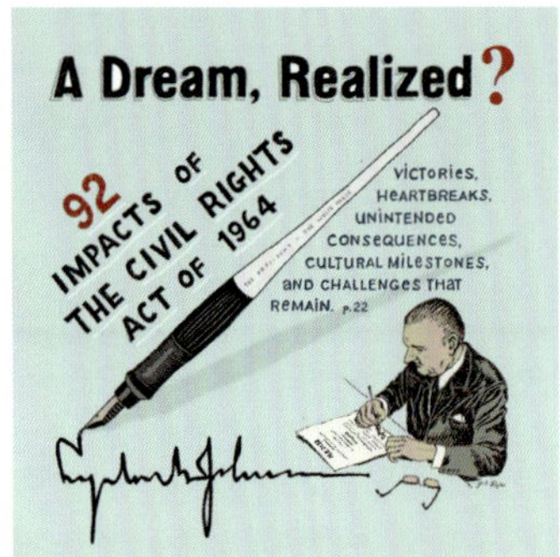


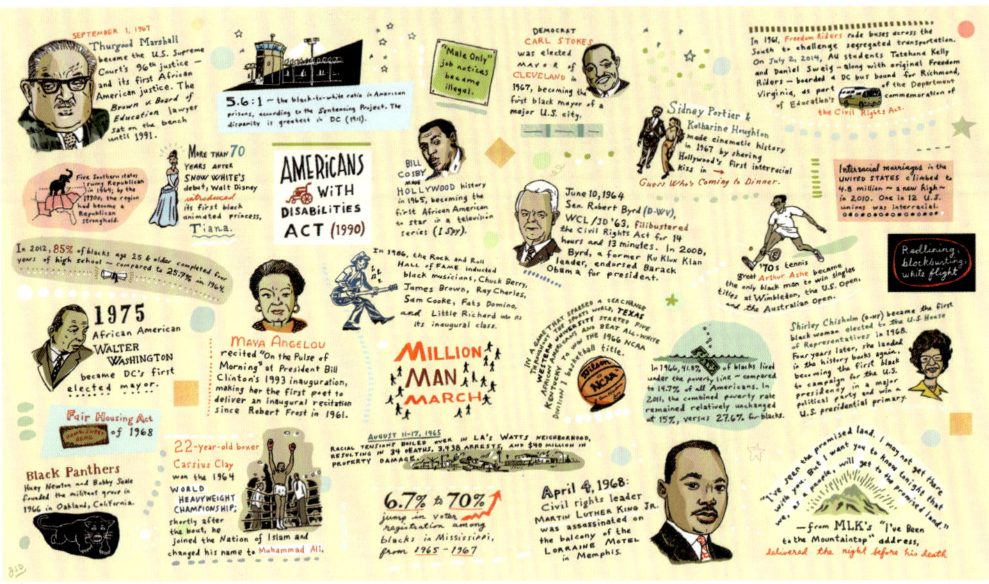


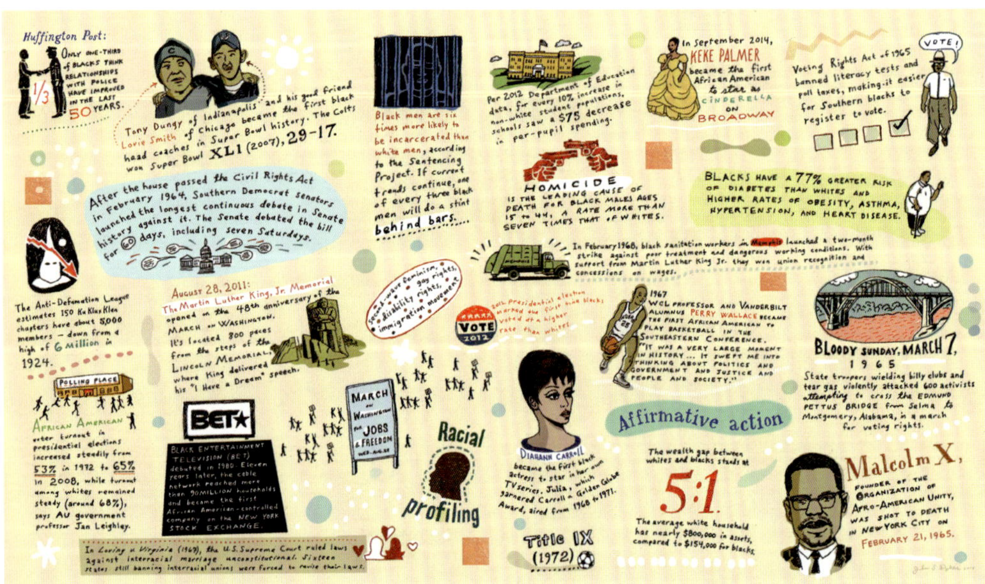


MERIT *John S. Dykes*

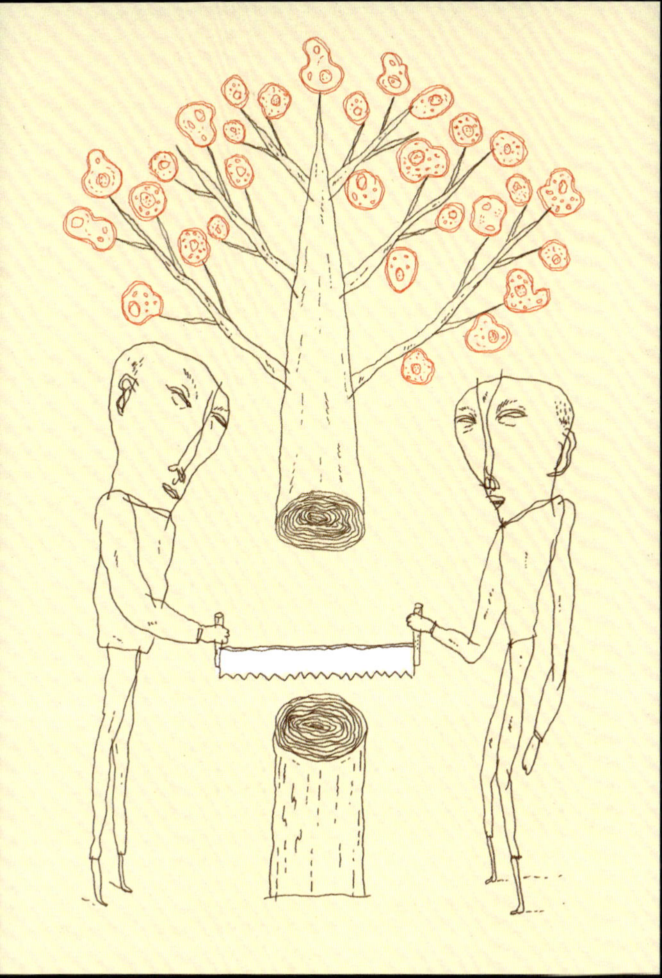

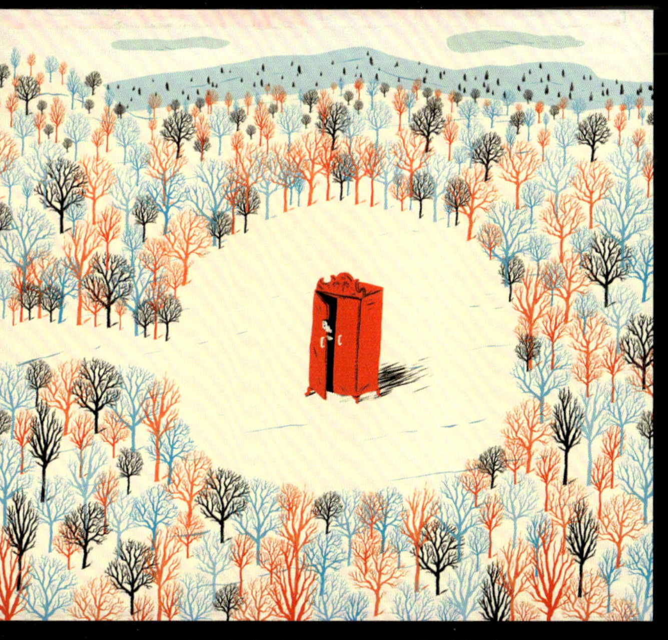

(1) MERIT *Jordin Isip*    (B) MERIT *Paul Blow*

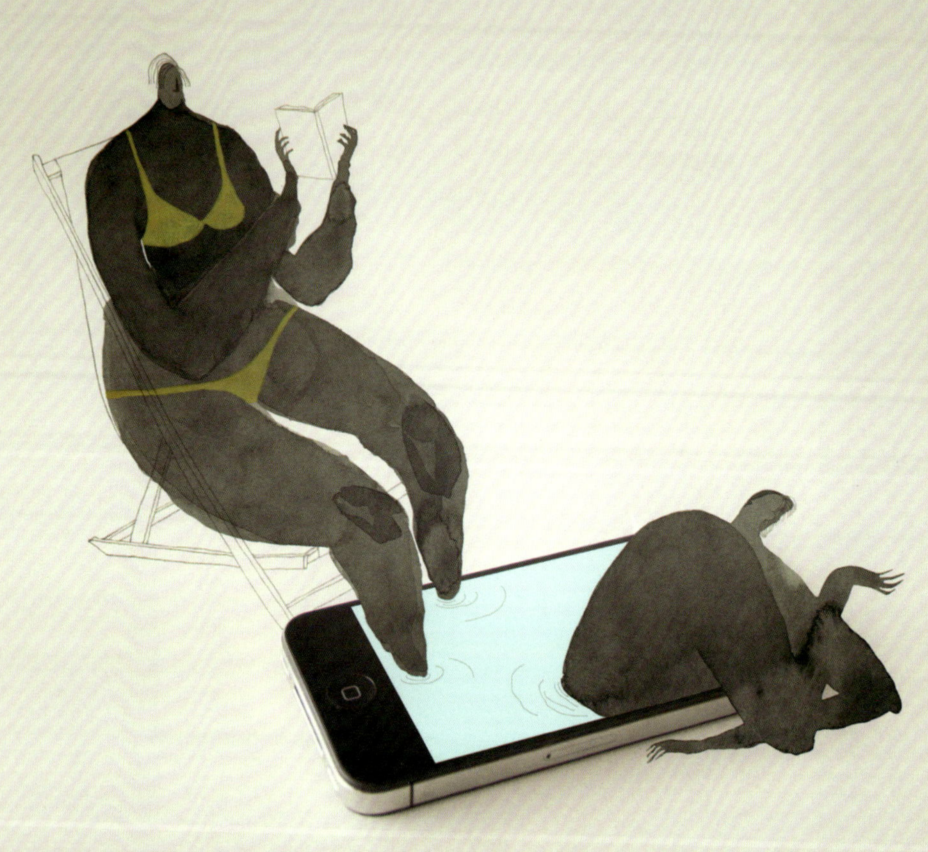



MERIT *Ailadi*

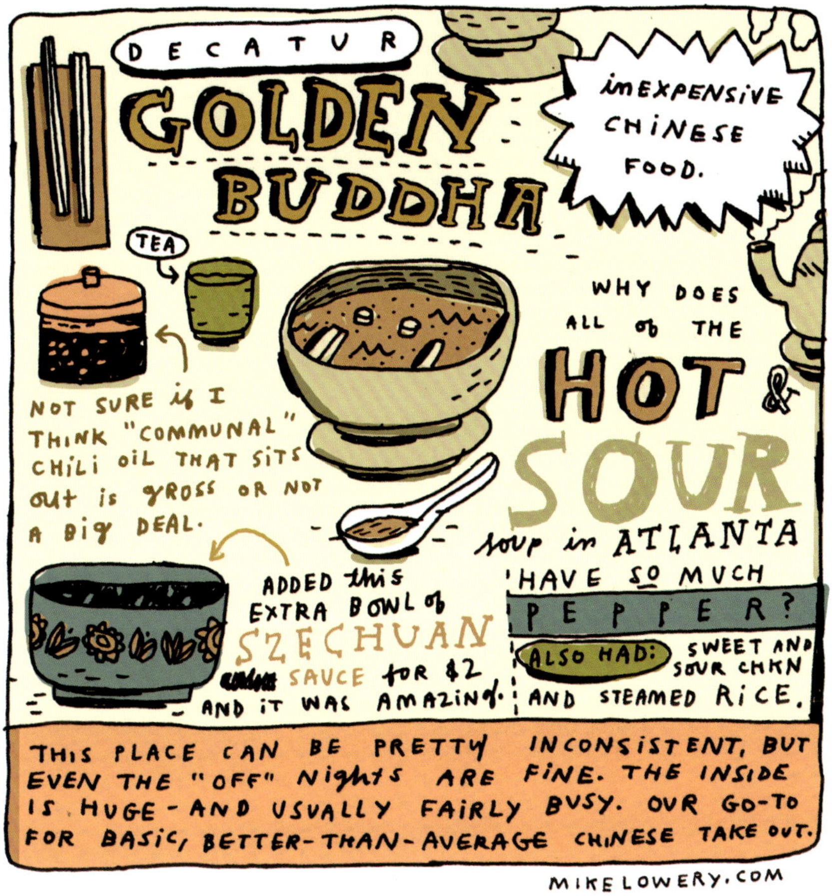

DECATUR
GOLDEN BUDDHA
inEXPENSIVE CHINESE FOOD.
TEA
NOT SURE if I THINK "COMMUNAL" CHILI OIL THAT SITS OUT IS GROSS OR NOT A BIG DEAL.
ADDED this EXTRA BOWL of SZECHUAN SAUCE for $2 AND IT WAS AMAZING.
WHY DOES ALL of THE HOT & SOUR soup in ATLANTA HAVE SO MUCH PEPPER?
ALSO HAD: SWEET AND SOUR CHKN AND STEAMED RICE.
THIS PLACE CAN BE PRETTY INCONSISTENT, BUT EVEN THE "OFF" NIGHTS ARE FINE. THE INSIDE IS HUGE - AND USUALLY FAIRLY BUSY. OUR GO-TO FOR BASIC, BETTER-THAN-AVERAGE CHINESE TAKE OUT.
MIKELOWERY.COM

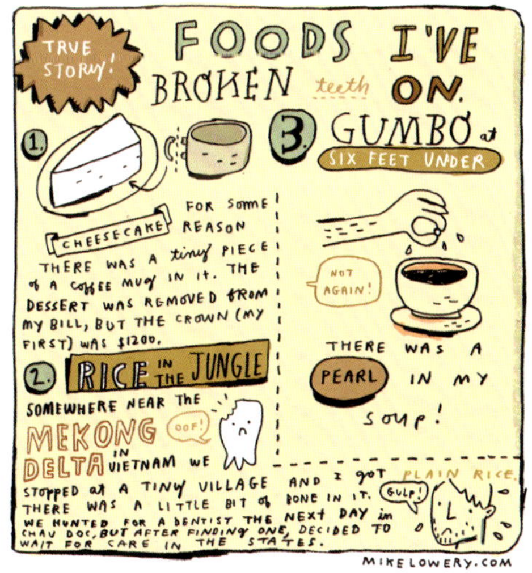
TRUE STORY!
FOODS I'VE BROKEN teeth ON.
1.
CHEESECAKE
3 GUMBO at SIX FEET UNDER
FOR SOME REASON THERE WAS A tiny PIECE of A COFFEE MUG IN IT. THE DESSERT WAS REMOVED FROM MY BILL, BUT THE CROWN (MY FIRST) WAS $1200.
NOT AGAIN!
2. RICE IN THE JUNGLE
SOMEWHERE NEAR THE MEKONG DELTA IN VIETNAM WE
OOF!
THERE WAS A PEARL IN MY SOUP!
STOPPED AT A TINY VILLAGE THERE WAS A LITTLE BIT of BONE IN IT. WE HUNTED FOR A DENTIST THE NEXT DAY in CHAU DOC, BUT AFTER FINDING ONE, DECIDED TO WAIT FOR CARE IN THE STATES.
AND I GOT PLAIN RICE IN IT. GULP!
MIKELOWERY.COM

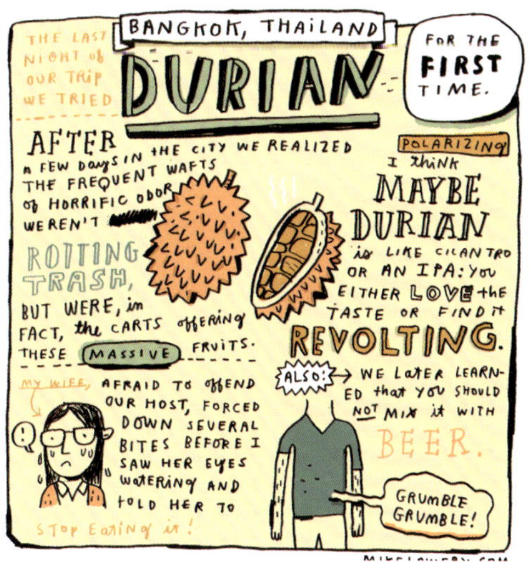
BANGKOK, THAILAND
THE LAST NIGHT of OUR TRIP WE TRIED
DURIAN
FOR THE FIRST TIME.
AFTER A FEW DAYS IN THE CITY WE REALIZED THE FREQUENT WAFTS of HORRIFIC ODOR WEREN'T ROTTING TRASH, BUT WERE, in FACT, the CARTS offering THESE MASSIVE FRUITS.
POLARIZING
I think MAYBE DURIAN is LIKE CILANTRO OR AN IPA: YOU EITHER LOVE the TASTE OR FIND IT REVOLTING.
MY WIFE, AFRAID TO OFFEND OUR HOST, FORCED DOWN SEVERAL BITES BEFORE I SAW HER EYES WATERING AND TOLD HER TO STOP EATING IT!
ALSO: WE LATER LEARNED THAT YOU SHOULD NOT MIX IT WITH BEER.
GRUMBLE GRUMBLE!
MIKELOWERY.COM

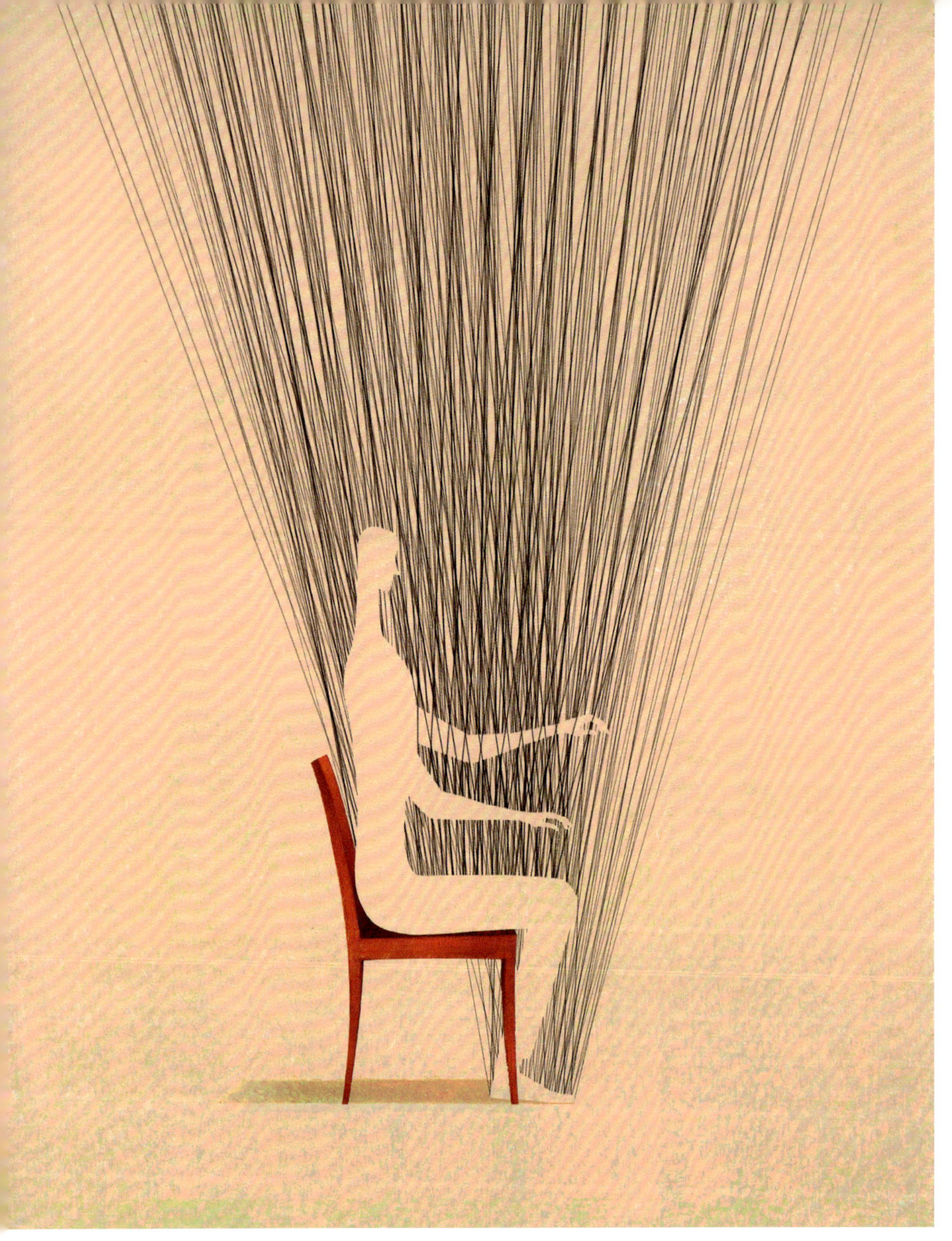



MERIT *Jon Krause*

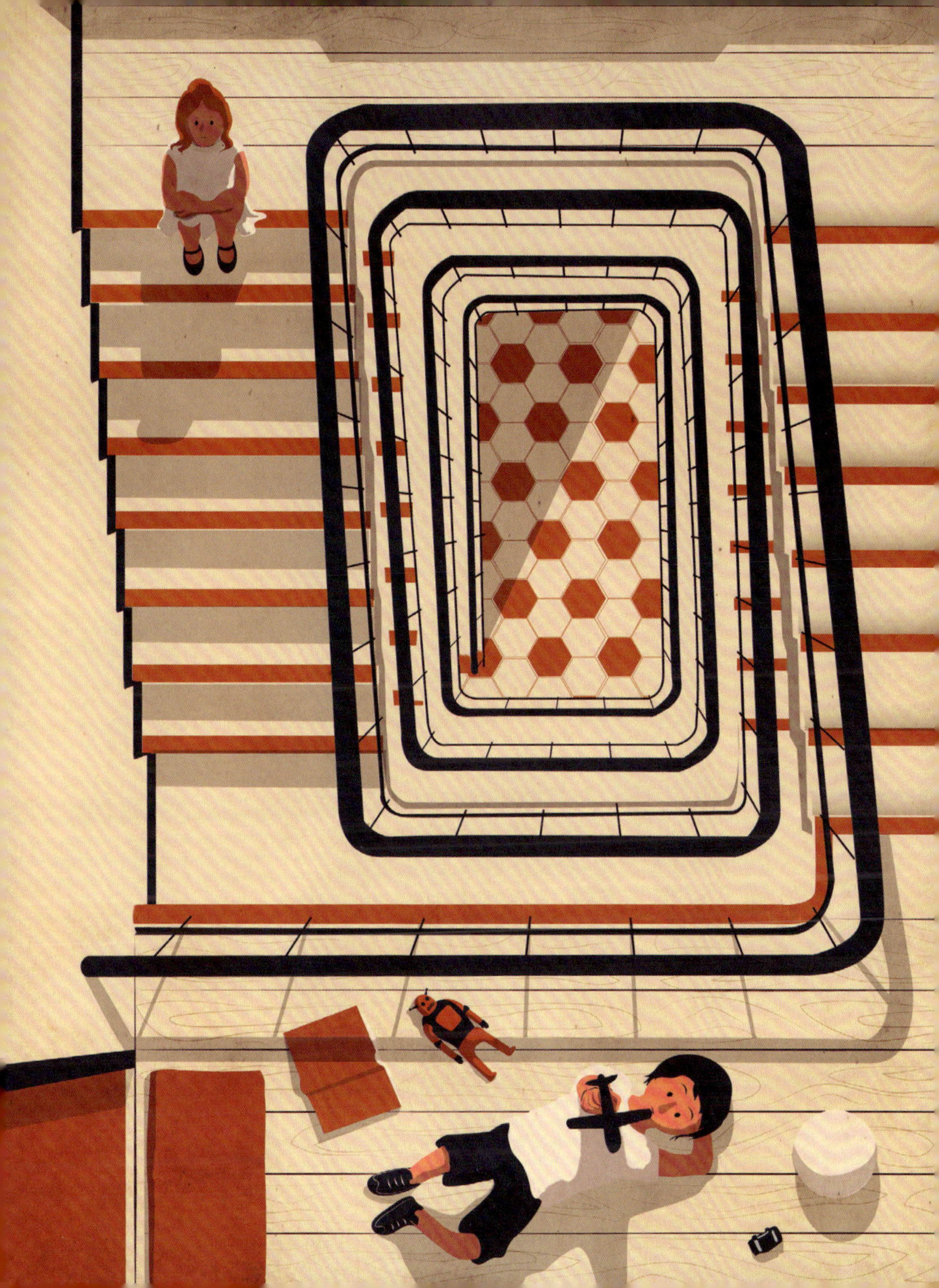

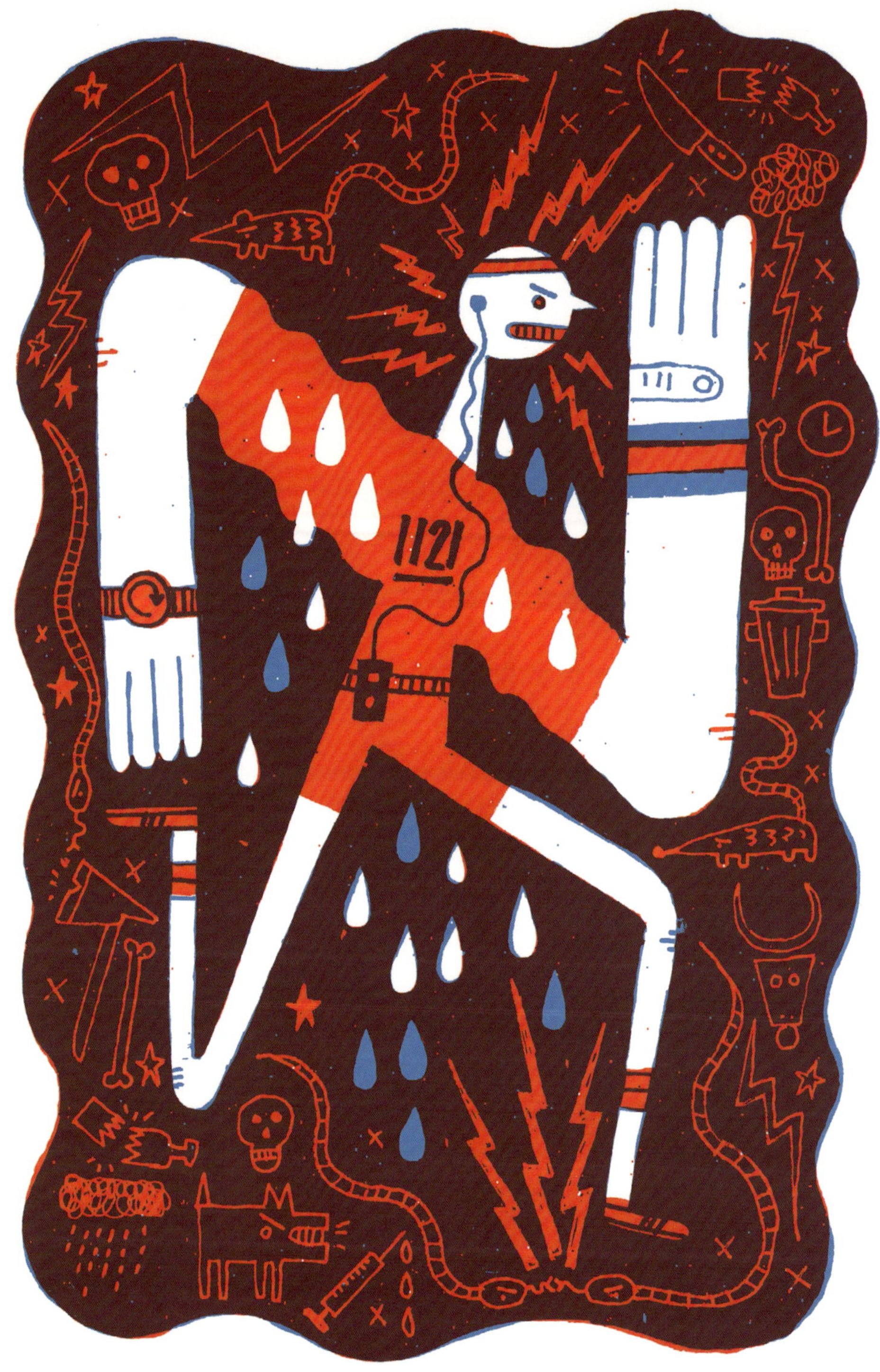

MERIT *Benoit Tardif*

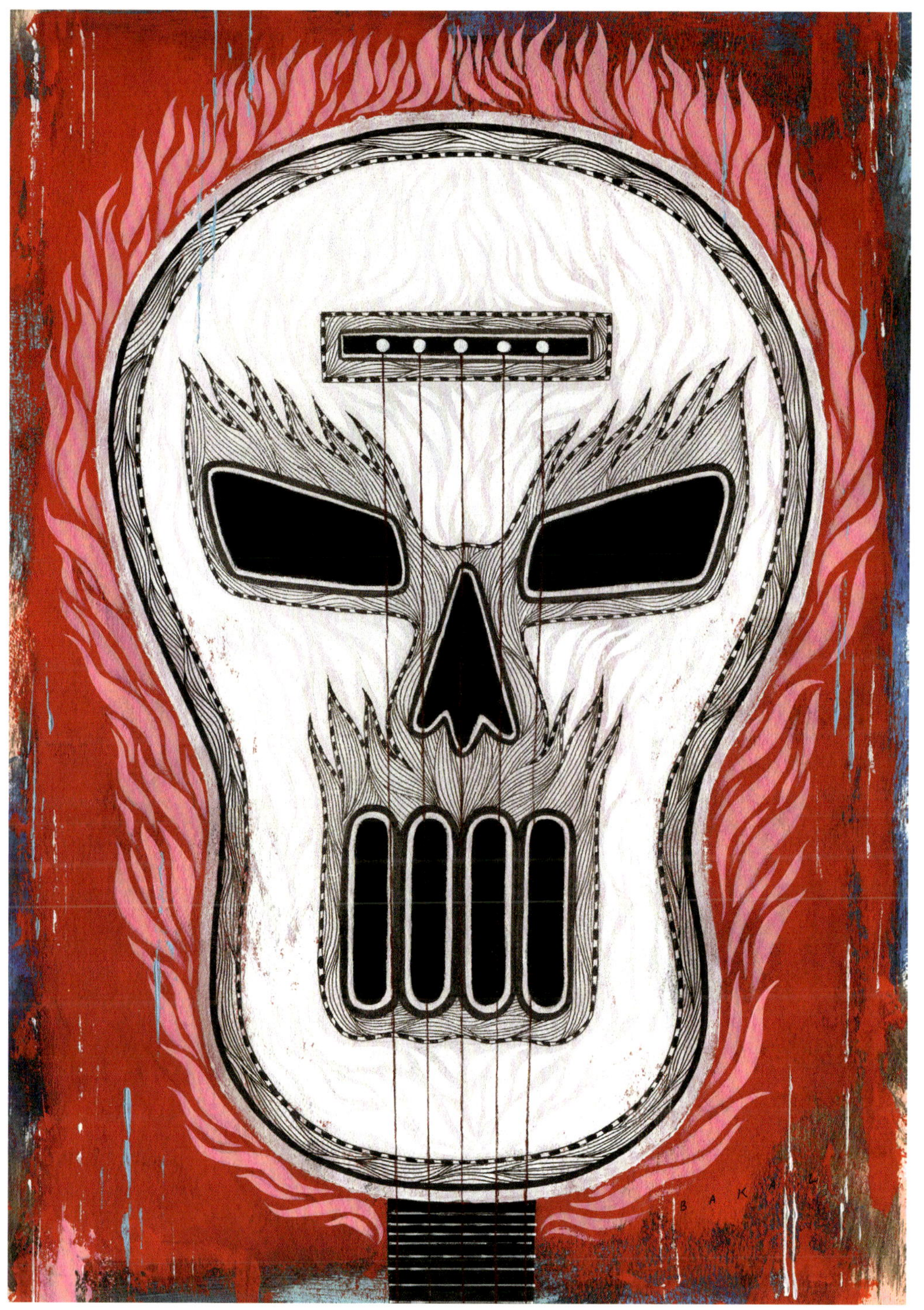



MERIT *Scott Bakal*

119

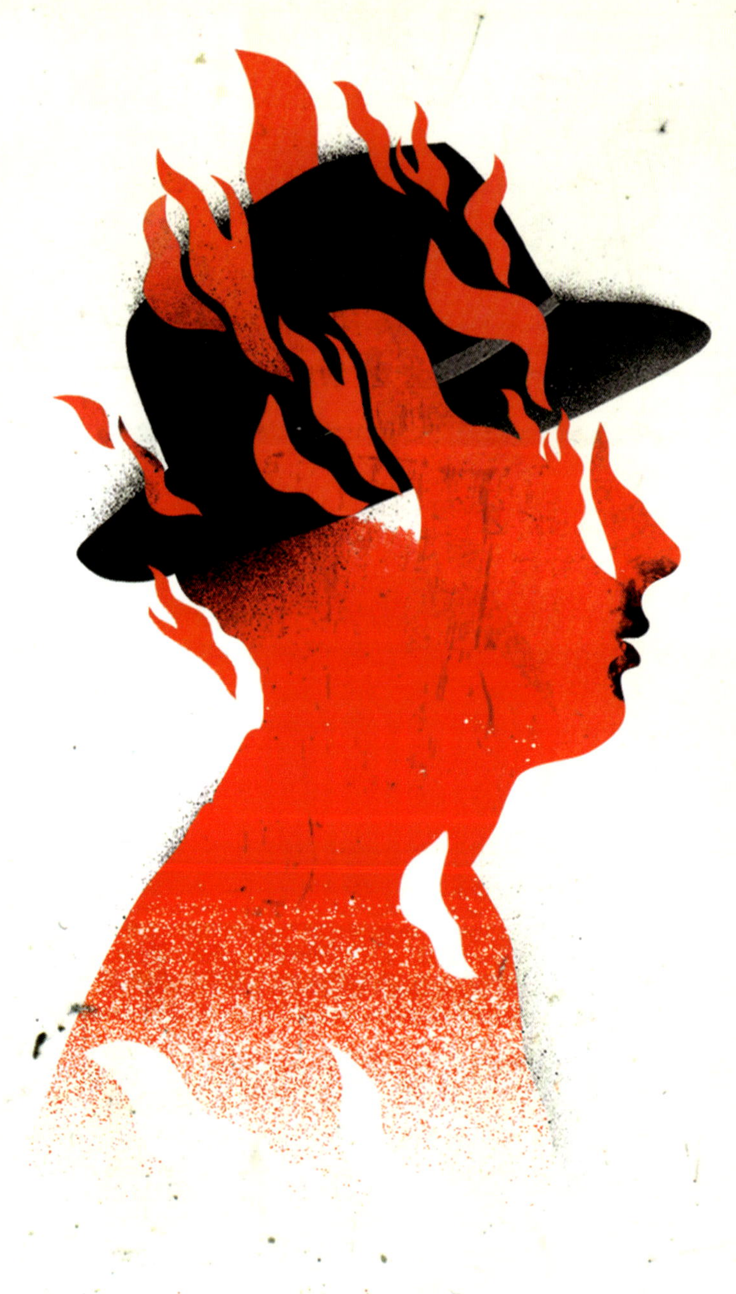



MERIT *Emmanuel Polanco*

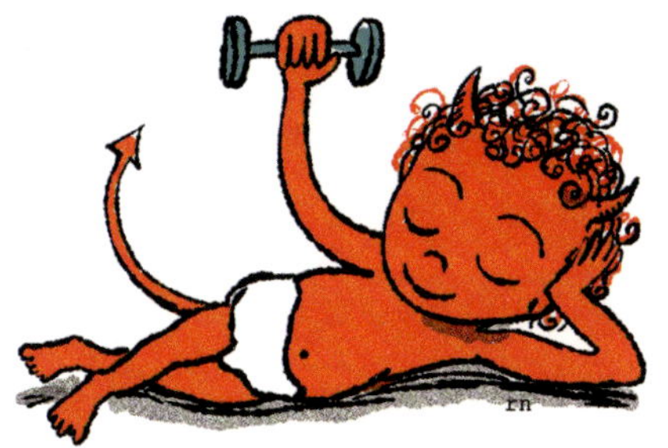

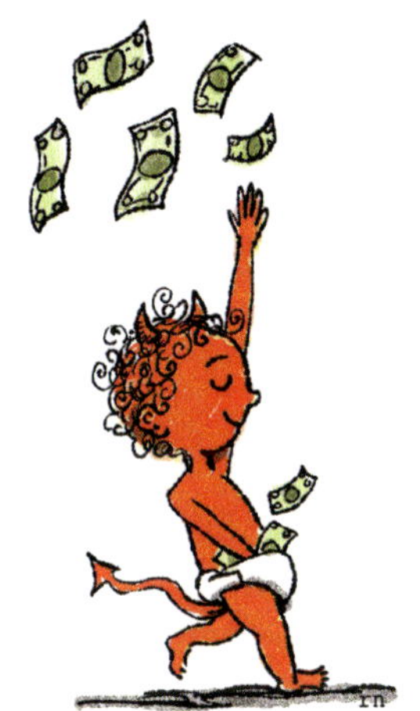

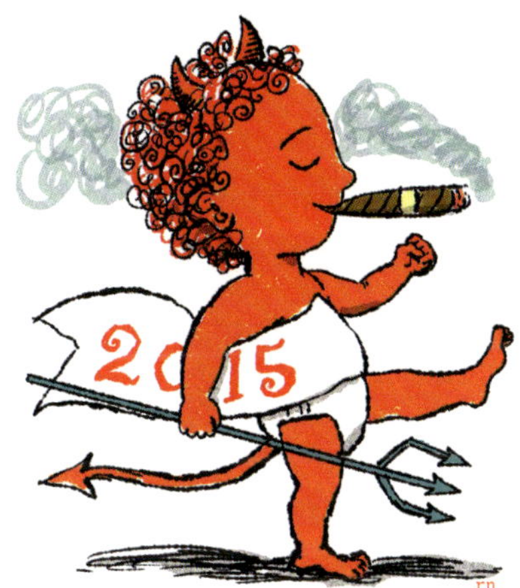


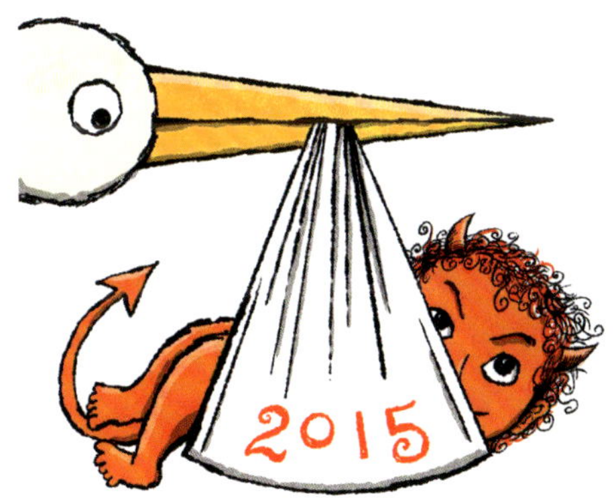


MERIT *Robert Neubecker*

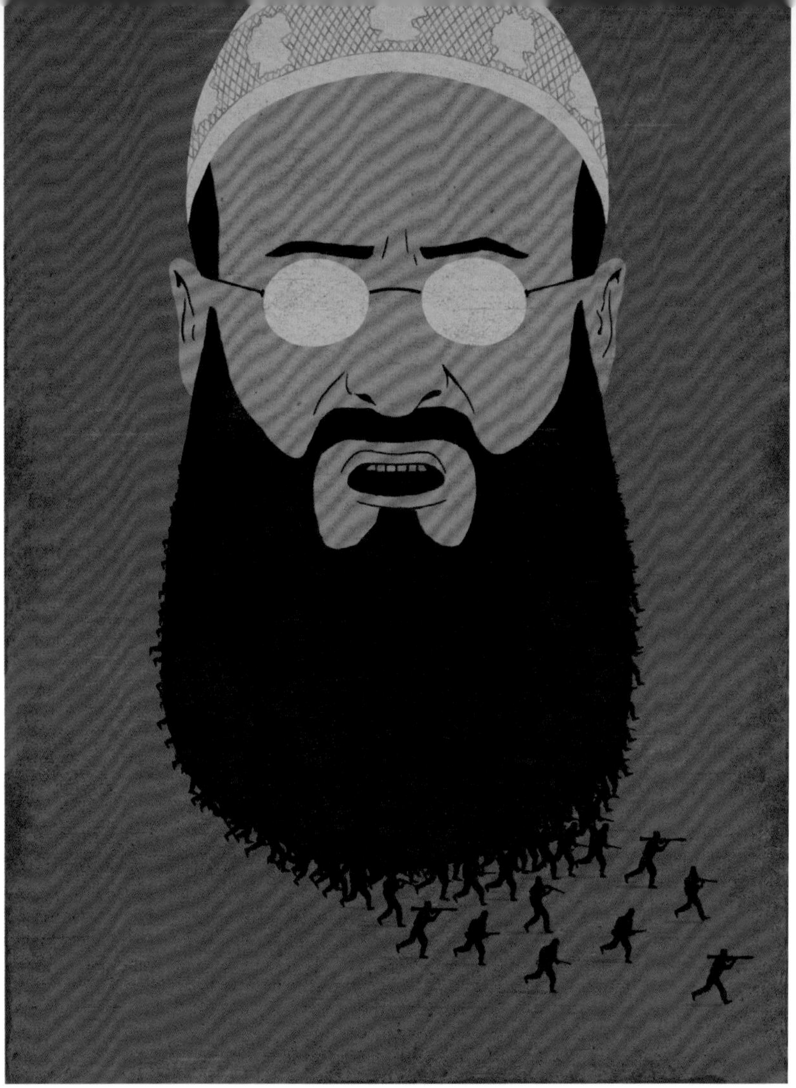

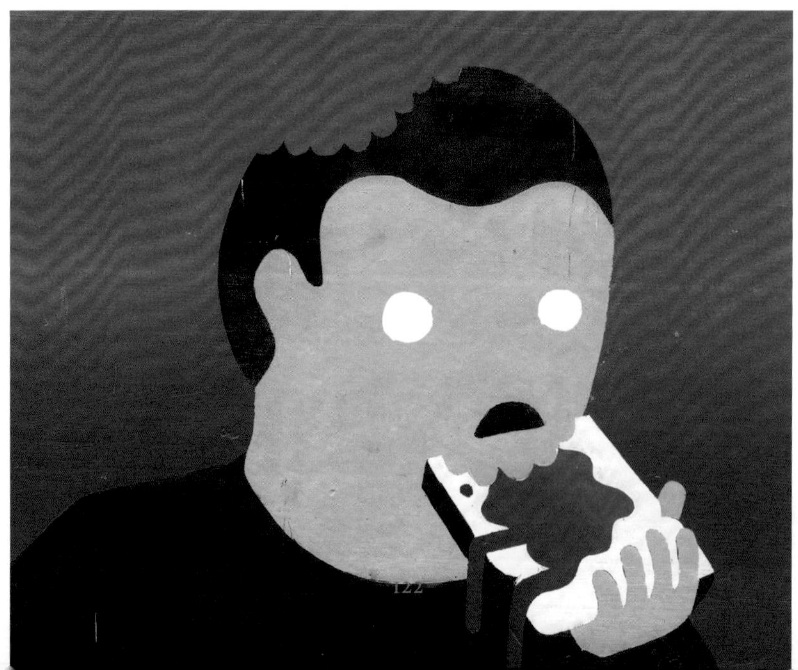

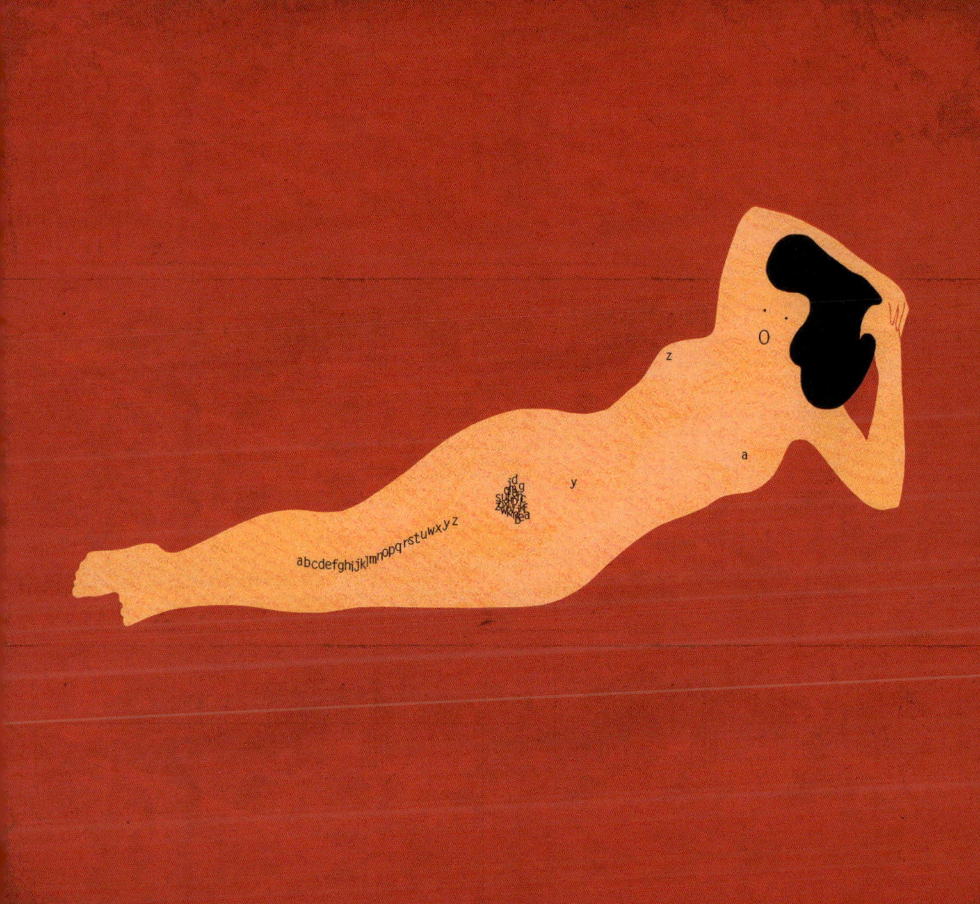

abcdefghijklmnopqrstuwxyz

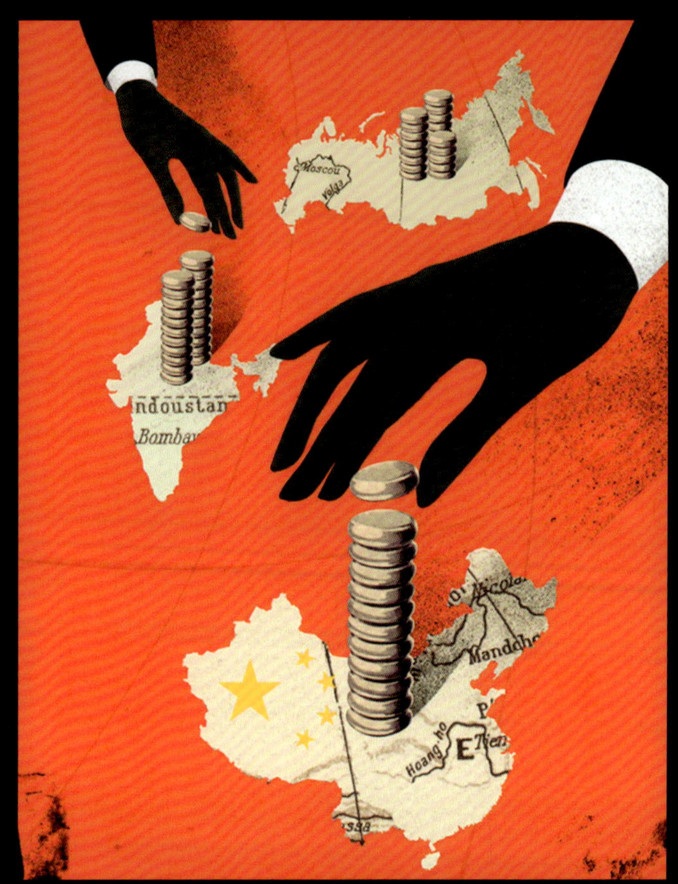


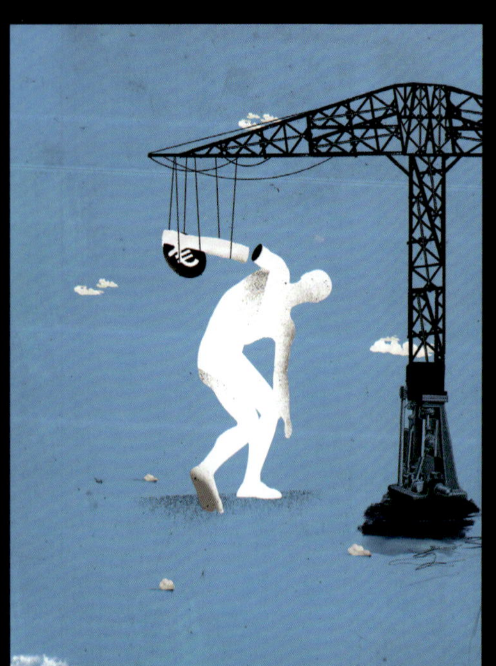

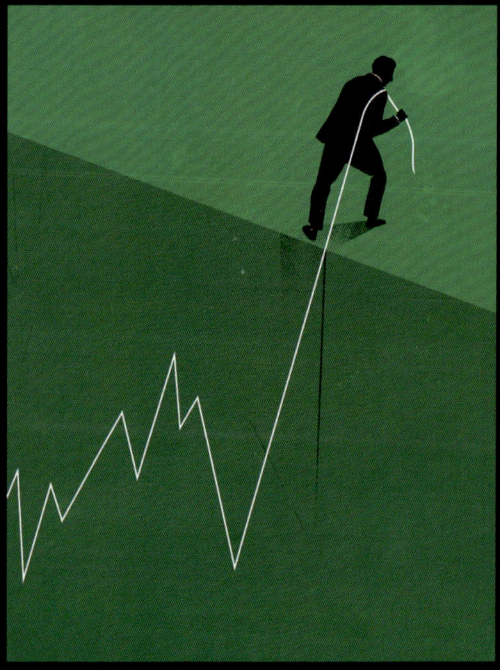

MERIT *Emmanuel Polanco*

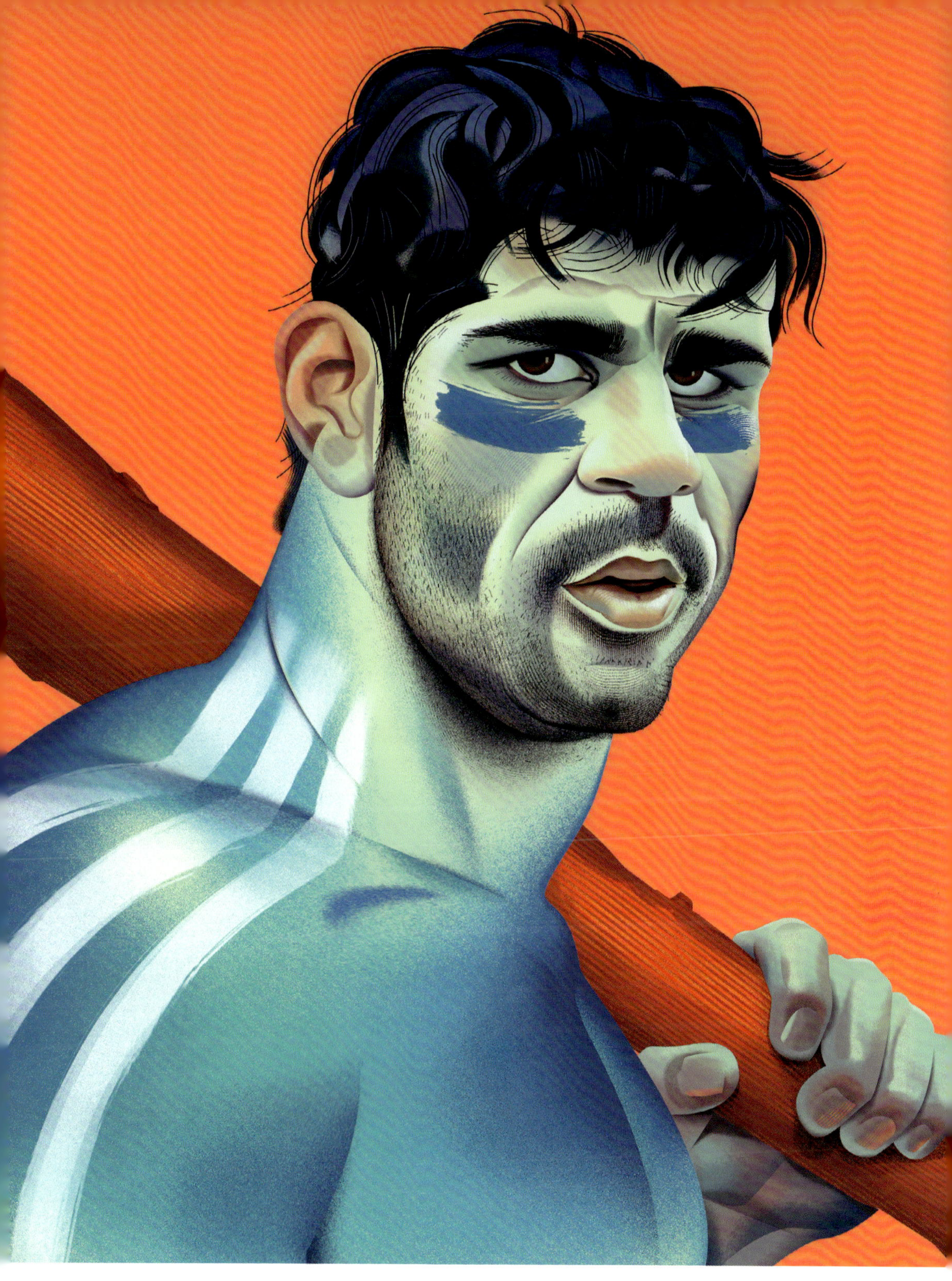



MERIT *Nigel Buchanan*

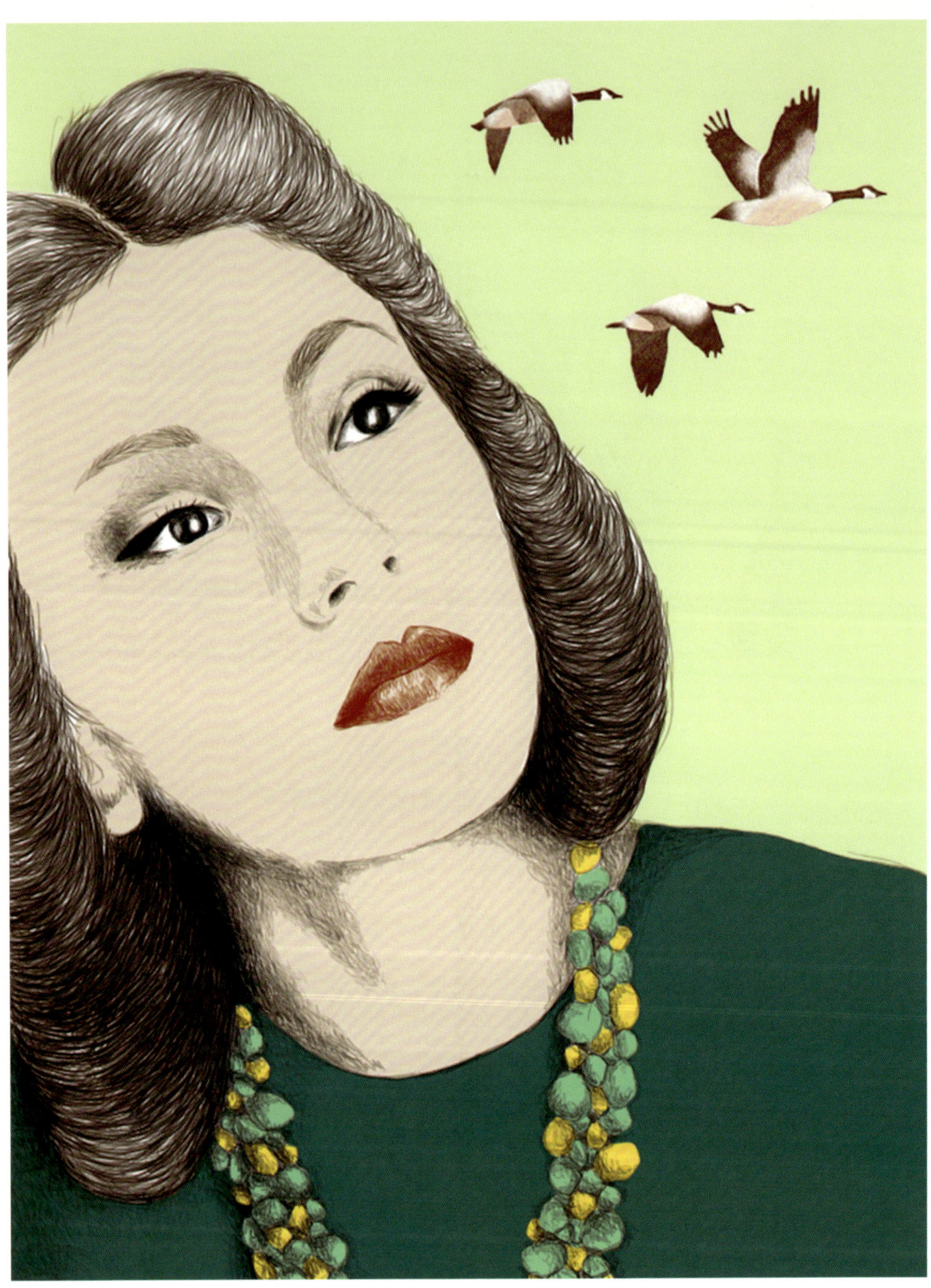



MERIT *Neta Rabinovitch*

126

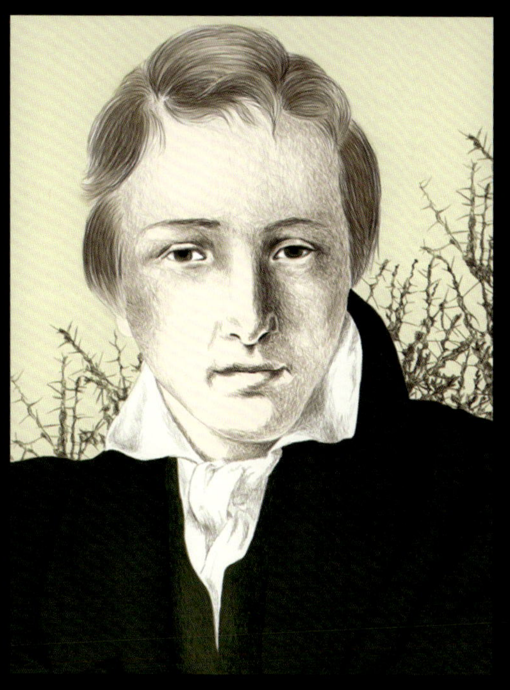
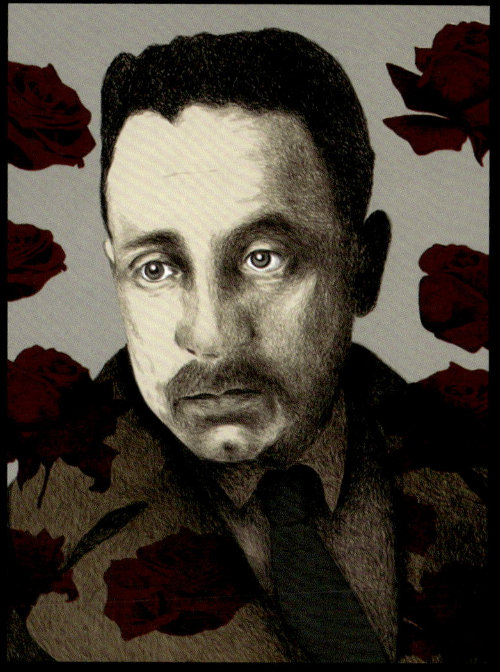
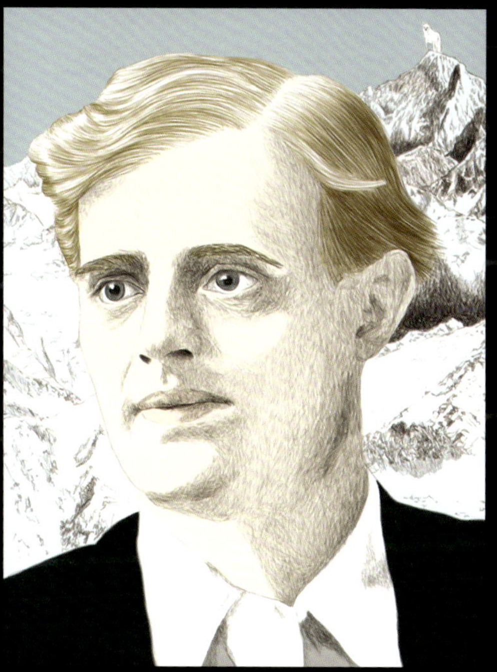
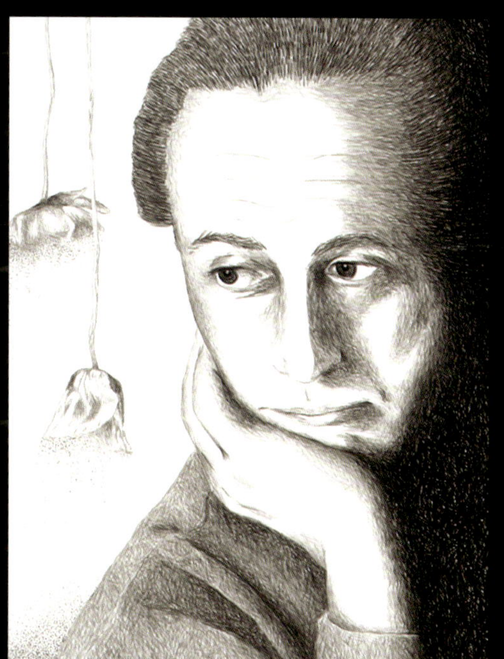

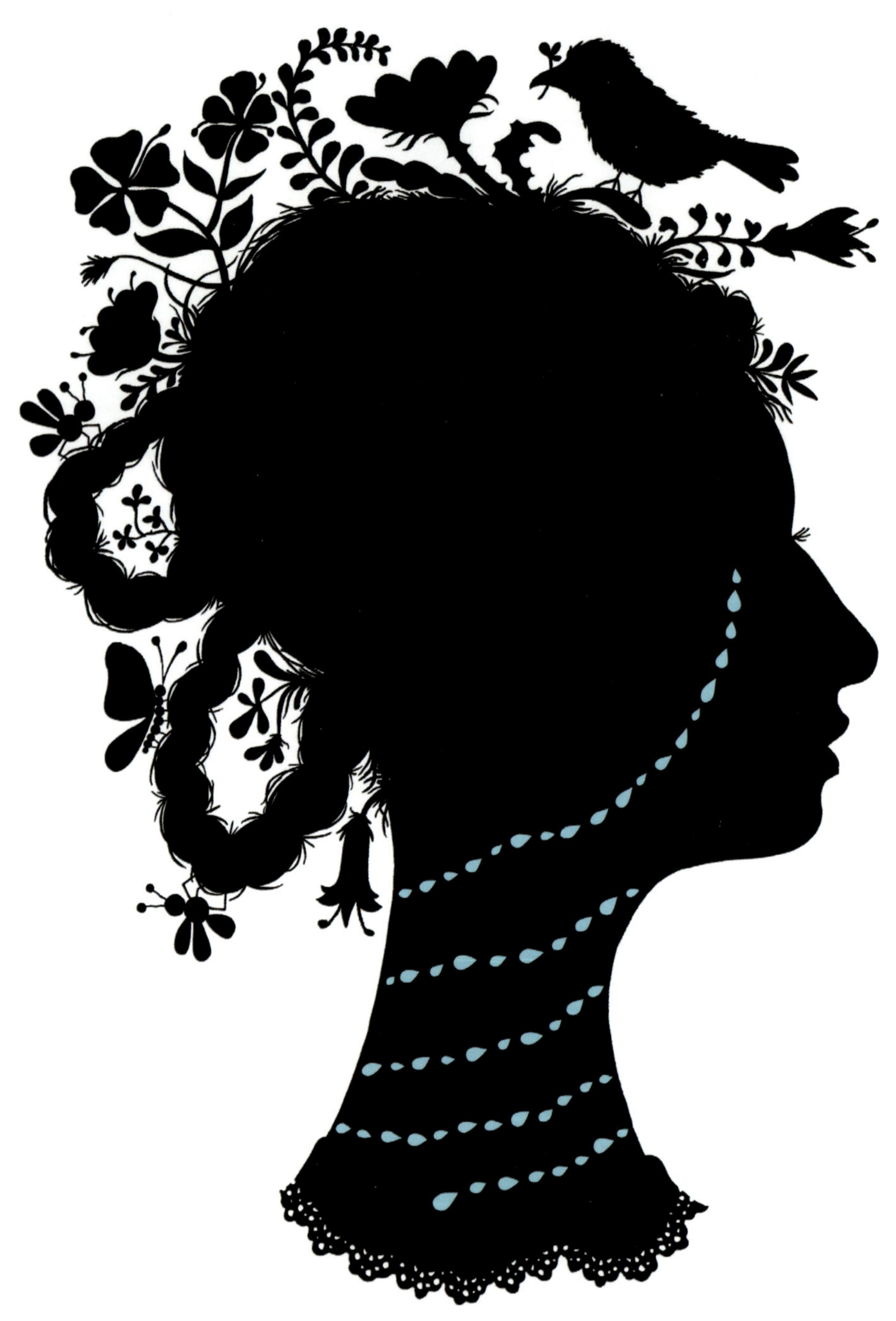



MERIT *Melinda Beck*

128

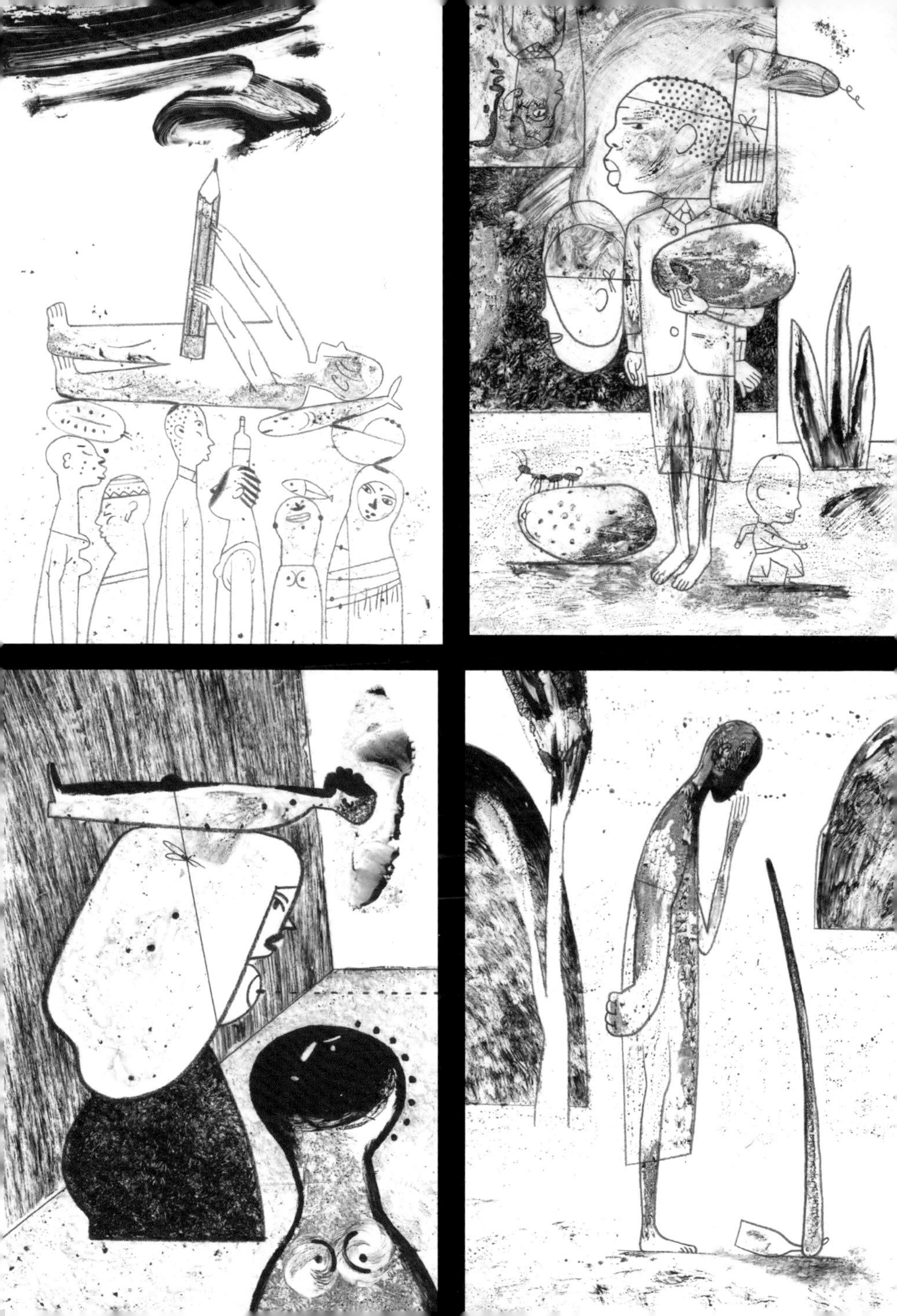

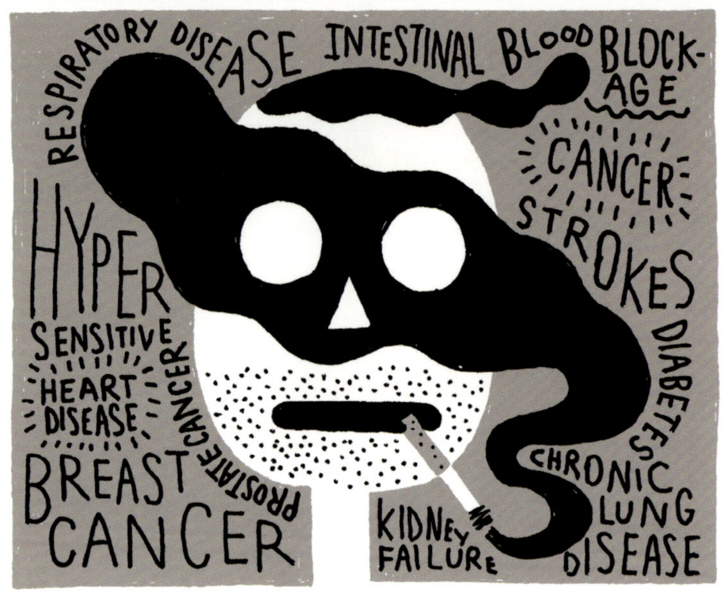


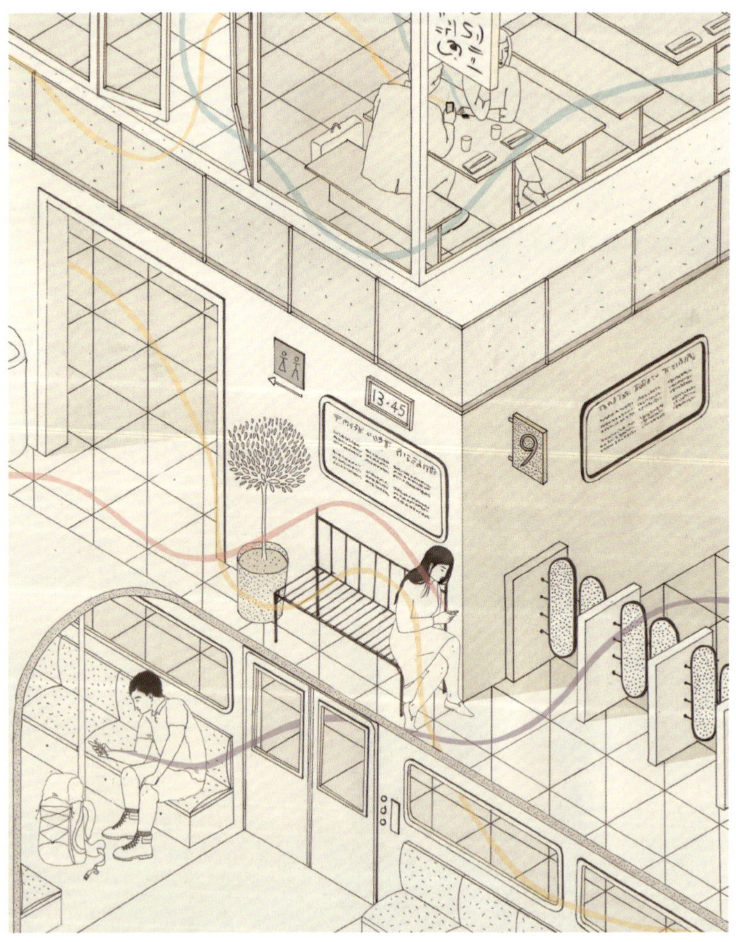


(T) **MERIT** *Benoit Tardif*   (B) **MERIT** *Harriet Lee-Merrion*

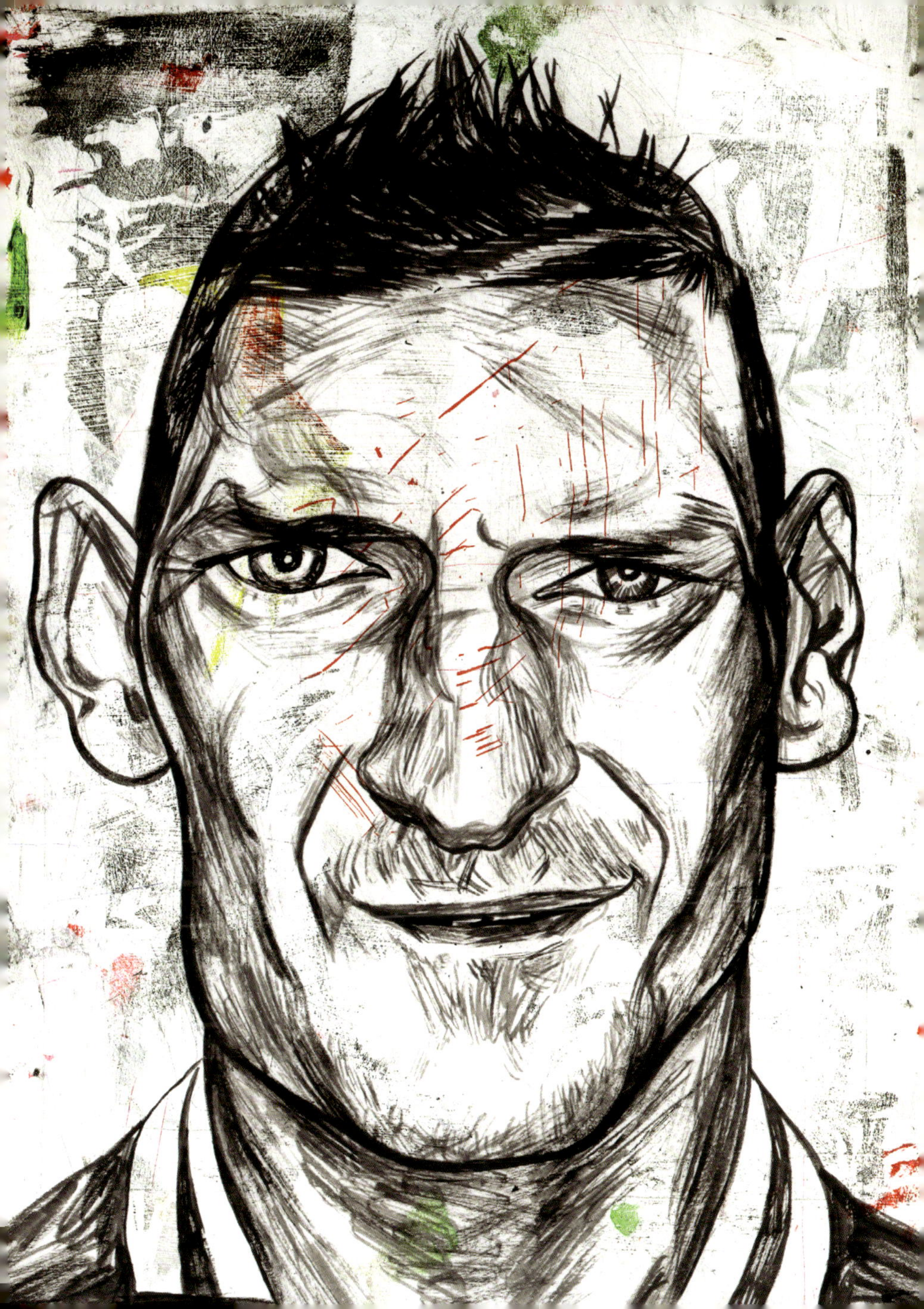

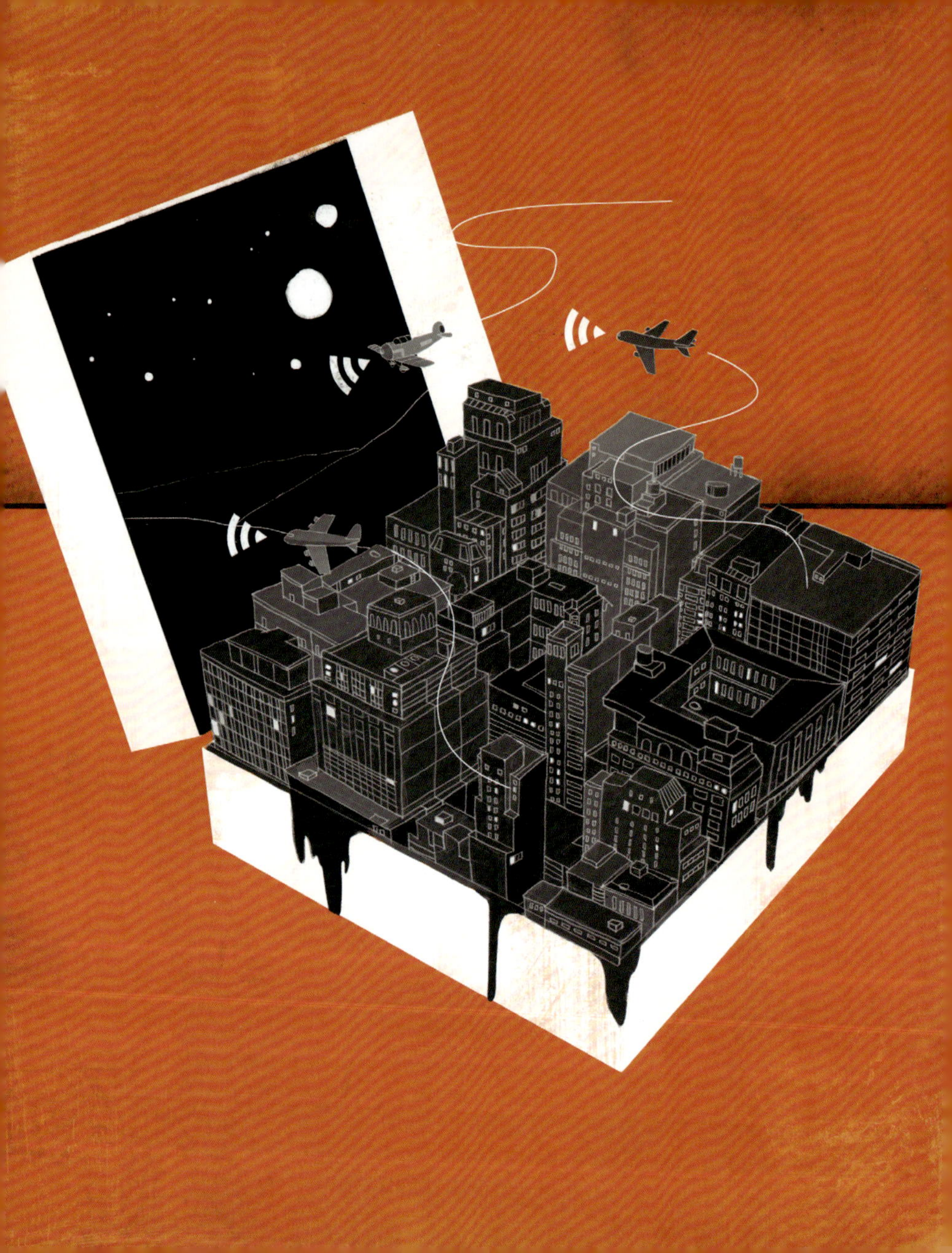

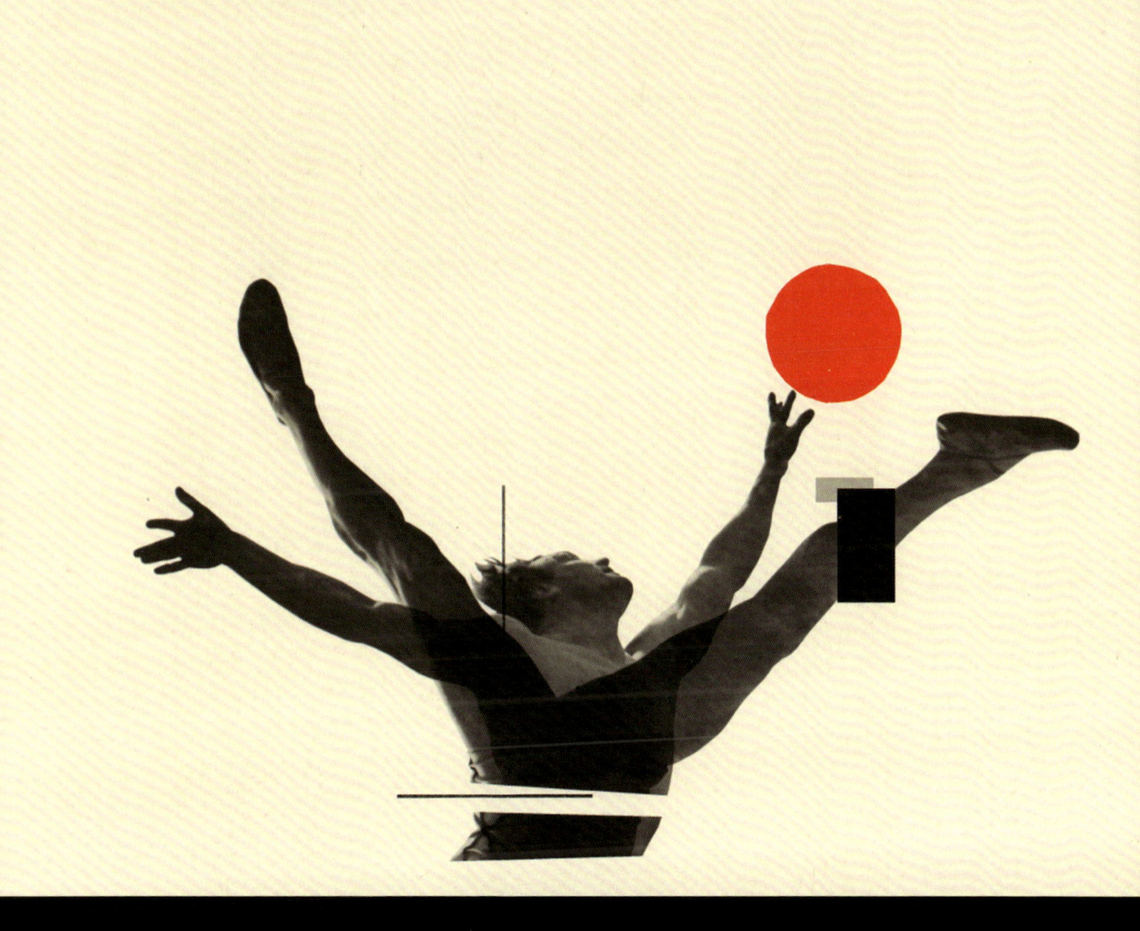

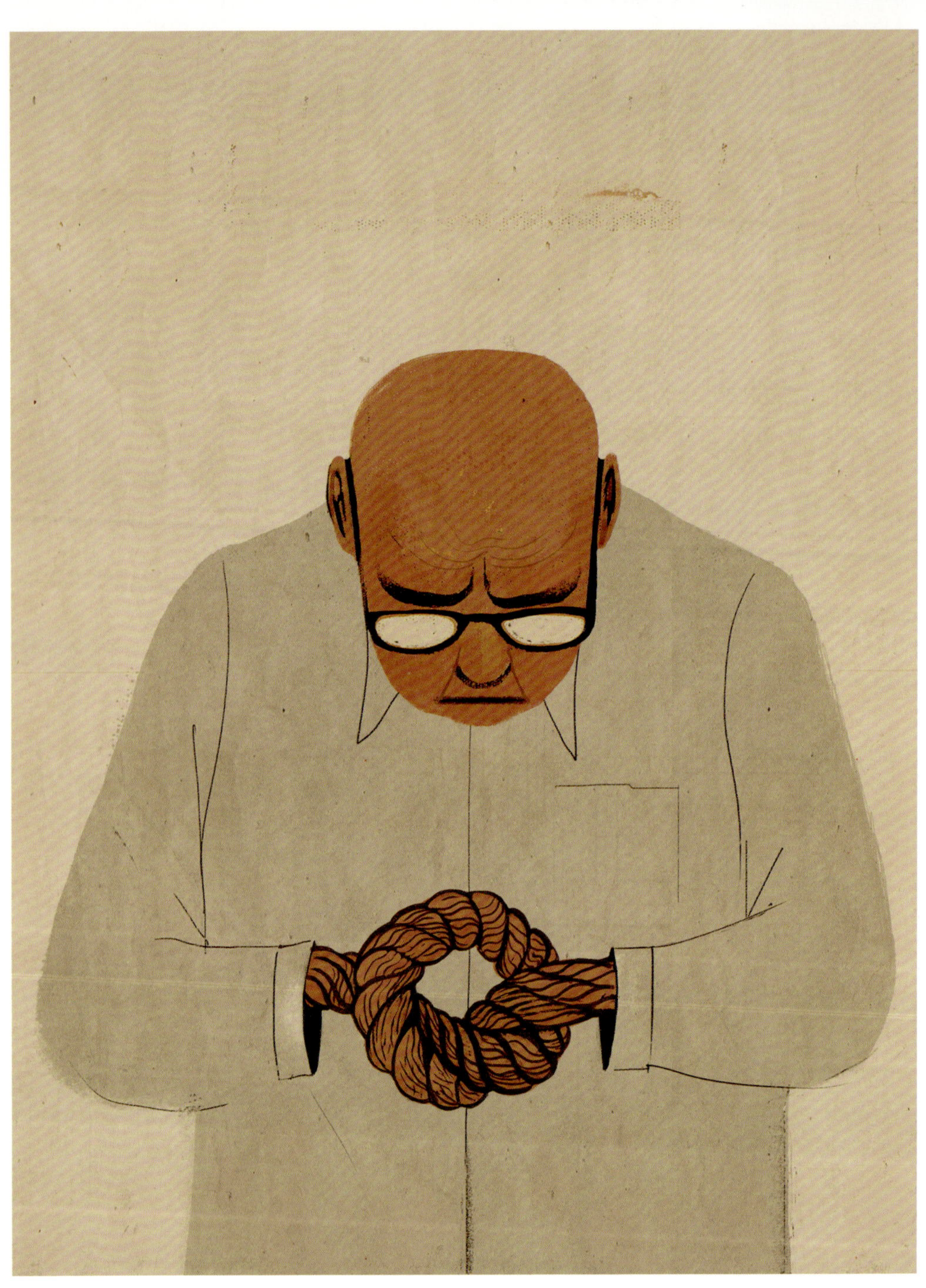



MERIT *Beppe Giacobbe*

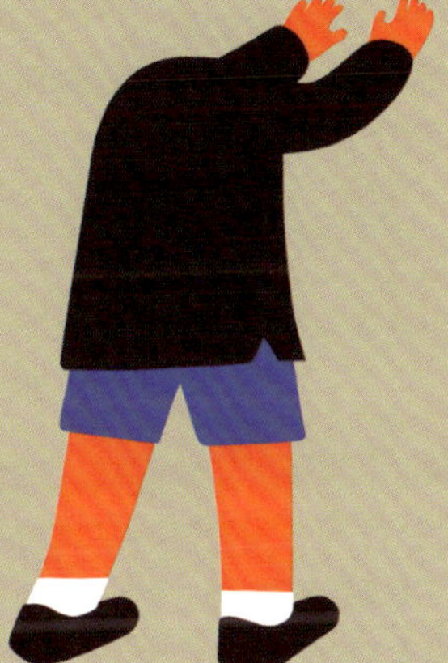

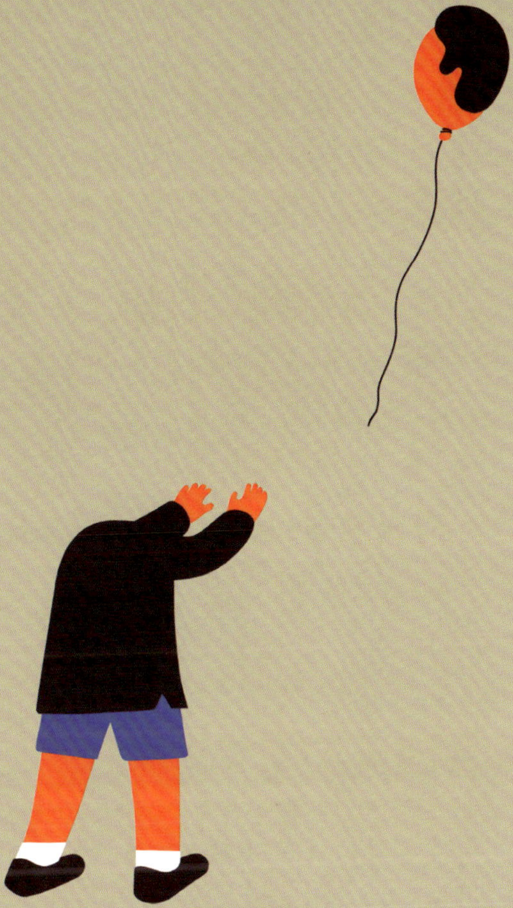

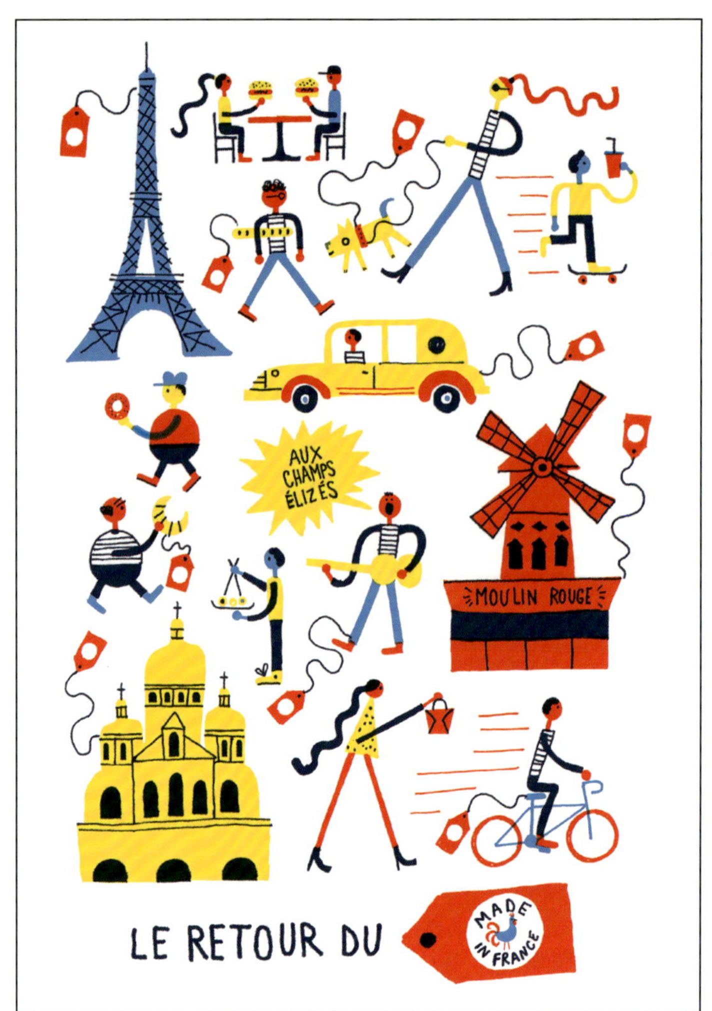


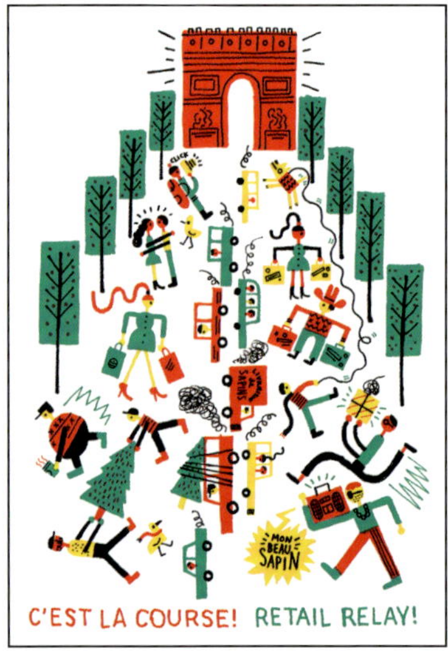


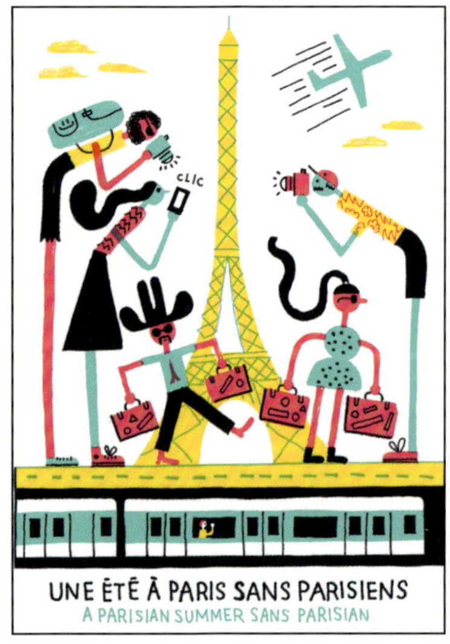


MERIT *Benoit Tardif*

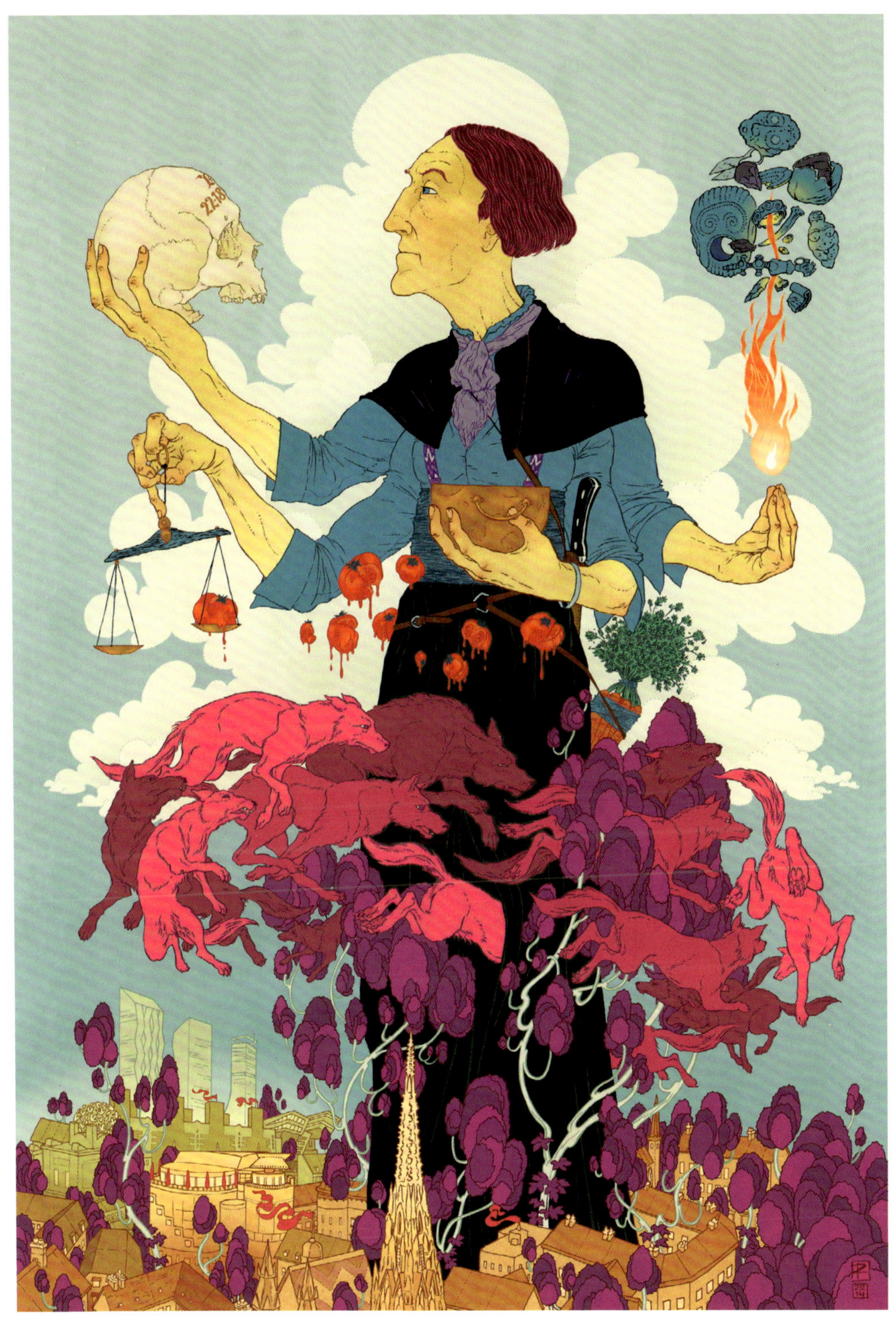



MERIT *Peter Diamond*

137

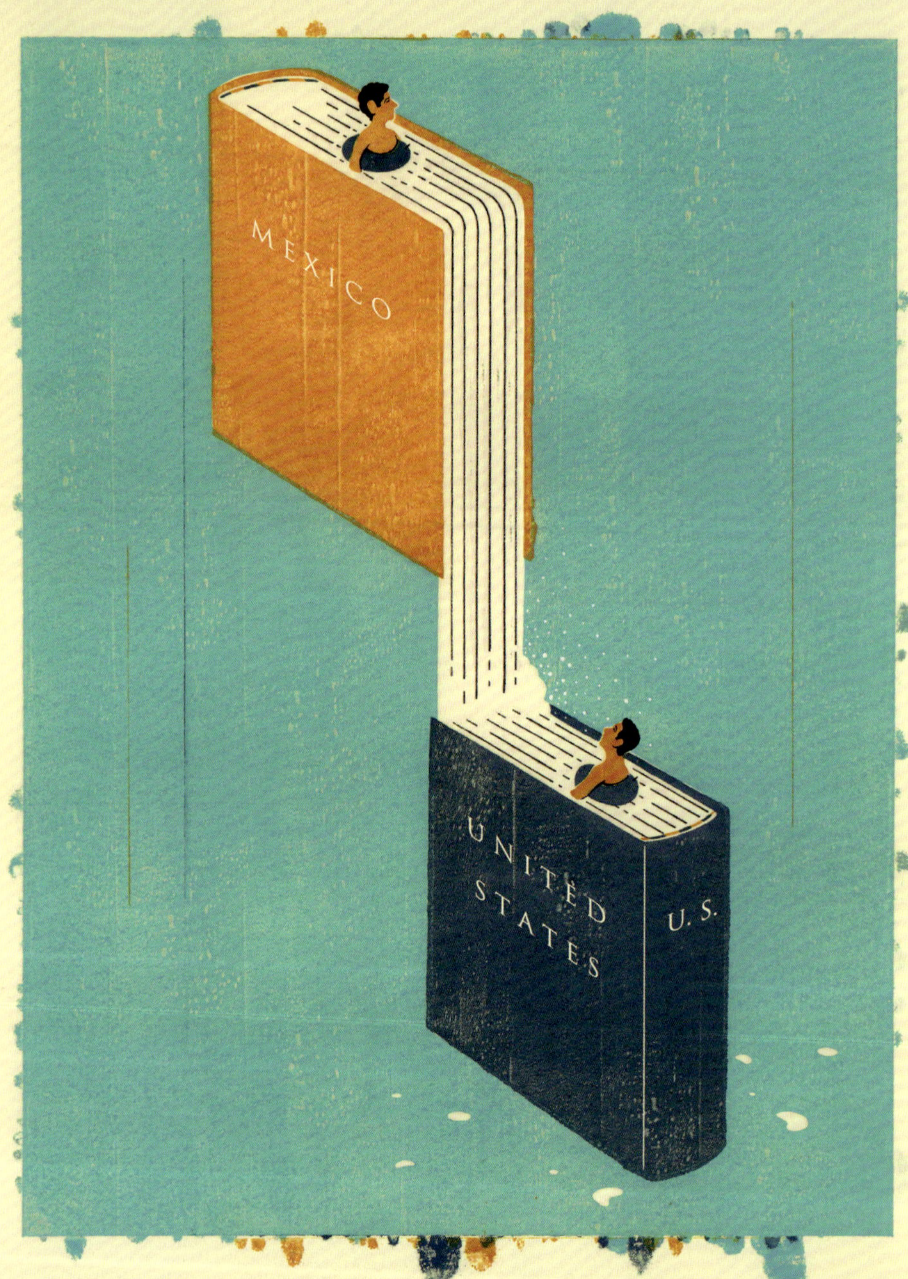

MEXICO
UNITED STATES
U.S.

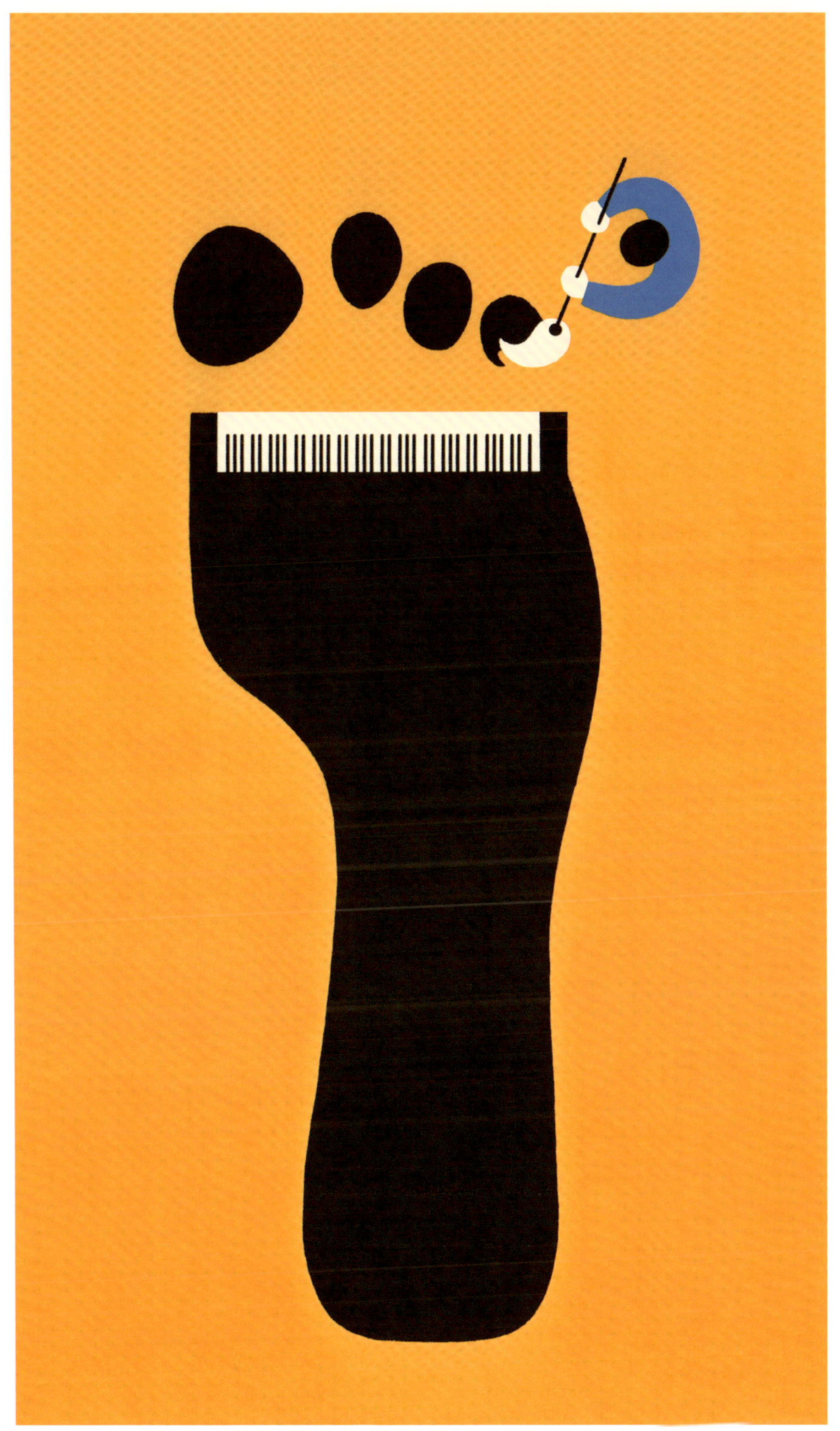



MERIT *Miguel Porlan*

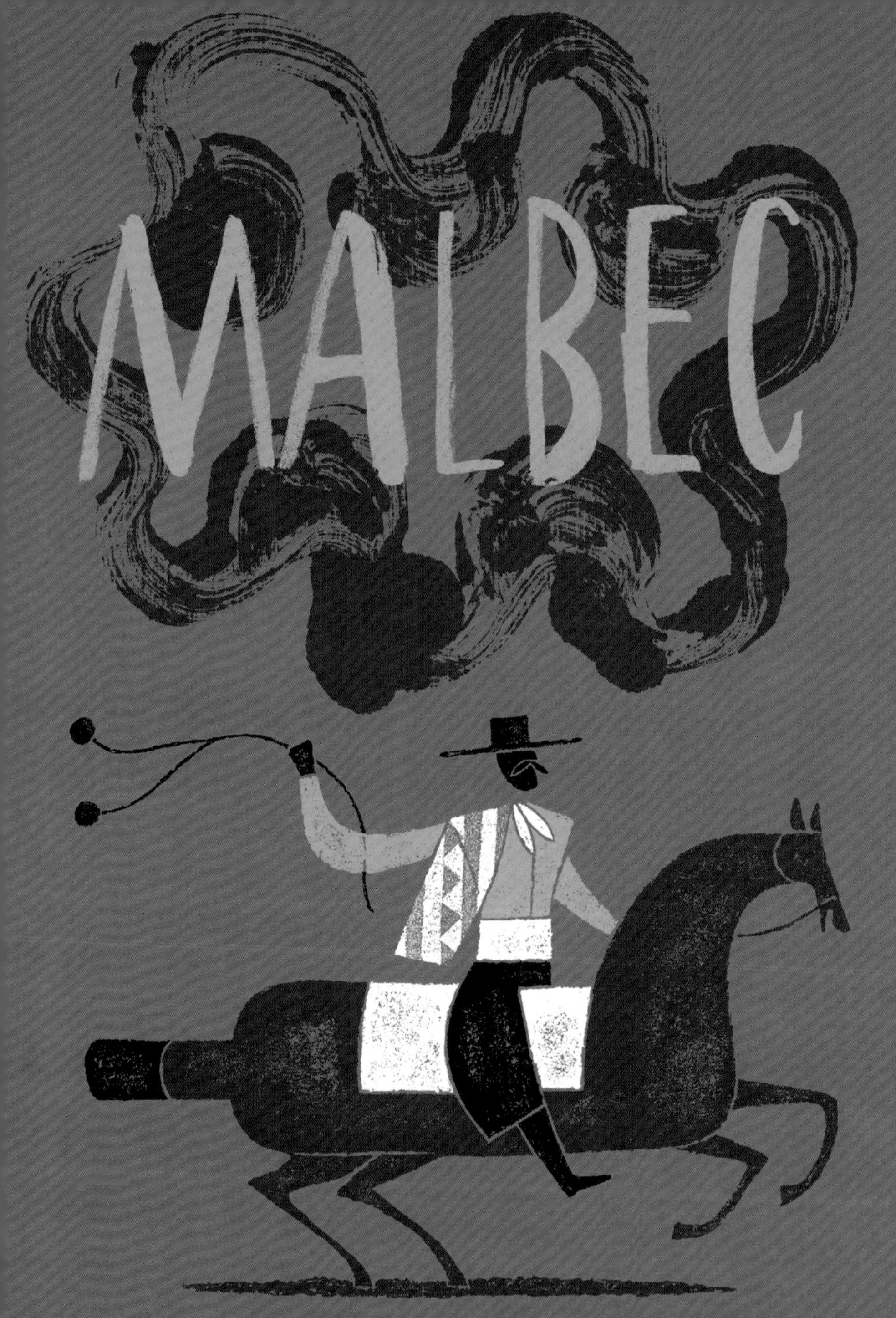
MALBEC

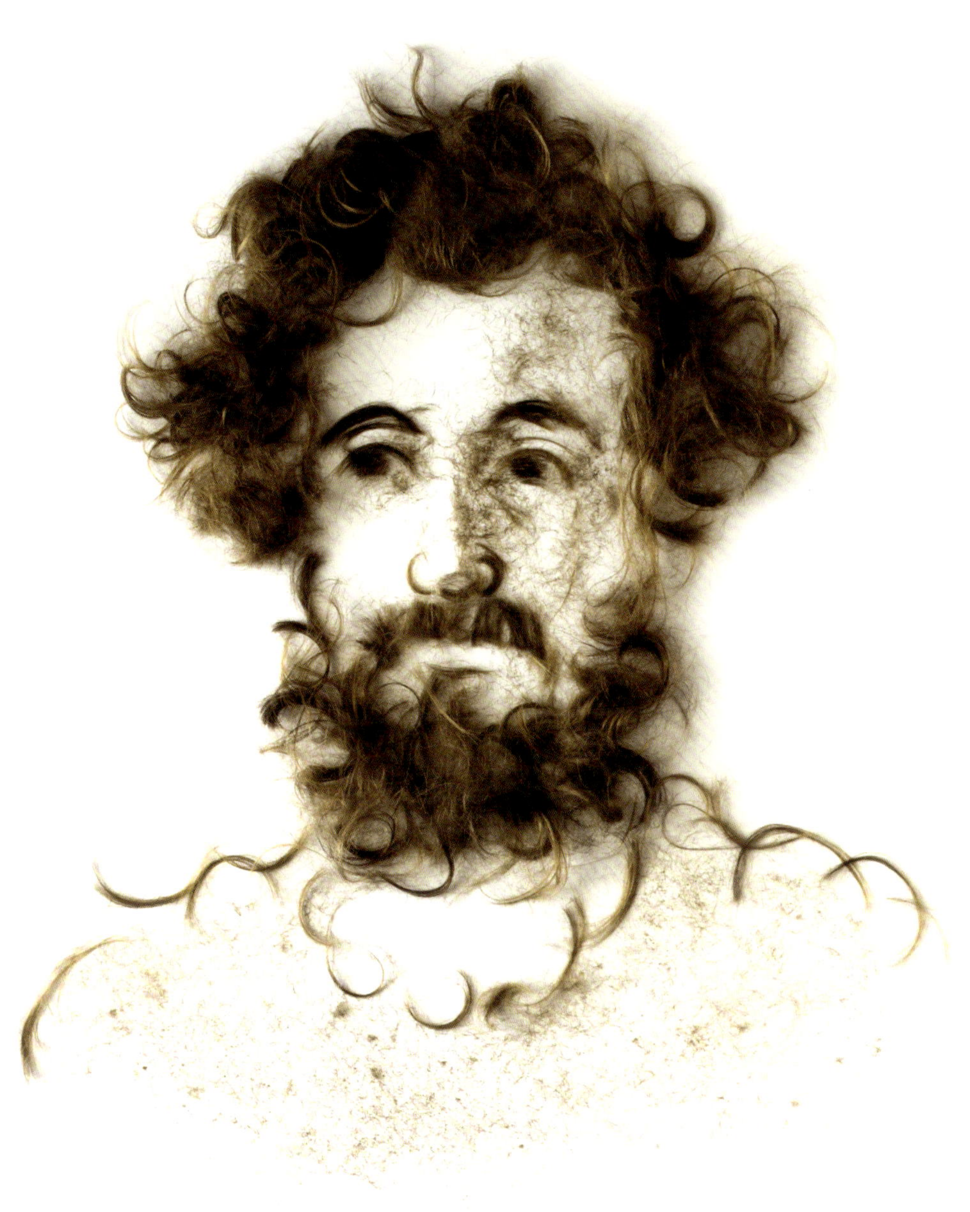

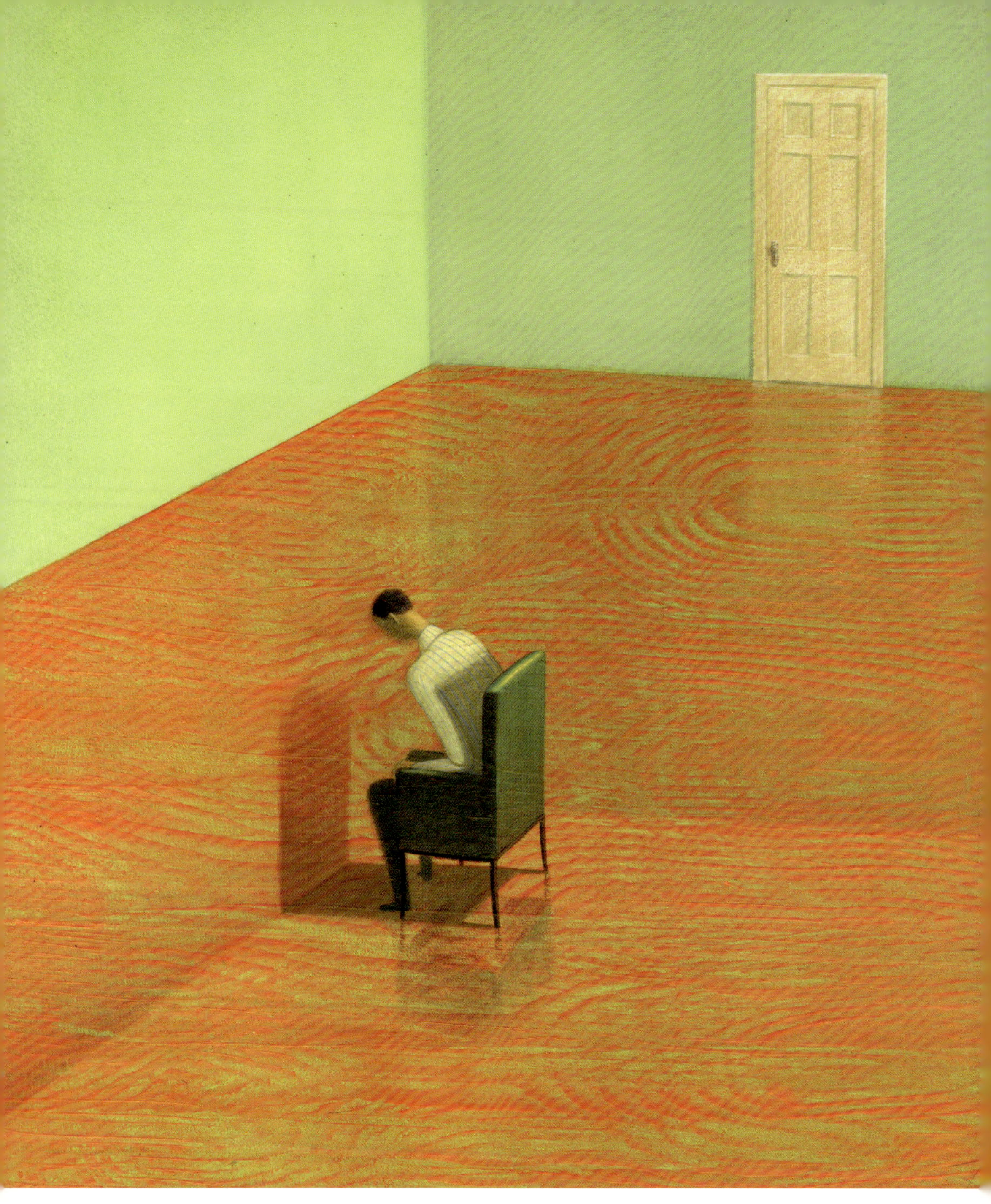



MERIT *Jon Krause*

142

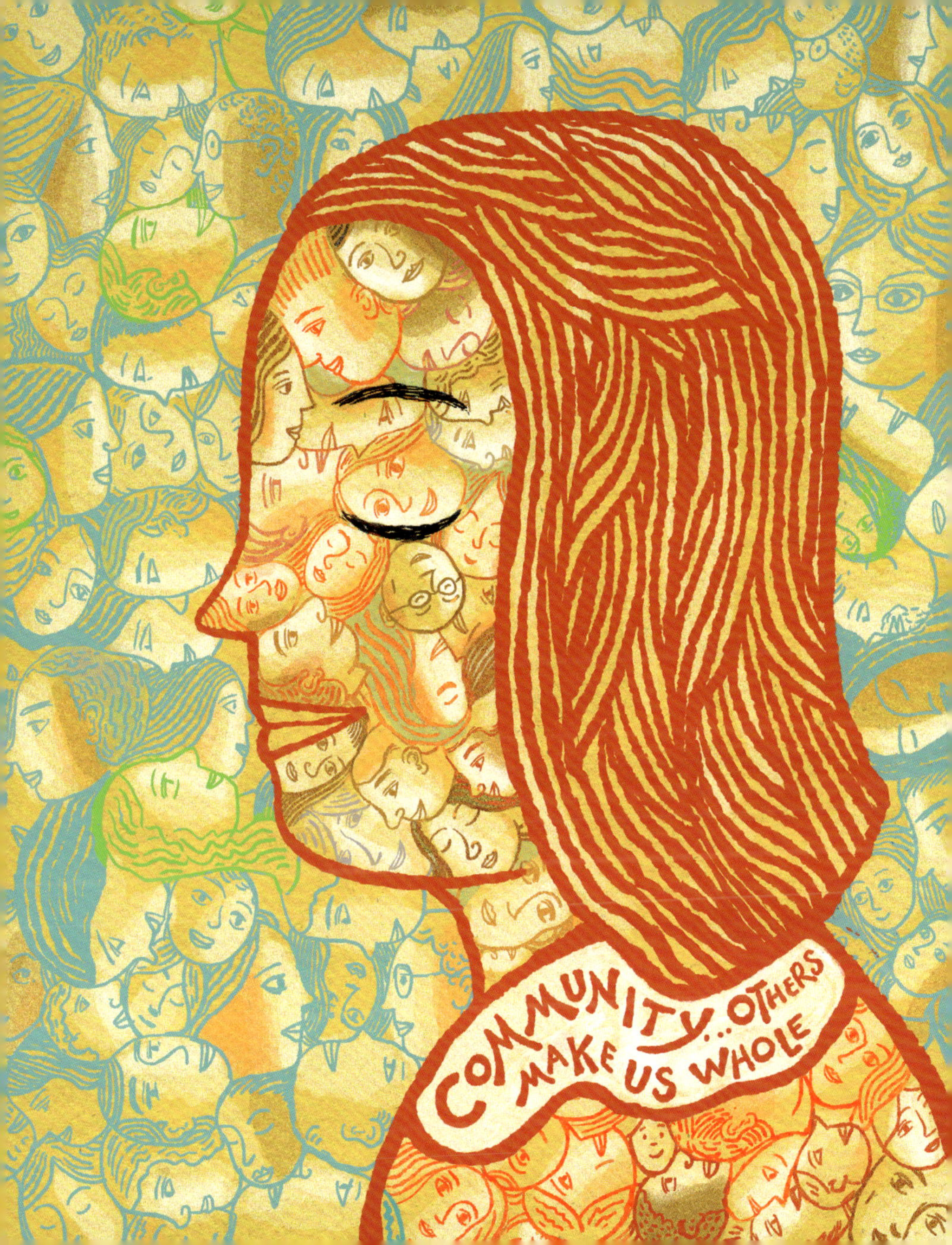

COMMUNITY...OTHERS MAKE US WHOLE

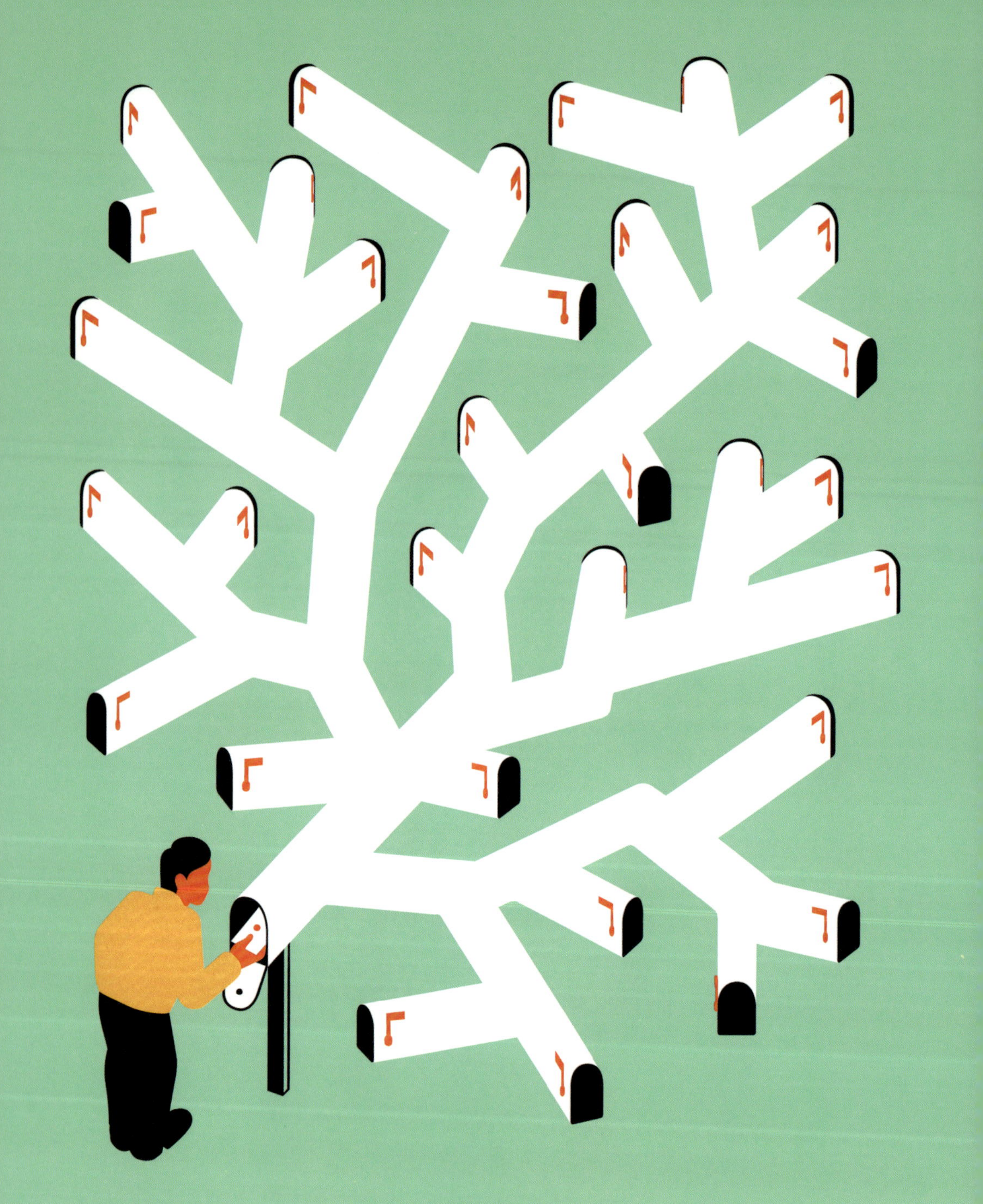



MERIT *Miguel Montaner*

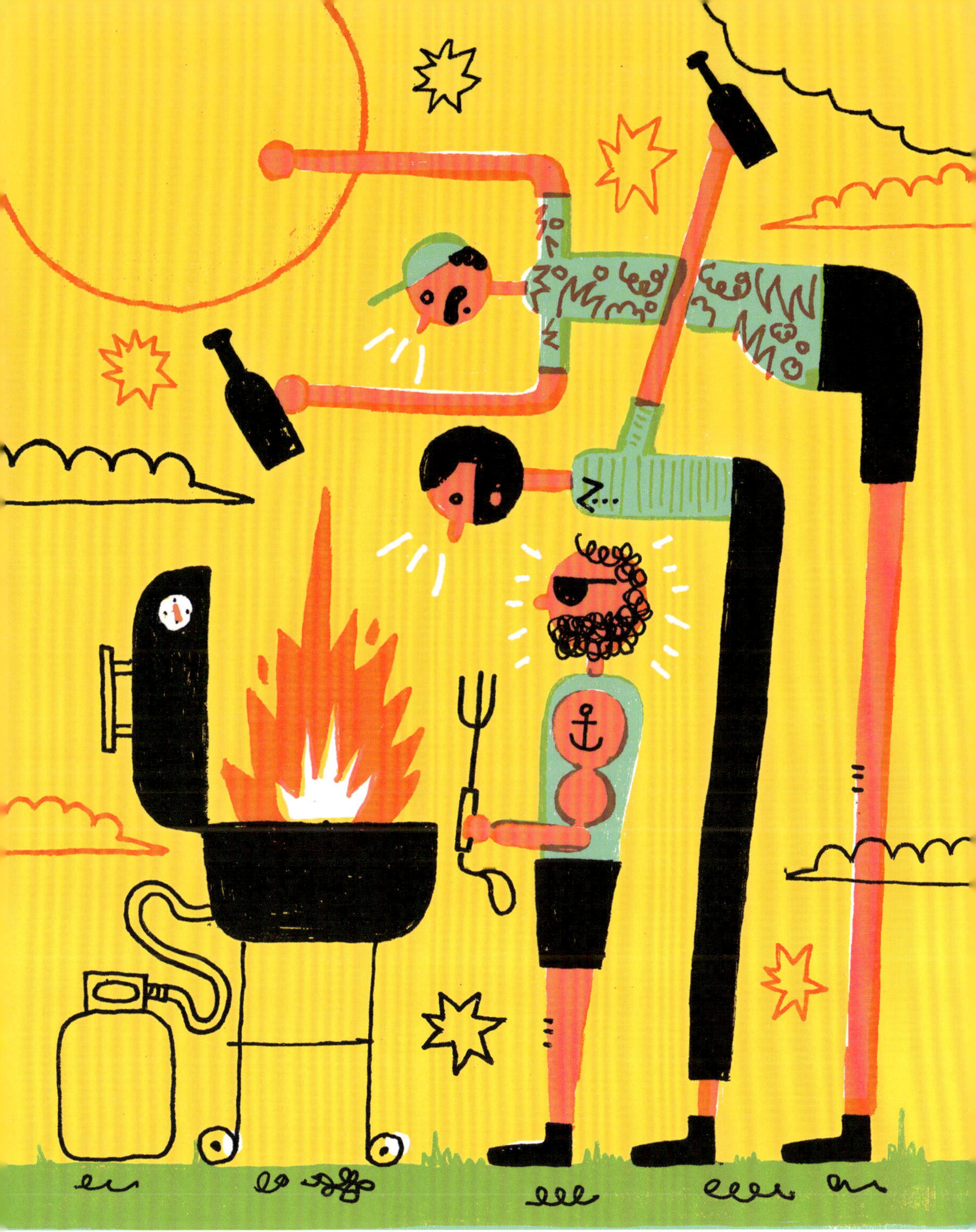

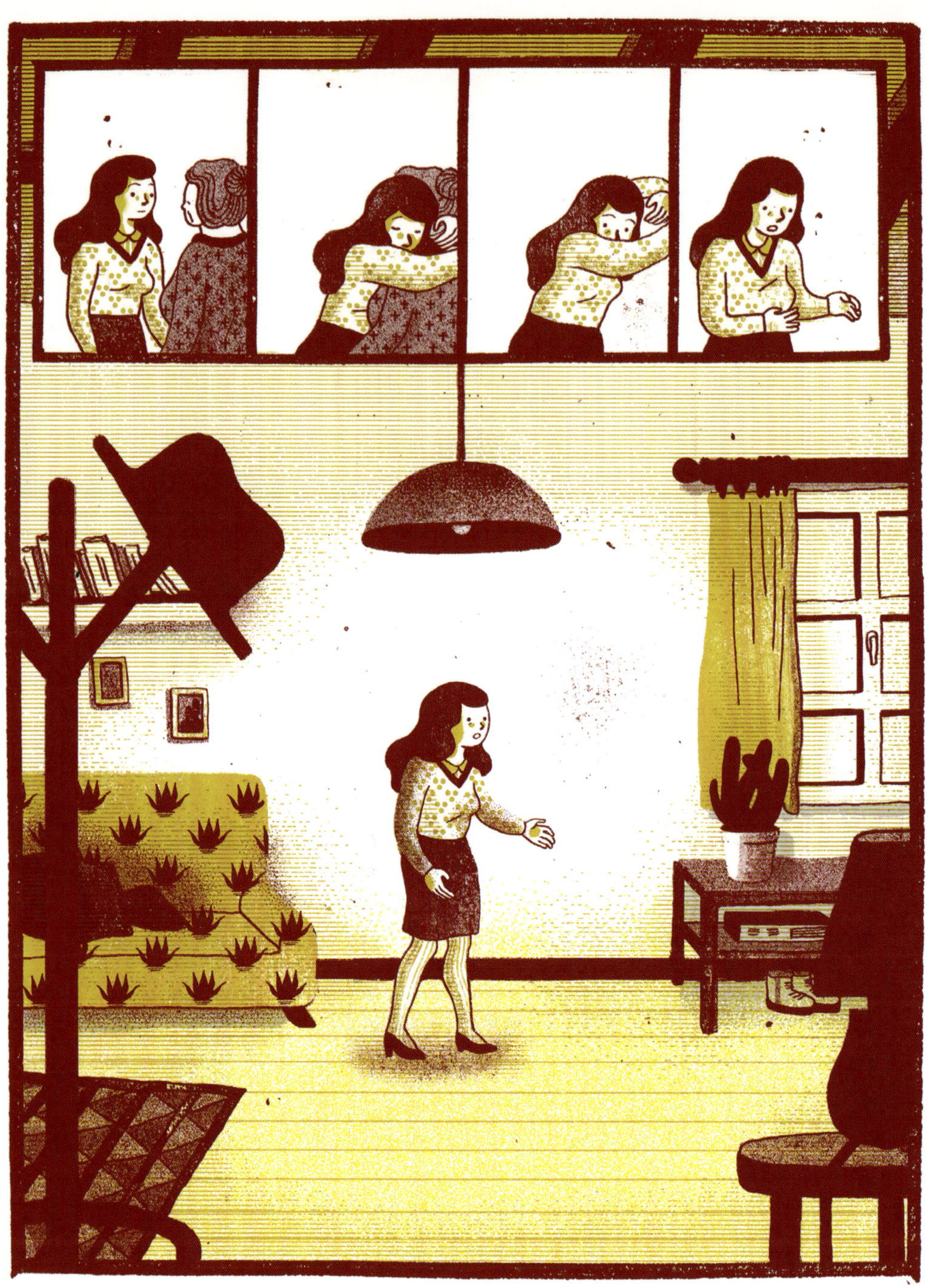



MERIT *Cristina Spanò*

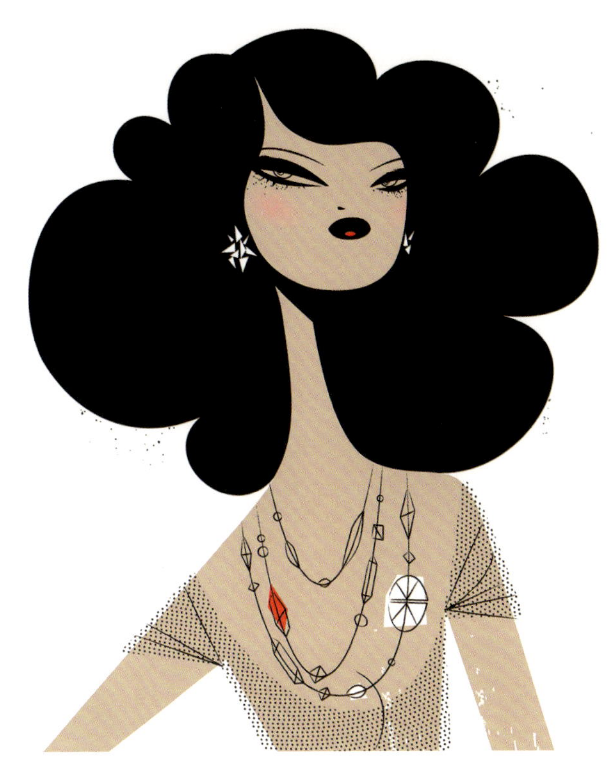

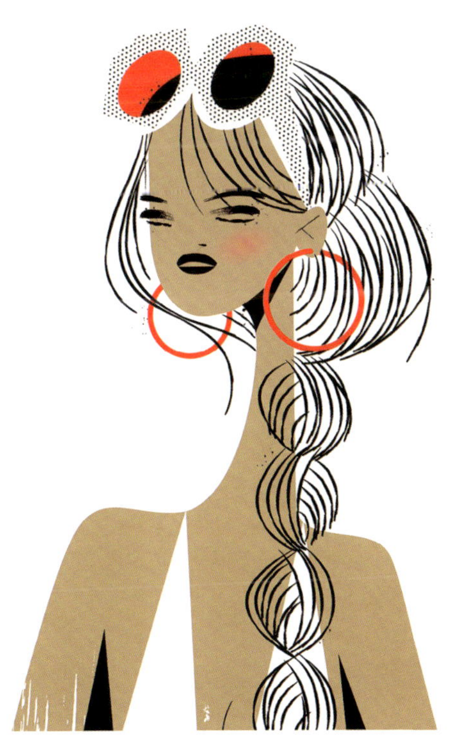

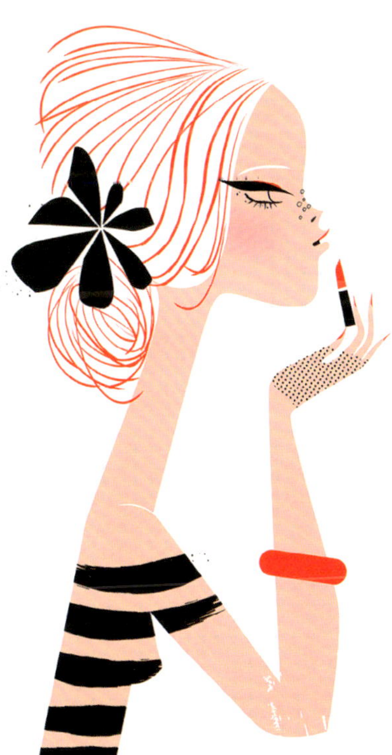



MERIT *Kirsten Ulve*

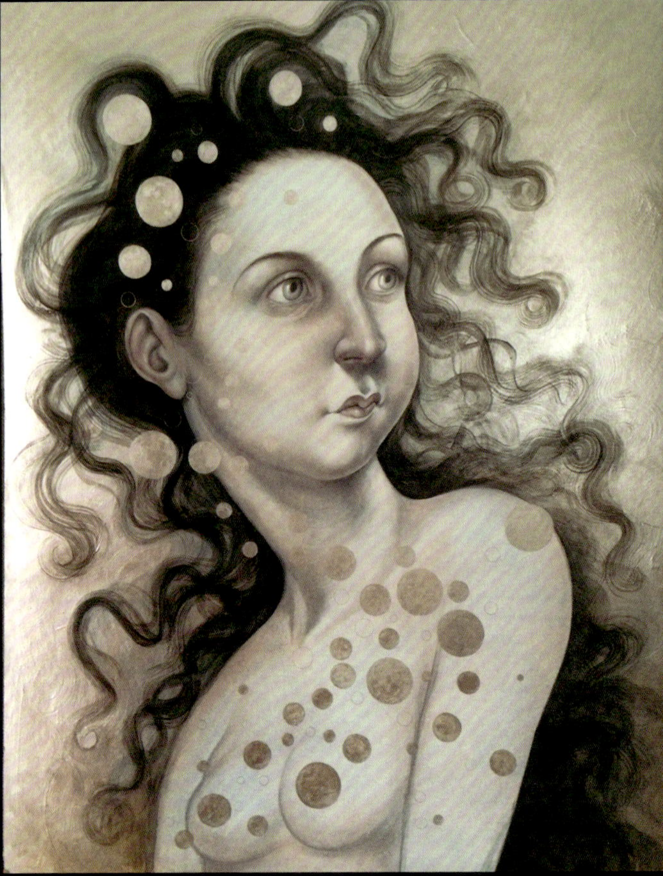

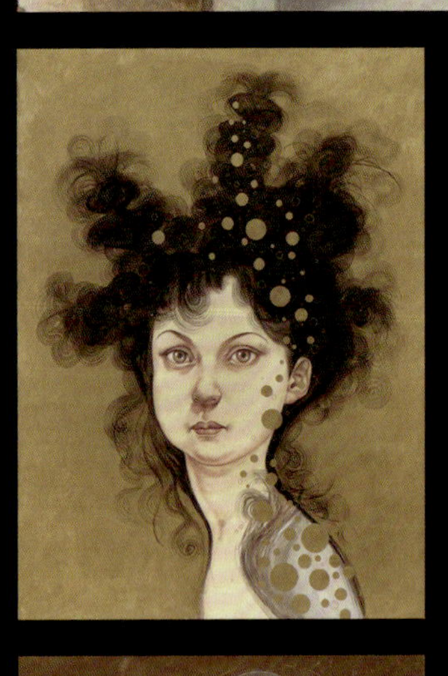

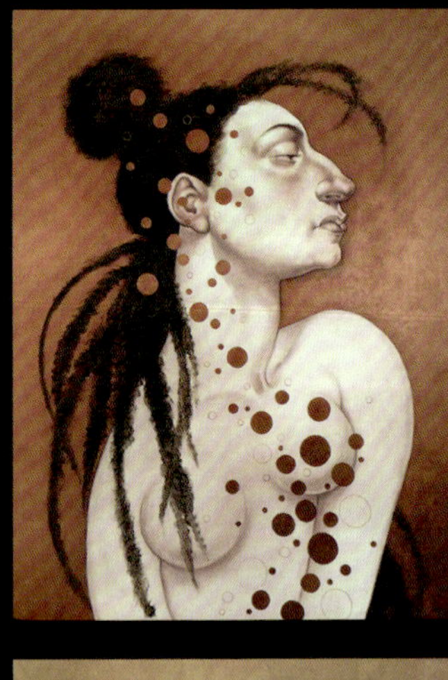

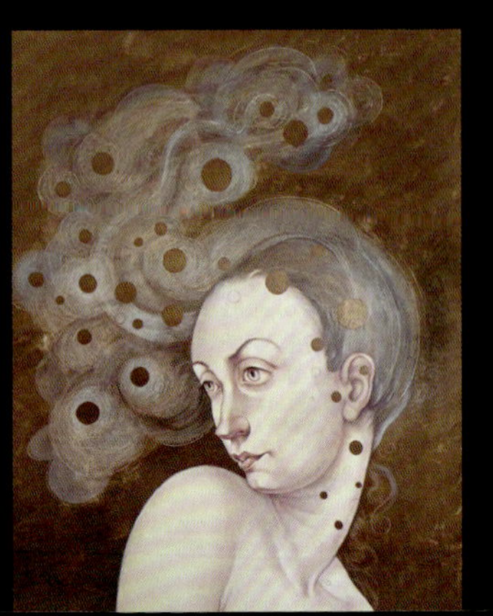

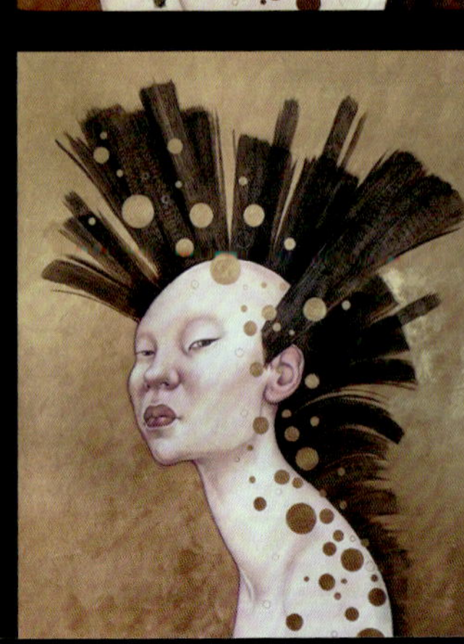

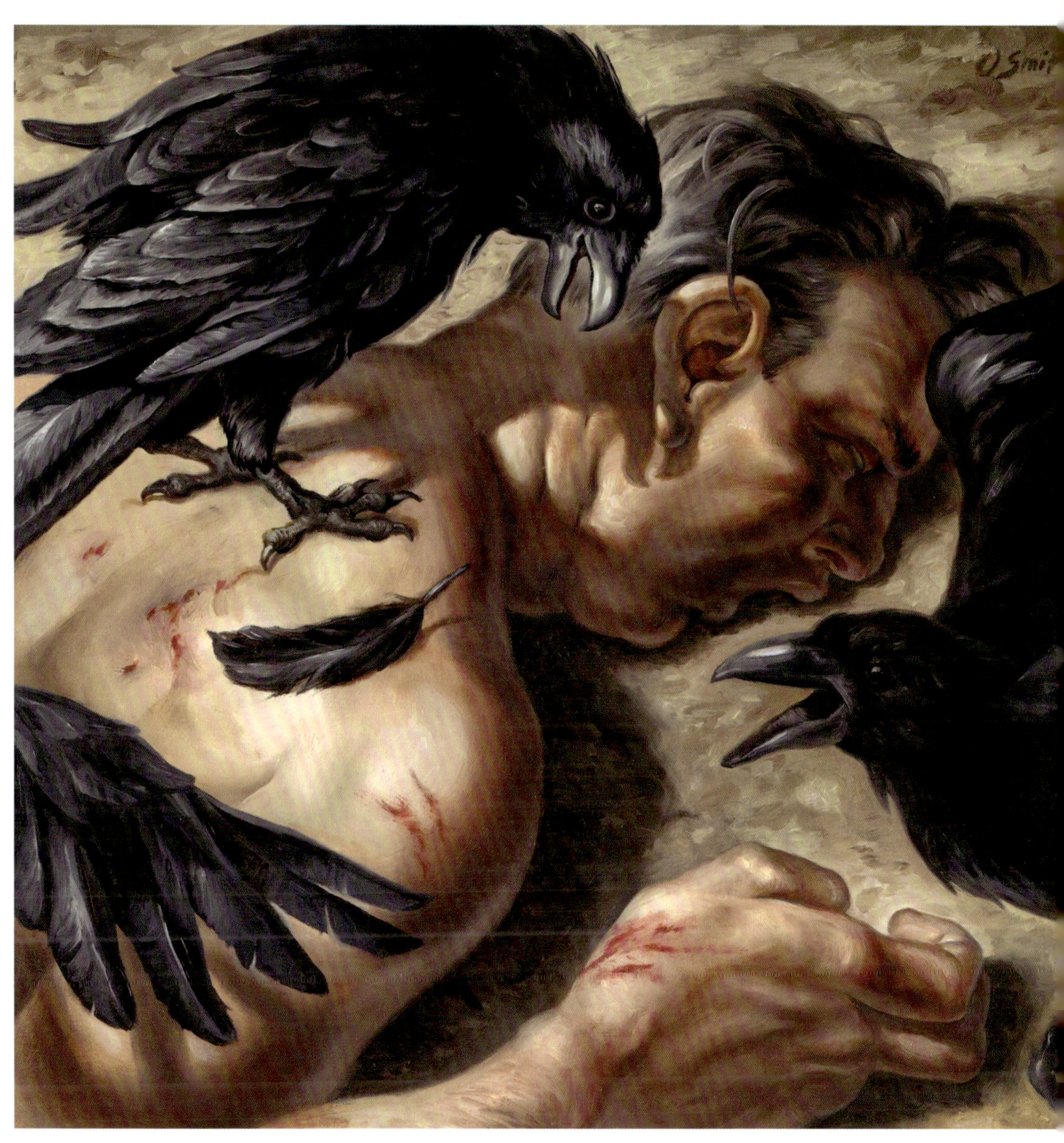



(L) MERIT *Anita Kunz*   (R) MERIT *Owen Smith*

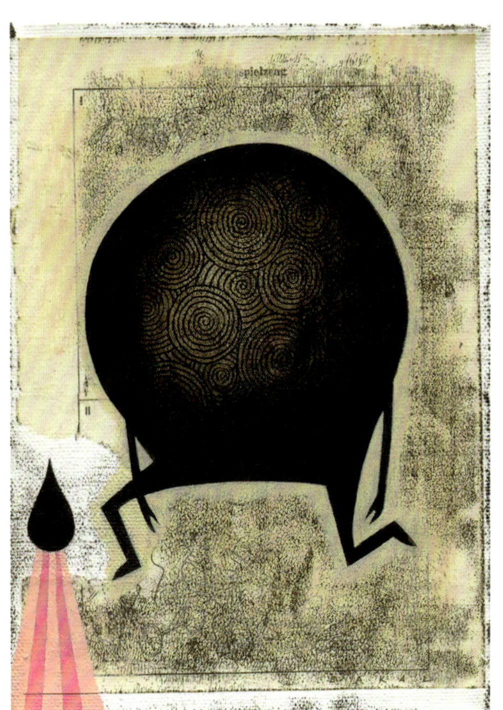

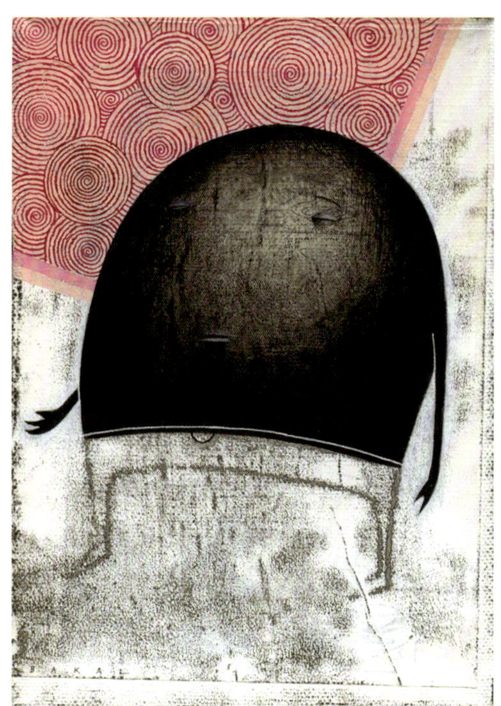

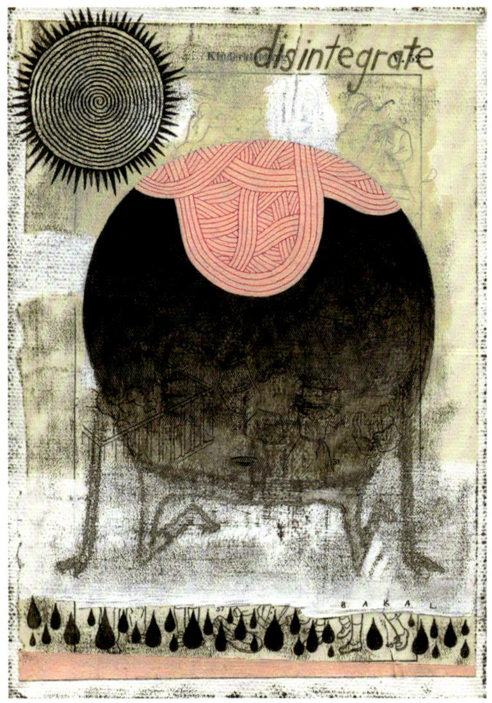

disintegrate
BAKAL


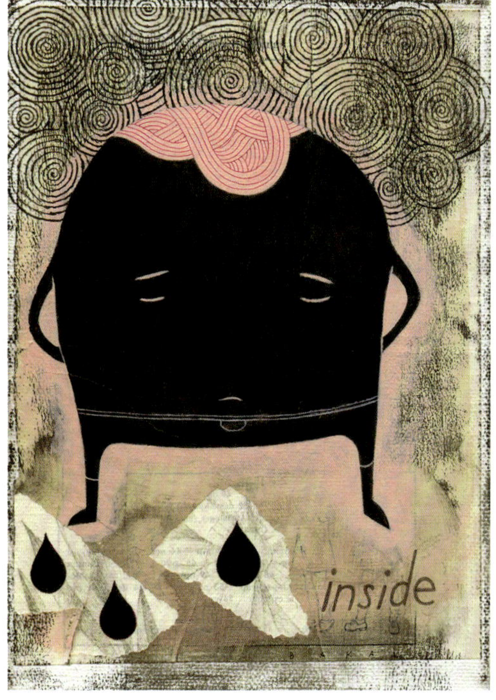

inside

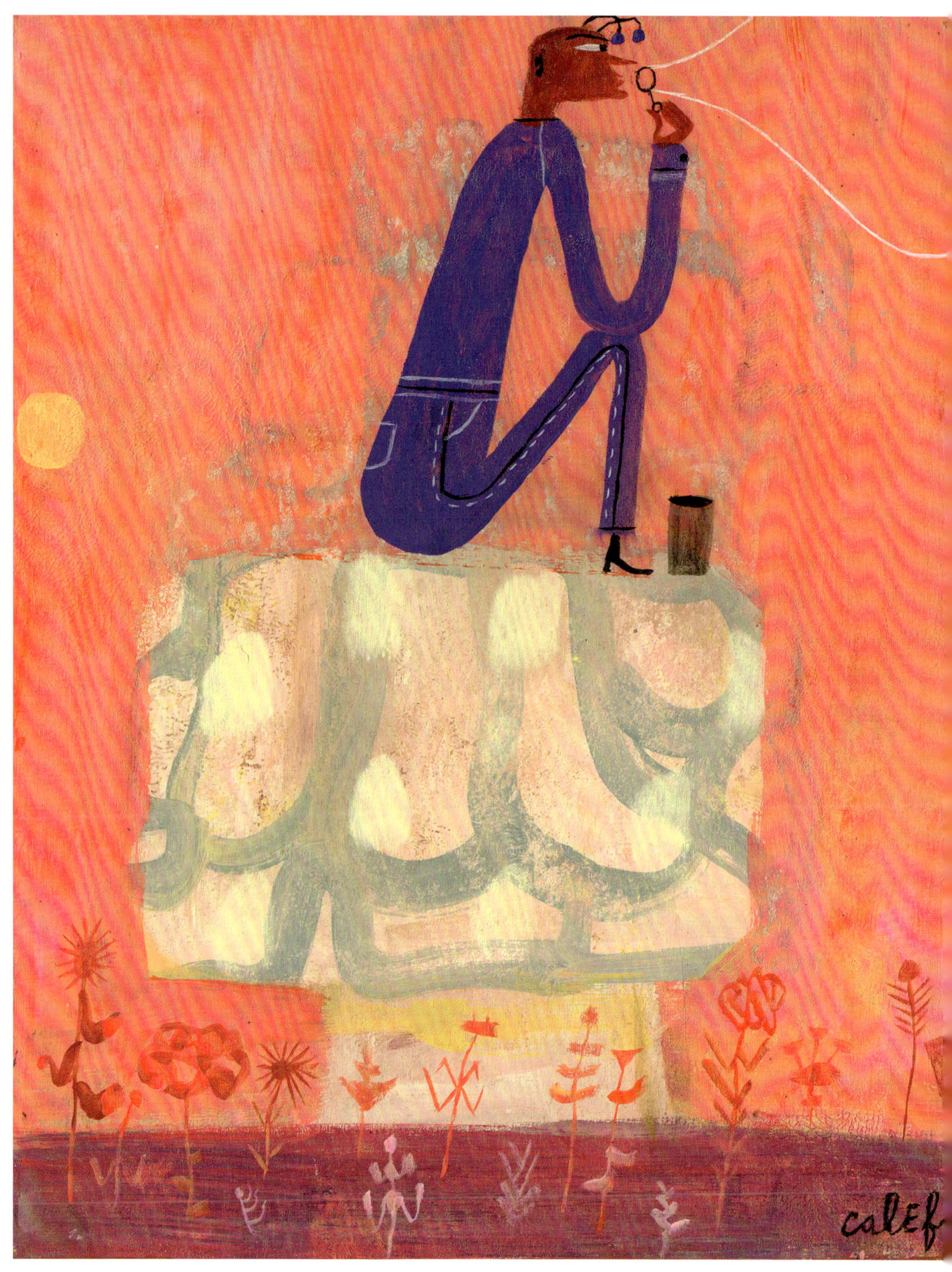



MERIT *Calef Brown*

151

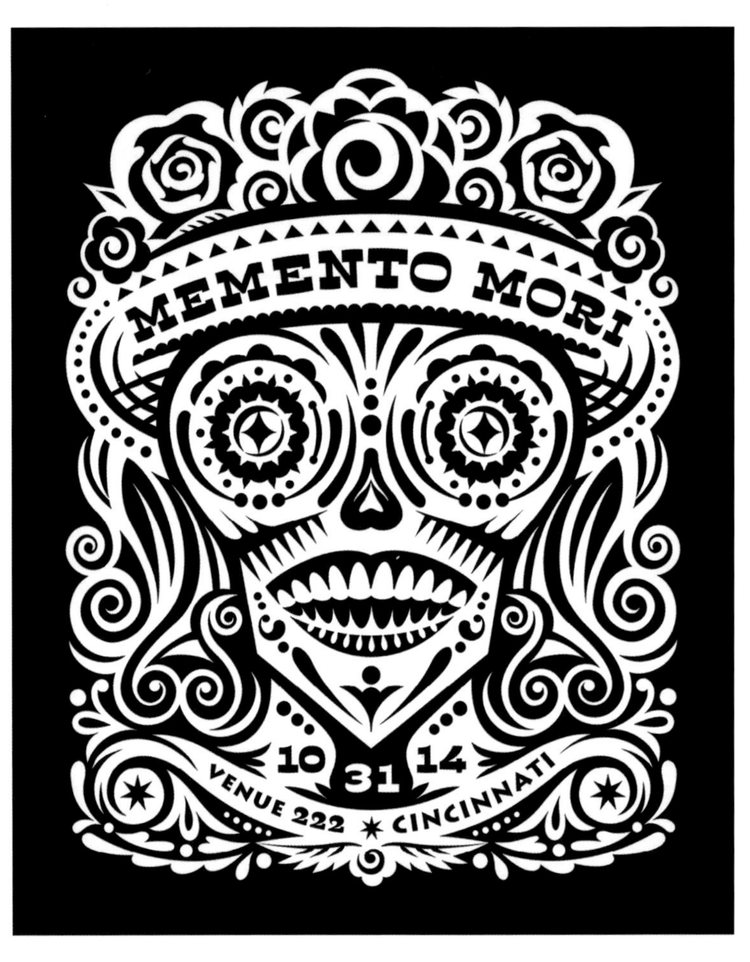


MERIT *Jean Tuttle*

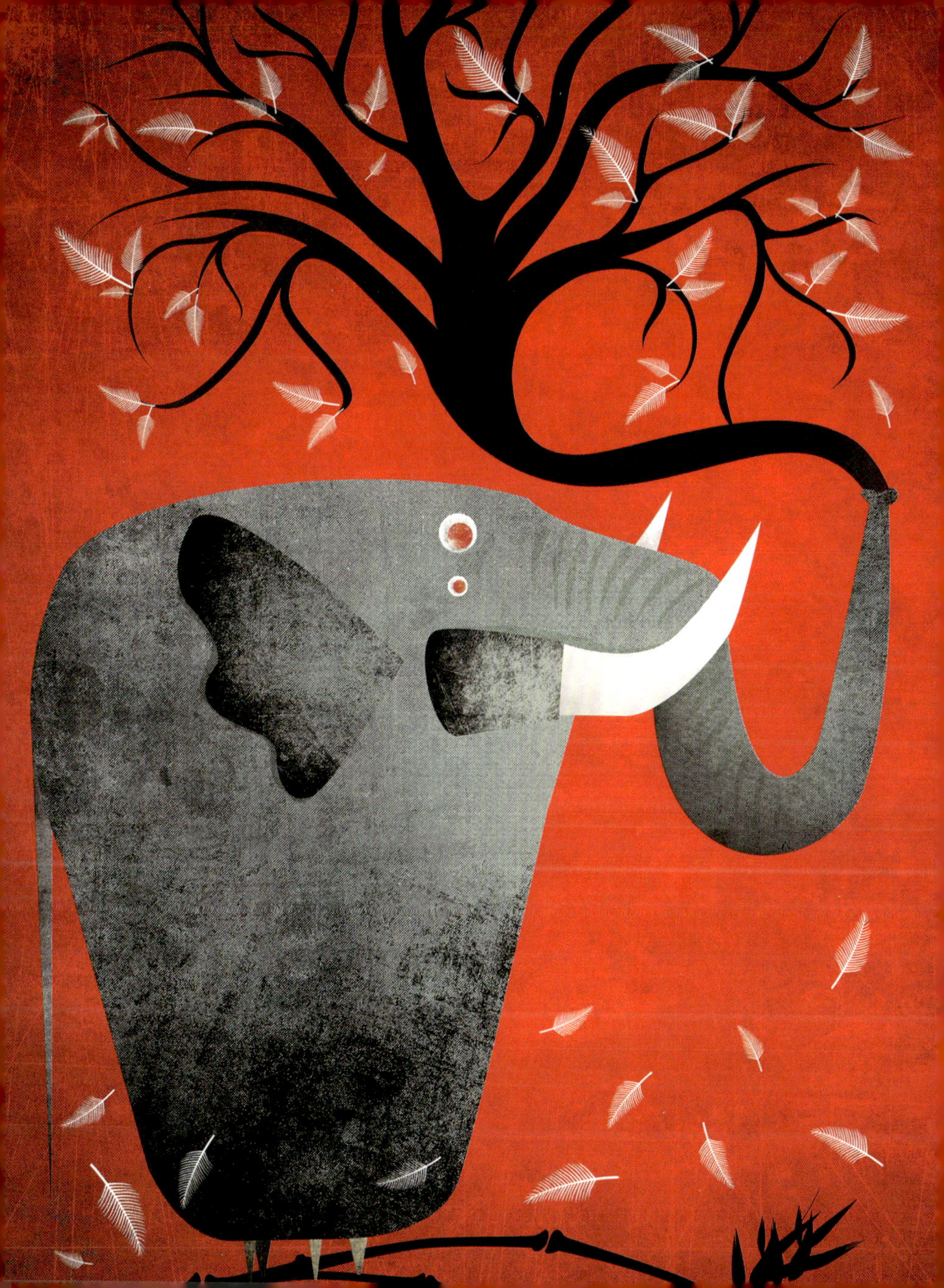

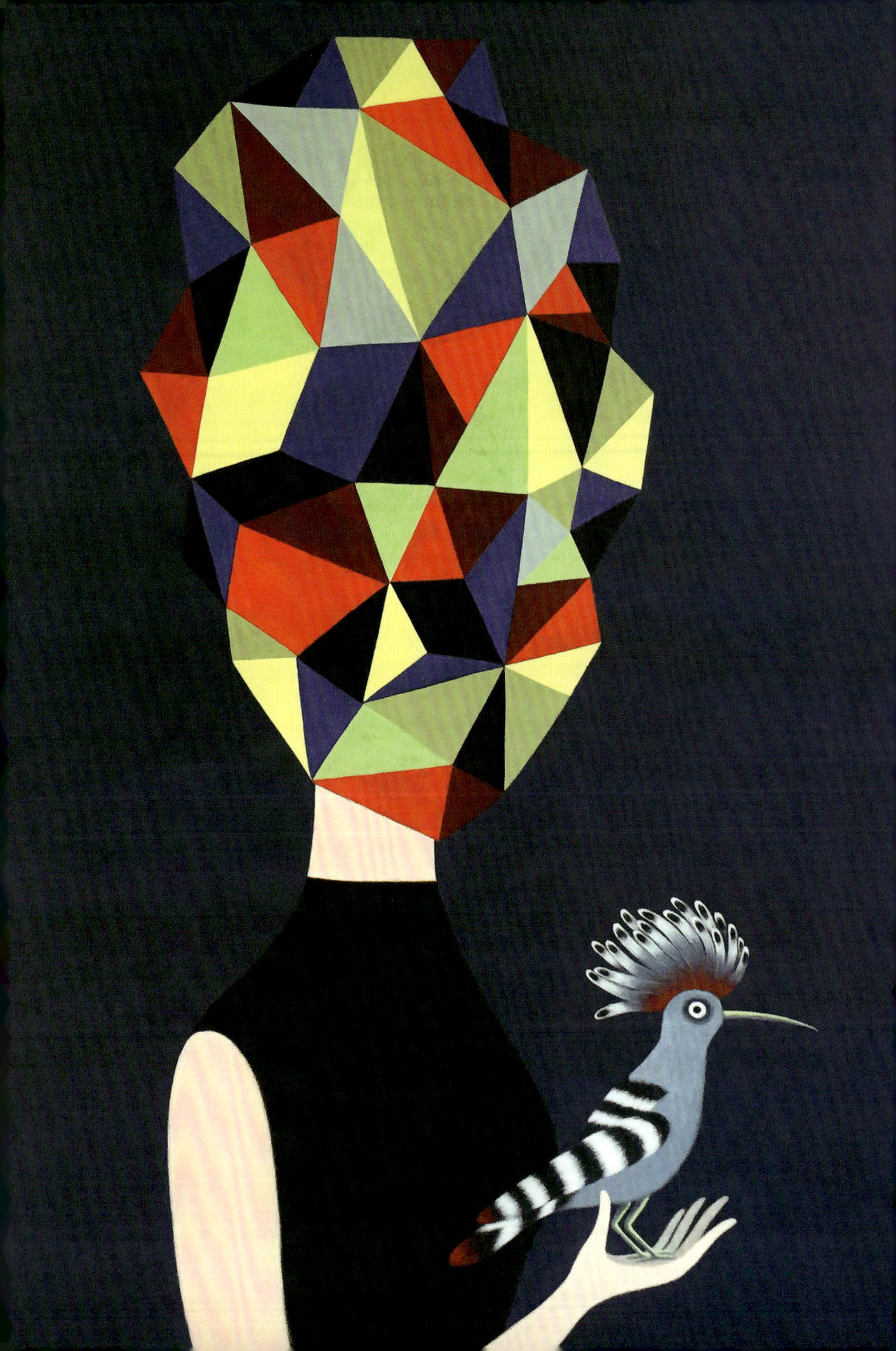

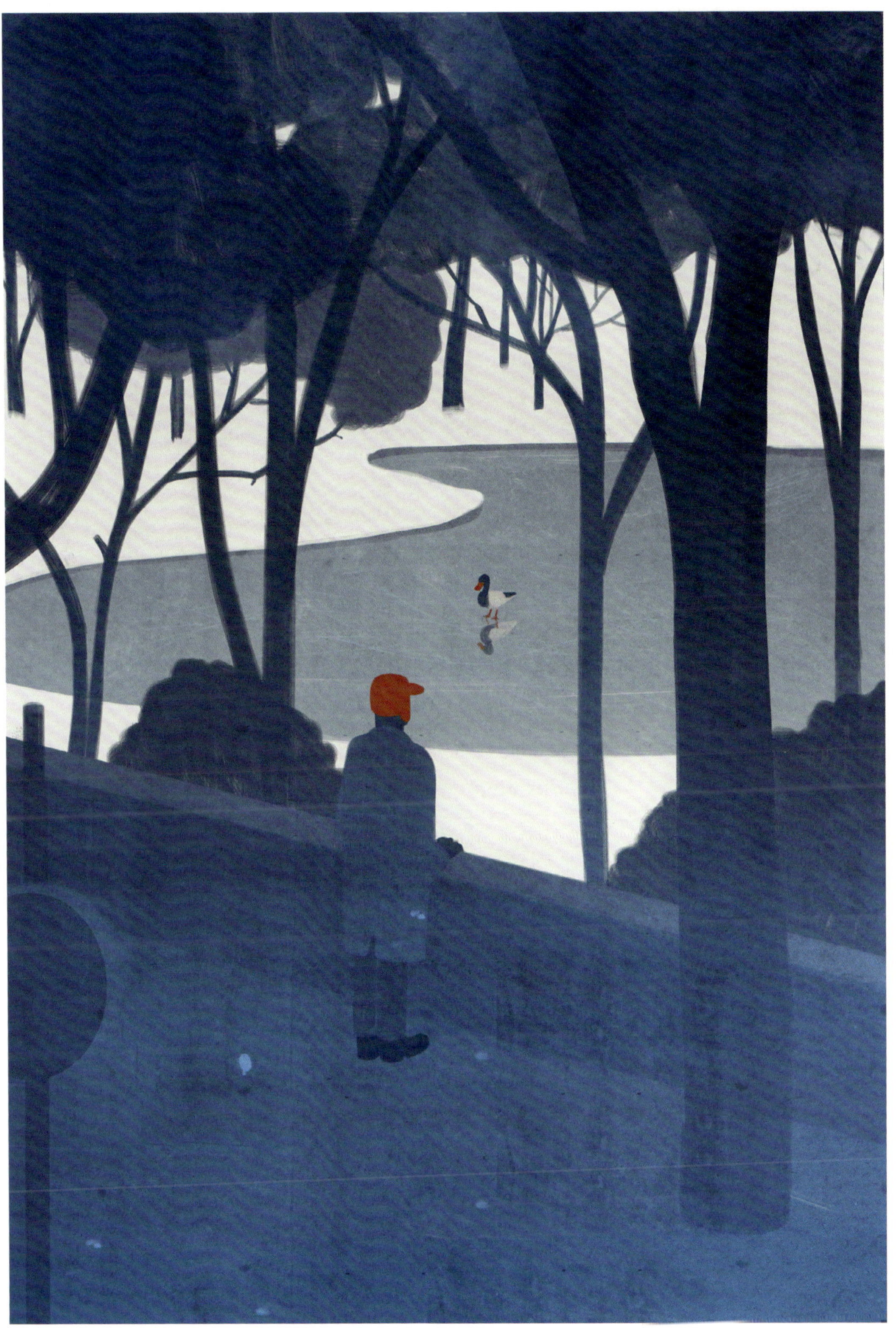



(L) MERIT *Valeria Petrone*   (R) MERIT *Emiliano Ponzi*

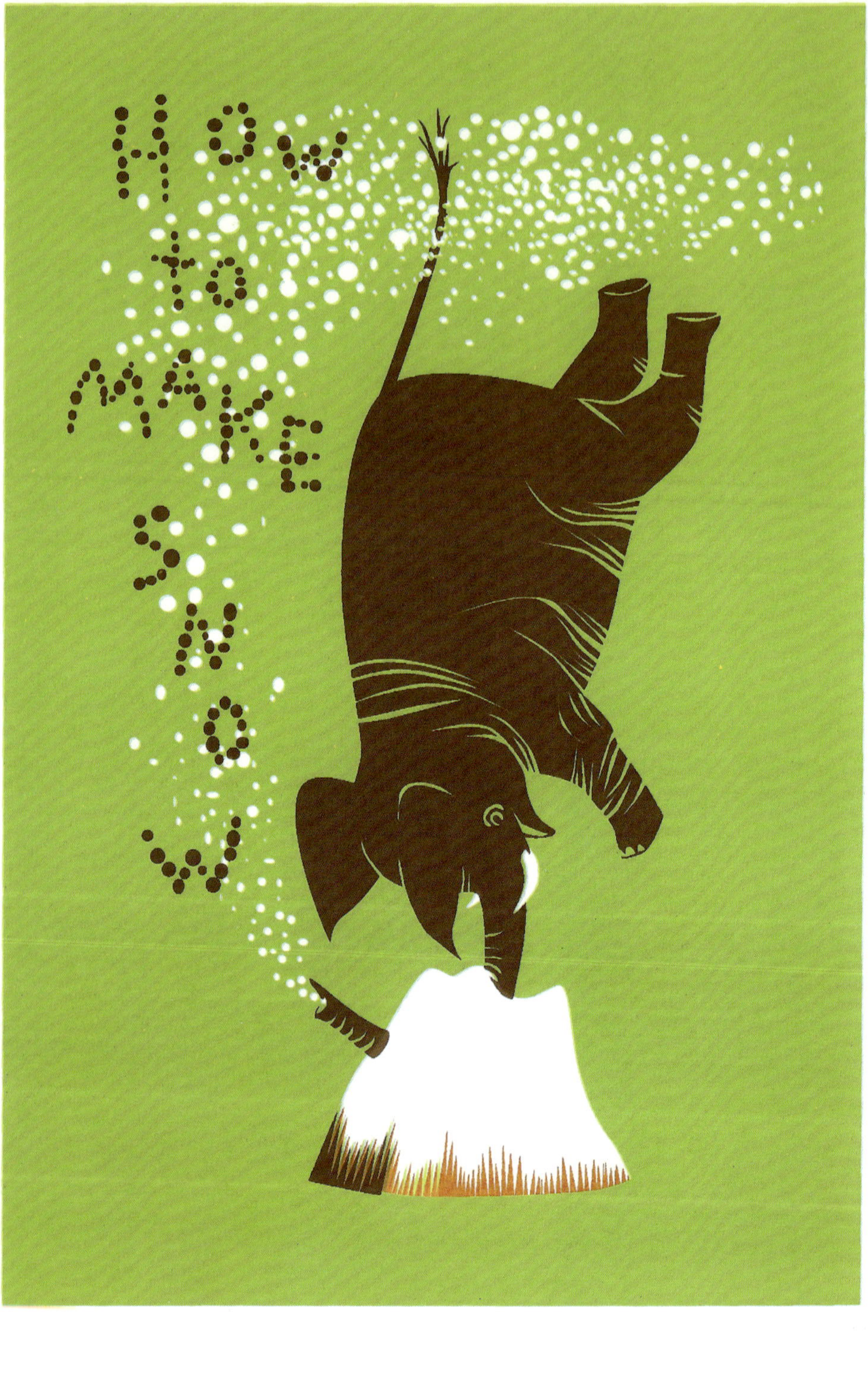

MERIT *Monika Aichele*

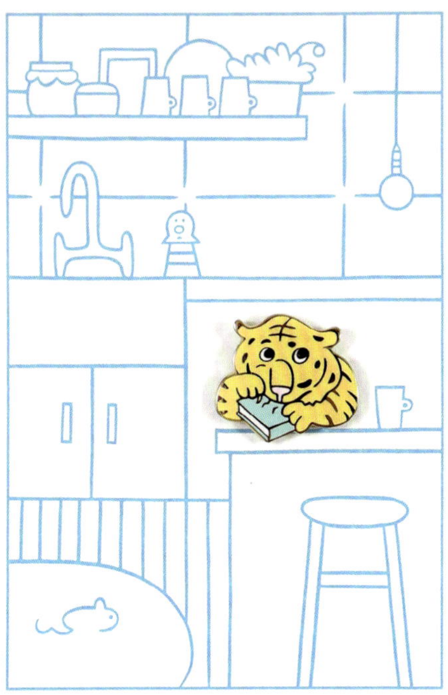

*The Snack* by Evah Fan

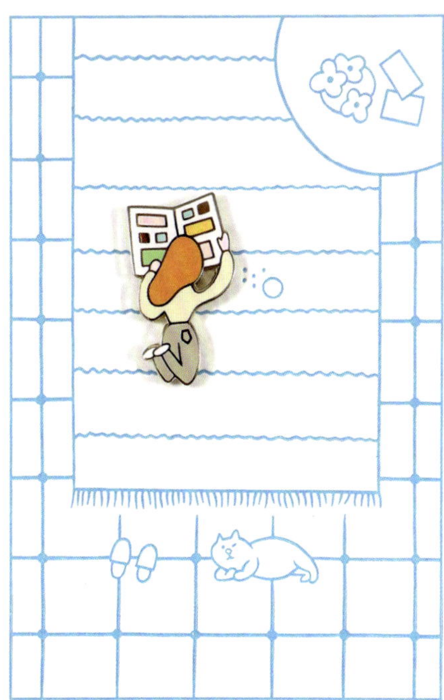

*The Funnies* by Evah Fan

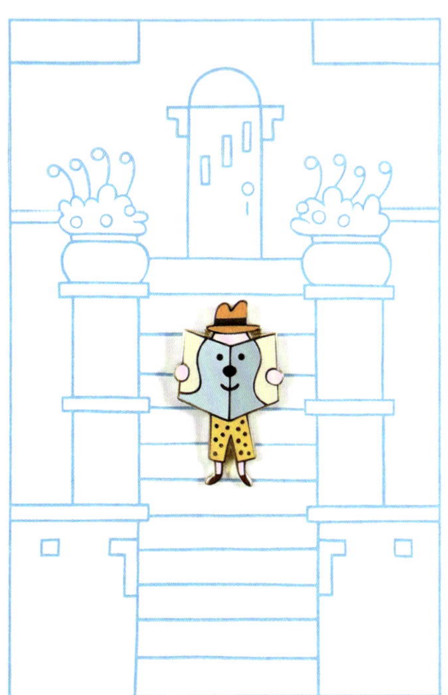

*The Scout* by Evah Fan

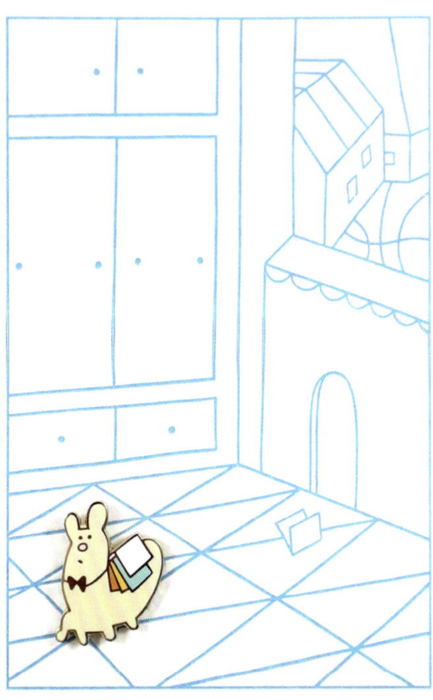

*The Sneak* by Evah Fan



MERIT *Evah Fan*

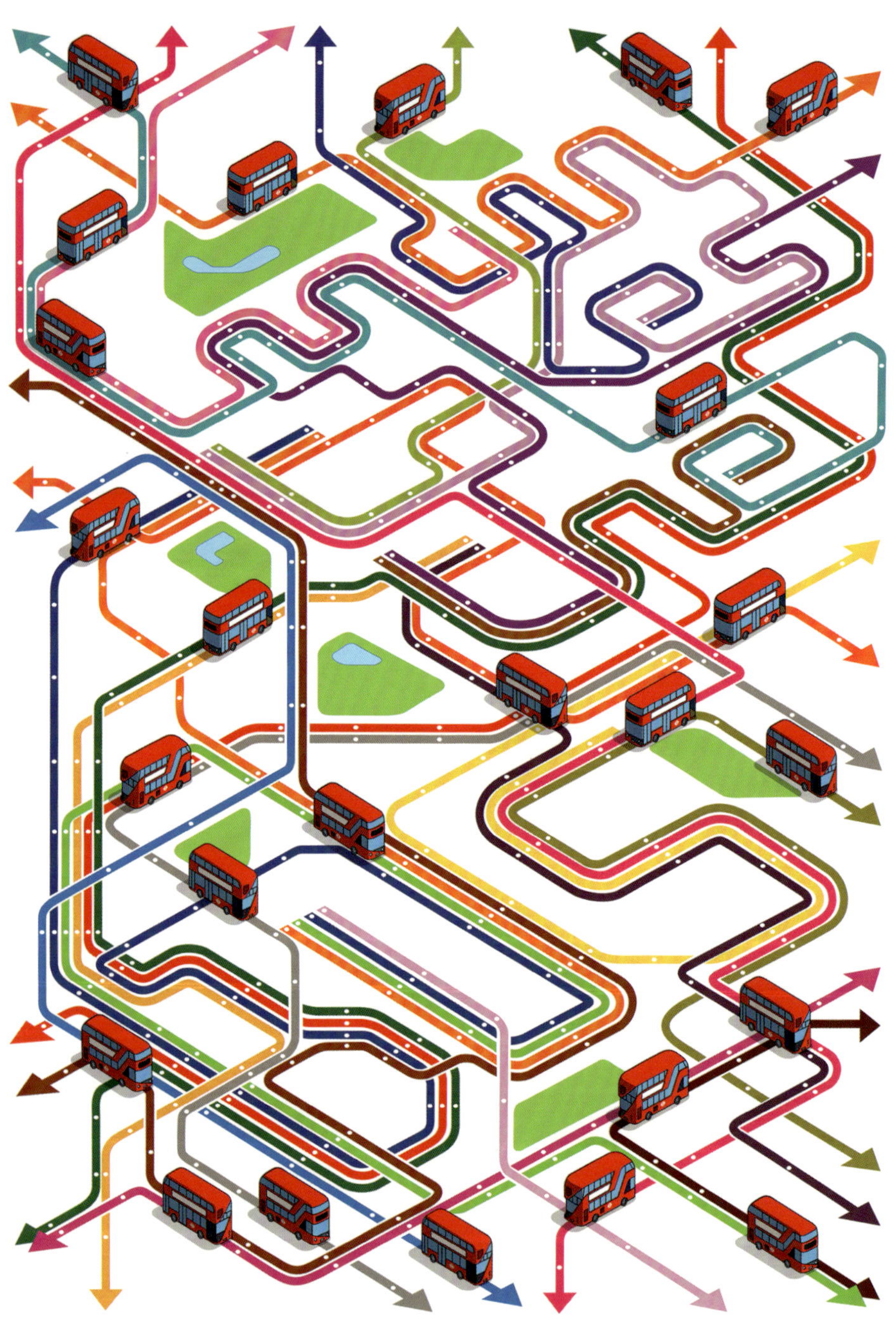



(L) MERIT *Rod Hunt*    (R) MERIT *Mark Smith*

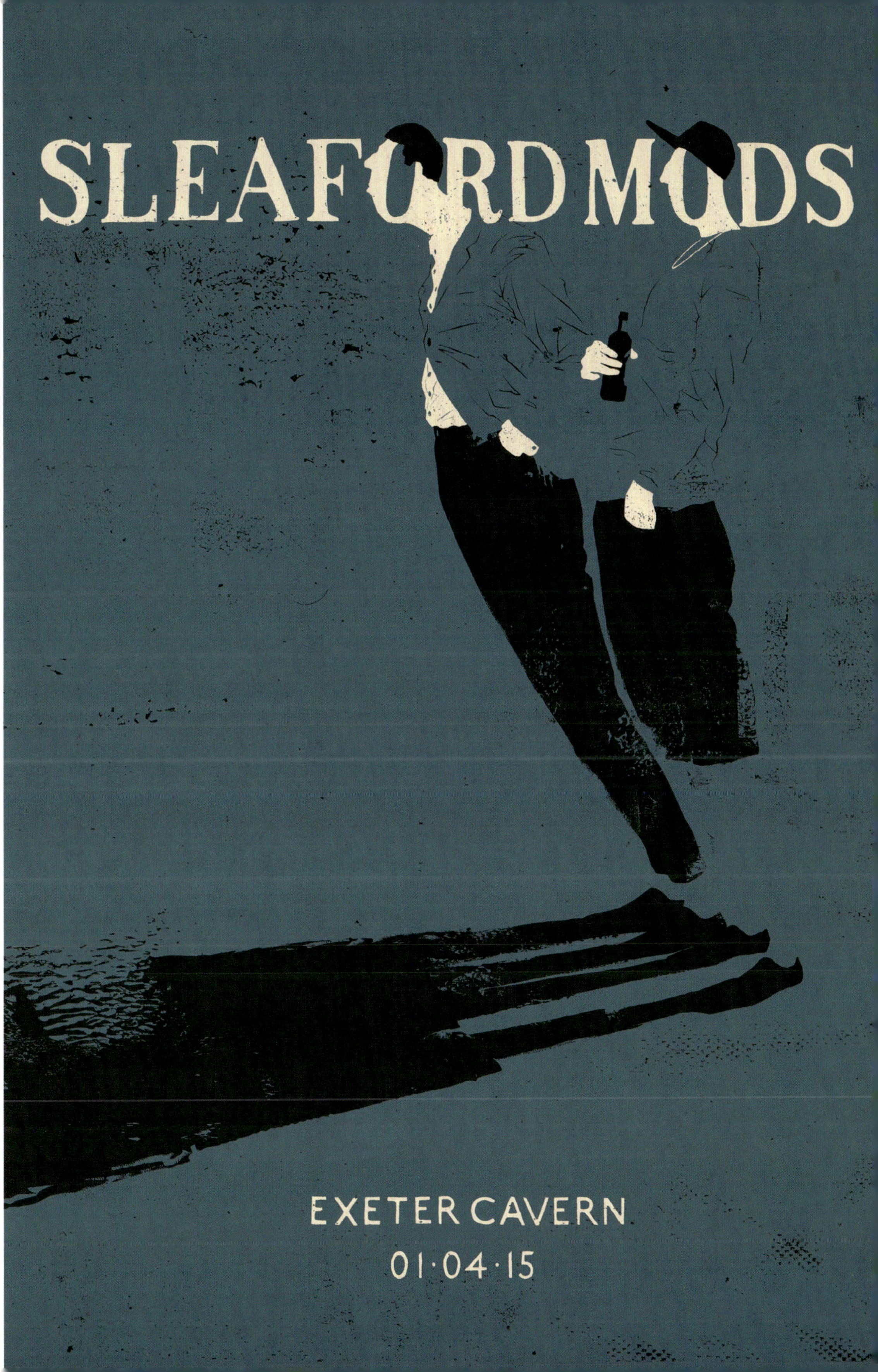

# SLEAFORD MODS

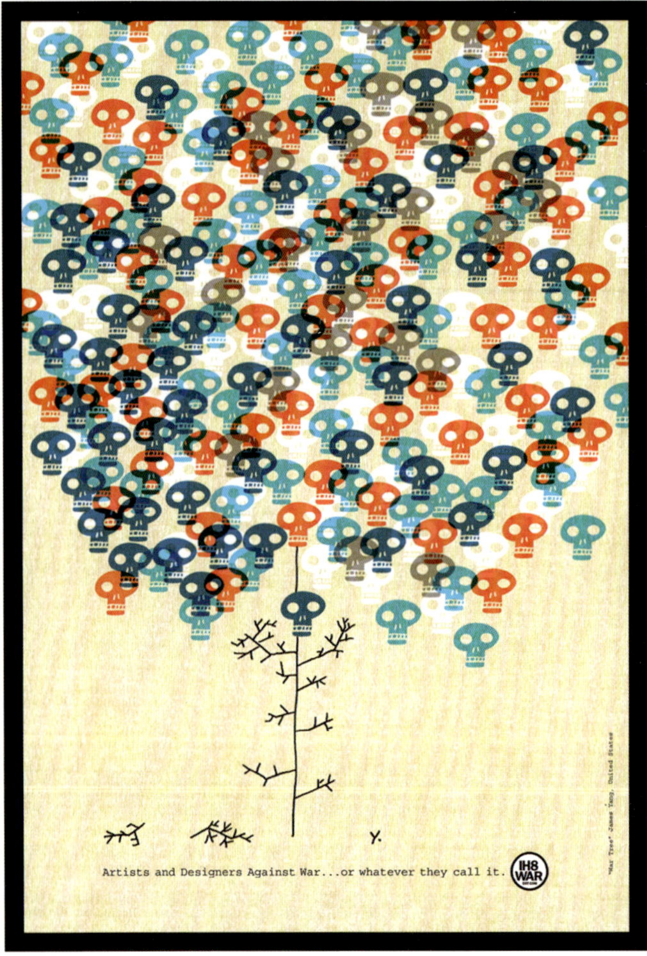


Artists and Designers Against War...or whatever they call it.
IH8 WAR


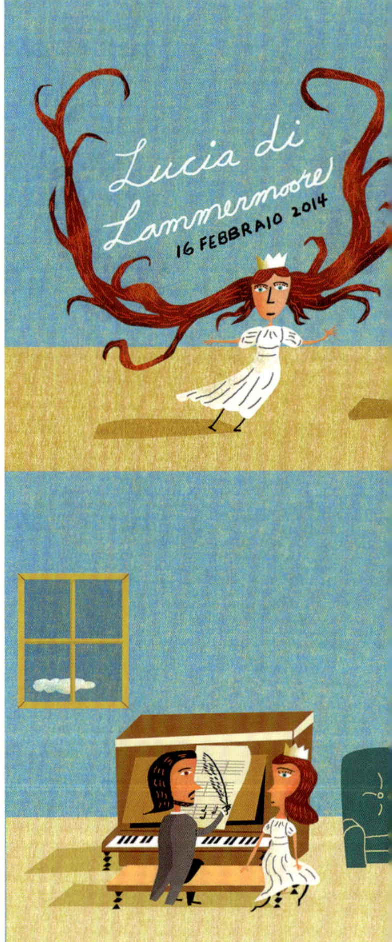


Lucia di Lammermoore
16 FEBBRAIO 2014

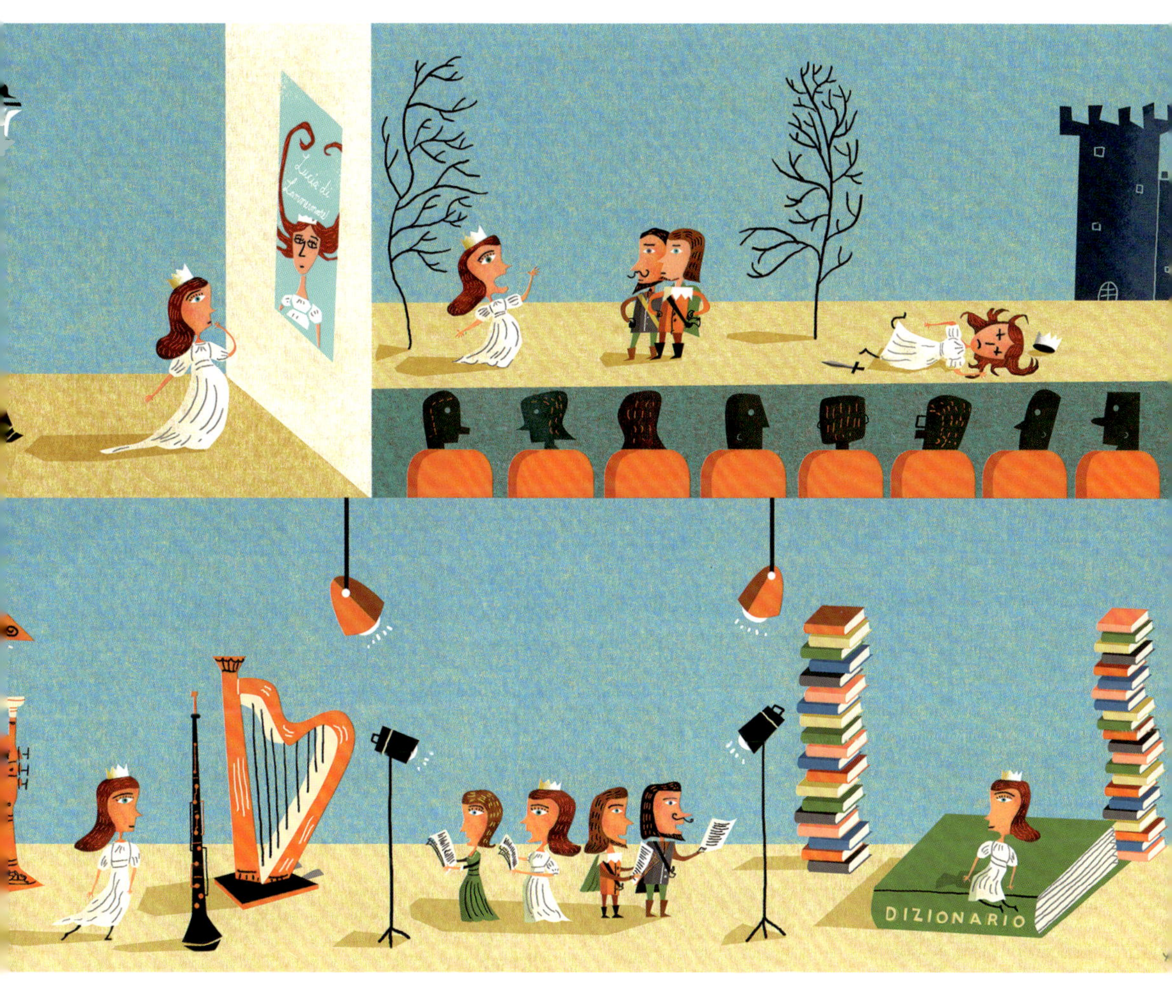




MERIT *James Yang*

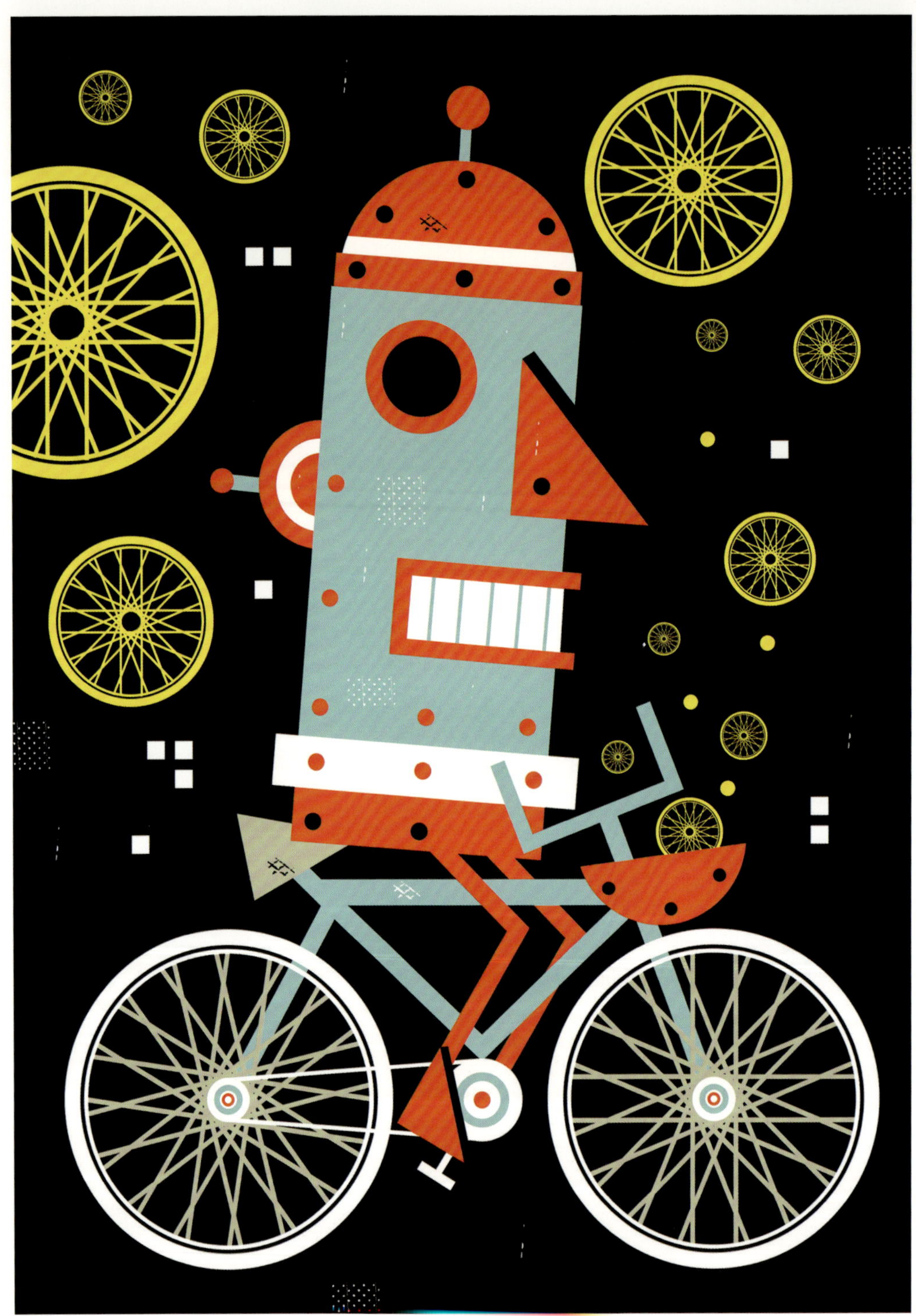



MERIT *Daniel Bueno*

# PIXINGUINHA

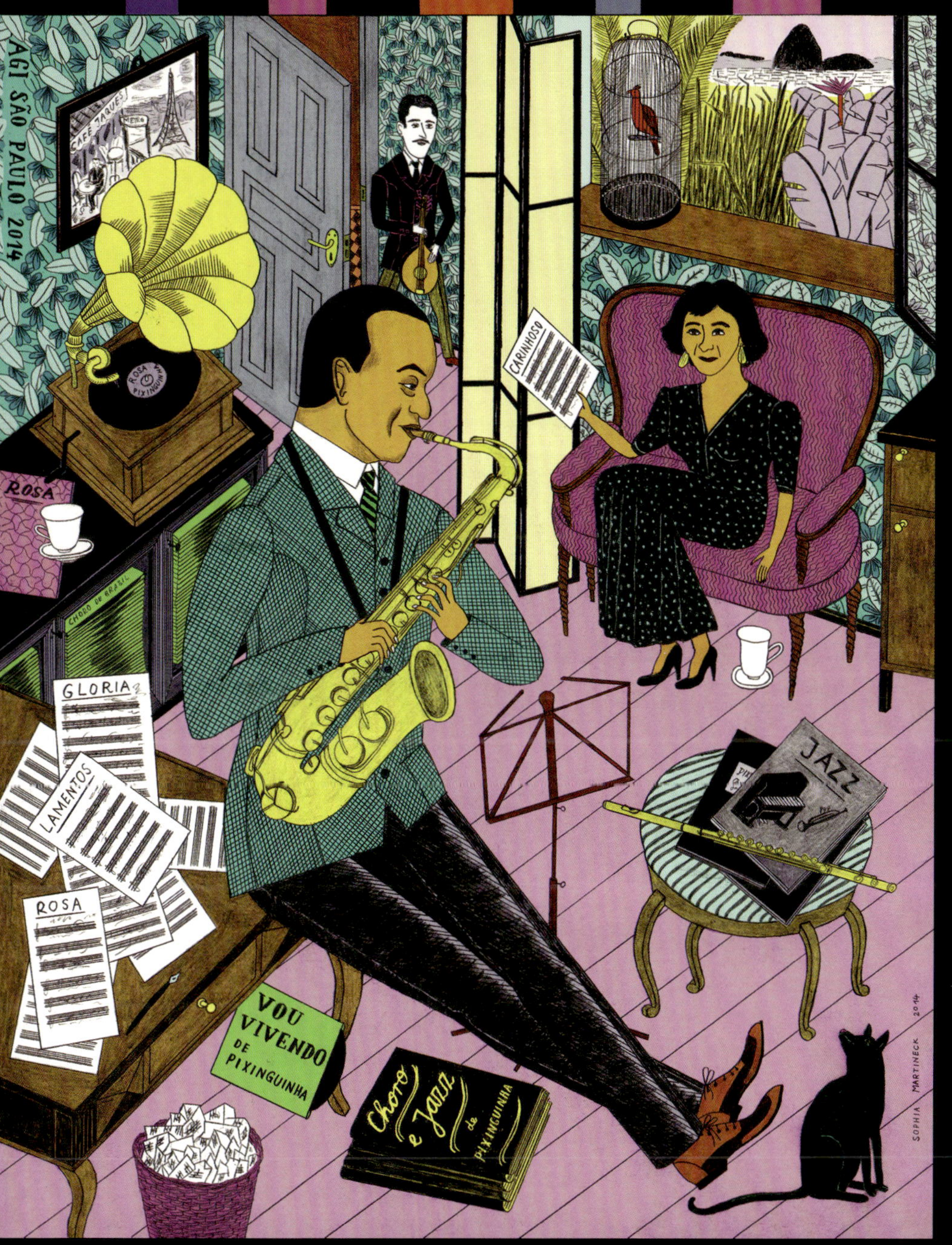

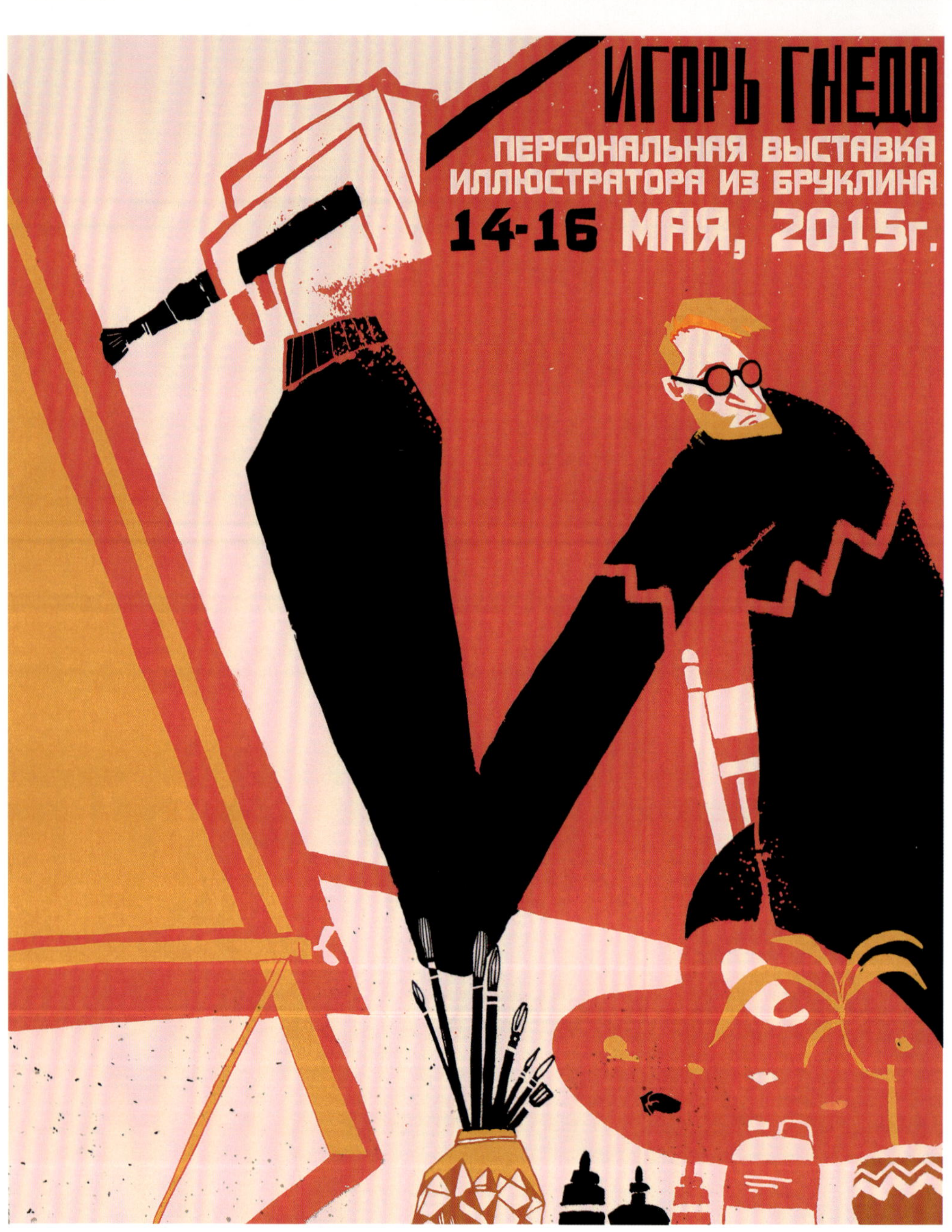


MERIT *Igor Gnedo*

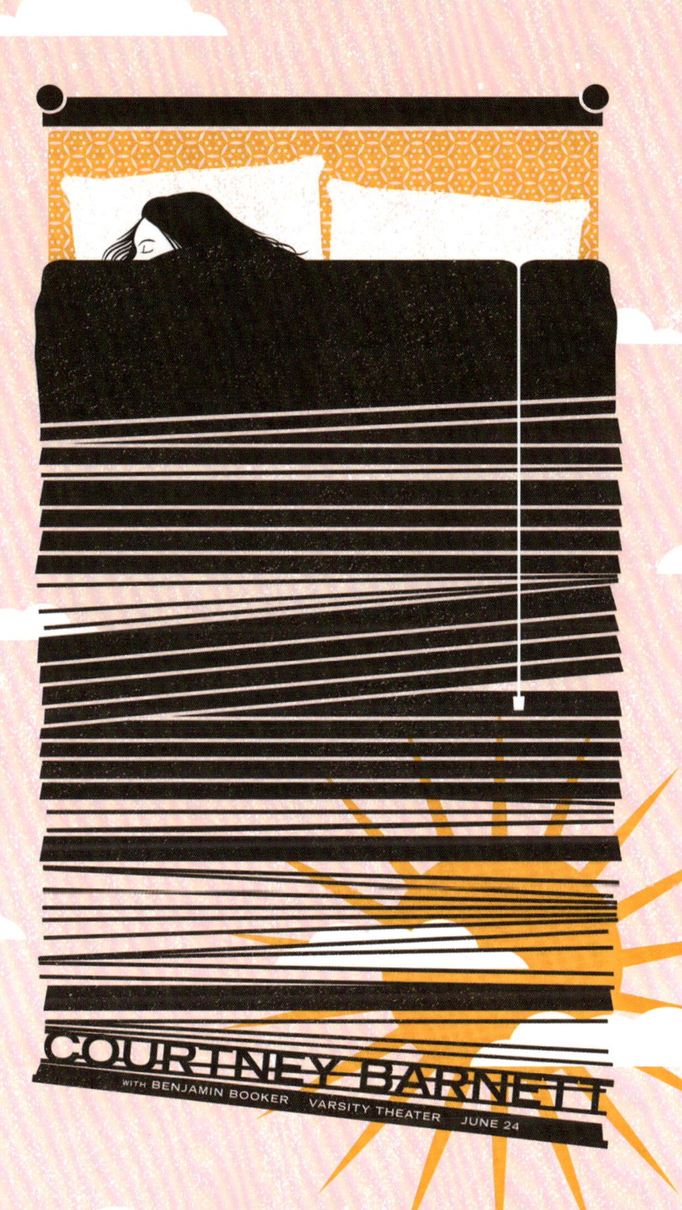

COURTNEY BARNETT
WITH BENJAMIN BOOKER   VARSITY THEATER   JUNE 24

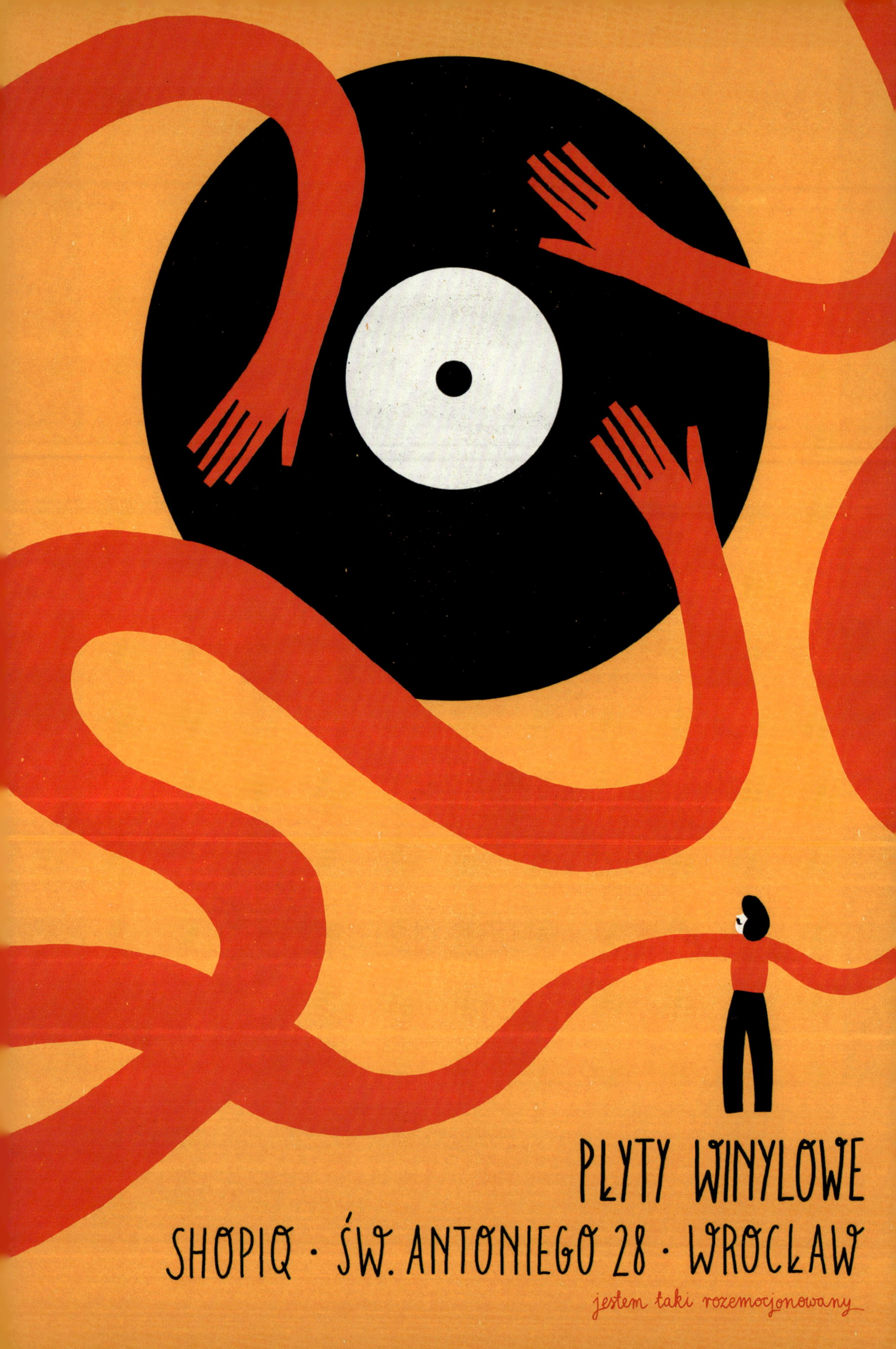

PŁYTY WINYLOWE
SHOPIQ · ŚW. ANTONIEGO 28 · WROCŁAW
jestem taki rozemocjonowany

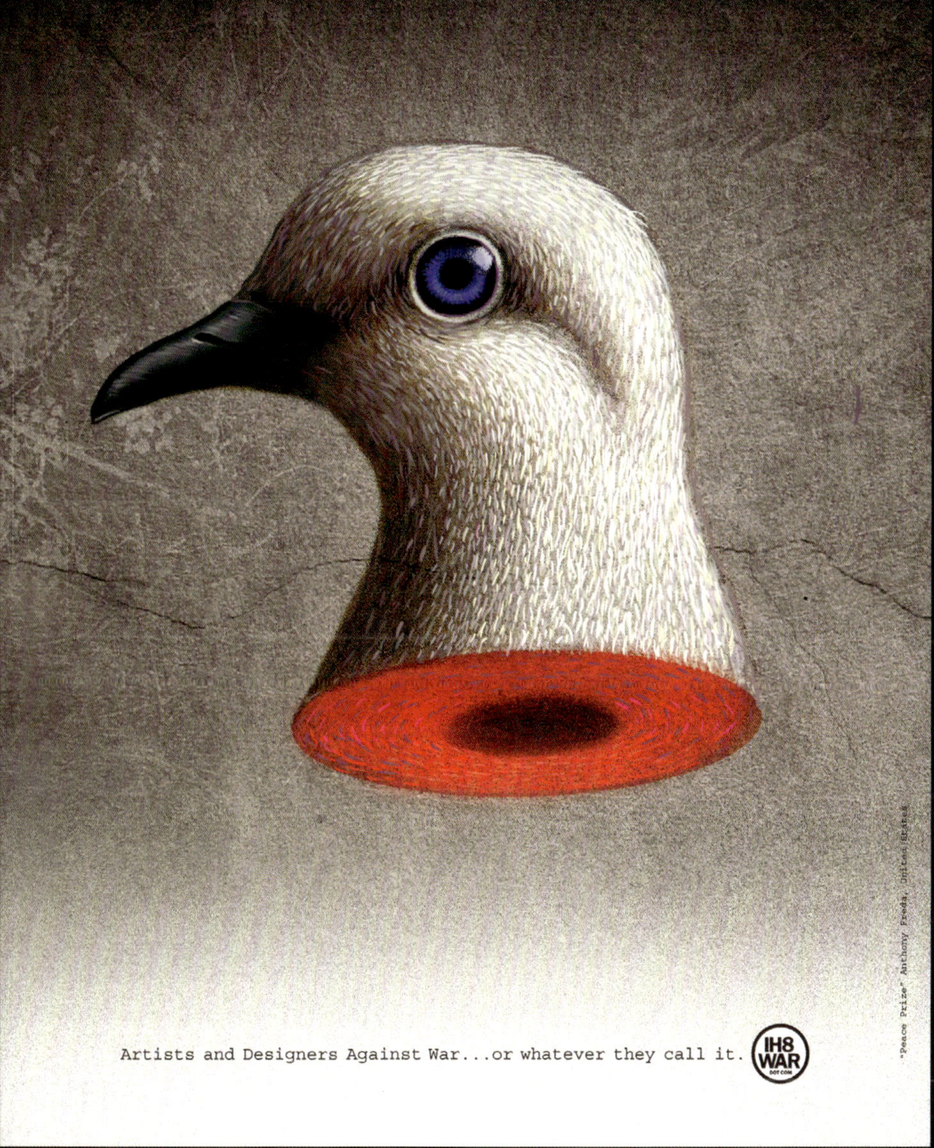

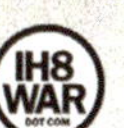


(L) MERIT *Joanna Gniady*    (R) MERIT *Anthony Freda*

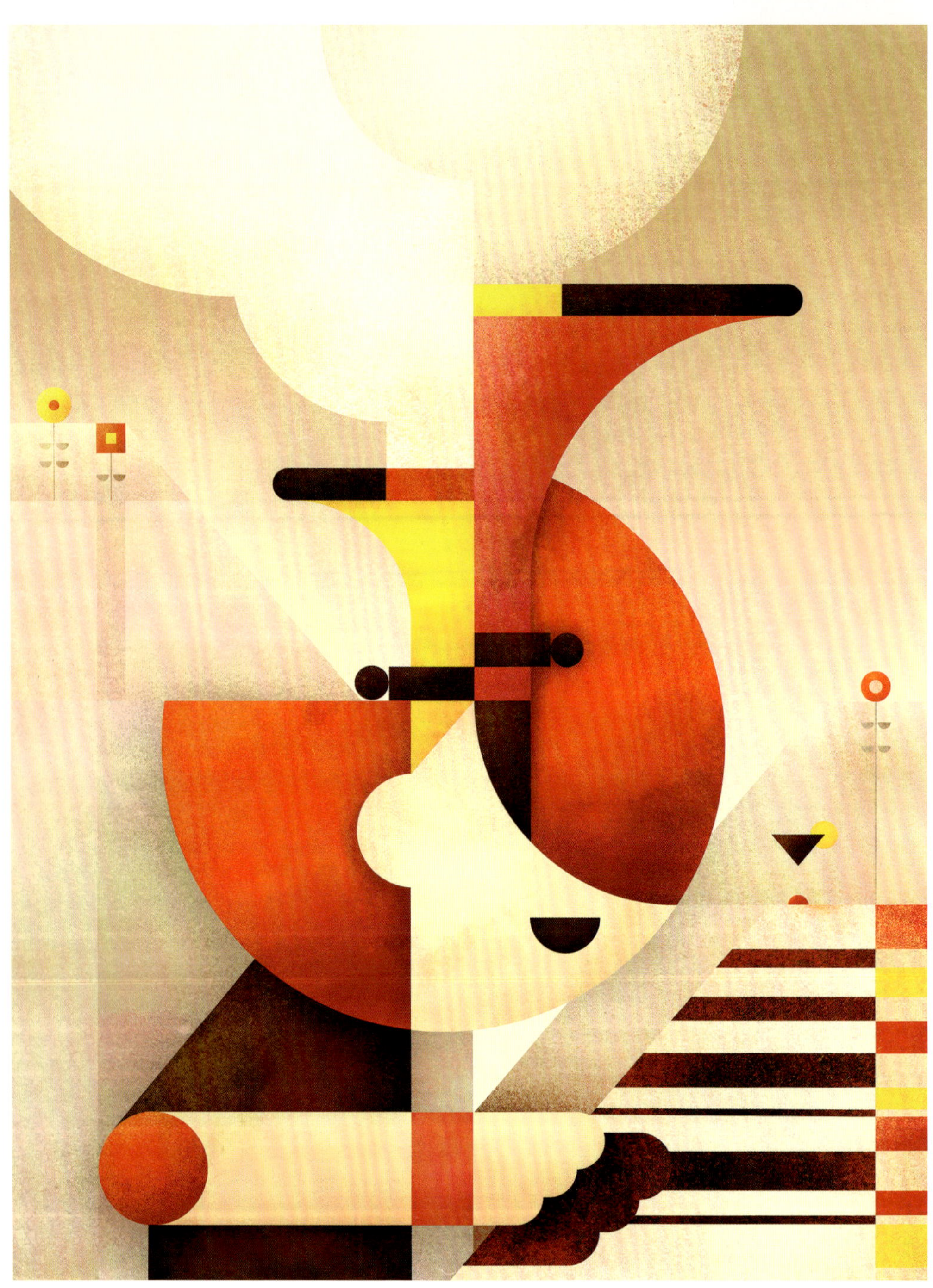

MERIT *Antony Squizzato*

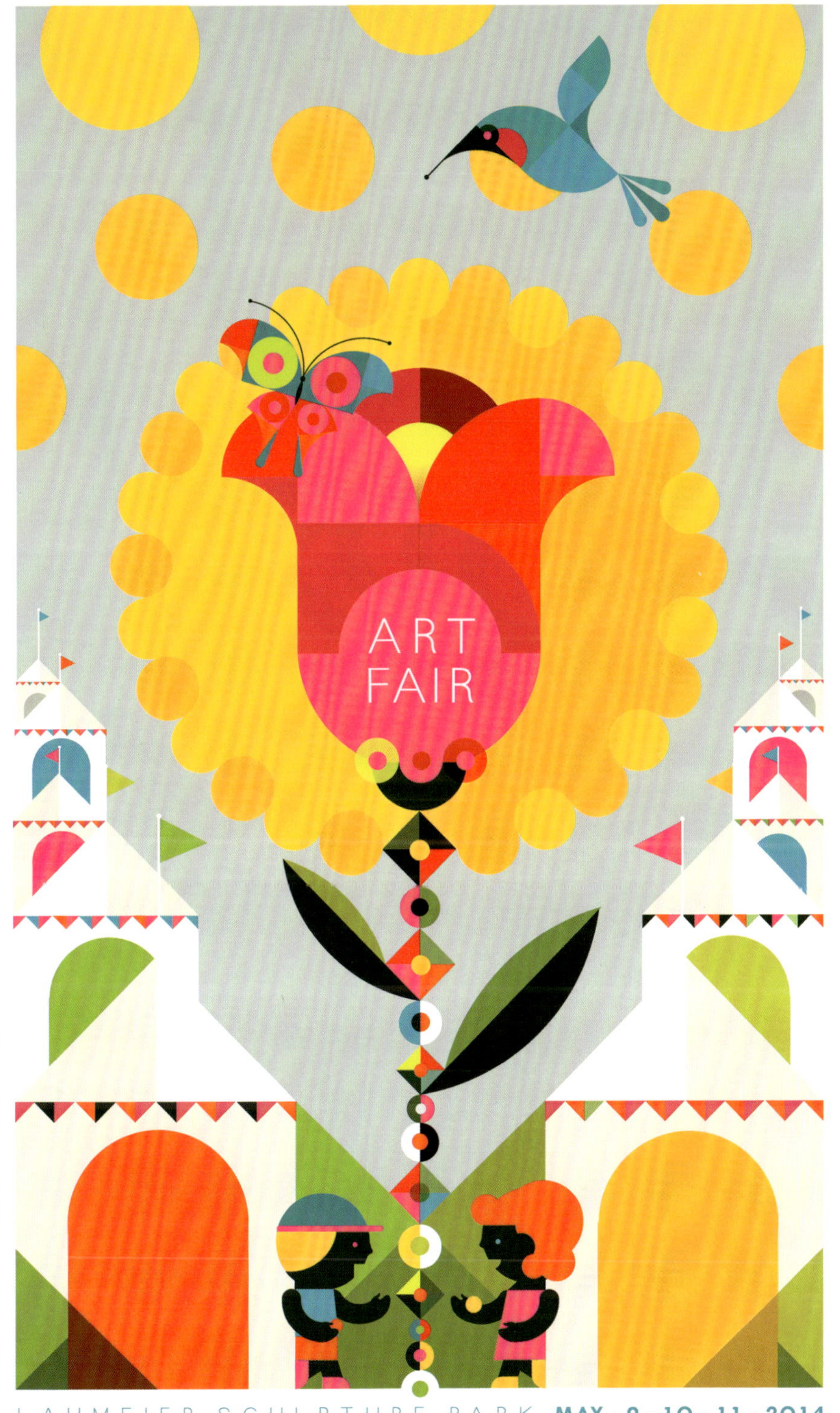

ART
FAIR
LAUMEIER SCULPTURE PARK   MAY · 9 · 10 · 11 · 2014
MERIT Carlos Zamora

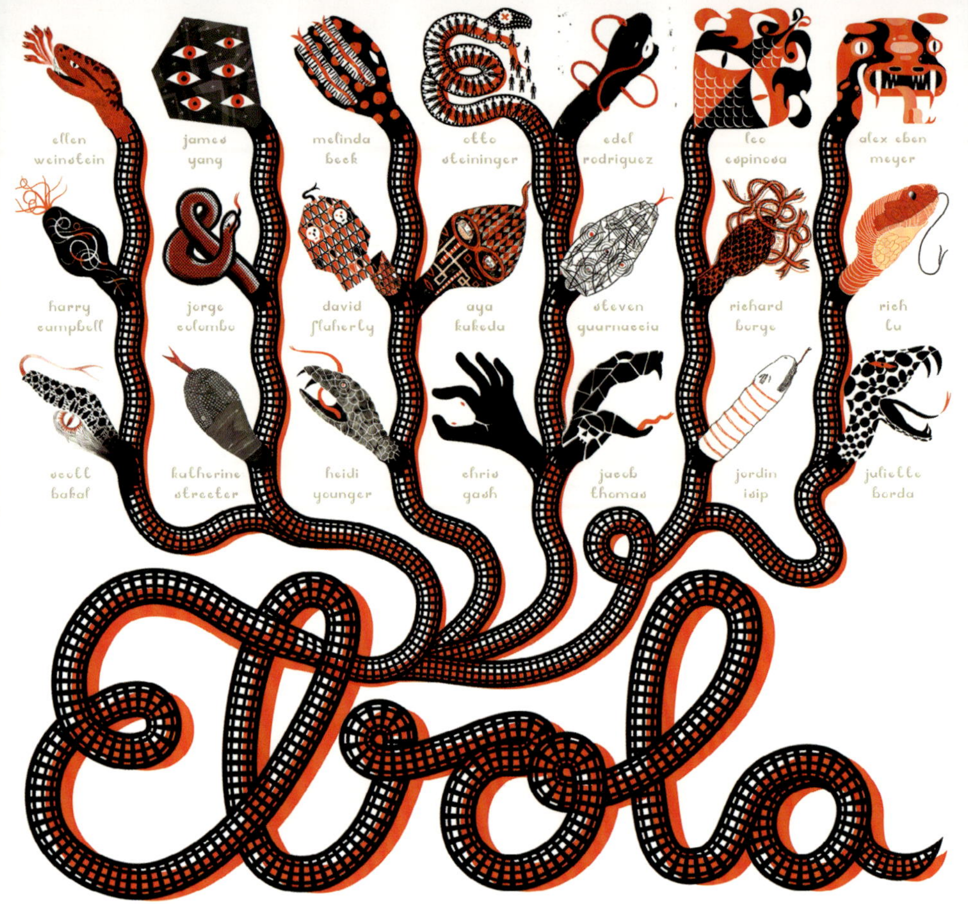

ellen
weinstein
james
yang
melinda
beck
otto
steininger
edel
rodriguez
leo
espinosa
alex eben
meyer
harry
campbell
jorge
colombo
david
flaherty
aya
kakeda
steven
guarnaccia
richard
borge
rich
lu
scott
bakal
katherine
streeter
heidi
younger
chris
gash
jacob
thomas
jordin
isip
juliette
borda
Ebola

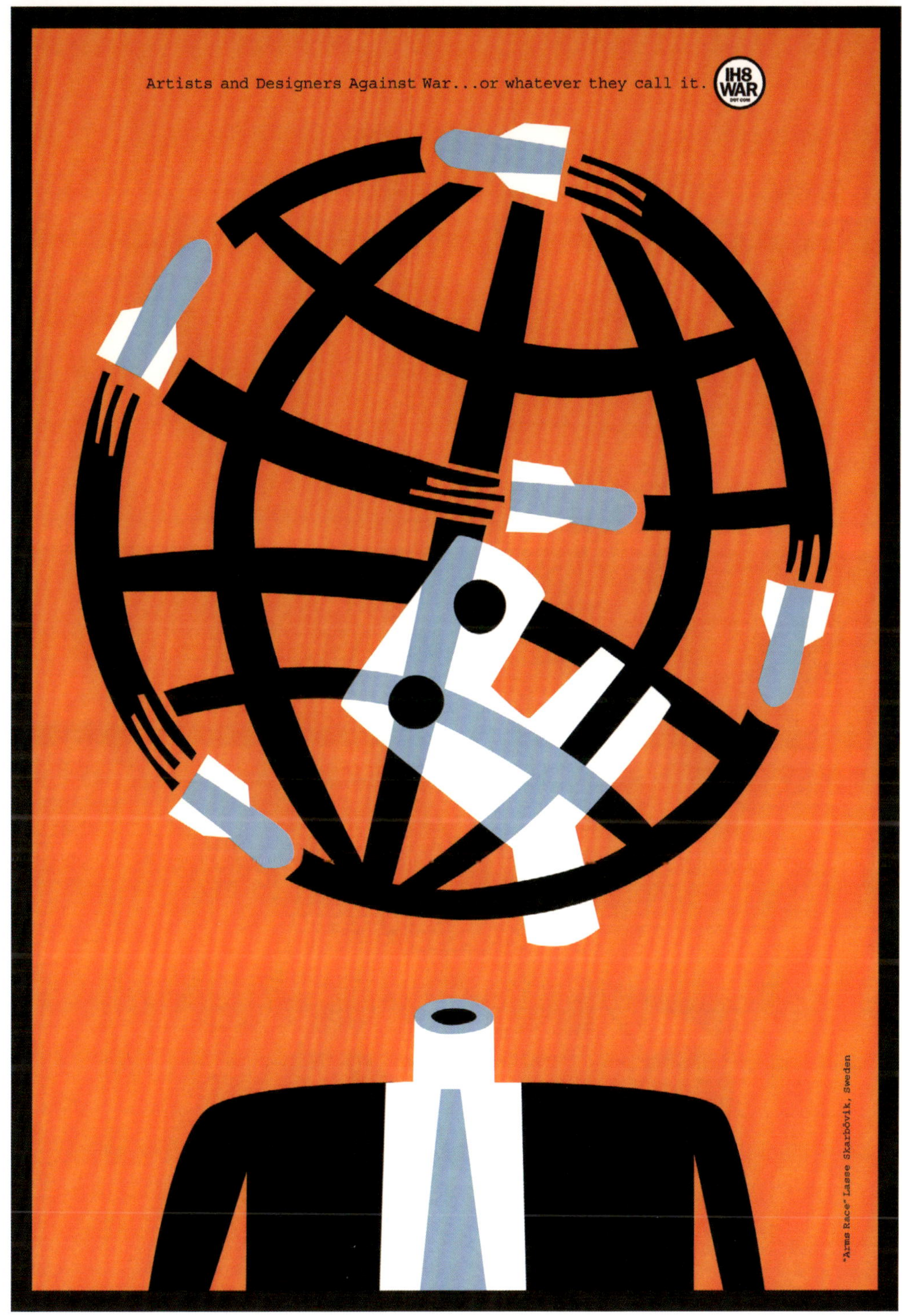


GOLD *Lasse Skarbövik*

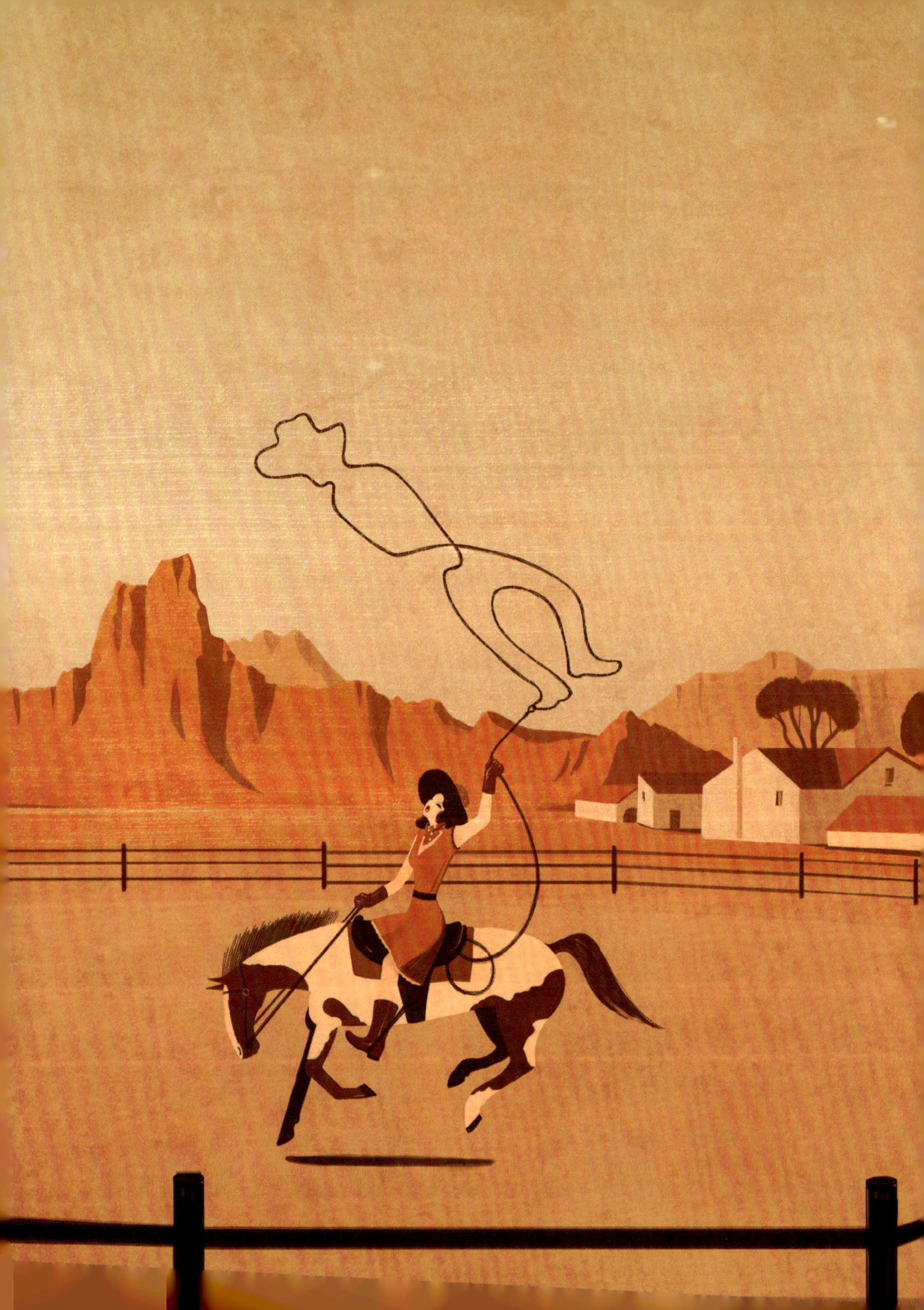

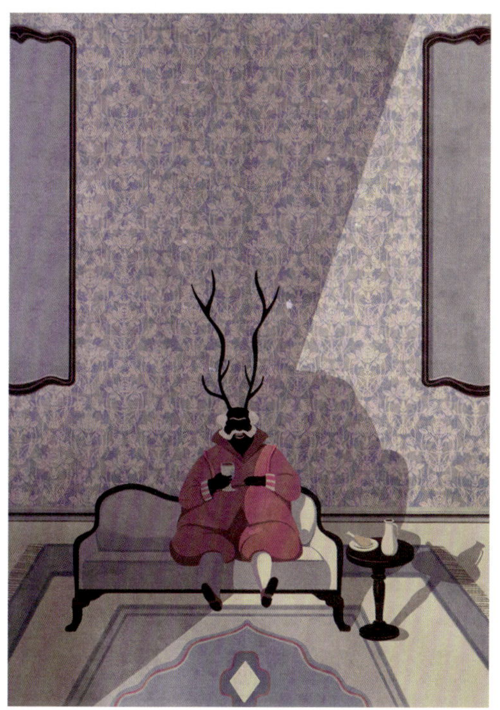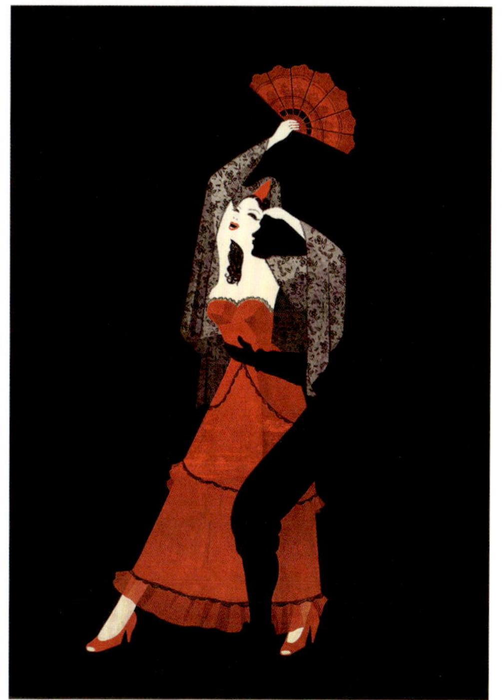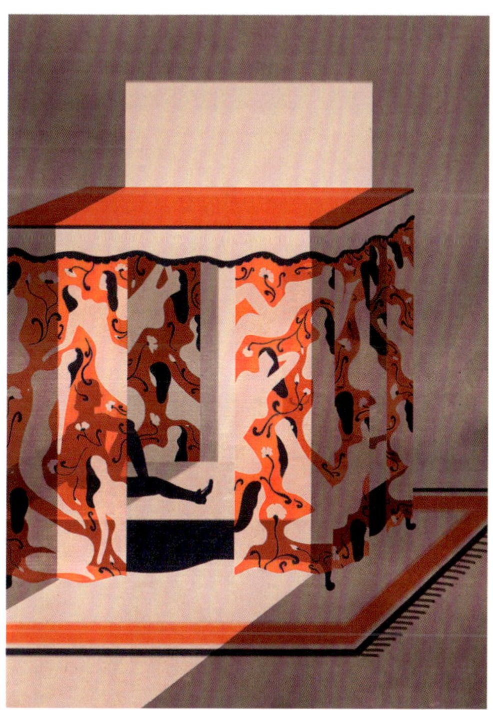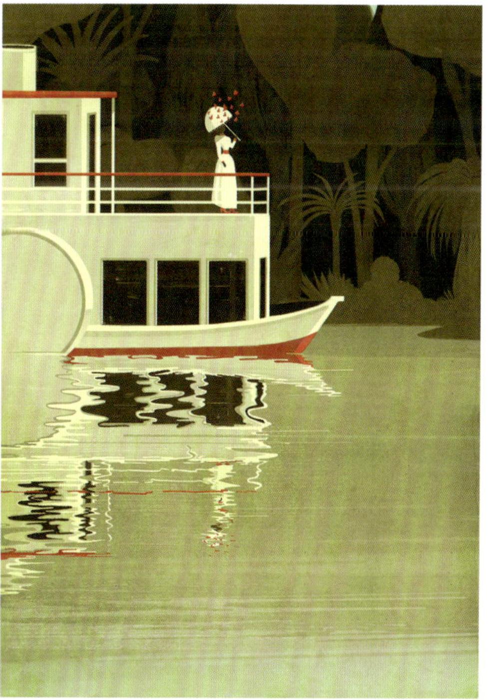



MERIT *Emiliano Ponzi*

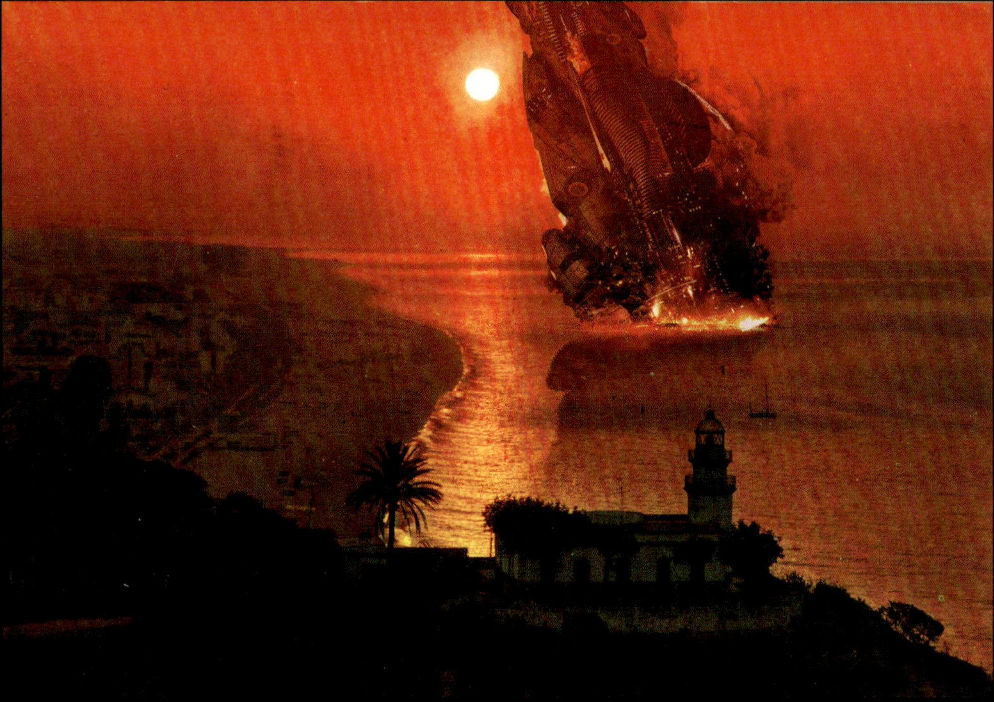

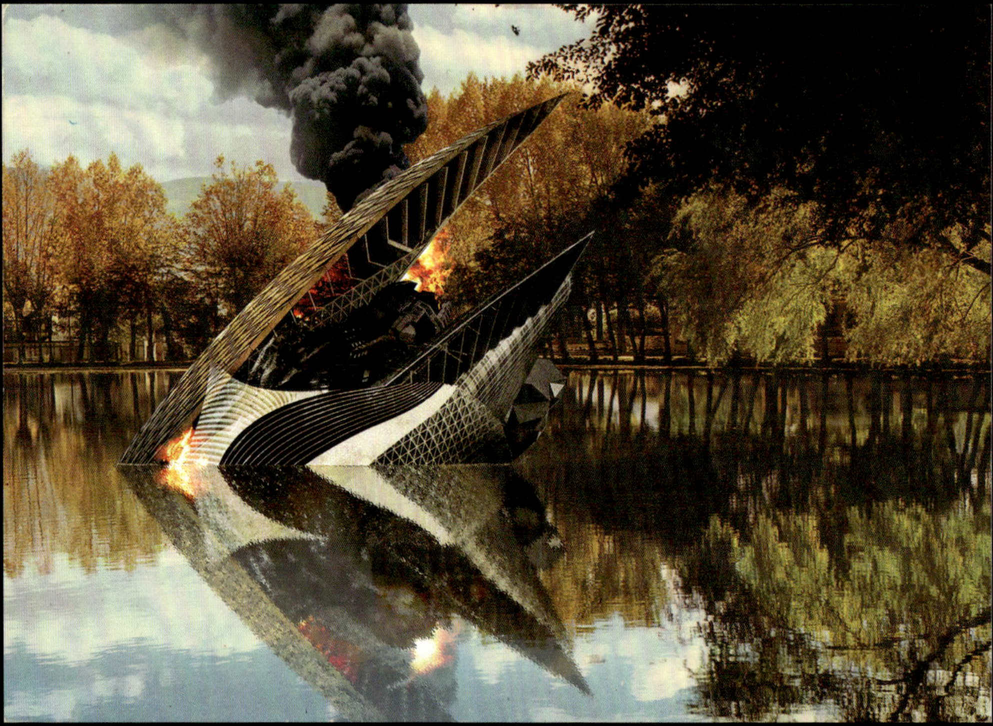

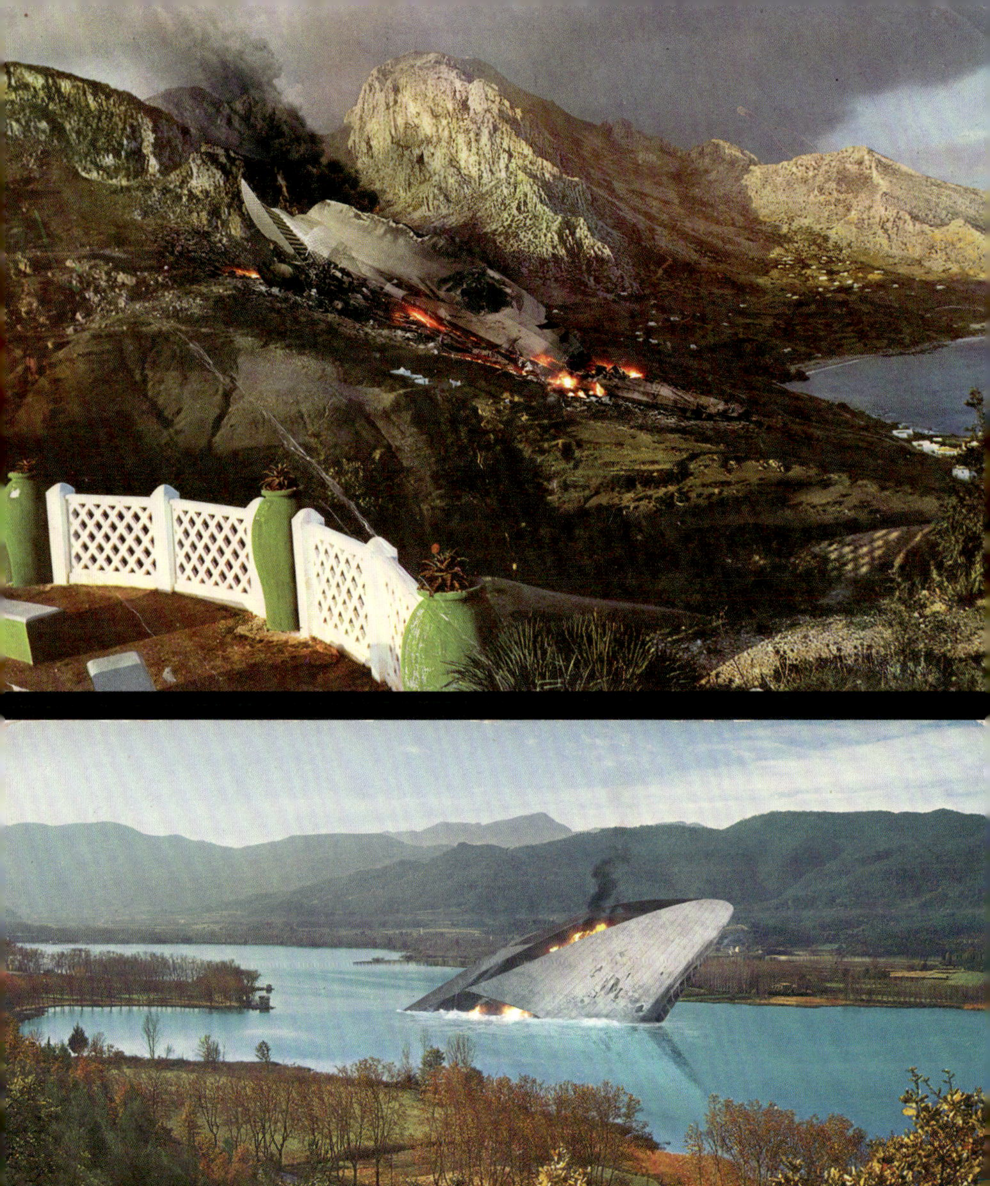

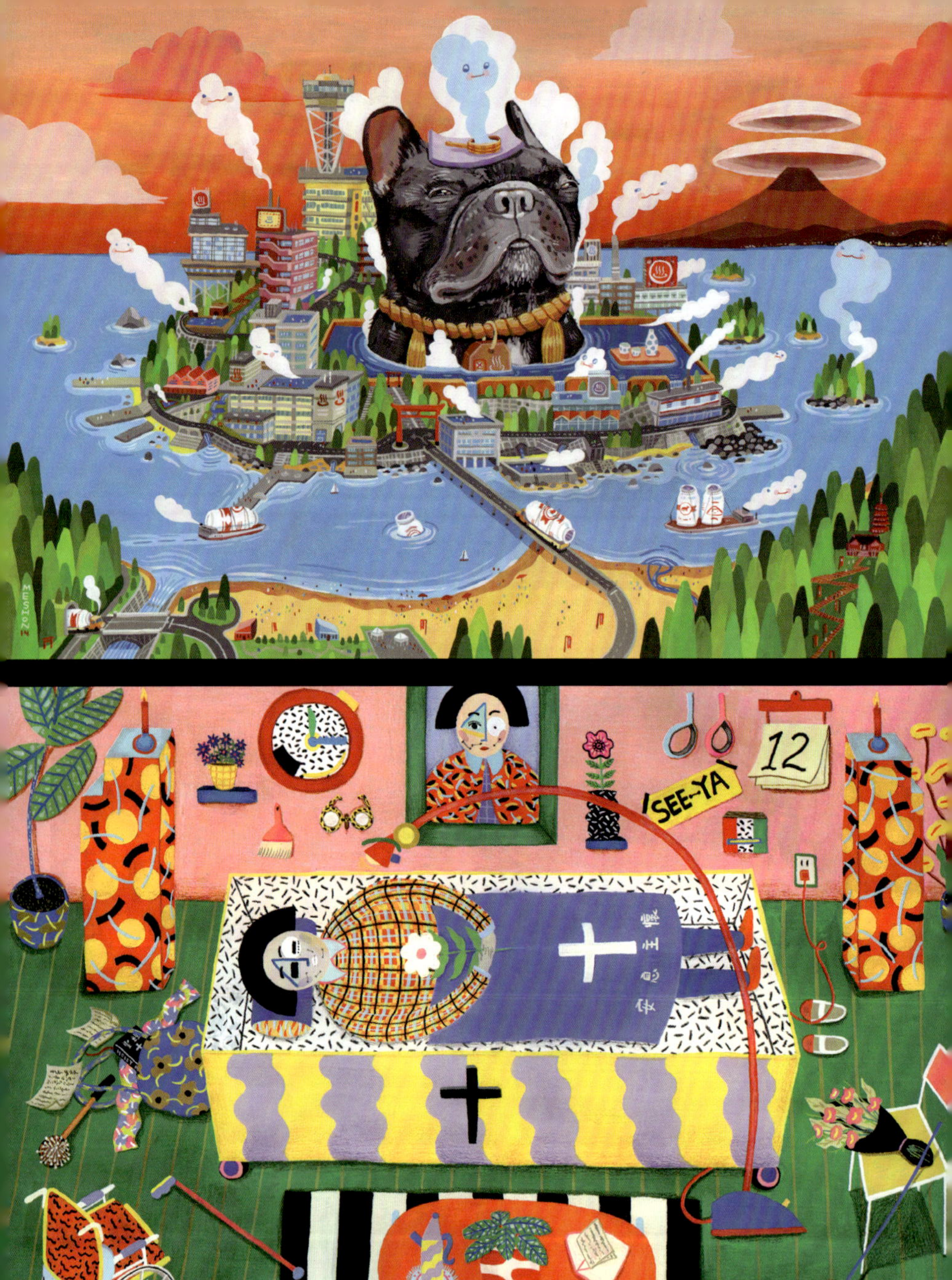
SEE-YA
12

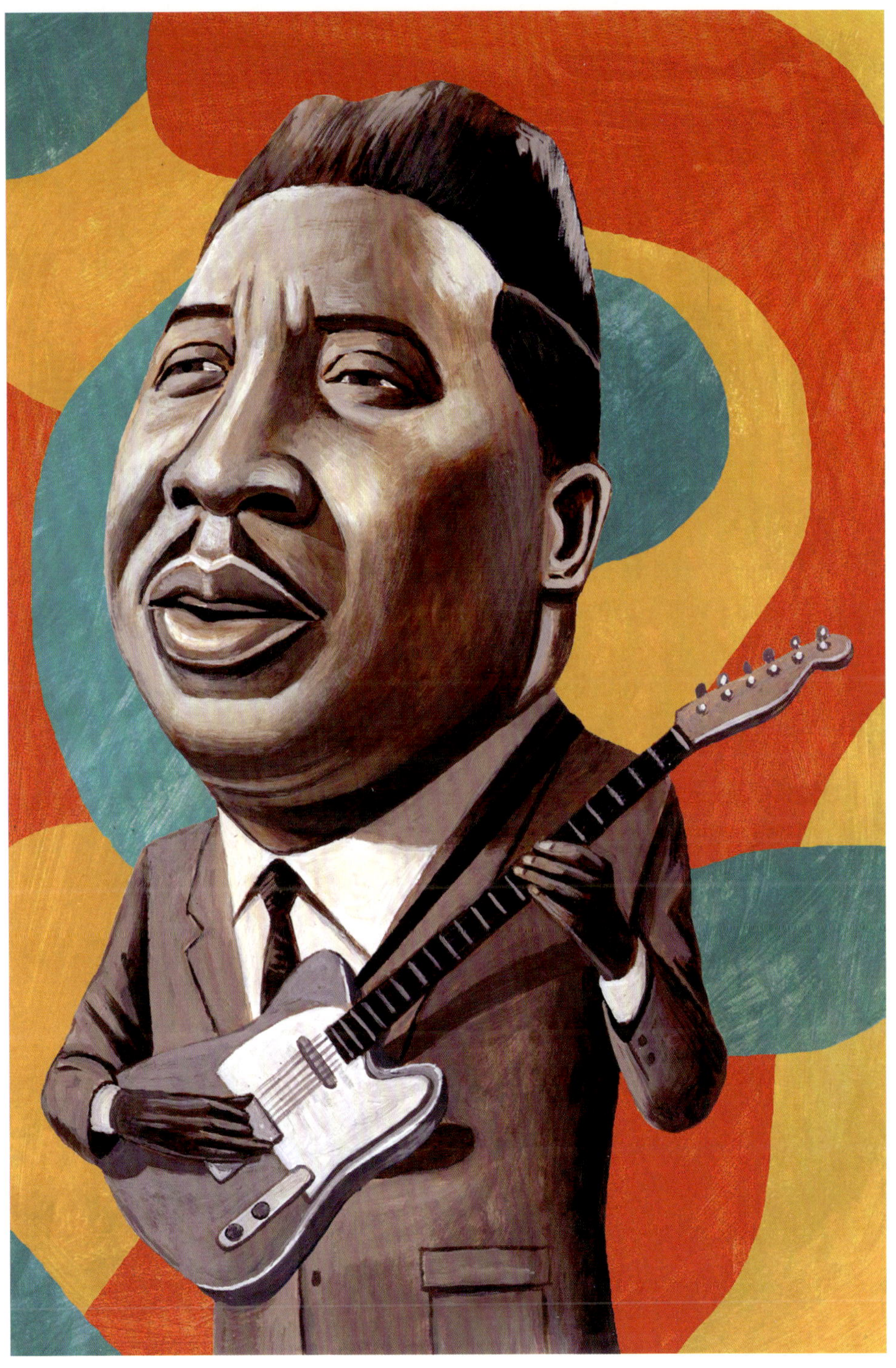



MERIT *Charlie Powell*

177

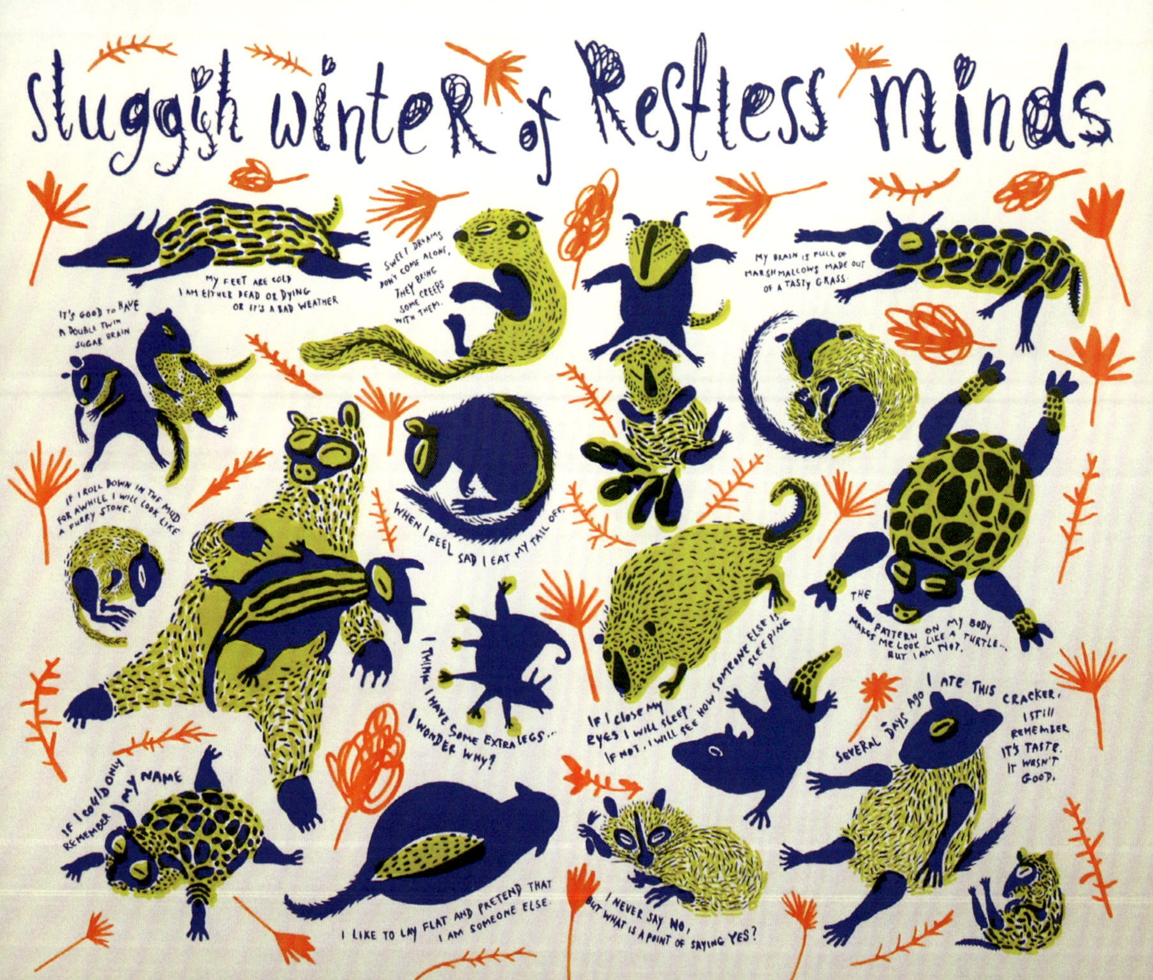




(L) BRONZE *Natalya Balnova*    (R) MERIT *Oren Haskins*

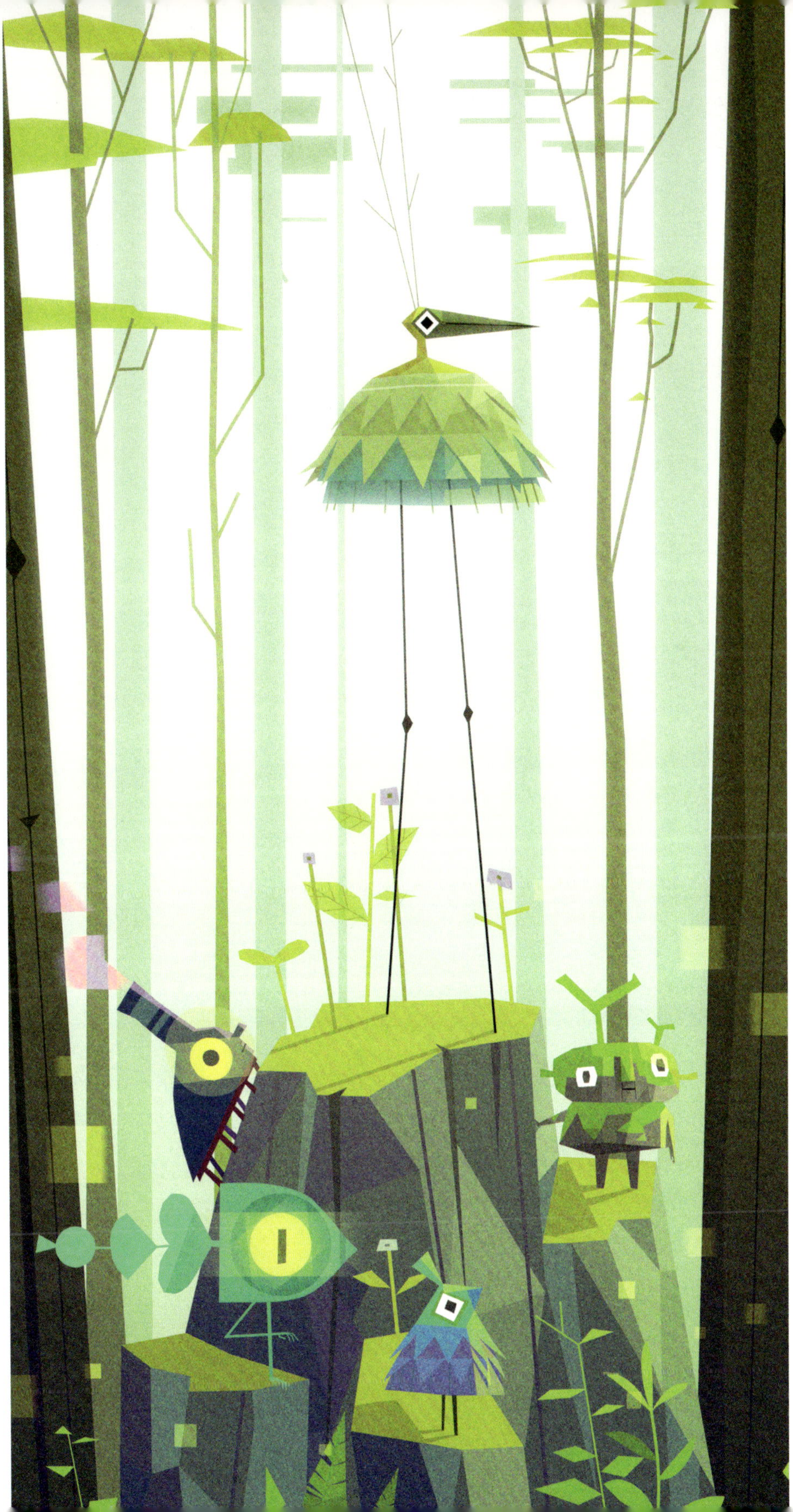

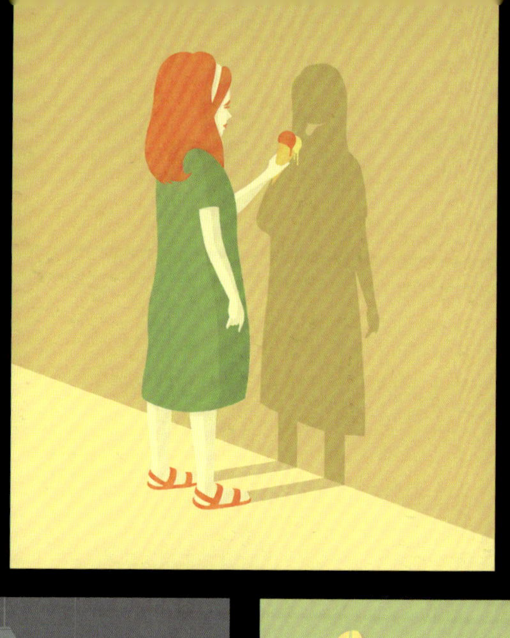
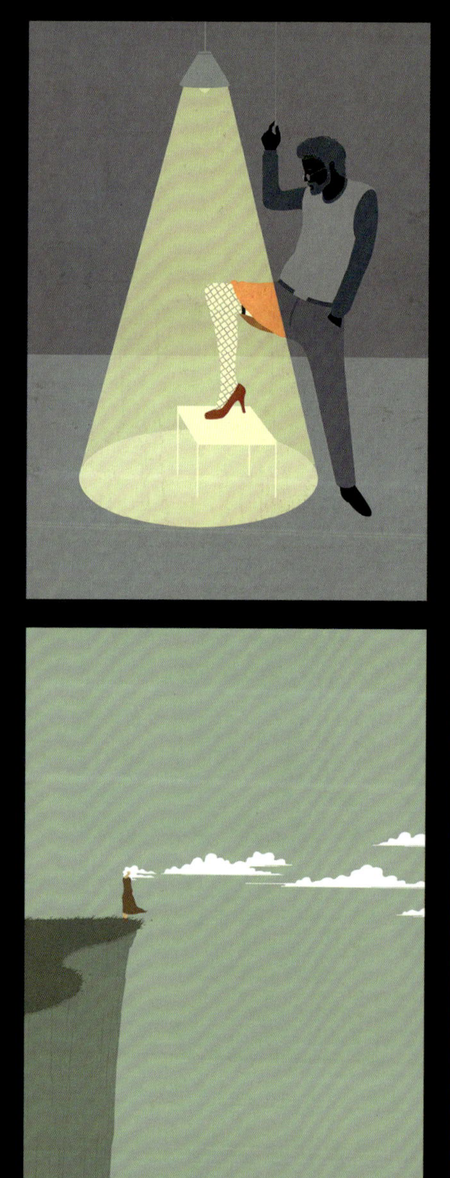
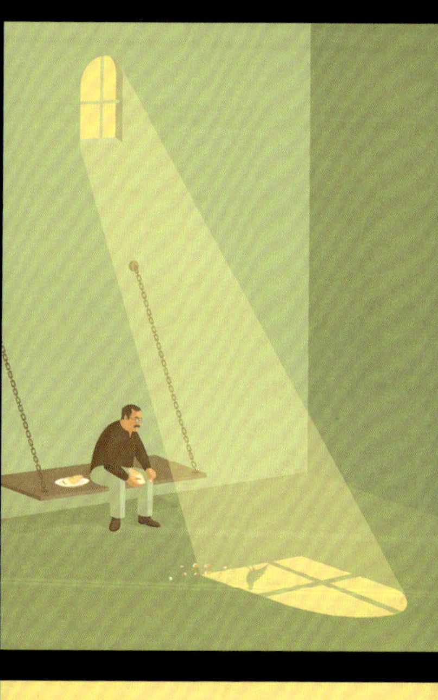
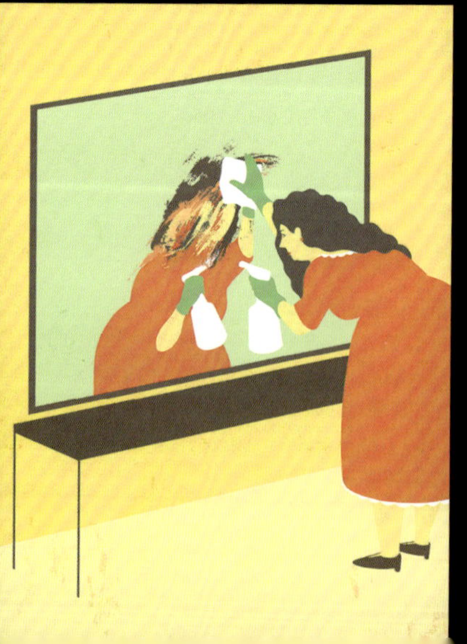

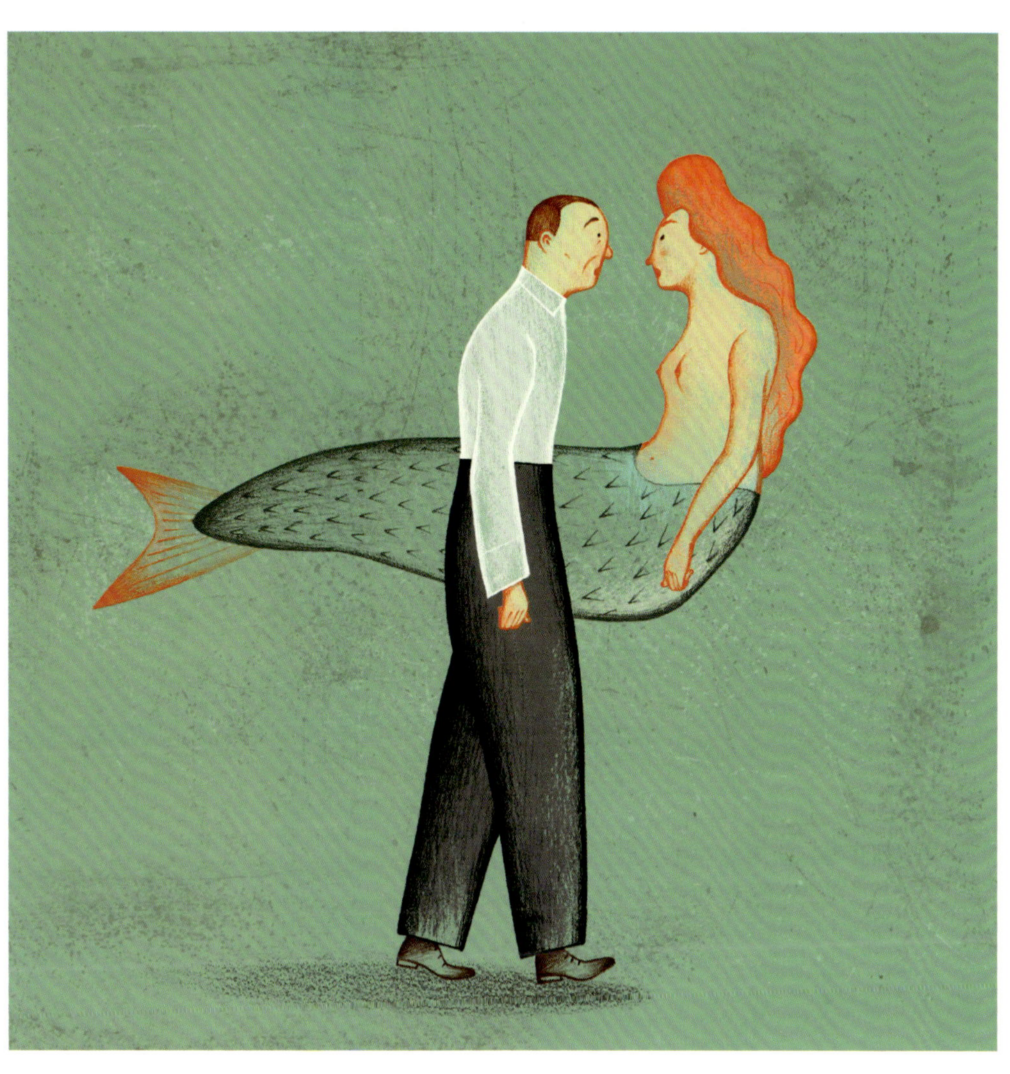



(L) MERIT *Stephan Schmitz*    (R) MERIT *Marie Lafrance*

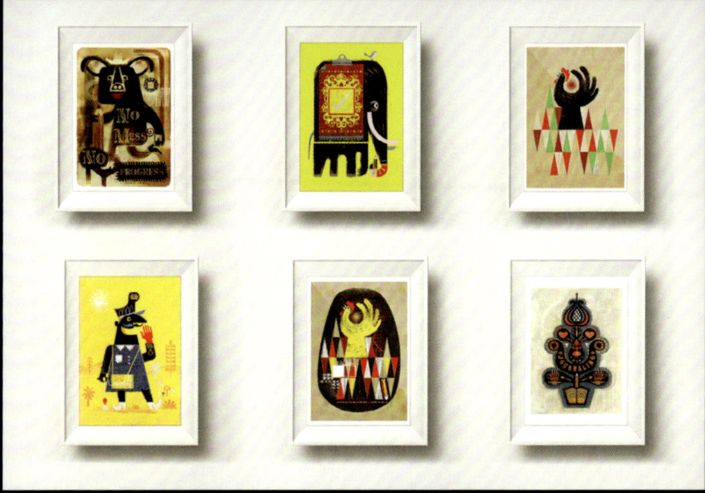

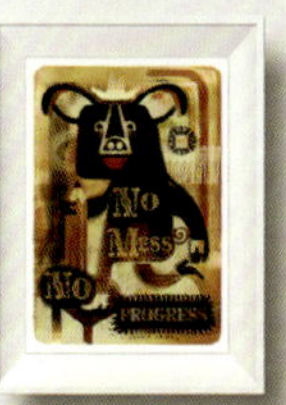
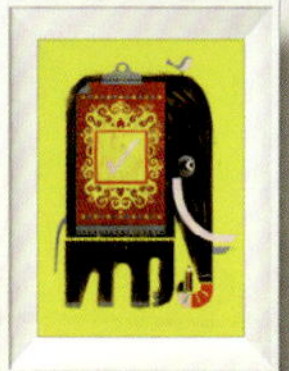
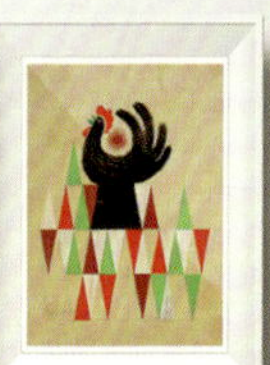
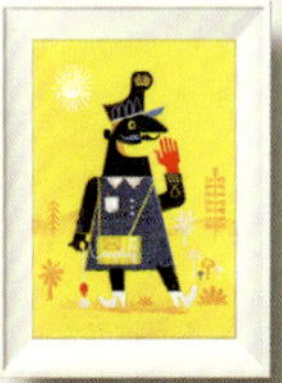
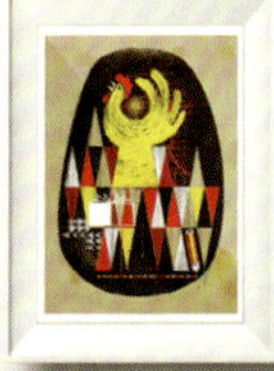
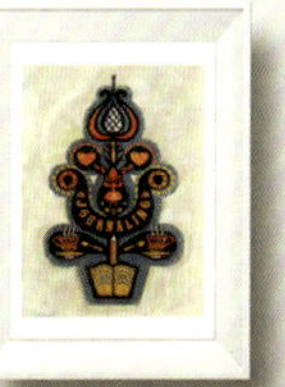

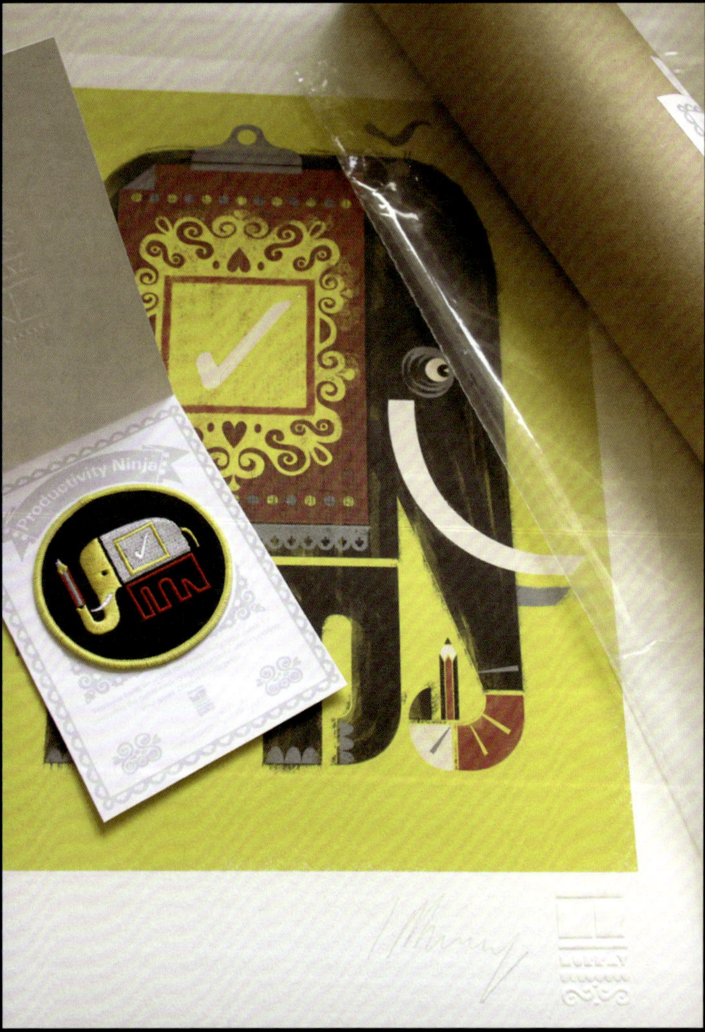

MERIT *Ian Murray*

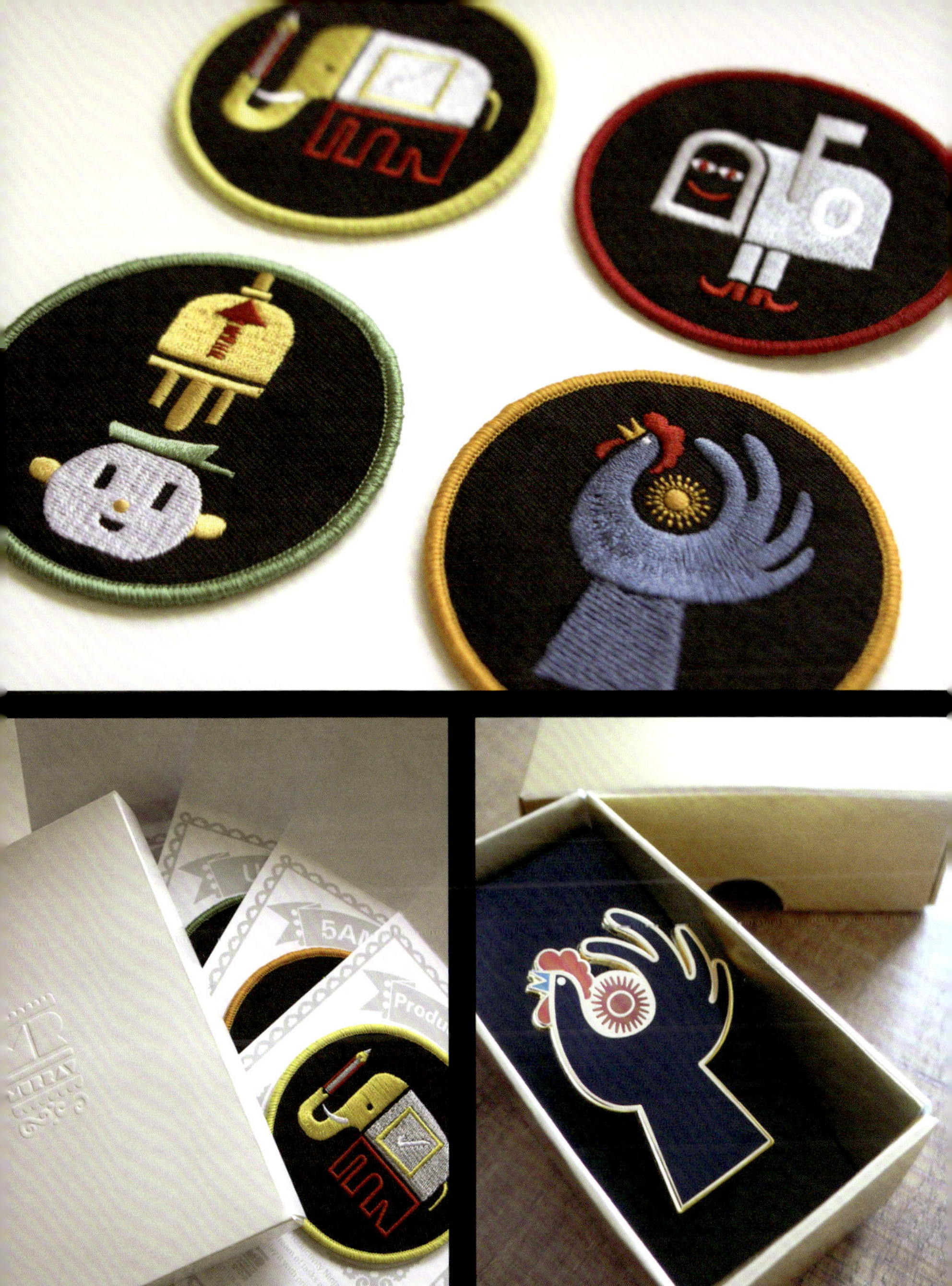

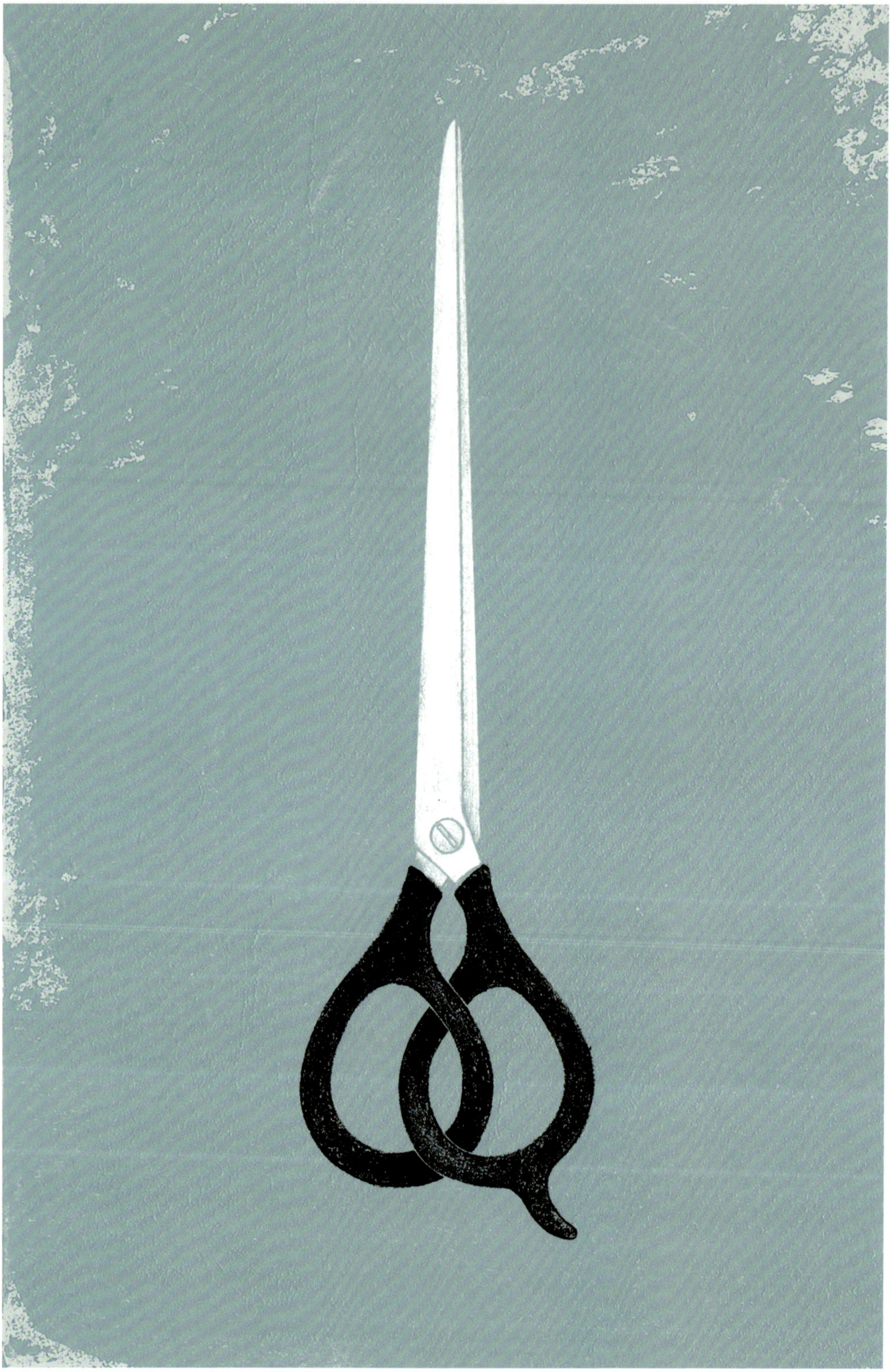

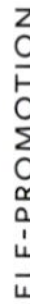

MERIT *Carlo Giambarresi*

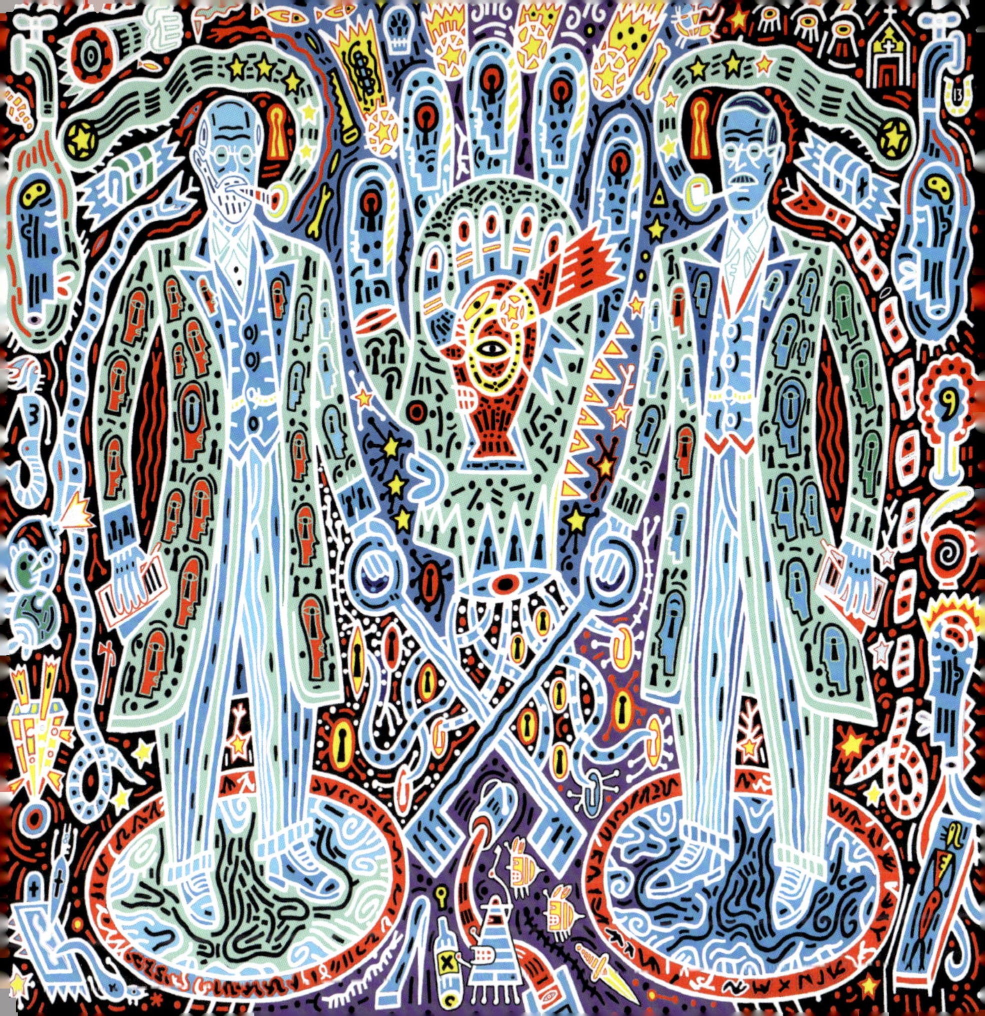

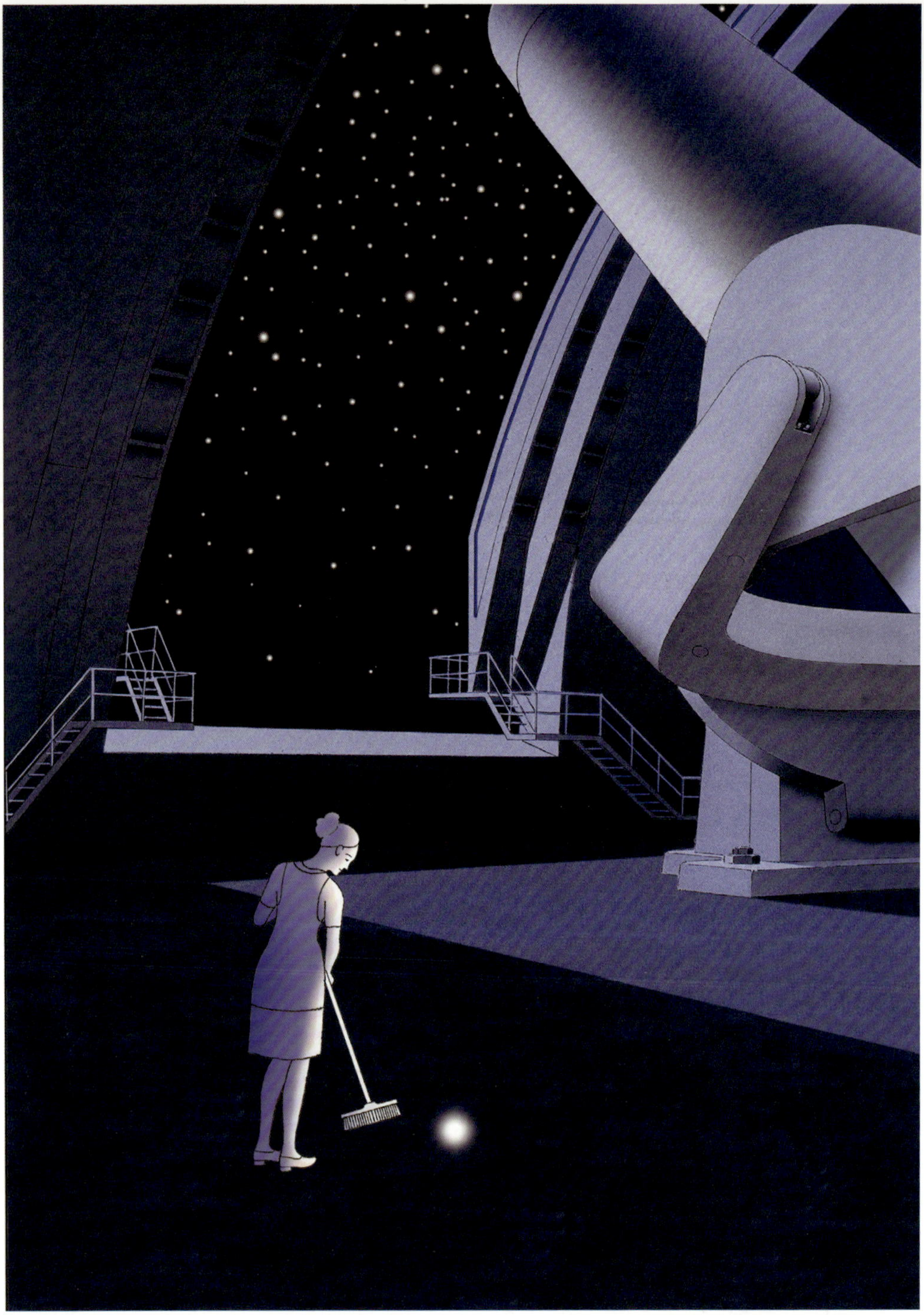

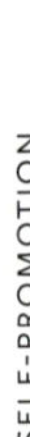

MERIT *Guy Billout*

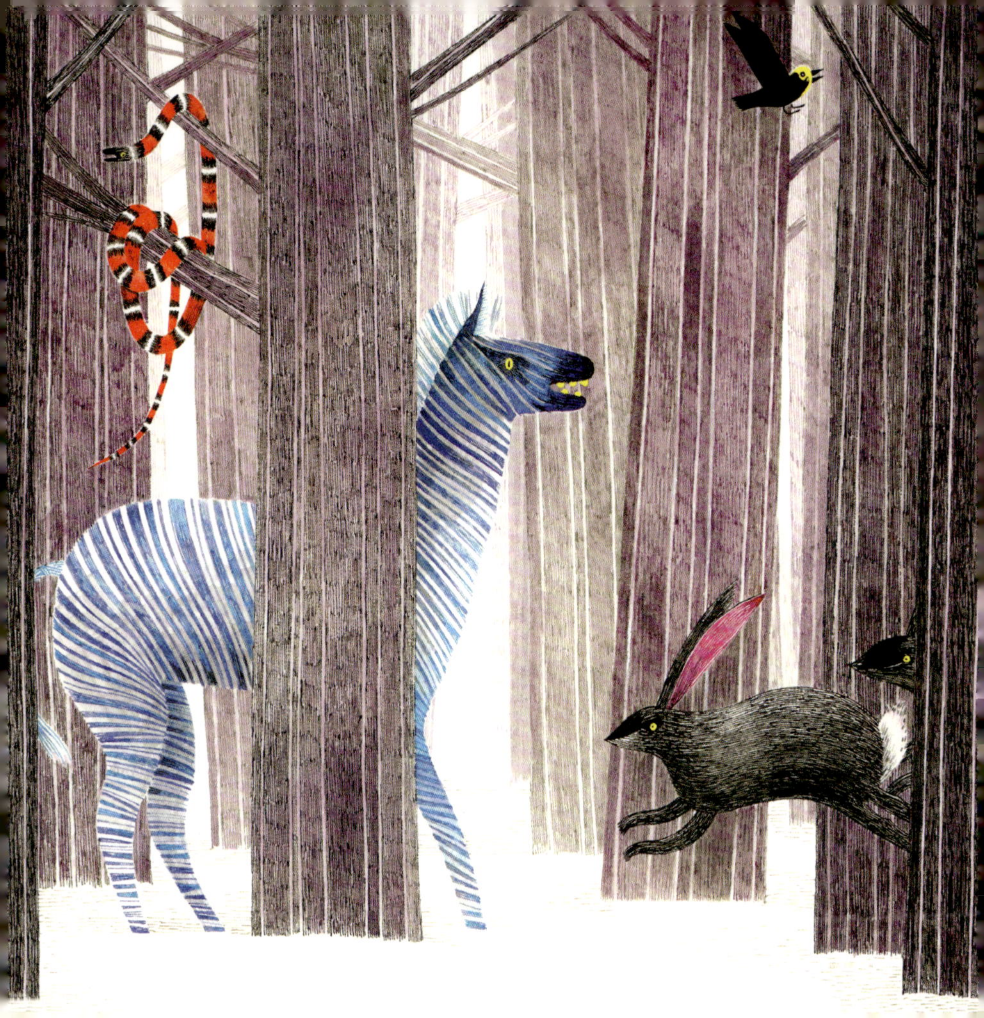

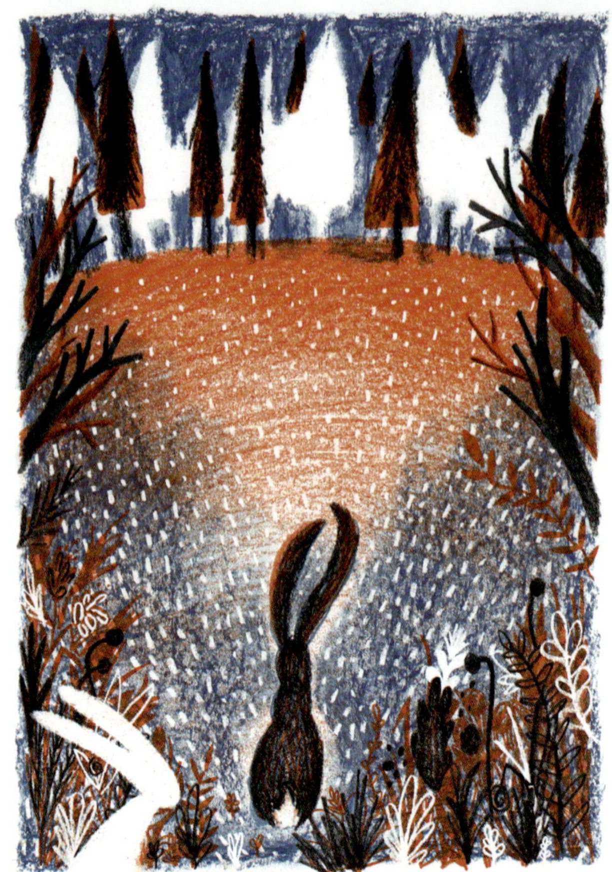
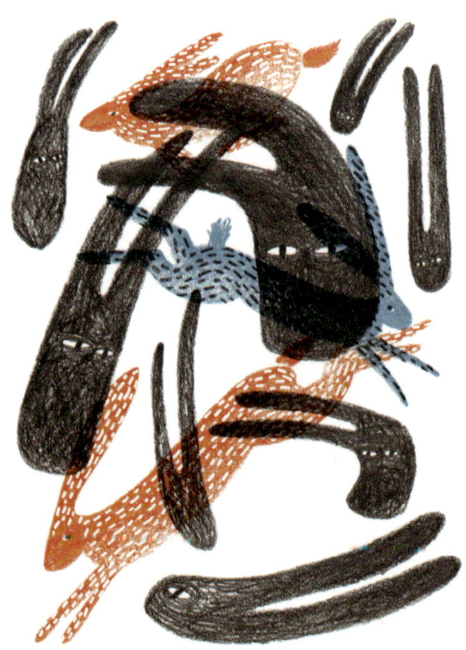
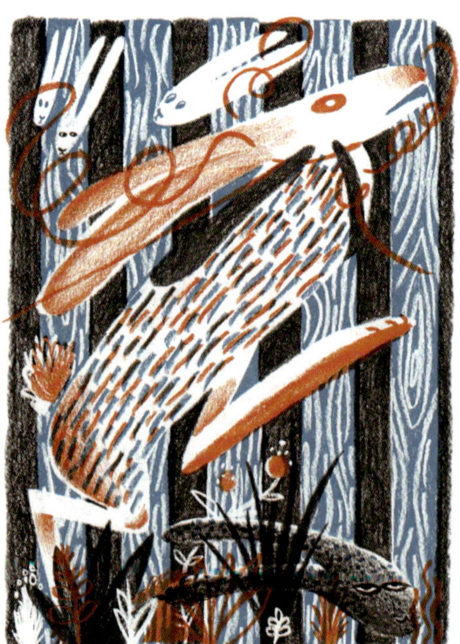

MERIT *Daniel Gray*

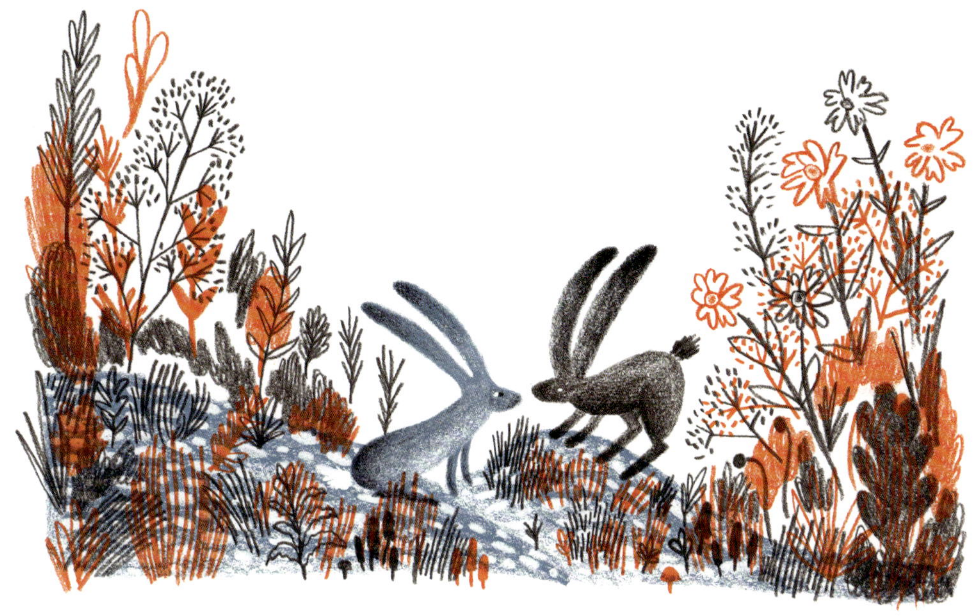

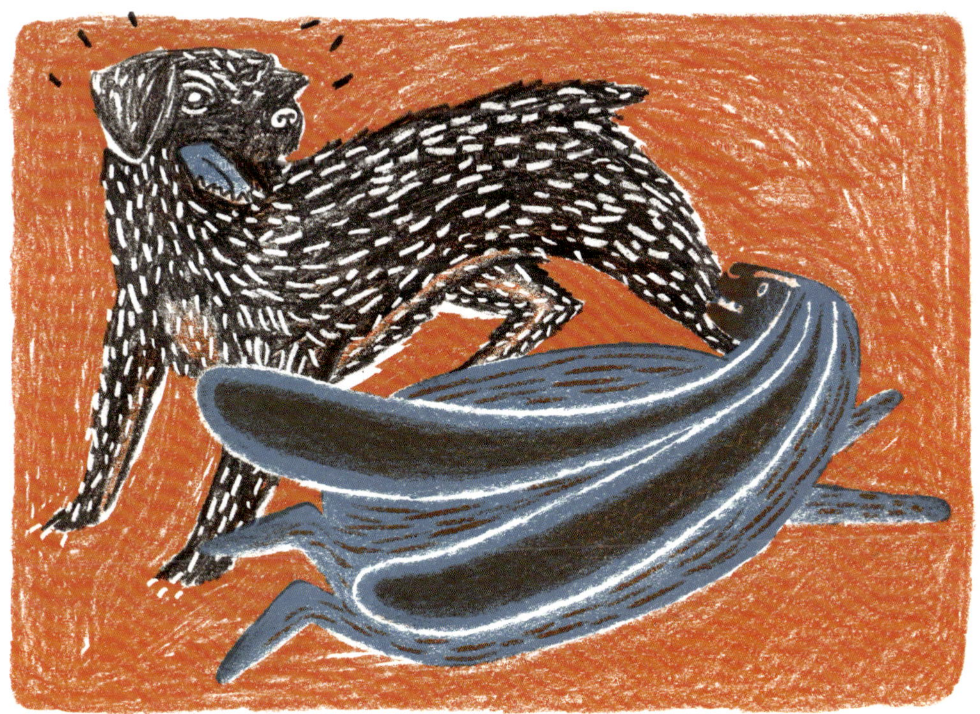

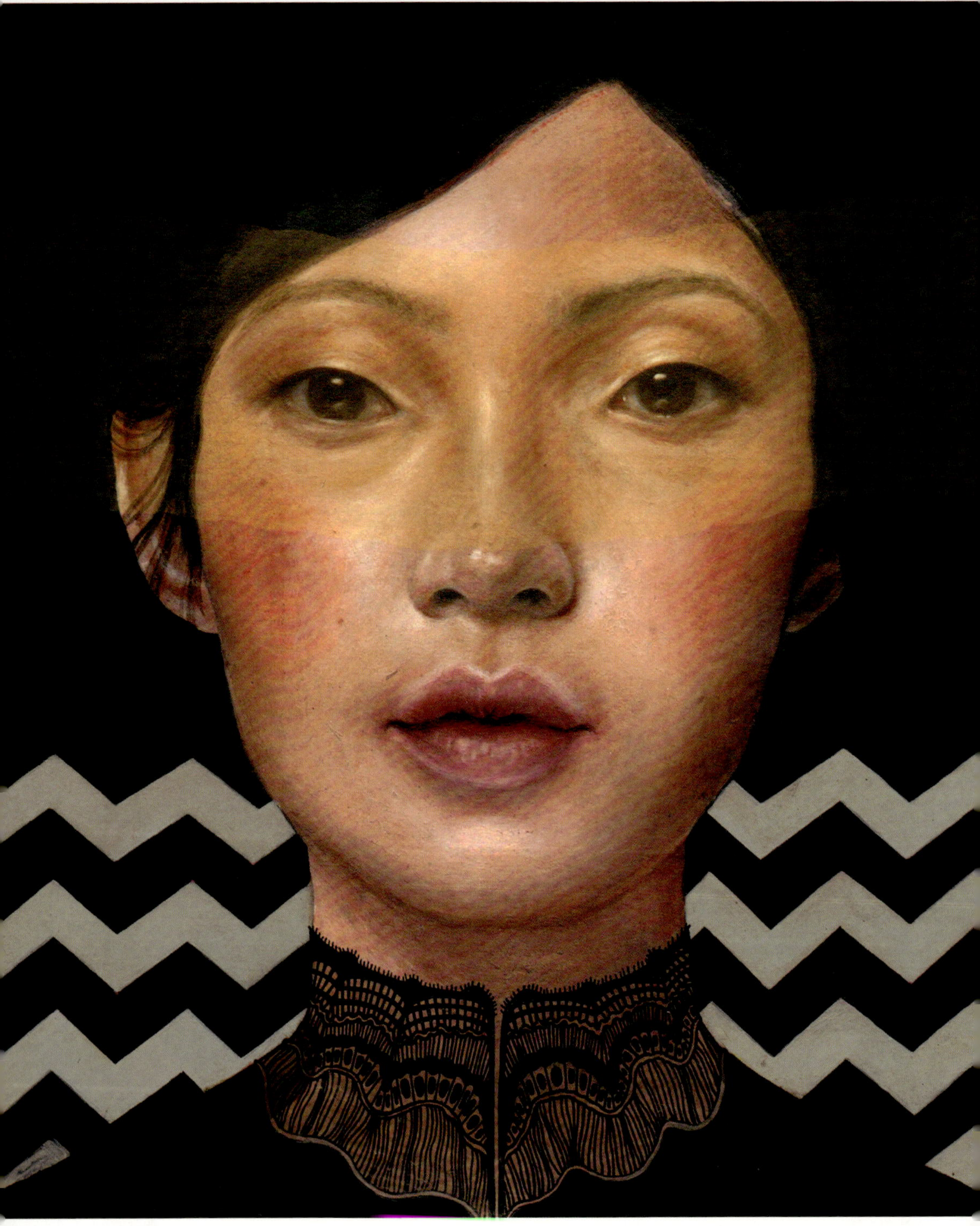



190

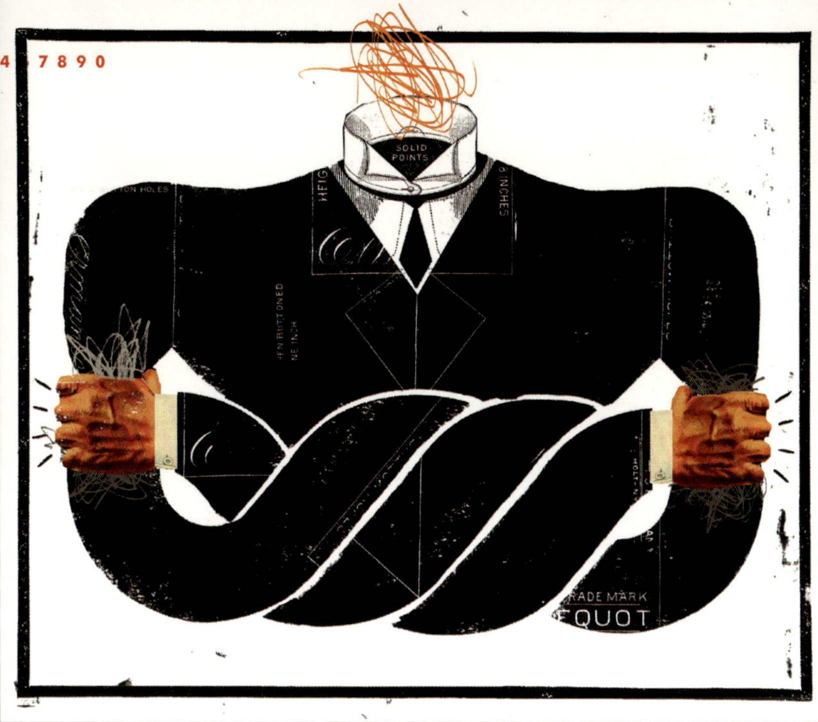

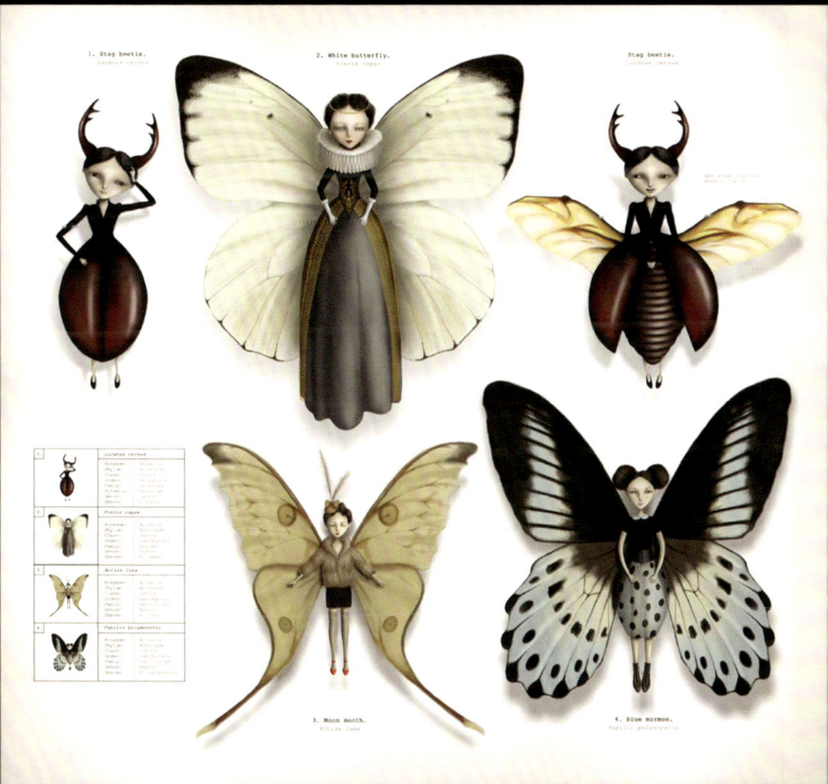

SOLID POINTS
TRADE MARK
EQUOT
4 7890

1. Stag beetle.
Lucanus cervus
2. White butterfly.
Pieris rapae
Stag beetle.
Lucanus cervus
3. Moon month.
Actias luna
4. Blue mormon.
Papilio polymnestor

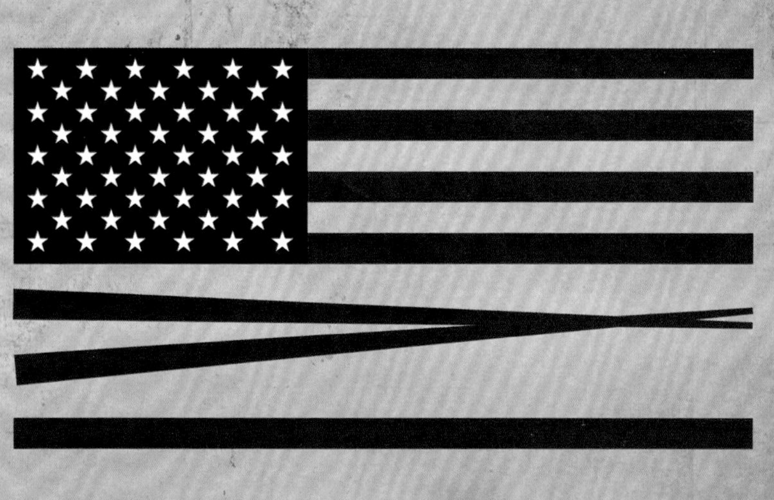

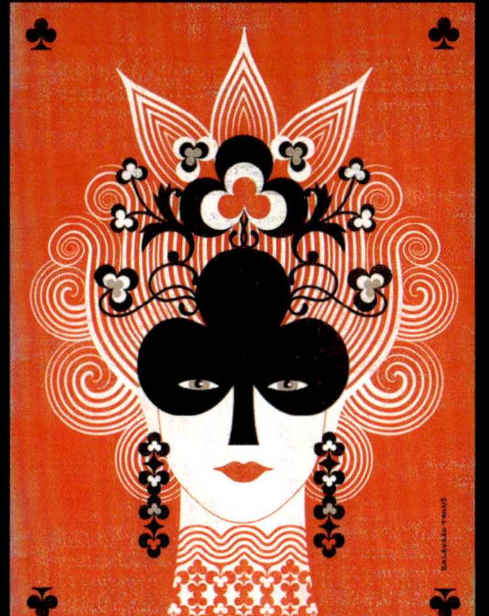

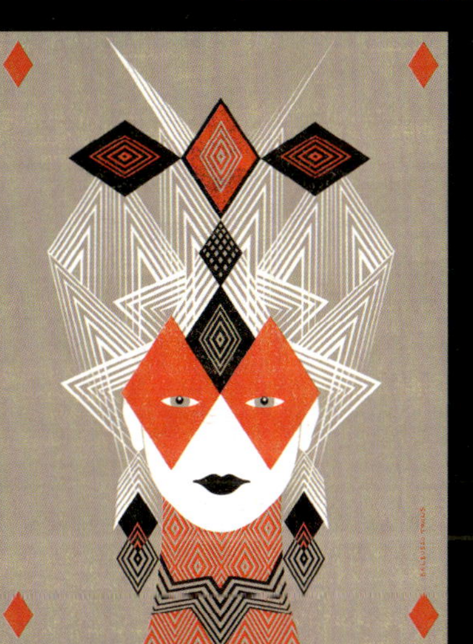

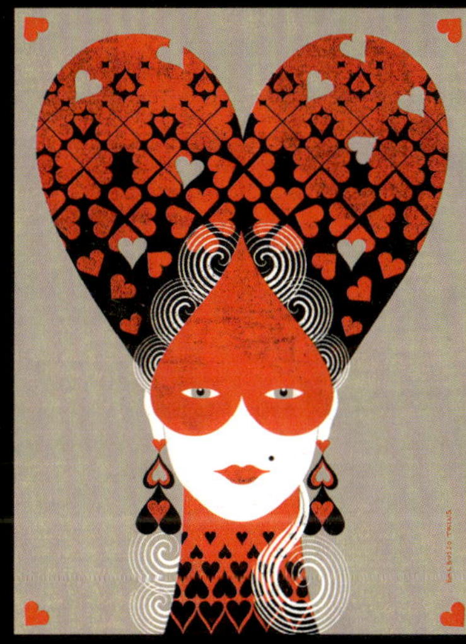

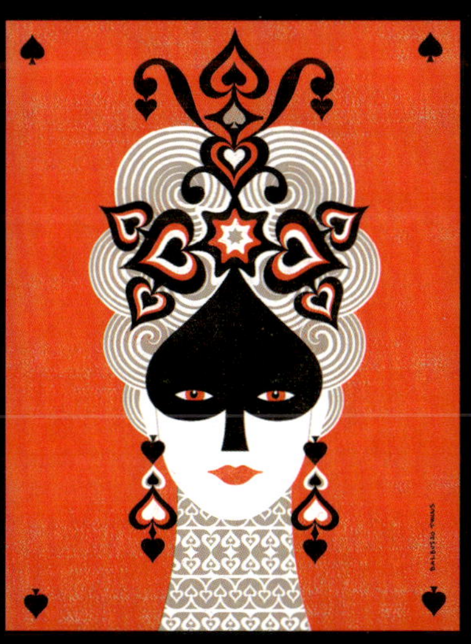

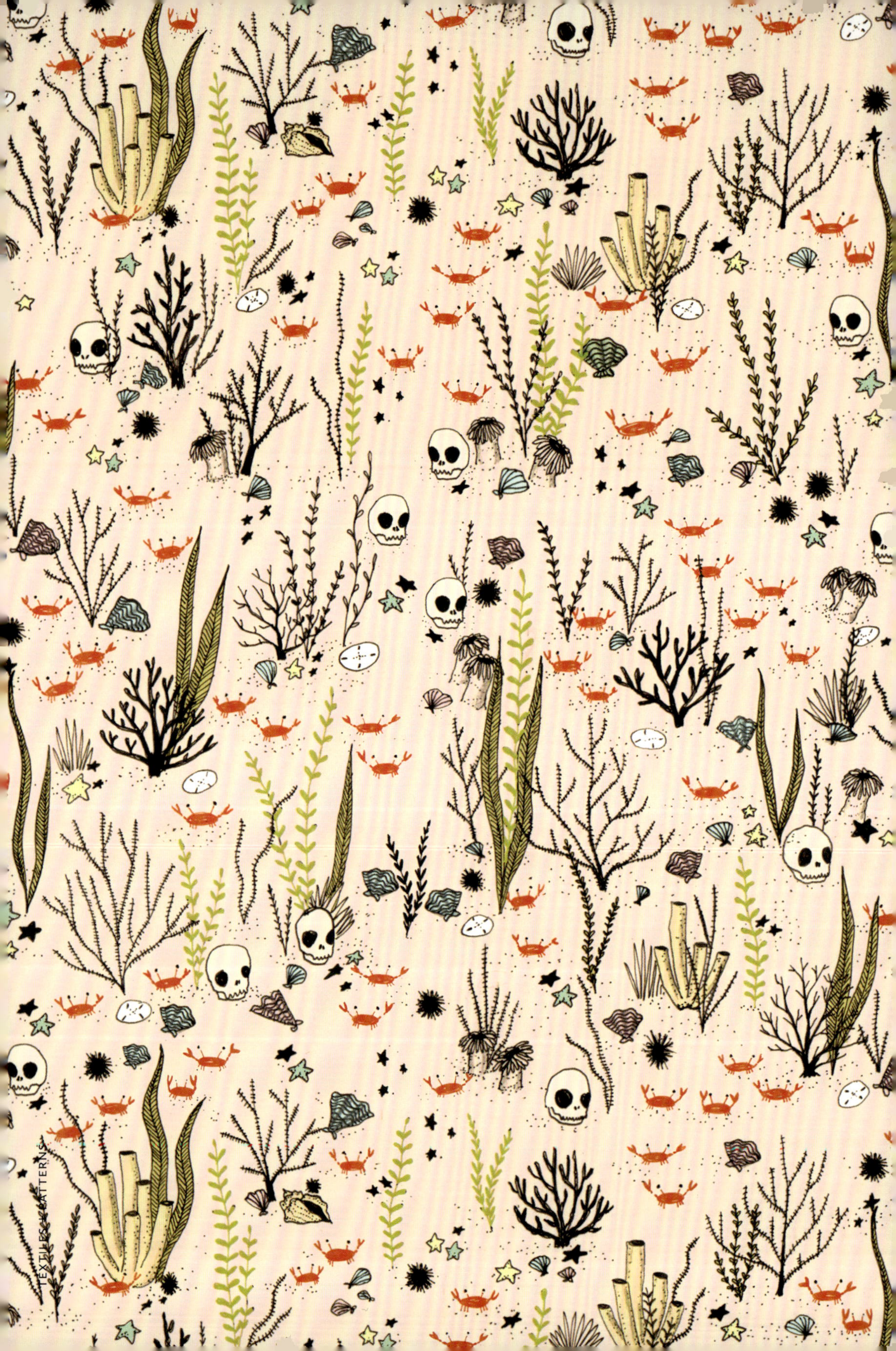
TEXTILES PATTERNS

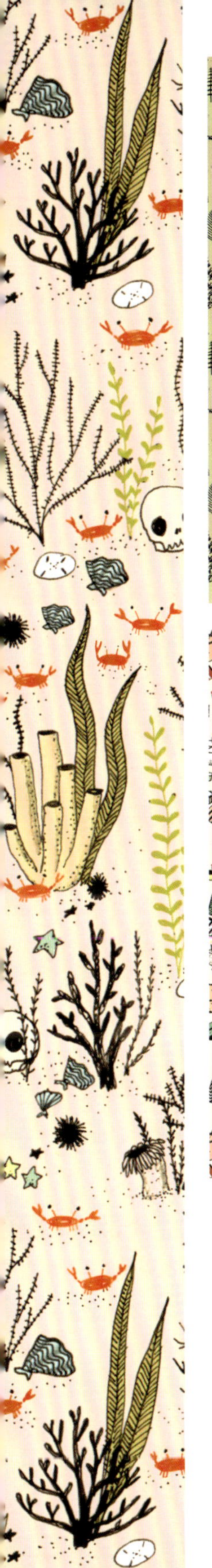

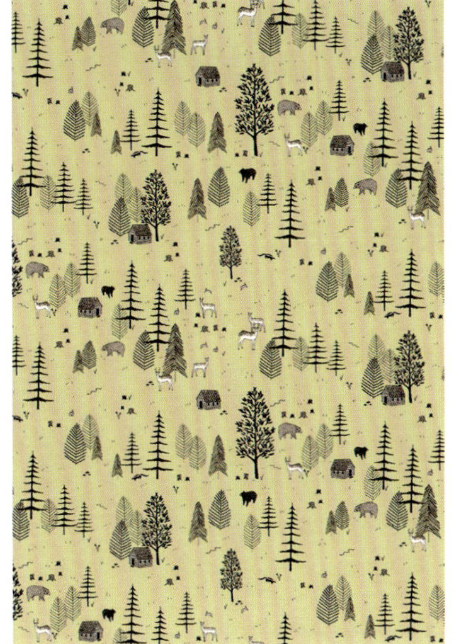

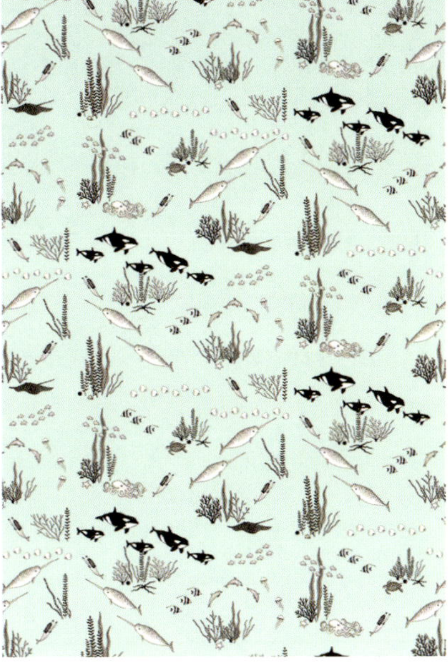

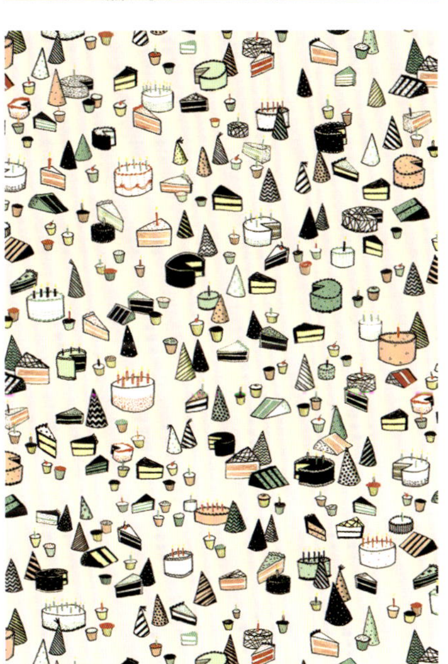

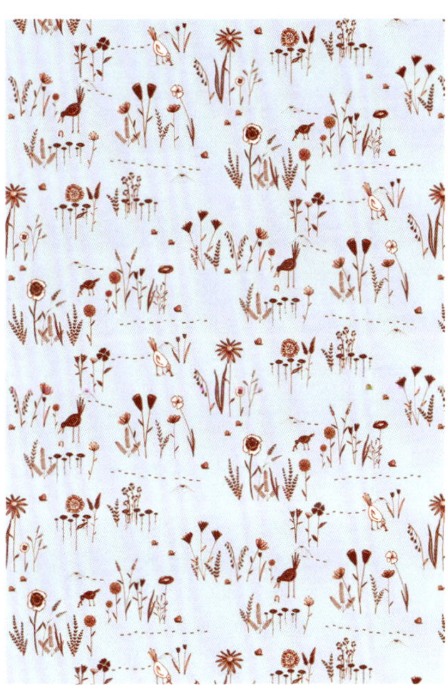

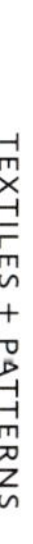

MERIT *Mai Ly Degnan*

195

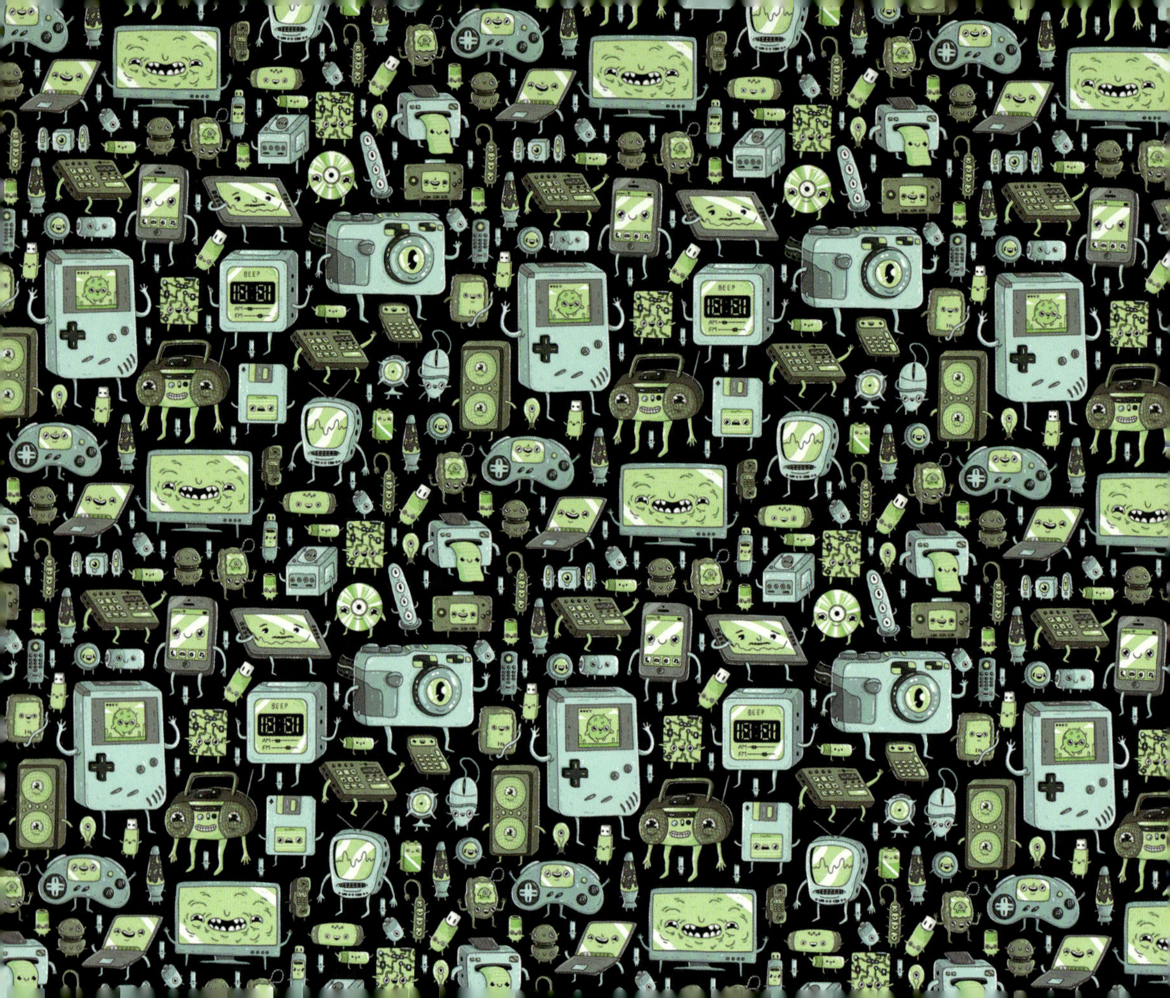

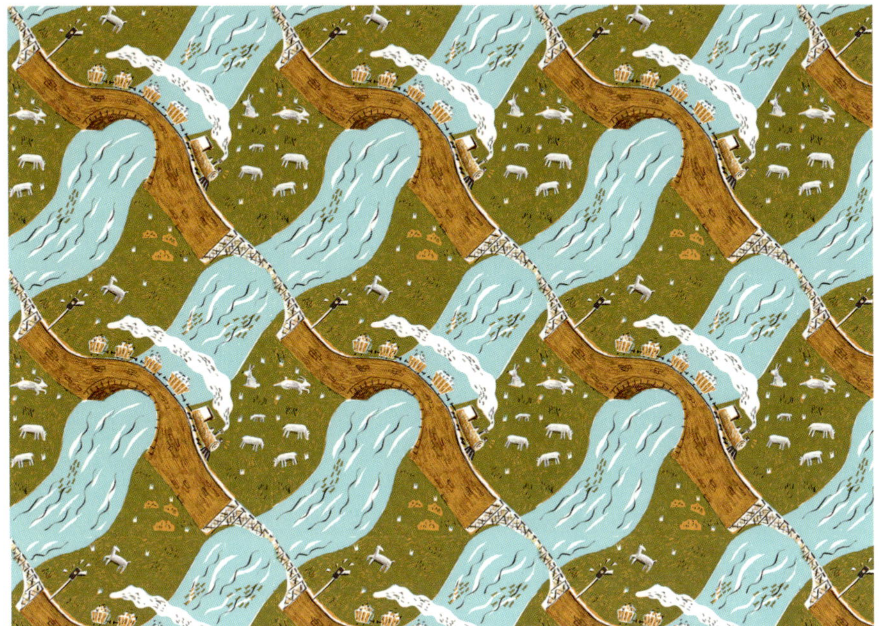

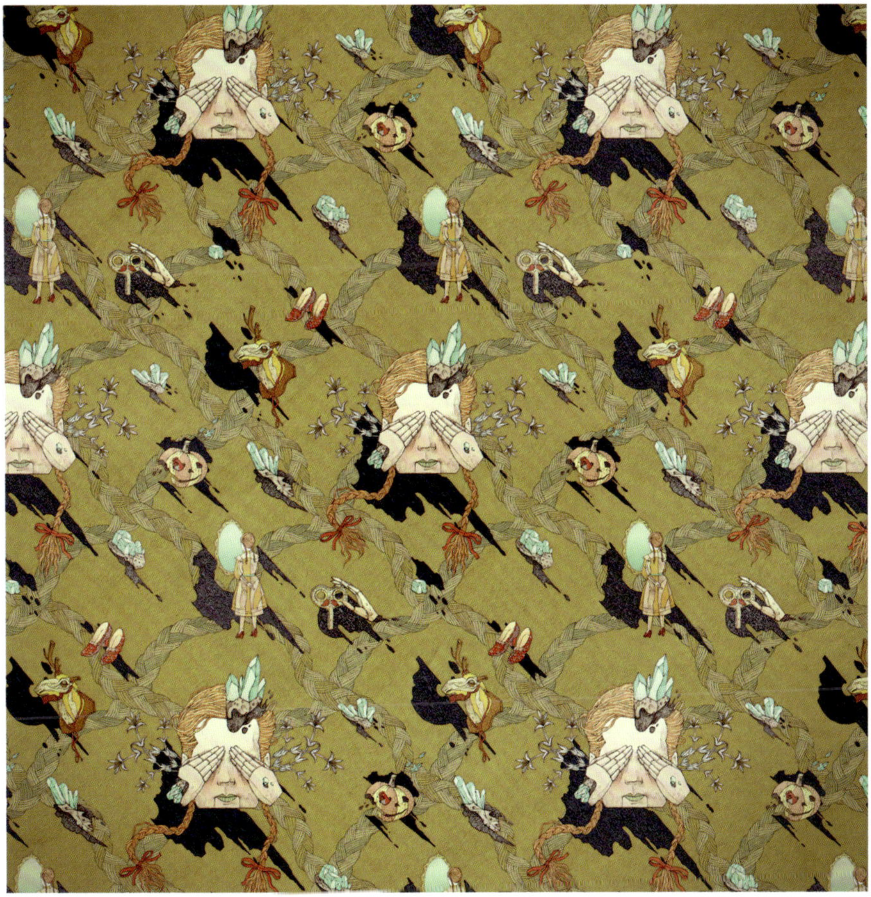

(T) MERIT *Toby Rampton*    (B) MERIT *Summerise*

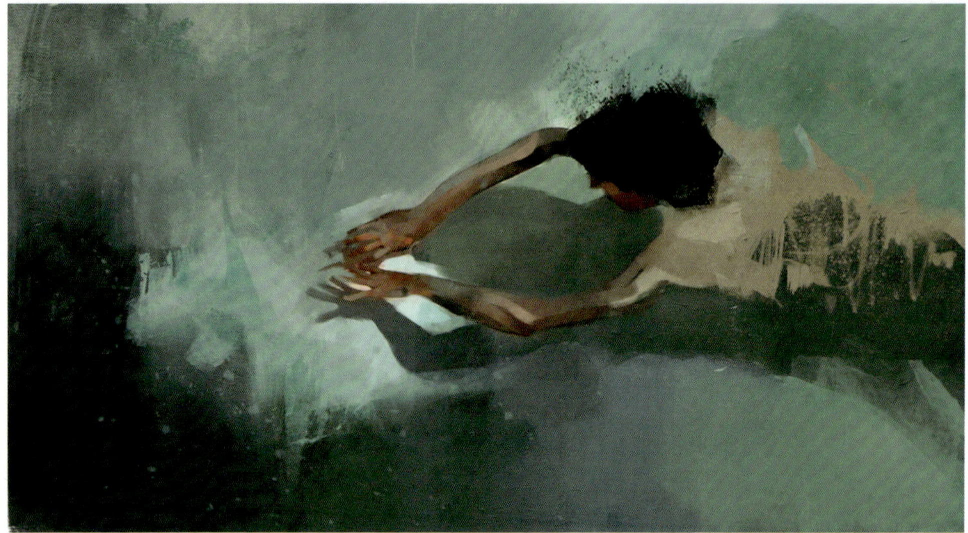

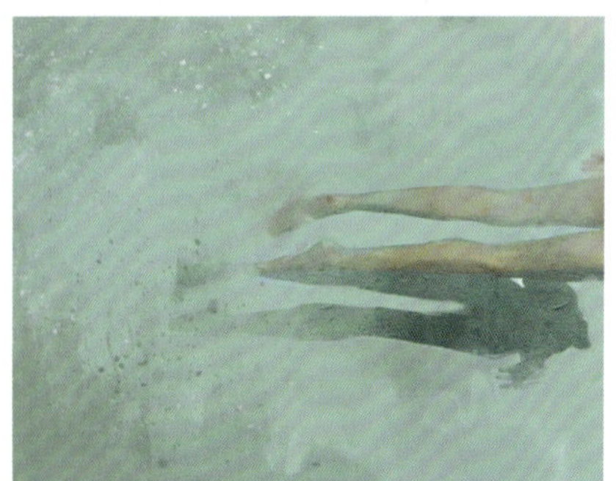

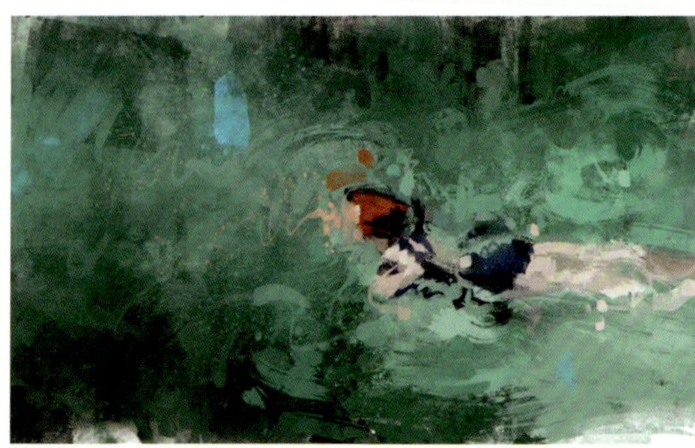

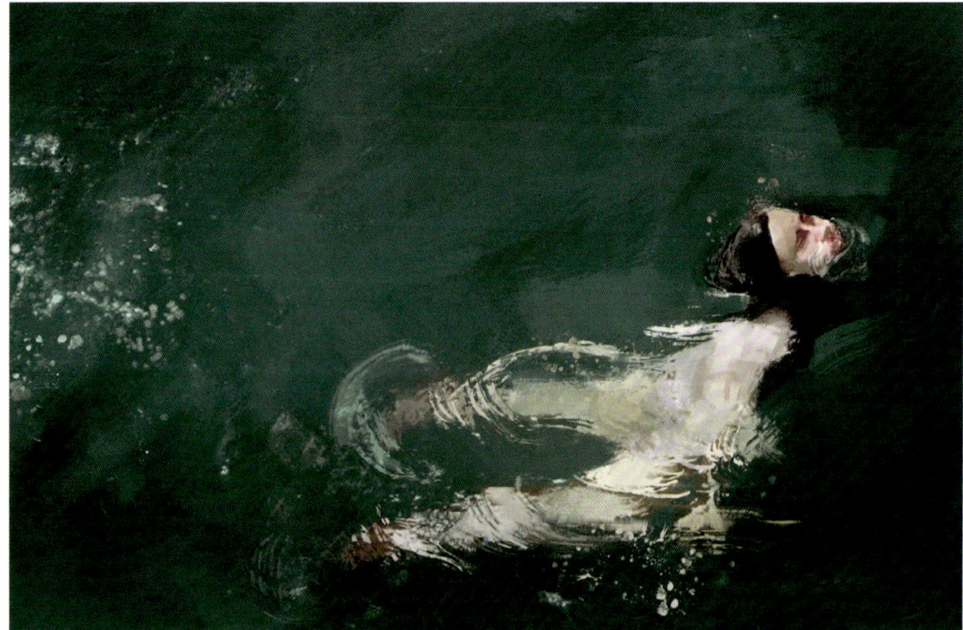

MERIT *Pedro Covo*

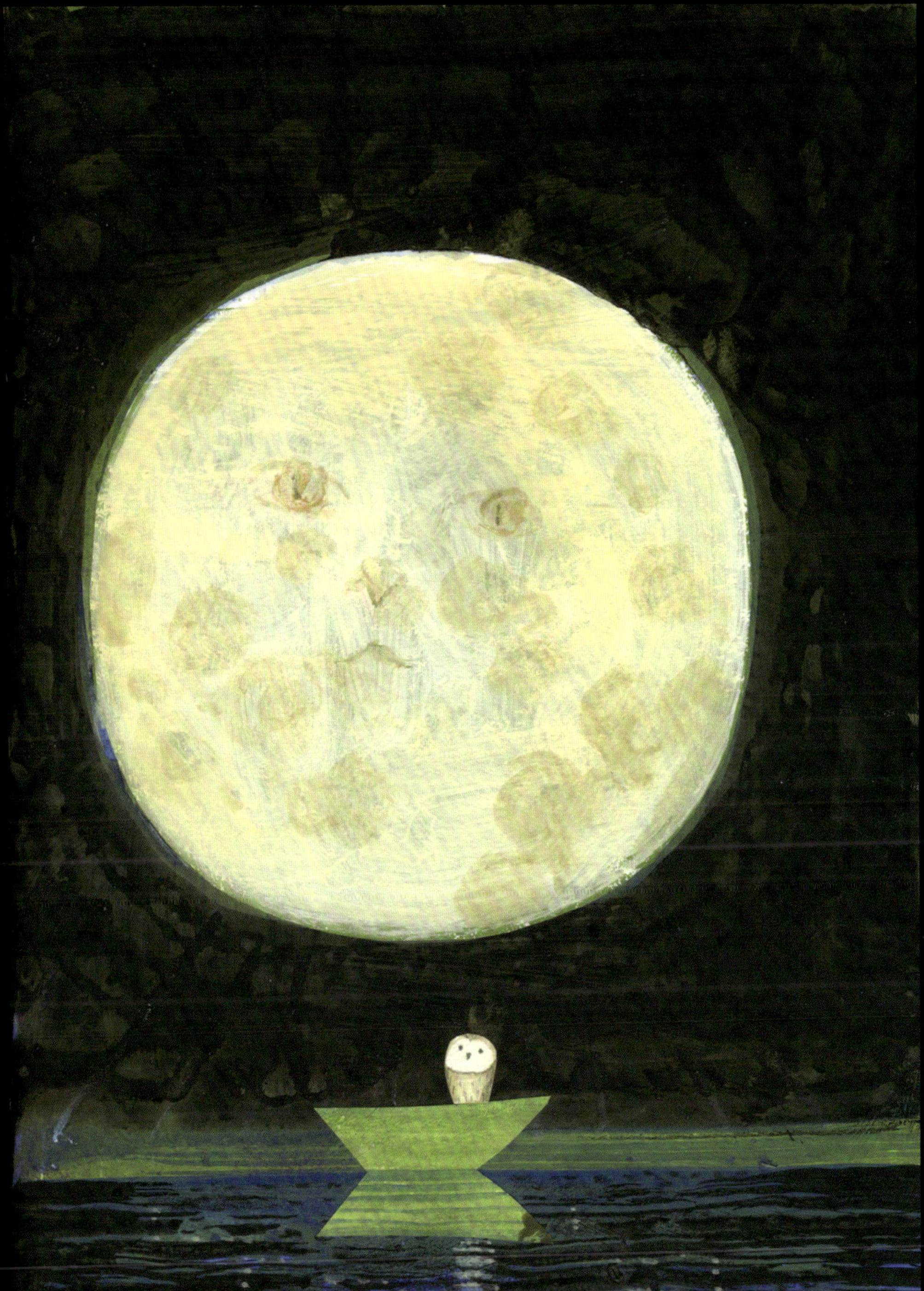

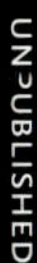



MERIT *Rob Dunlavey*

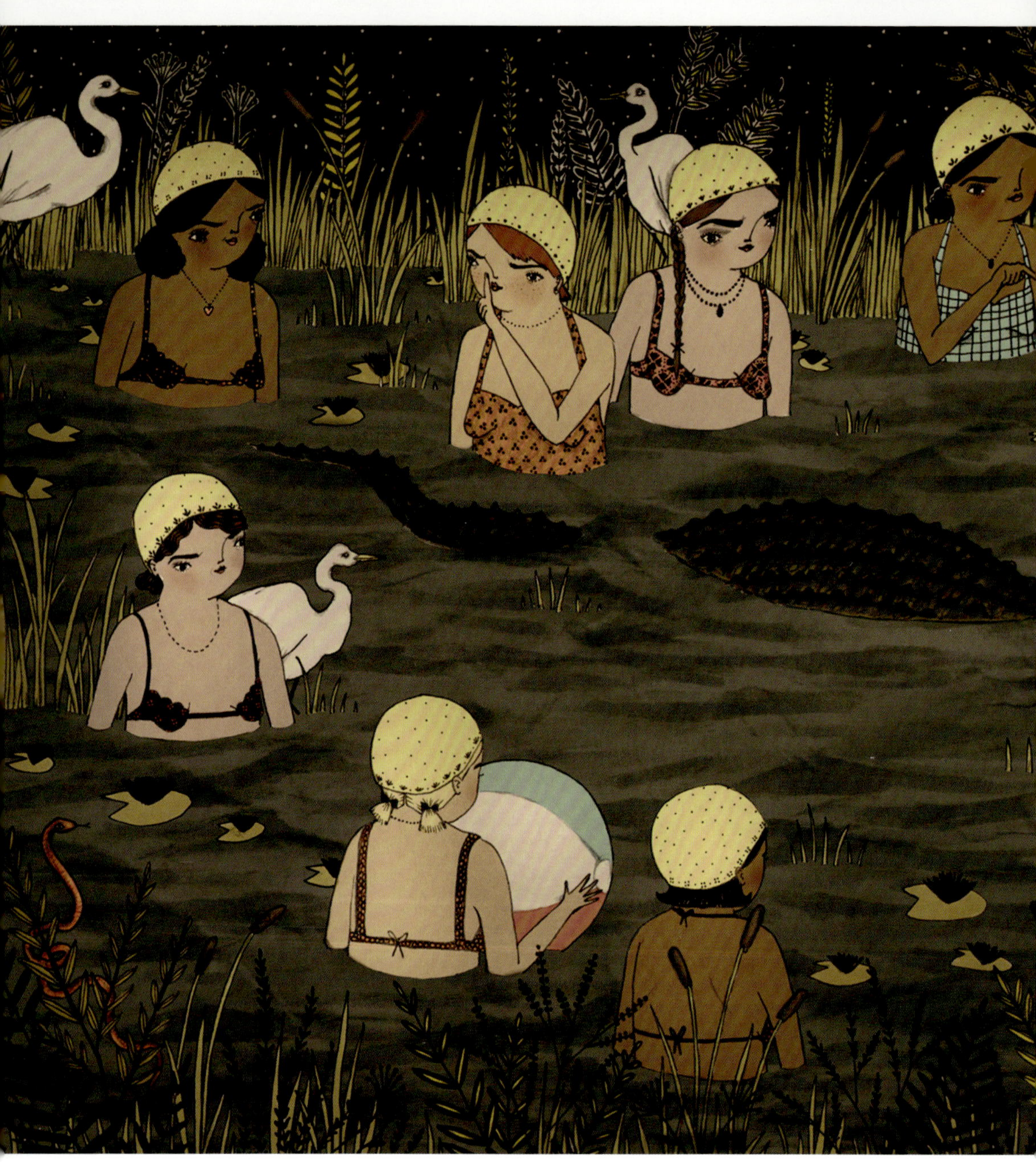

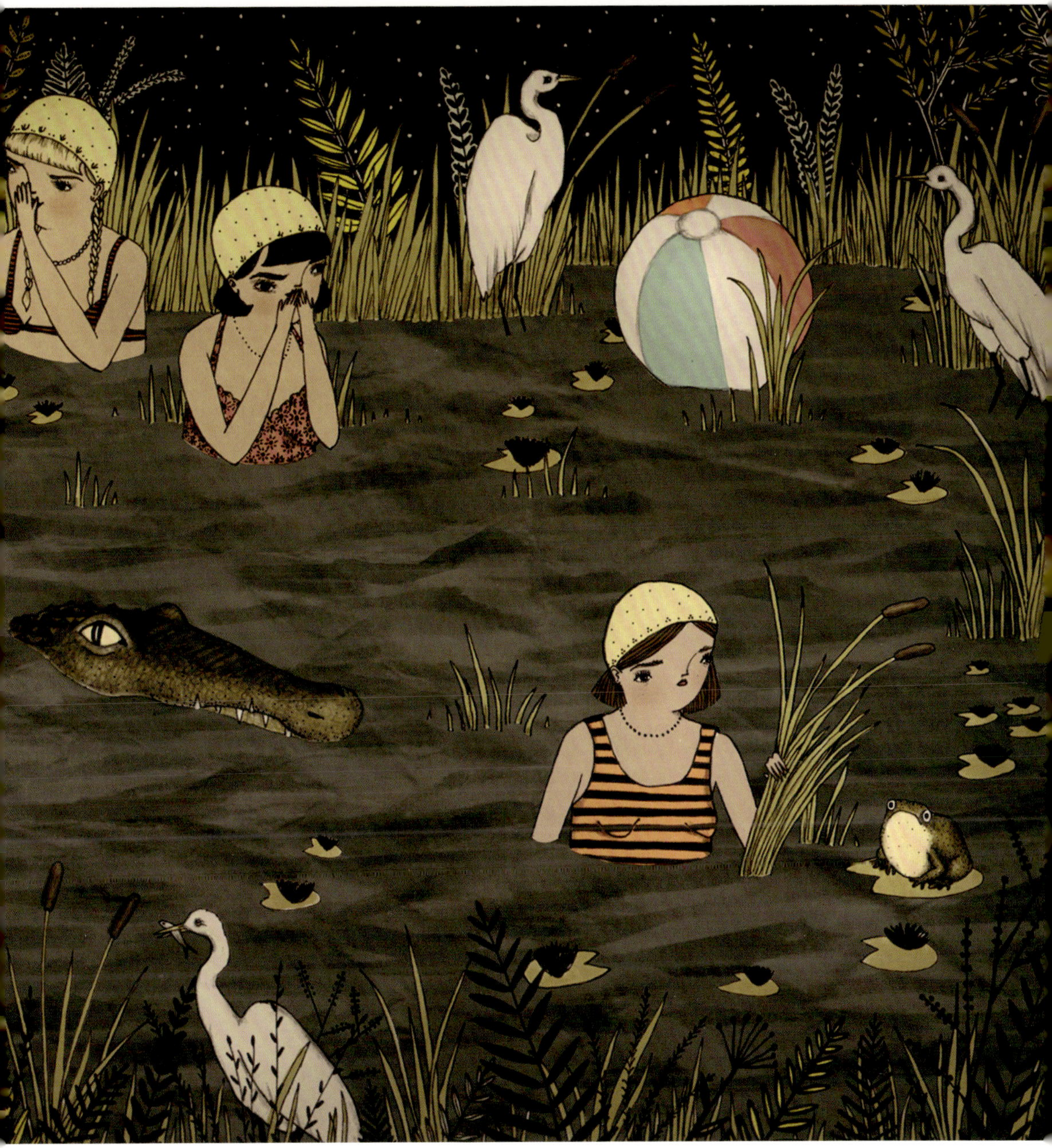

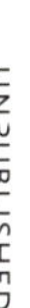

UNPUBLISHED

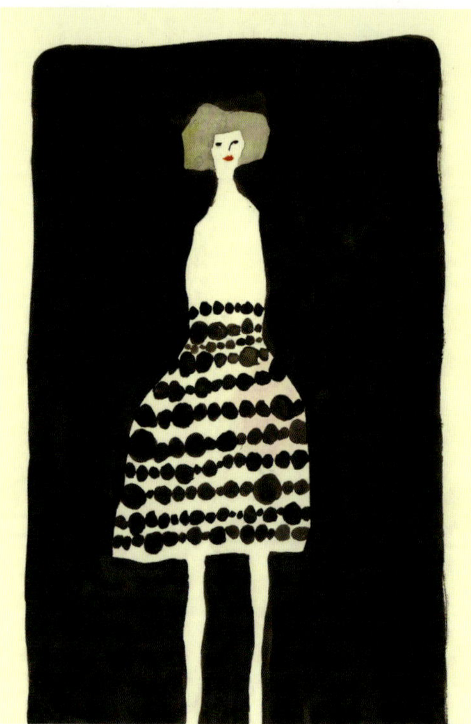
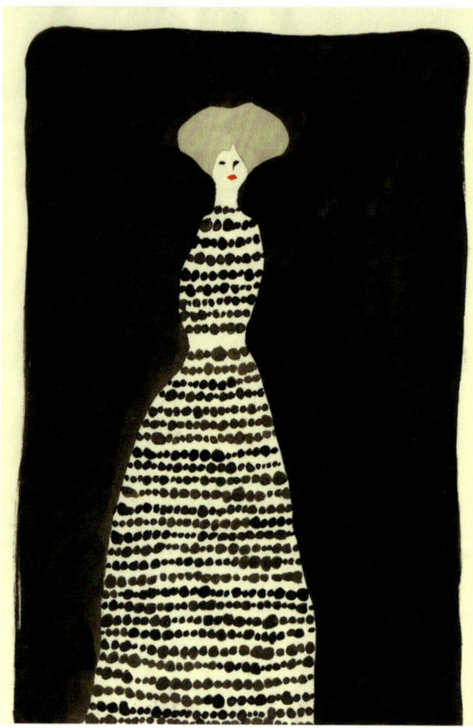
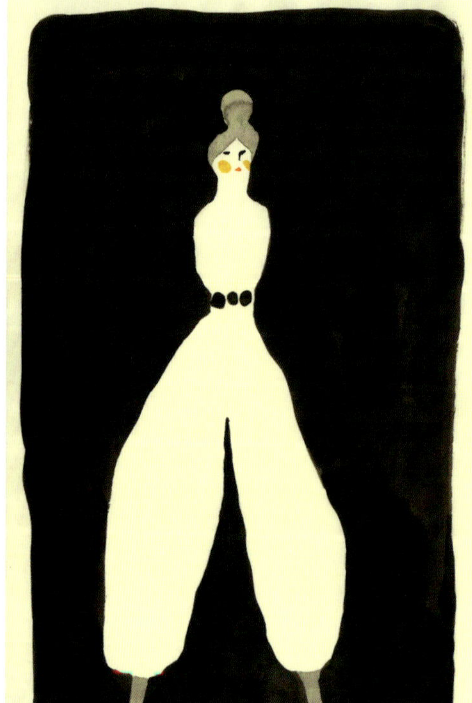
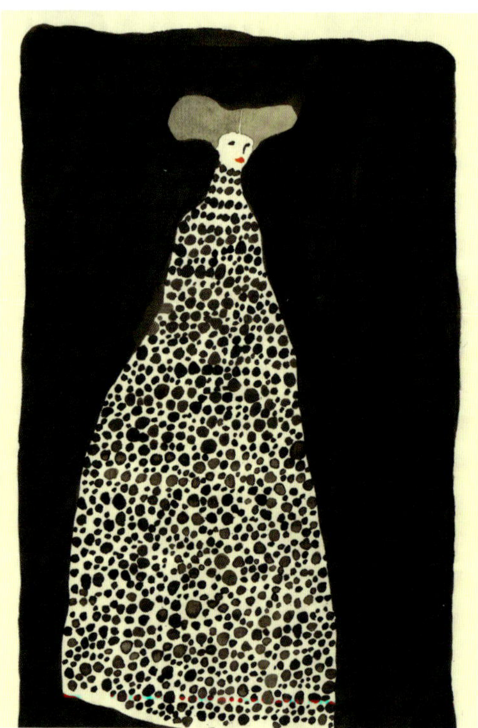

MERIT *Nomoco*

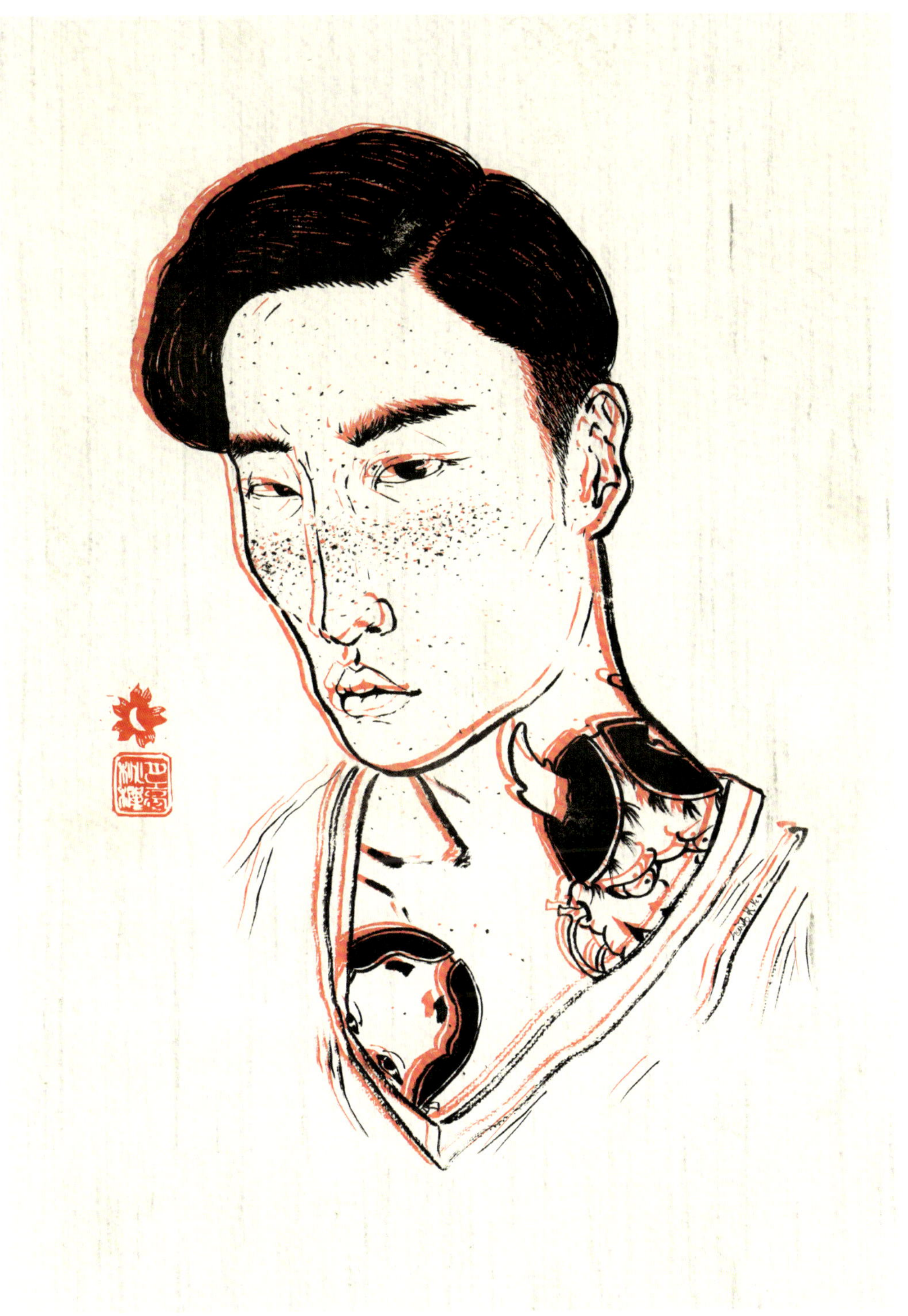

MERIT *Luna Kirsche*

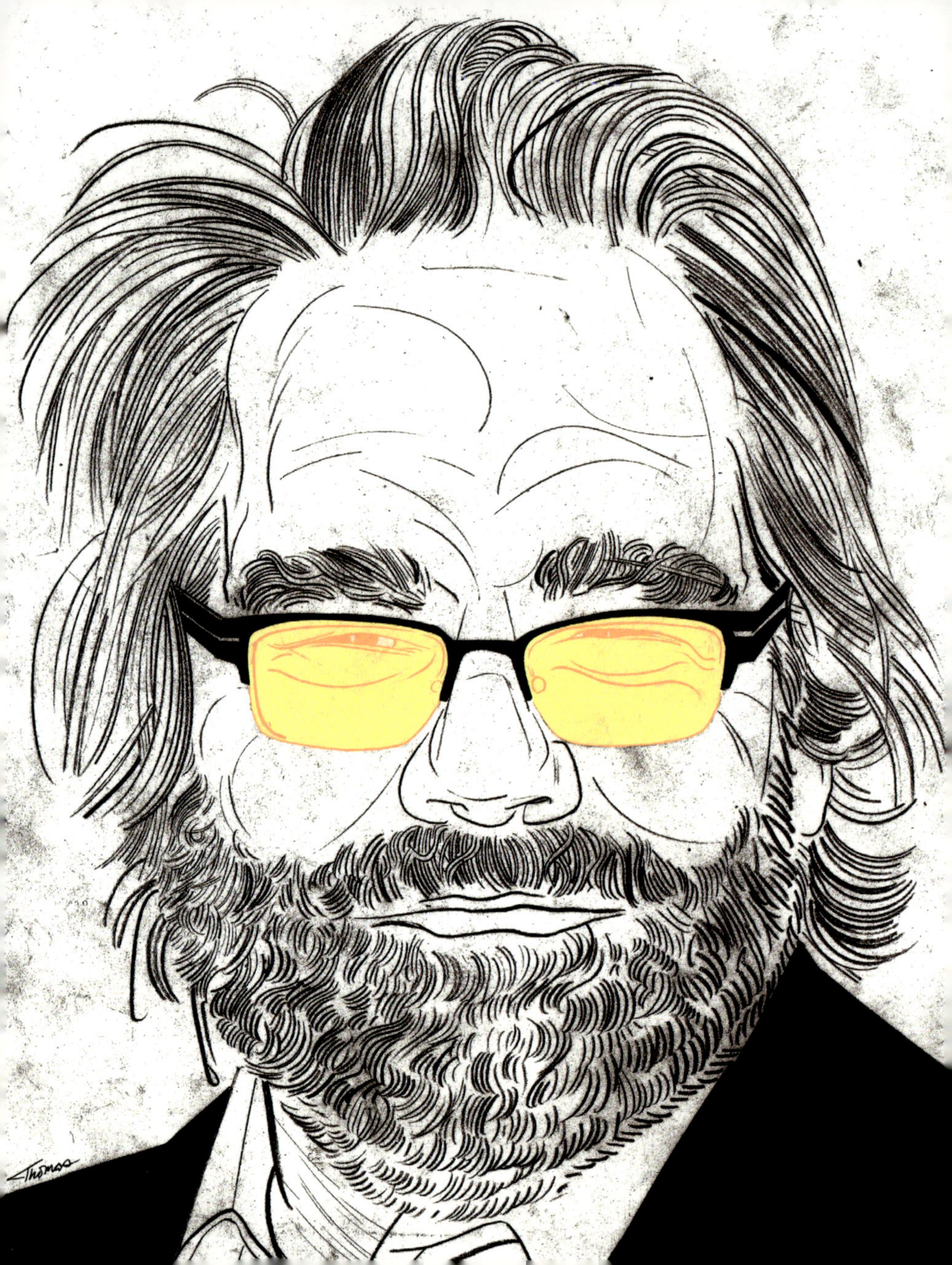

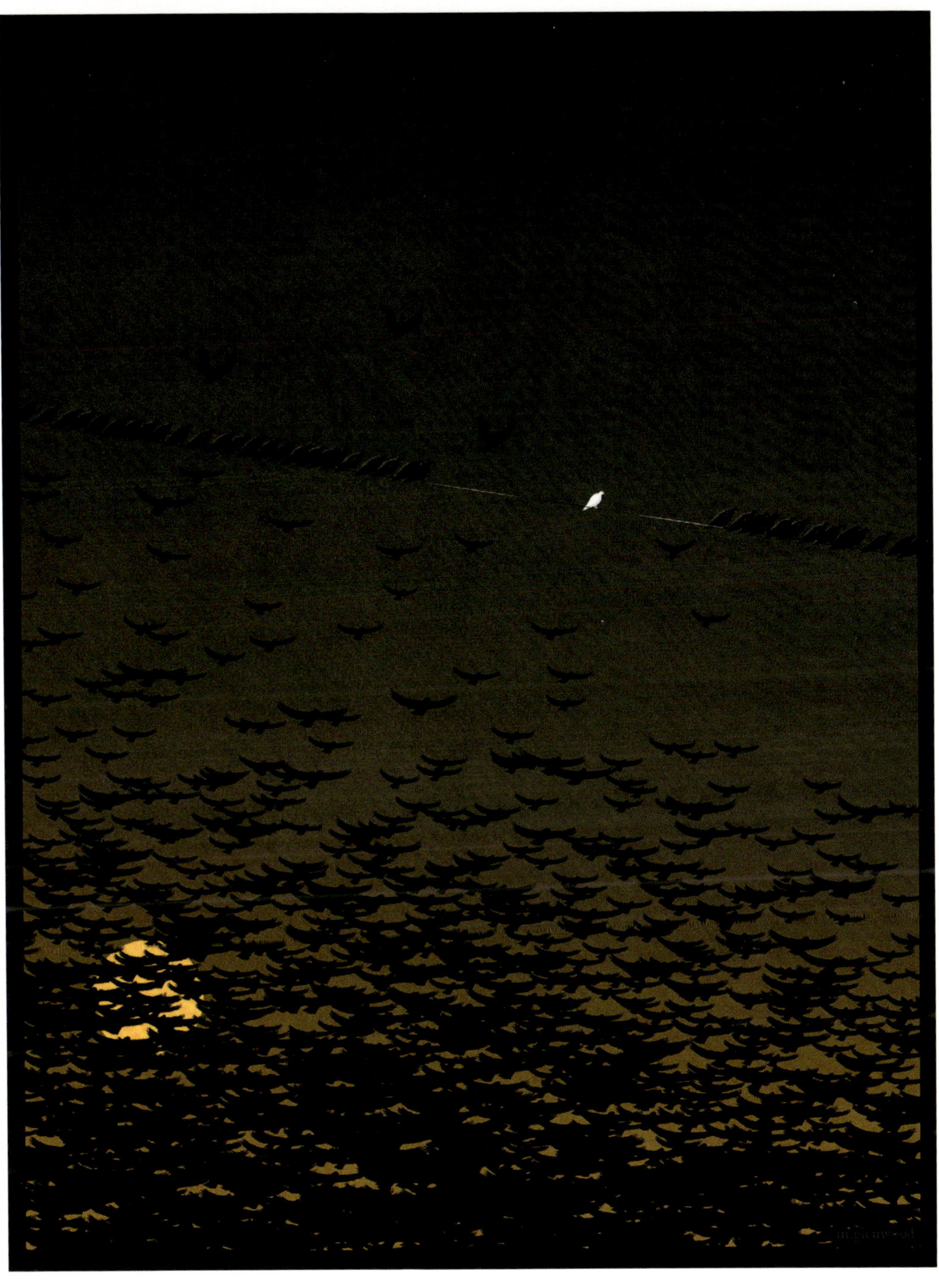

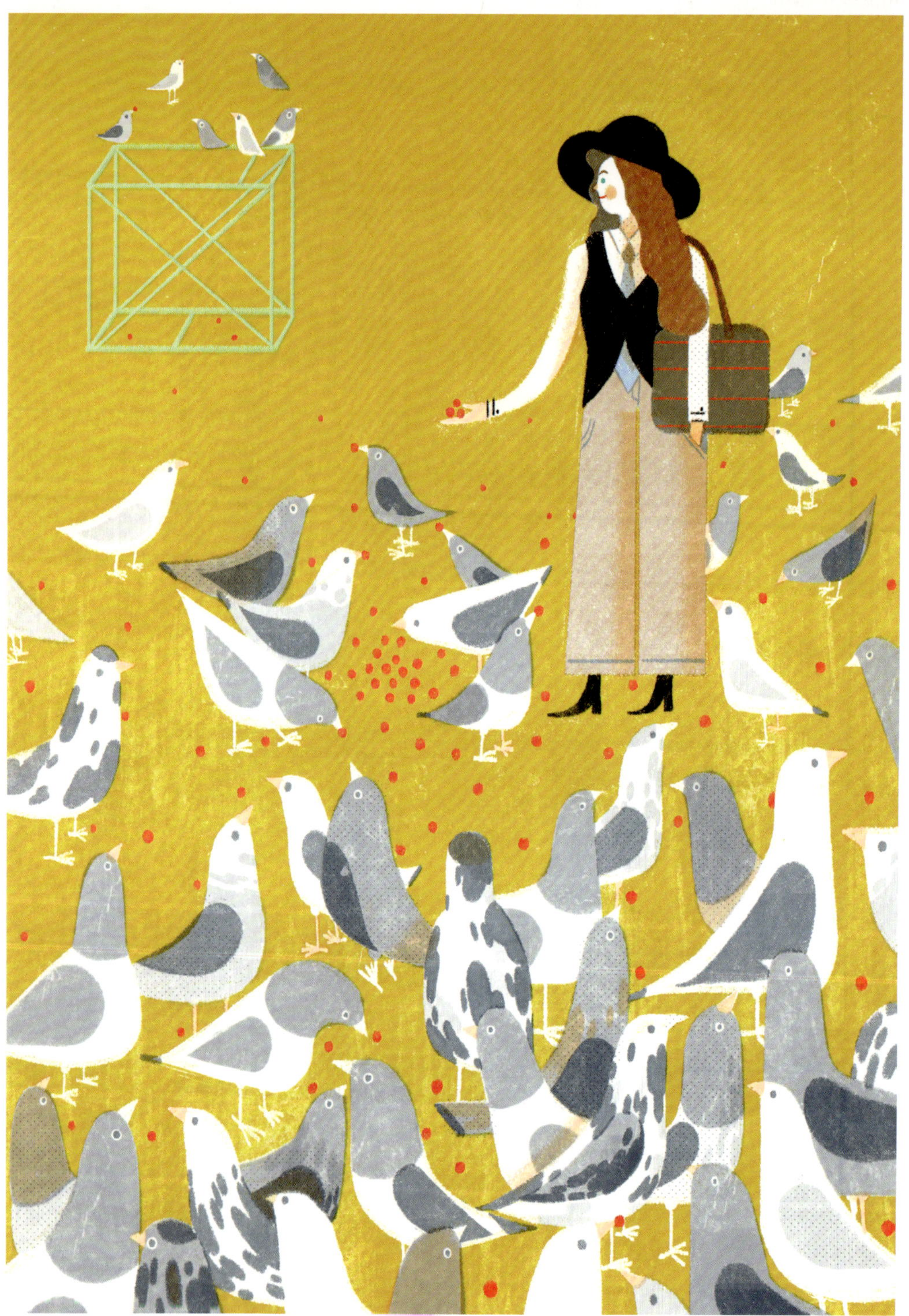

MERIT *Lisk Feng*

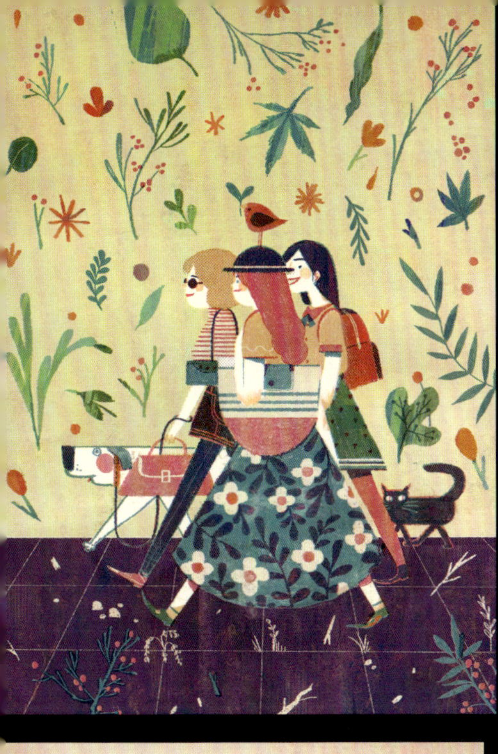
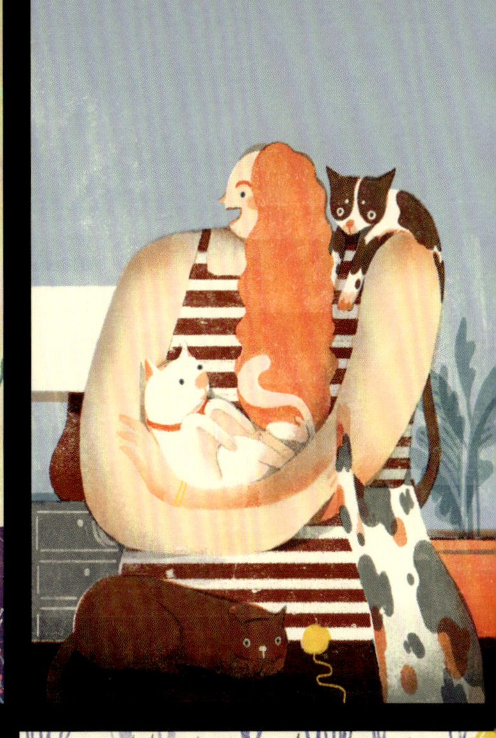
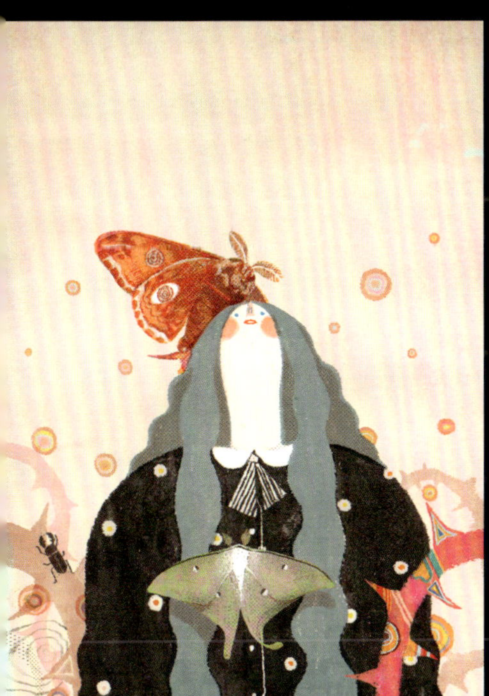
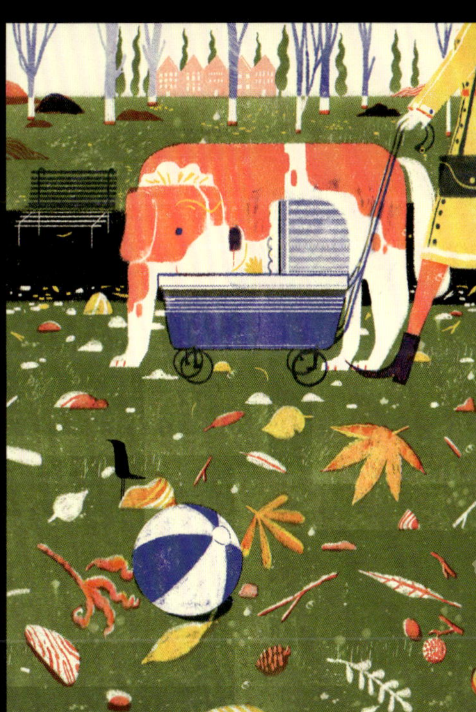

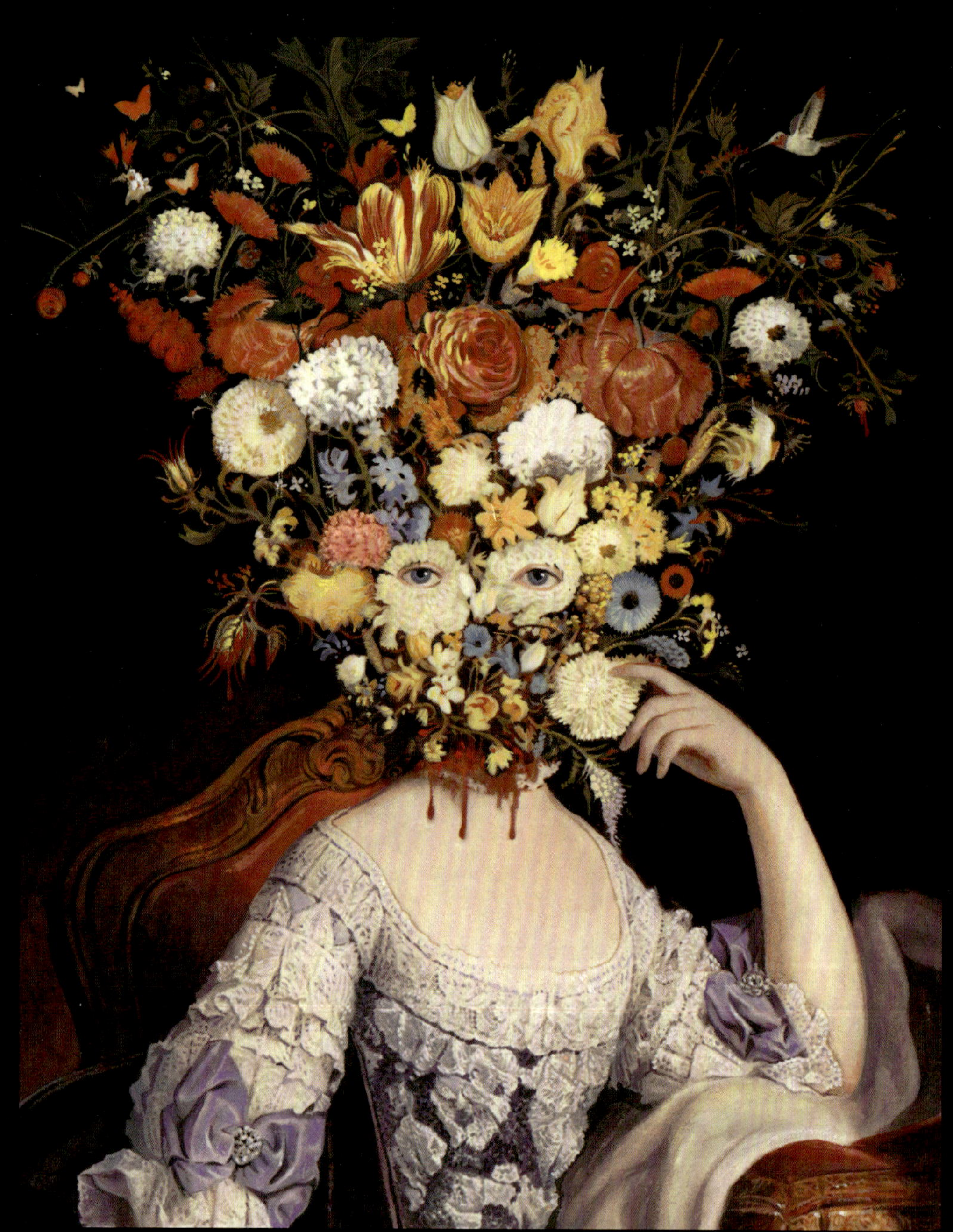


MERIT *Bill Mayer*

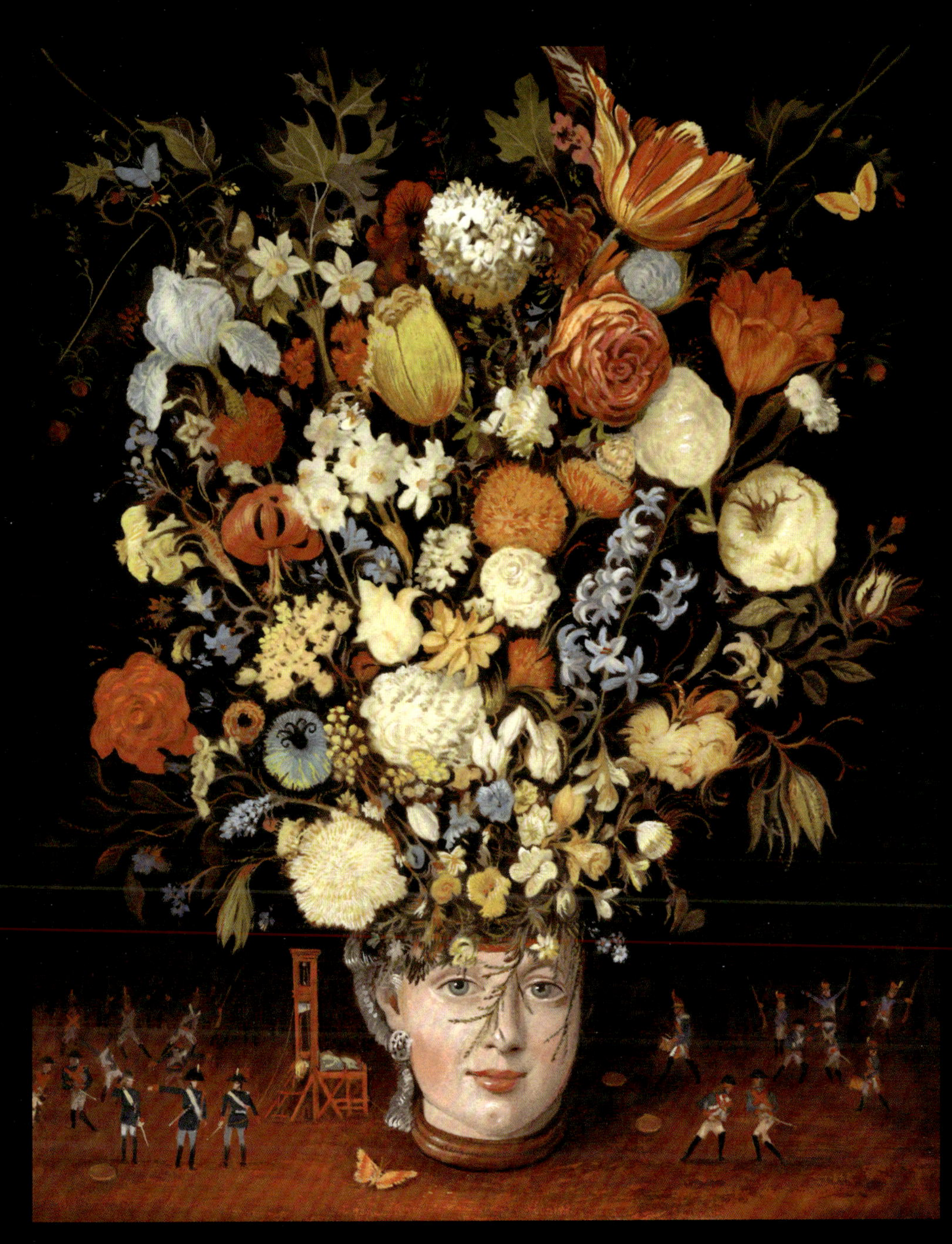

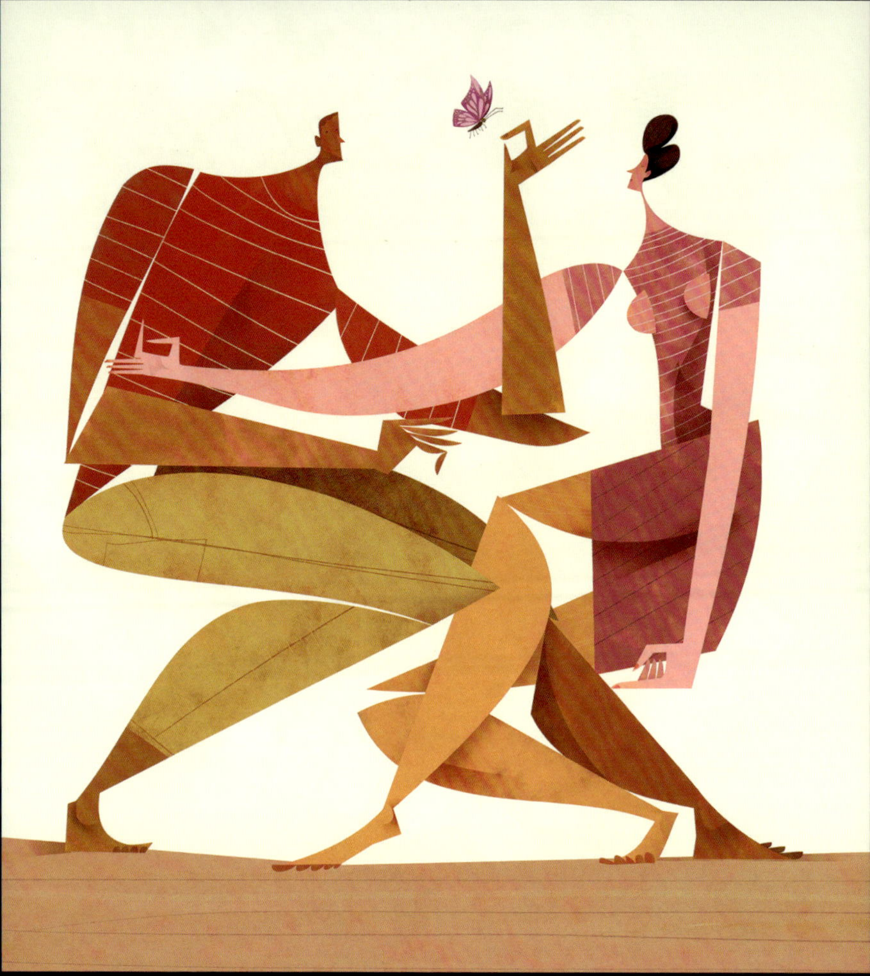

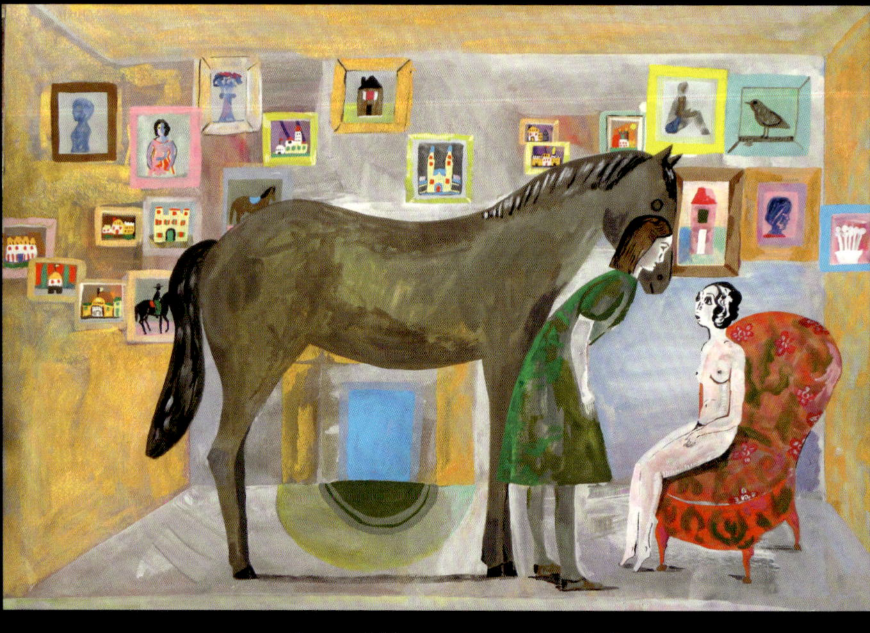

(T) MERIT Gregory Baldwin   (B) MERIT Karen Barbour

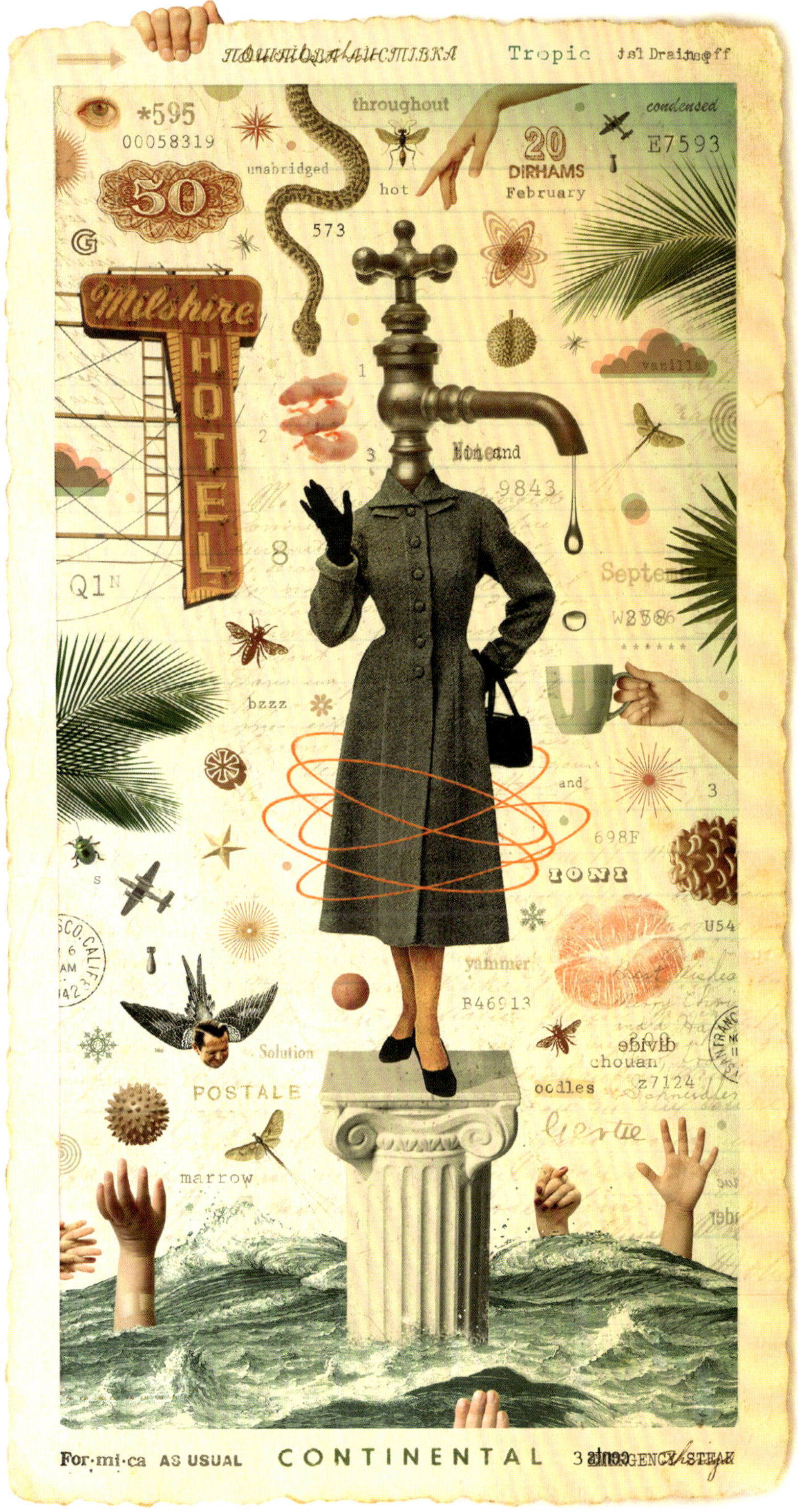


MERIT *Michael Waraksa*

211

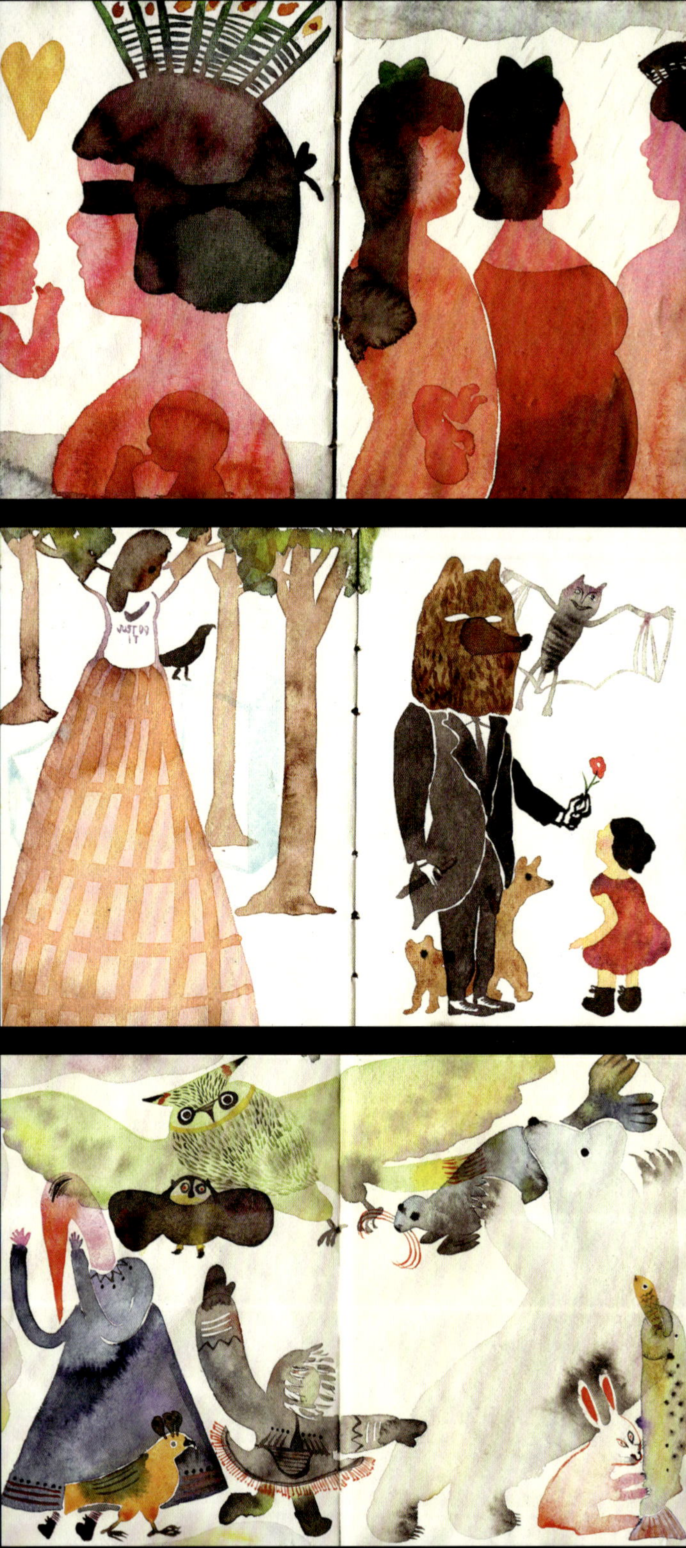

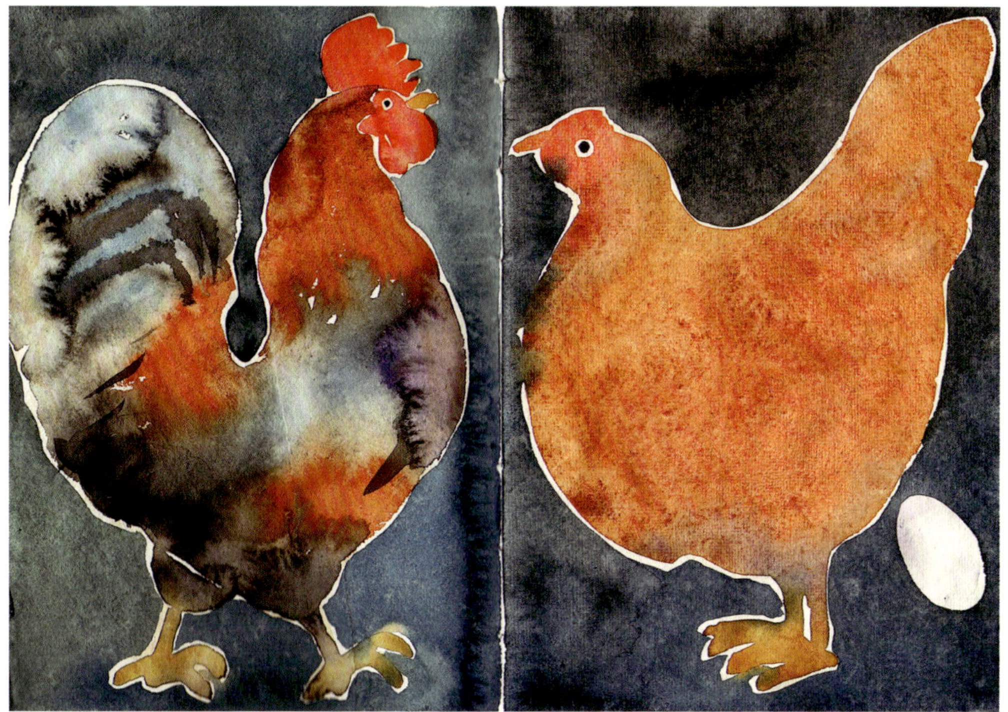

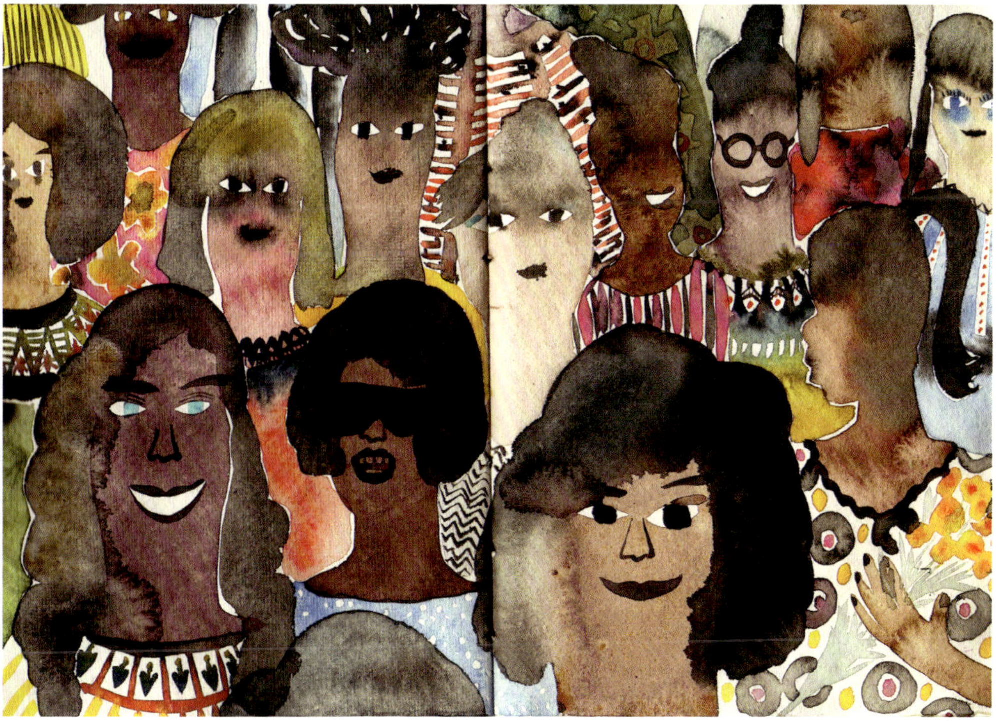

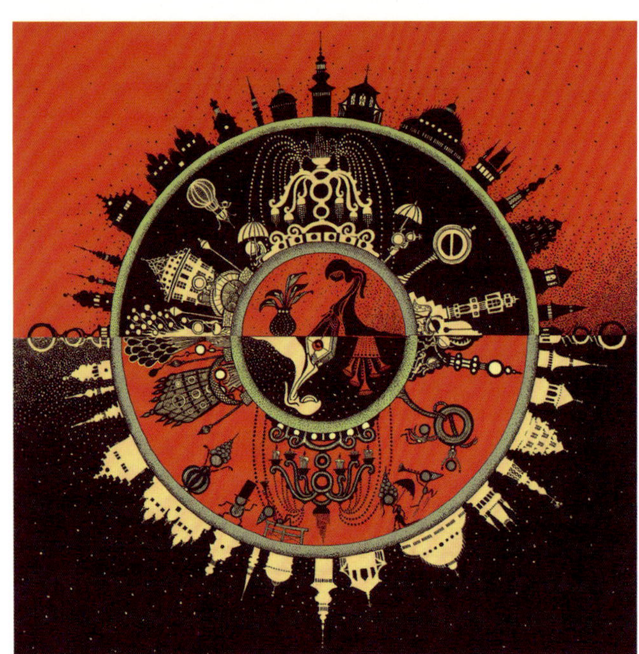
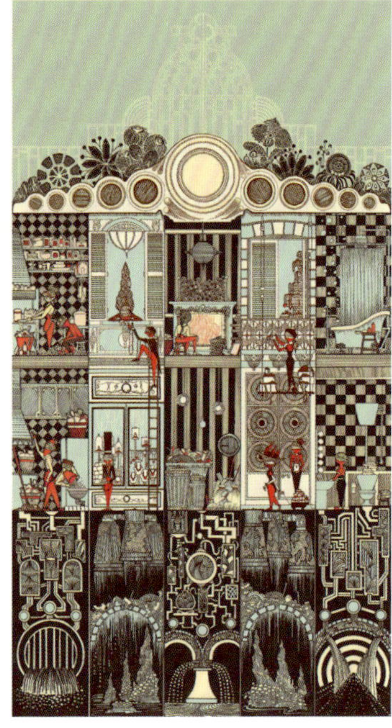
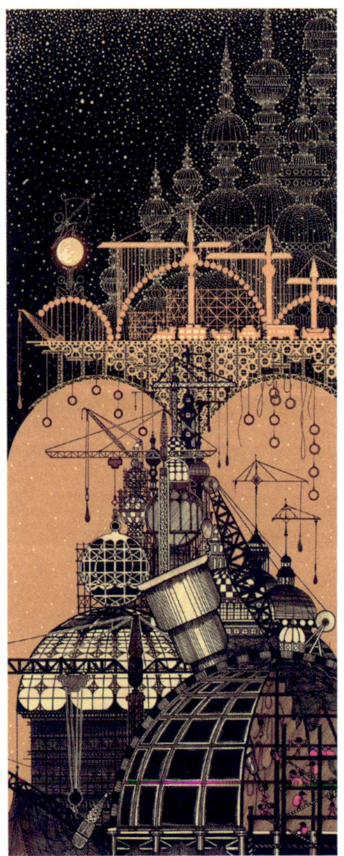
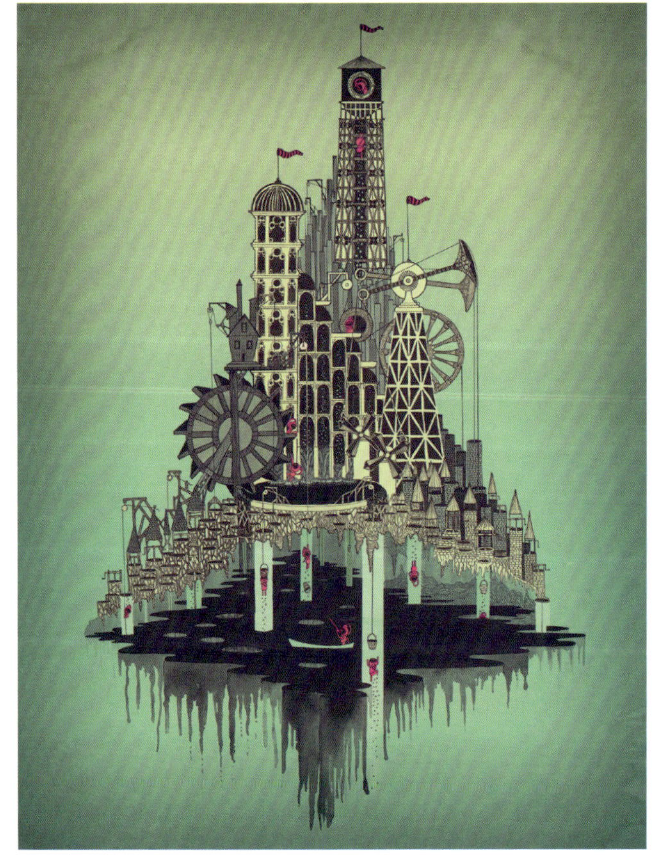

MERIT *Liisa Aaltio*

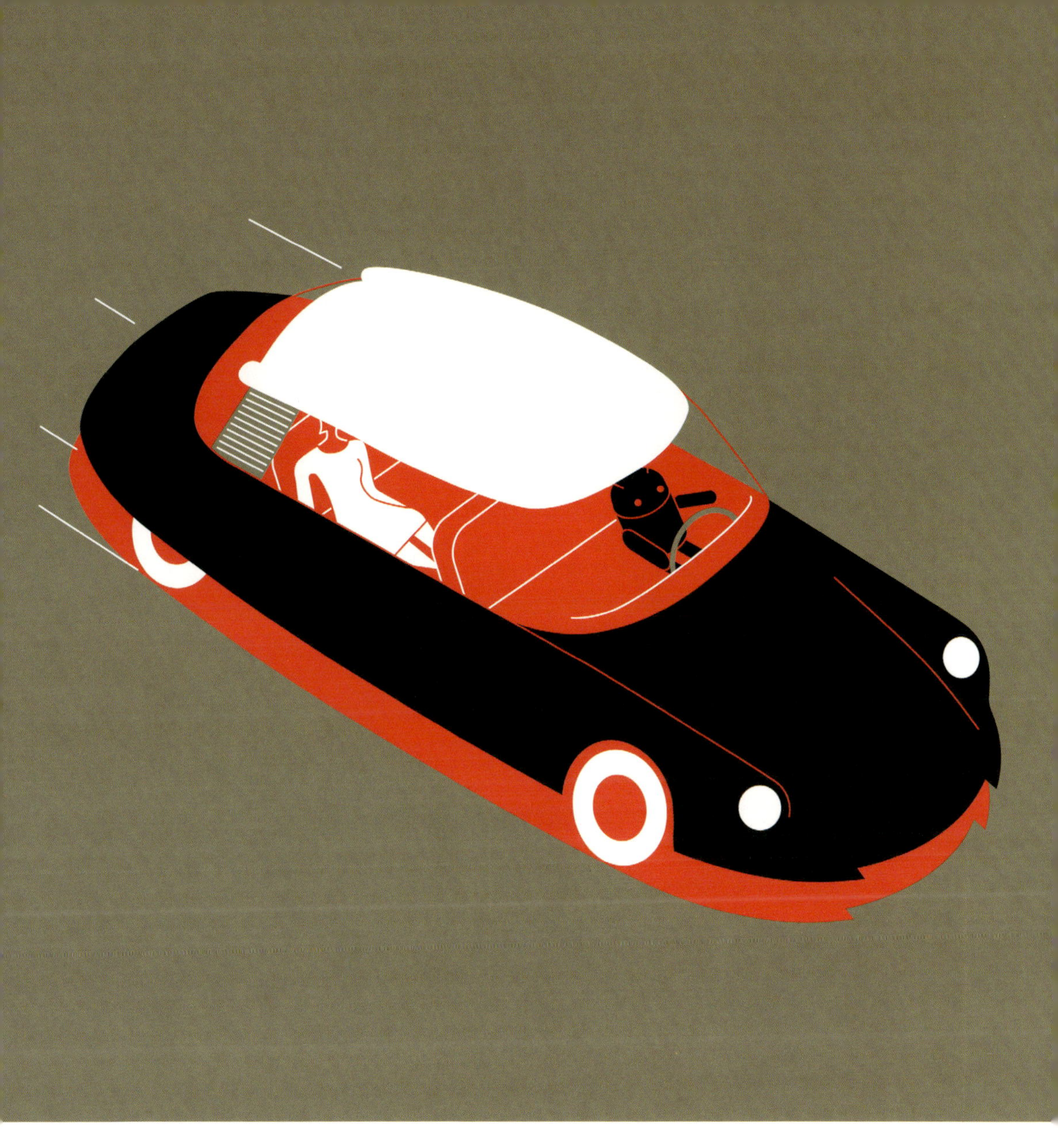



MERIT *Otto Steininger*

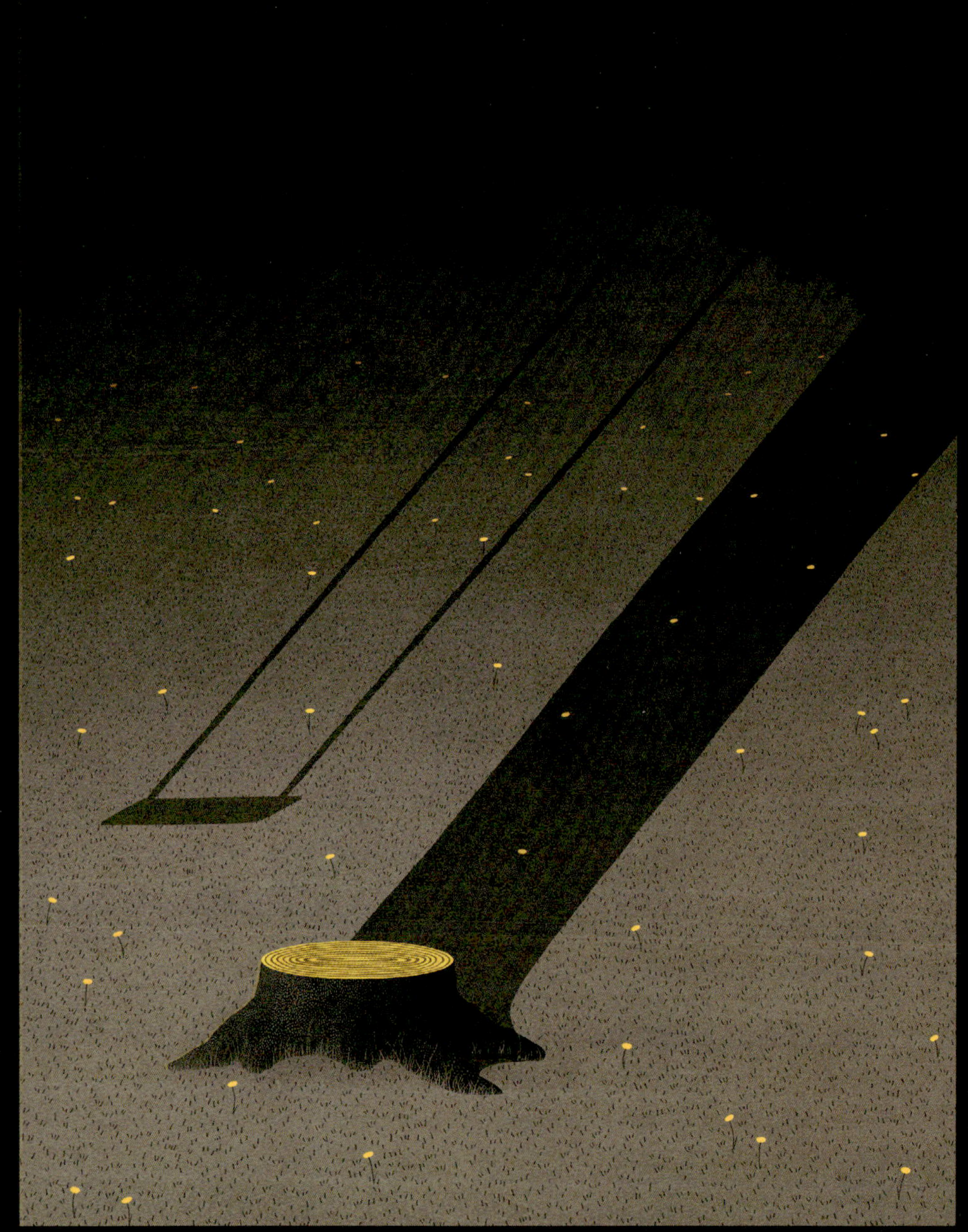

MERIT *Michael Glenwood Gibbs*

**PICTURE BOOK SHOW**

218    BOOK COVERS

220    BOOKS PUBLISHED

248    BOOKS UNPUBLISHED

257    ILLUSTRATION PUBLISHED

264    ILLUSTRATION UNPUBLISHED

278    EDUCATIONAL MATERIALS

280    EDITORIAL

283    MISCELLANEOUS

288    YOUNG ADULT

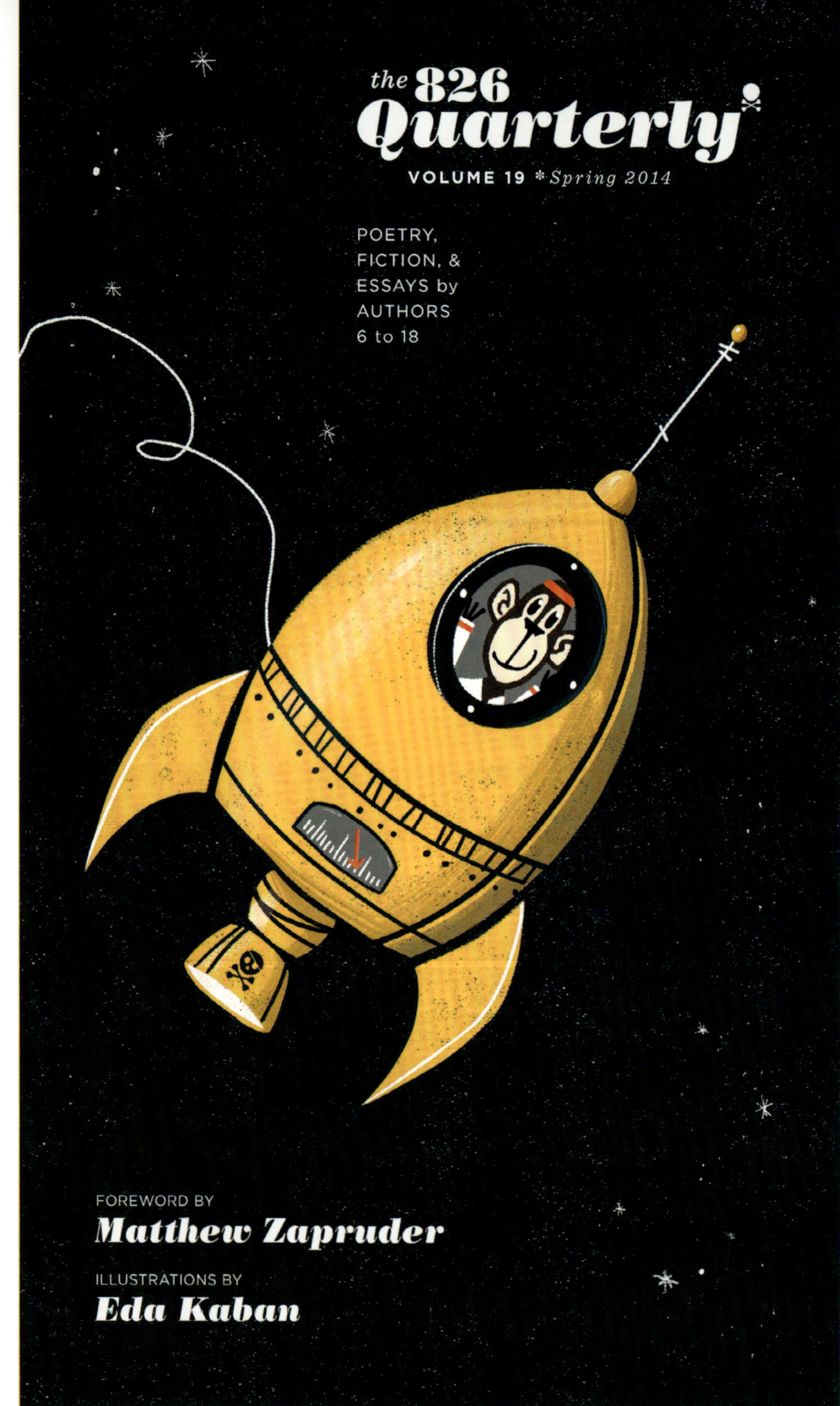




MERIT *Eda Kaban*

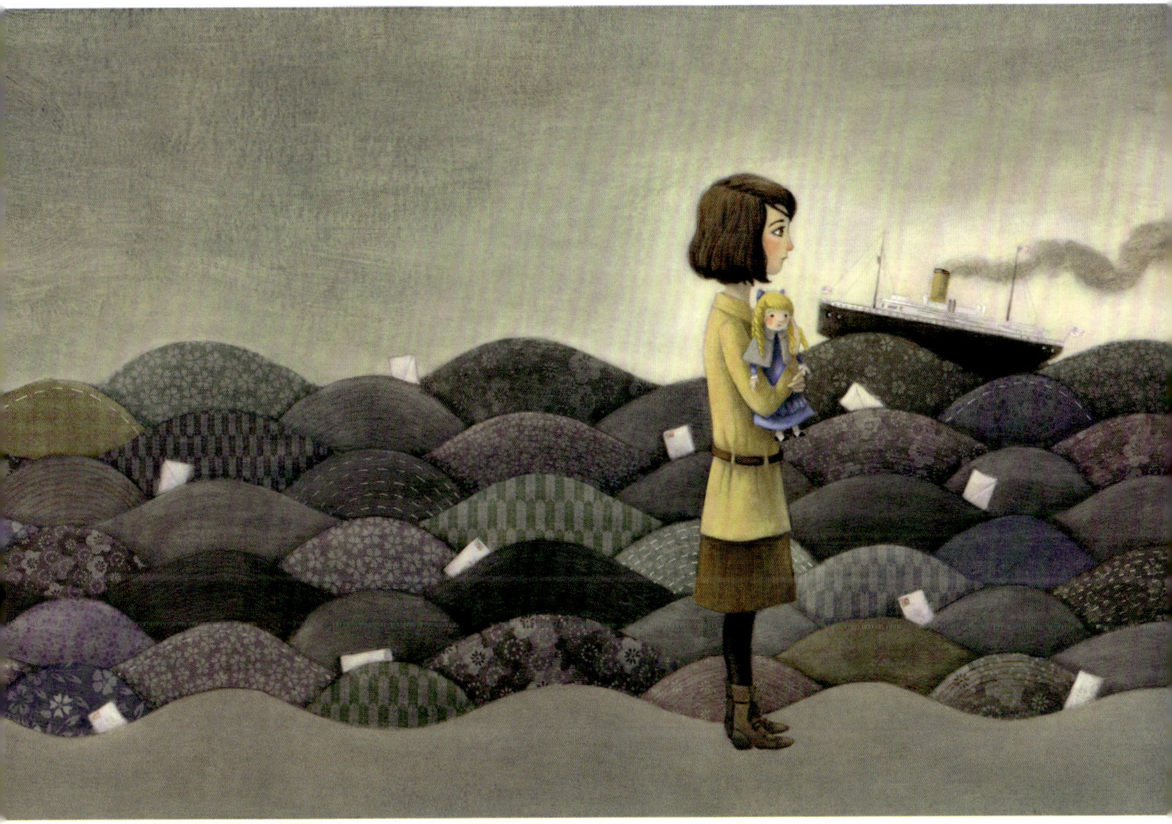

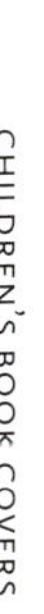

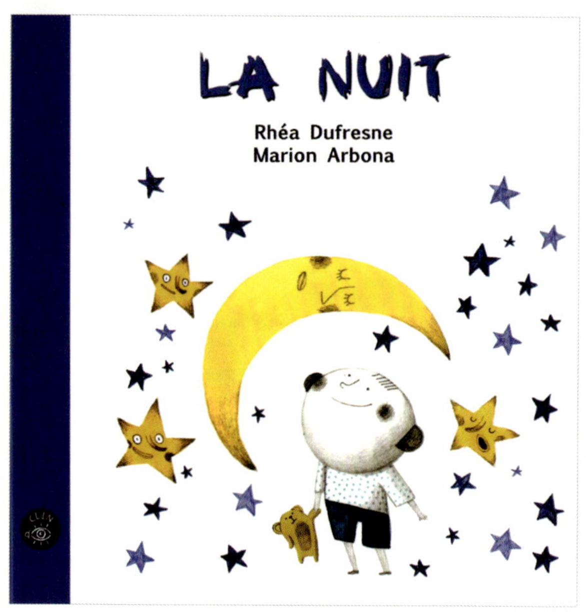


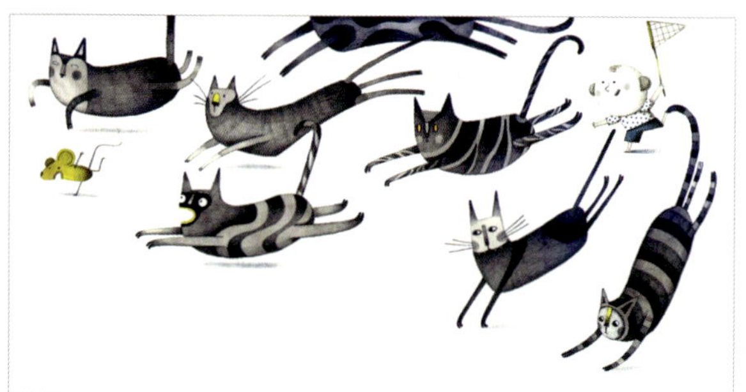

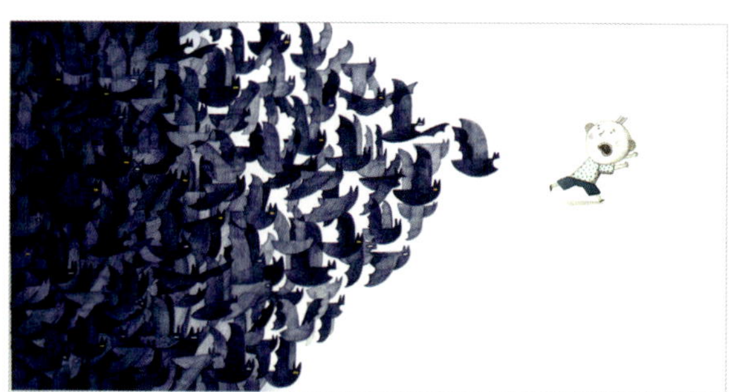

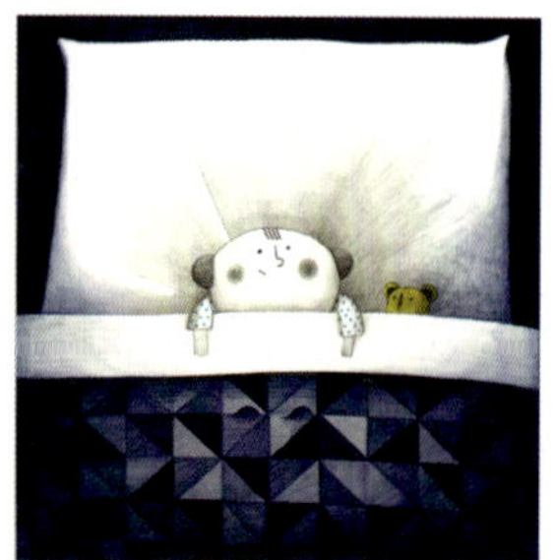

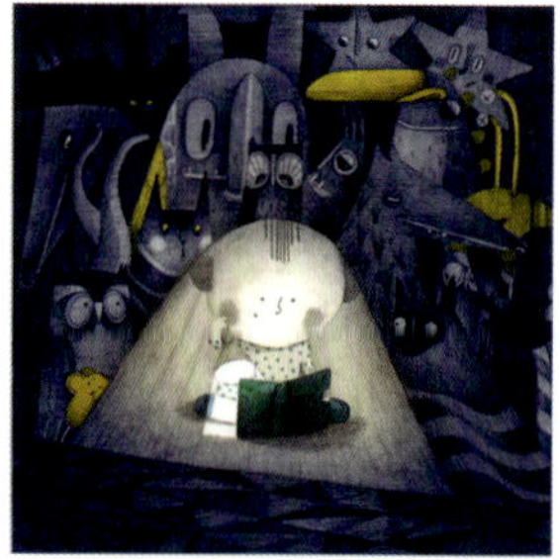

BRONZE *Marion Arbona*

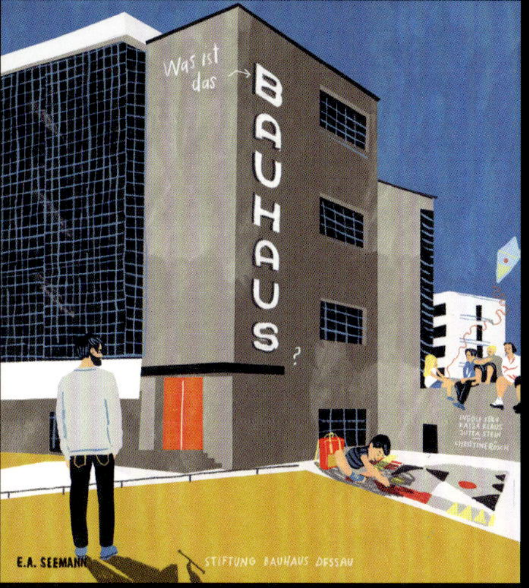

Was ist das BAUHAUS?
E.A. SEEMANN
STIFTUNG BAUHAUS DESSAU


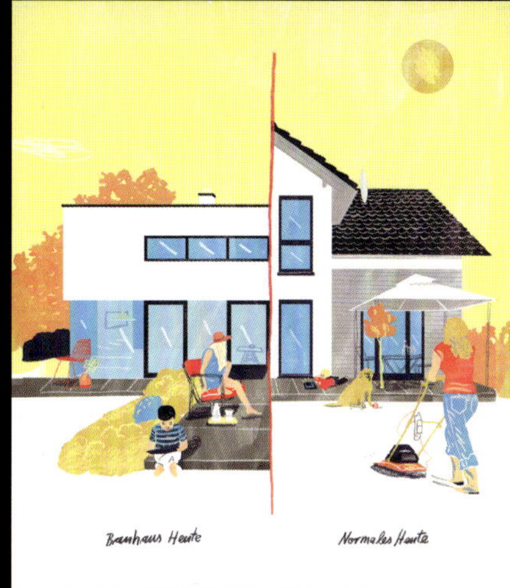

Bauhaus Heute
Normales Heute


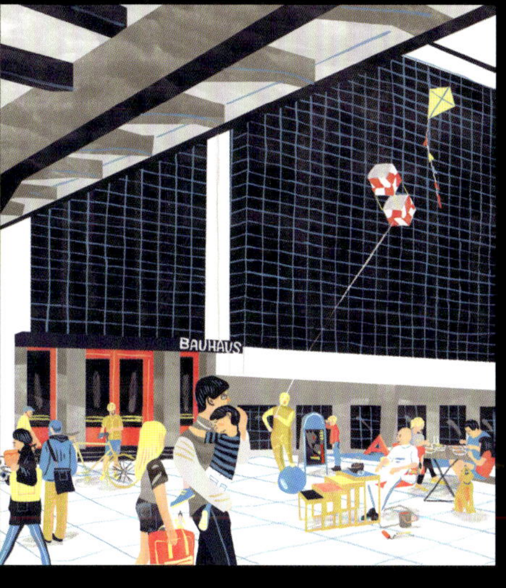

BAUHAUS


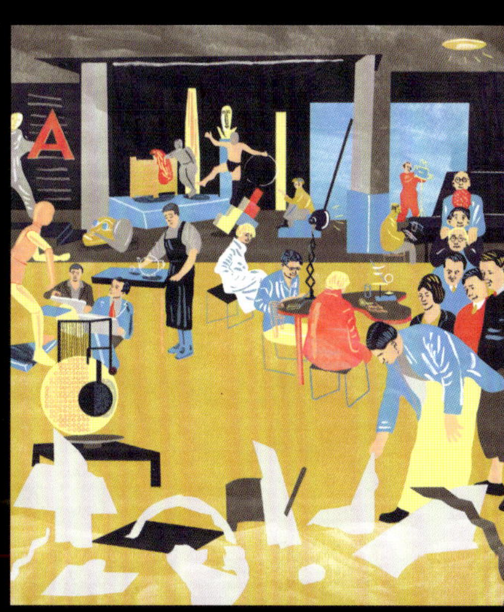

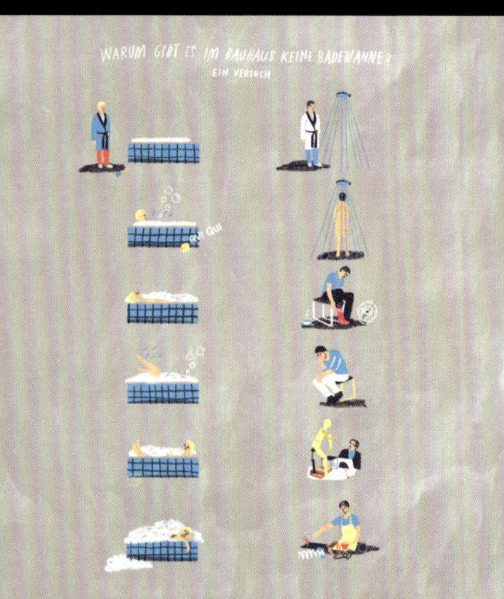

WARUM GIBT ES IM BAUHAUS KEINE BADEWANNE?
EIN VERSUCH


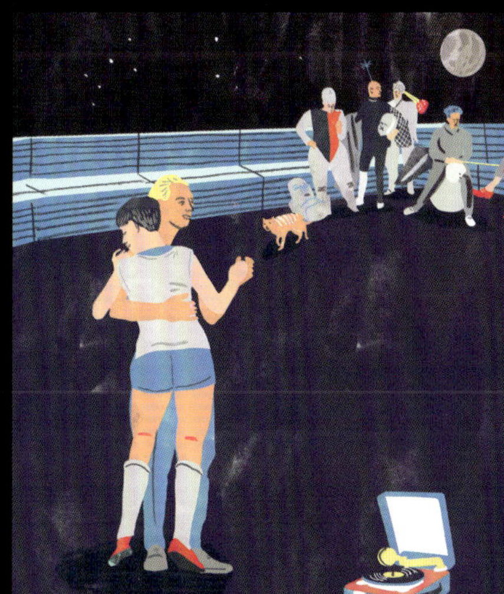

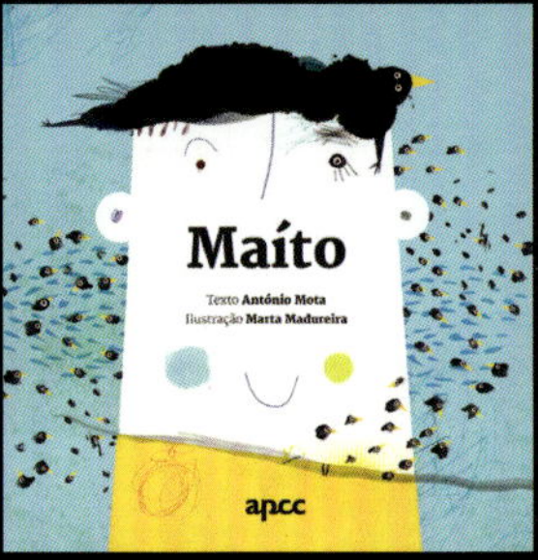


Em cima da tília estavam os seus pais, que não paravam de lhes
dizer, saltitando de ramo em ramo:
— Força, filhas! Não tenham medo! É tão perigoso ficarem aí.
E os melros respondiam:
— Eu não quero abandonar o ninho. Estou muito bem aqui!
— Eu não sei se vou conseguir!
— É tão difícil esta vida!
É claro que se entendiam em melrês, que é a língua assobiada que
só os melros sabem usar.
Um rapaz que se chamava Francisco, e tinha num pombal trinta
e dois pombos-correios, achou que seria boa ideia apanhá-los.
— Deixa os melros em paz, Francisco. Deixa-os aprender o voar —
aconselhou o professor Ramiro.
Nesse dia o Francisco e os colegas prestaram pouca atenção às aulas,
estavam mais interessados em ver os melrinhos a voar.
Quando as aulas terminaram, os melros tinham desaparecido.
— Voaram, voaram há bocadinho, eu vi, eu vi! — disse o Francisco,
e toda a gente acreditou. Até o professor.

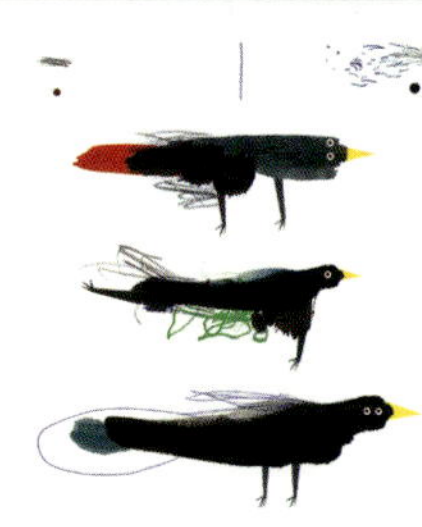

**3.**

Todas as coisas mudam.
A escola da Pedrinha do Sol fechou há muitos anos, o professor
Ramiro reformou-se e agora os alunos, que se chamam Tiago,
Maria e Carolina, no tempo de aulas entram numa carrinha que
os leva para o Centro Escolar Número Cento e Vinte e Sete, que fica
longe. Vão de manhã cedo e regressam ao fim da tarde.
Como passam junto da escola, numa grande correria, ainda não
descobriram que o canteiro da antiga escola se transformou num
silvado, o recreio numa mata, e as três roseiras já não existem.
Também não sabem que há muitos, muitos anos, num dia quente
de Maio quando os alunos entraram no recreio da escola da Pedrinha
do Sol, viram que já lá havia três melros pequeninos, aflitos por não
saberem voar.

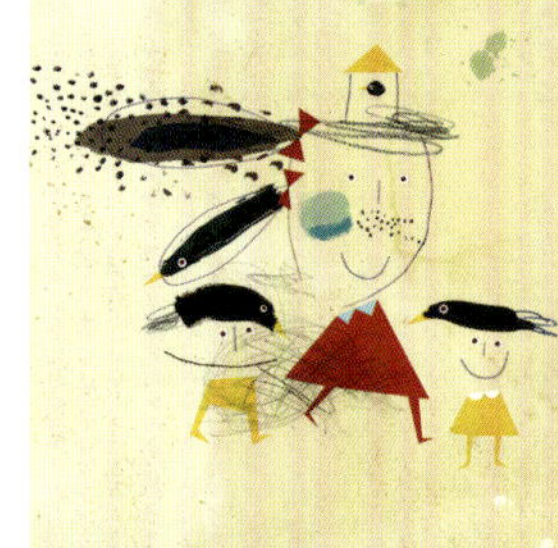

**5.**

No terceiro manhã restava um melro muito trôpego, muito triste,
quase mudo. Estava encostado ao muro e quase não tinha forças
para fechar o bico.
— O que teria acontecido ao outro melrinho? — perguntou a Beatriz,
muito triste.
Foi o Tiago que deu a resposta. Disse que o outro melrito tinha
marchado para dentro da barriga da Princesa. A Princesa era uma
gata branca, muito comprida e muito independente, implacável
caçadora de ratos e pássaros.

— Temos de salvar o último melro. Quem me quer ajudar? —
perguntou a Beatriz.
Quando o professor Ramiro apareceu, encontrou os alunos muito
silenciosos, amontoados à volta de uma gaiola que o Francisco tinha
ido buscar a sua casa. Foi e veio numa grande corrida. Lá dentro,
com o bico aberto, muito aflito, muito fraquinho, estava o melro.
E o Francisco dava-lhe água com uma palhinha.
— Pode ser que ele aprenda a voar — disse o professor Ramiro. O
Francisco levou a gaiola para dentro da escola, pousou-a em cima
de um armário e reparou que o melro quase não se mexia.

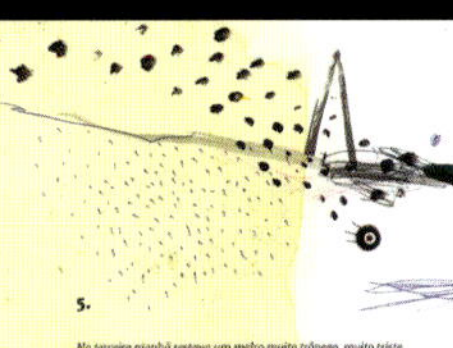

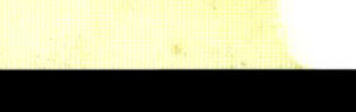

**7.**

No dia seguinte o melro voltou à escola a meio da manhã e pôs-se
a bicar no vidro de uma janela.
— Entra, Maíto! — disse o Francisco.
— Entra! — pediu a Beatriz.
— Entra! Entra! — pediram todos.
Mas o melro não quis entrar. Levantou voo, e foi pousar num ramo
da tília.
Mas não estava só.
Pousados em todos os ramos da tília, em todos os ramos do pinheiro,
em cima do telhado e nos fios do telefone, havia centenas e centenas
de melros.
E todos assobiavam, muito afinados.

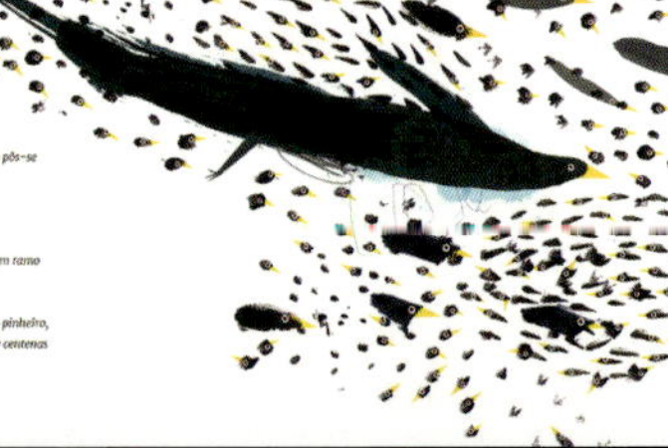

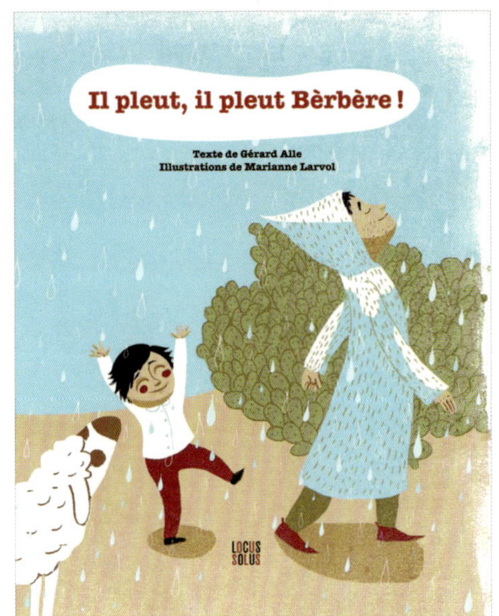

Il pleut, il pleut Bèrbère !
Texte de Gérard Alle
Illustrations de Marianne Larvol
LOCUS SOLUS


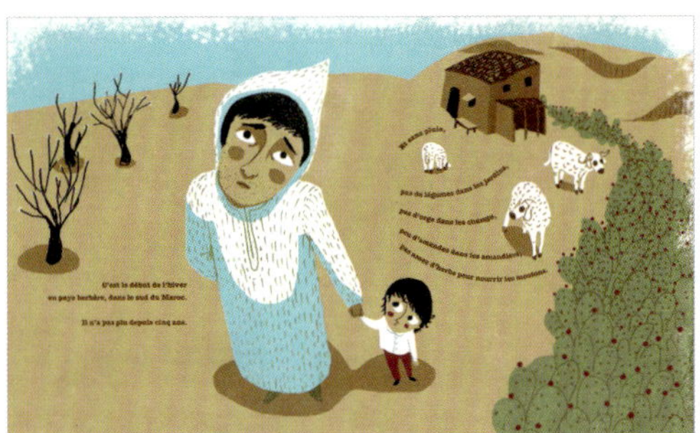

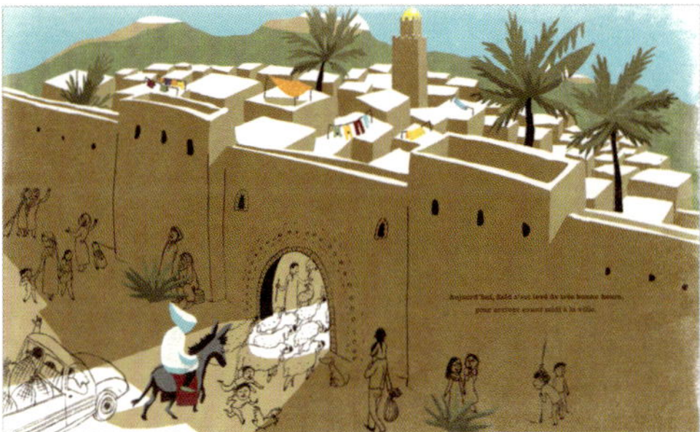

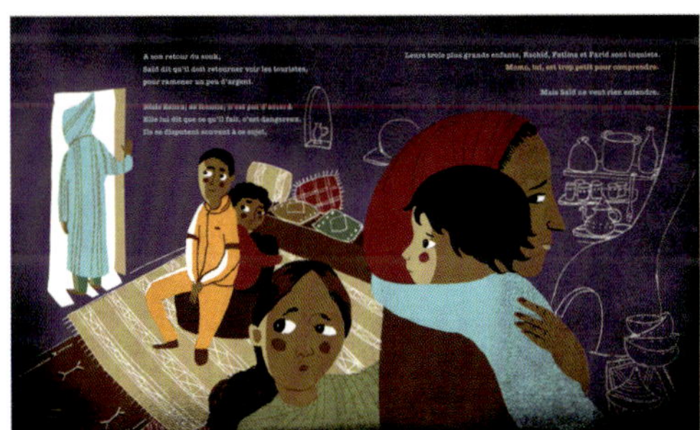

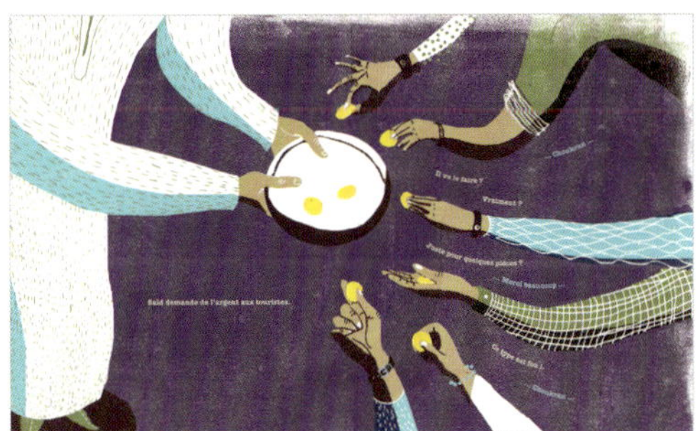

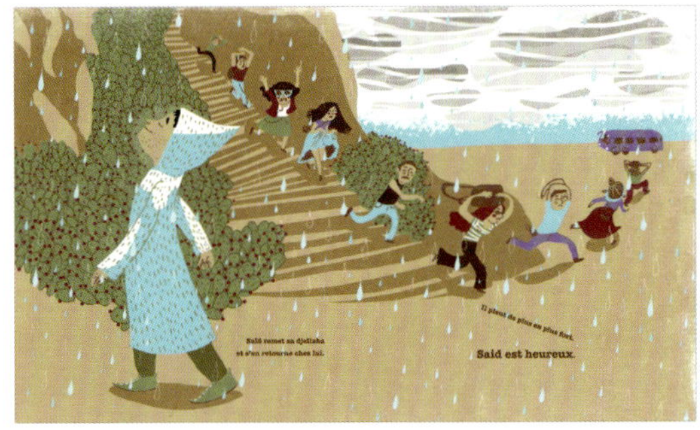

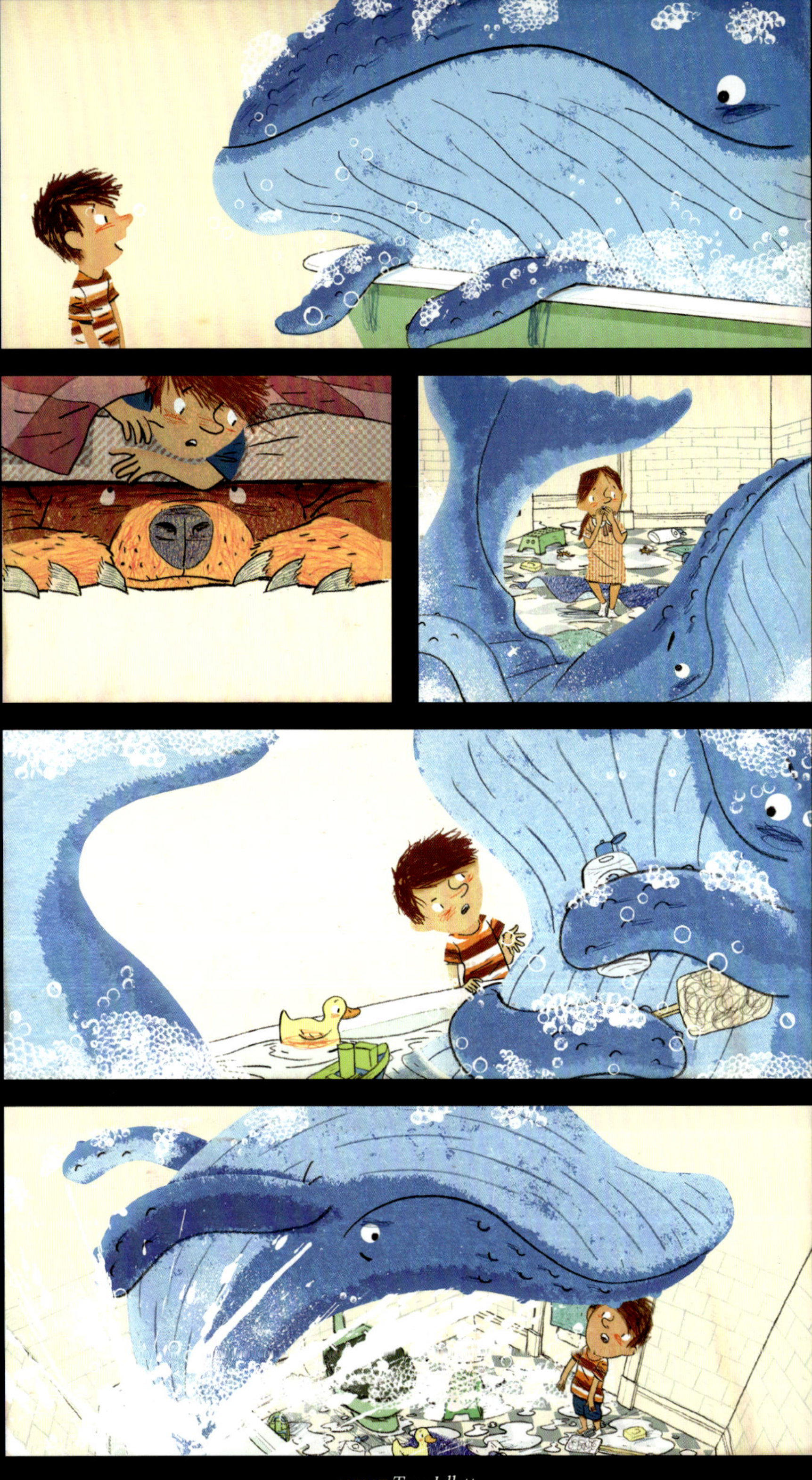

MERIT *Tom Jellett*

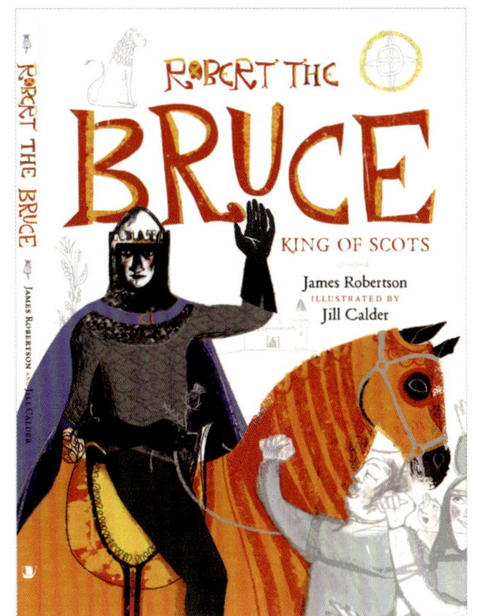

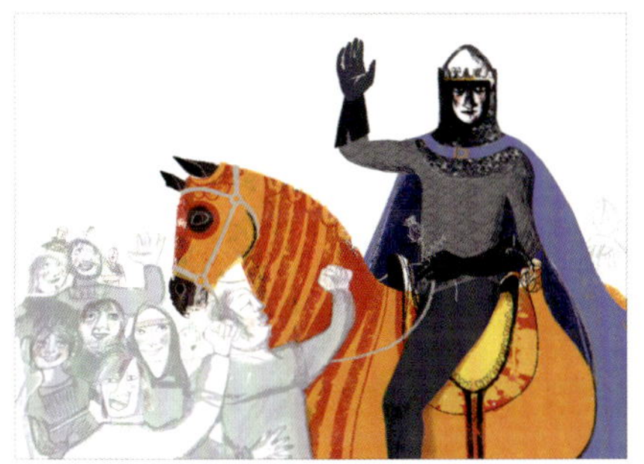

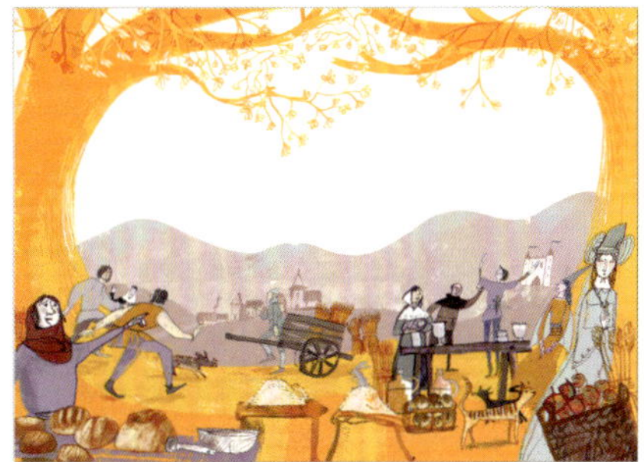

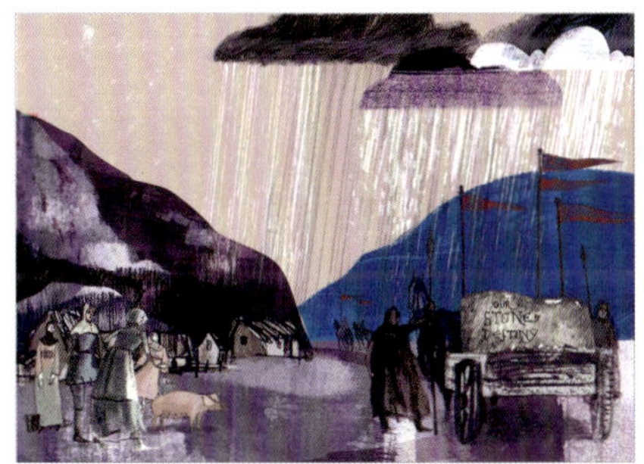

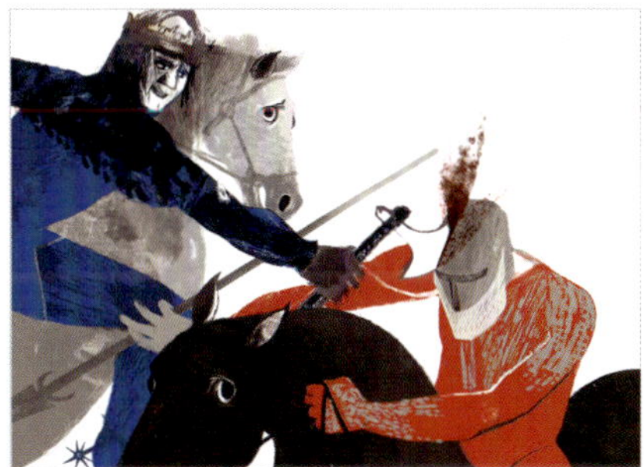

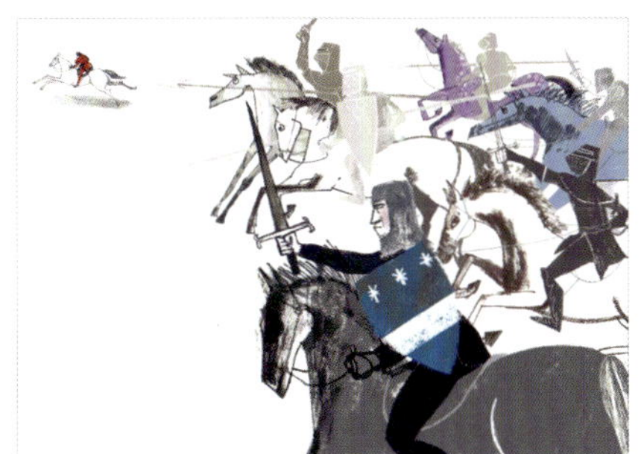

MERIT *Jill Calder*

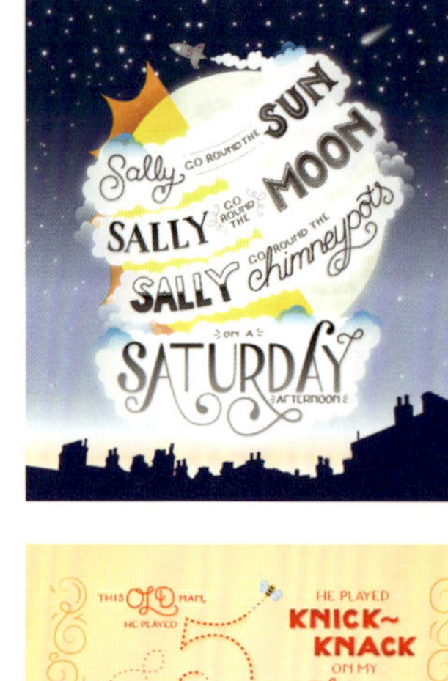
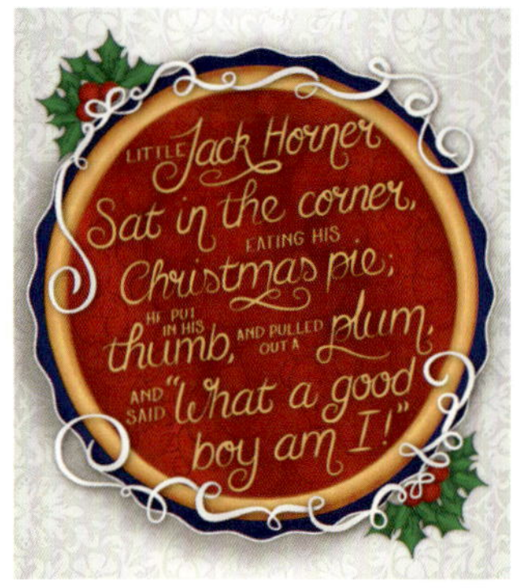
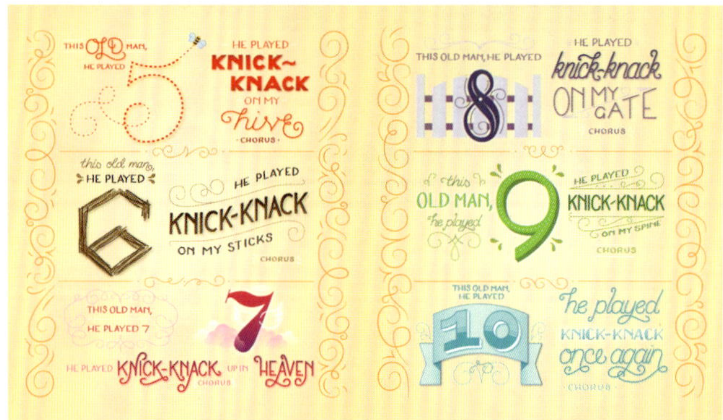
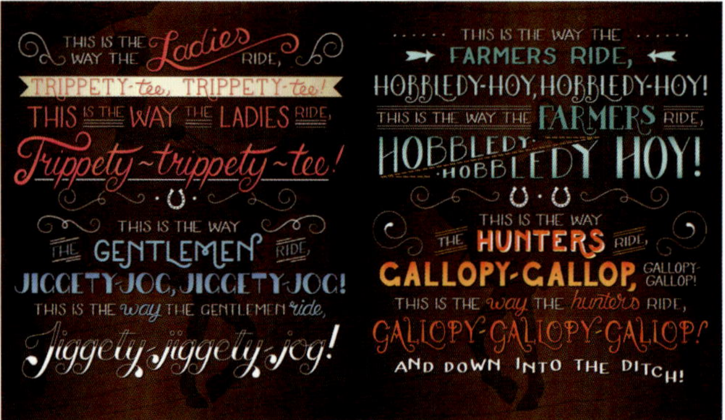
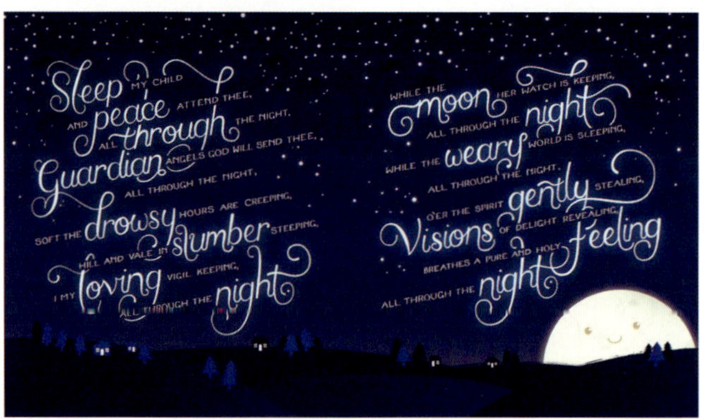

(L) MERIT *Jessica Matthews*    (R) MERIT *Jamie Hogan*

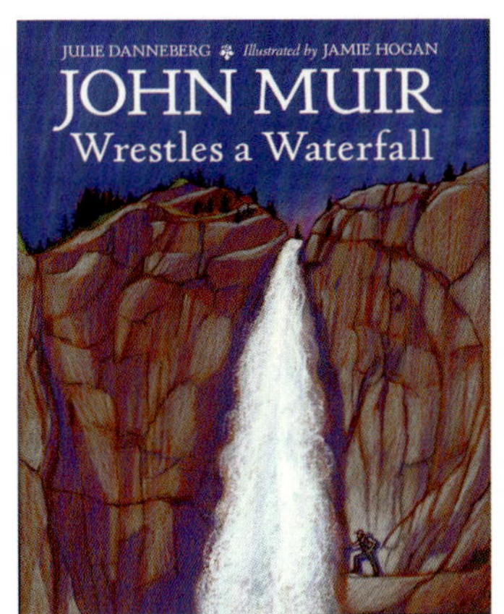

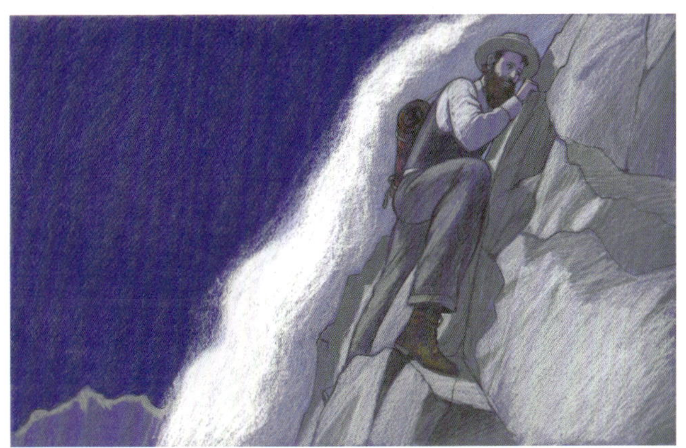

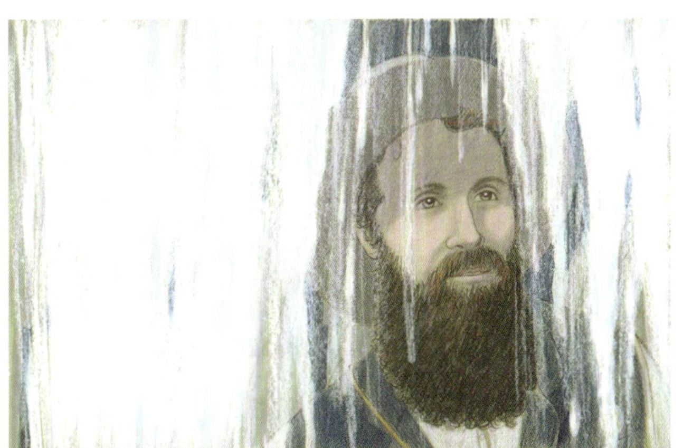

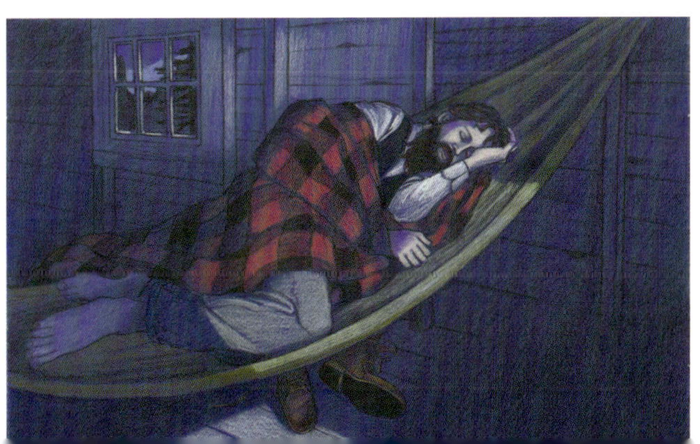

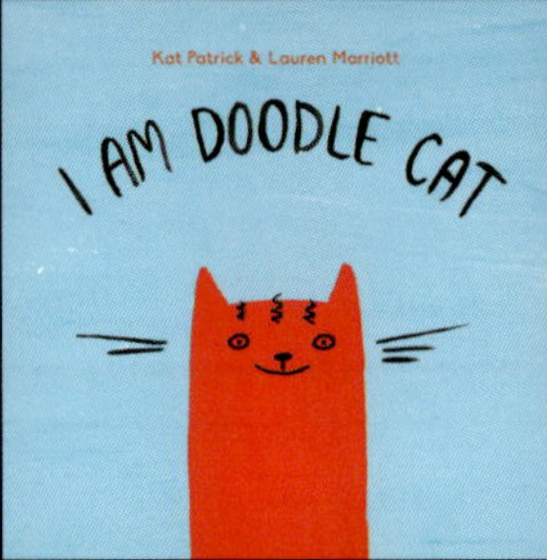


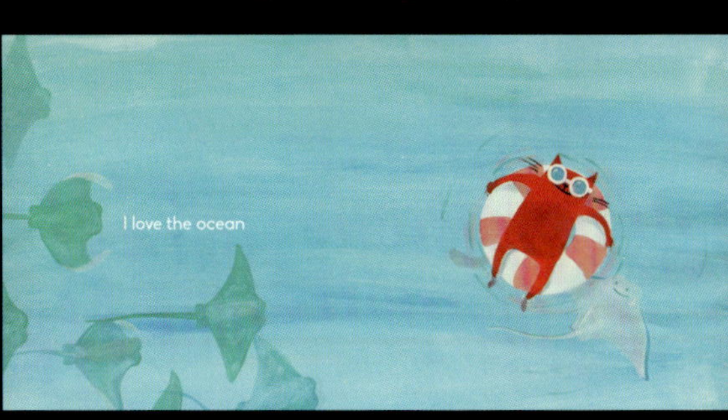


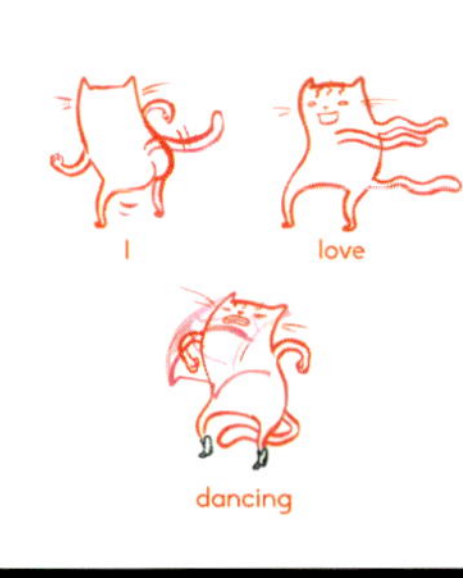


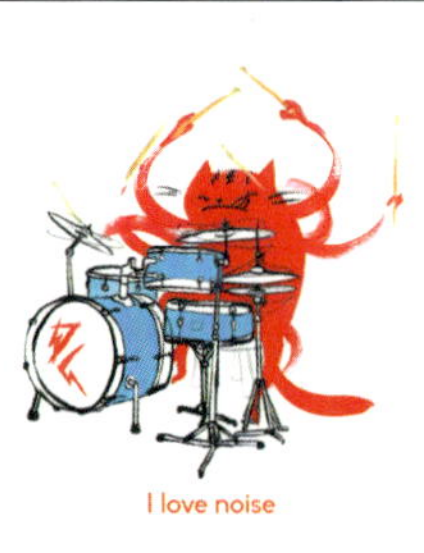


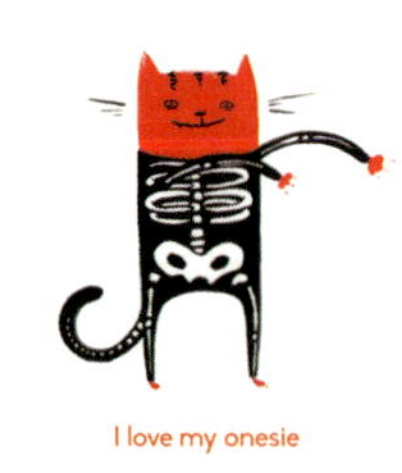


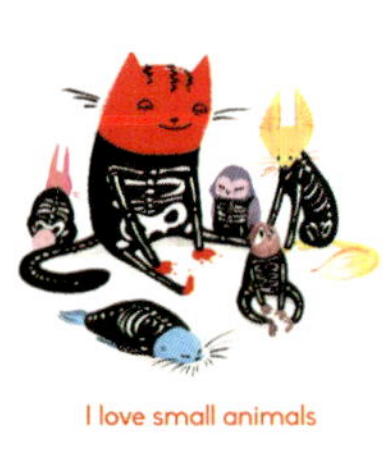


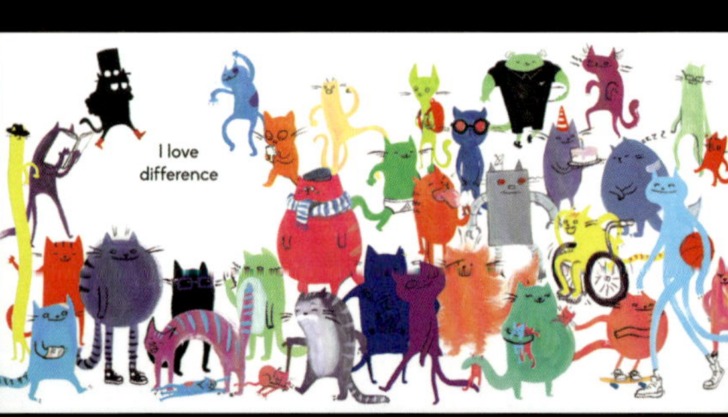


MERIT *Lauren Marriott*

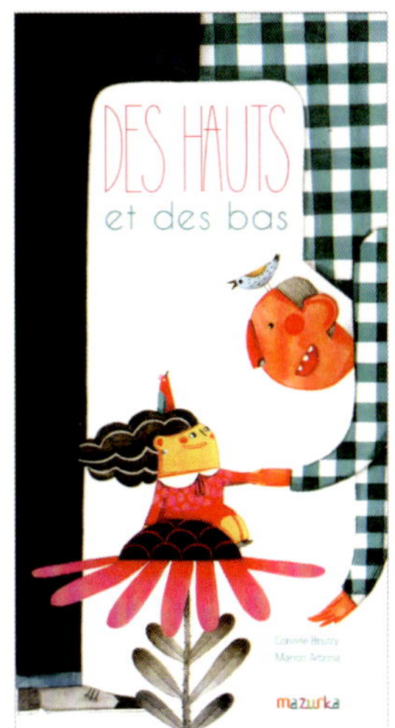

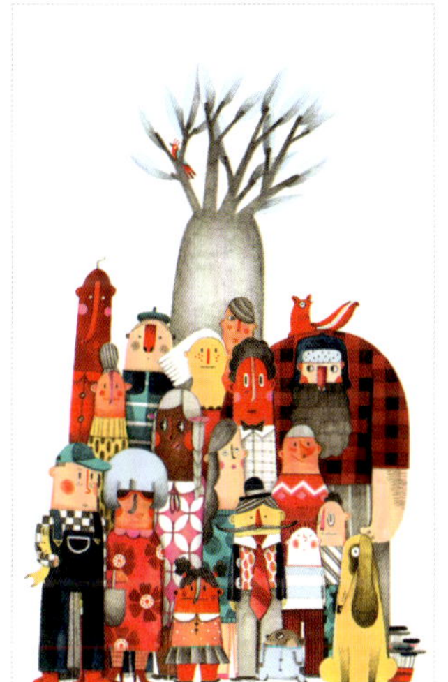

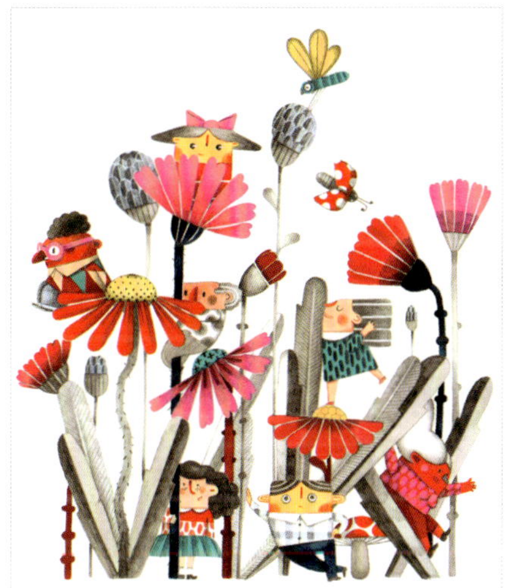

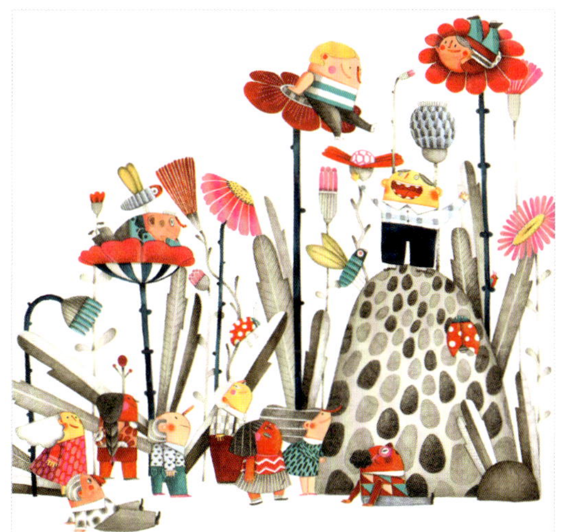

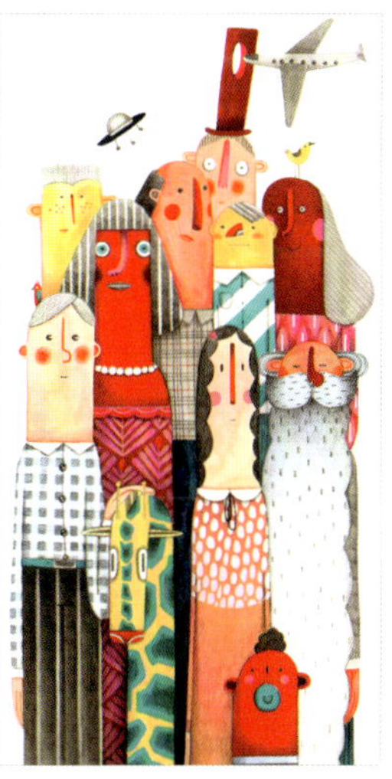

MERIT *Marion Arbona*

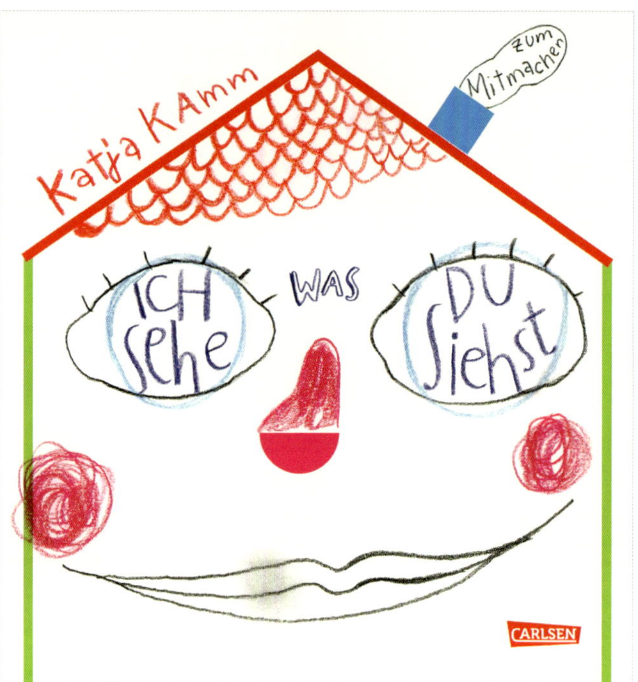


Katja Kamm
zum Mitmachen
ICH WAS DU
Sehe Siehst
CARLSEN


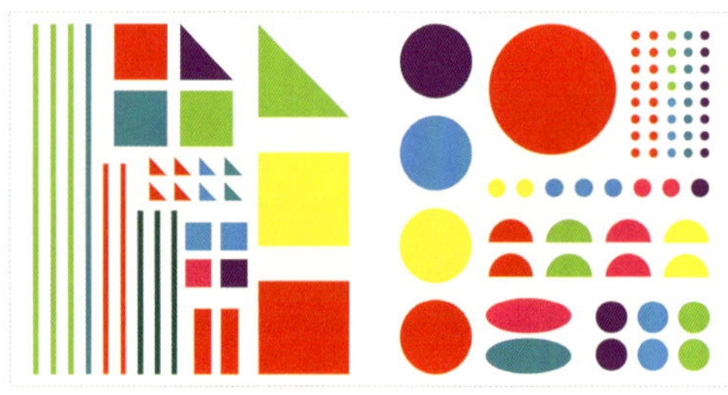

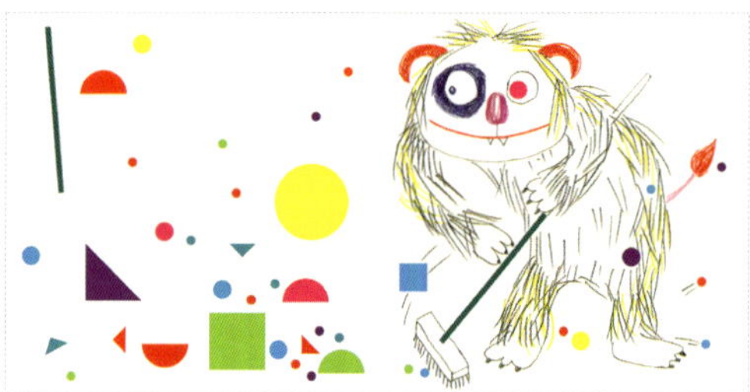

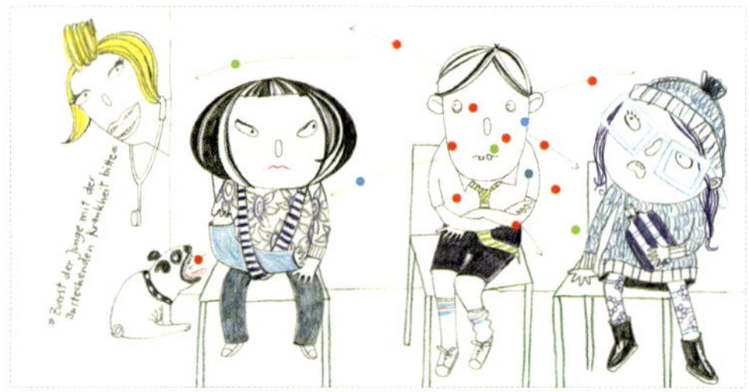

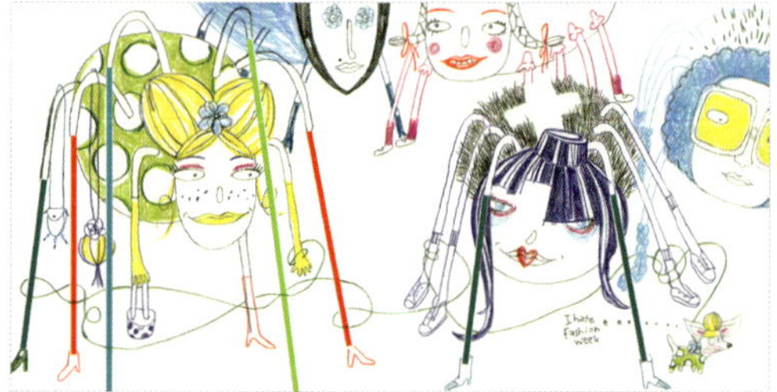

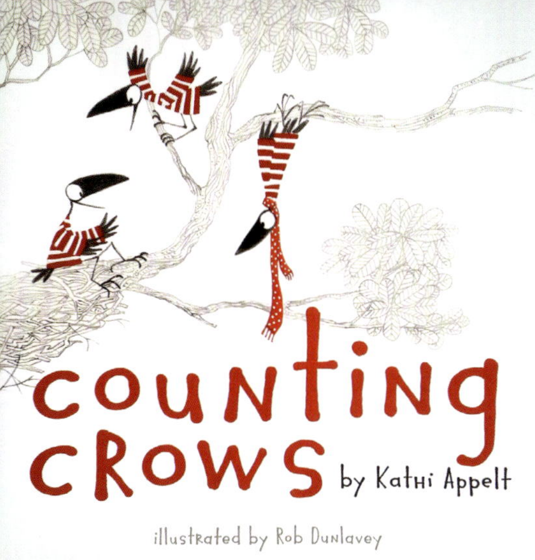

# counting crows

## CROWS

by Kathi Appelt

illustrated by Rob Dunlavey

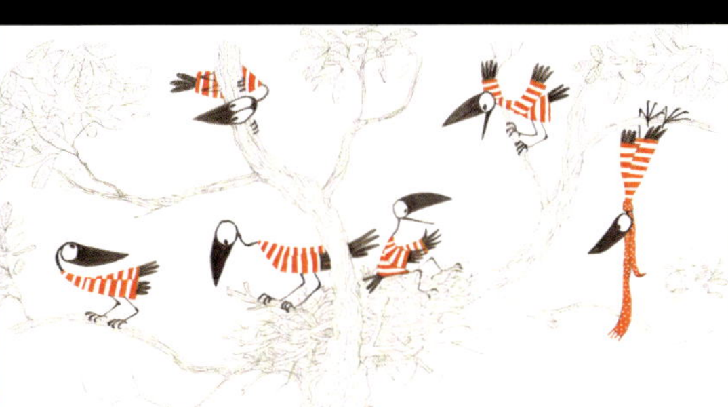

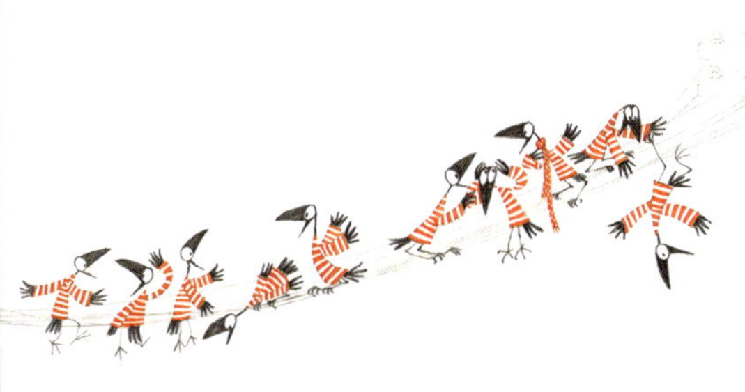

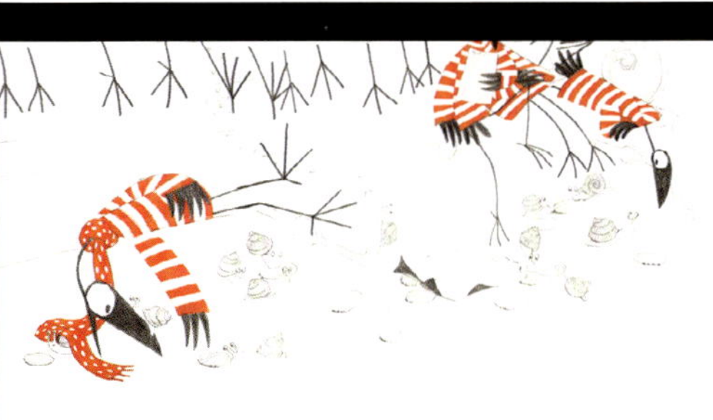

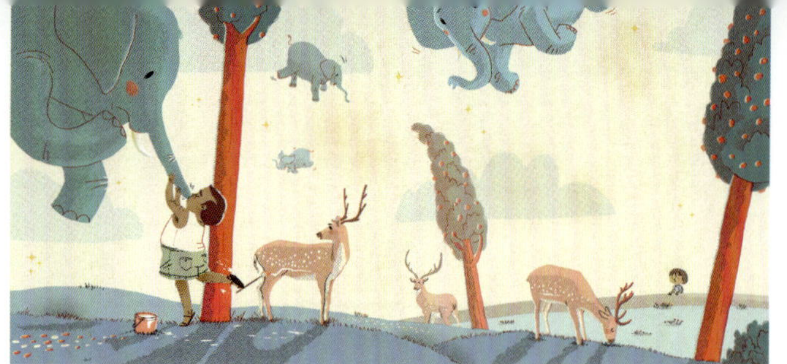

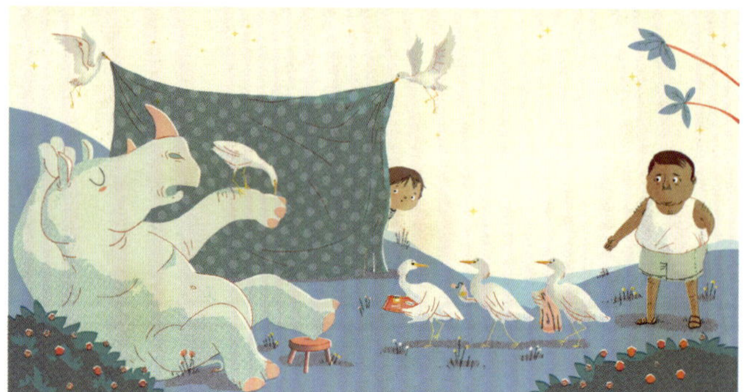

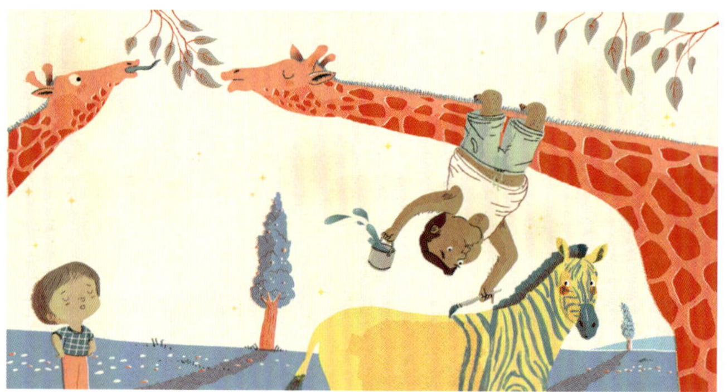

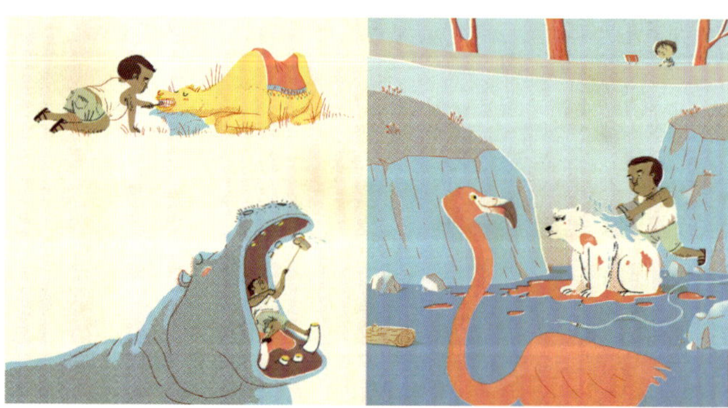

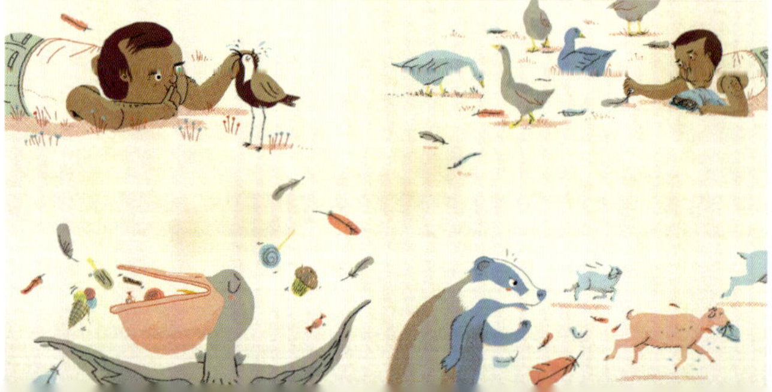

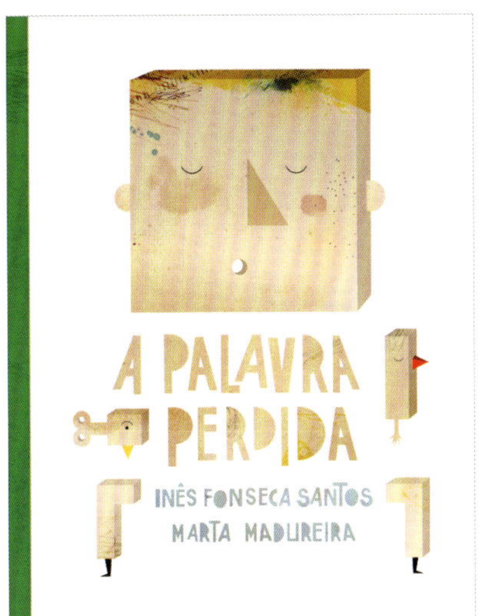


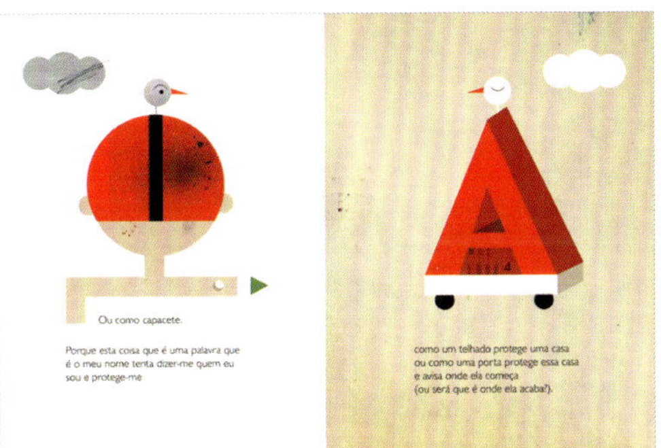


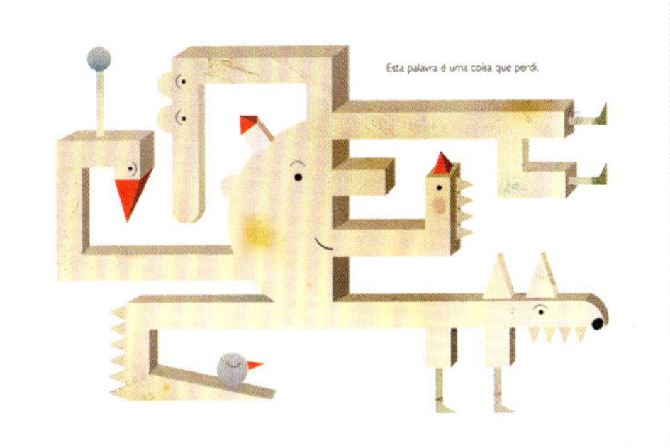


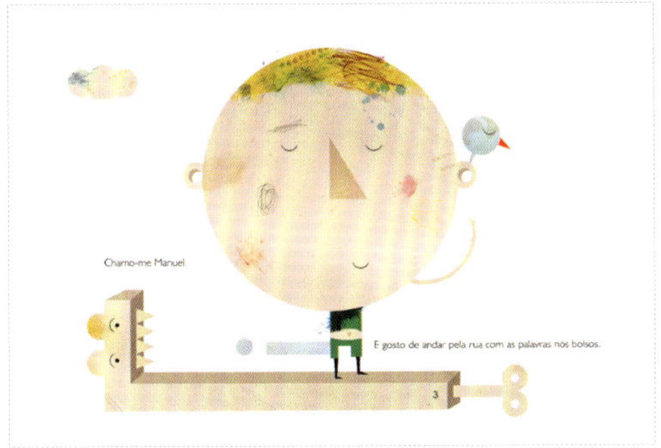


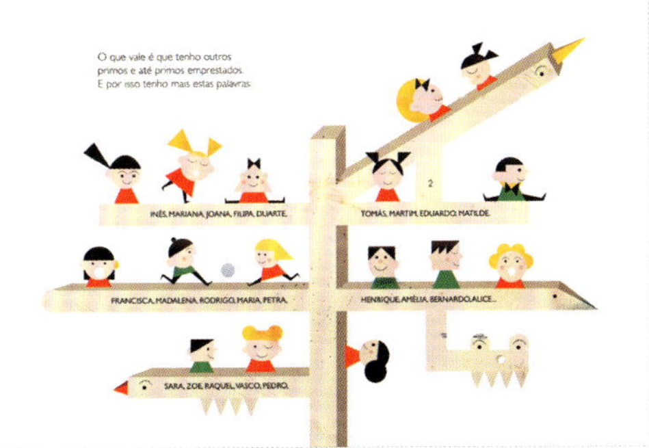


(L) MERIT *Shahar Kober*    (R) MERIT *Marta Madureira*

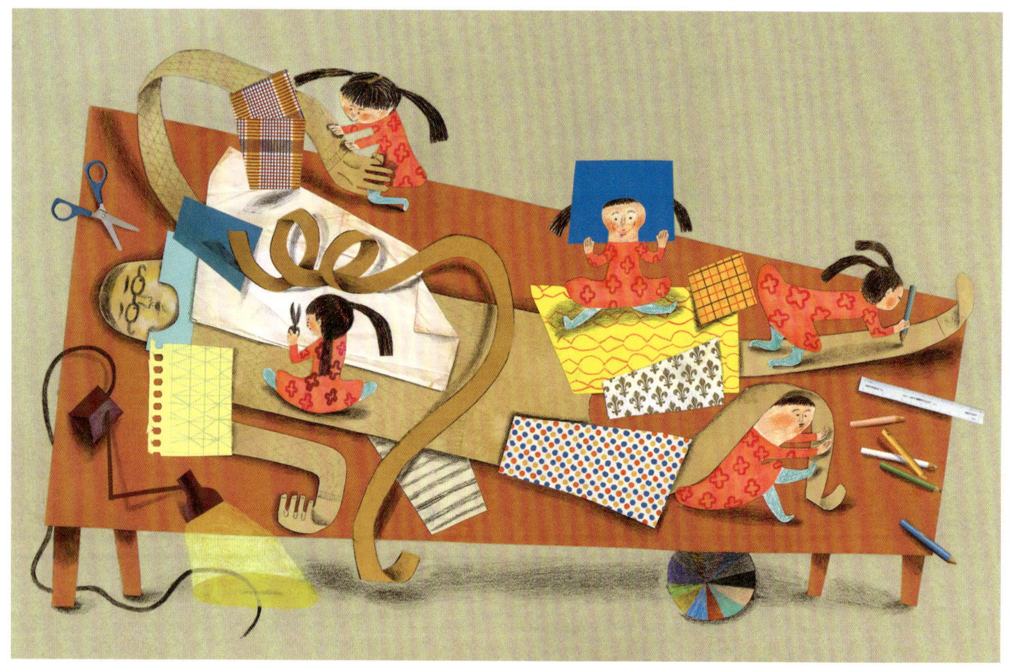

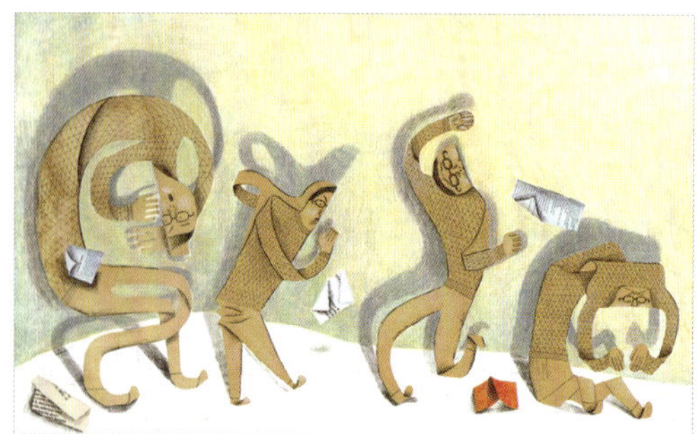

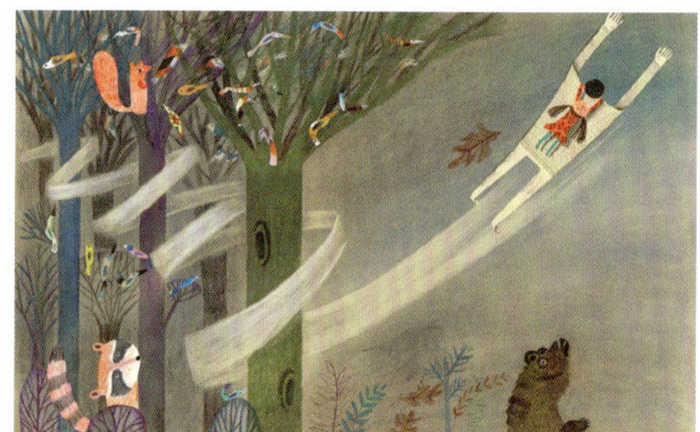

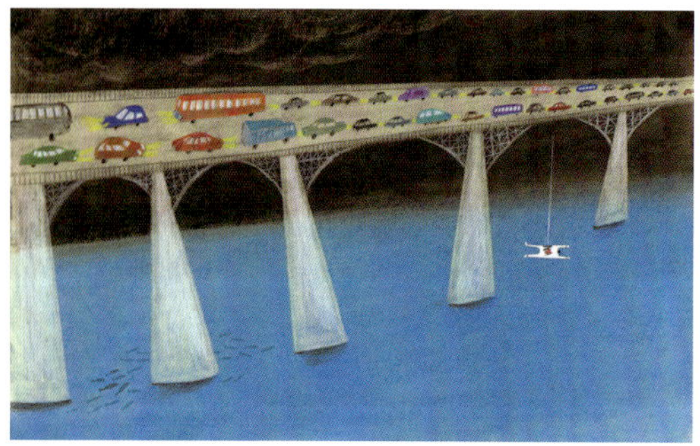

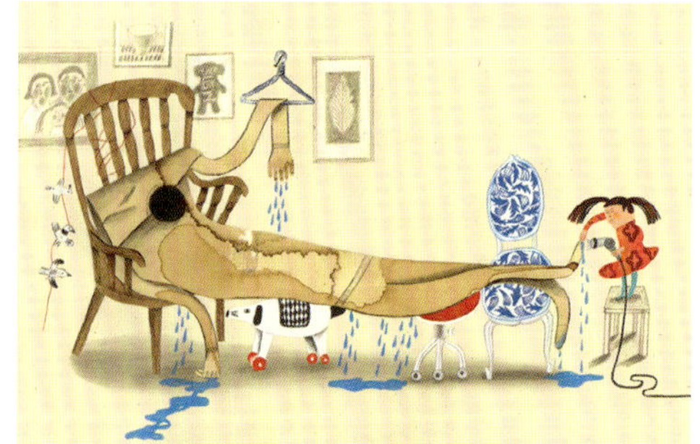

MERIT *Gee Eun Lee*

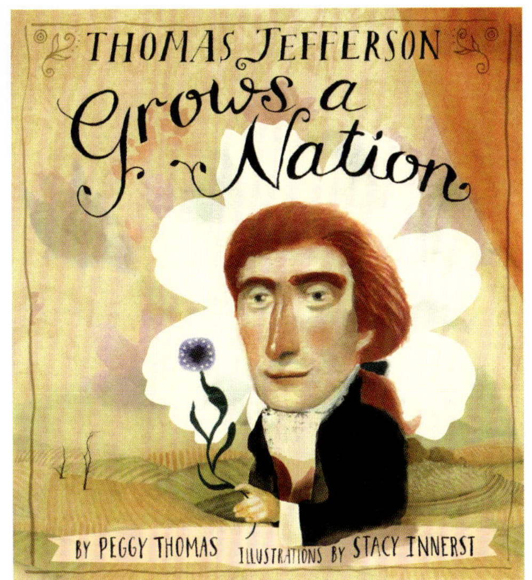


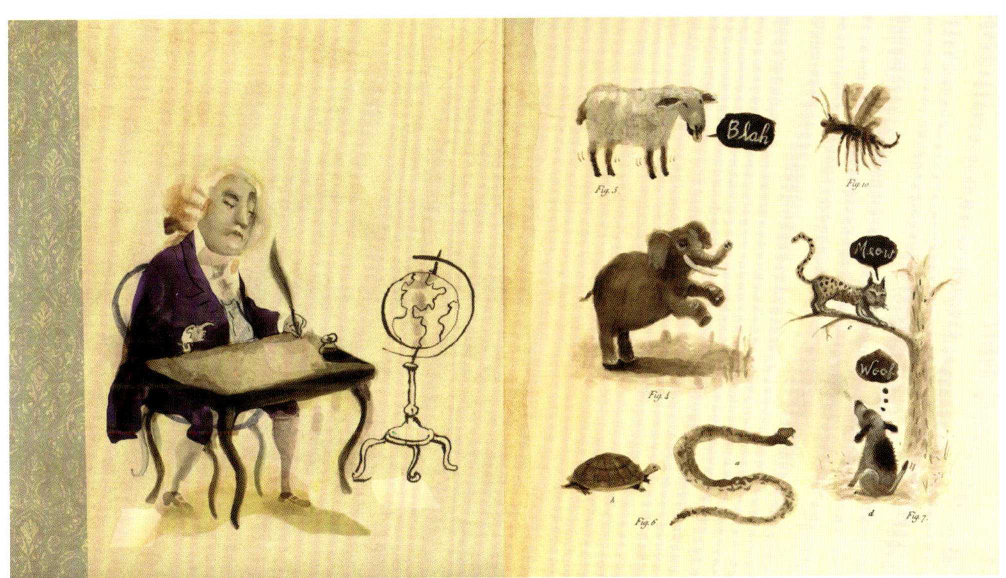


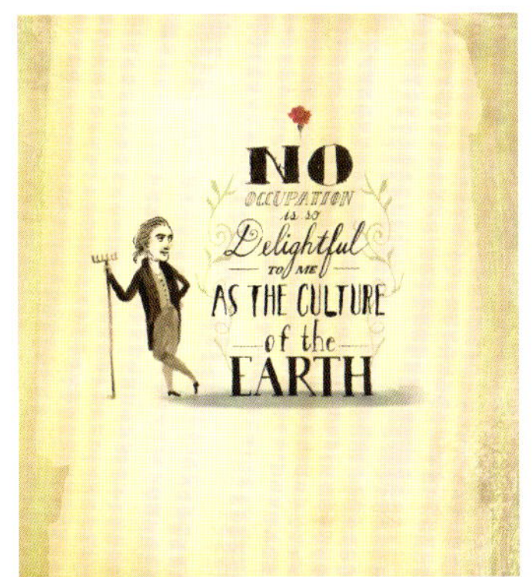


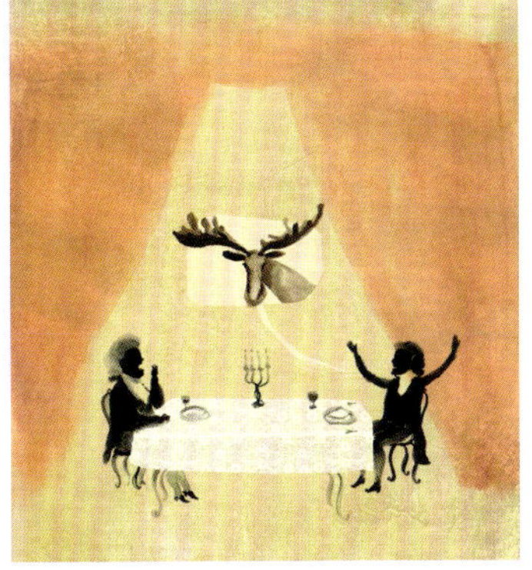

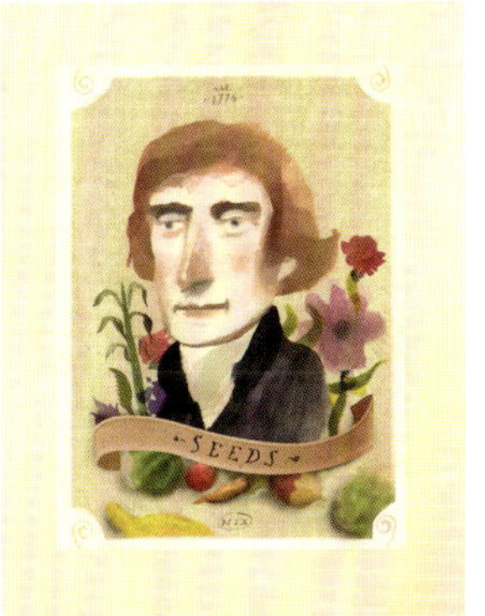


MERIT *Stacy Innerst*

235

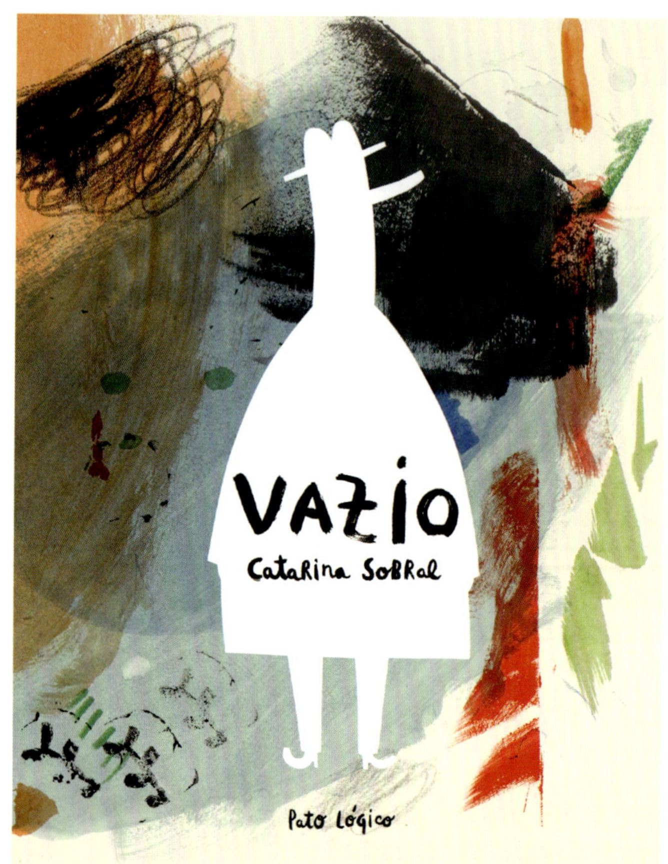


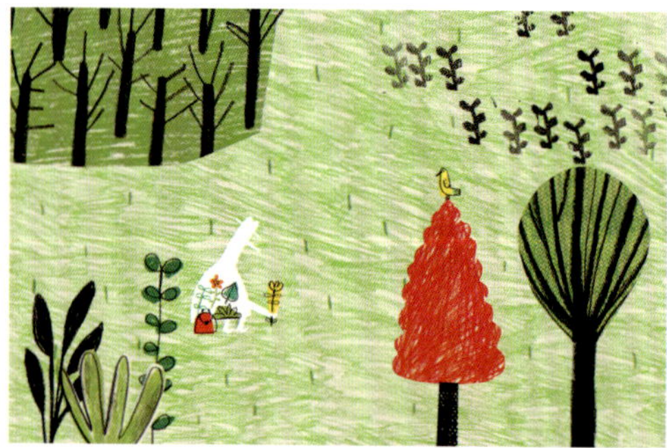

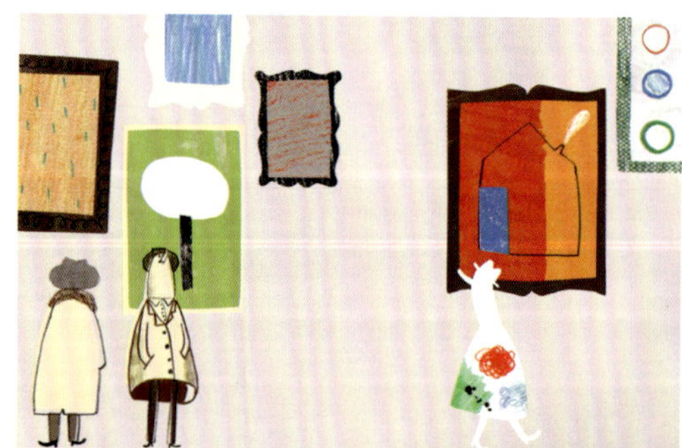

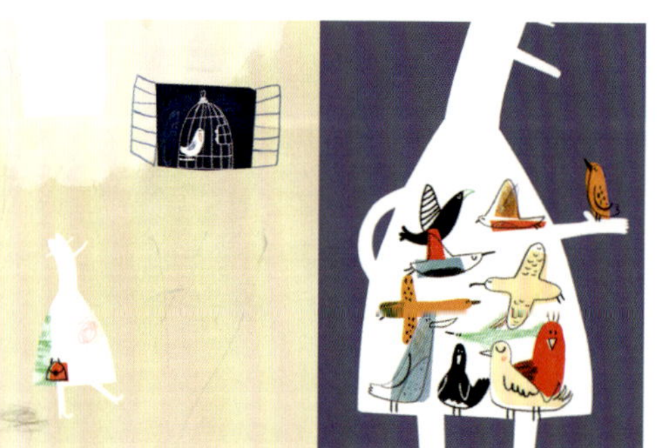

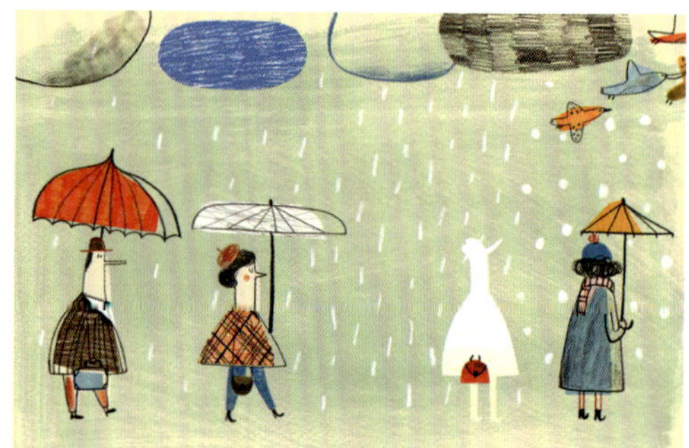

**BEST OF SHOW** *Catarina Sobral*

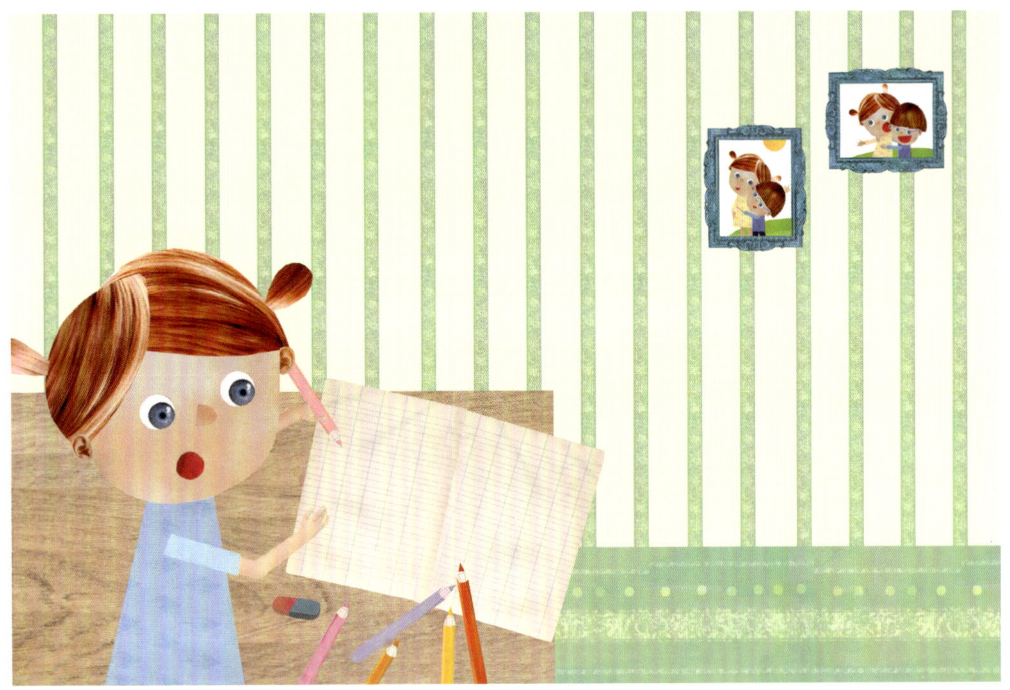

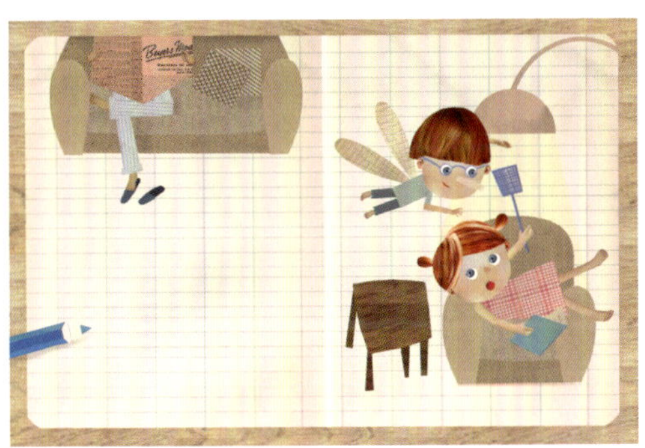

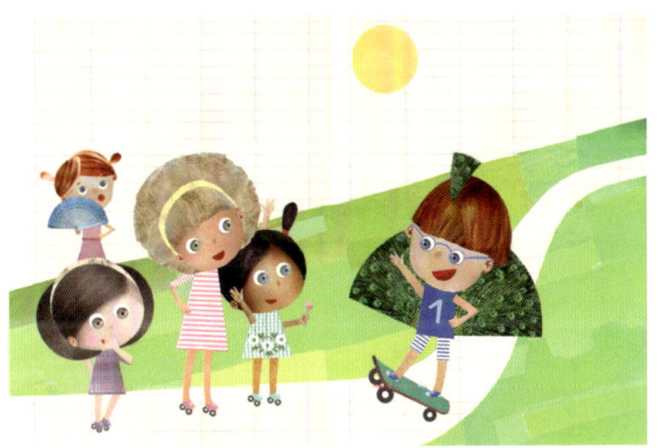

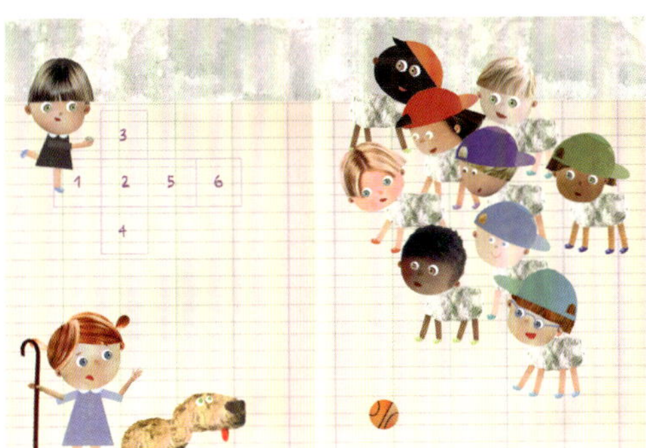

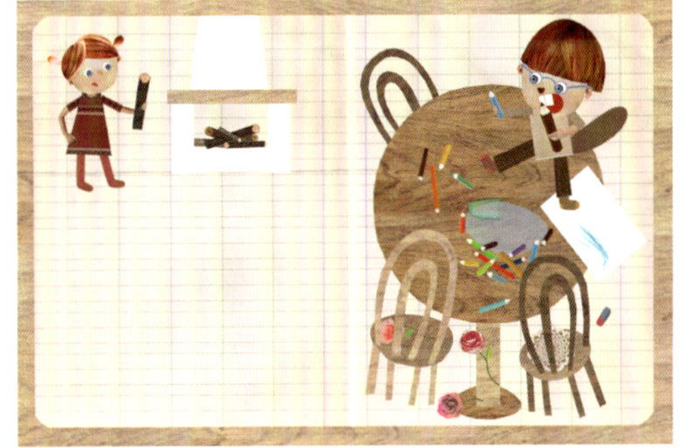

MERIT *Silvia Bonanni*

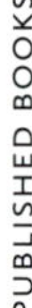

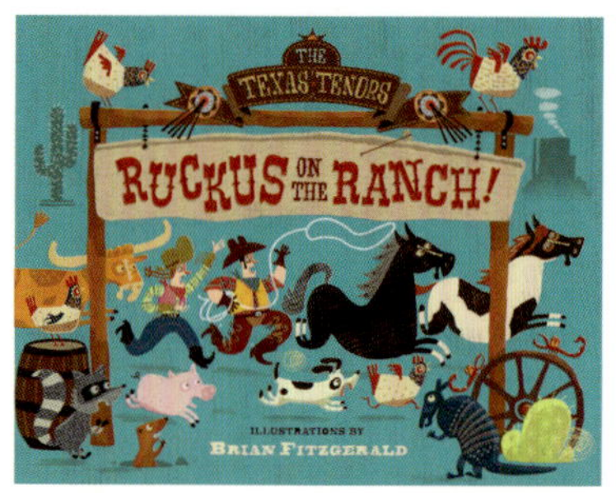

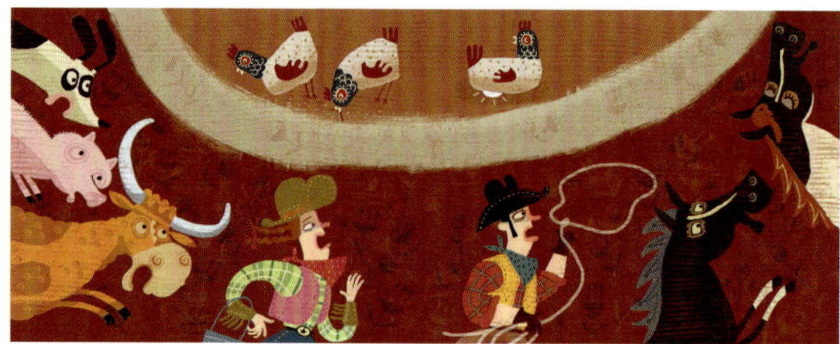

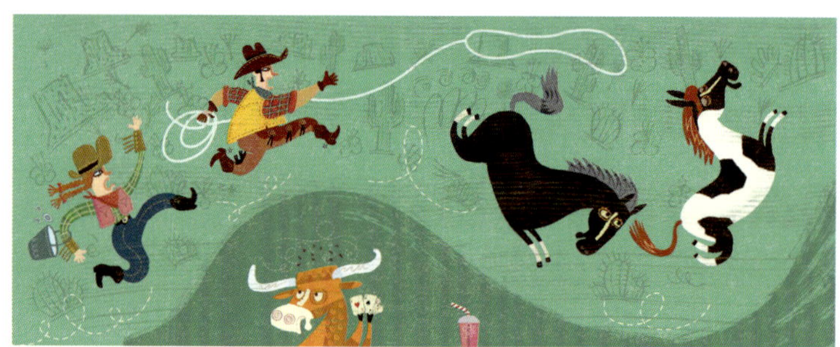

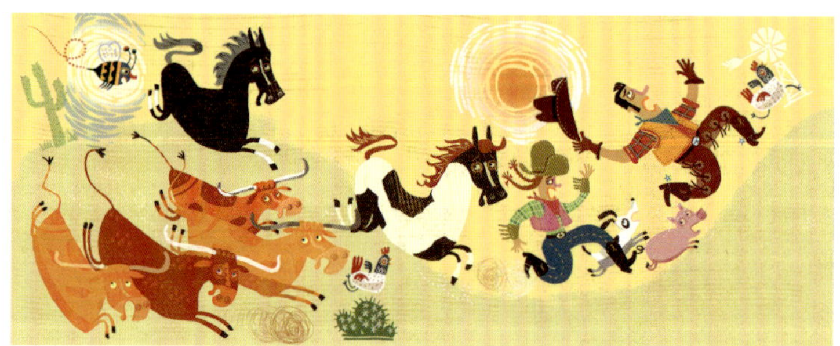

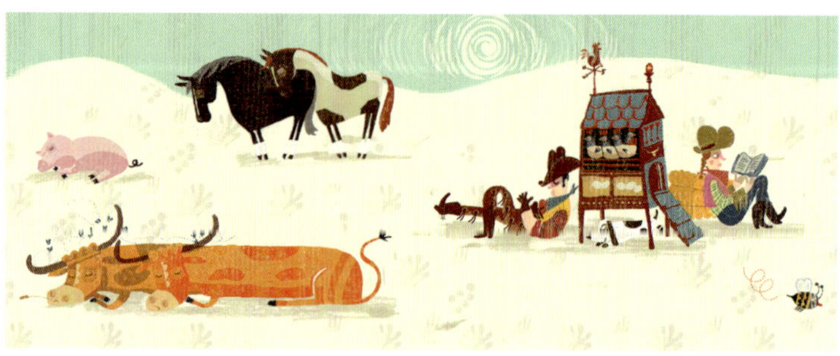

MERIT *Brian Fitzgerald*

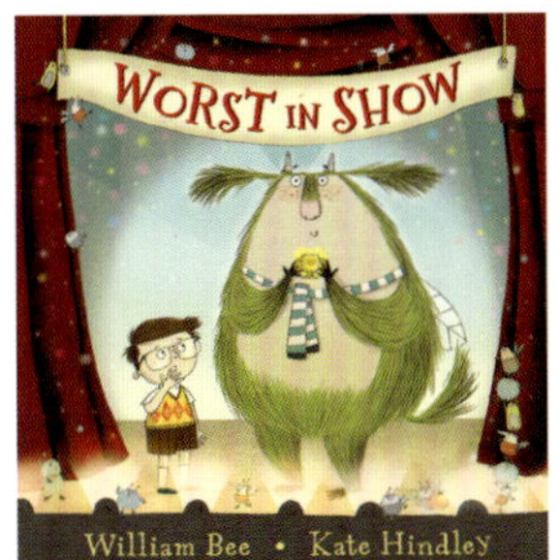


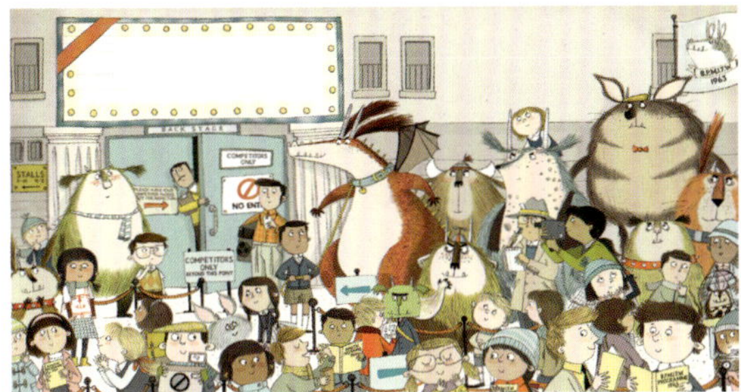

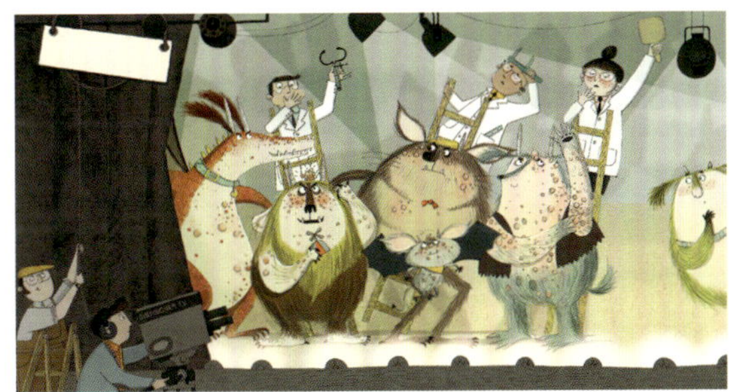

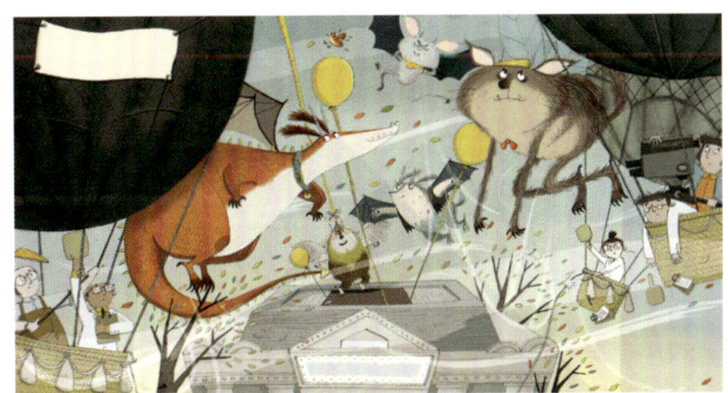

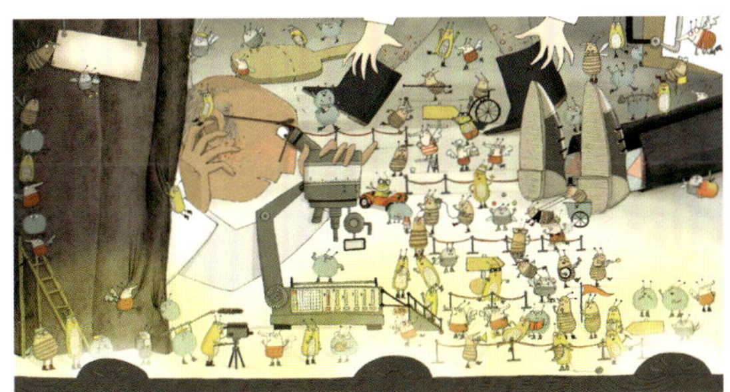

**SILVER** *Kate Hindley*

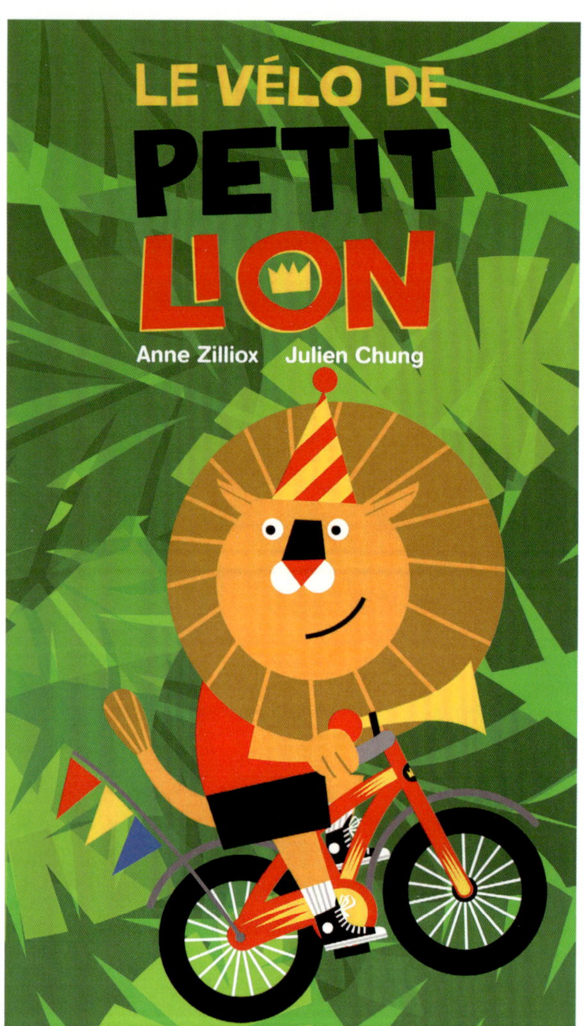


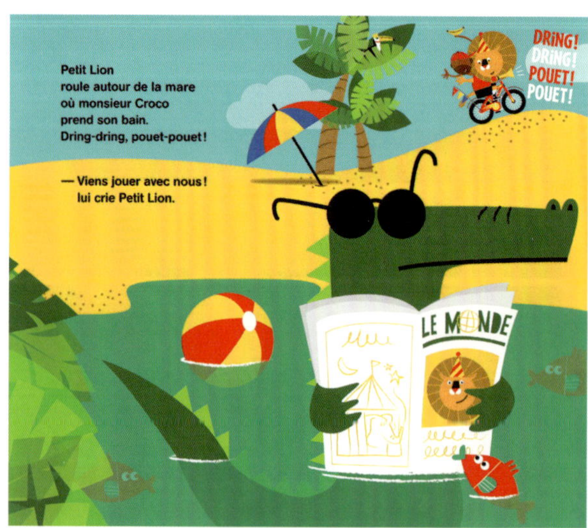


MERIT *Julien Chung*

240

Et hop !
Tout mouillé, monsieur Croco
saute sur le dos de Ouistiti.

Ensemble, ils partent – oh là là ! –
chez monsieur Éléphant.

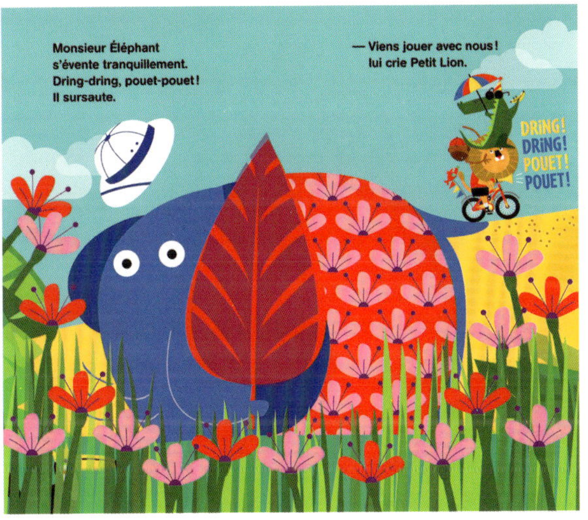



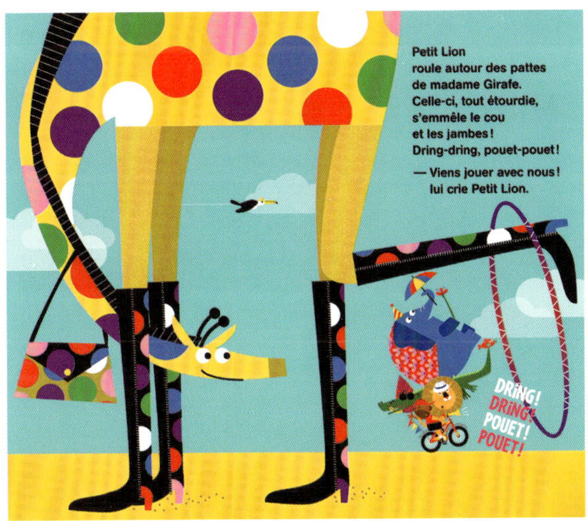

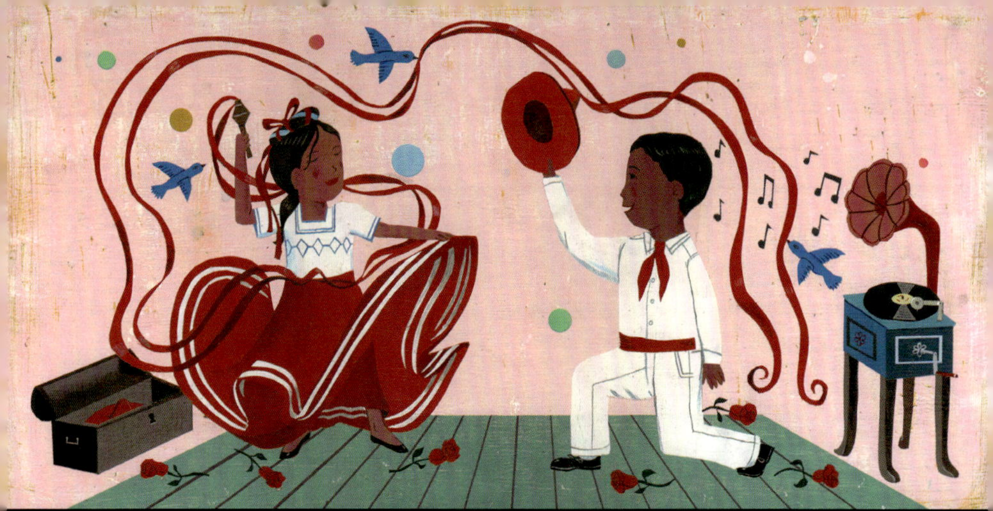

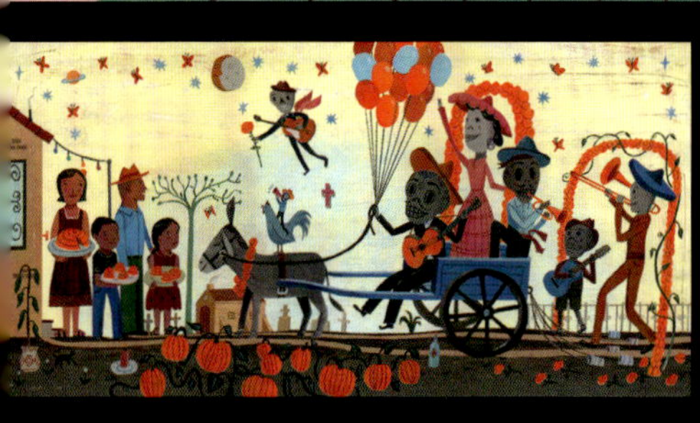

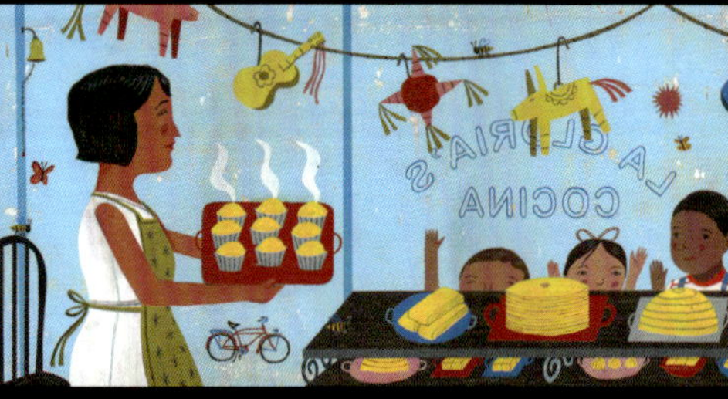
LA GLORIA'S
COCINA

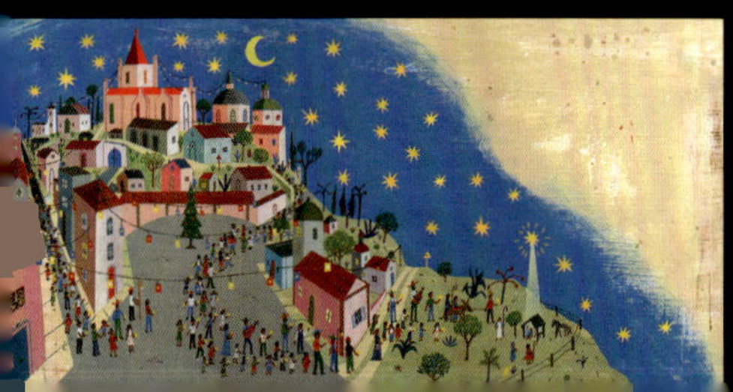

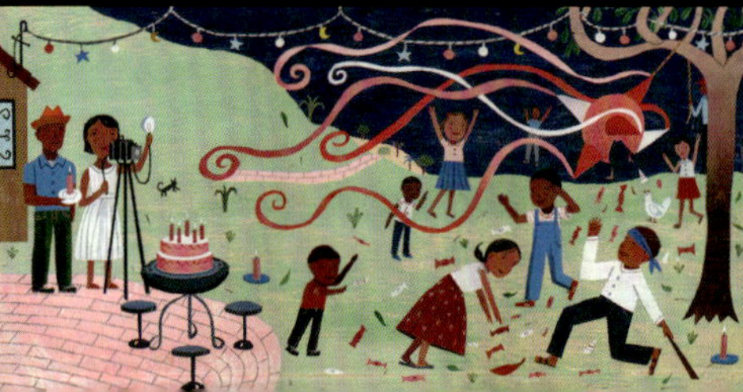

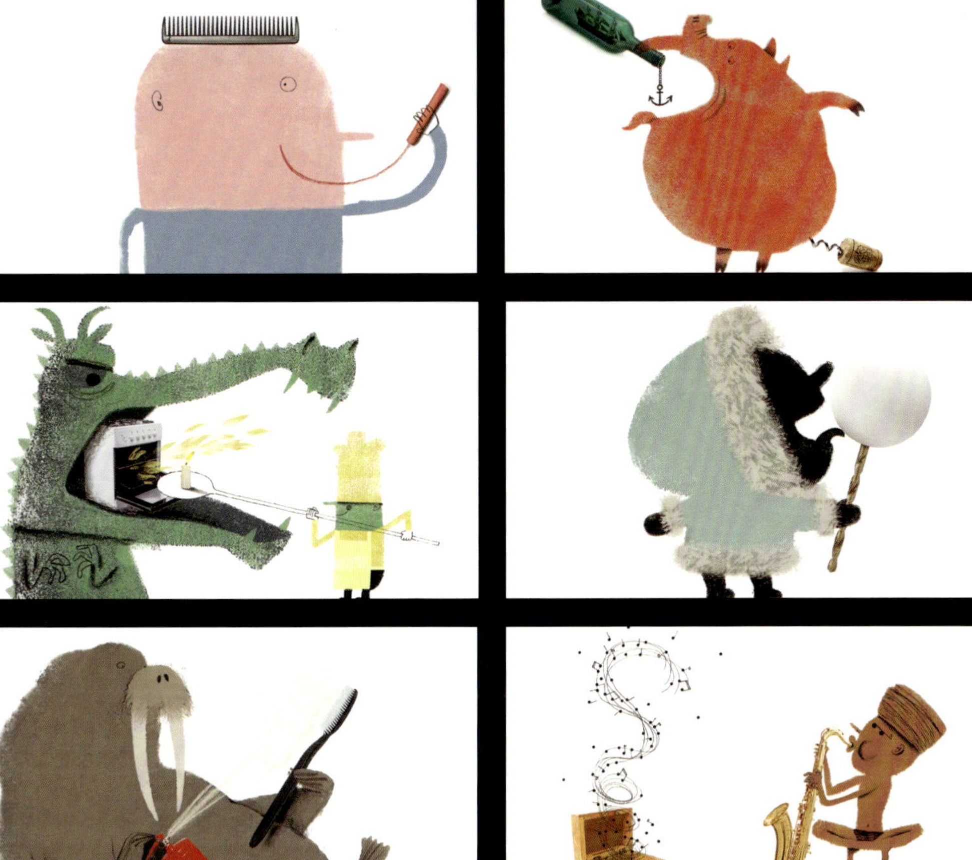

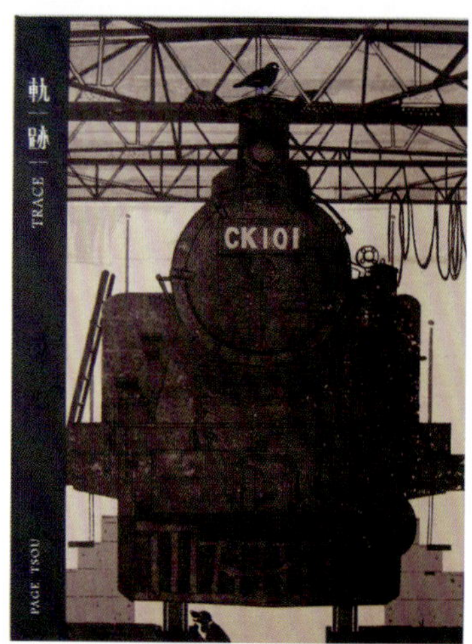


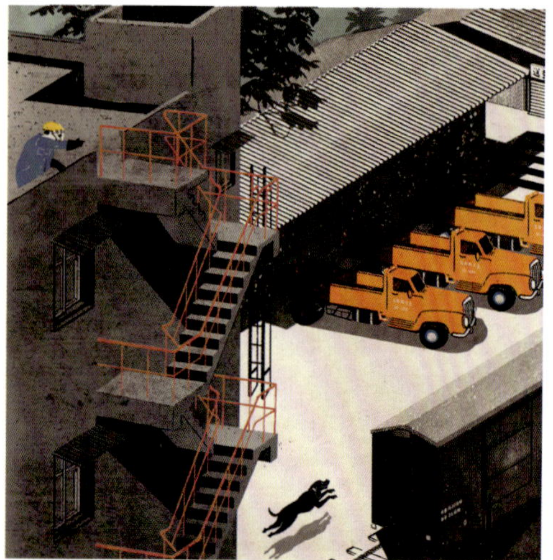

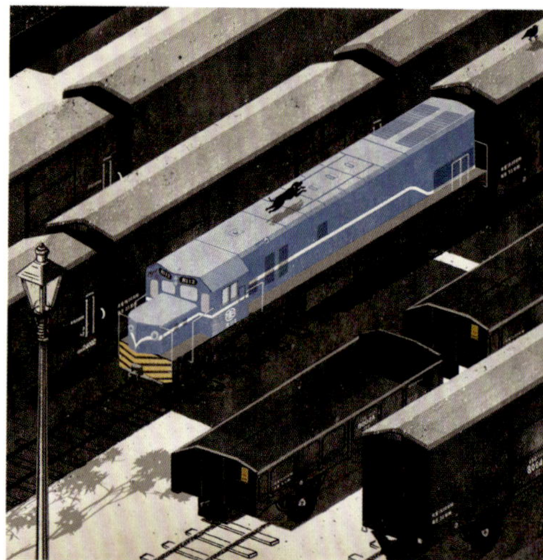

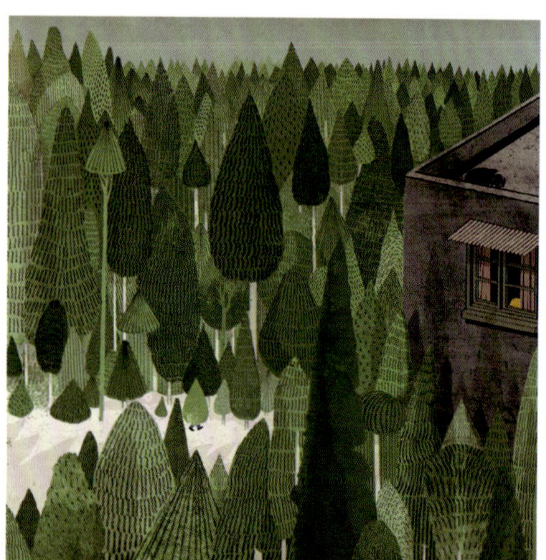

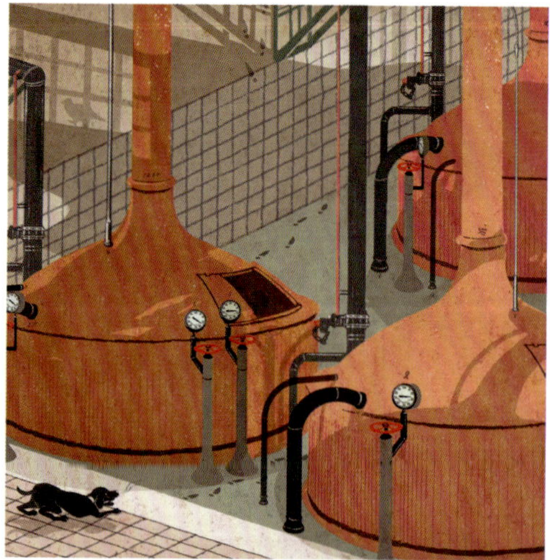

GOLD *Page Tsou*

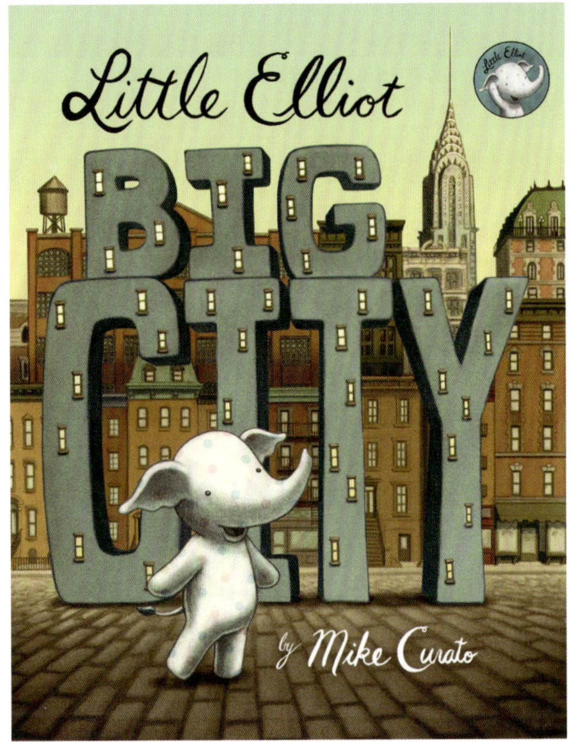


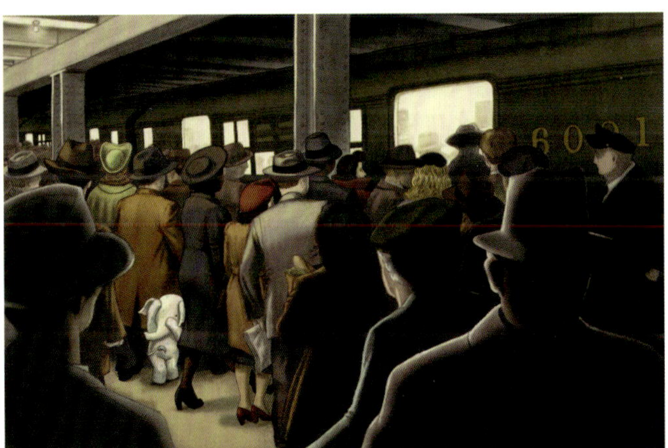
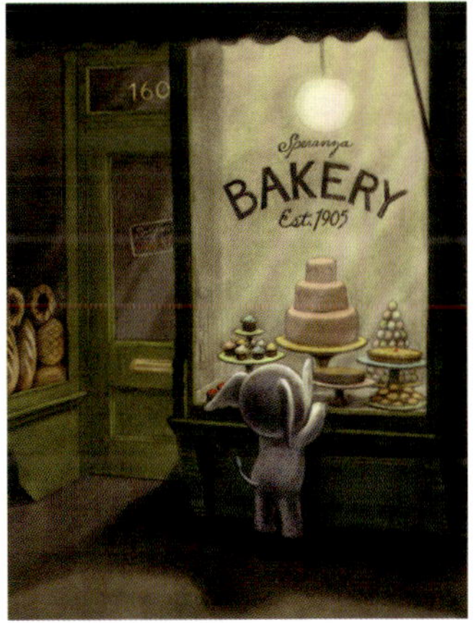


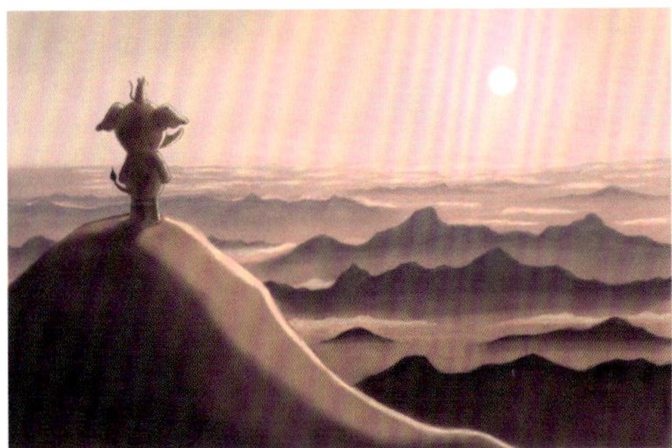
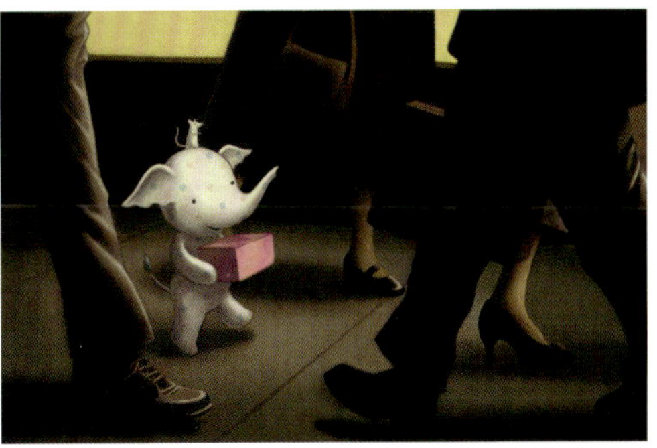

**MERIT** *Mike Curato*

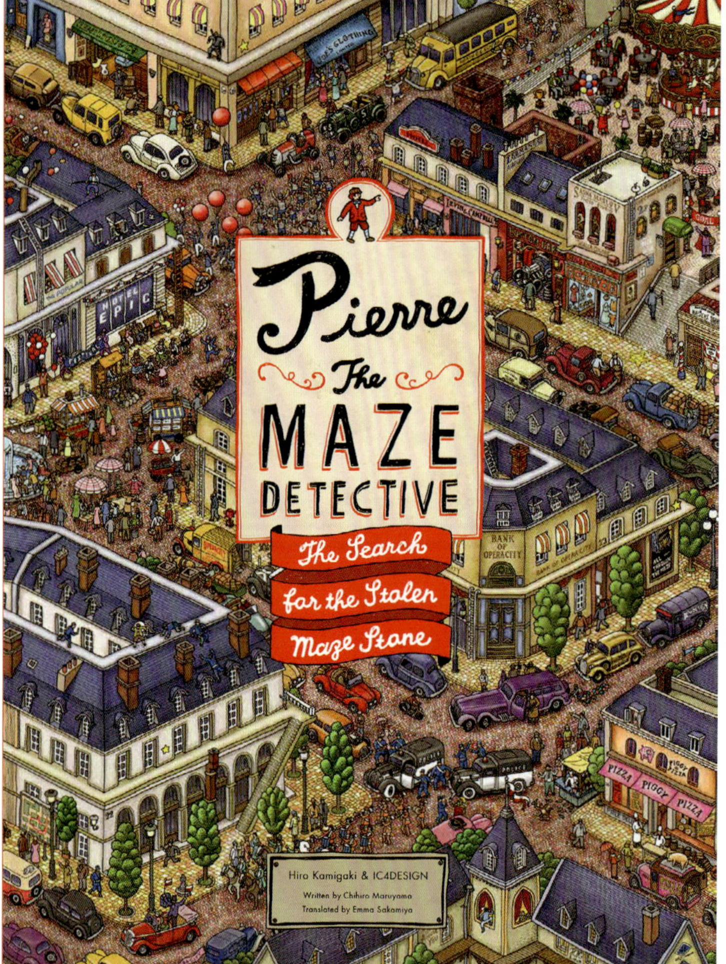


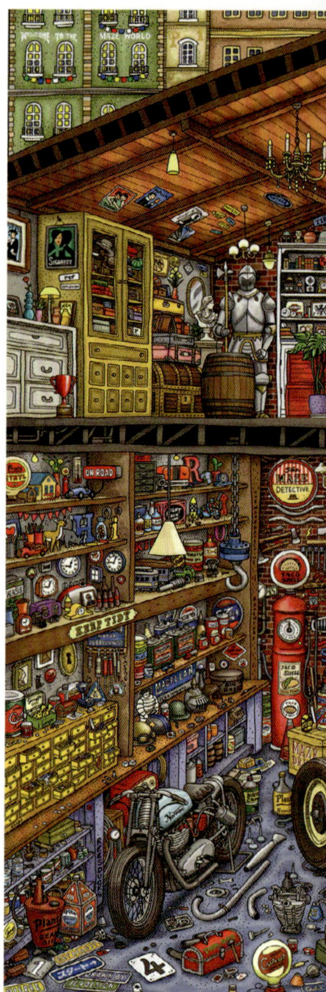

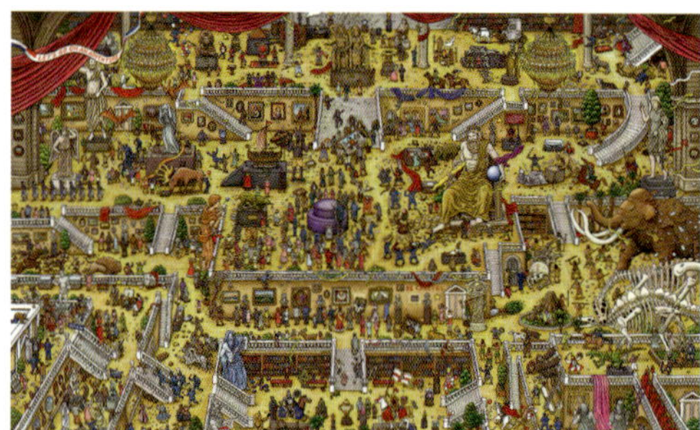

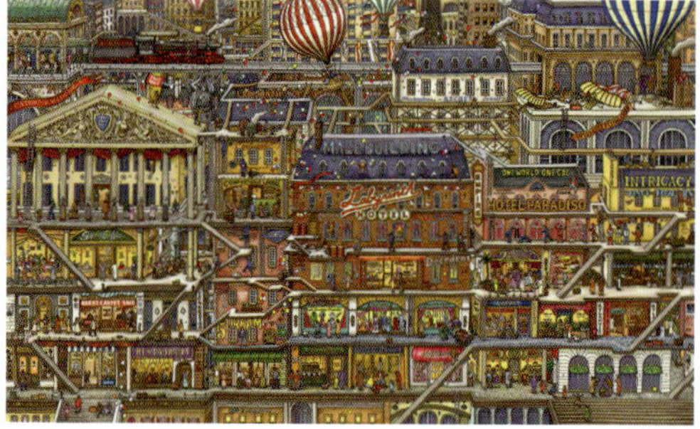

MERIT *IC4Design*

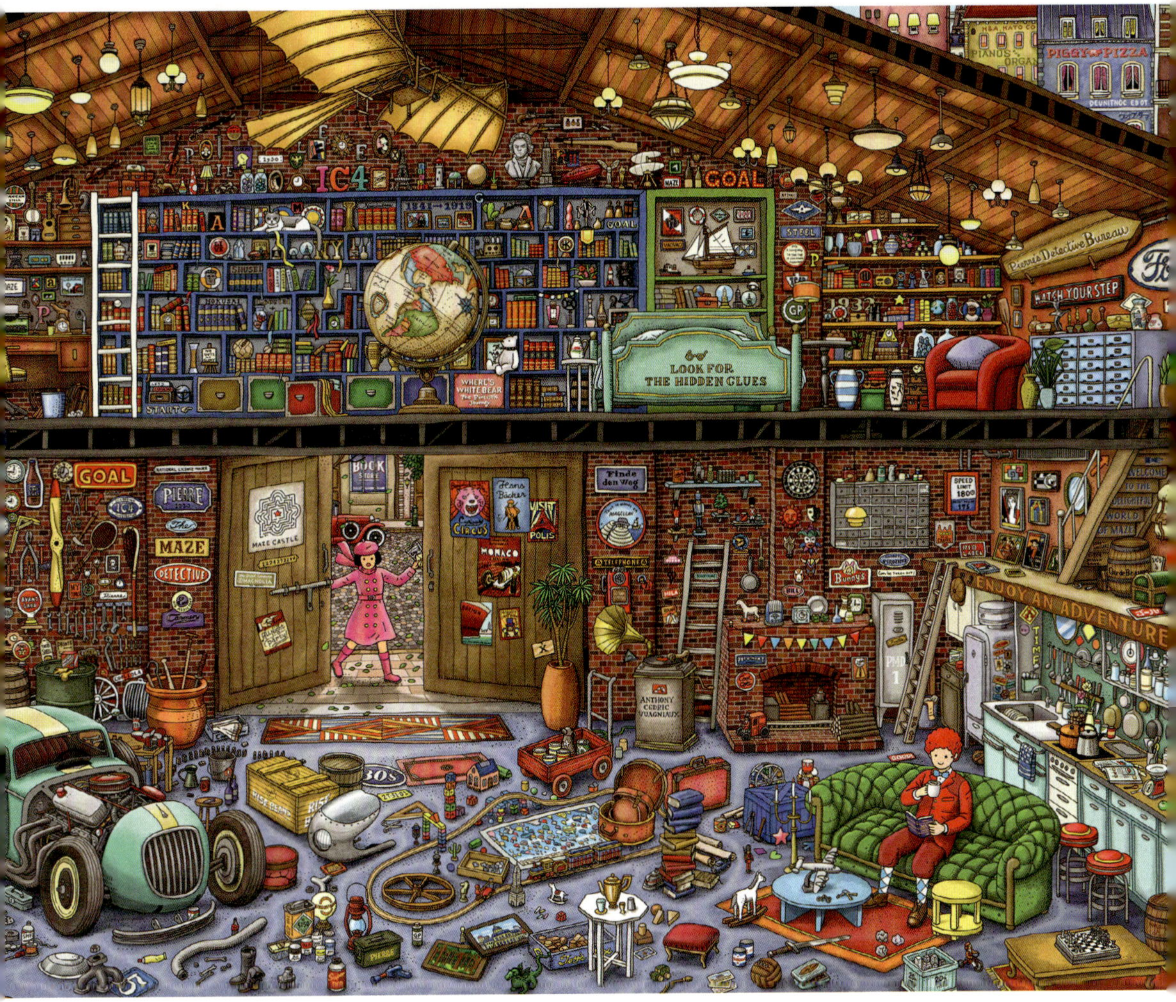

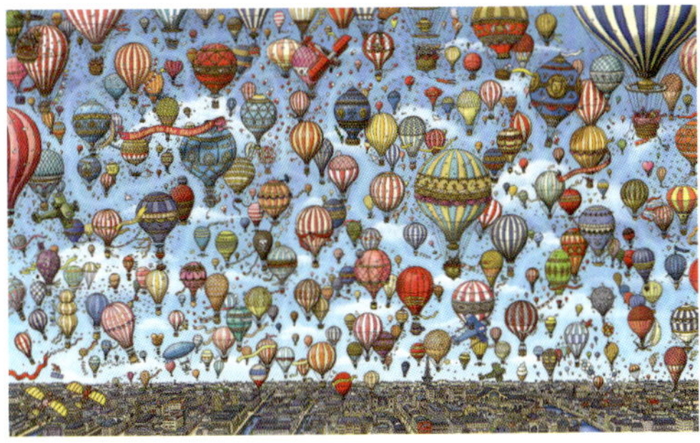

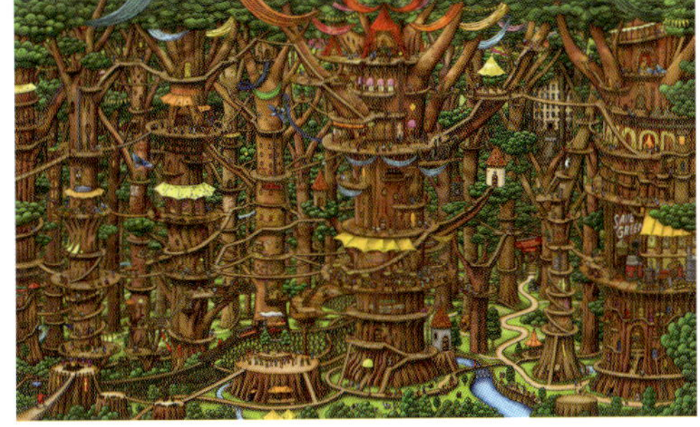



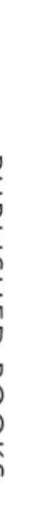
PUBLISHED BOOKS

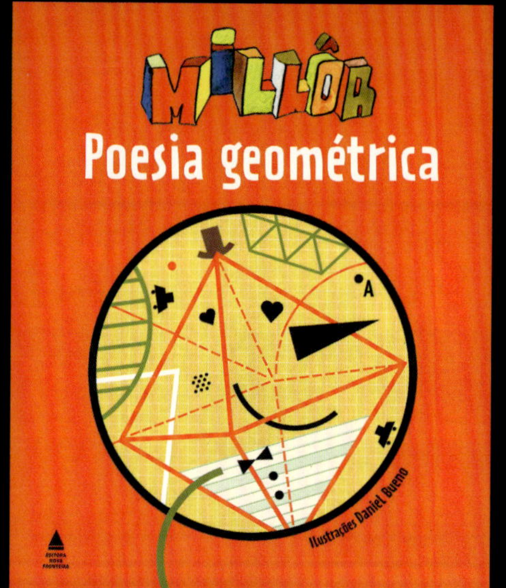


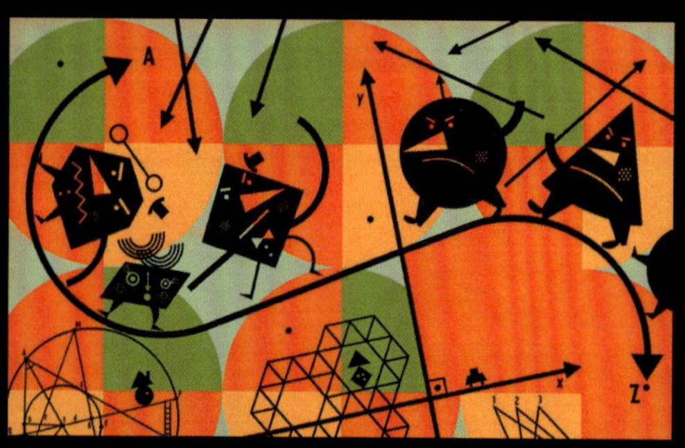

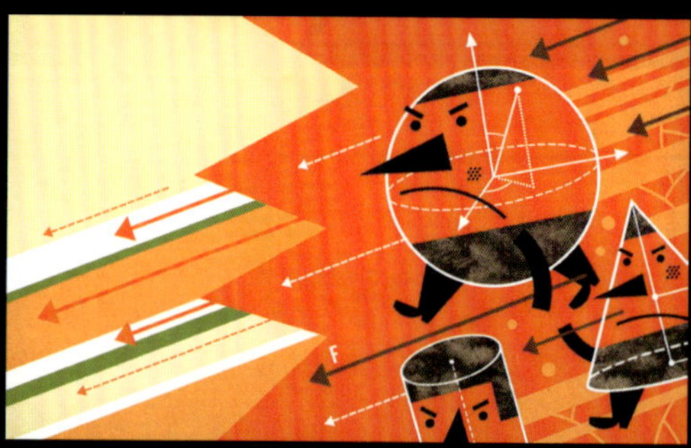

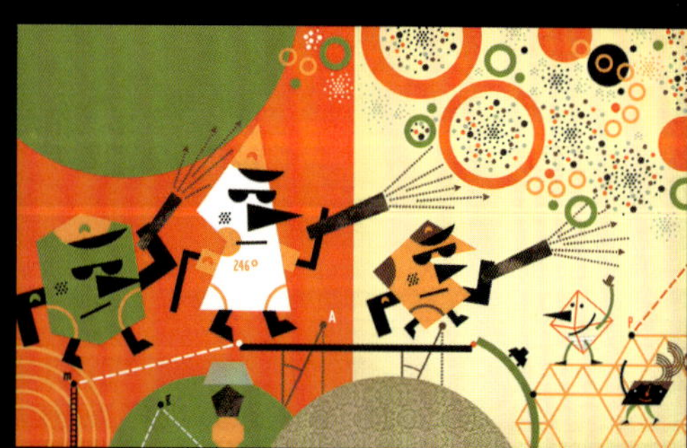

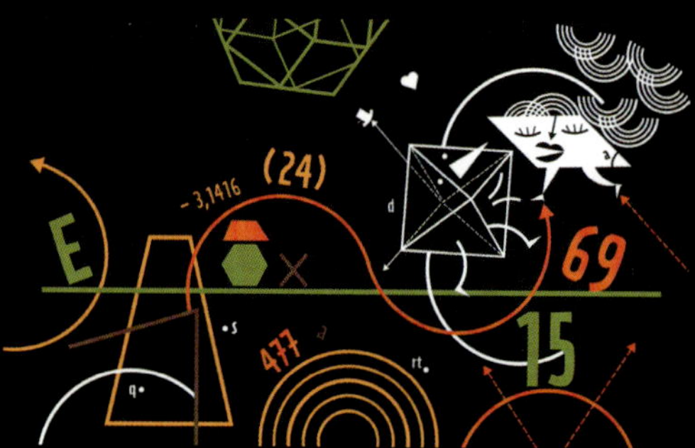

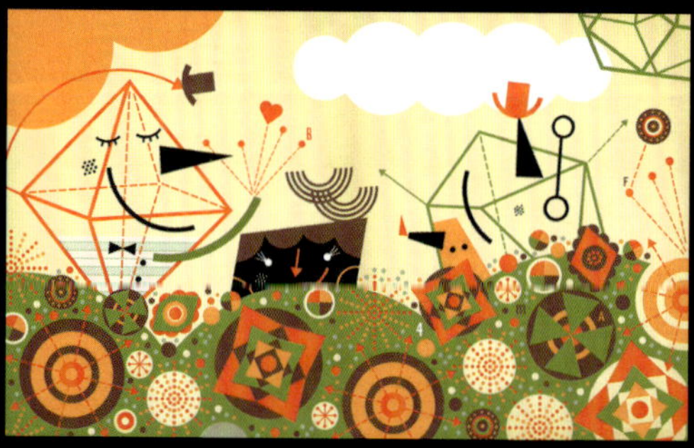

BRONZE *Daniel Bueno*

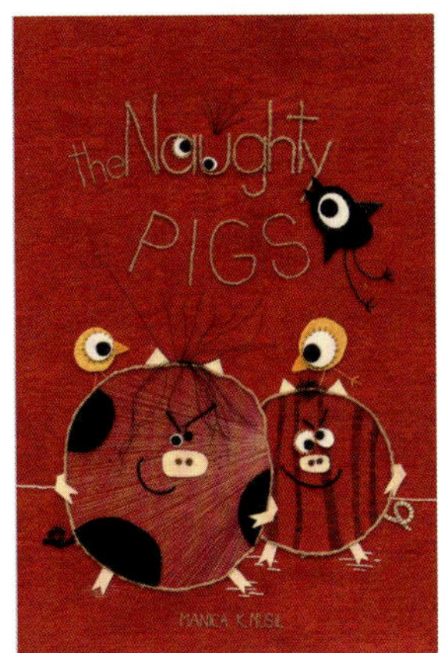


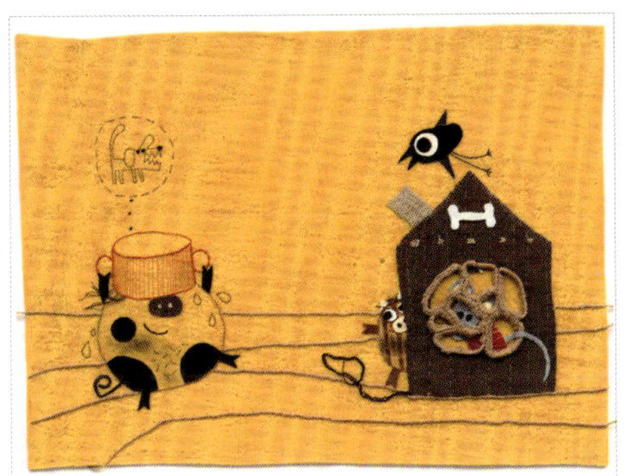

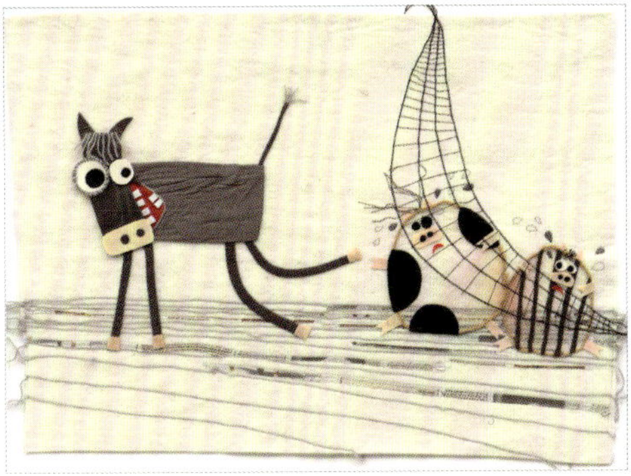

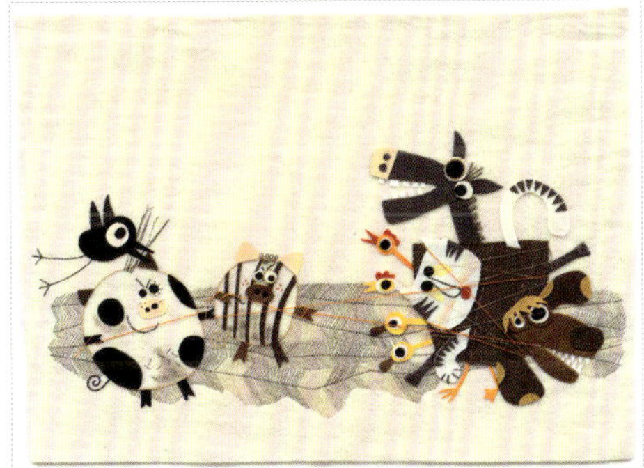

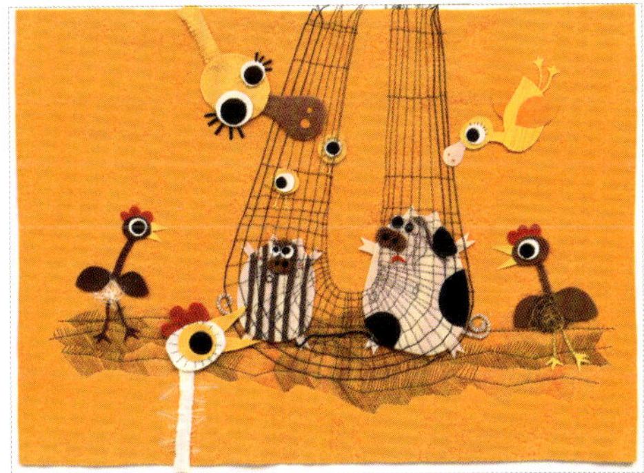

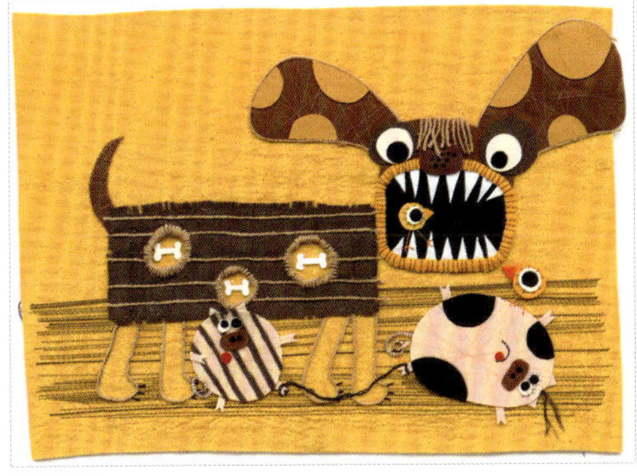

MERIT *Manica K. Musil*

249

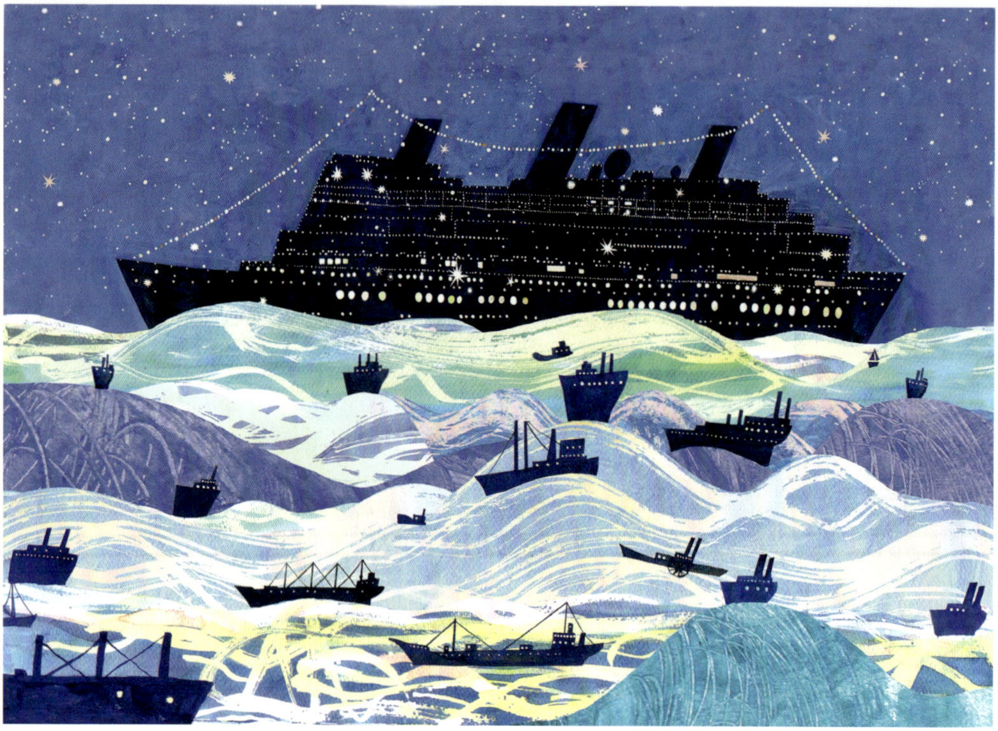

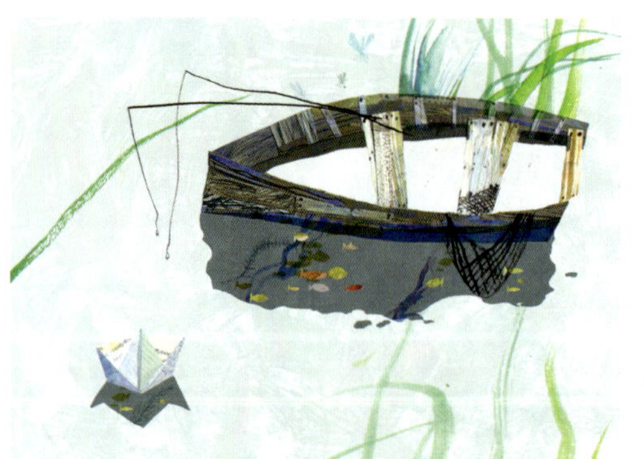

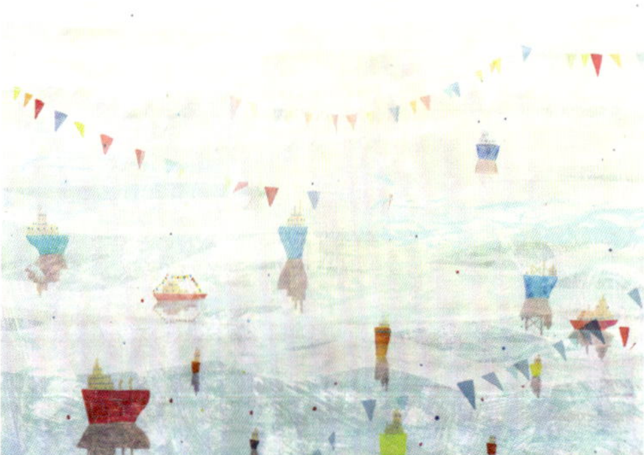

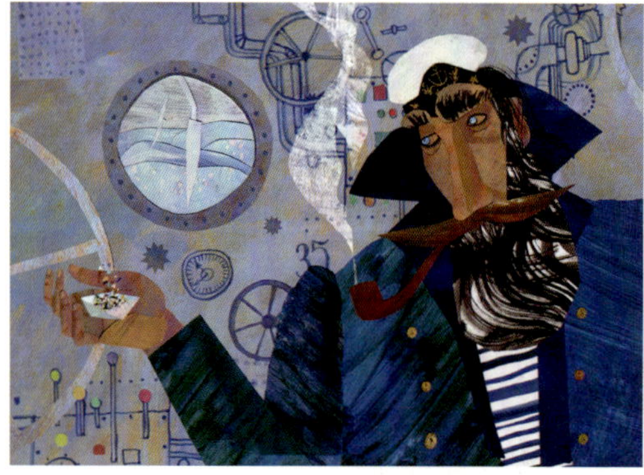

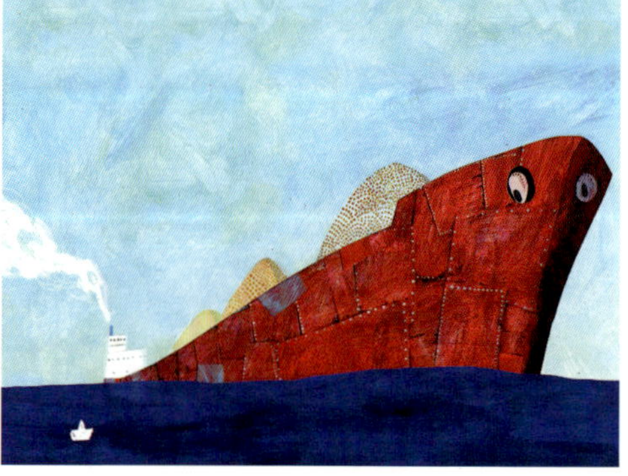

MERIT *Victoria Antolini*

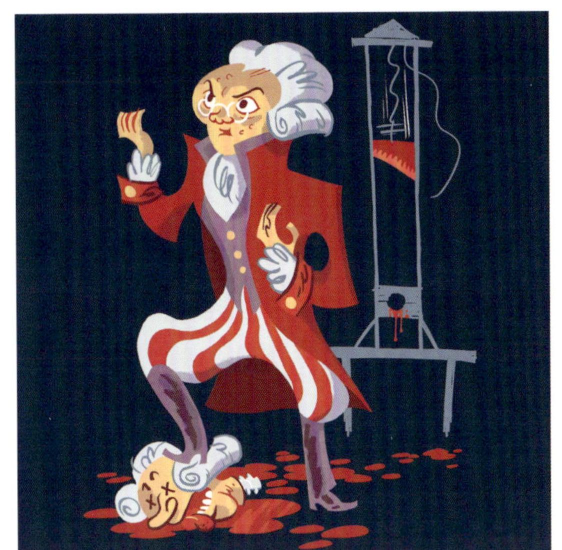

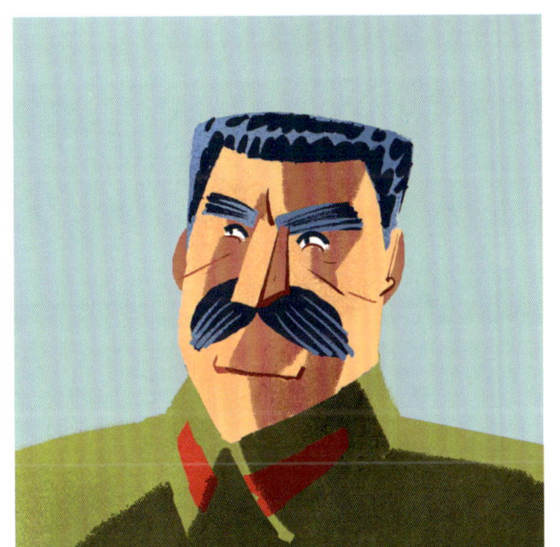

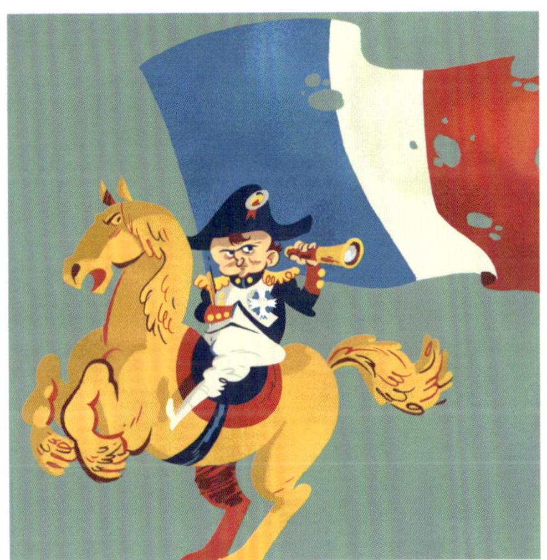

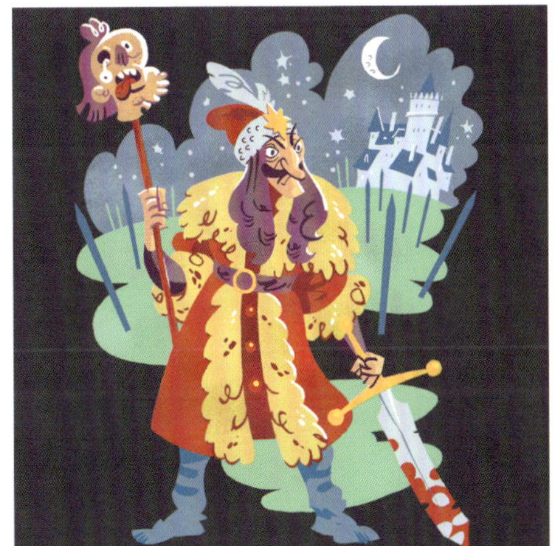

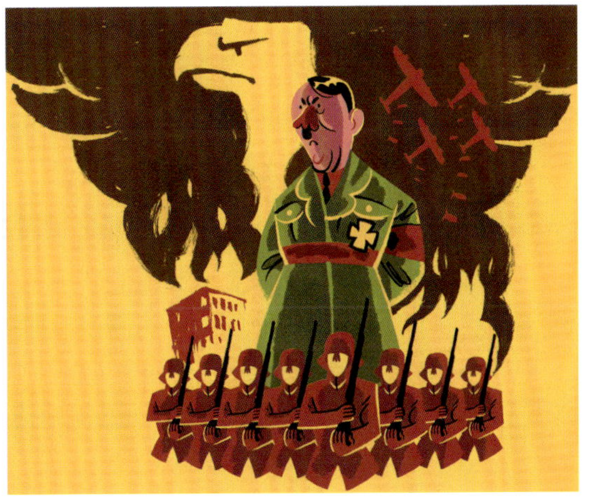

MERIT *Jan Bielecki*

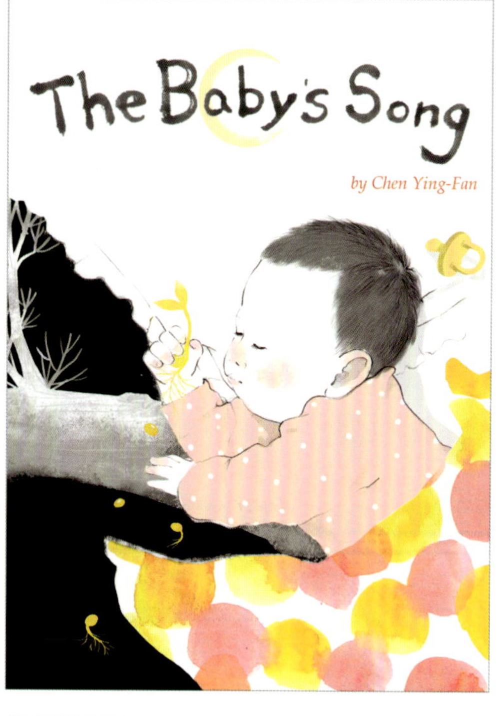



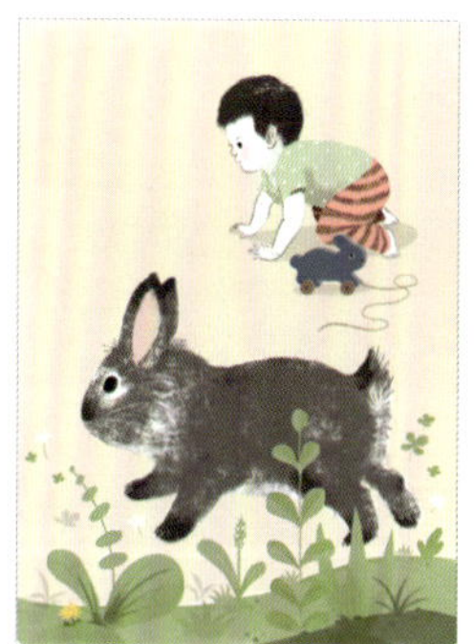
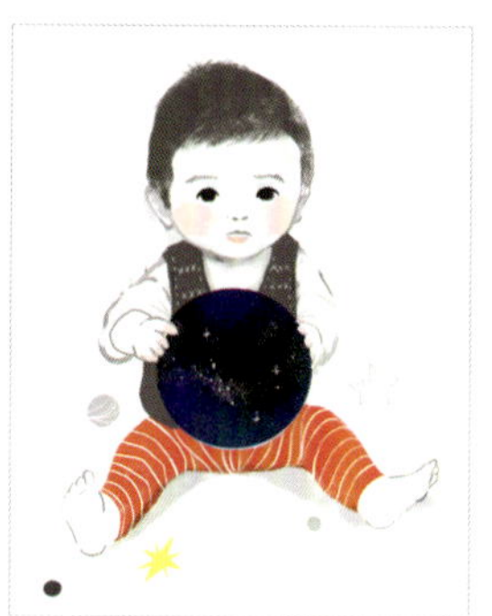
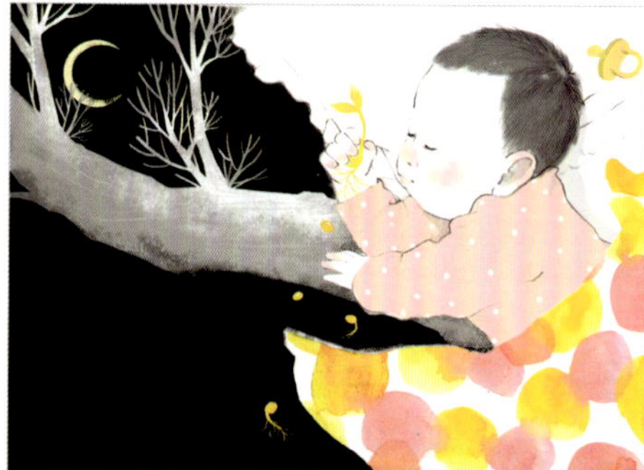
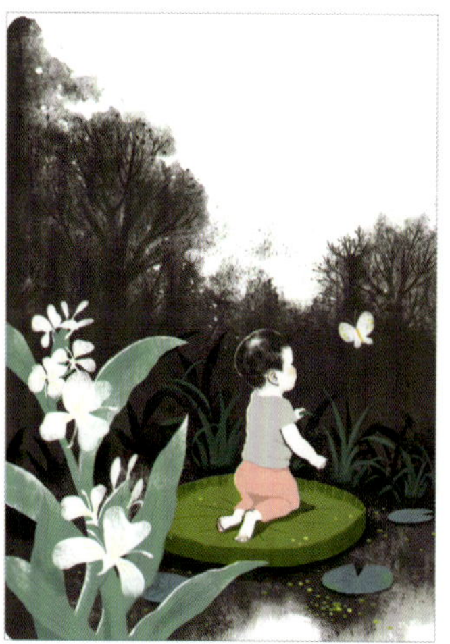
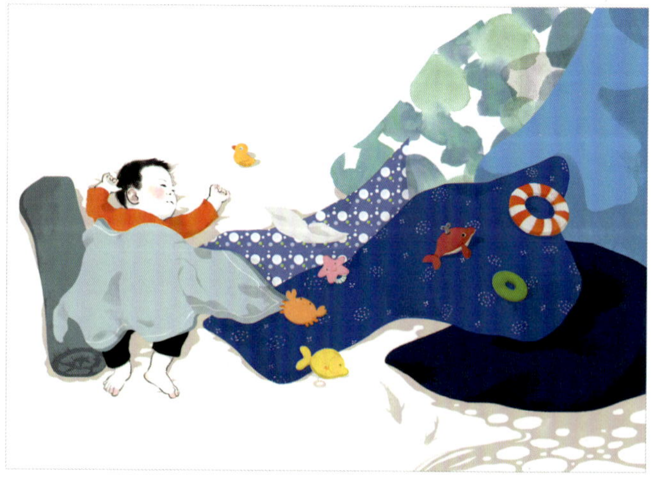

MERIT *Chen Ying-Fan*

252

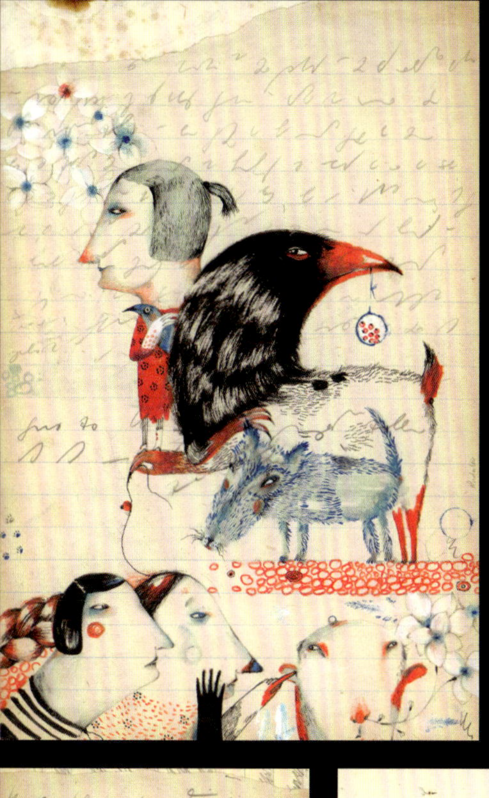
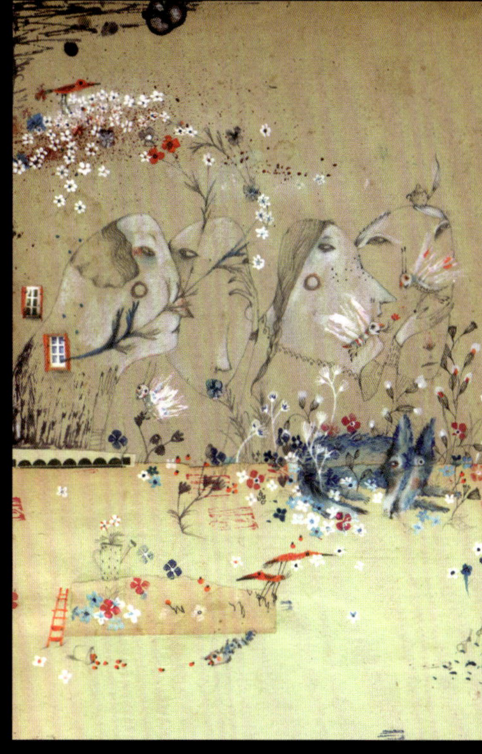
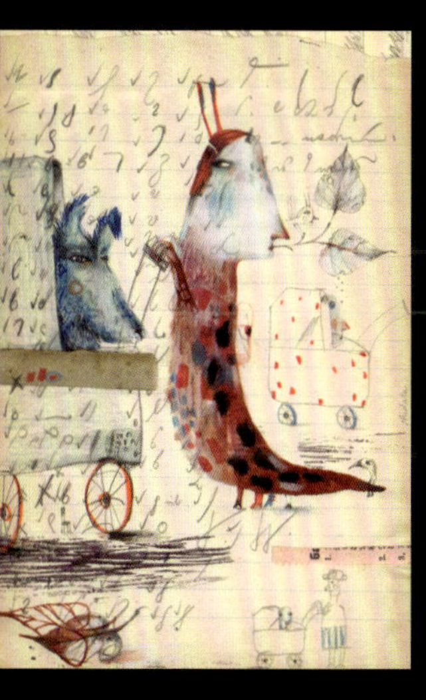
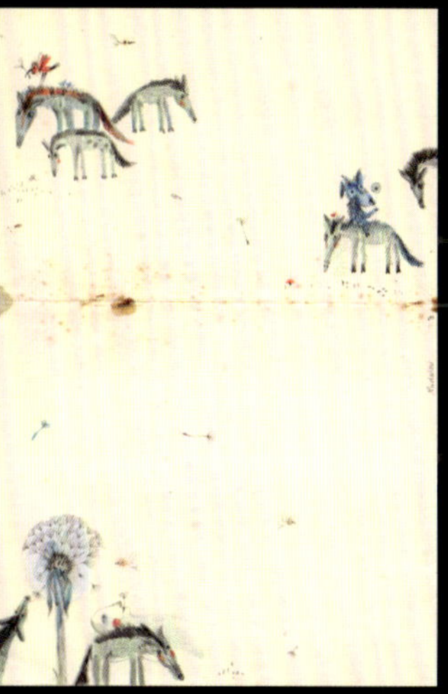
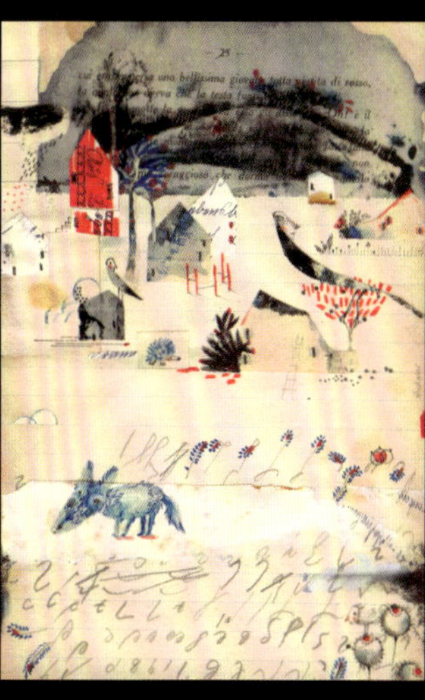

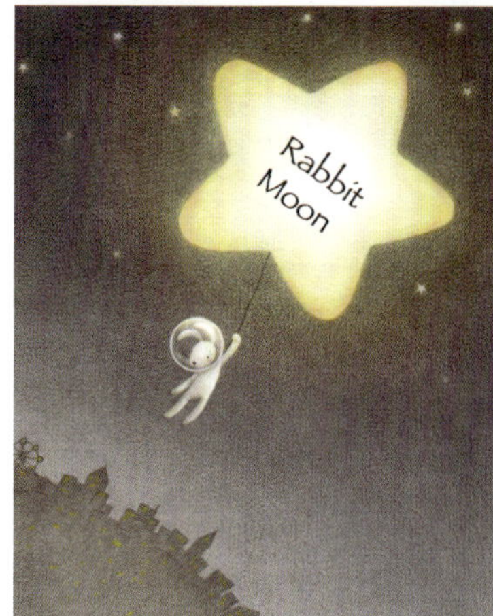



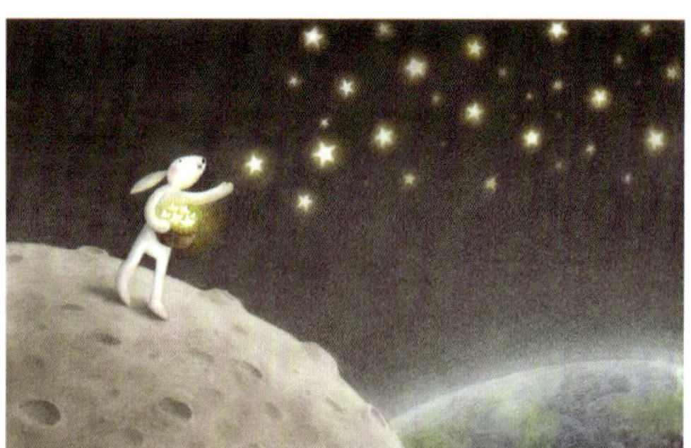

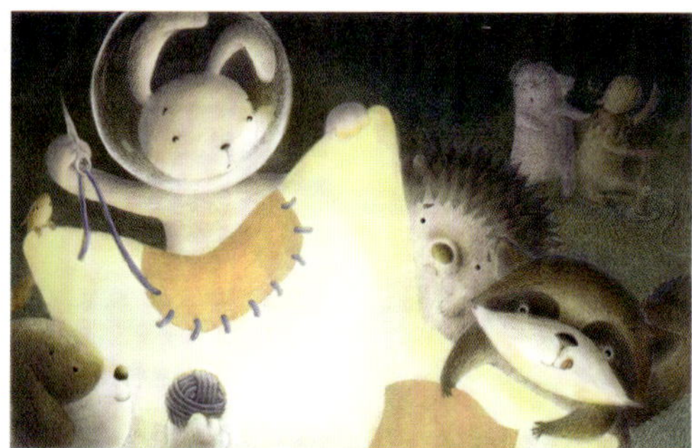

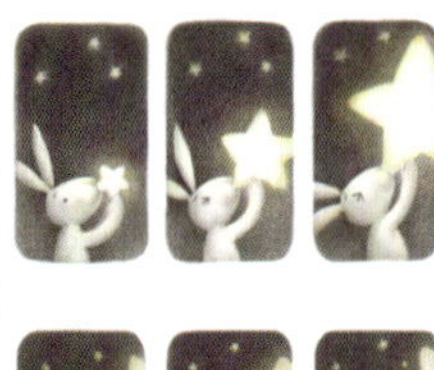

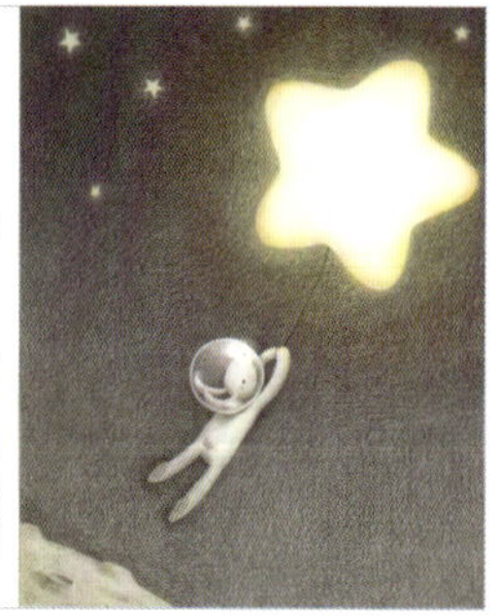

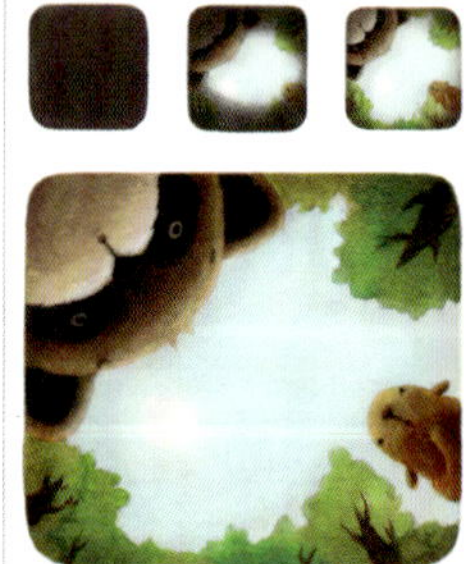

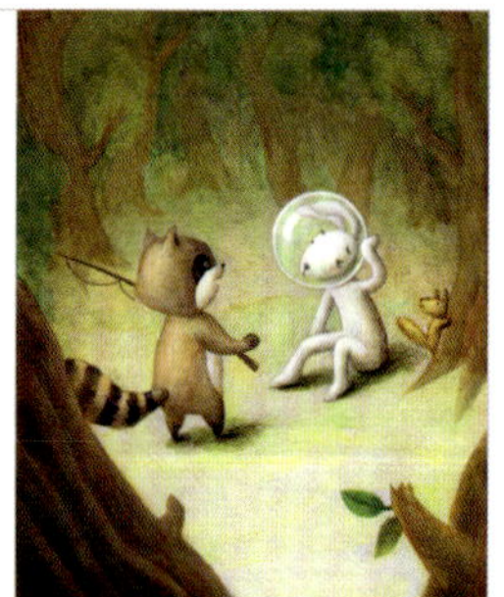

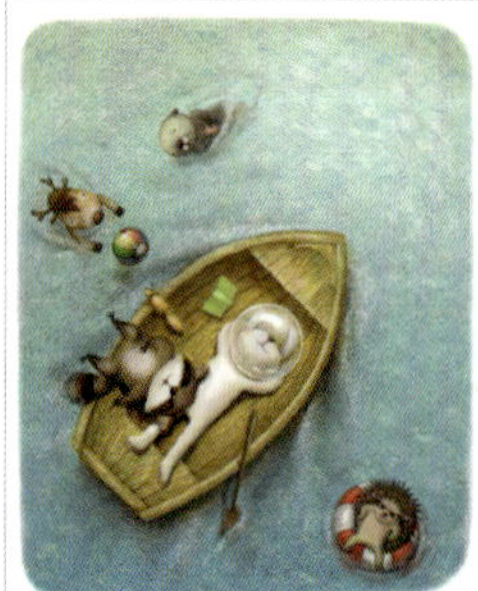

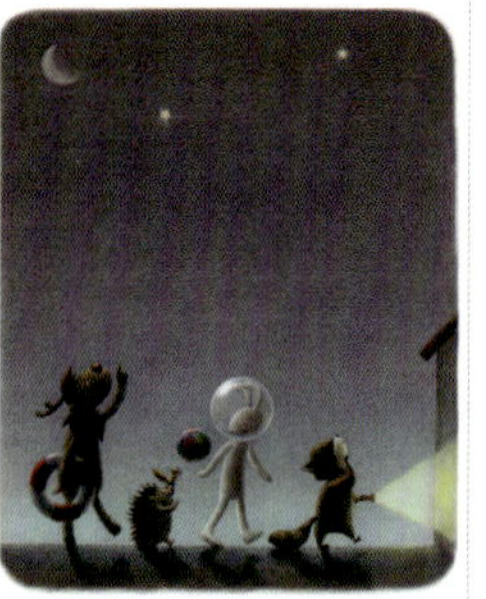

MERIT *Jean Ji In Kim*

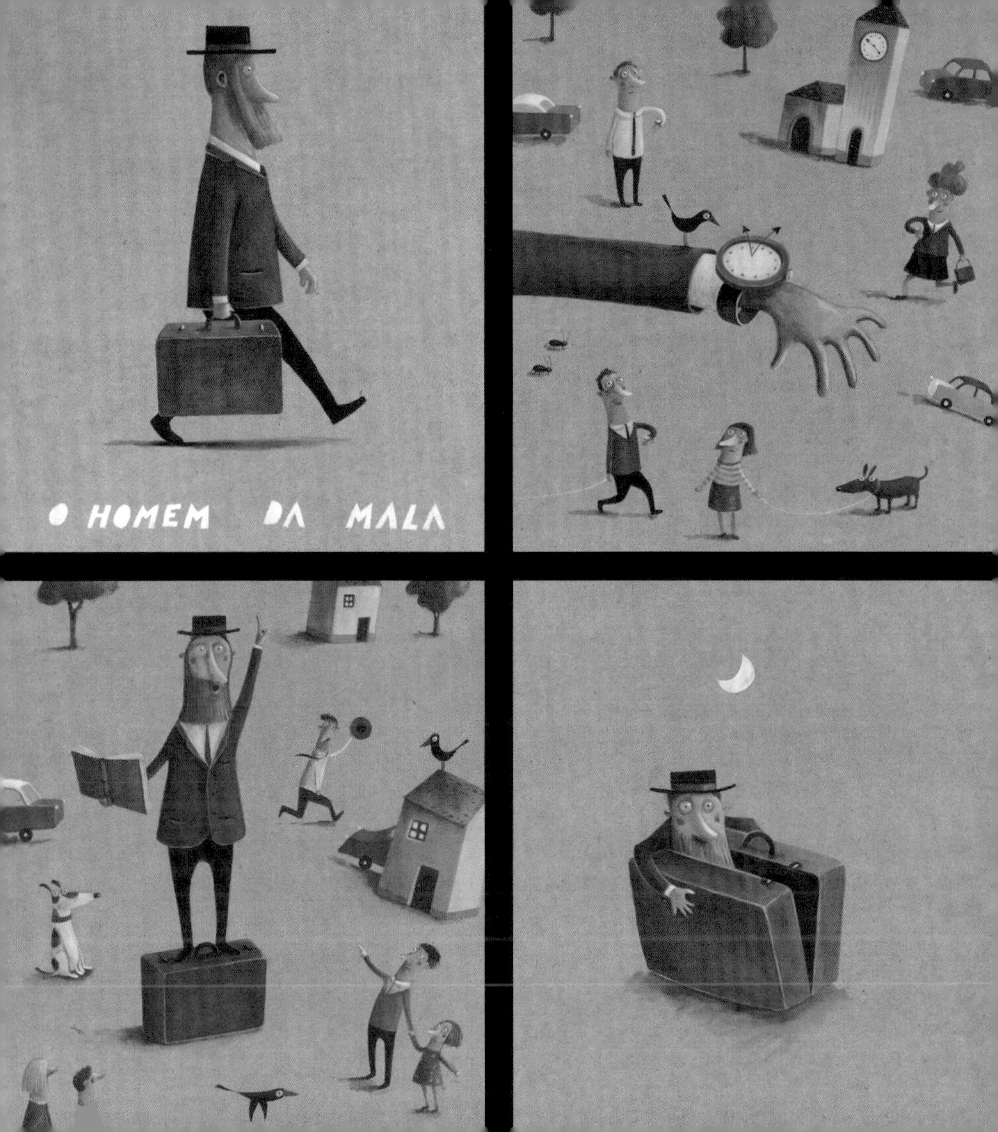

O HOMEM DA MALA

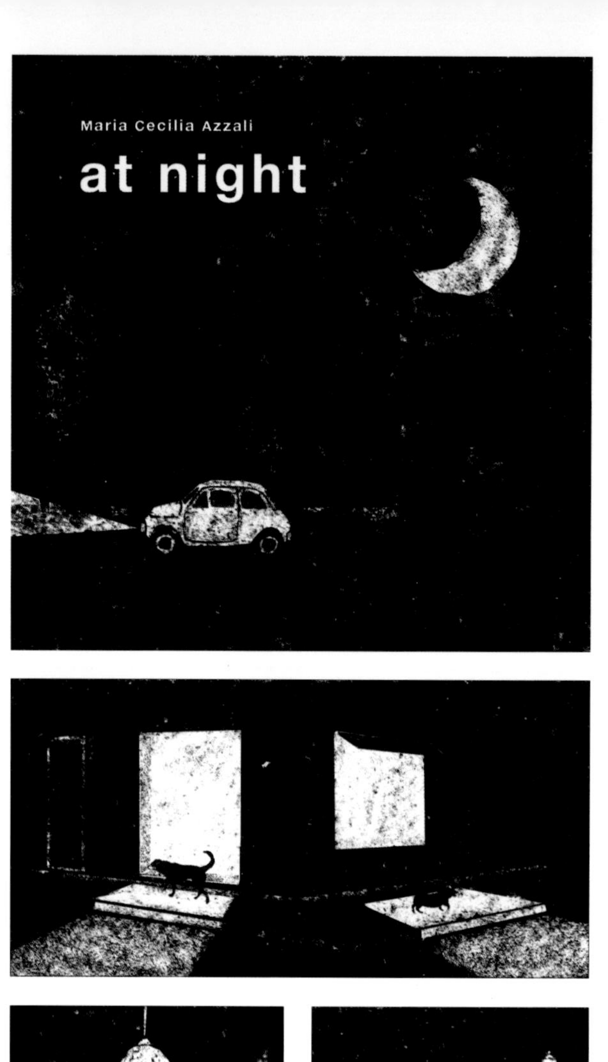


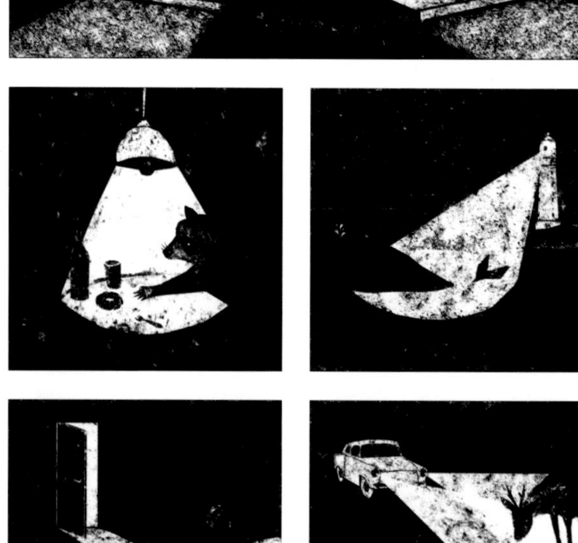



MERIT *Maria Cecilia Azzali*

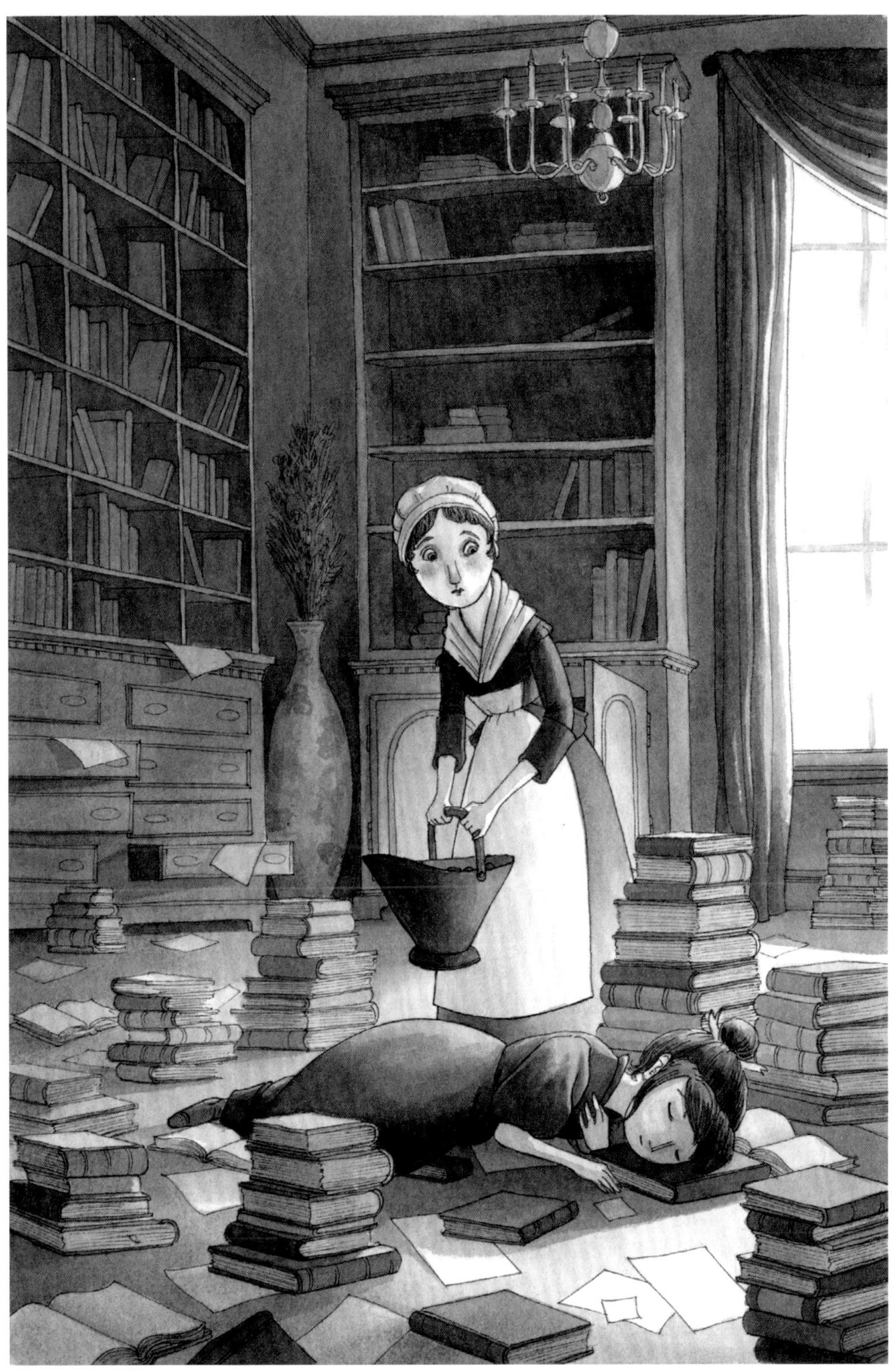

DISTINGUISHED MERIT *Kelly Murphy*

257

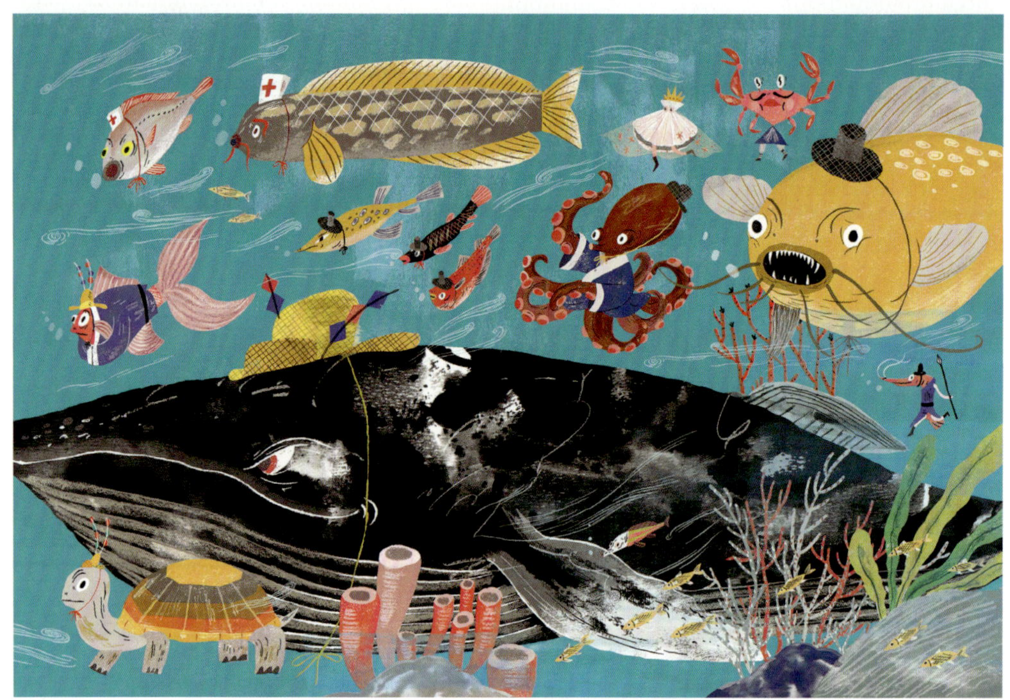

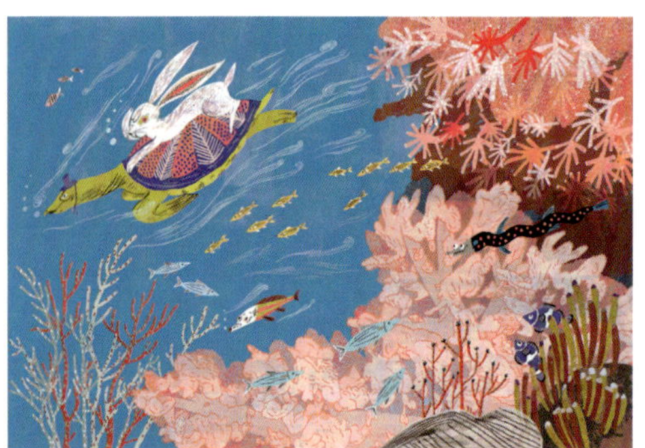

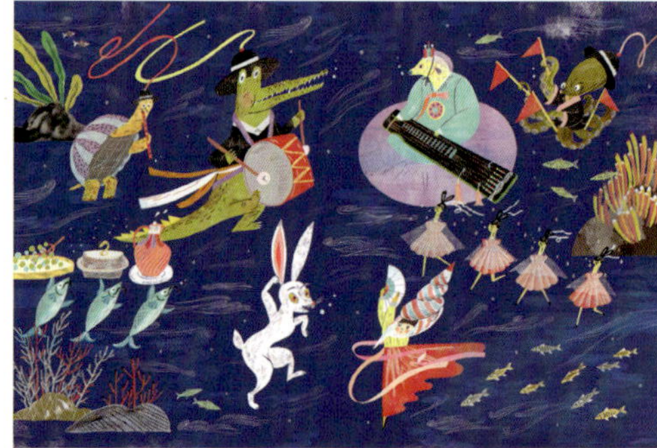

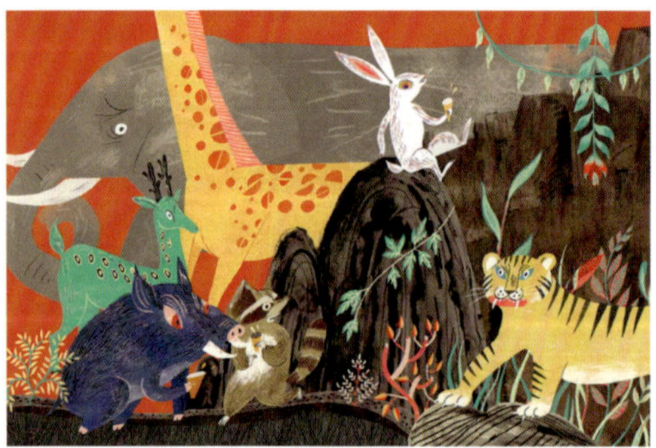

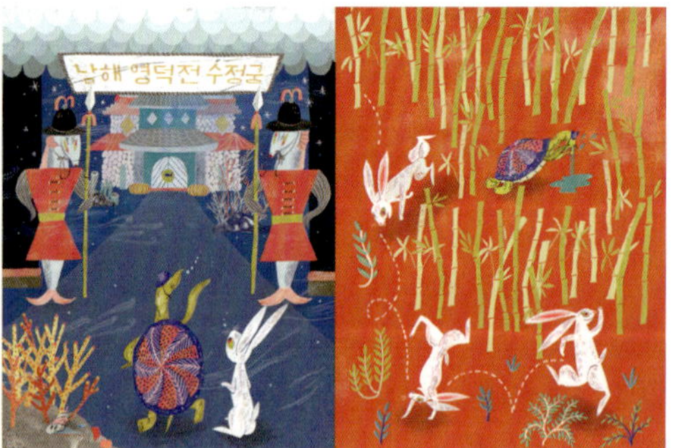




MERIT *Yeji Yun*

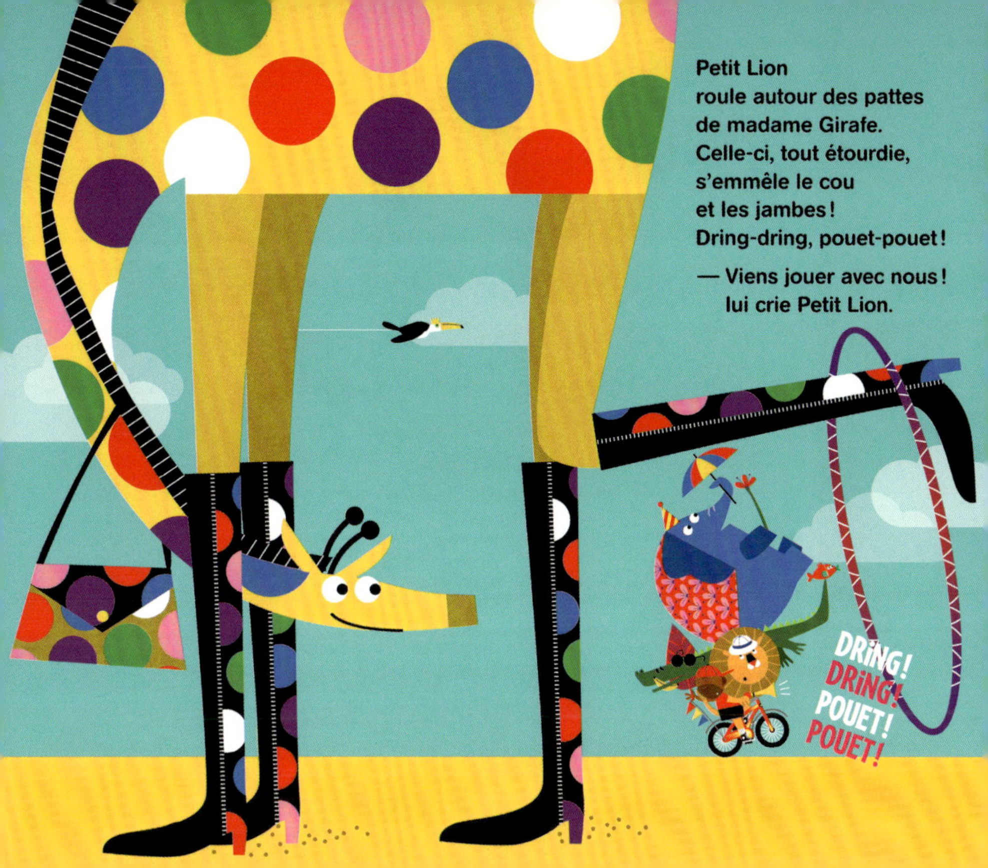

Petit Lion
roule autour des pattes
de madame Girafe.
Celle-ci, tout étourdie,
s'emmêle le cou
et les jambes !
Dring-dring, pouet-pouet !

— Viens jouer avec nous !
lui crie Petit Lion.

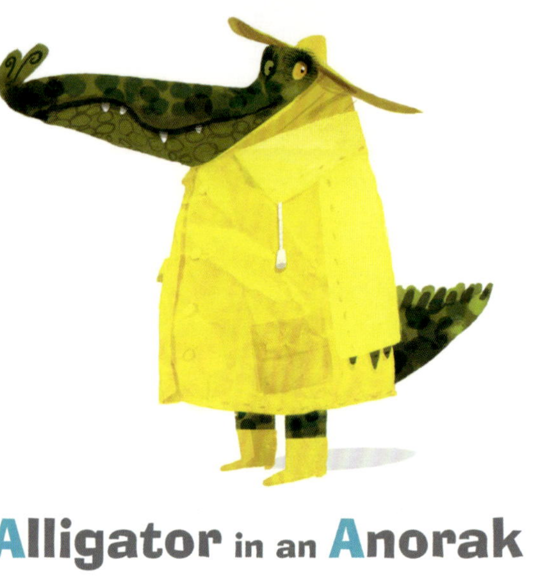

# **Alligator** in an **Anorak**

**Tiger** in a **Tent**

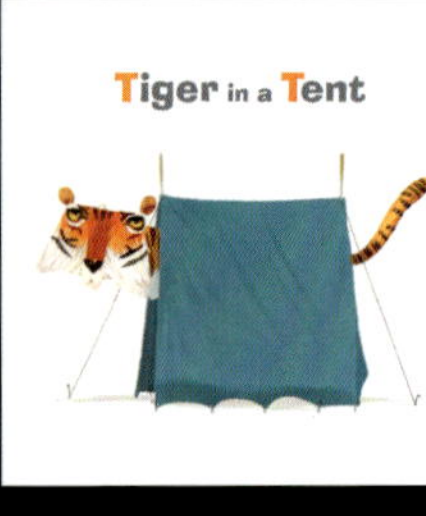

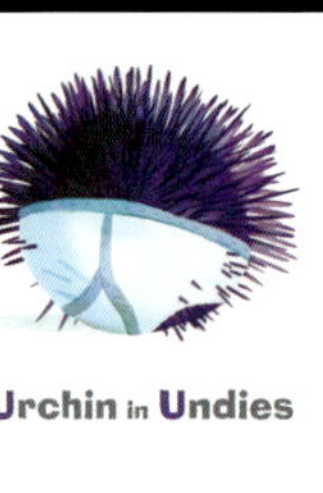

**Urchin** in **Undies**

**Hippo** in a **Helicopter**

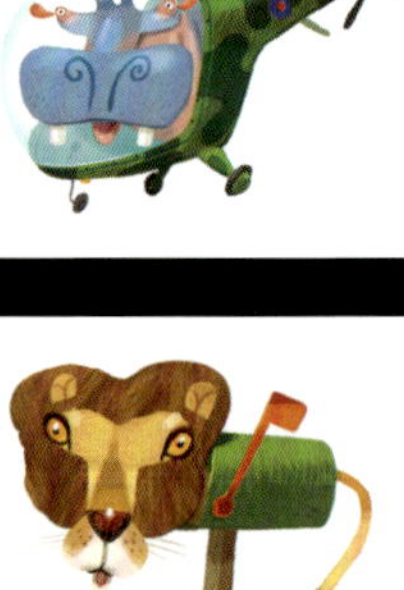

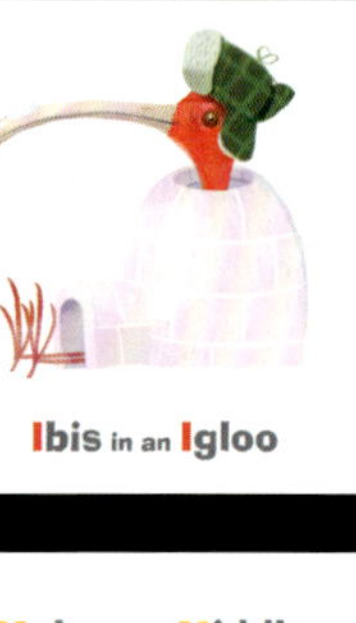

**Ibis** in an **Igloo**

**Yak** in a **Yacht**

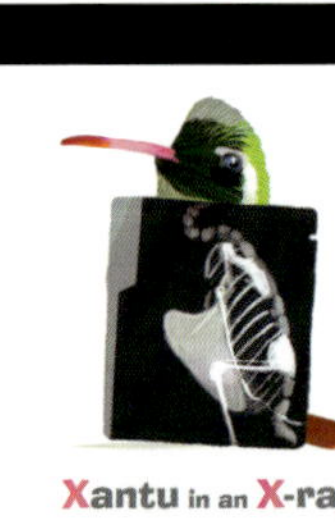

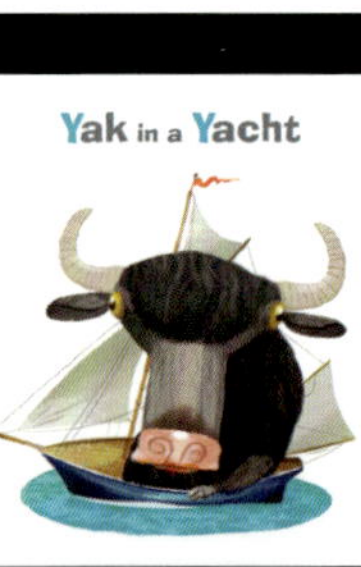

**Xantu** in an **X-ray**

**Mole** in the **Middle**

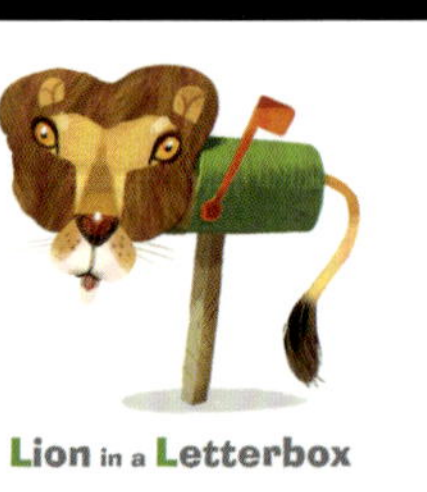

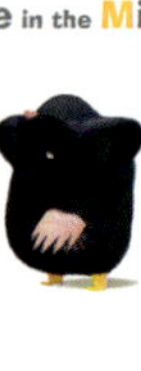

**Lion** in a **Letterbox**

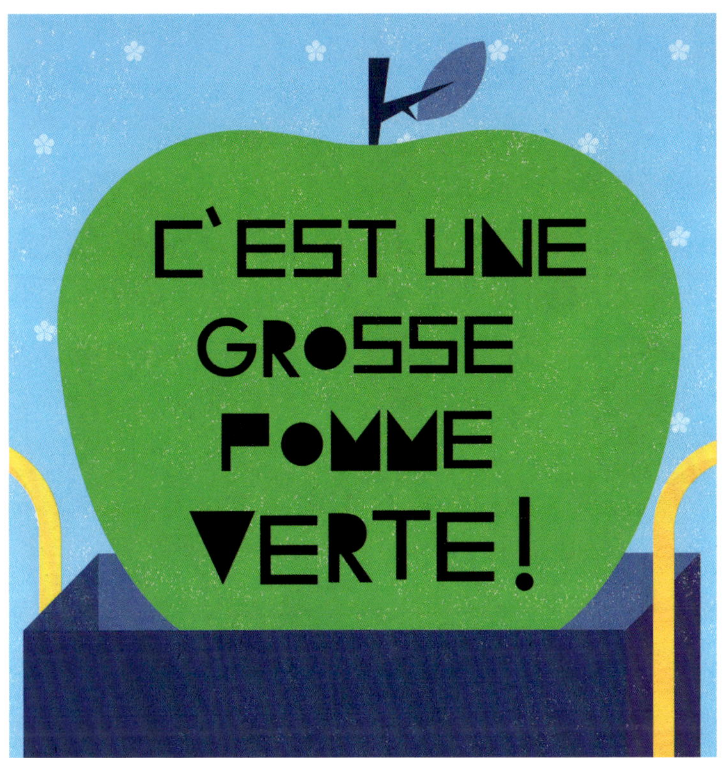


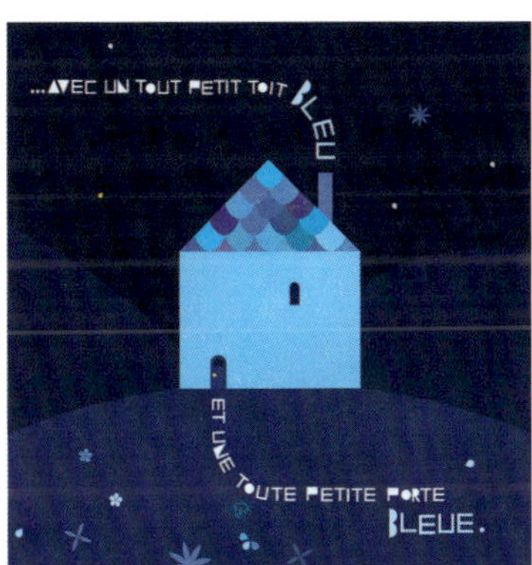


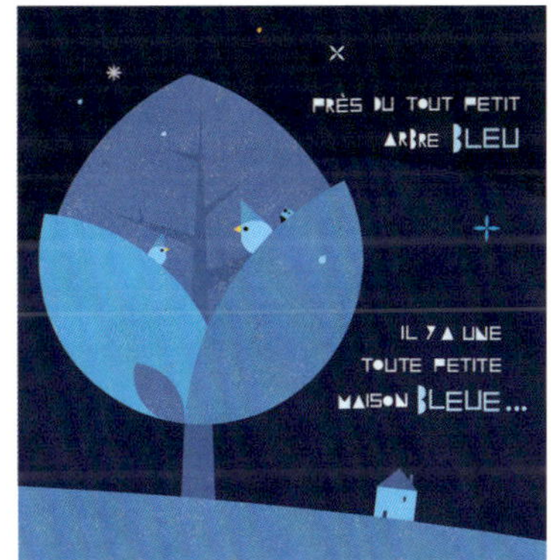


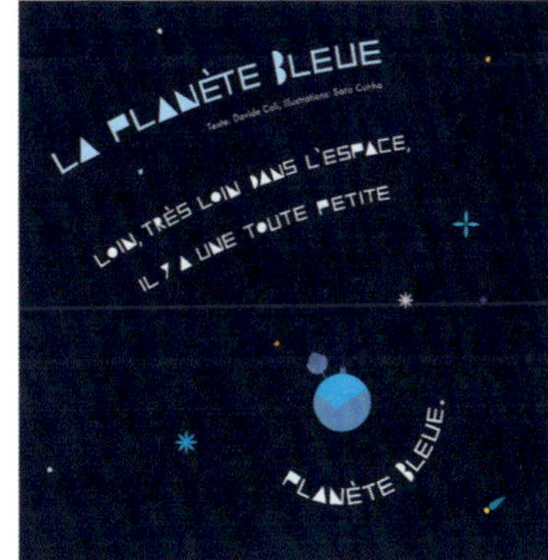


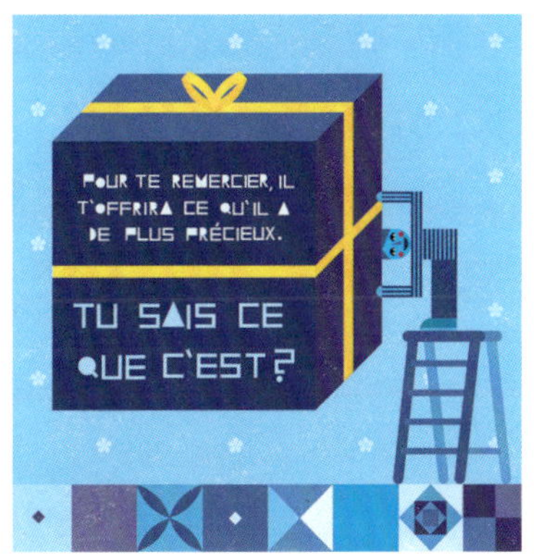


MERIT Sara Cunha

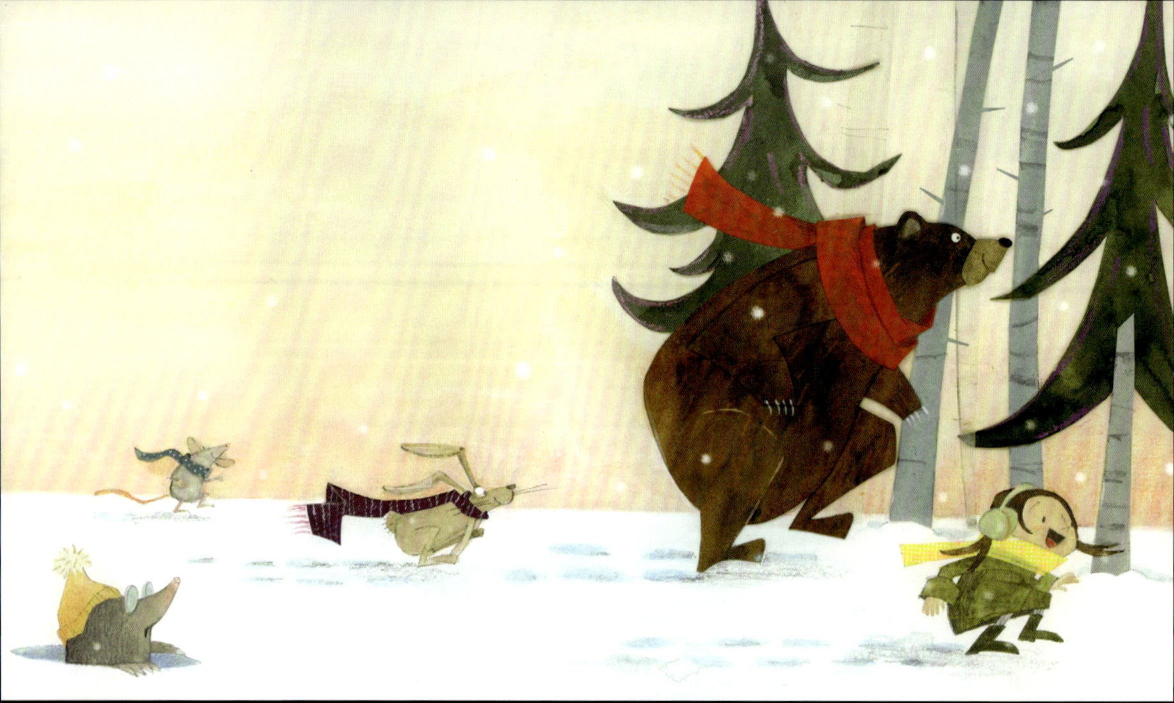

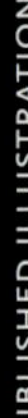



MERIT *Isabel Roxas*

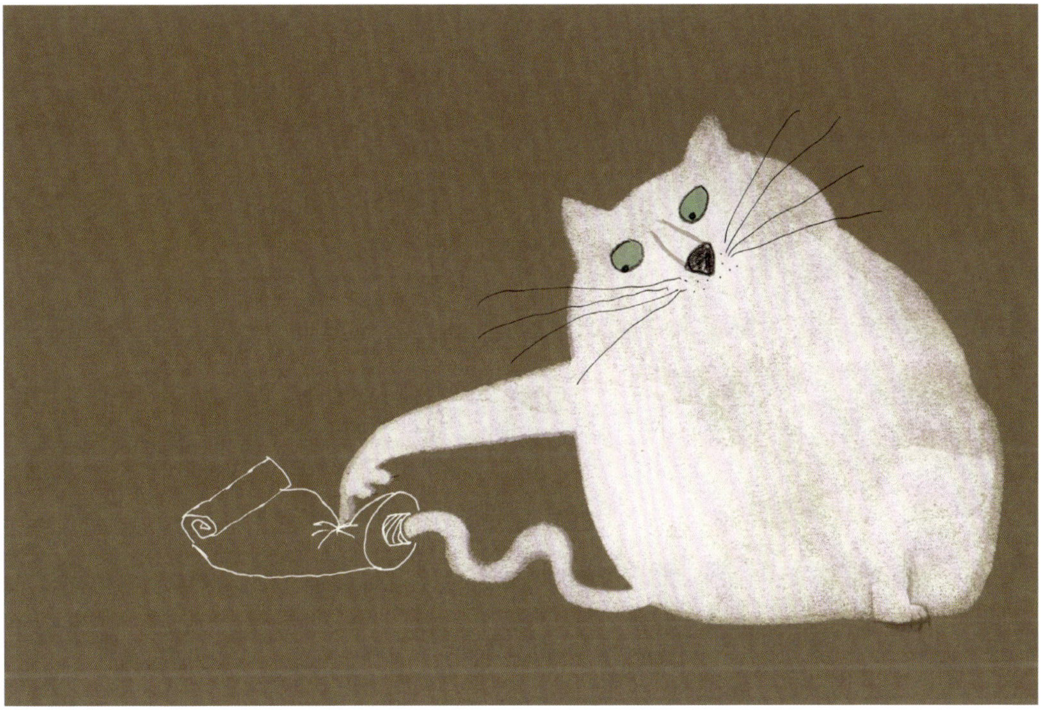

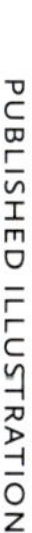

MERIT *Klaas Verplancke*

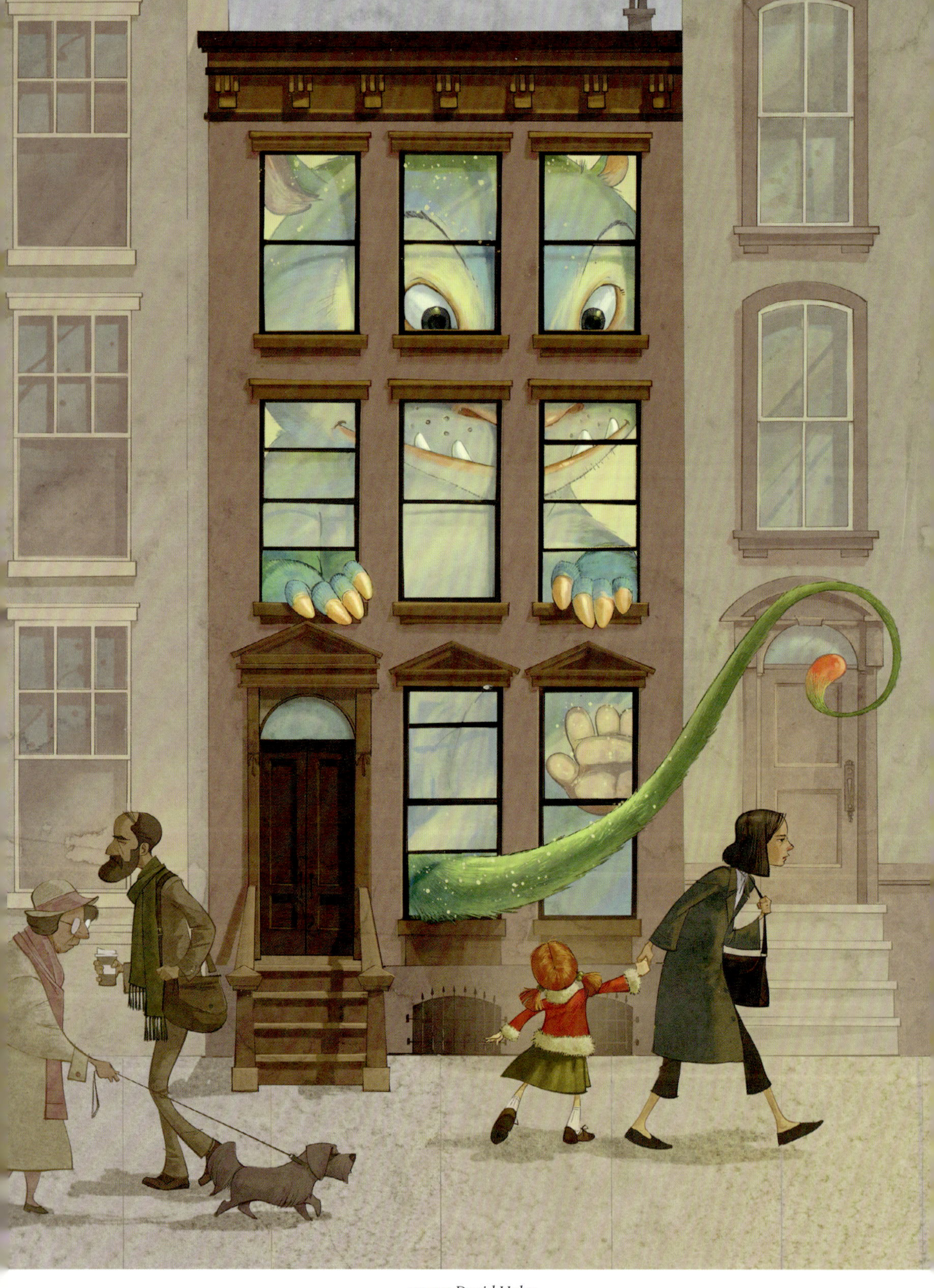

MERIT *David Hohn*

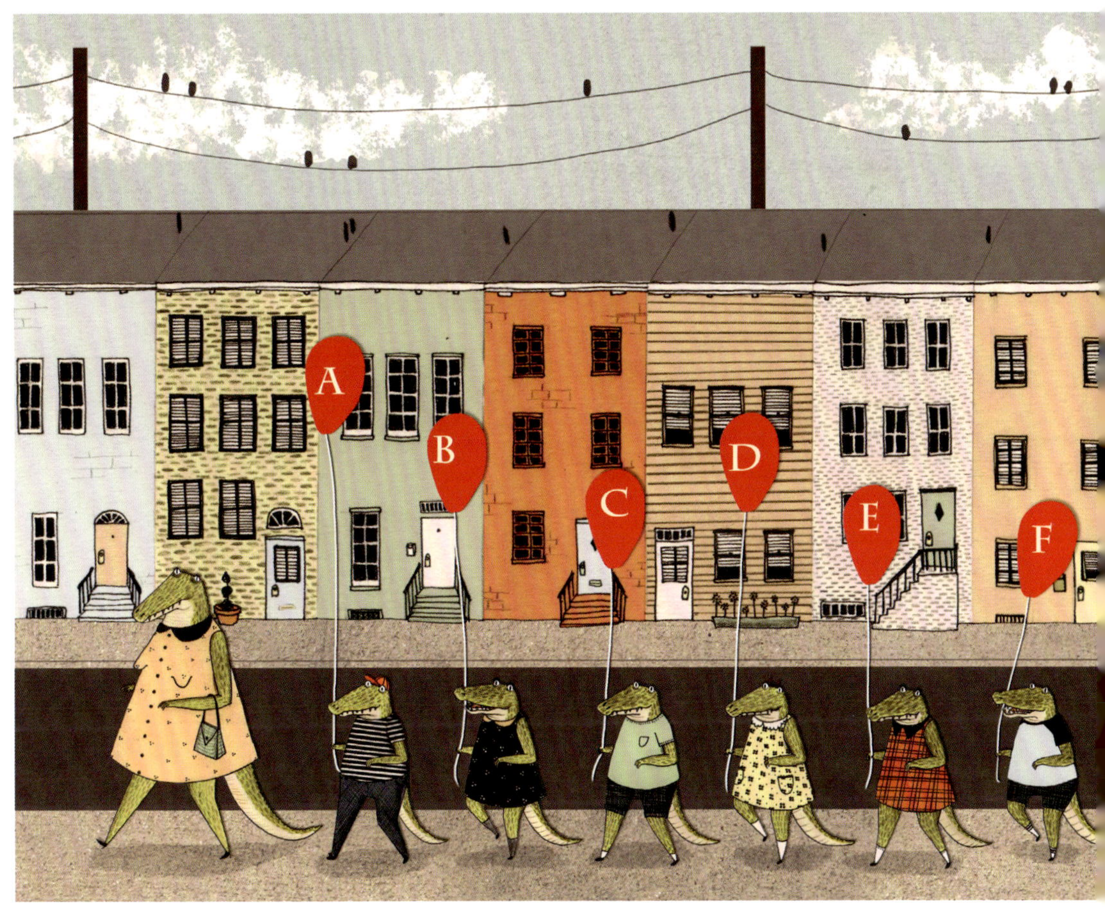


MERIT *Mai Ly Degnan*

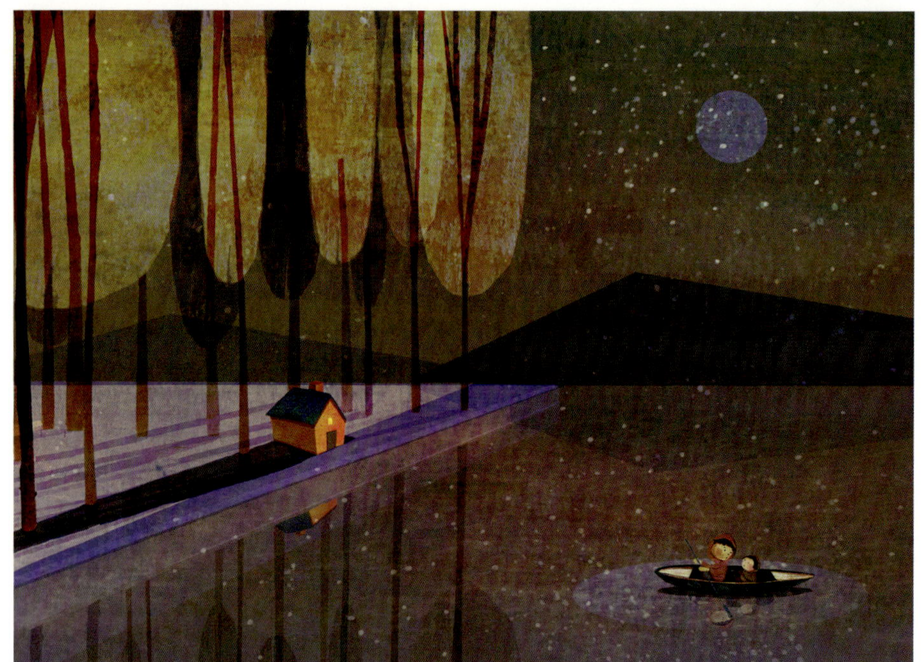

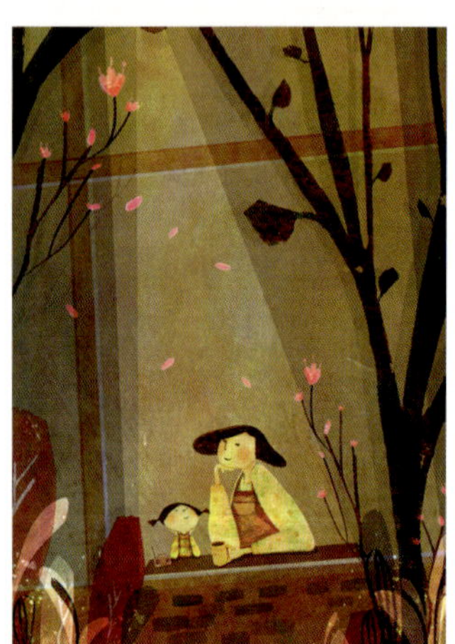

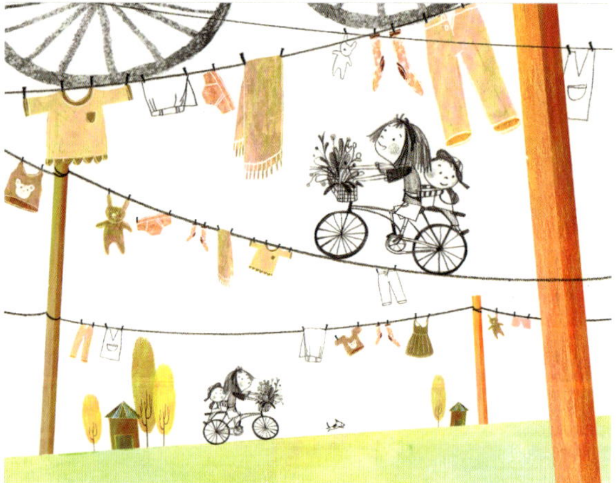

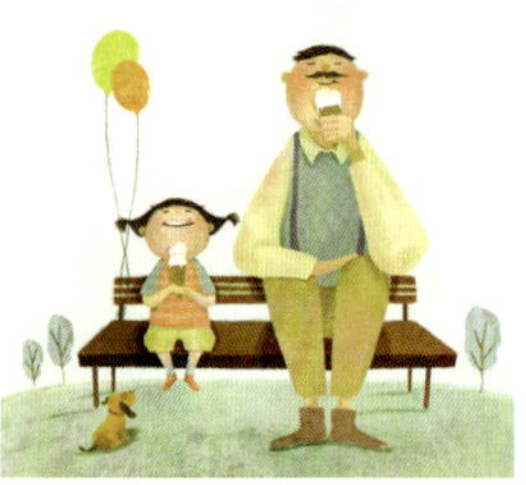


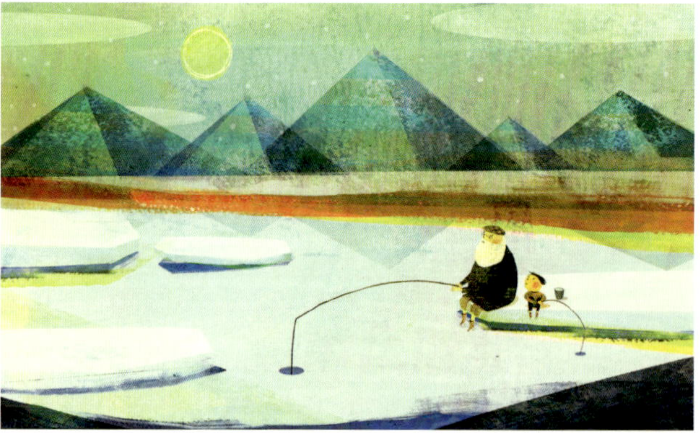

(L) MERIT *Jaime Jimyung Kim*   (R) MERIT *Sara Corbett*

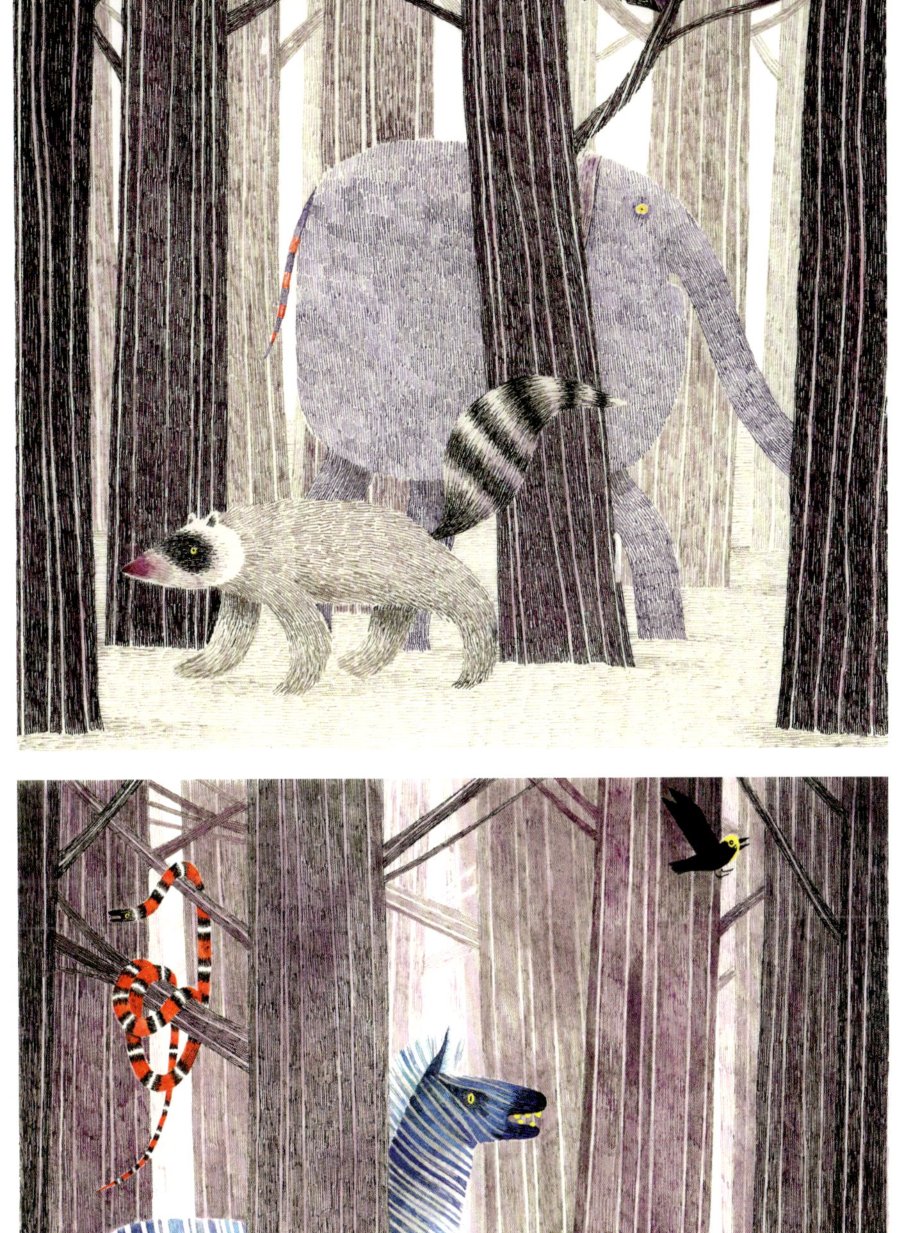

UNPUBLISHED ILLUSTRATION

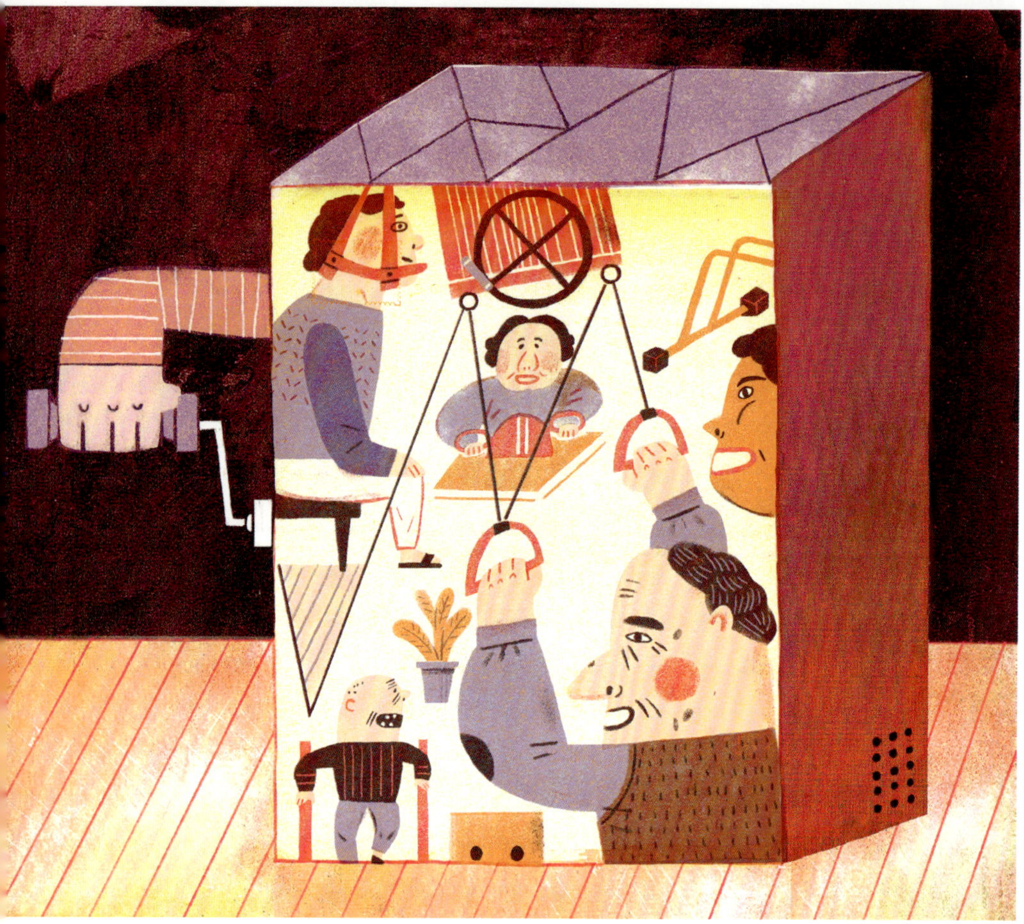

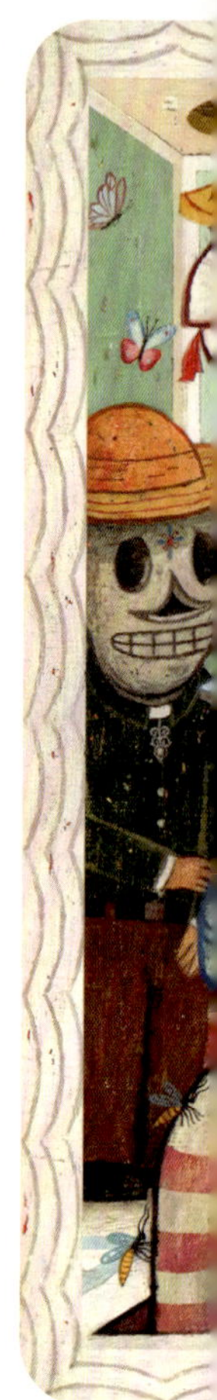

MERIT *Huang Ling Hsing*

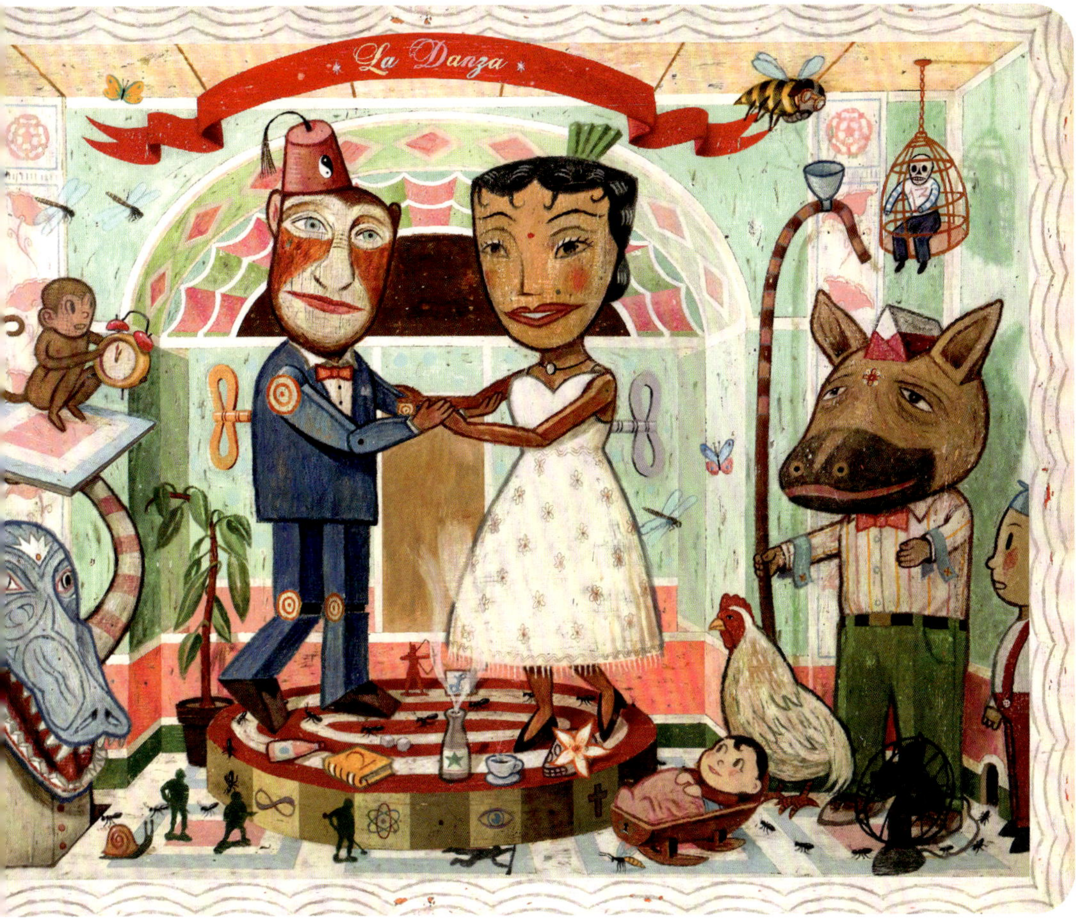

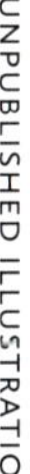




MERIT *John Parra*

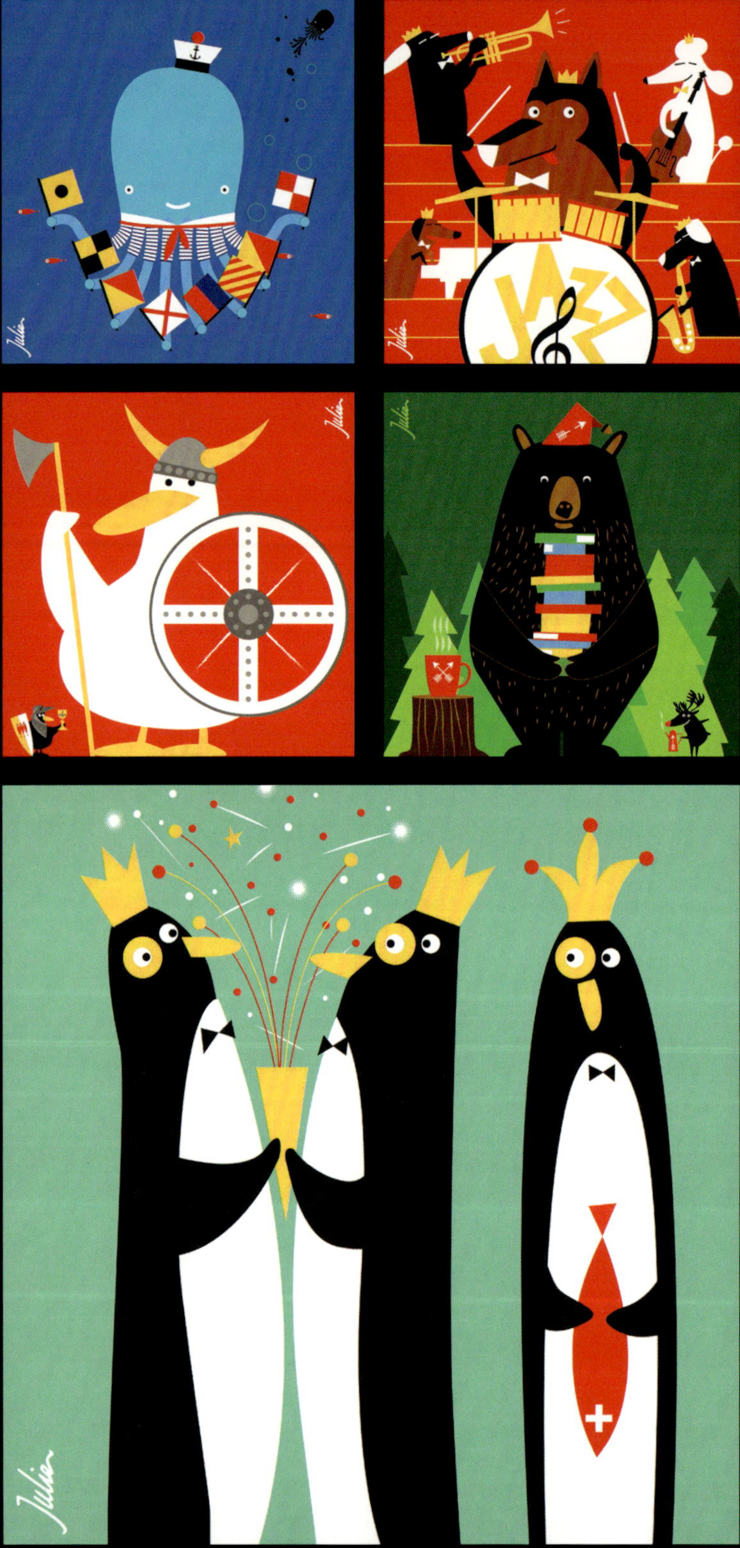

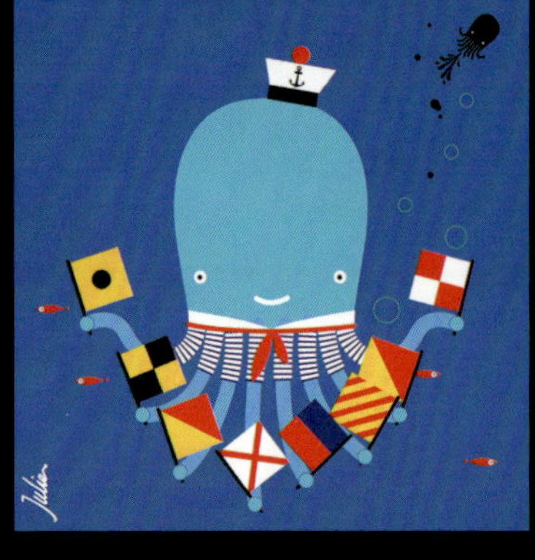
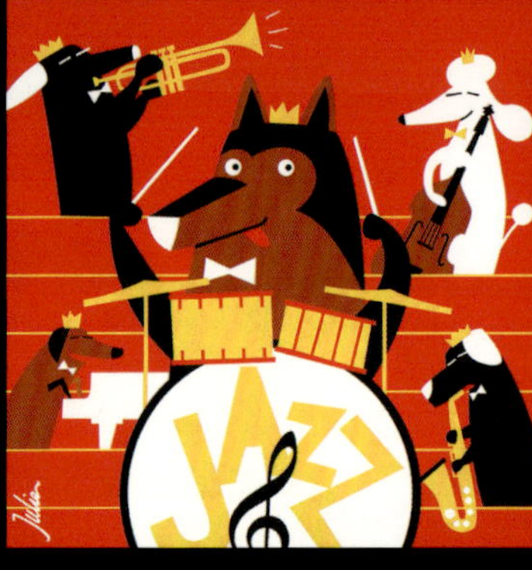
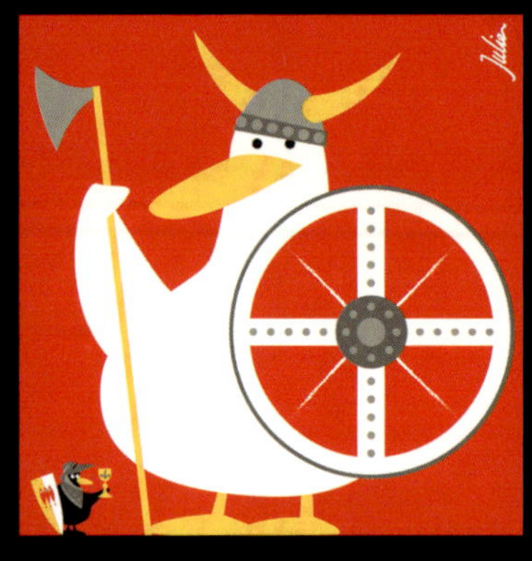
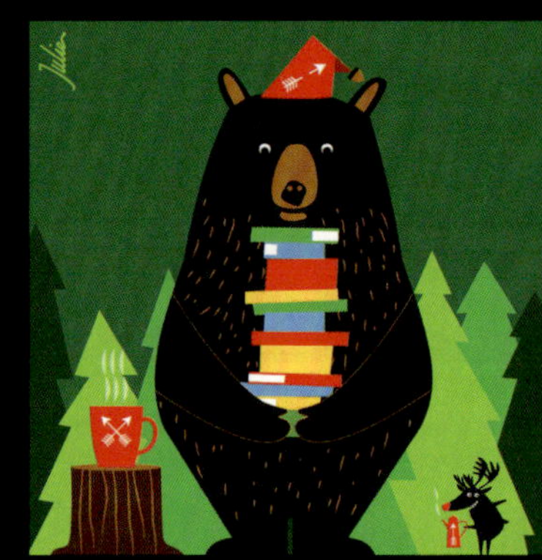

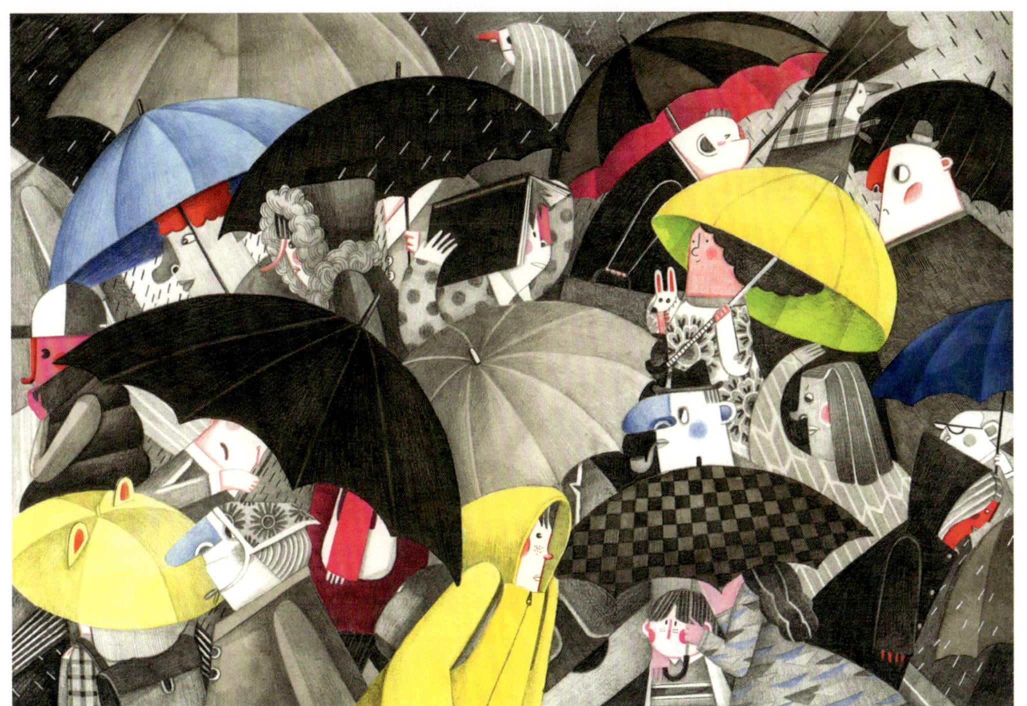

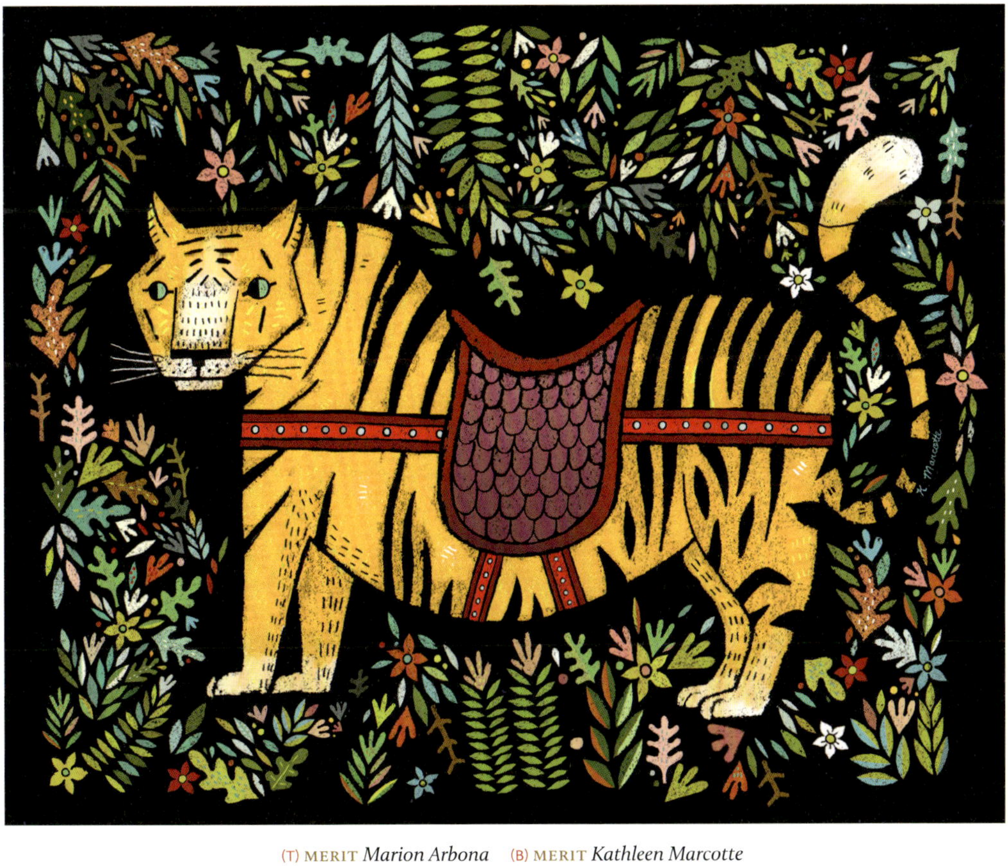

(T) MERIT *Marion Arbona*    (B) MERIT *Kathleen Marcotte*

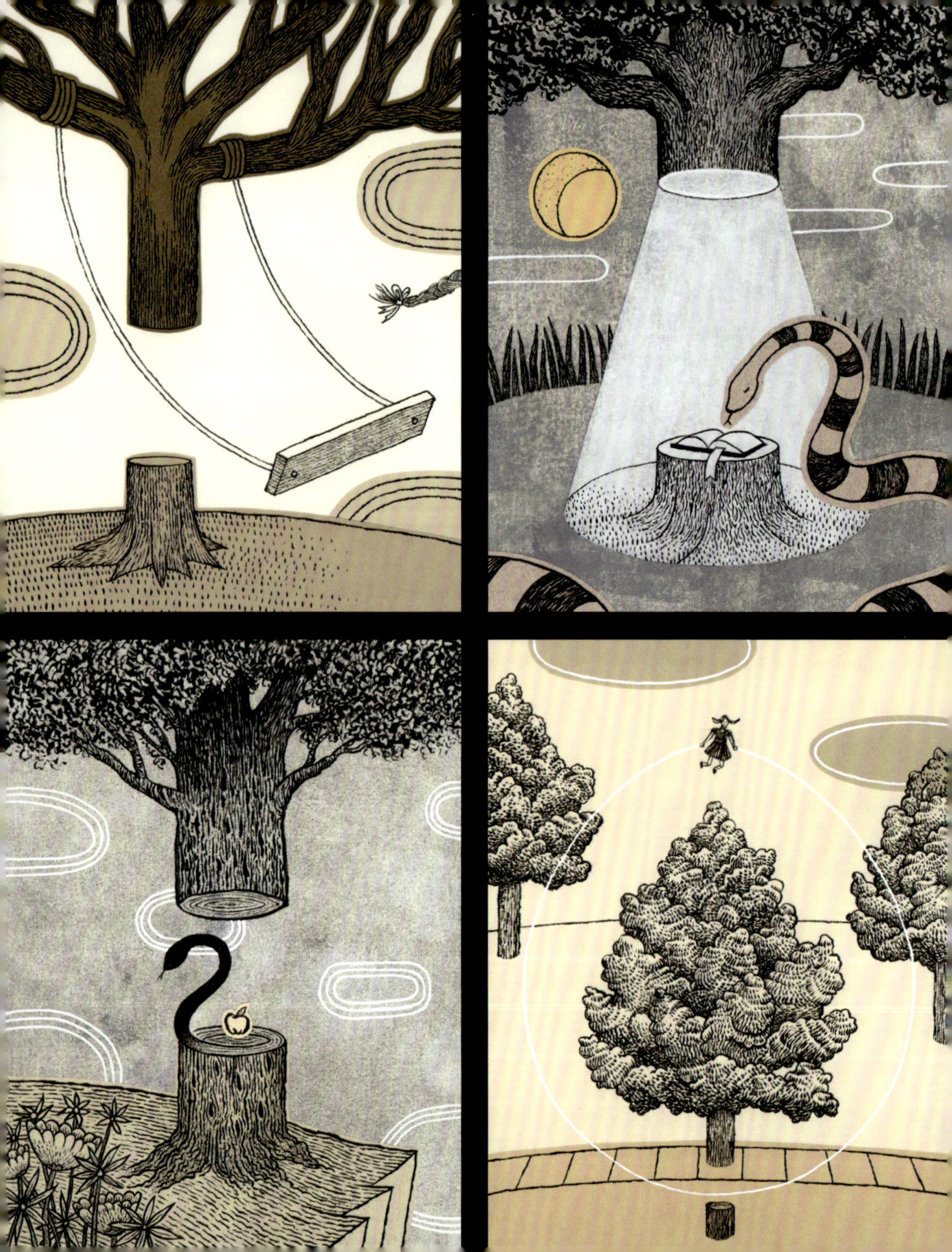

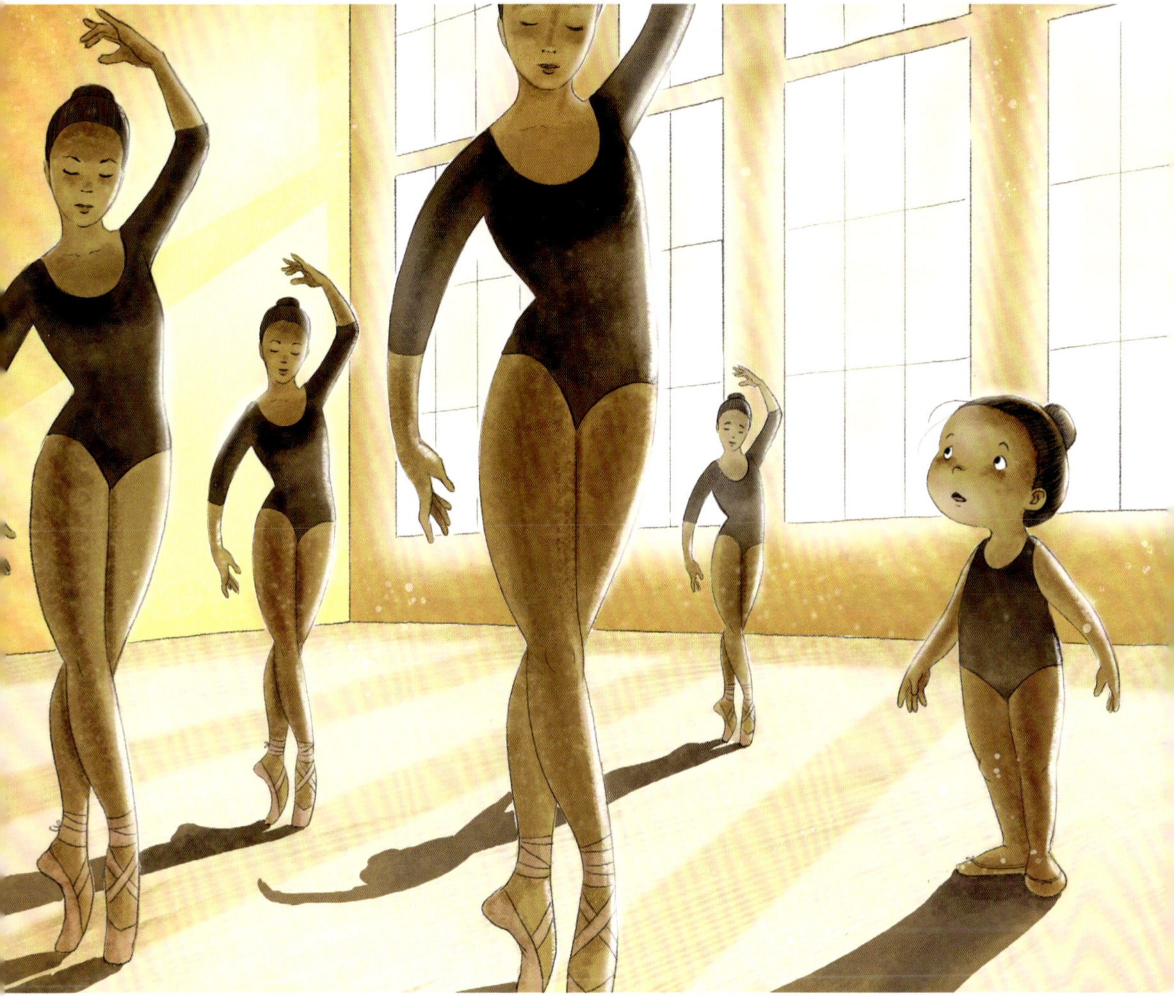

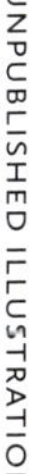
UNPUBLISHED ILLUSTRATION

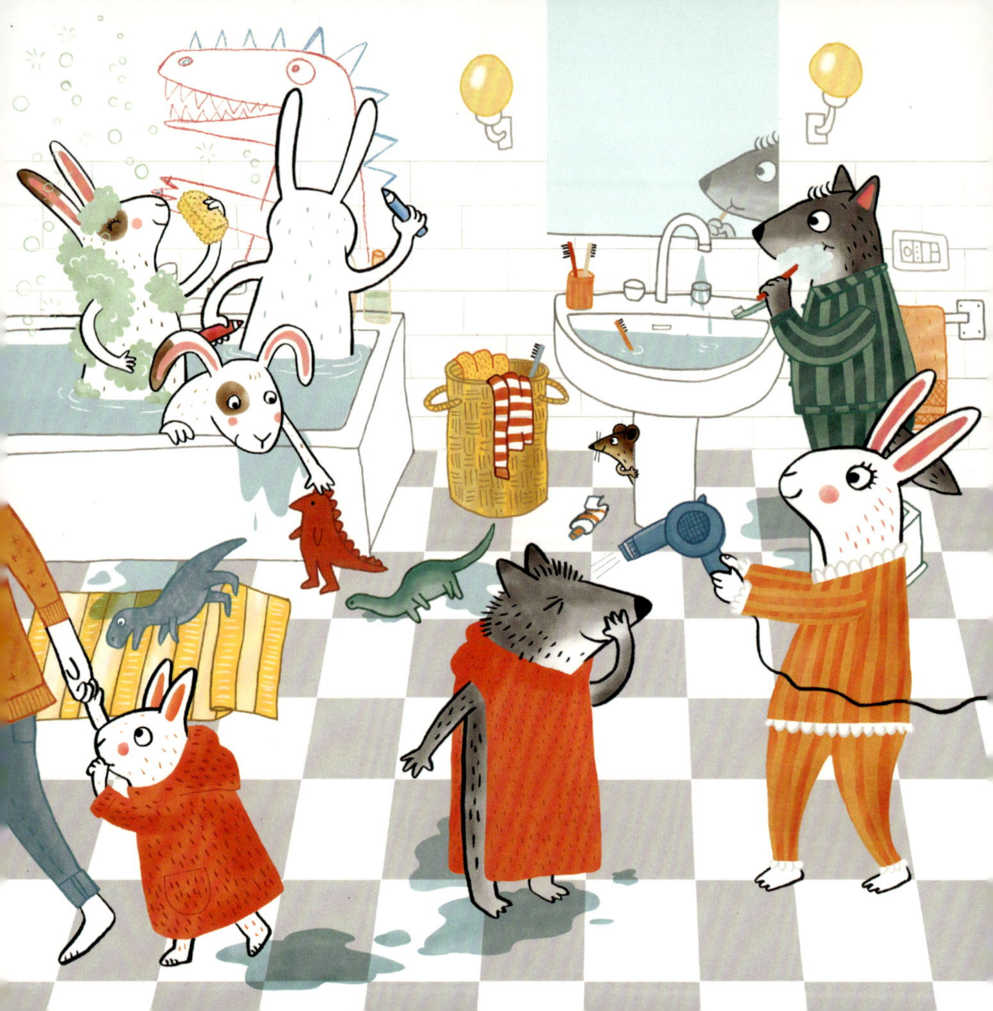

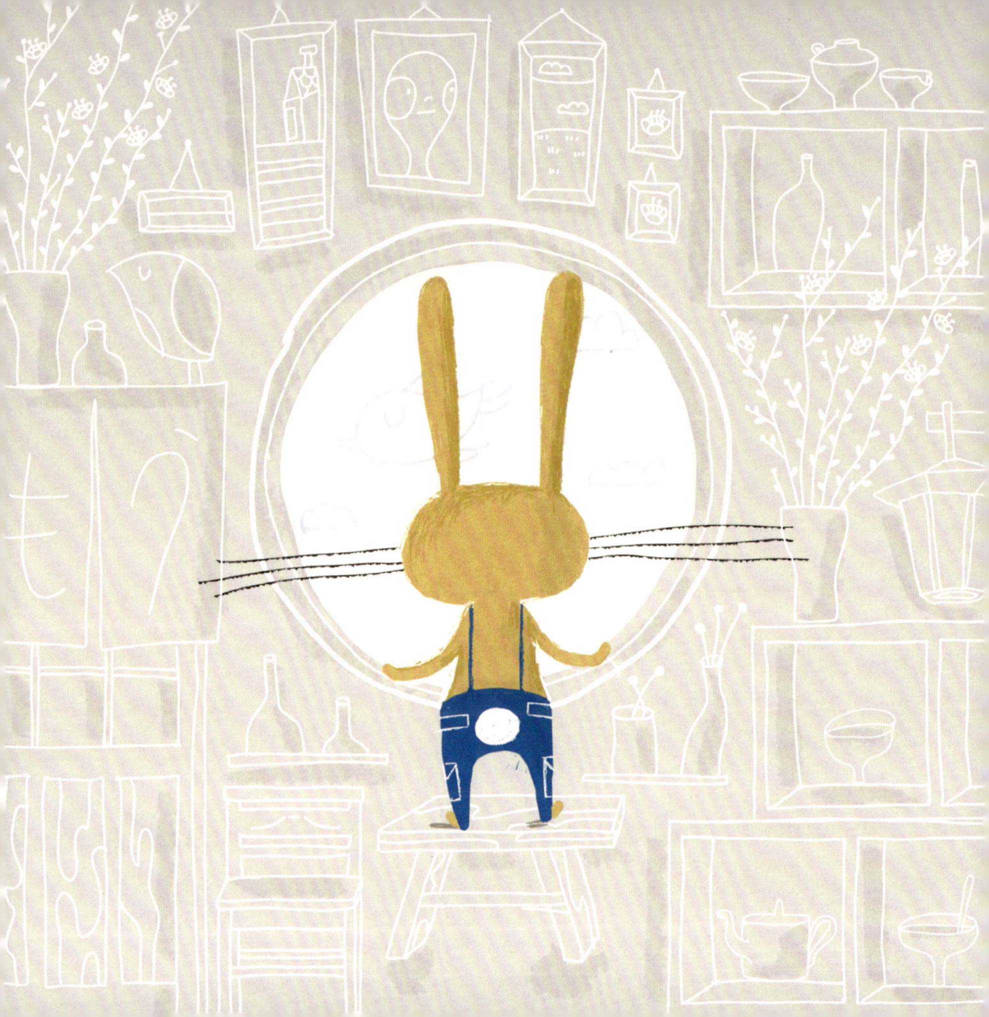

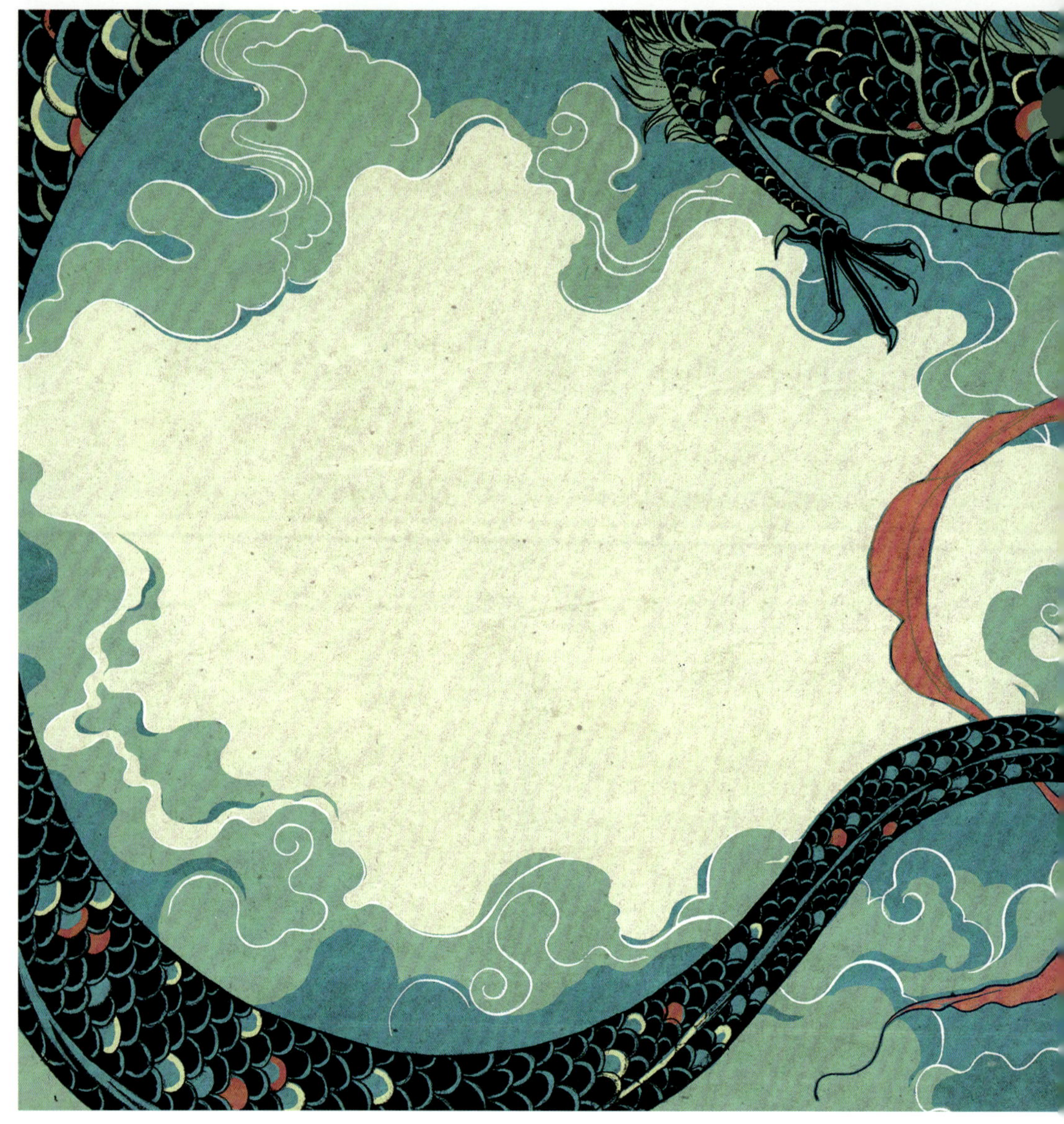

BRONZE *Rongyuan Ma*

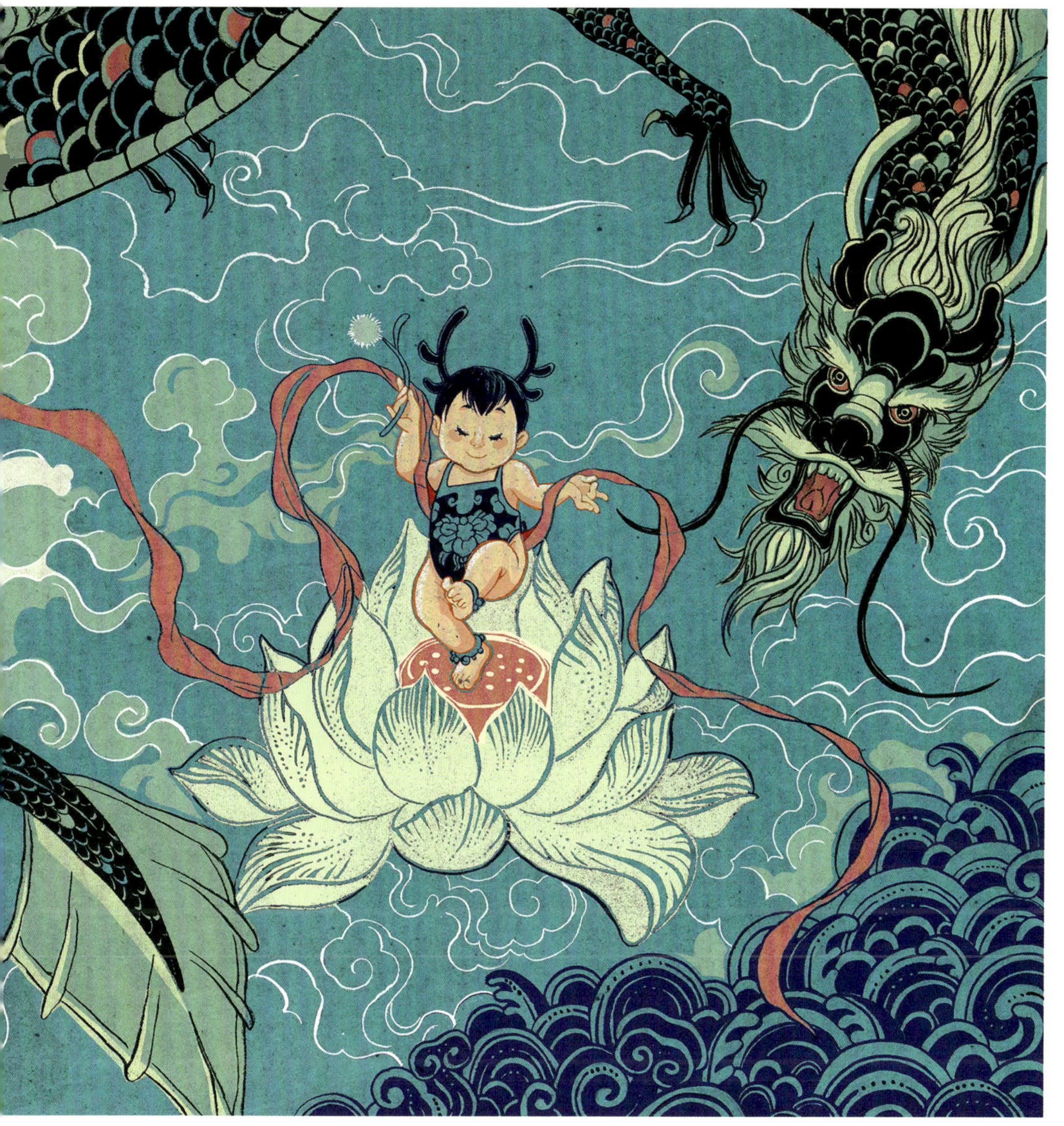

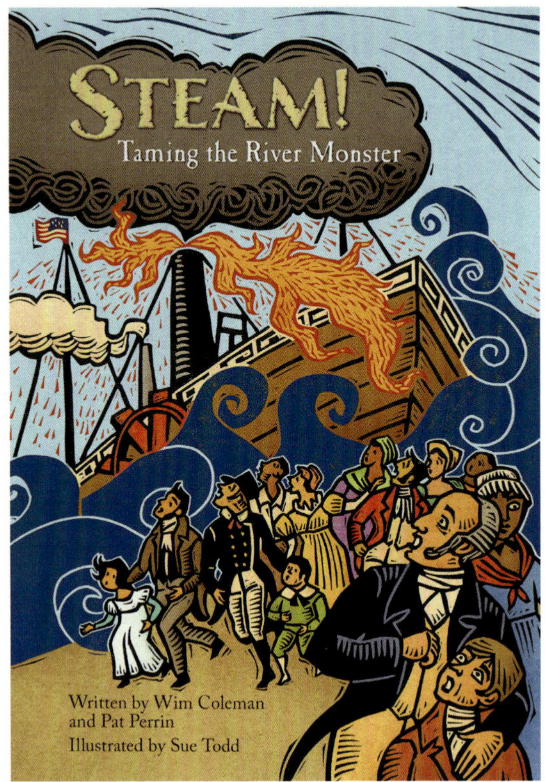


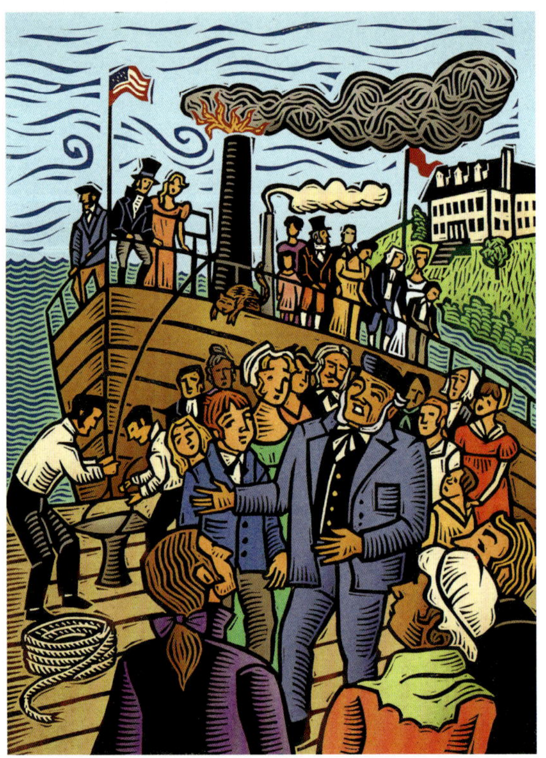

MERIT *Sue Todd*

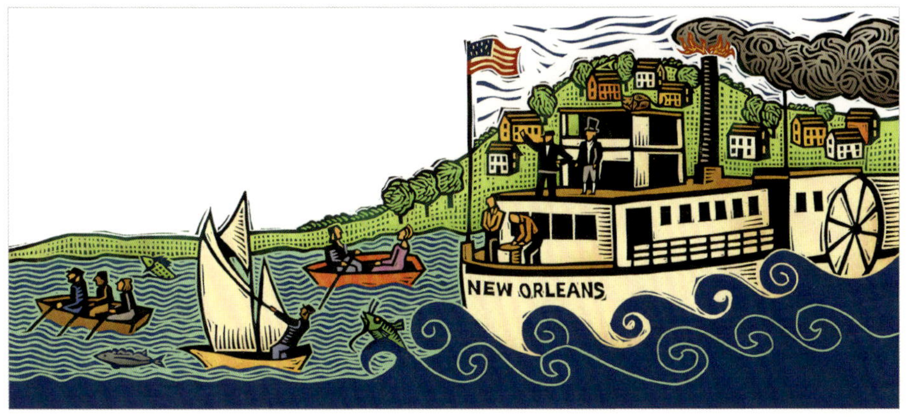

NEW ORLEANS


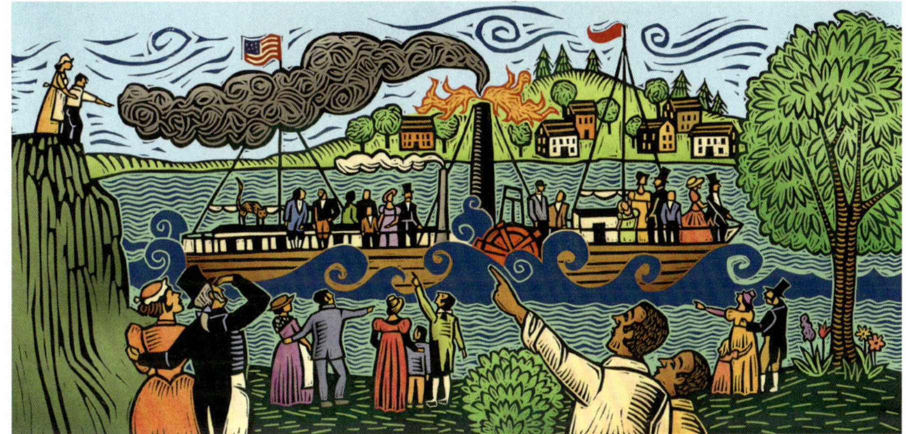

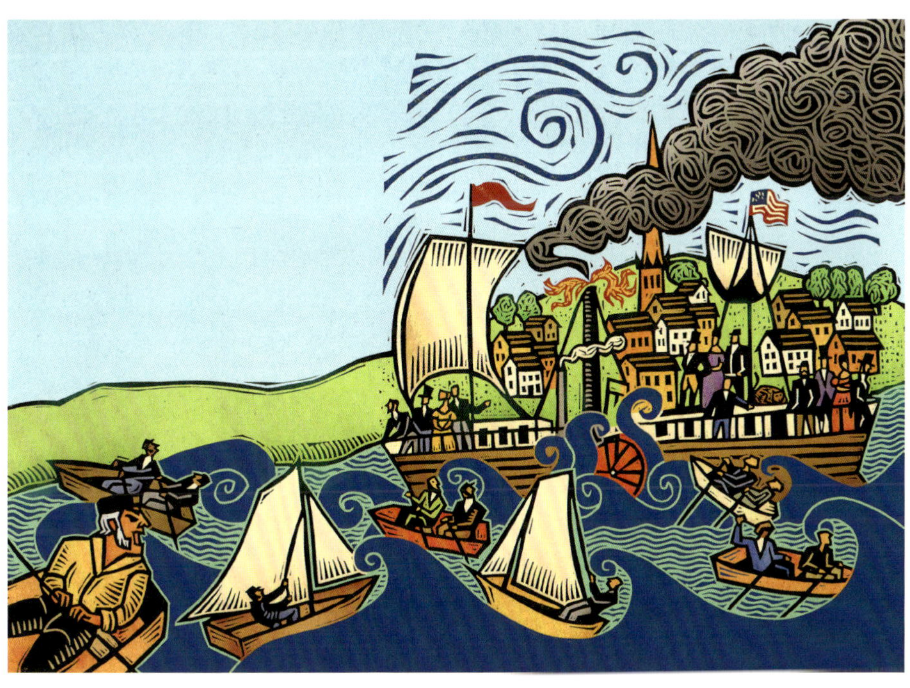

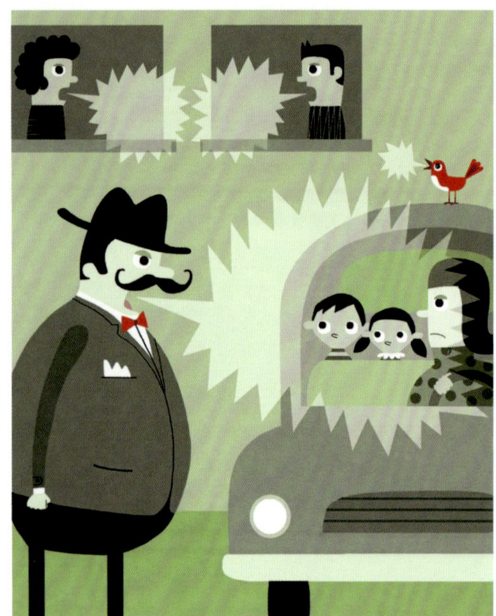
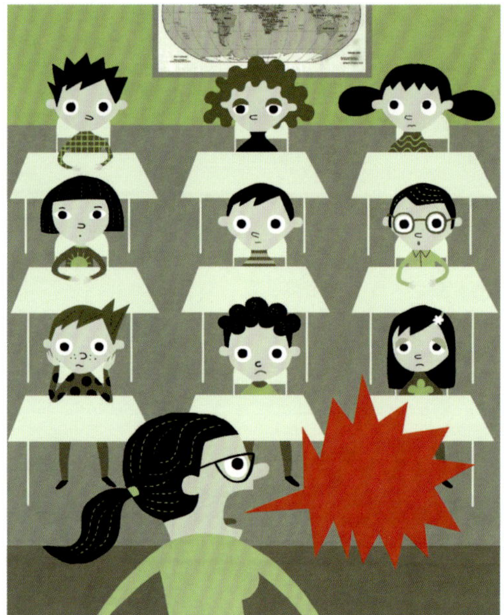
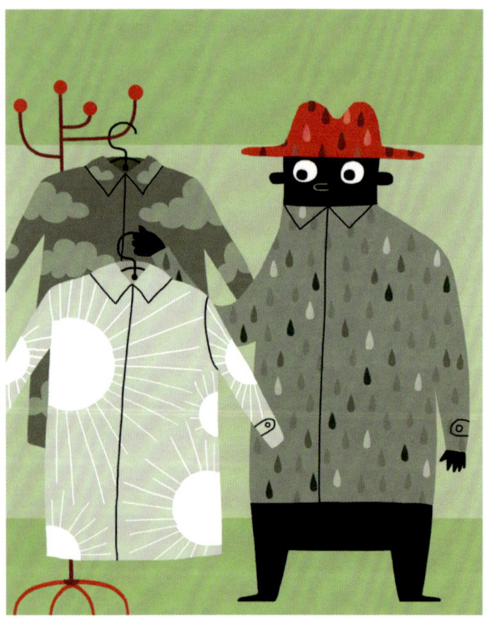
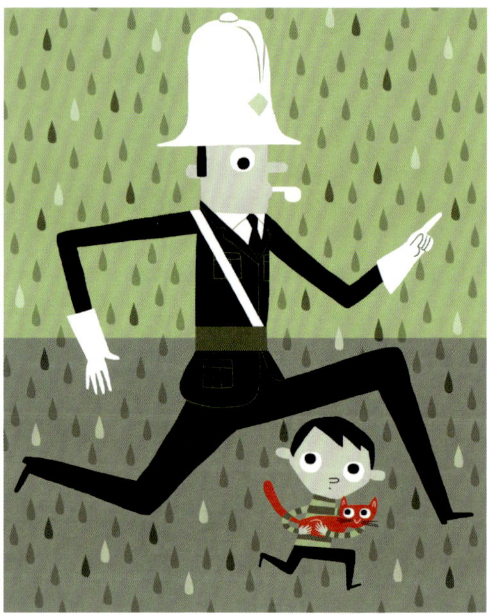

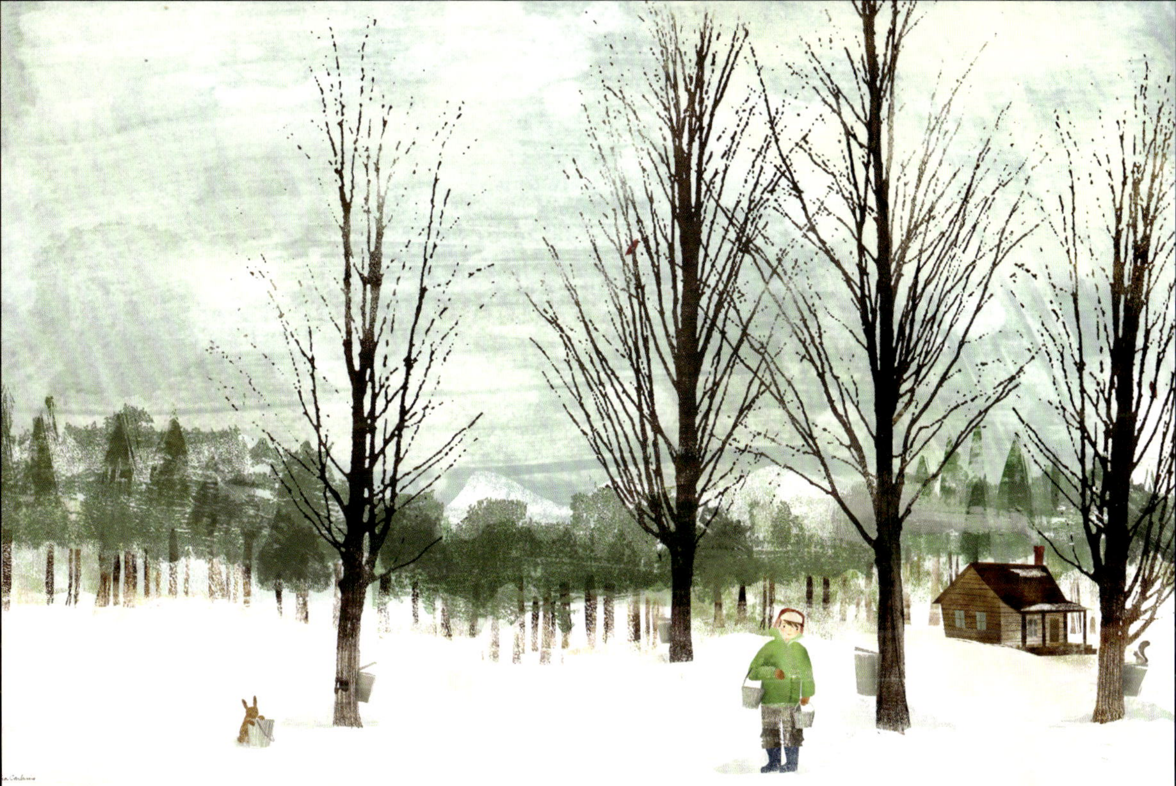

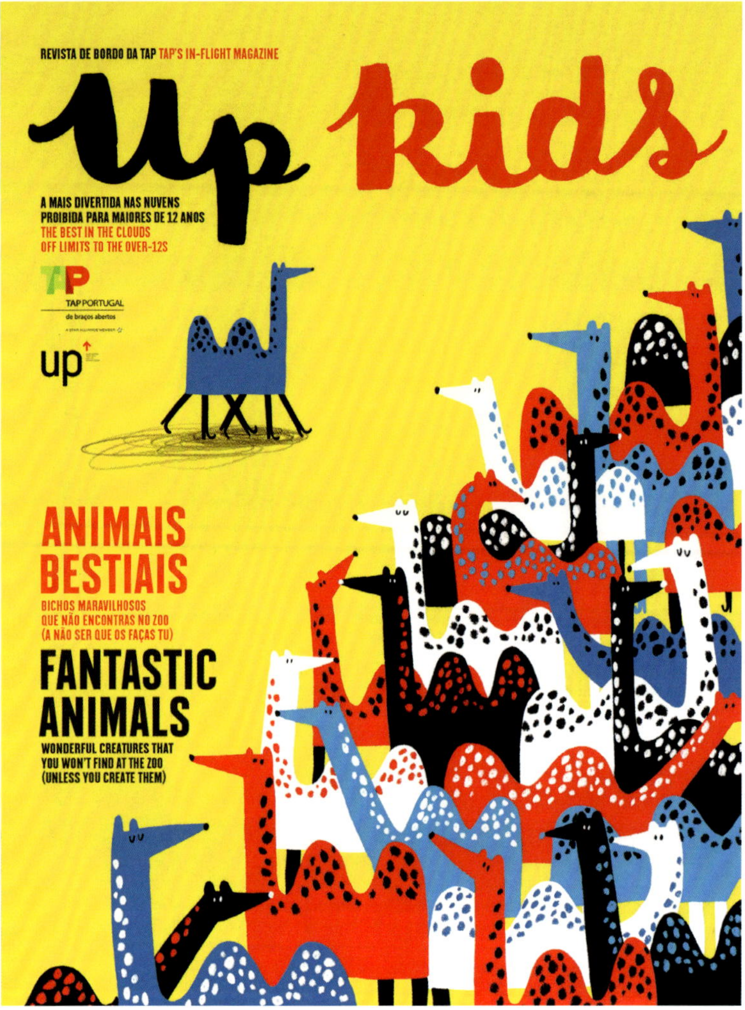

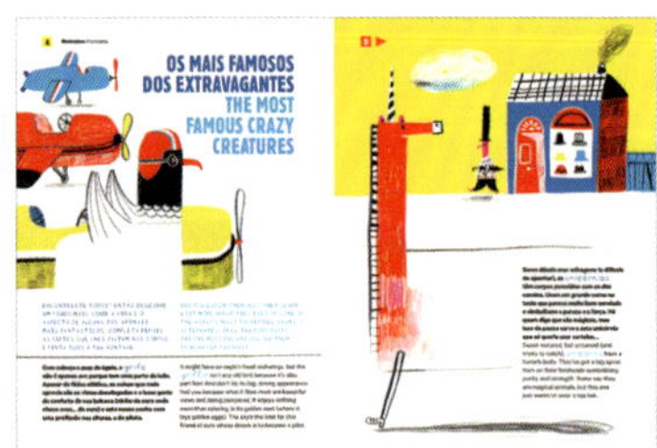


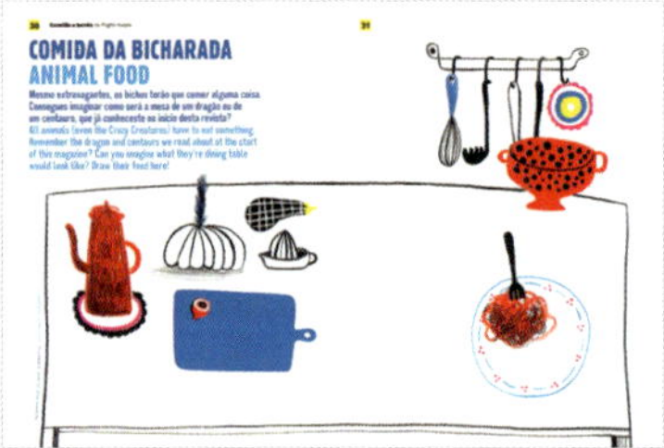


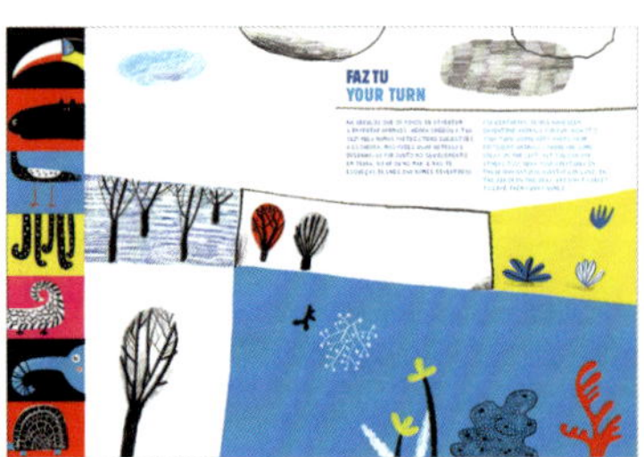


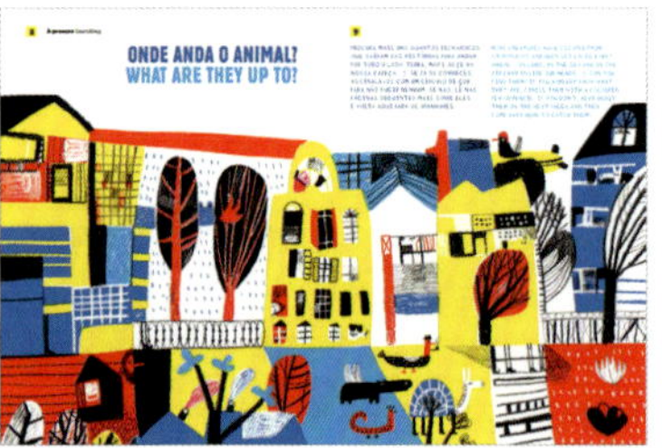


SILVER *Catarina Sobral*

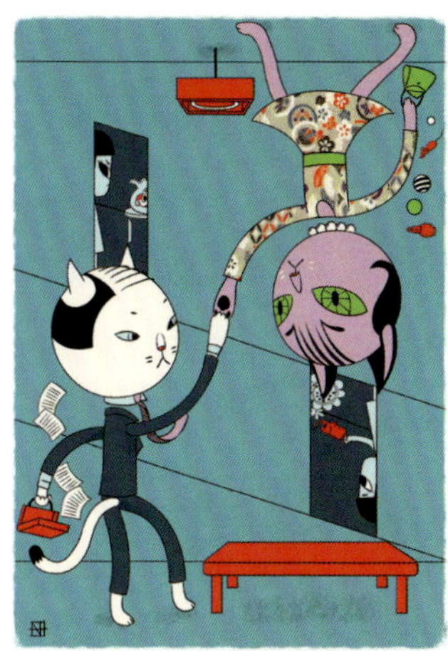
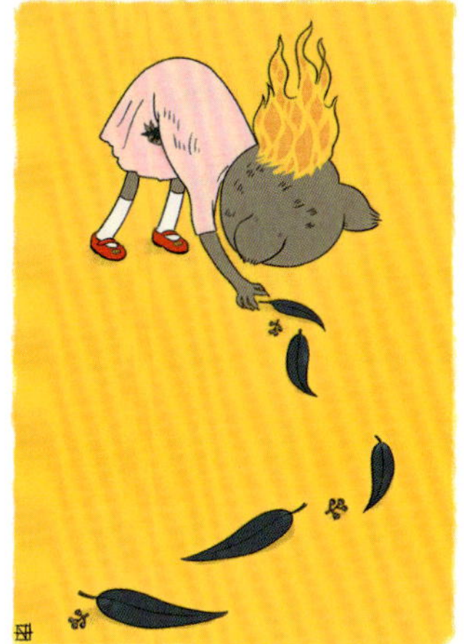
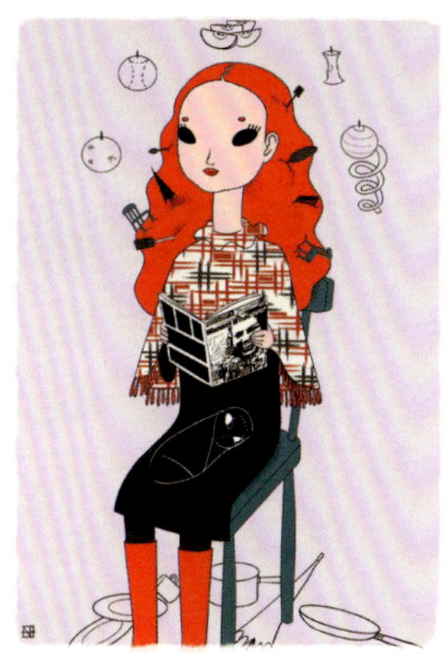
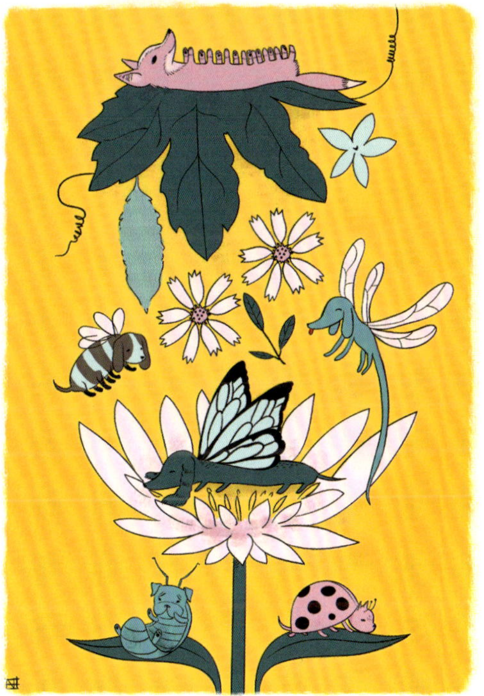
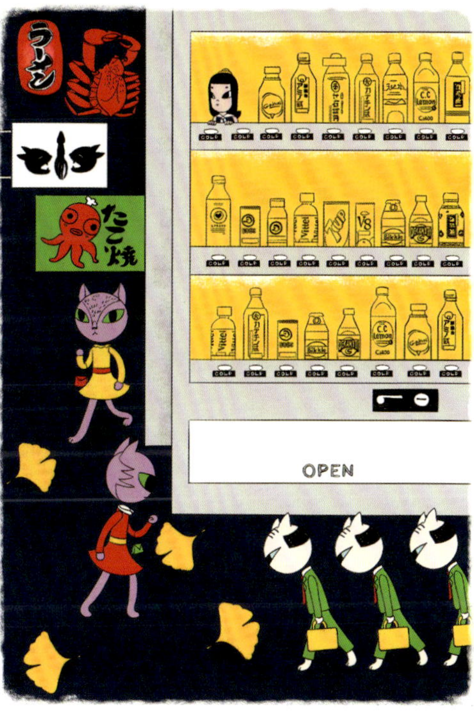



MERIT *Andrea Innocent*

283

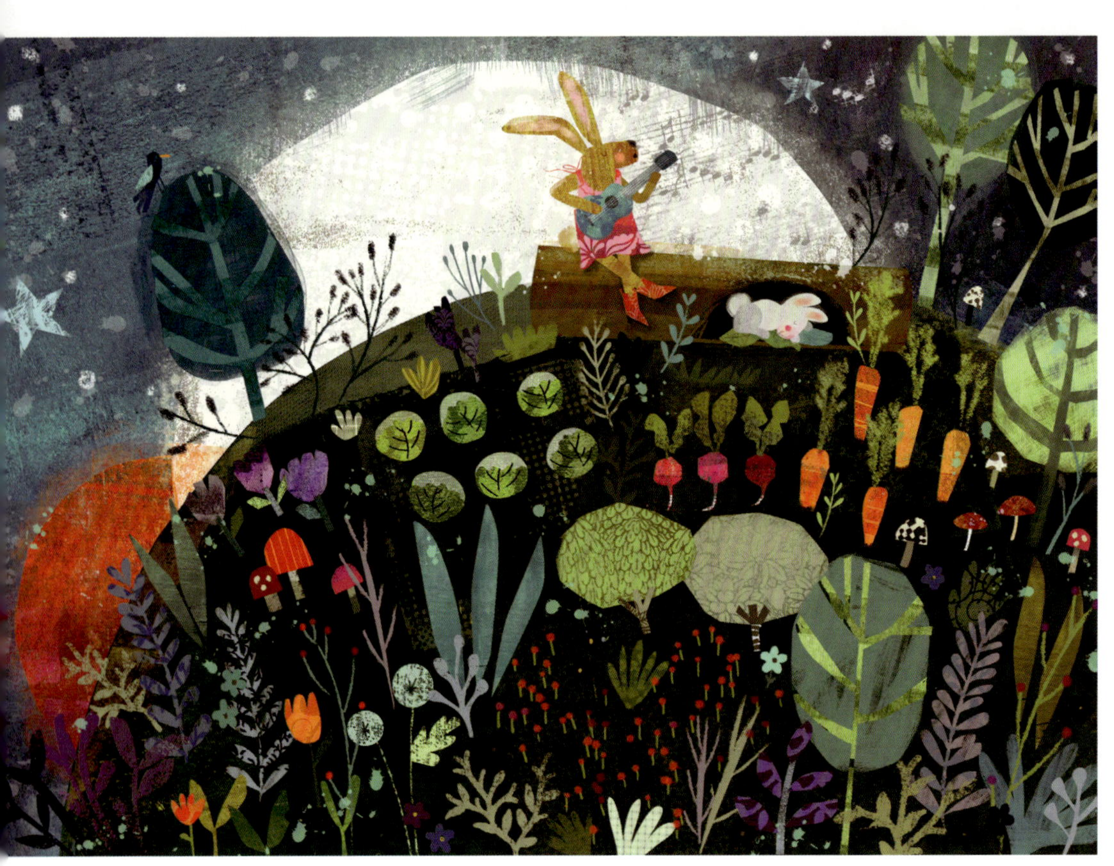

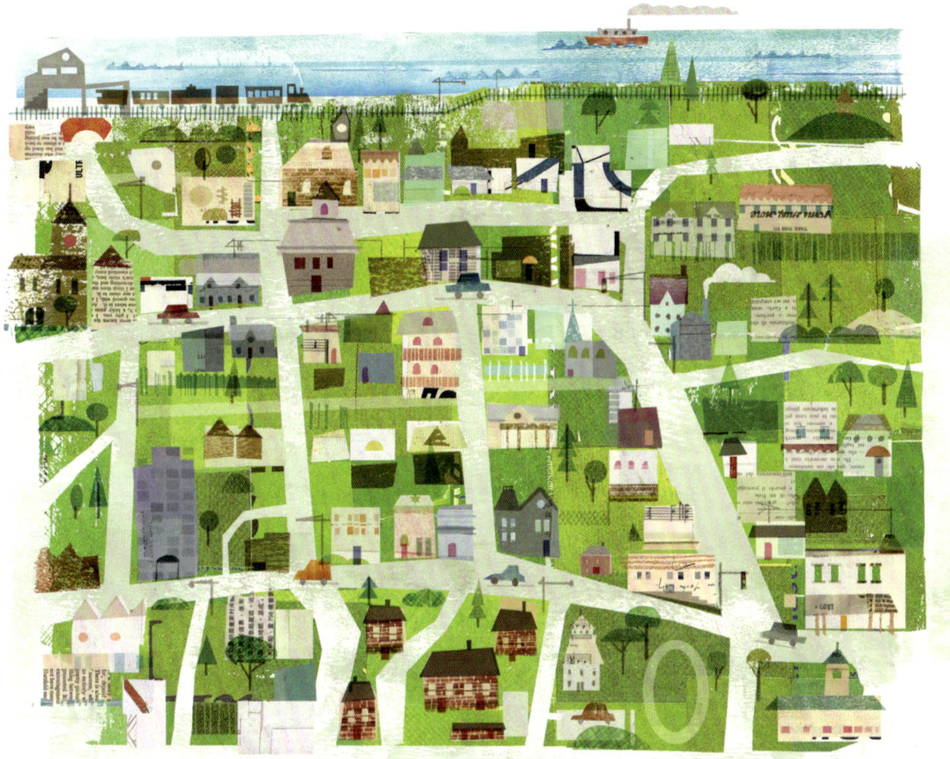

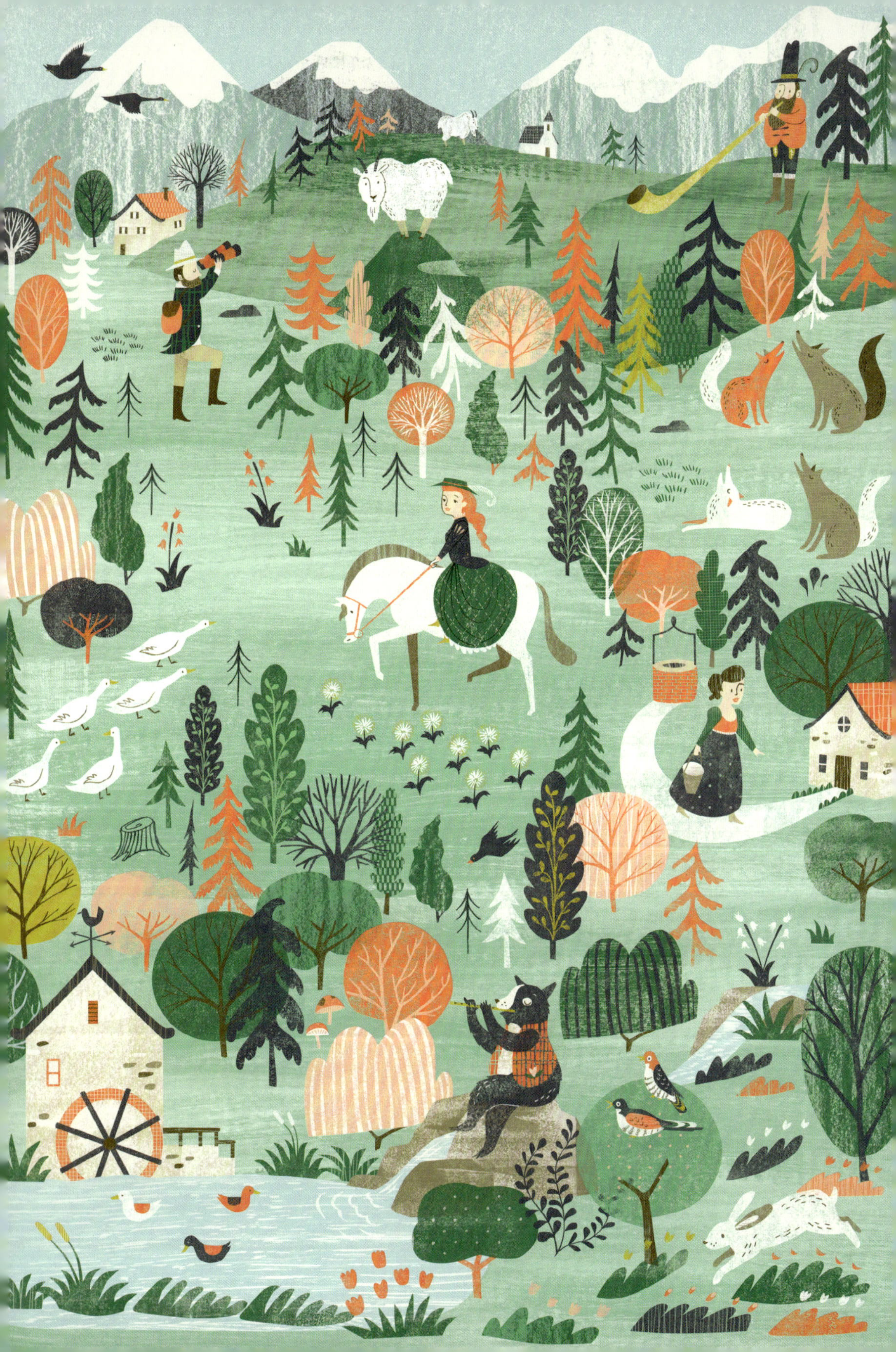

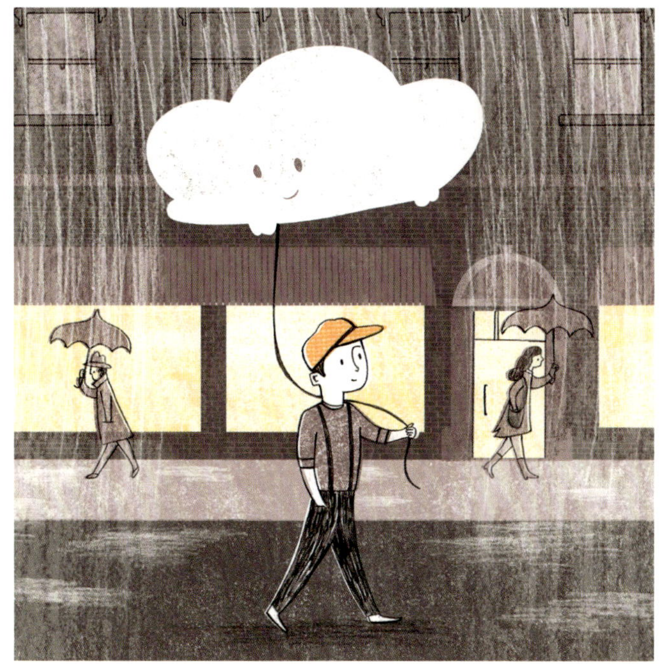
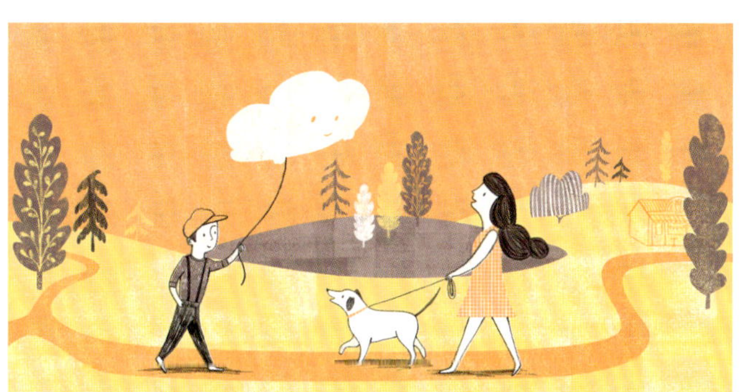
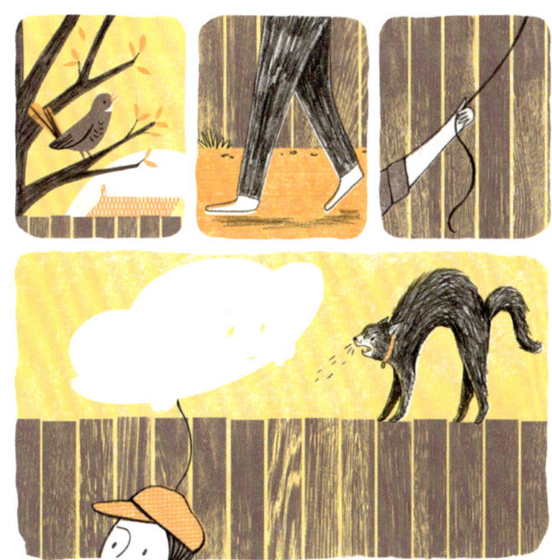
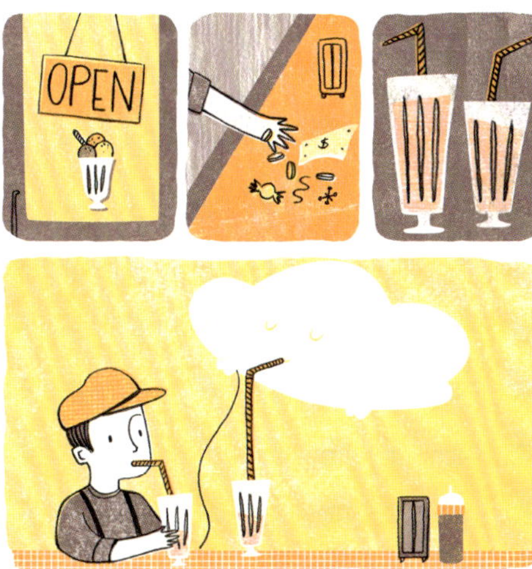


(L) MERIT *Angela Keoghan*  (R) MERIT *Angela Keoghan*

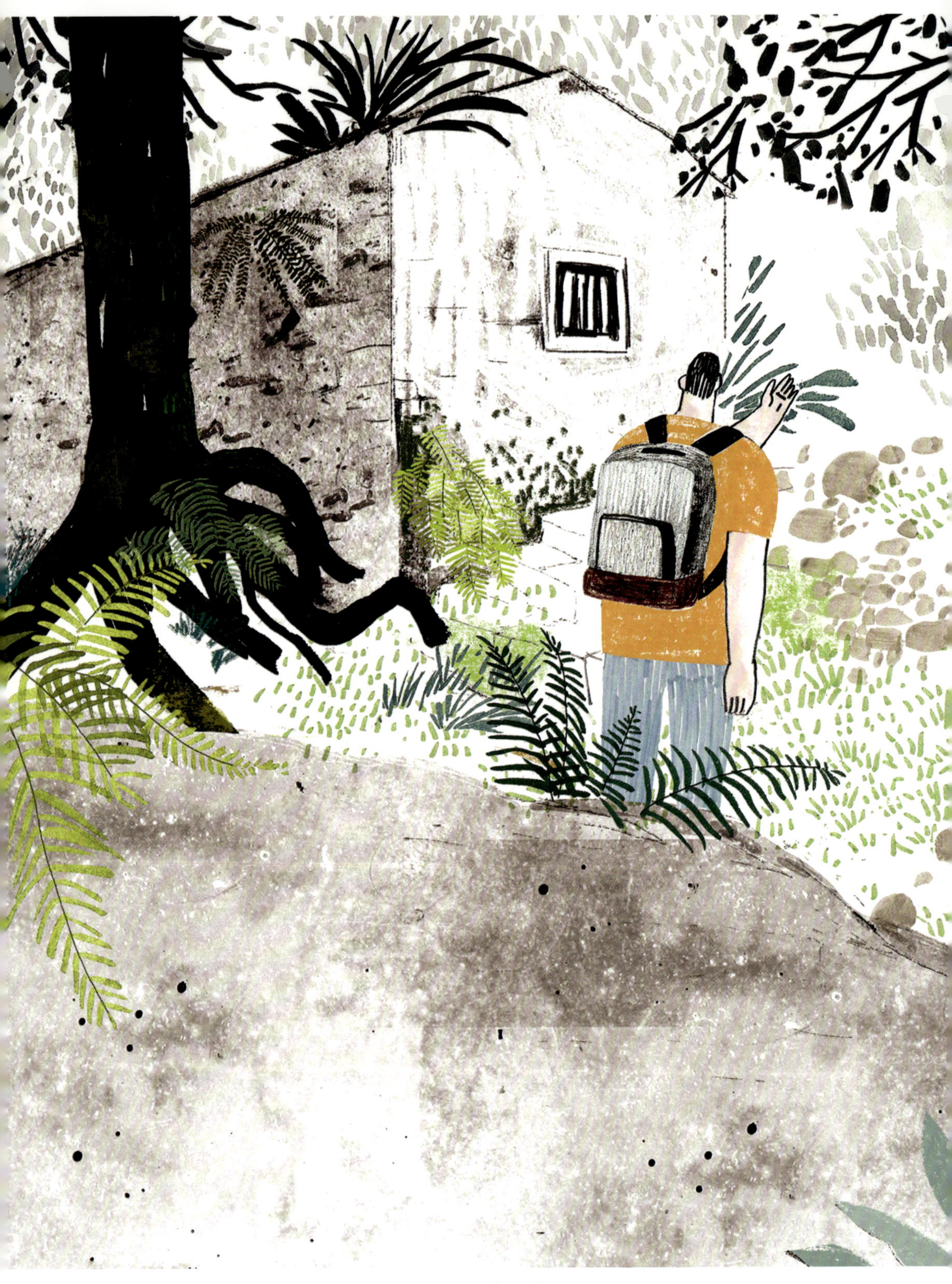

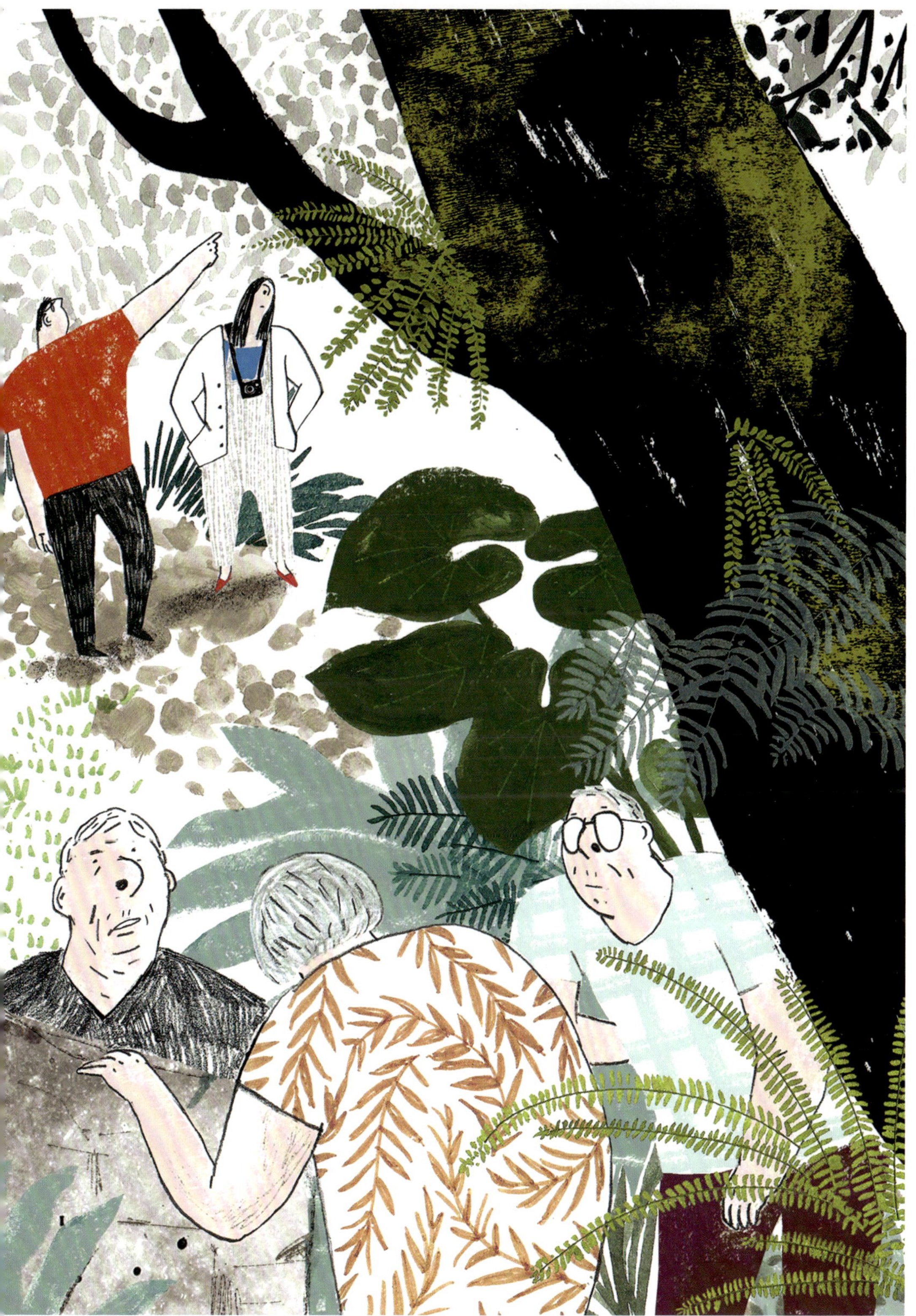

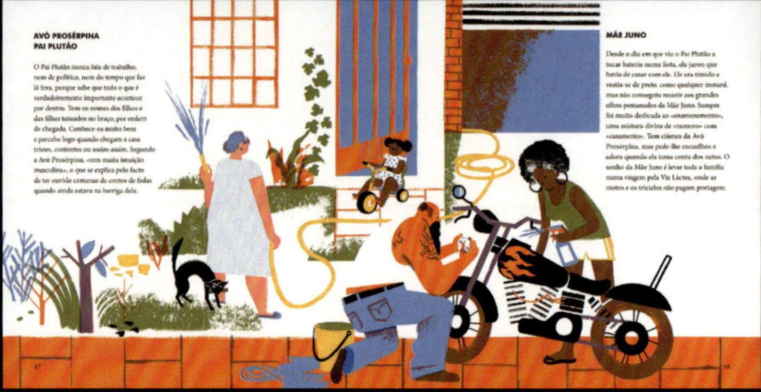

### AVÓ PROSÉRPINA
### PAI PLUTÃO

O Pai Plutão nunca fala de trabalho, nem de política, nem do tempo que faz lá fora, porque sabe que tudo o que é verdadeiramente importante acontece por dentro. Tem os nomes dos filhos e das filhas tatuados no braço, por ordem de chegada. Conhece-os muito bem e percebe logo quando chegam a casa tristes, contentes ou assim-assim. Segundo a Avó Prosérpina, «tem muita intuição masculina», o que se explica pelo facto de ter ouvido centenas de contos de fadas quando ainda estava na barriga dela.

### MÃE JUNO

Desde o dia em que viu o Pai Plutão a tocar bateria numa festa, ela jurou que havia de casar com ele. Ele era tímido e vestia-se de preto, como qualquer motard, mas não conseguiu resistir aos grandes olhos pestanudos da Mãe Juno. Sempre foi muito dedicada ao «enamoramento», uma mistura divina de «namoro» com «casamento». Tem ciúmes da Avó Prosérpina, mas pede-lhe conselhos e adora quando ela ioma conta dos netos. O sonho da Mãe Juno é levar toda a família numa viagem pela Via Láctea, onde as motos e os triciclos não pagam portagem.

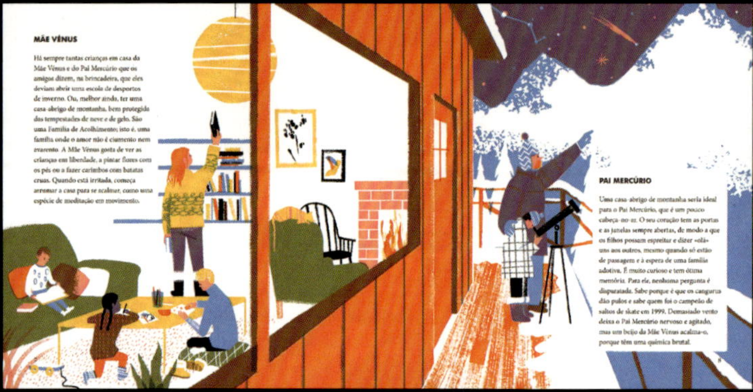

### MÃE VÉNUS

Há sempre tantas crianças em casa da Mãe Vénus e do Pai Mercúrio que os amigos dizem, na brincadeira, que eles deviam abrir uma escola de desportos de inverno. Ou, melhor ainda, ter uma casa-abrigo de montanha, bem protegida das tempestades de neve e de gelo. São uma família de Acolhimento; isto é, uma família onde o amor não é ciumento nem invejoso. A Mãe Vénus gosta de ver as crianças em liberdade, a pintar flores com os pés ou a fazer carimbos com batatas cruas. Quando está irritada, começa a arrumar a casa para se acalmar, como uma espécie de meditação em movimento.

### PAI MERCÚRIO

Uma casa-abrigo de montanha seria ideal para o Pai Mercúrio, que é um pouco cabeça-no-ar. O seu coração tem as portas e as janelas sempre abertas, de modo a que os filhos possam espreitar e dizer «olá» uns aos outros, mesmo quando só estão de passagem e à espera de uma família adotiva. É muito curioso e tem ótima memória. Para ele, nenhuma pergunta é disparatada. Sabe porque é que os cangurus dão pulos e sabe quem foi o campeão de saltos de skate em 1999. Demasiado vento deixa o Pai Mercúrio nervoso e agitado, mas um beijo da Mãe Vénus acalma-o, porque têm uma química brutal.

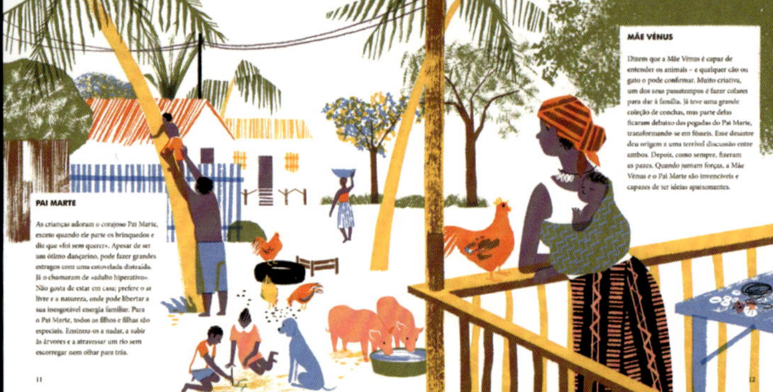

### PAI MARTE

As crianças adoram o corajoso Pai Marte, exceto quando ele parte os brinquedos e diz que «foi sem querer». Apesar de ser um ótimo dançarino, pode fazer grandes estragos com uma cotovelada distraída. Já o chamaram de «adulto hiperativo». Não gosta de estar em casa; prefere o ar livre e a natureza, onde pode libertar a sua inesgotável energia familiar. Para o Pai Marte, todos os filhos e filhas são especiais. Ensinou-os a nadar, a subir às árvores e a atravessar um rio sem escorregar nem olhar para trás.

### MÃE VÉNUS

Dizem que a Mãe Vénus é capaz de entender os animais – e qualquer cão ou gato o pode confirmar. Muito criativa, um dos seus passatempos é fazer colares para dar à família. Já teve uma grande coleção de conchas, mas parte delas ficaram debaixo das pegadas do Pai Marte, transformando-se em fósseis. Esse desastre deu origem a uma terrível discussão entre ambos. Depois, como sempre, fizeram as pazes. Quando juntam forças, a Mãe Vénus e o Pai Marte são invencíveis e capazes de ter ideias apaixonantes.

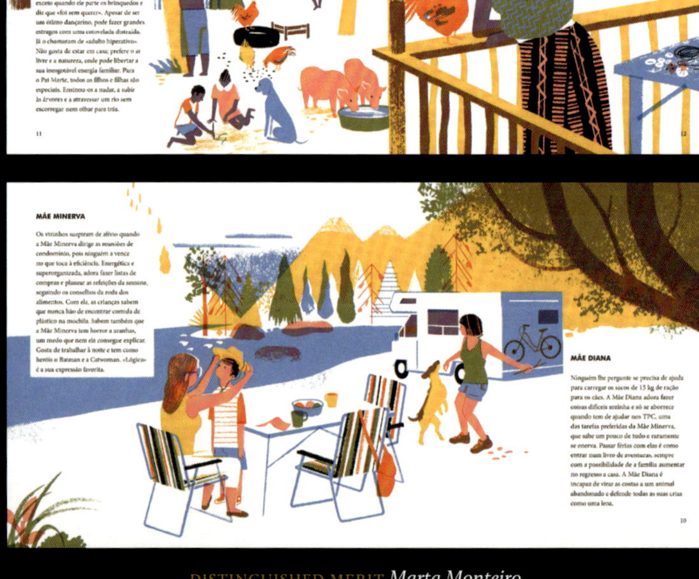

### MÃE MINERVA

Os vizinhos suspiram de alívio quando a Mãe Minerva dirige as reuniões de condomínio, pois ninguém a vence no que toca à eficiência. Enérgica e superorganizada, adora fazer listas de compras e planear as refeições da semana, seguindo os conselhos da roda dos alimentos. Com ela, as crianças sabem que nunca hão de encontrar comida de plástico na mochila. Sabem também que a Mãe Minerva tem horror a aranhas, um medo que nem ela consegue explicar. Gosta de trabalhar à noite e tem como heróis o Batman e a Catwoman. «Lógico» é a sua expressão favorita.

### MÃE DIANA

Ninguém lhe pergunte se precisa de ajuda para carregar os sacos de 15 kg de ração para os cães. A Mãe Diana adora fazer coisas difíceis sozinha e só se aborrece quando tem de ajudar nos TPC, uma das tarefas preferidas da Mãe Minerva, que sabe um pouco de tudo e raramente se enerva. Passar férias com elas é como entrar num livro de aventuras, sempre com a possibilidade de a família aumentar no regresso a casa. A Mãe Diana é incapaz de virar as costas a um animal abandonado e defende todas as suas crias como uma leoa.

DISTINGUISHED MERIT *Marta Monteiro*

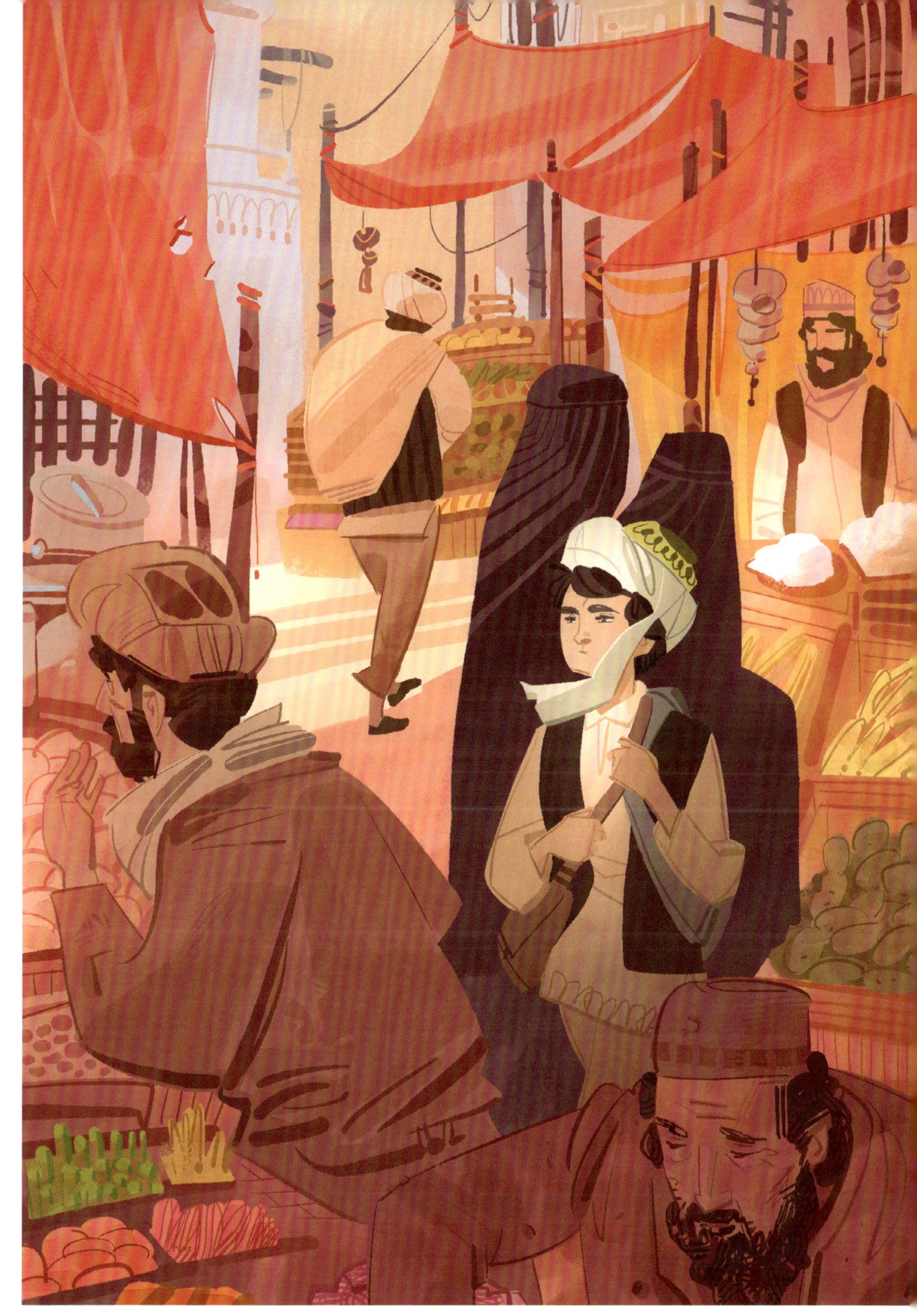

MERIT *Giovanni Da Re*

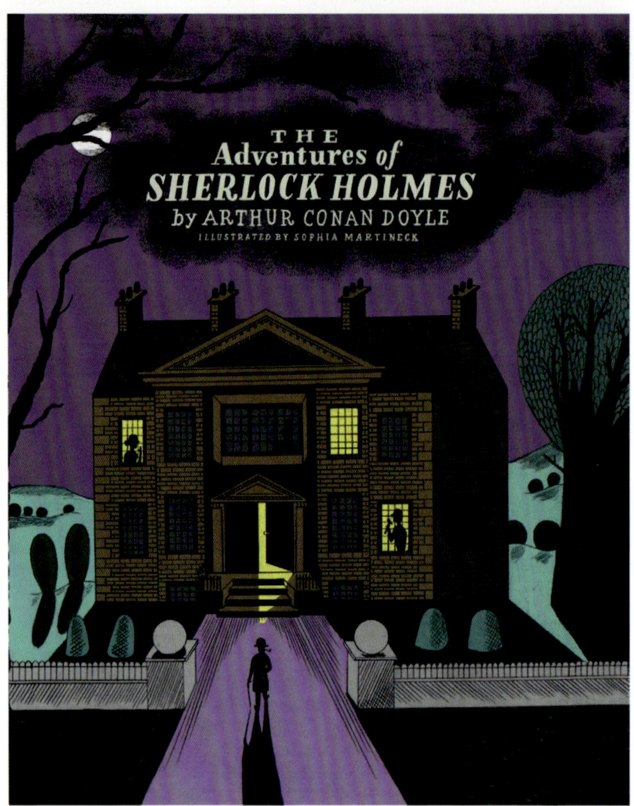

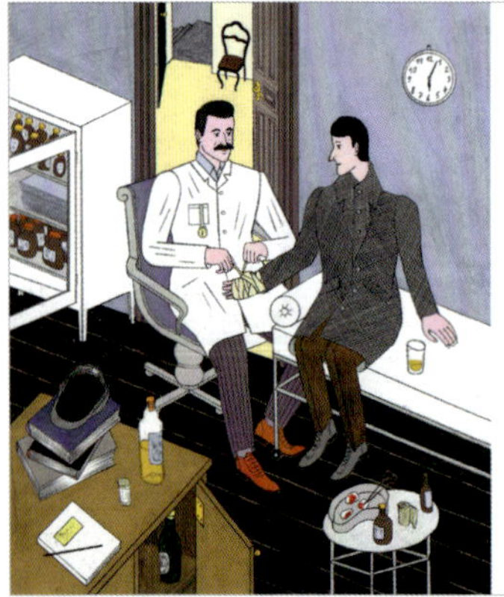

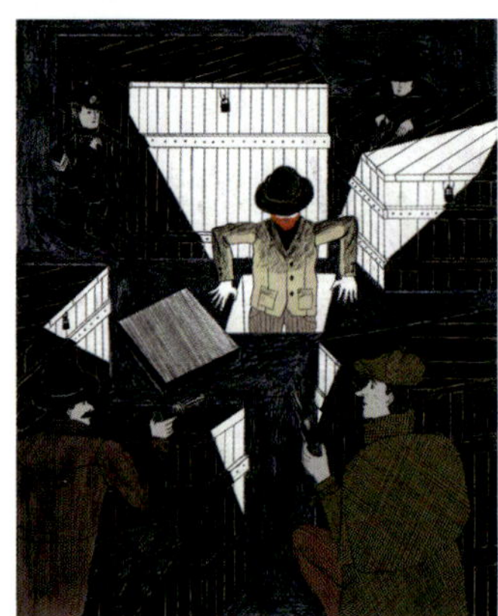

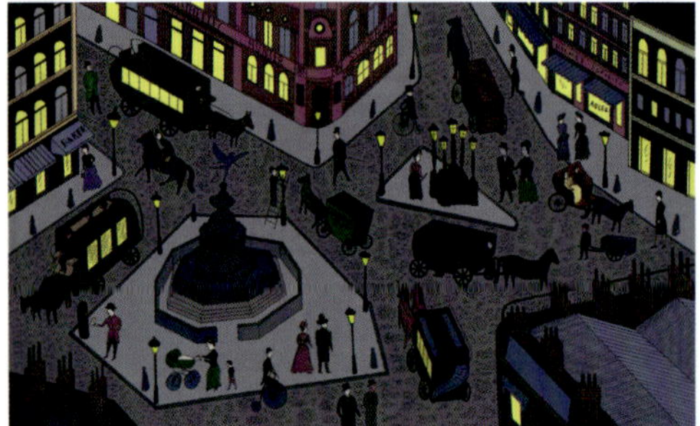

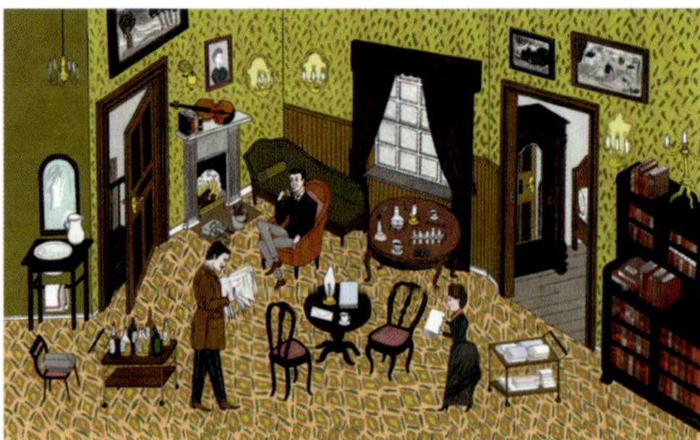



MERIT *Sophia Martineck*

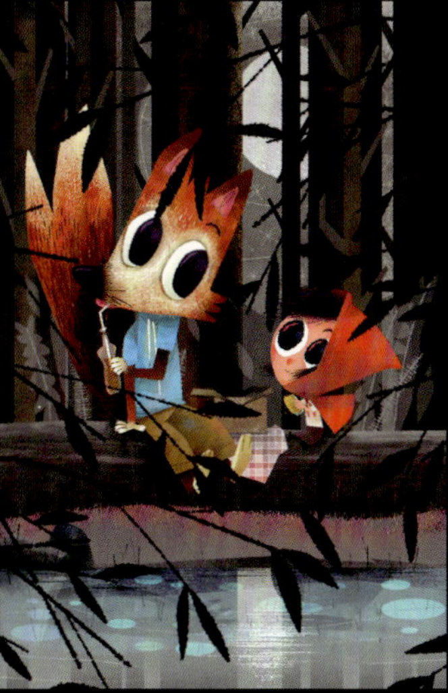

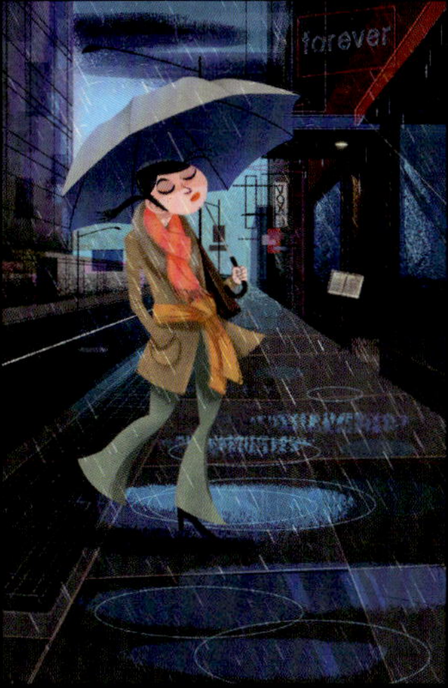

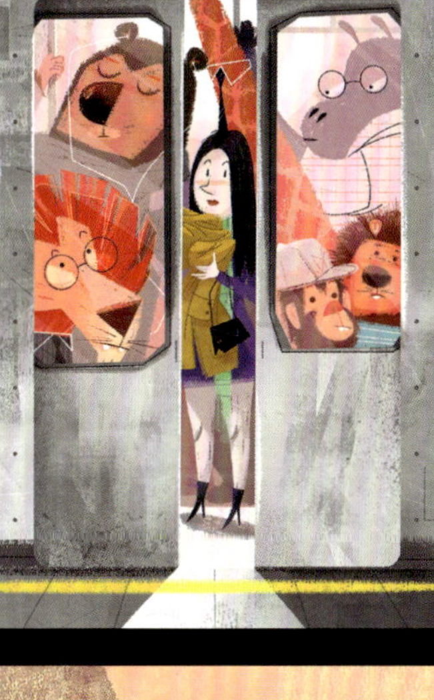

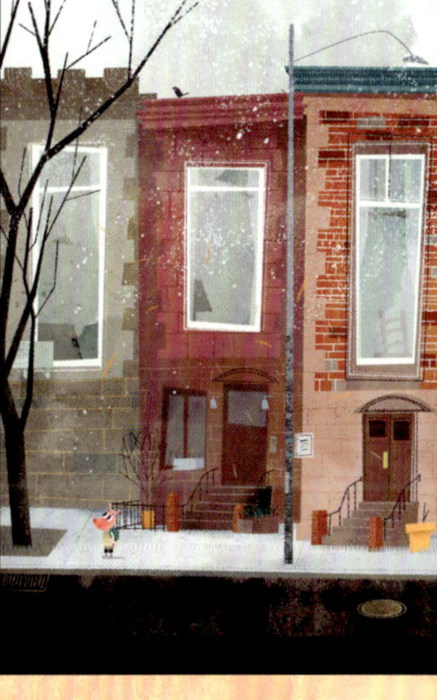

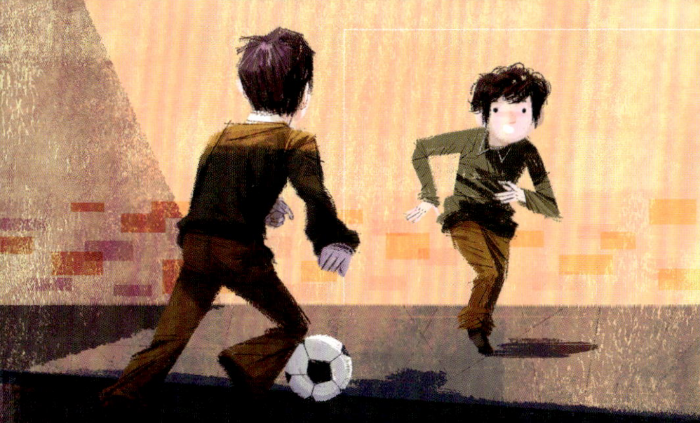

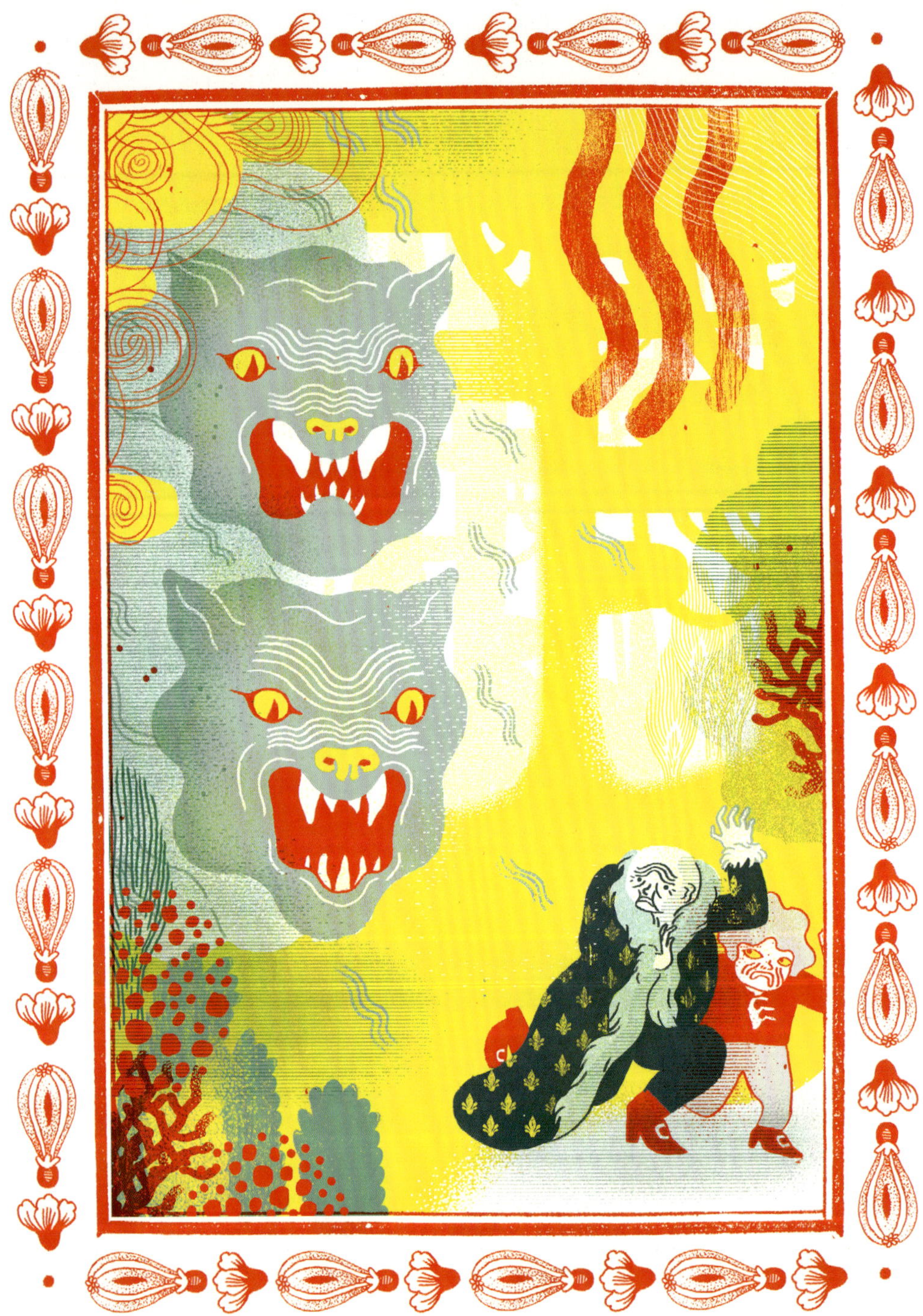



MERIT *Cristina Spanò*

**STUDENT SHOW**

382    BEST OF SHOW

316    GOLD

319    SILVER

330    SILVER

358    SILVER

378    SILVER

341    BRONZE

360    BRONZE

364    BRONZE

298    DISTINGUISHED MERIT

306    DISTINGUISHED MERIT

350    DISTINGUISHED MERIT

351    DISTINGUISHED MERIT

359    DISTINGUISHED MERIT

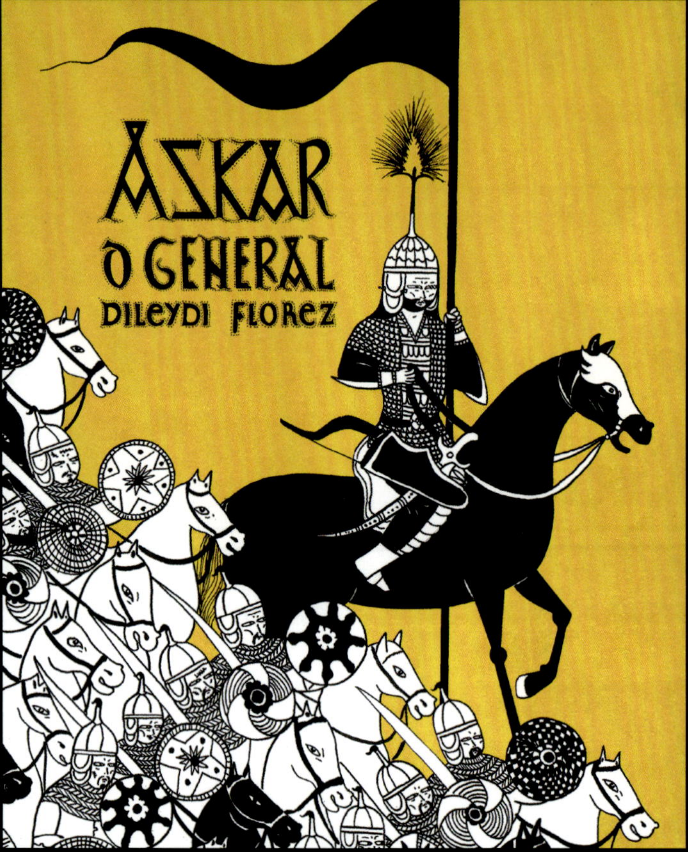

# ÁSKAR
## O GENERAL
### DILEYDI FLOREZ

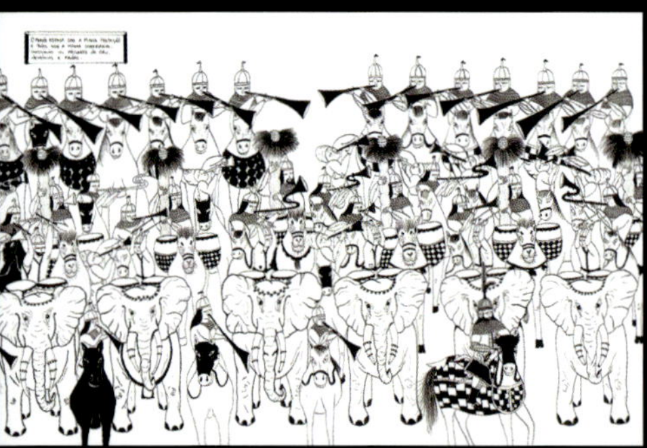
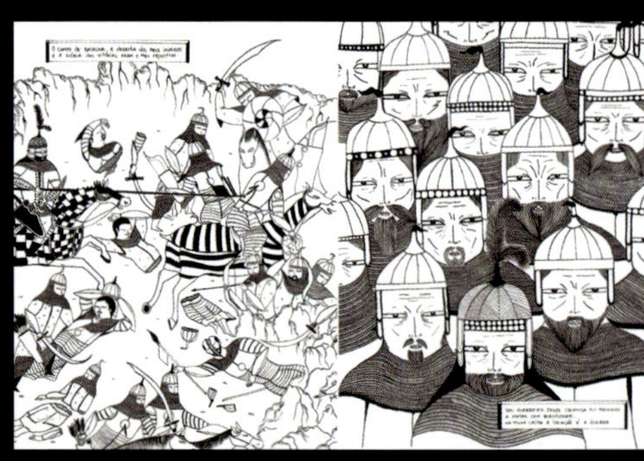
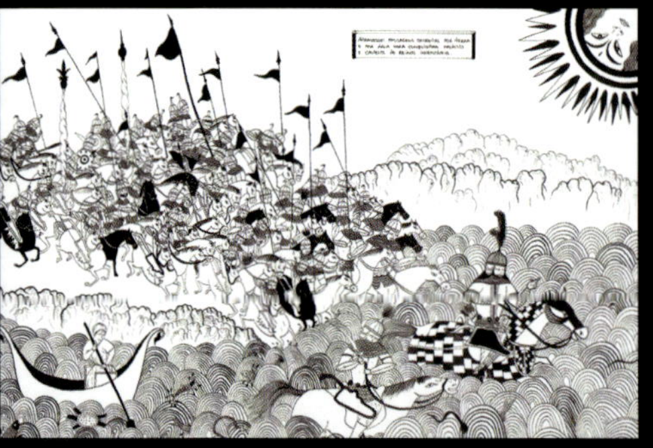
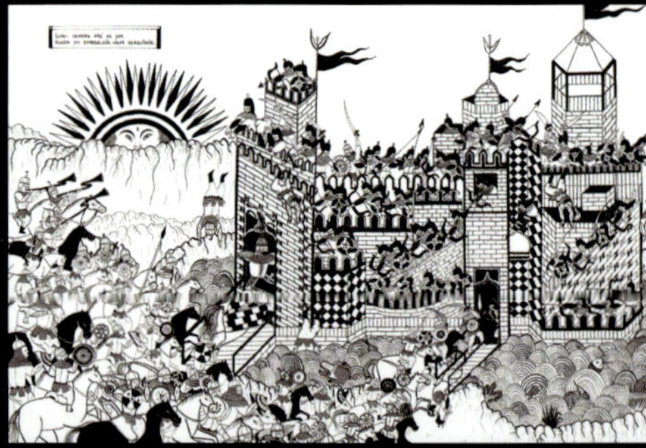

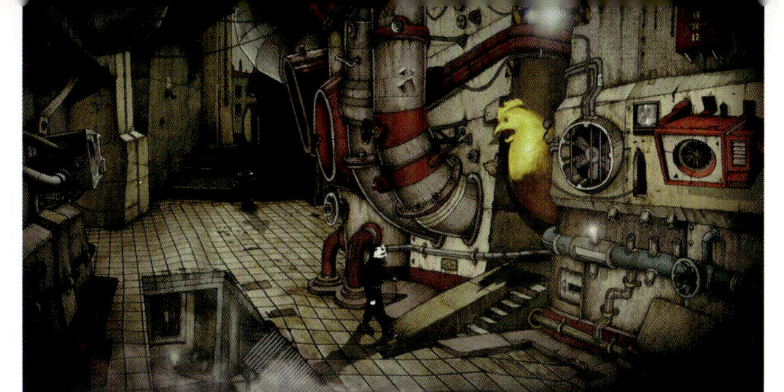

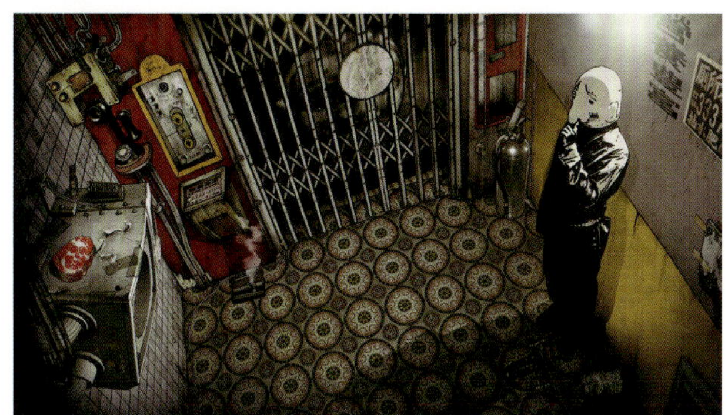

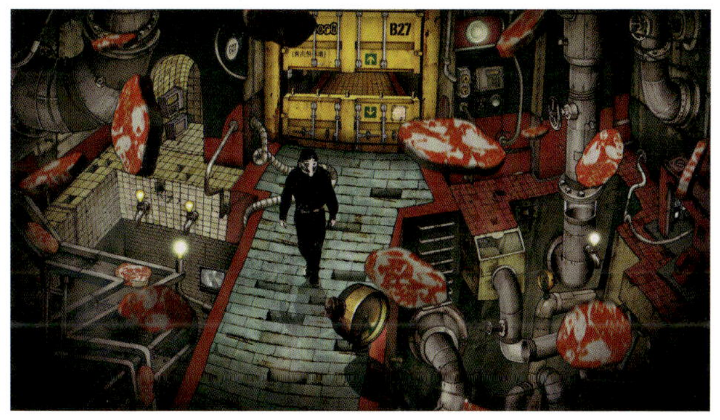
B27

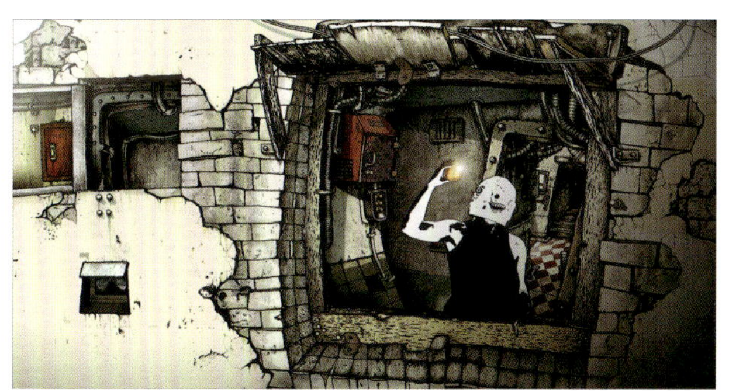

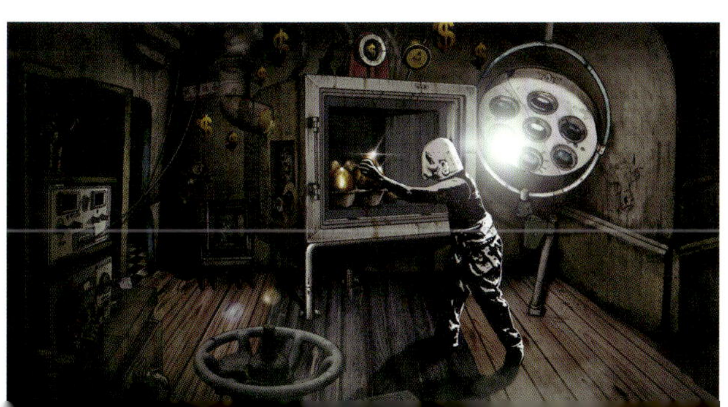

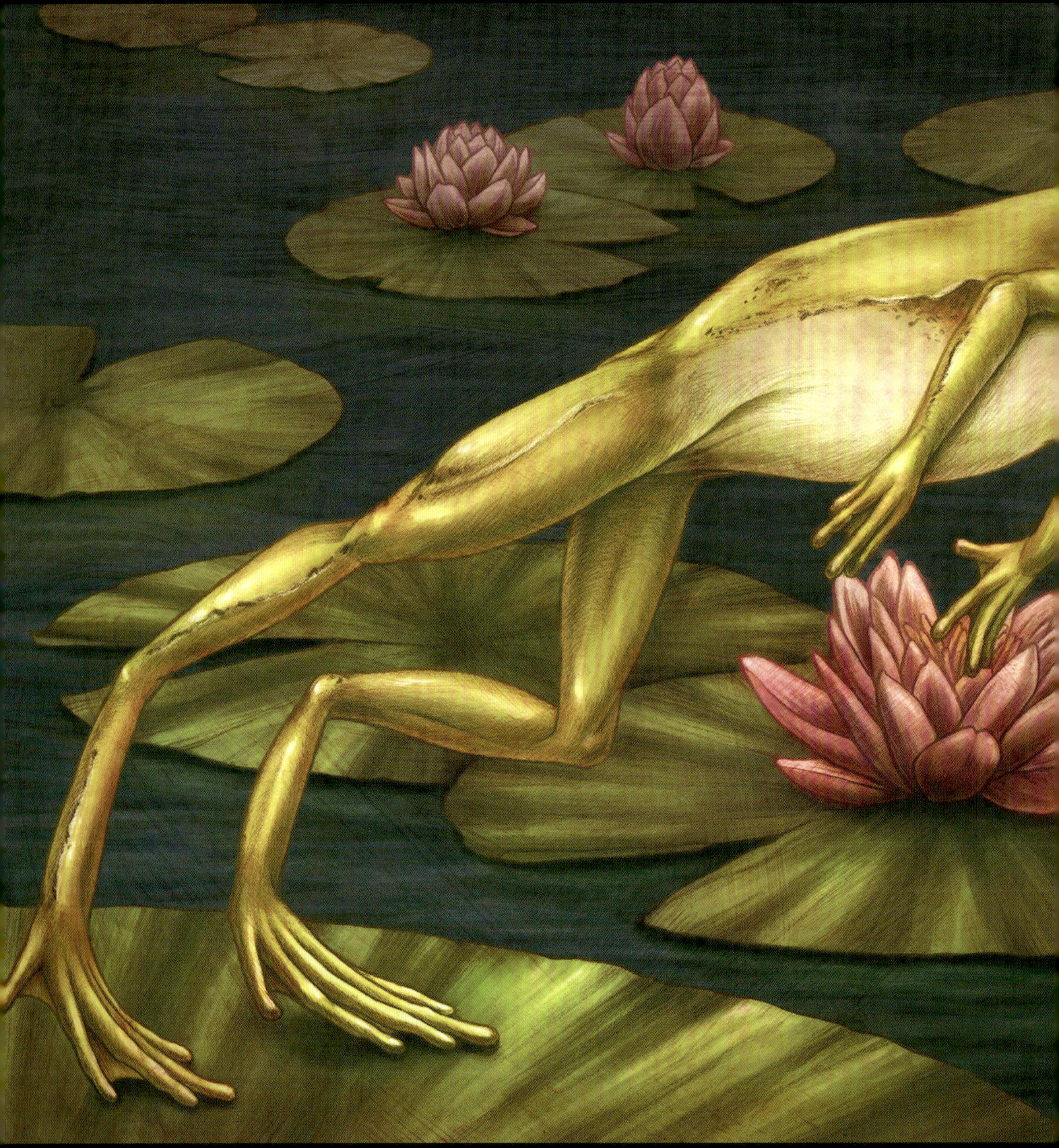

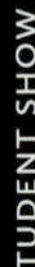

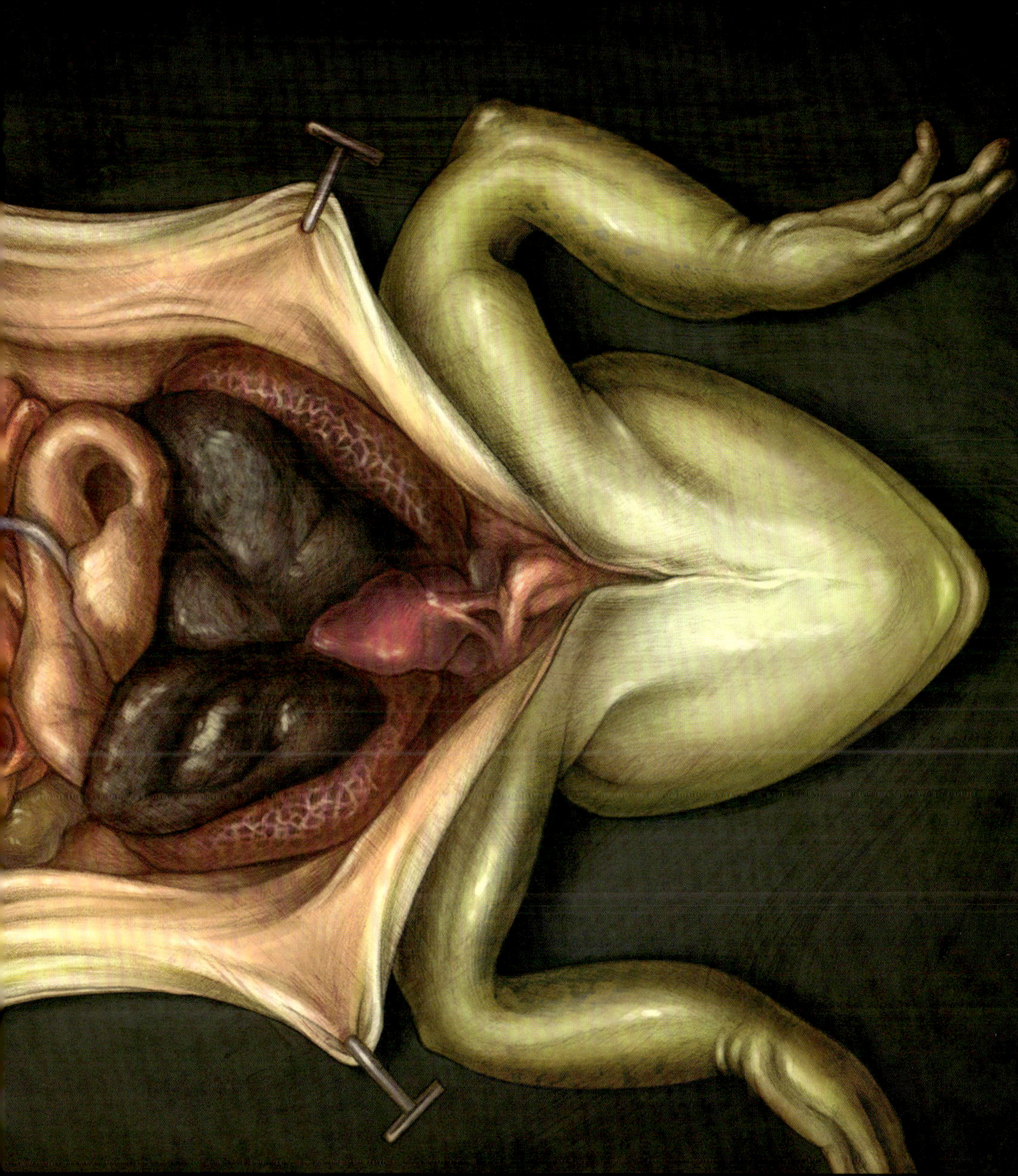

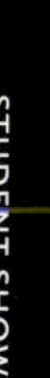
STUDENT SHOW

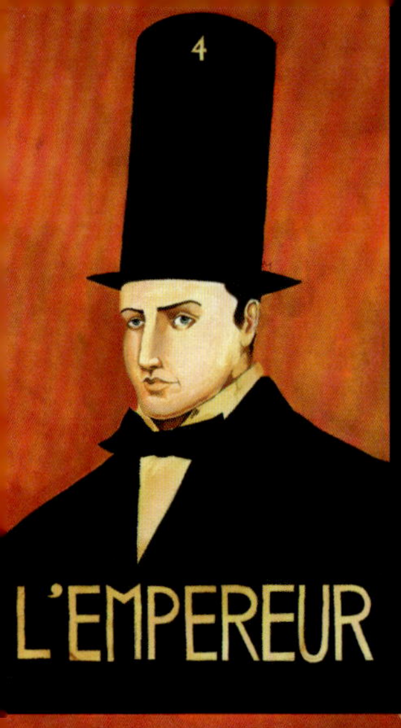

4
L'EMPEREUR

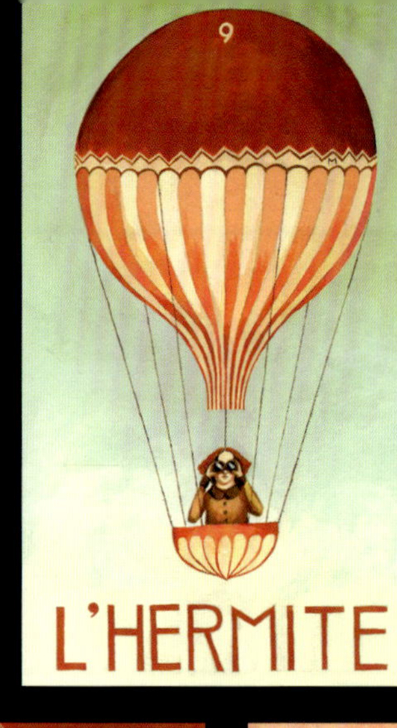

9
L'HERMITE

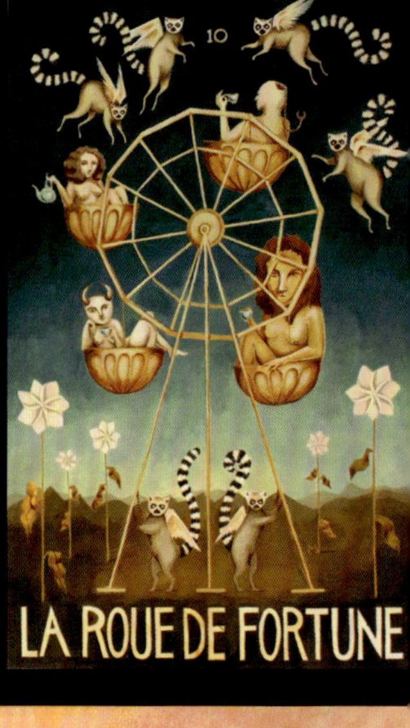

10
LA ROUE DE FORTUNE

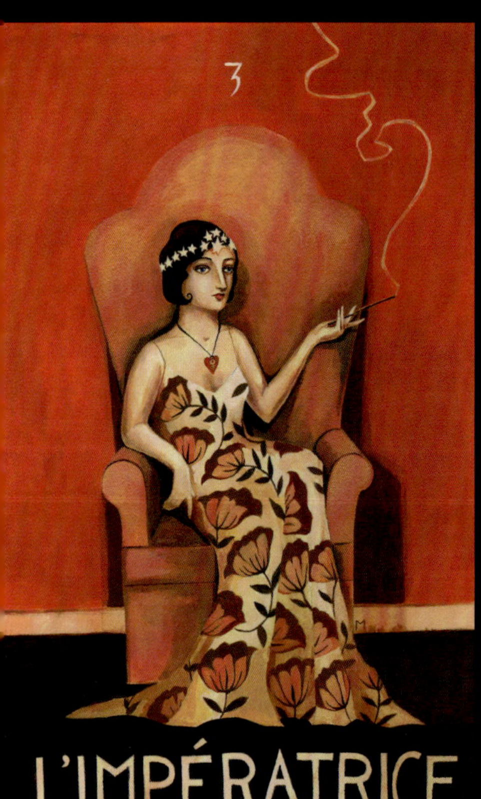

3
L'IMPÉRATRICE

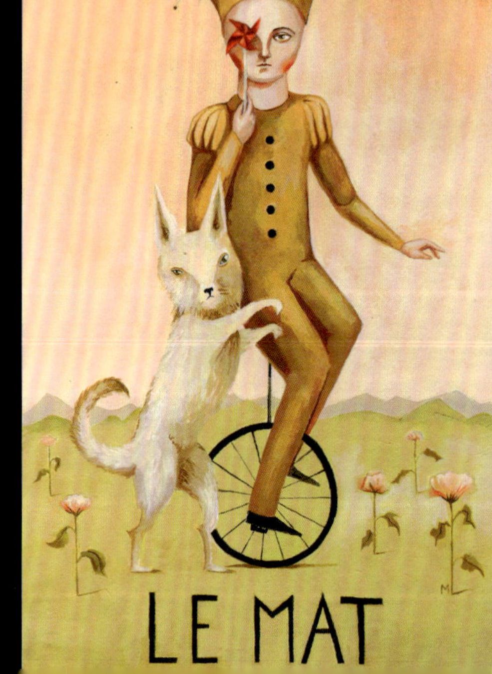

0
LE MAT

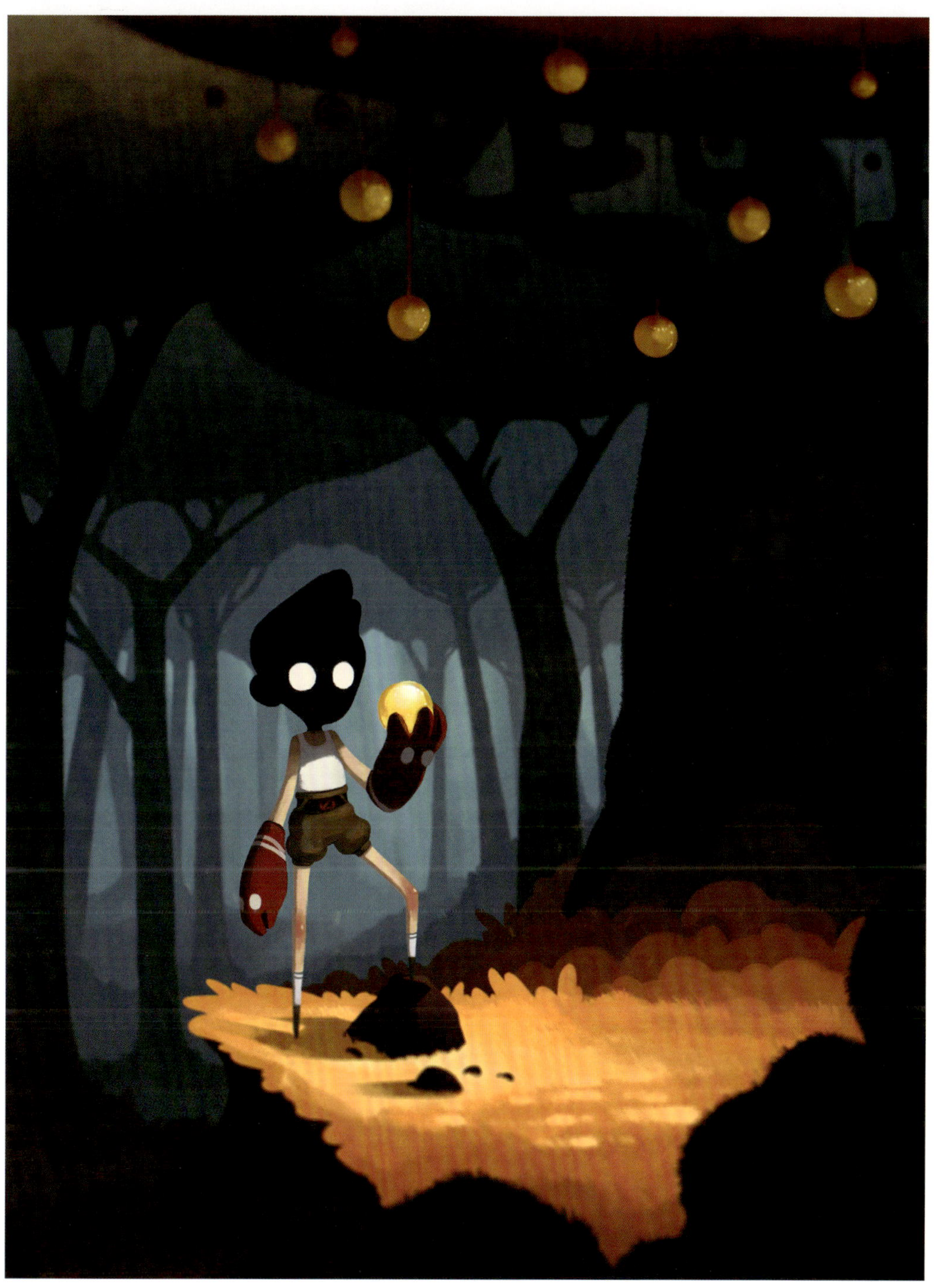

MERIT *Garrett Hamon*

301

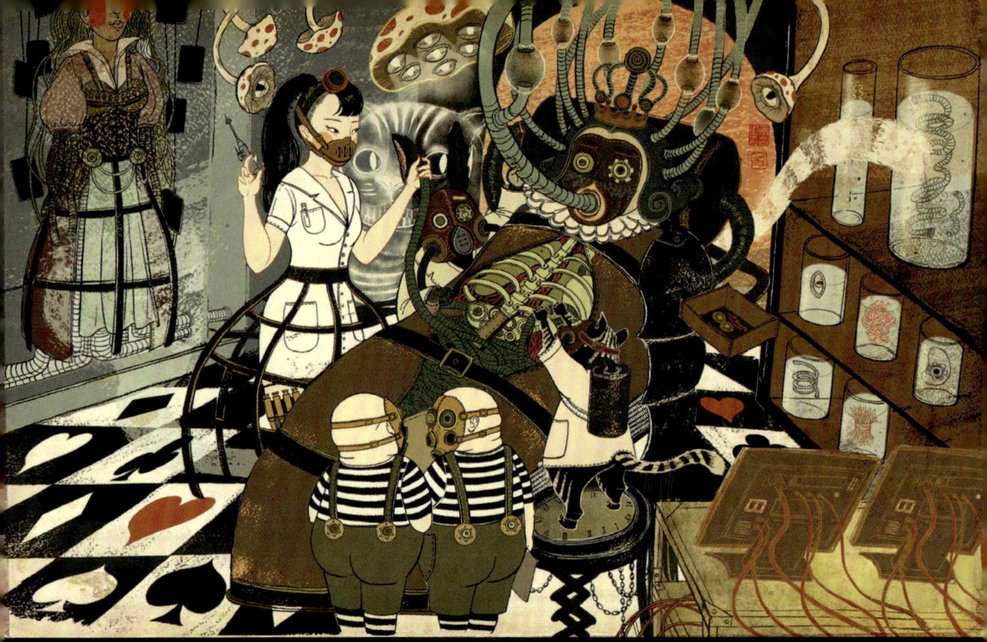

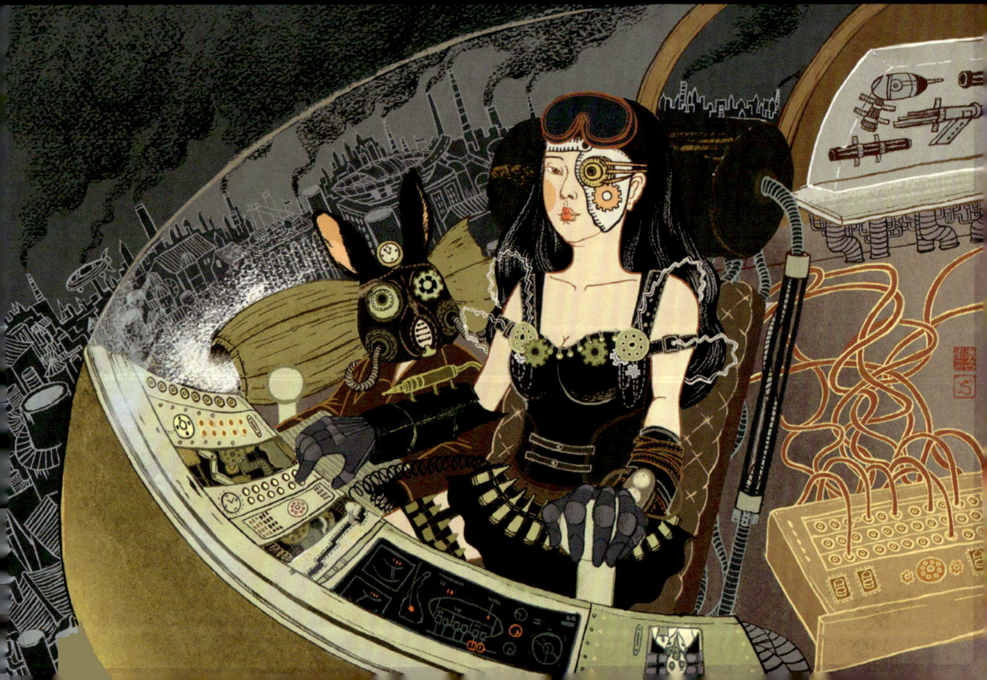

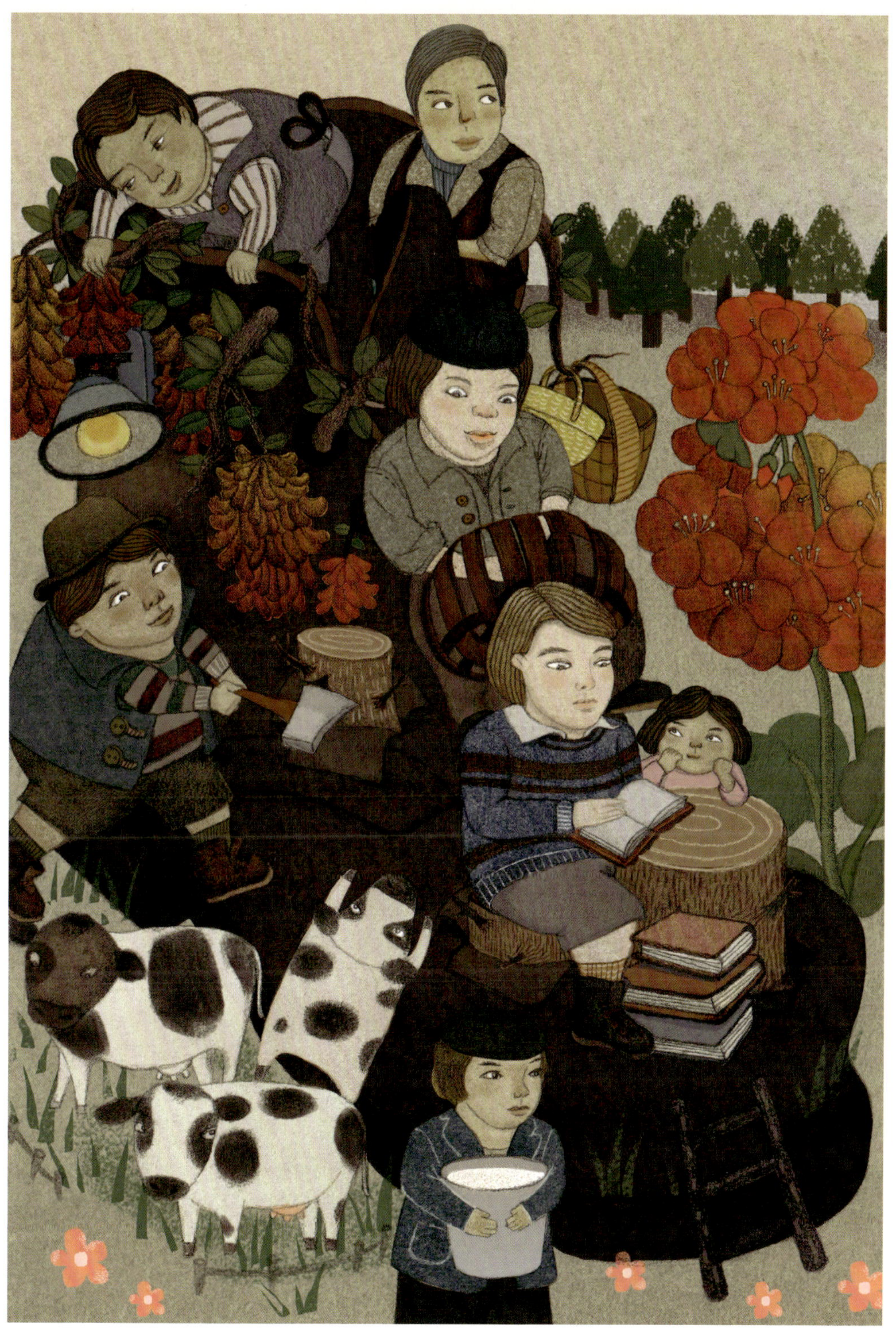



MERIT *Jing Li*

303

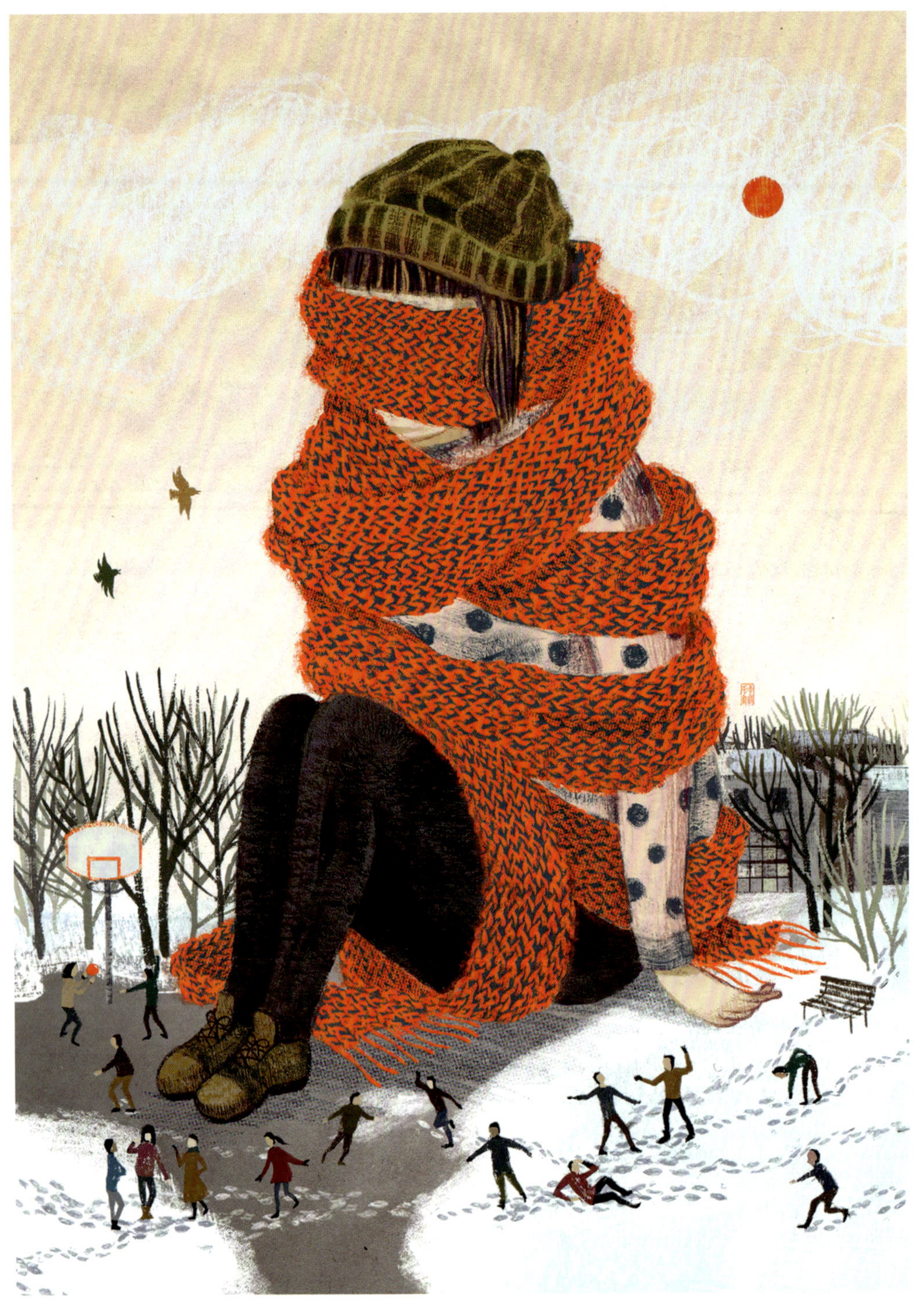

MERIT *Cornelia Li*

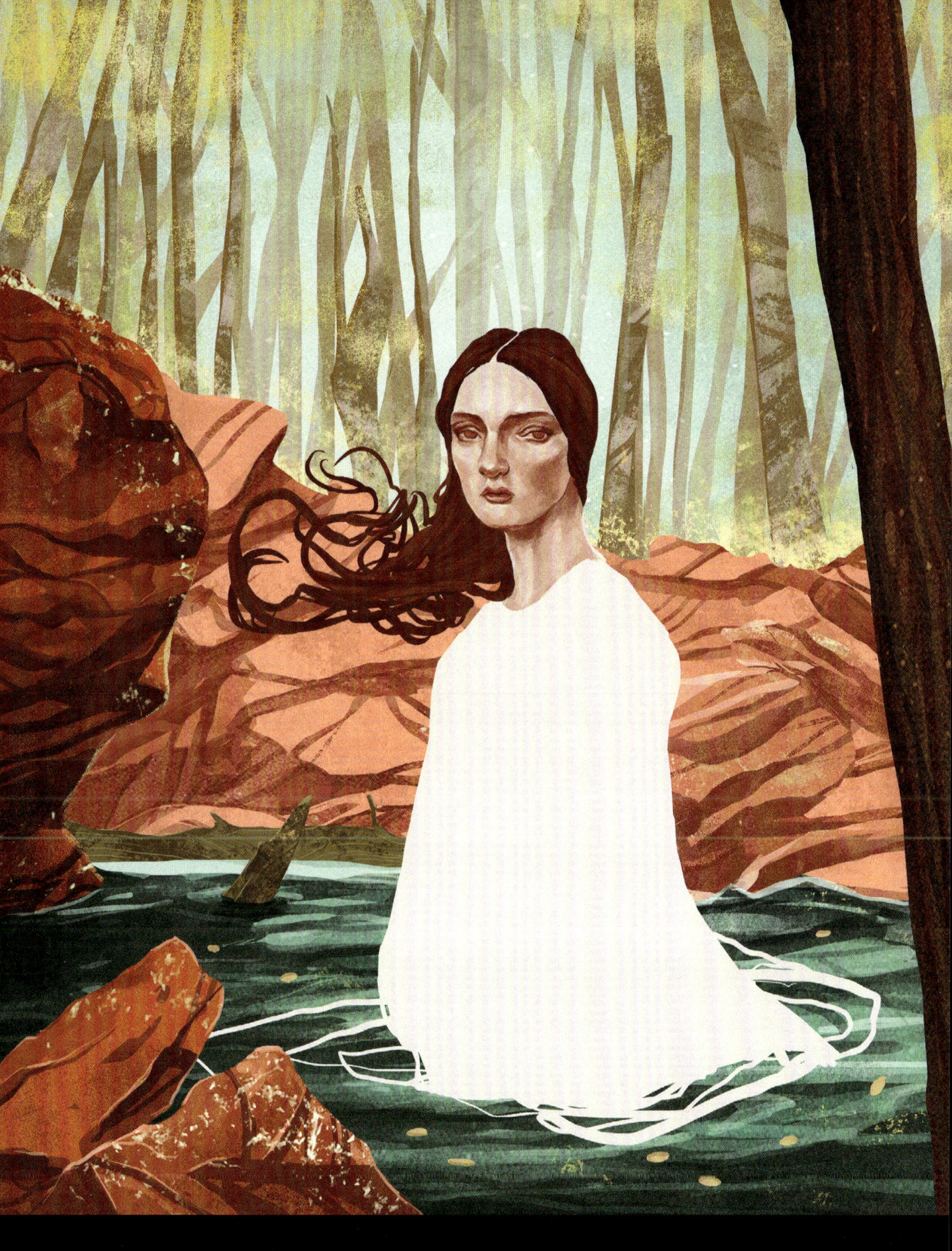
STUDEN

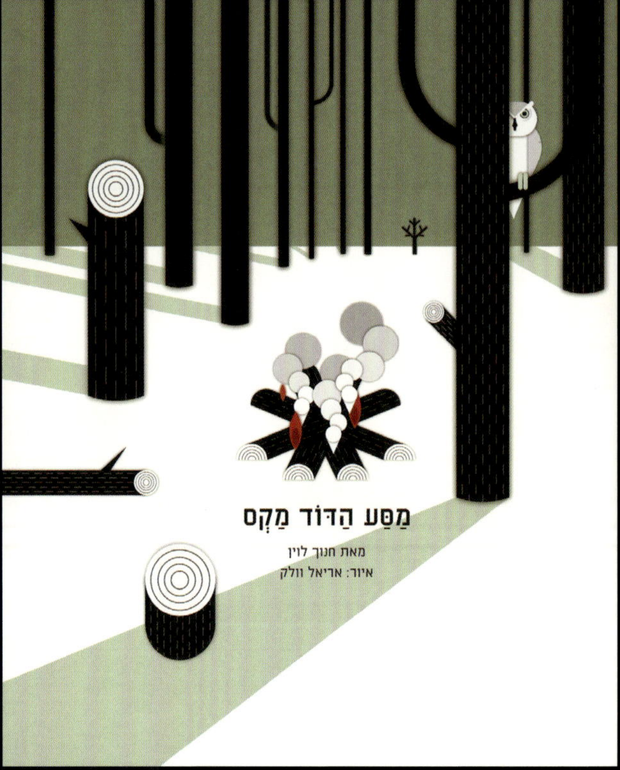

# מַסַּע הַדּוֹד מַקְס

מאת חנוך לוין

איור: אריאל וולק

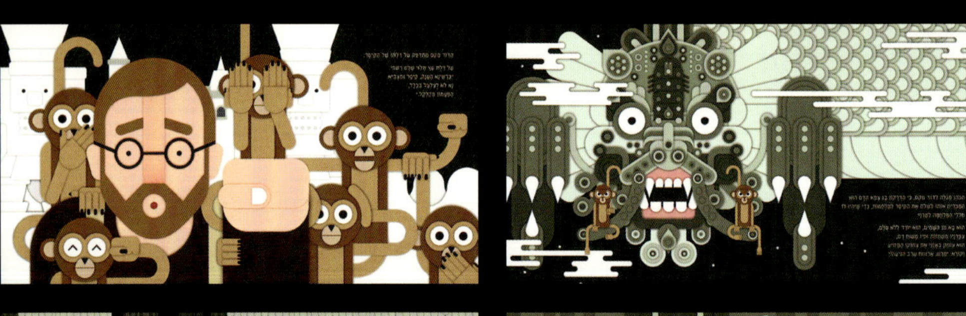

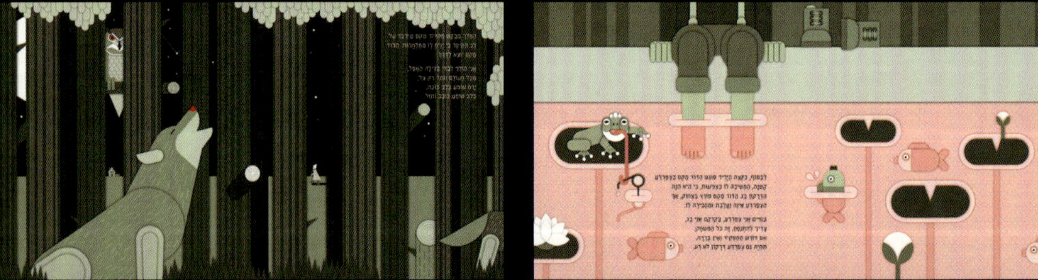

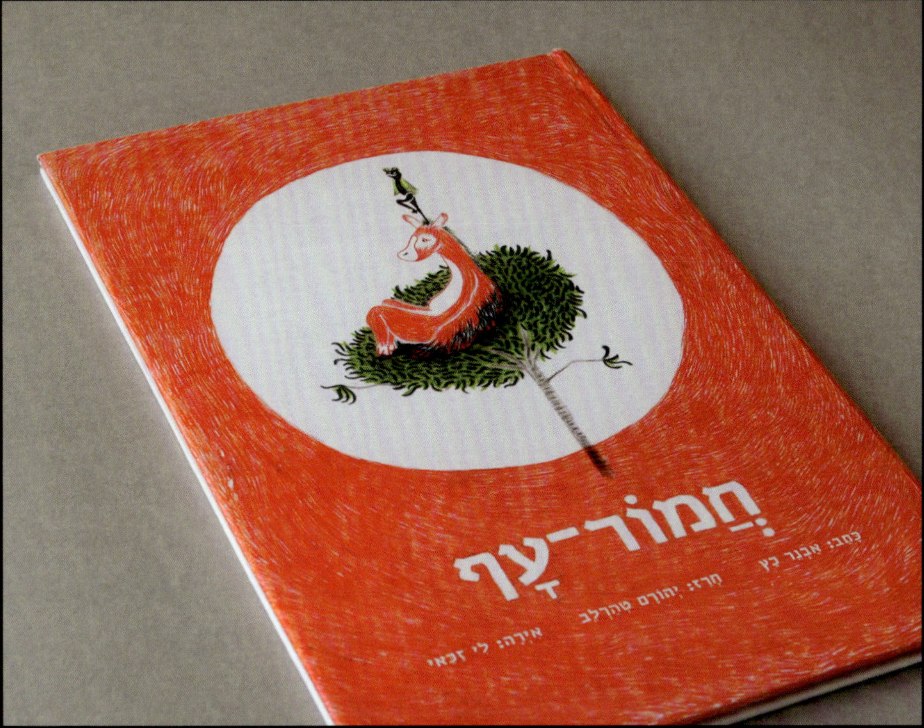

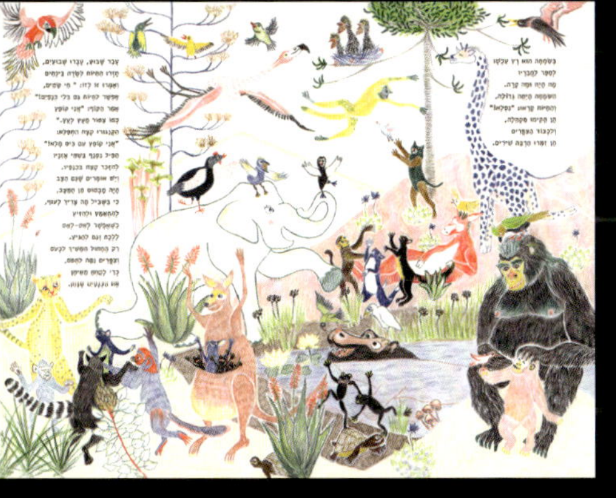
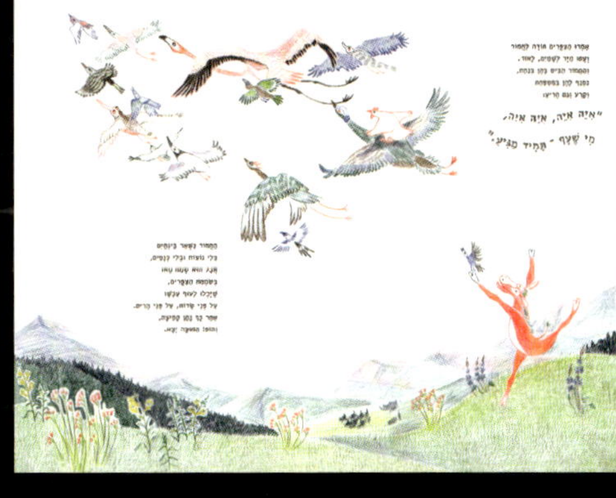
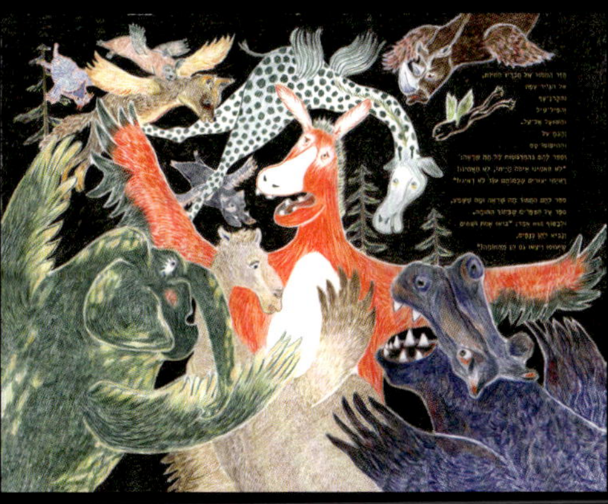
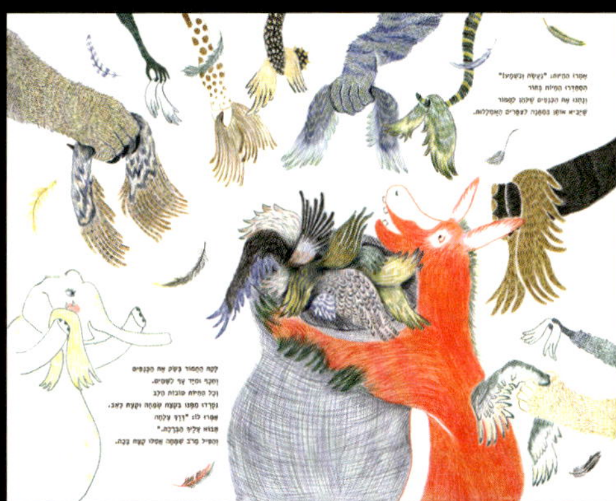

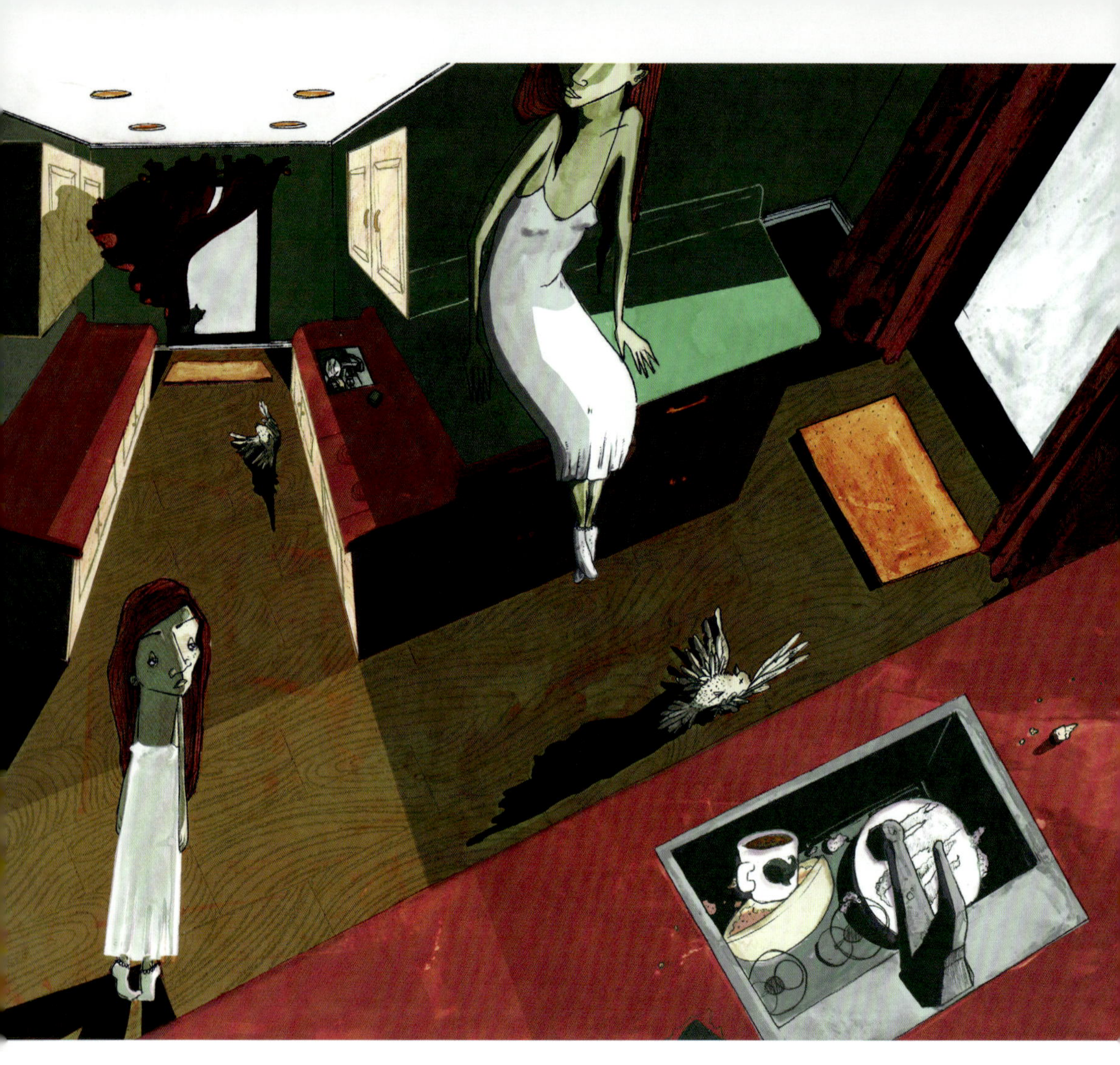



MERIT *Baily Crawford*

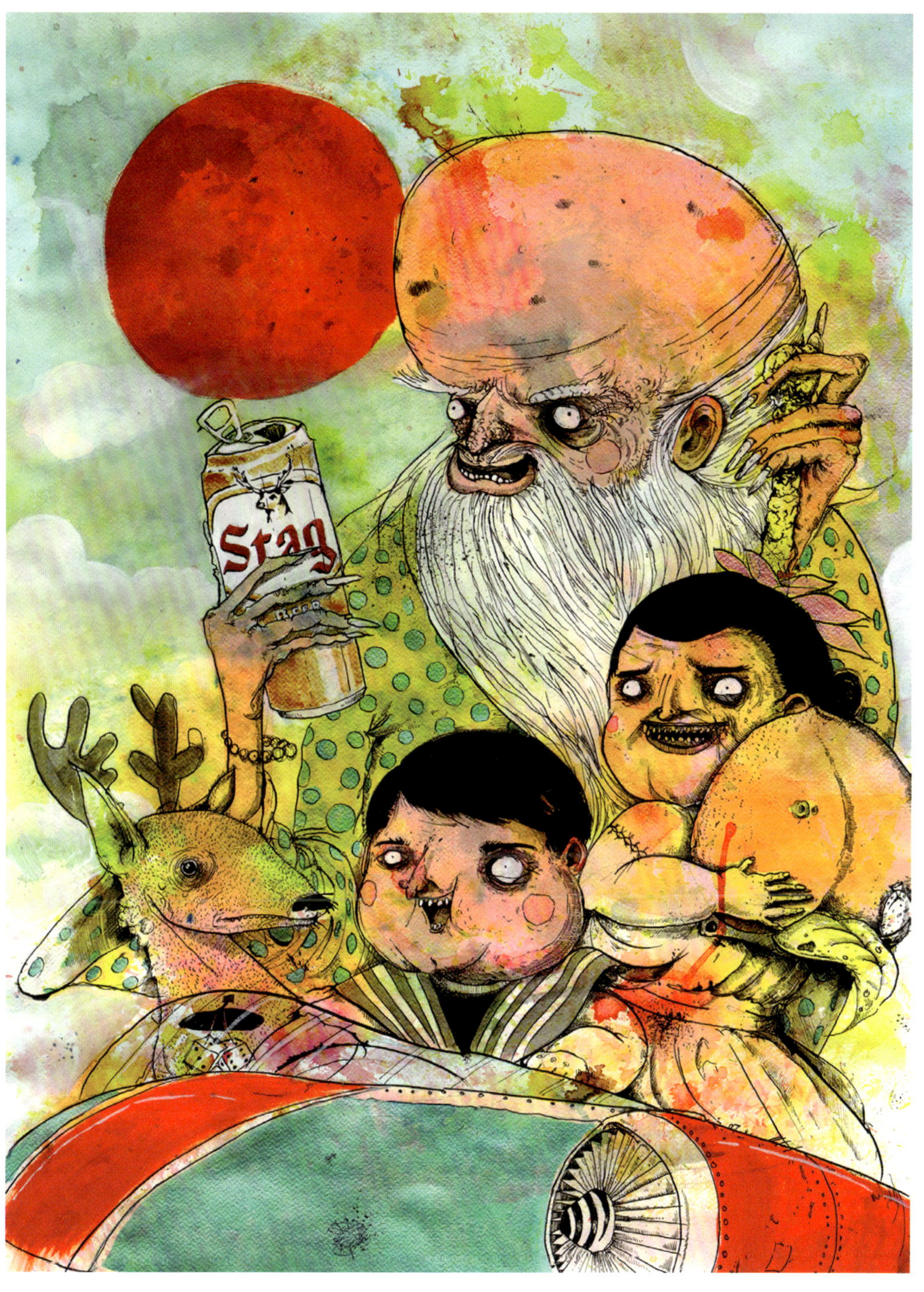



MERIT *Judge Bockman*

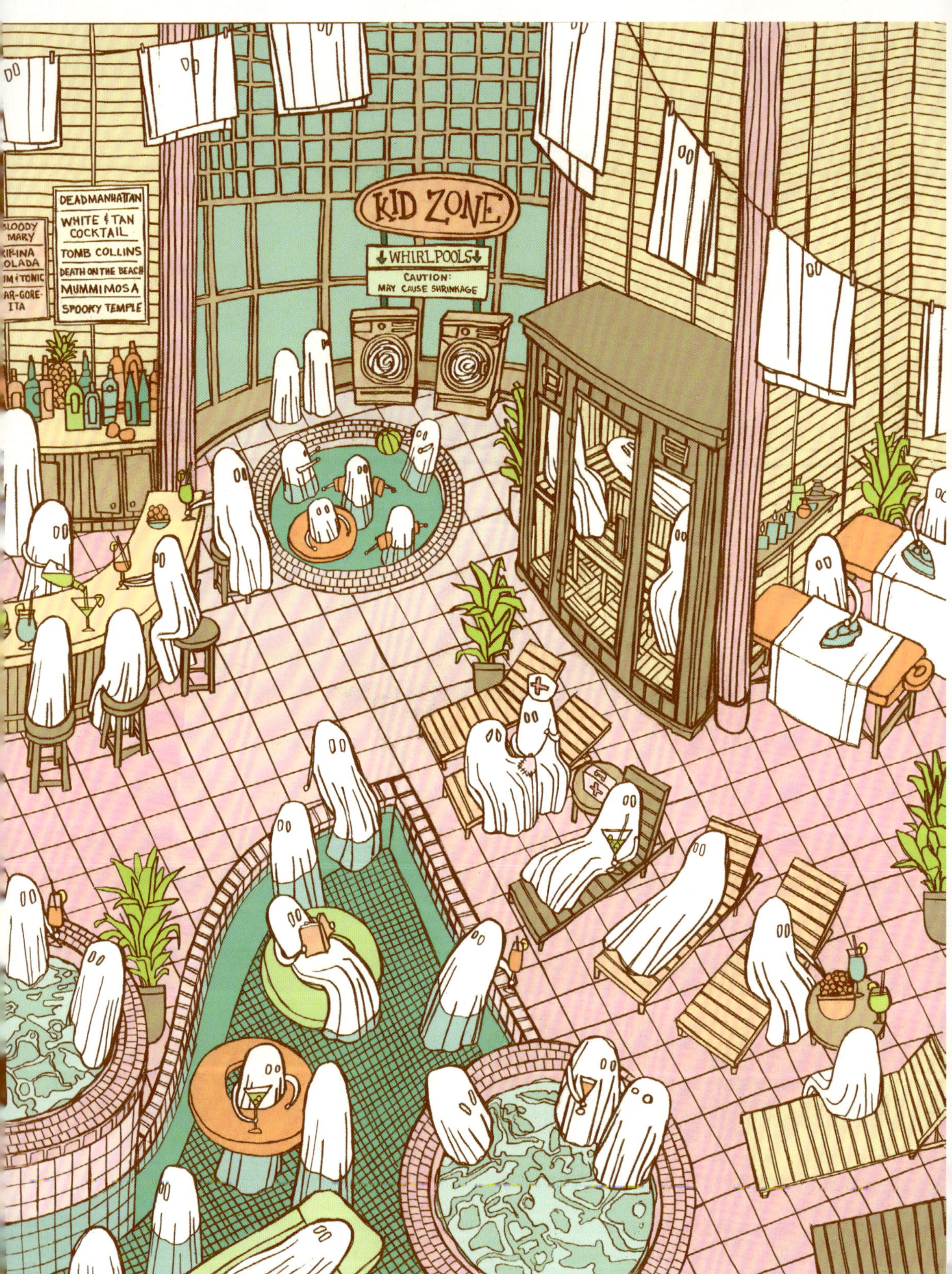


MERIT *Brenna Thummler*

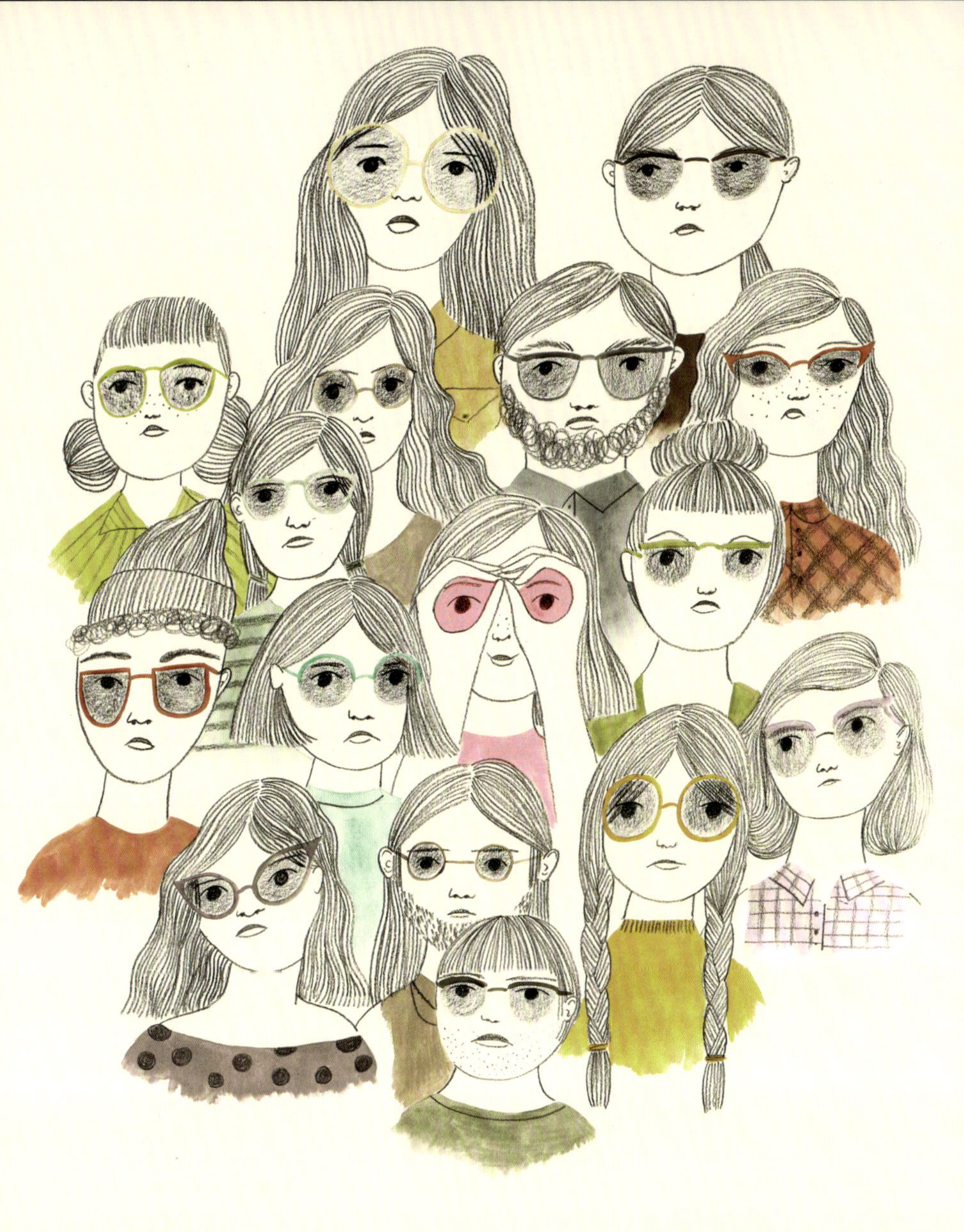

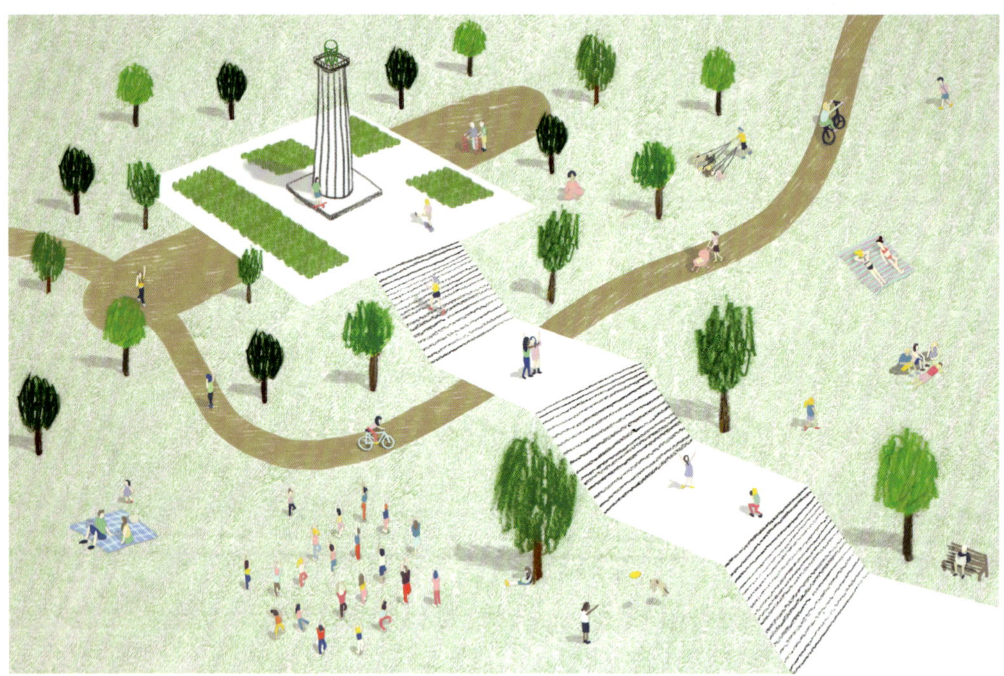

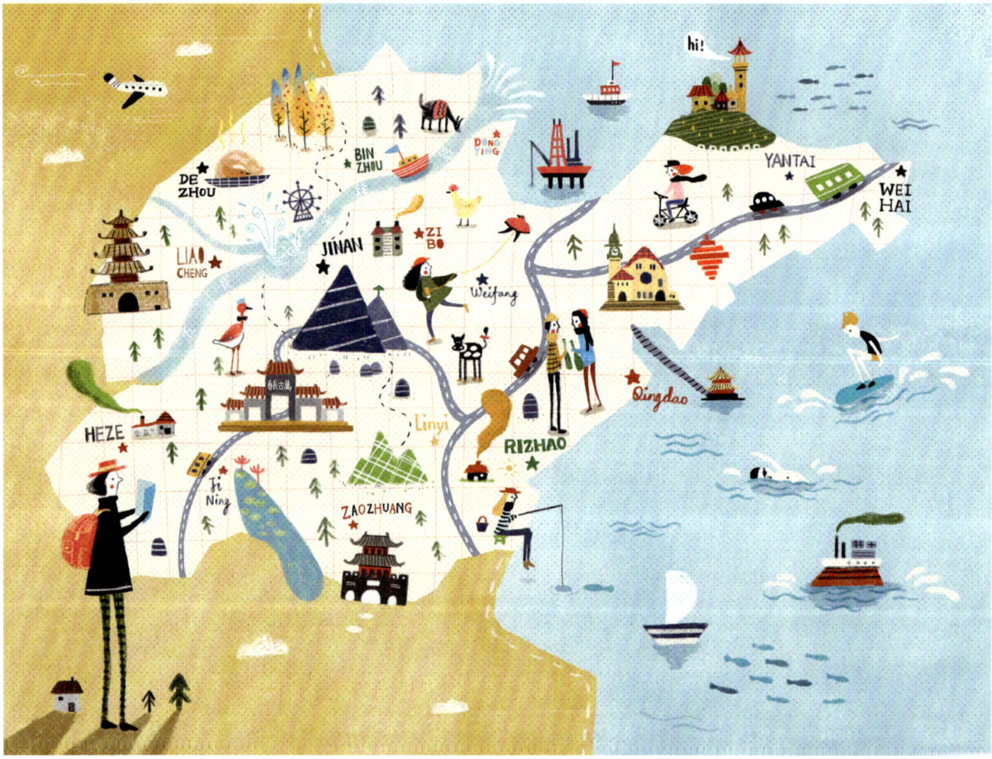

(T) MERIT *Grace Heejung Kim*　(B) MERIT *Yao Yu*

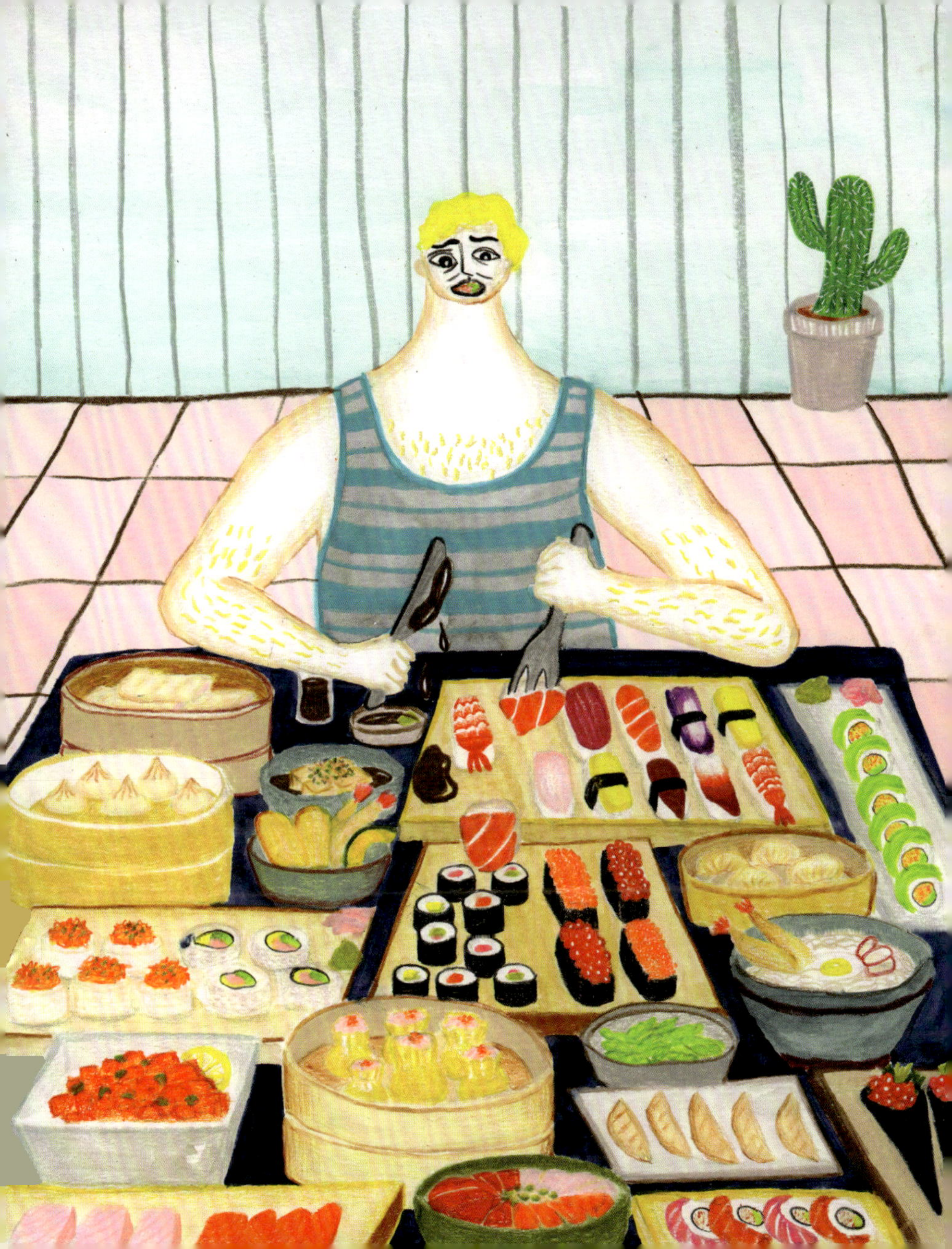

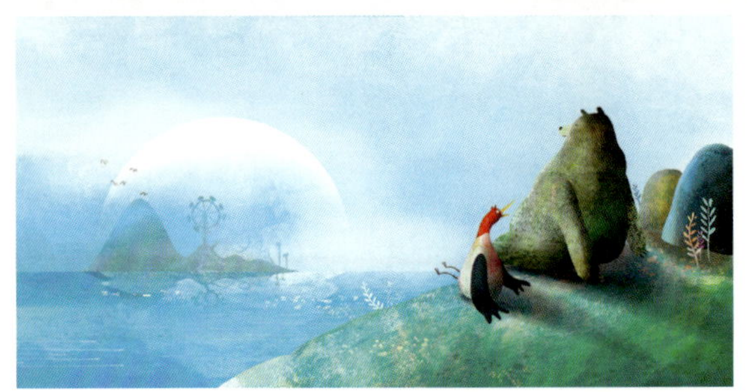
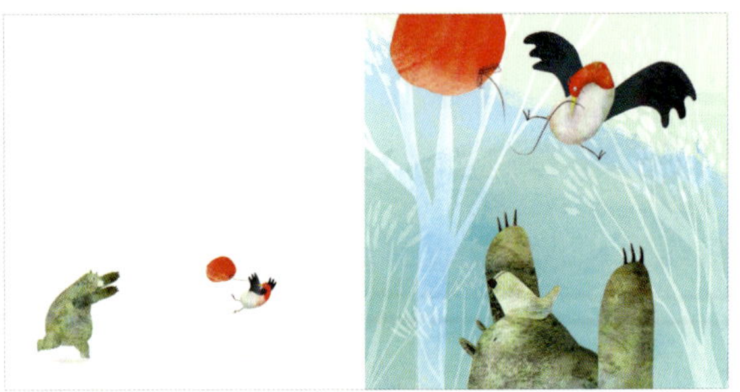
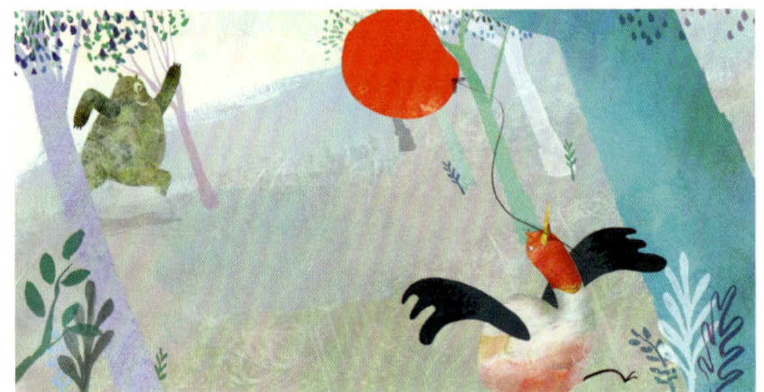
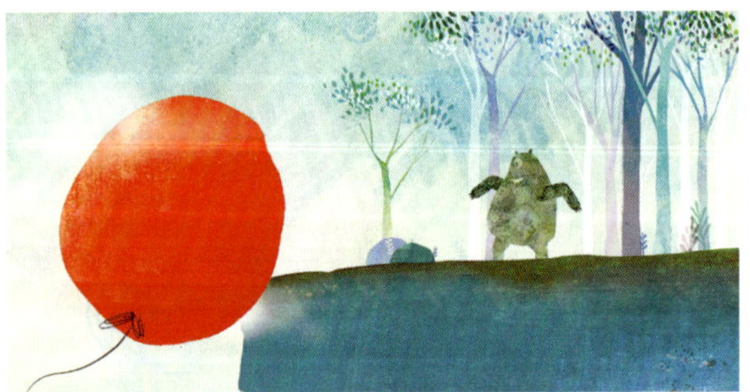
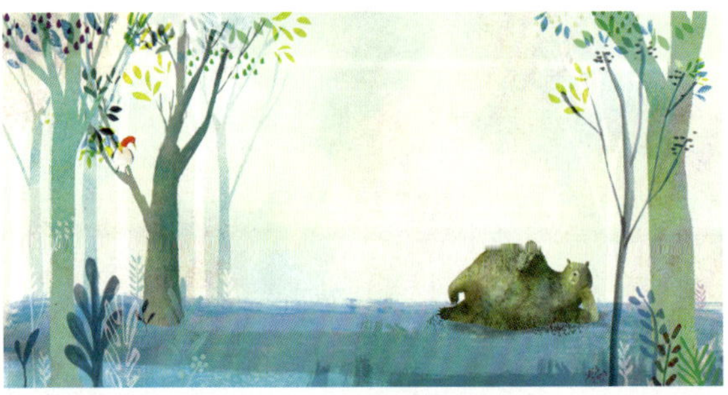



MERIT *Il Sung Na*

# Can you help me...?

SADIE HAN

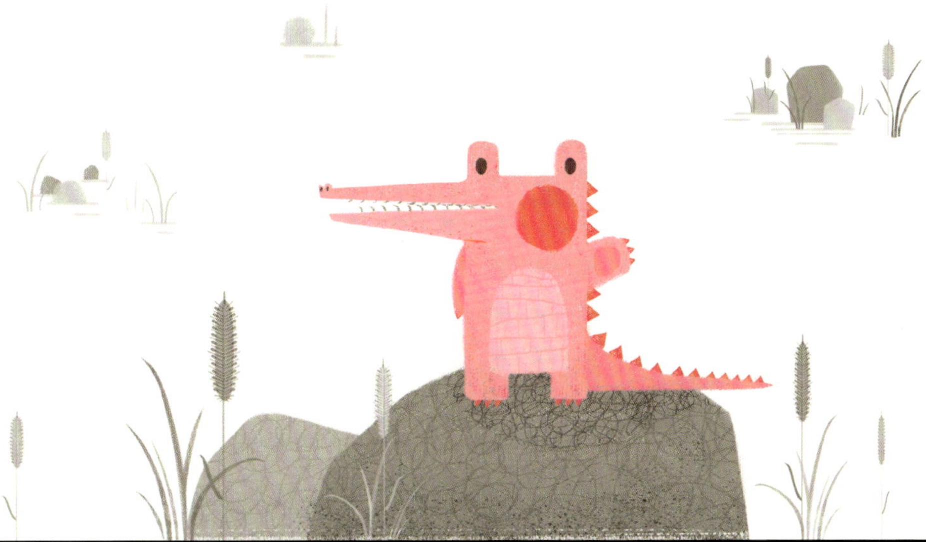

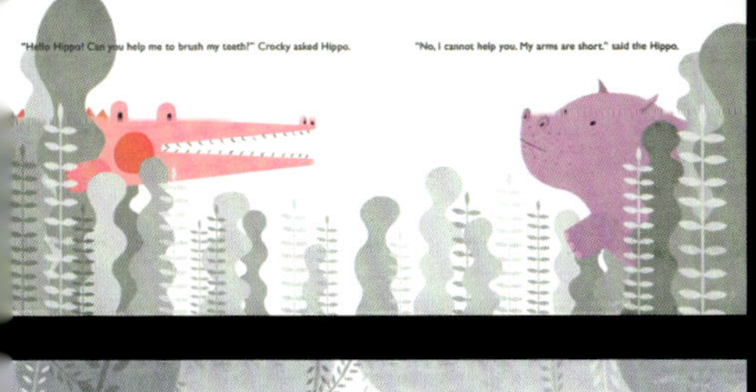


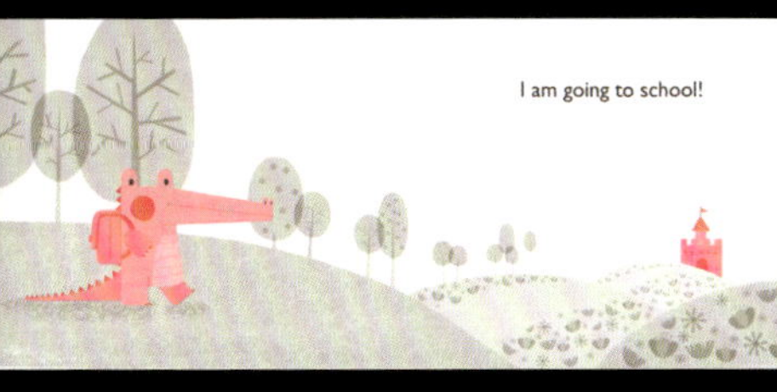


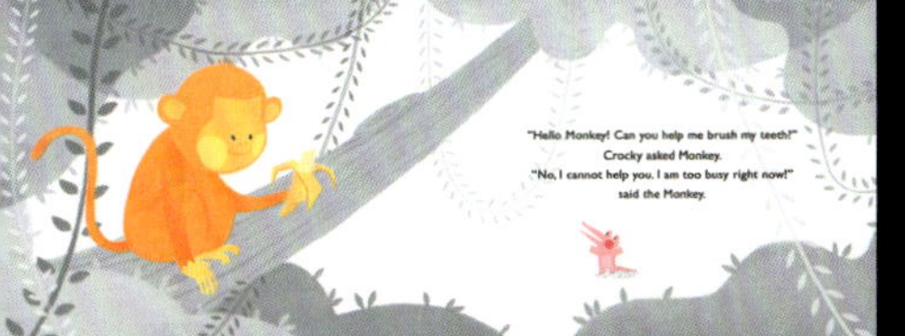


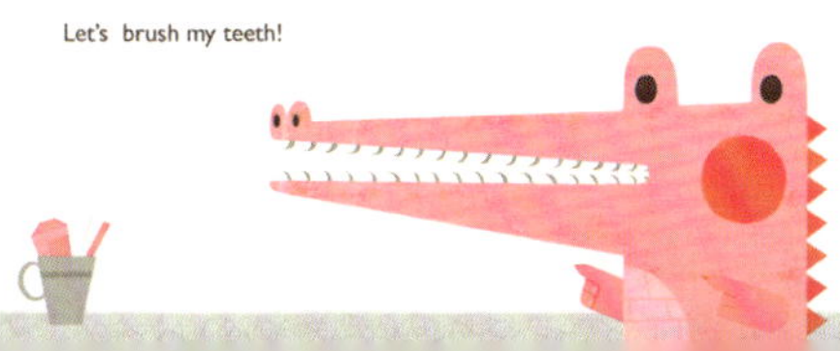

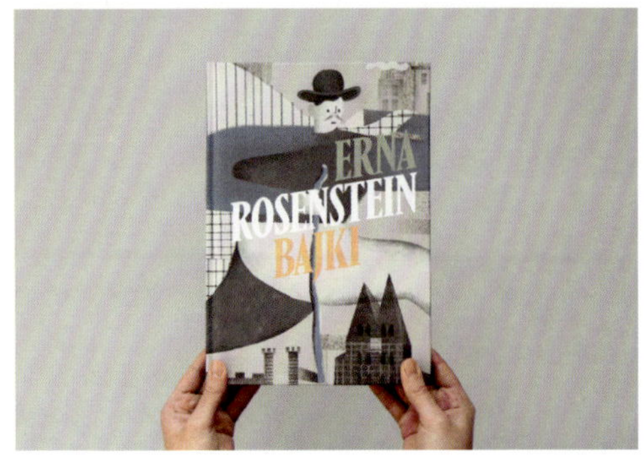

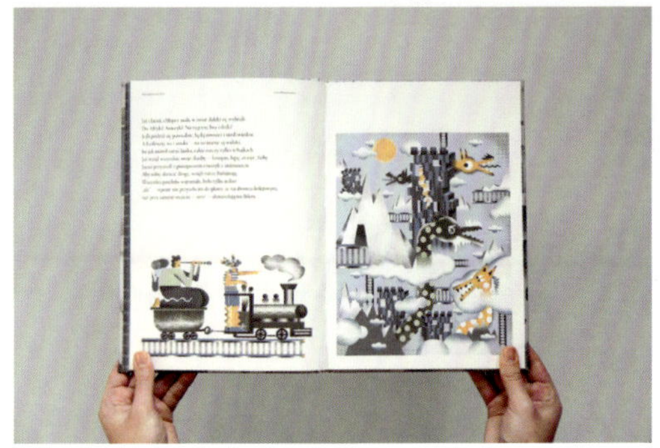

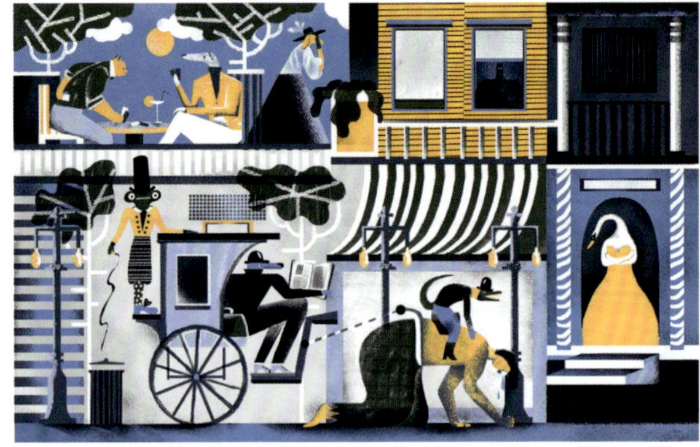

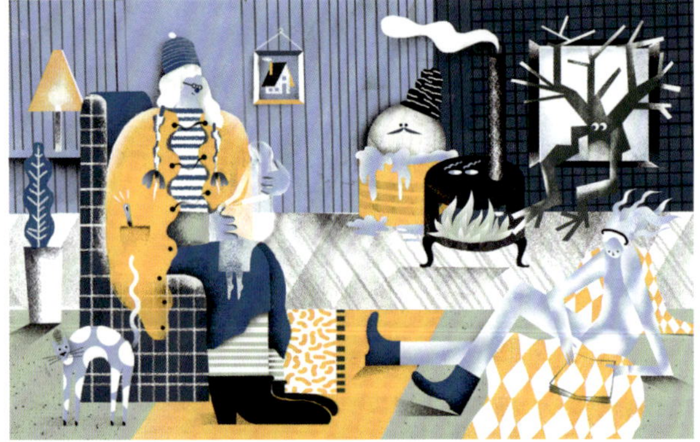

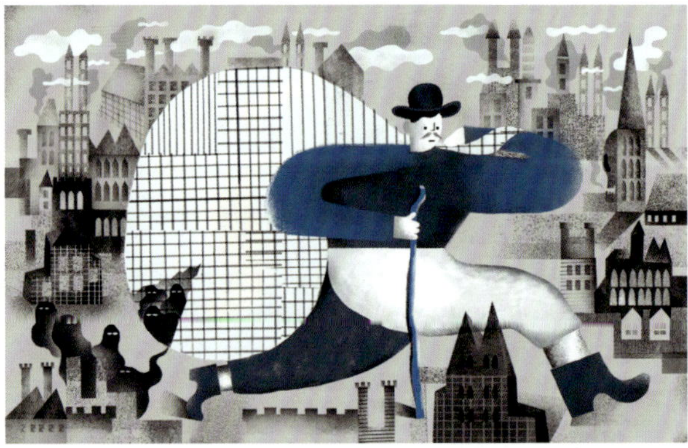

GOLD *Karol Banach*

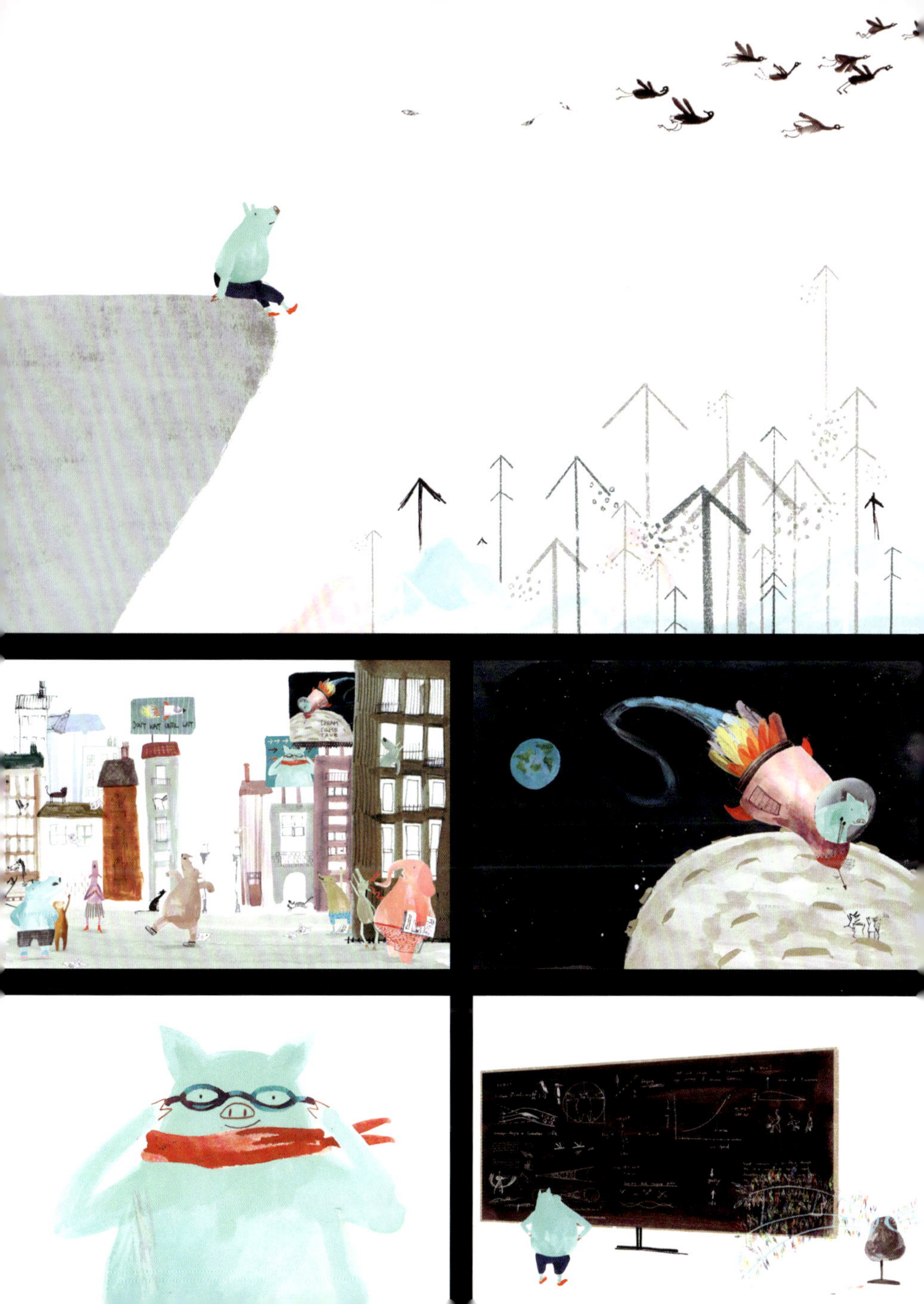

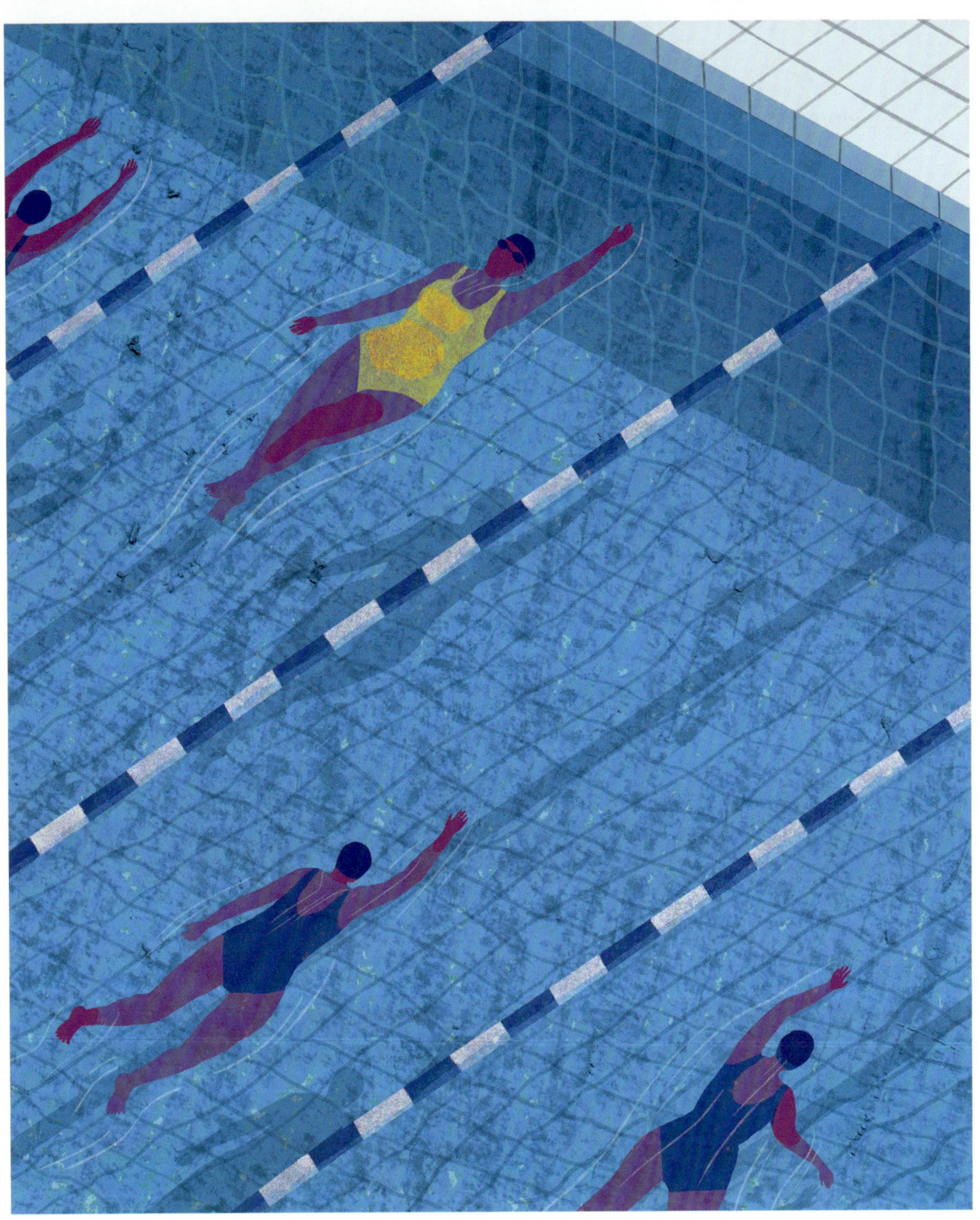

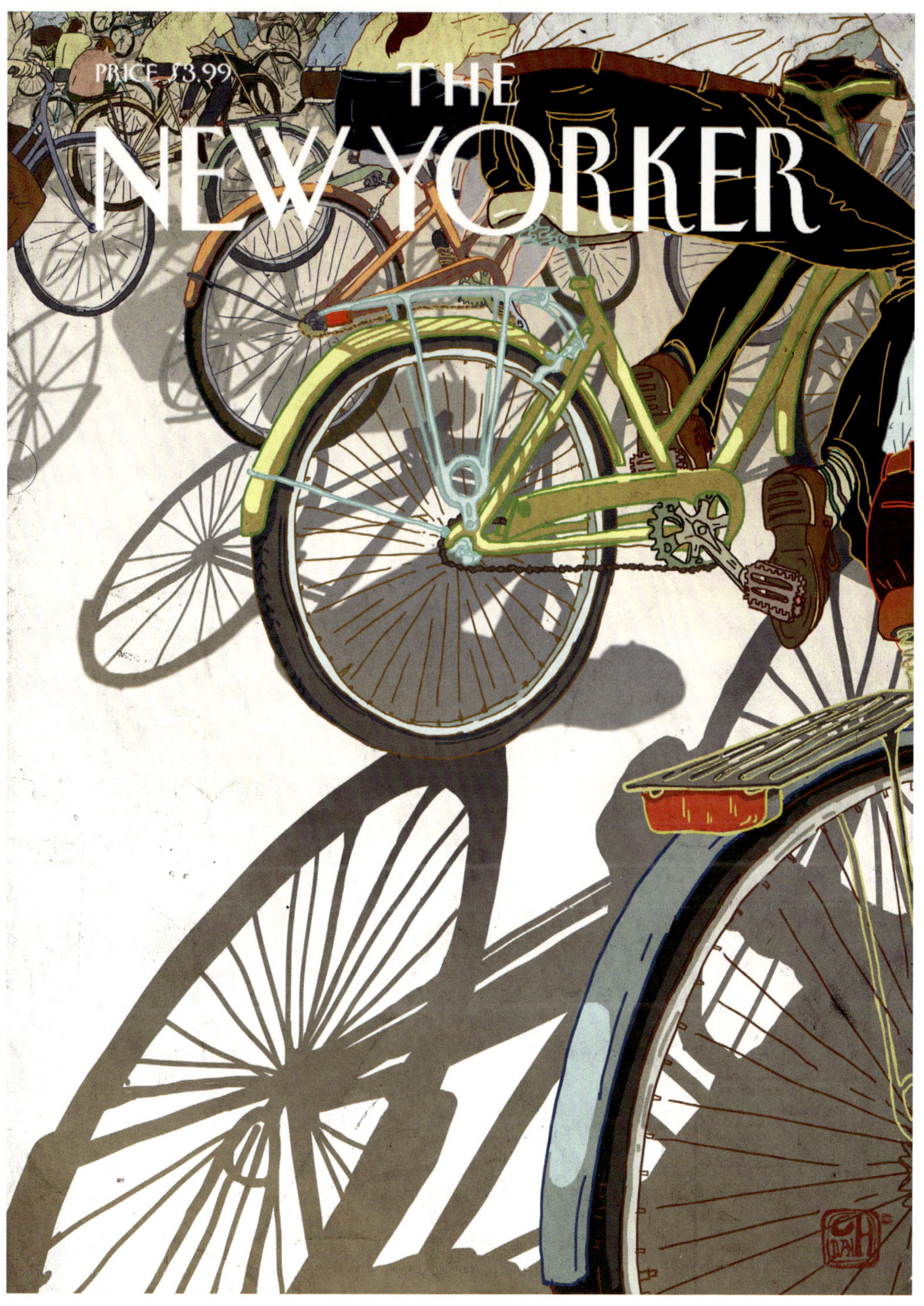

PRICE $3.99
THE
NEW YORKER

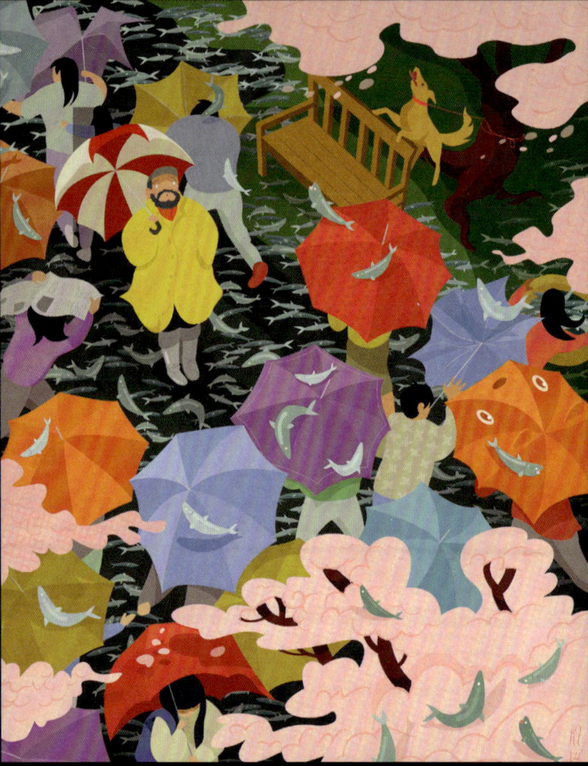

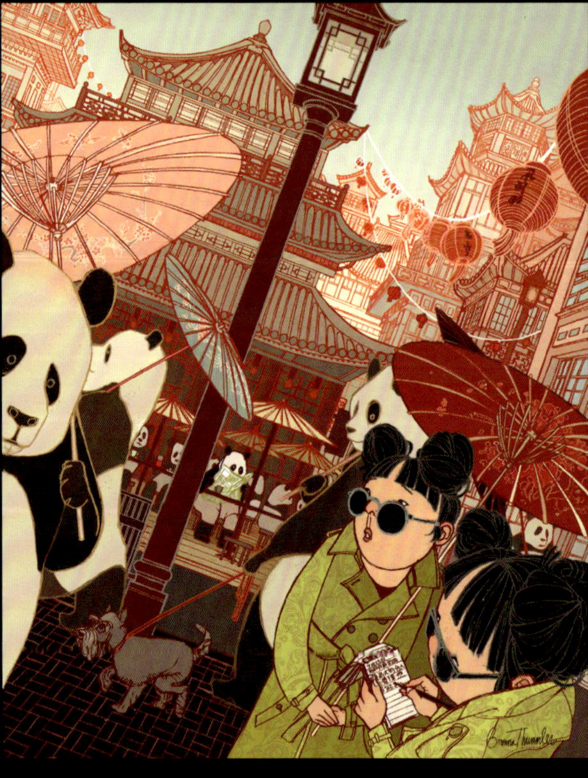

(T) MERIT Krystal Lauk   (B) MERIT Brenna Thummler

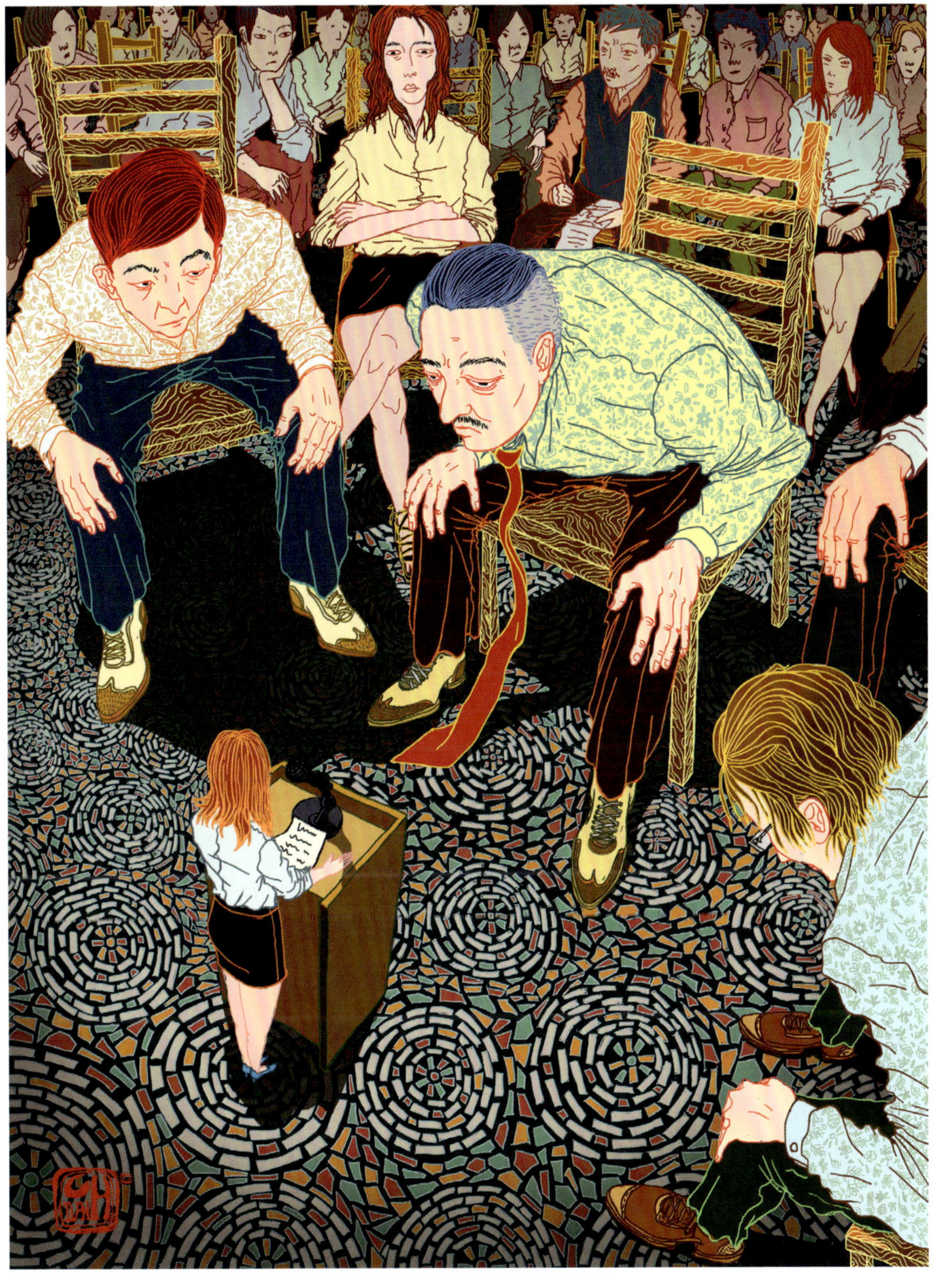

MERIT *Hong Chen*

321

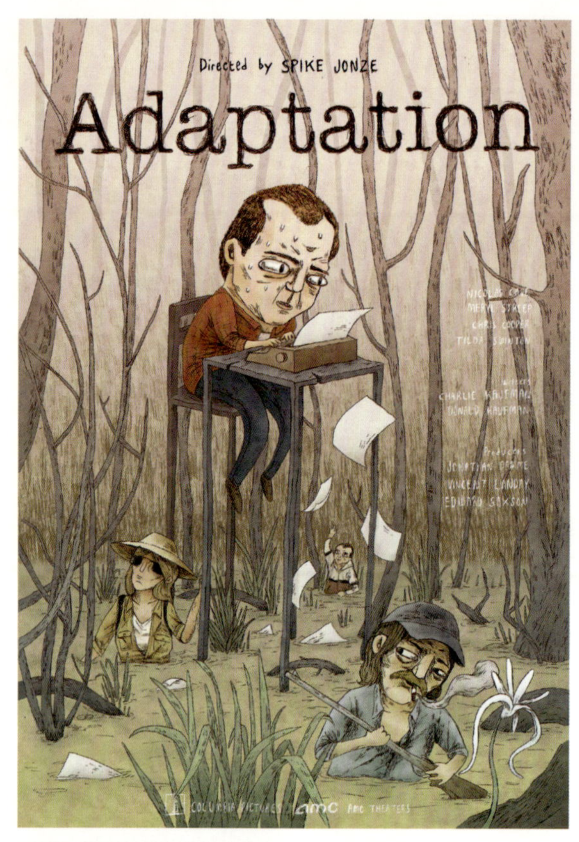


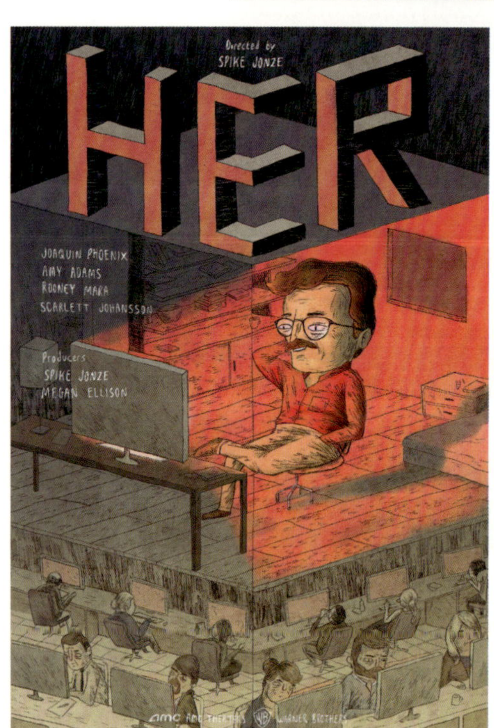


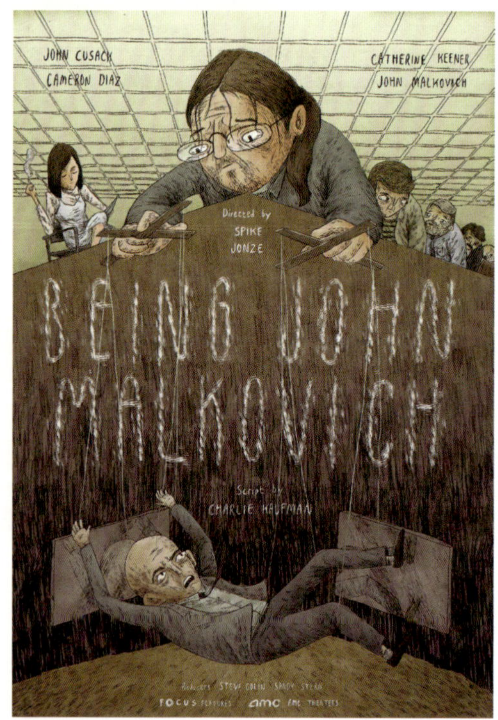


**MERIT** *Sivan Fiterman*

322

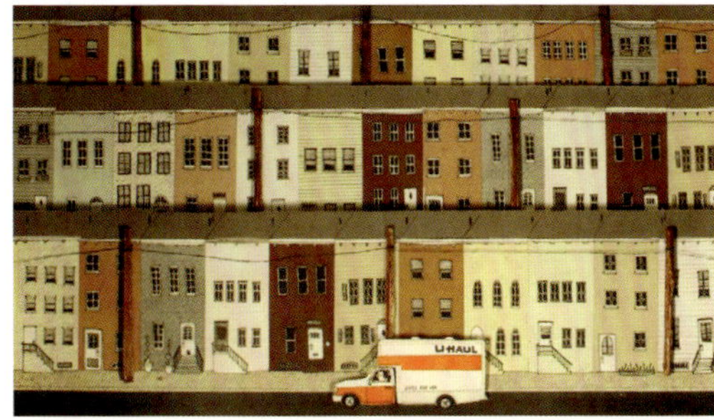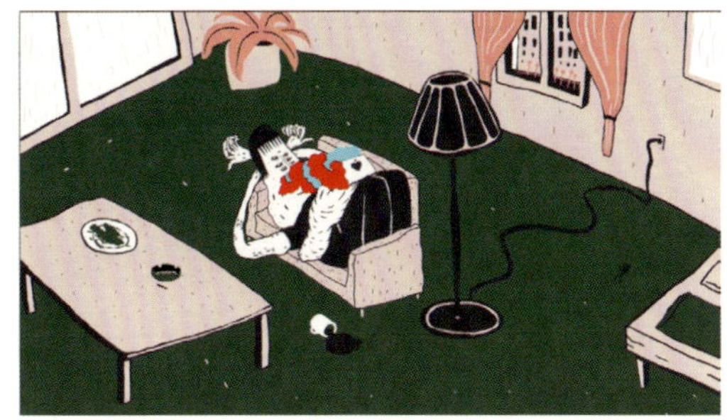

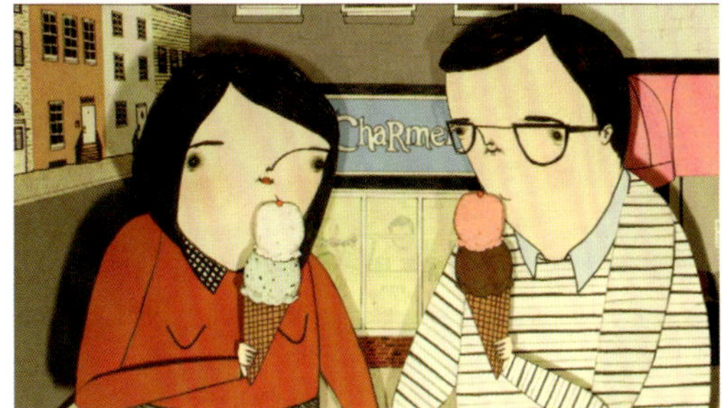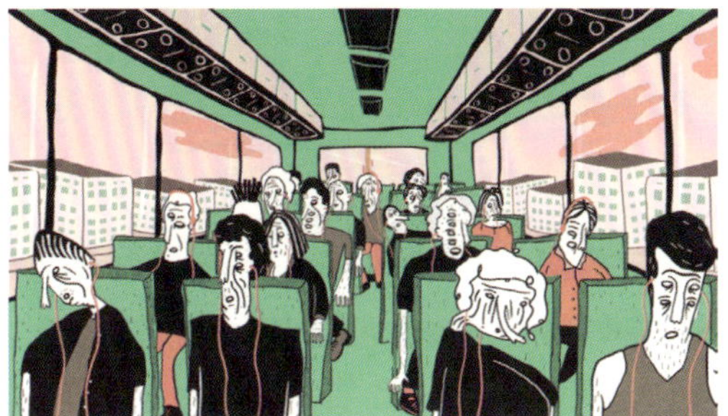

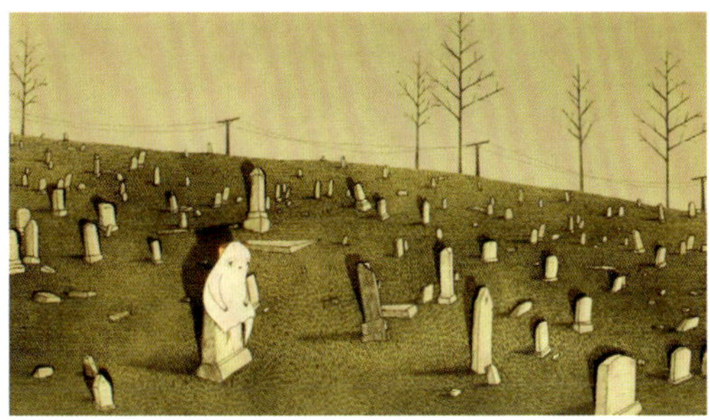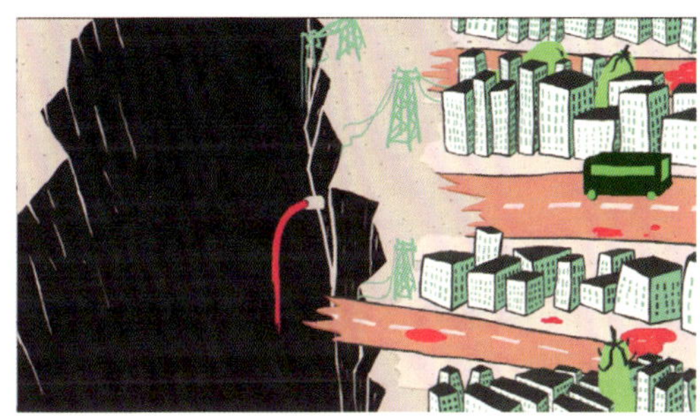

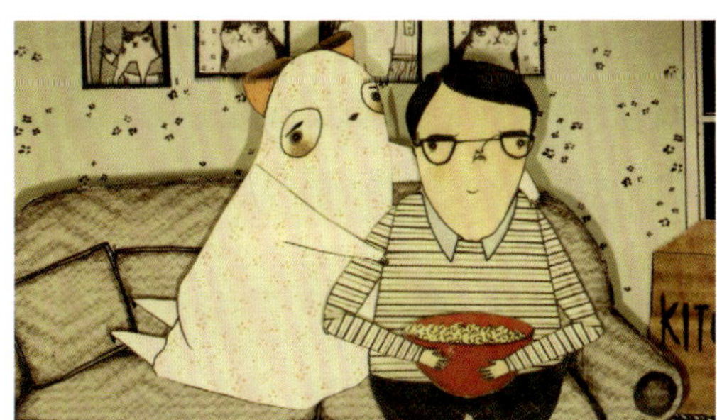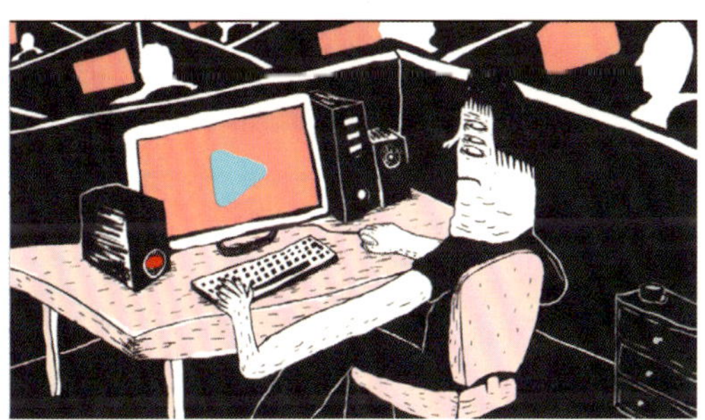

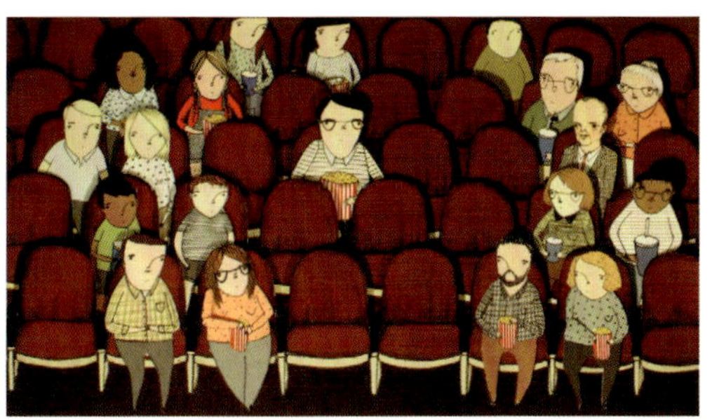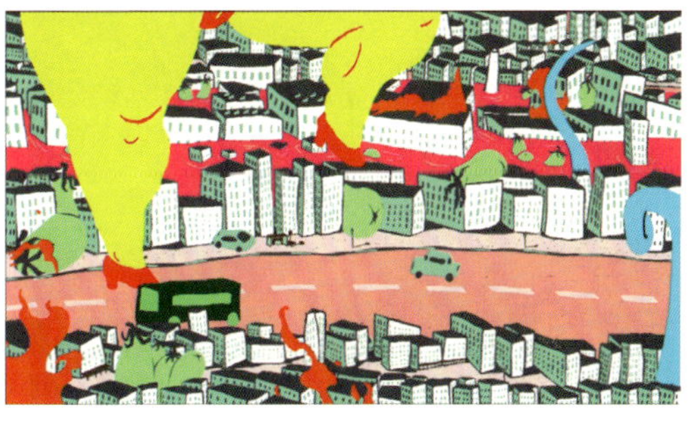

(L) MERIT *Mai Ly Degnan*   (R) MERIT *Ido Back & Tal Klein*

323

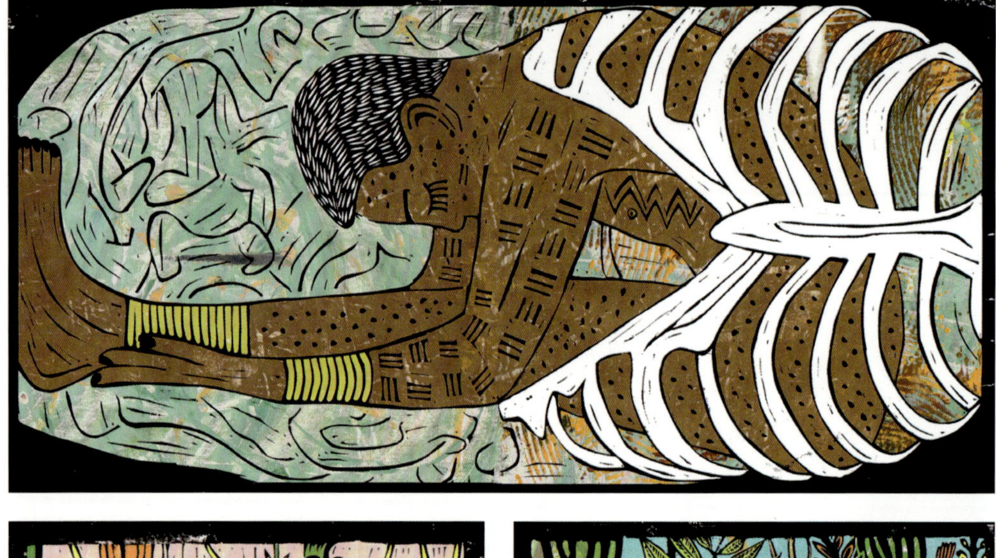

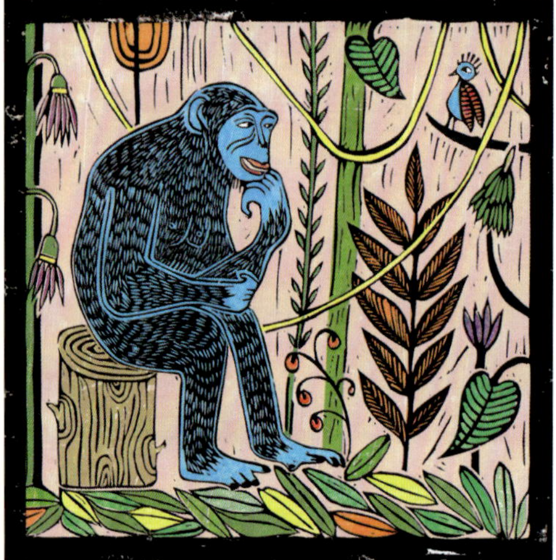

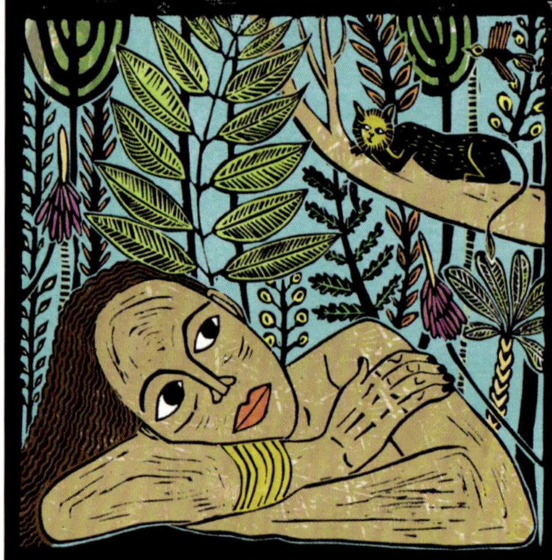

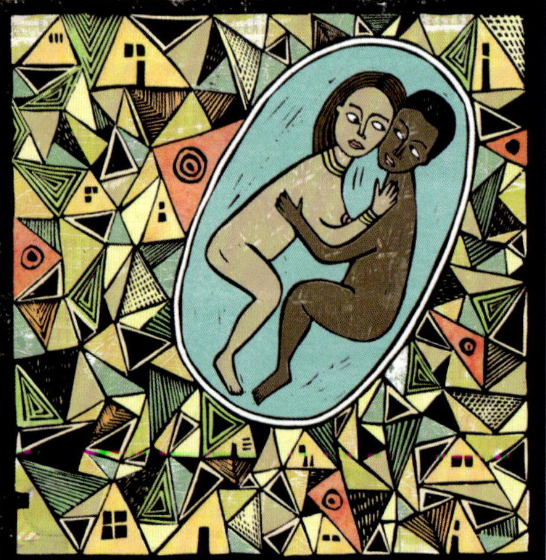

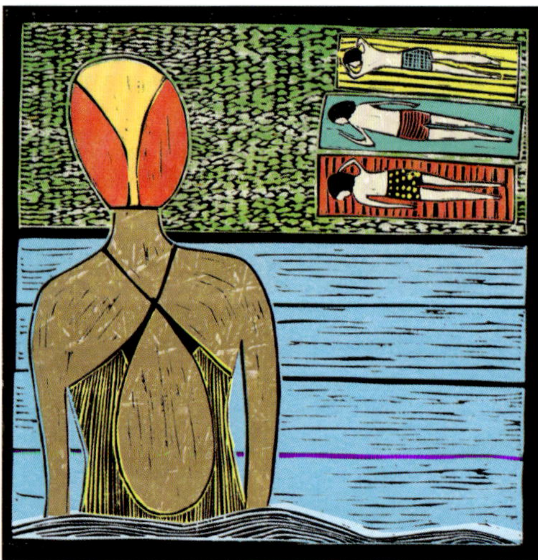

MERIT *Moran Yogev*

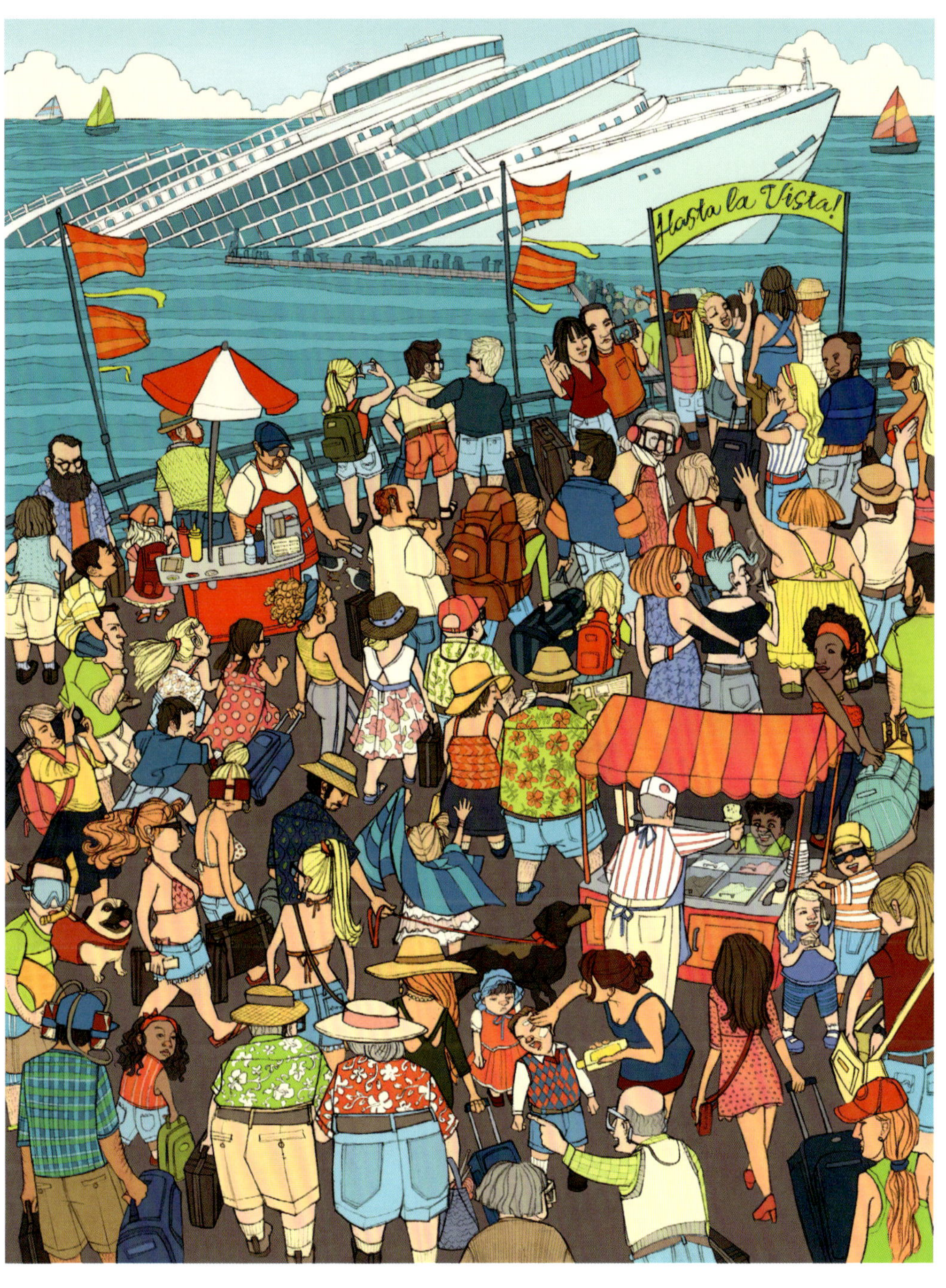


MERIT *Brenna Thummler*

325

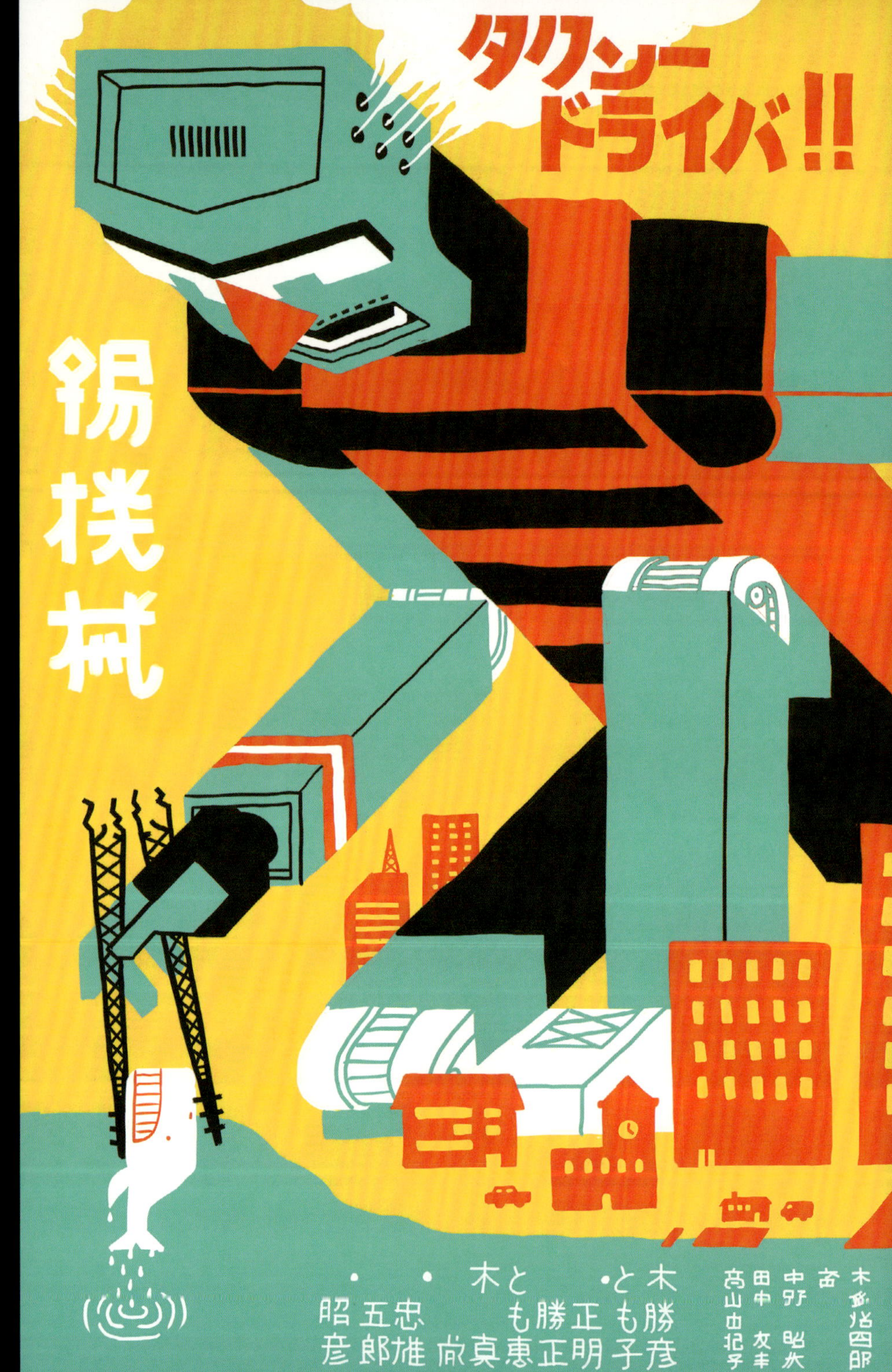
タクシー
ドライバ!!
錫楔杙
木と　・と木
も勝正も勝
真恵正明子彦
・・・
昭五忠
彦郎雄尚
古
木部治四郎
中野昭次
田中友幸
高山由妃子
ENT SHOW

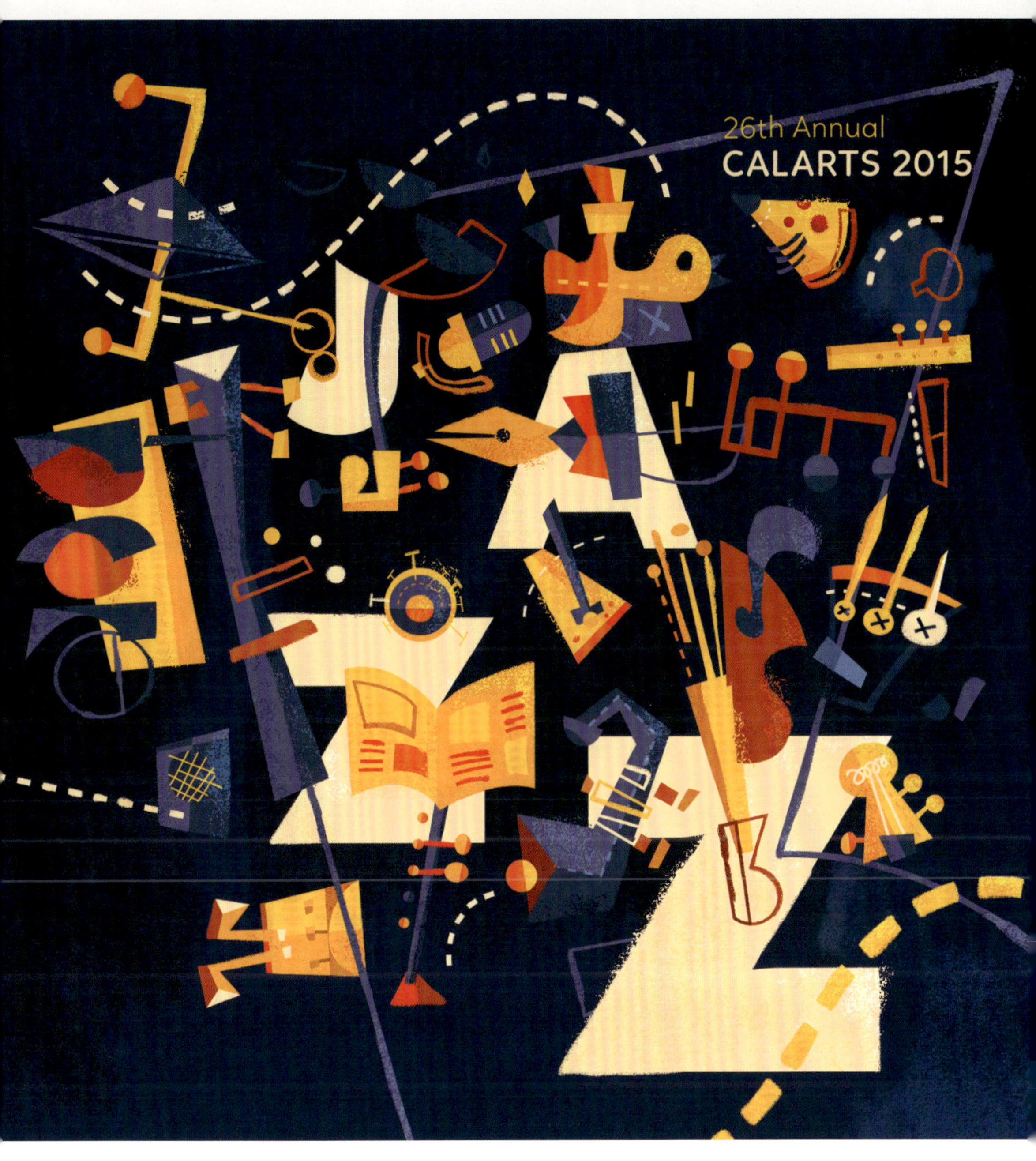




MERIT *Ray Yeunsu Shin*

327

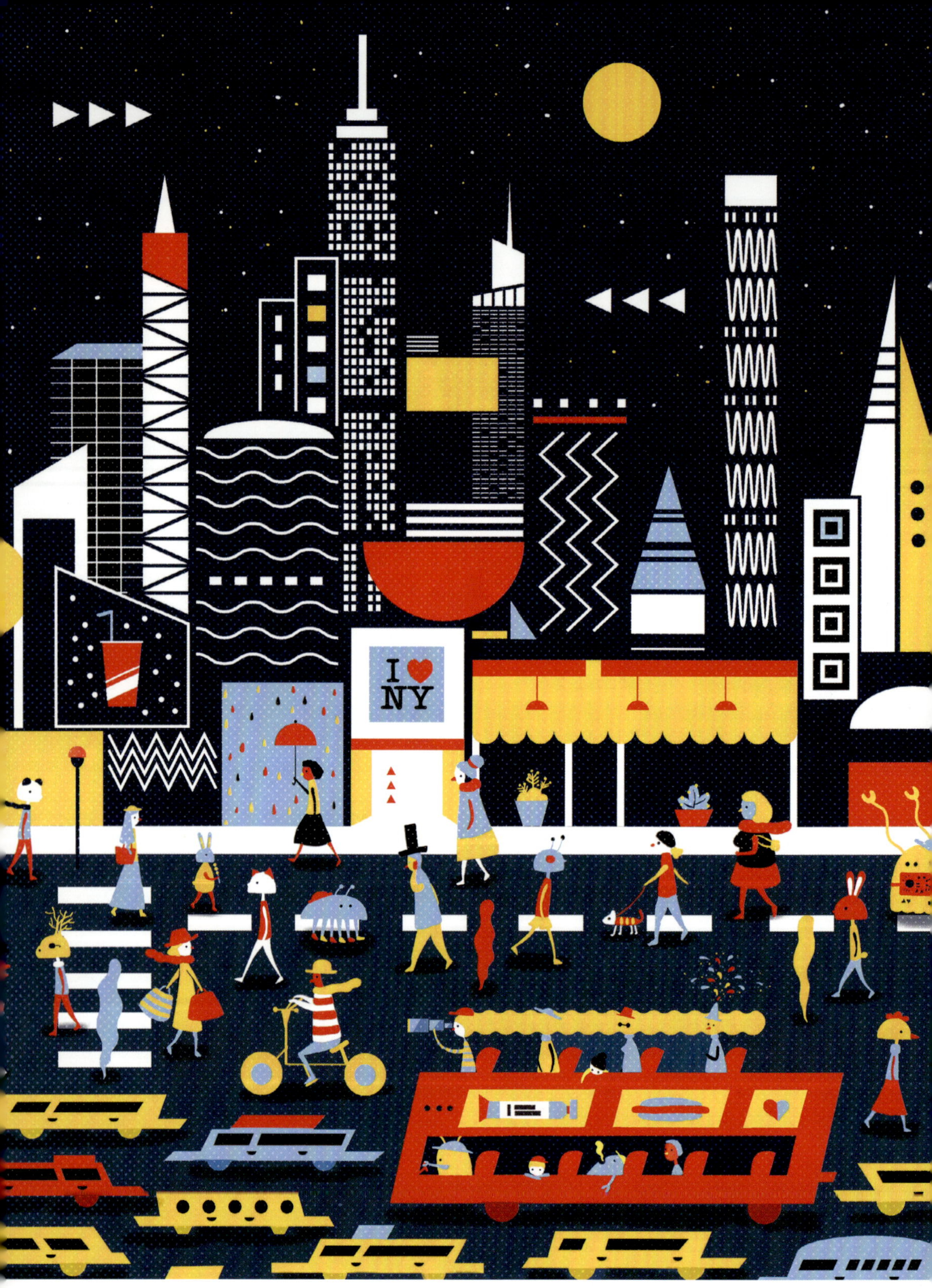


MERIT *Yao Yu*

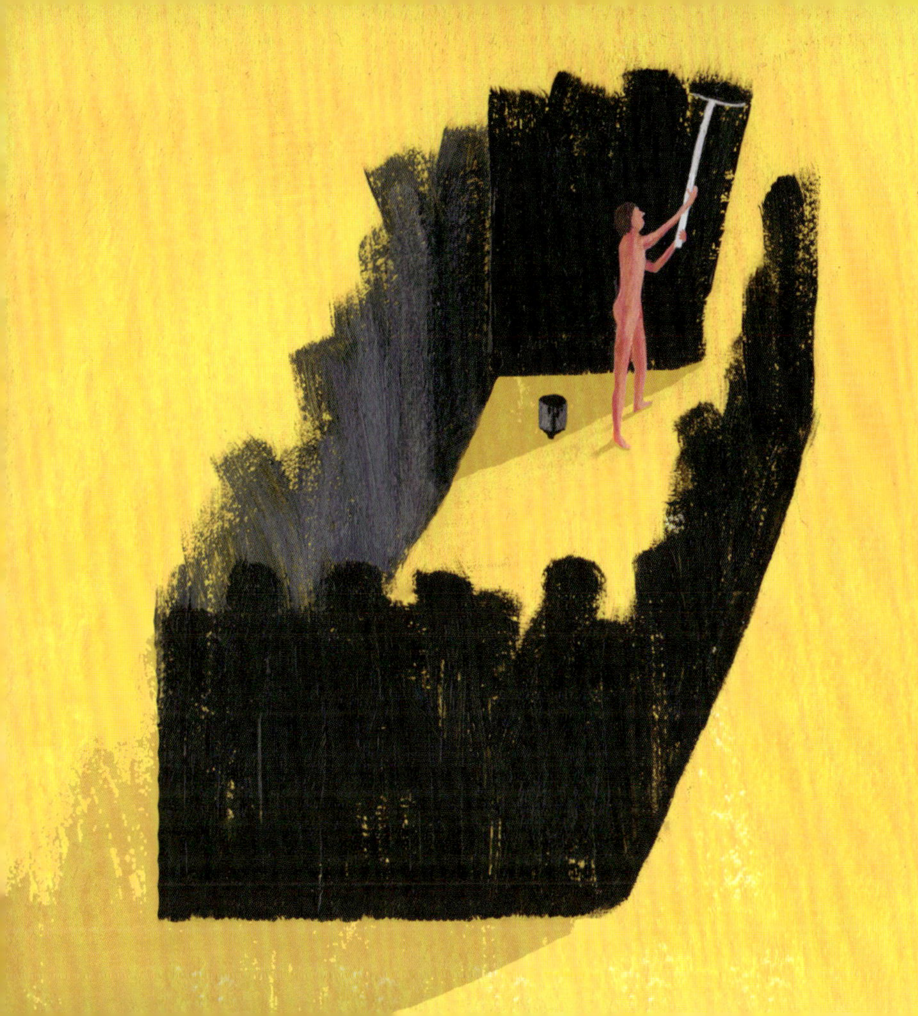

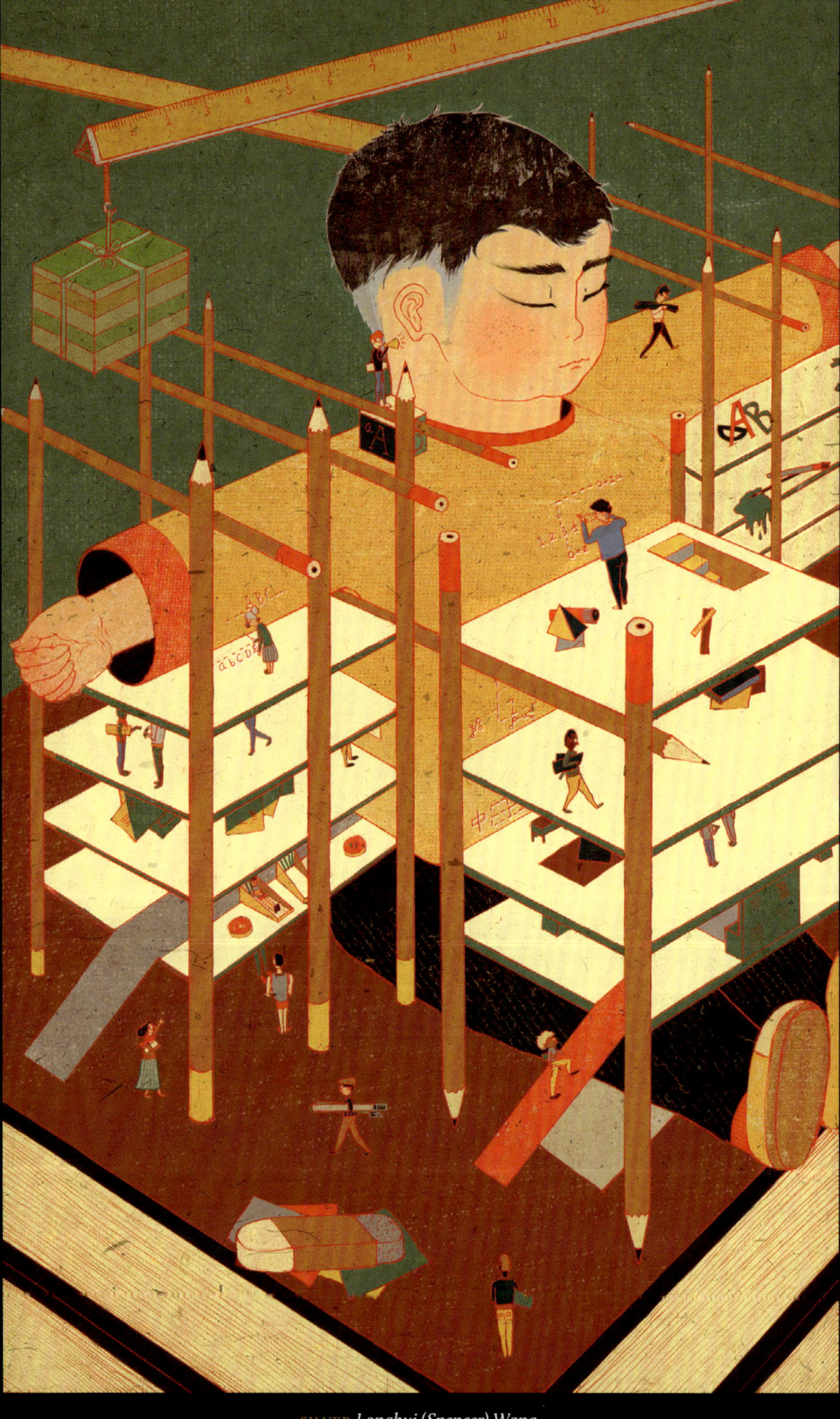

SILVER Longhui (Spencer) Wang

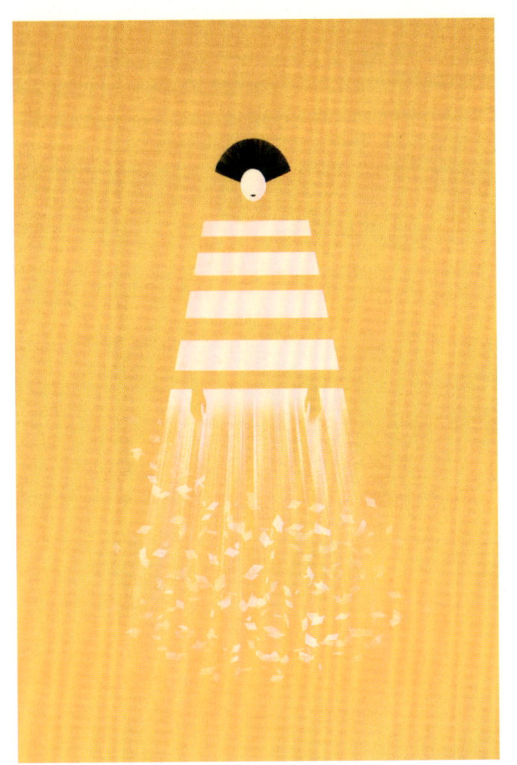
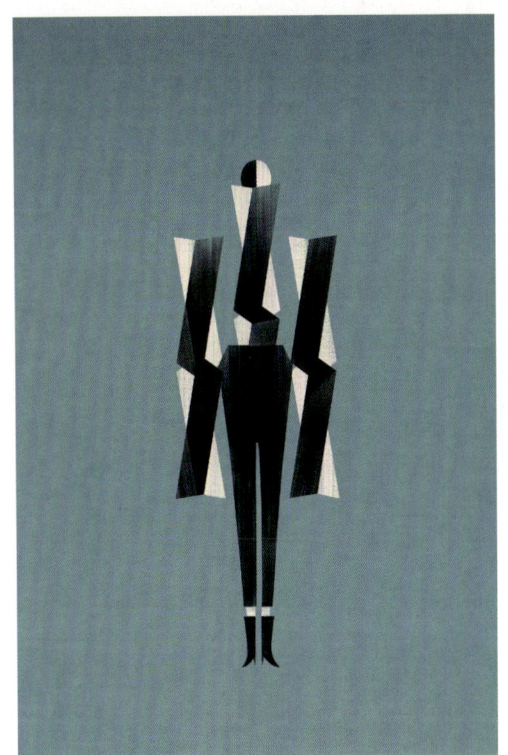
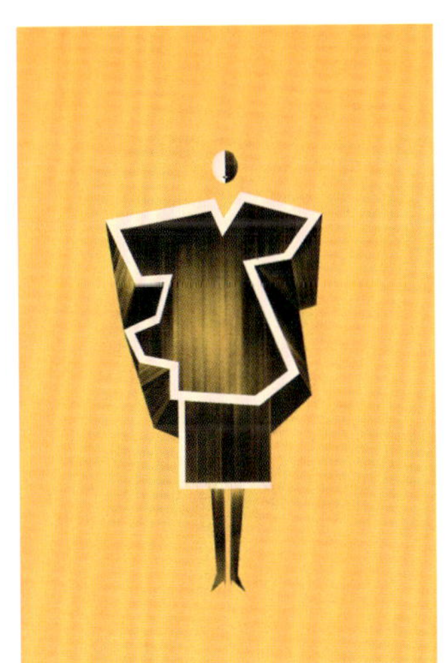
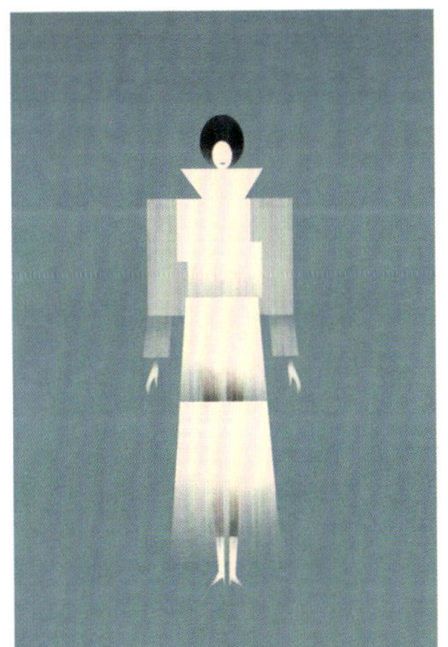
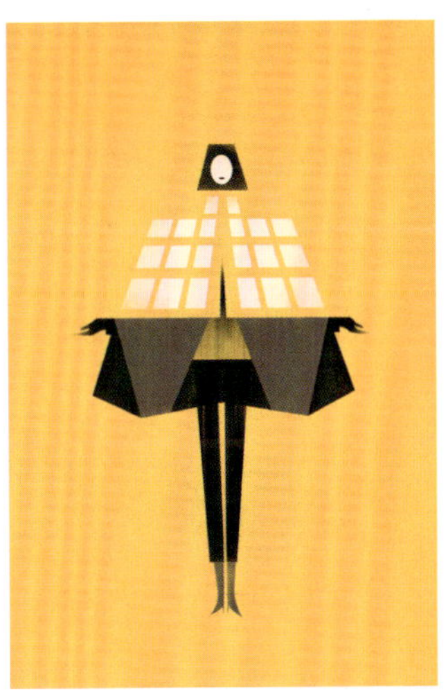

MERIT *Jasu Hu*

331

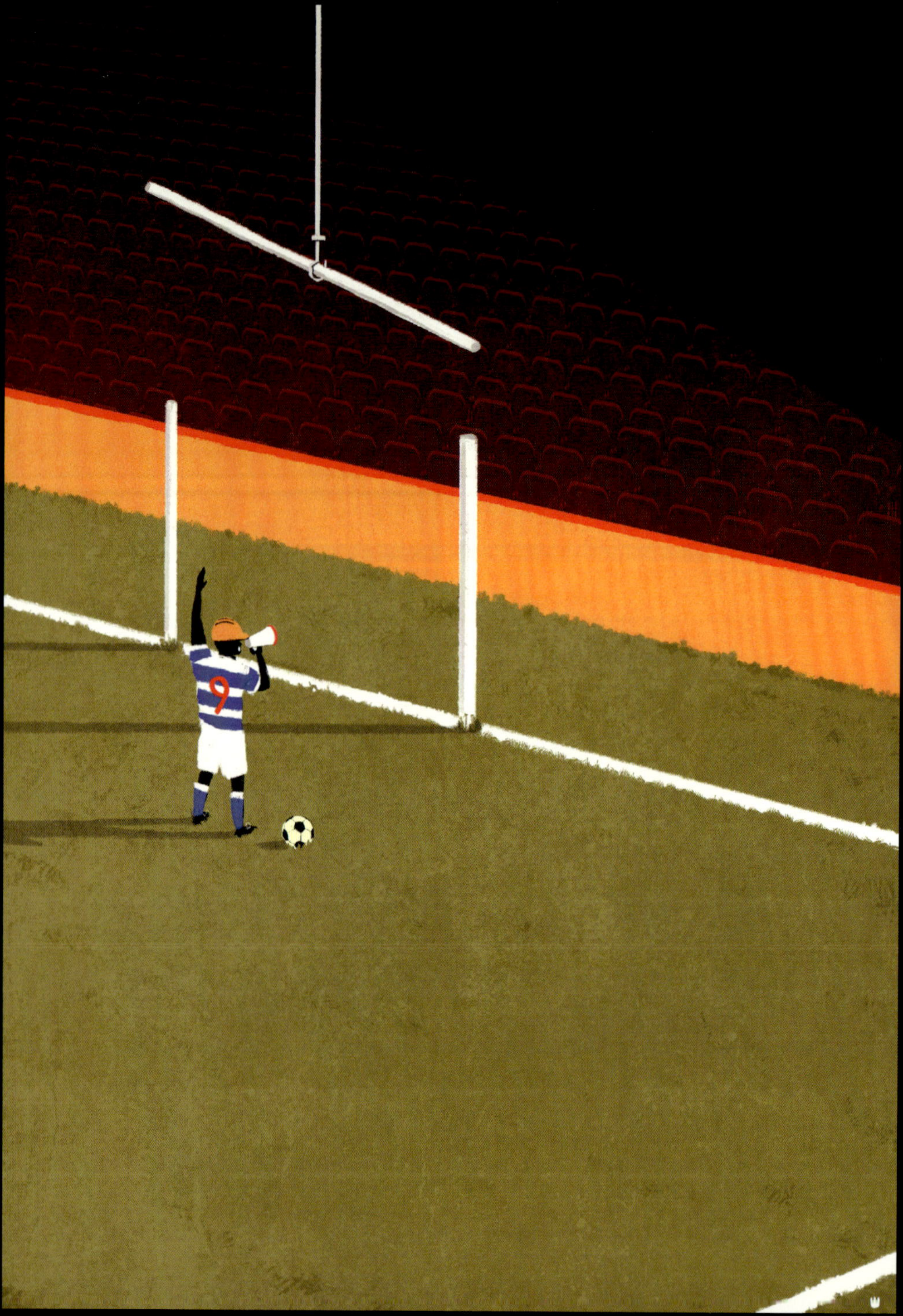

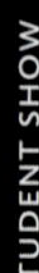

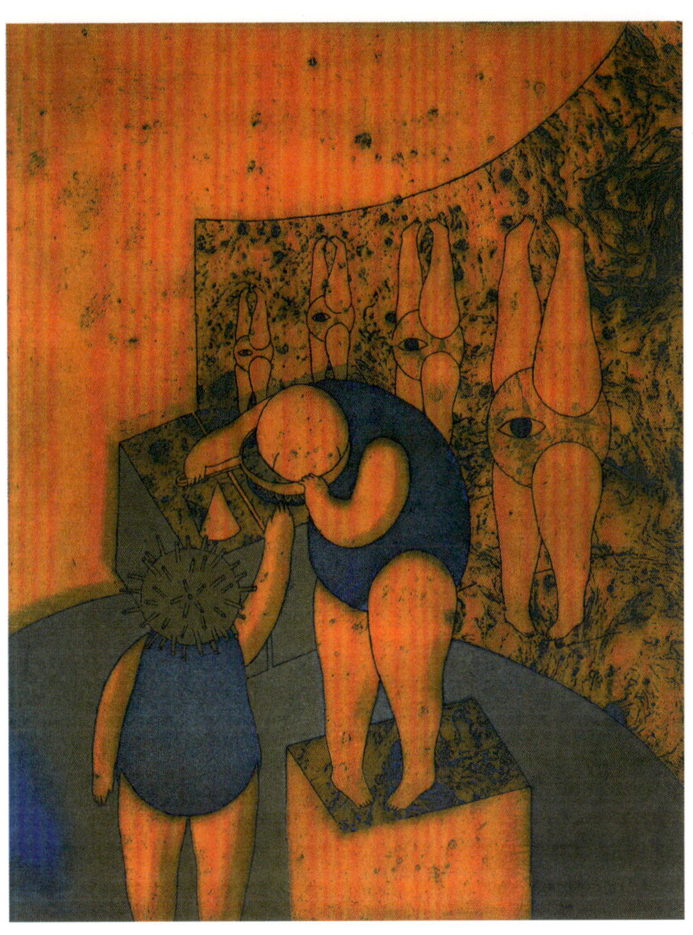

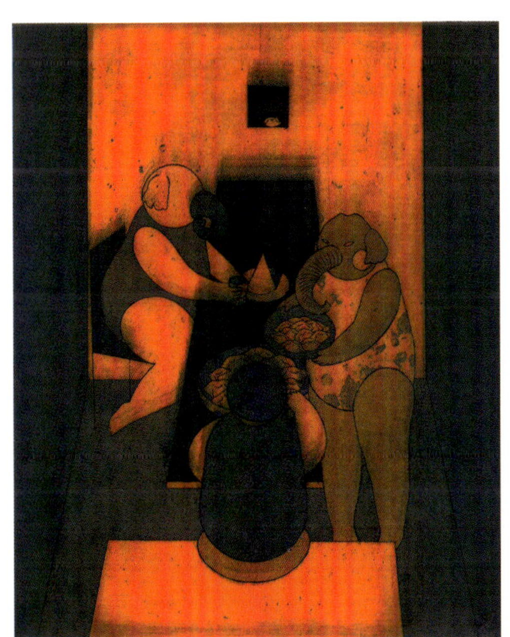

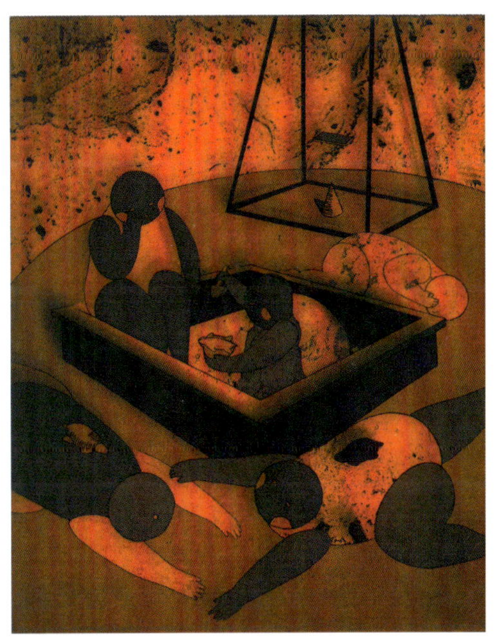

MERIT *Qiaoyi Shi*

333

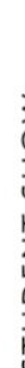

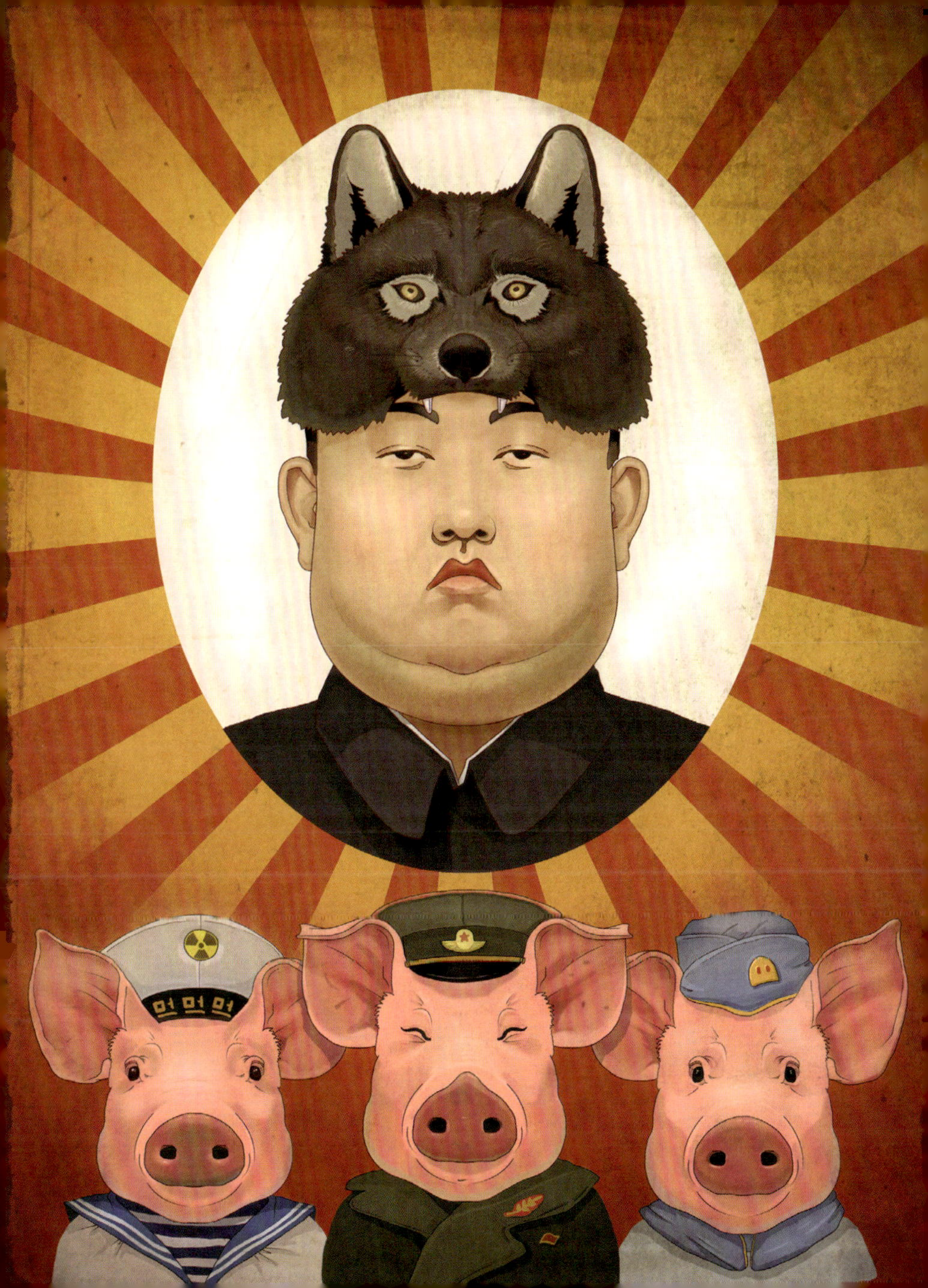

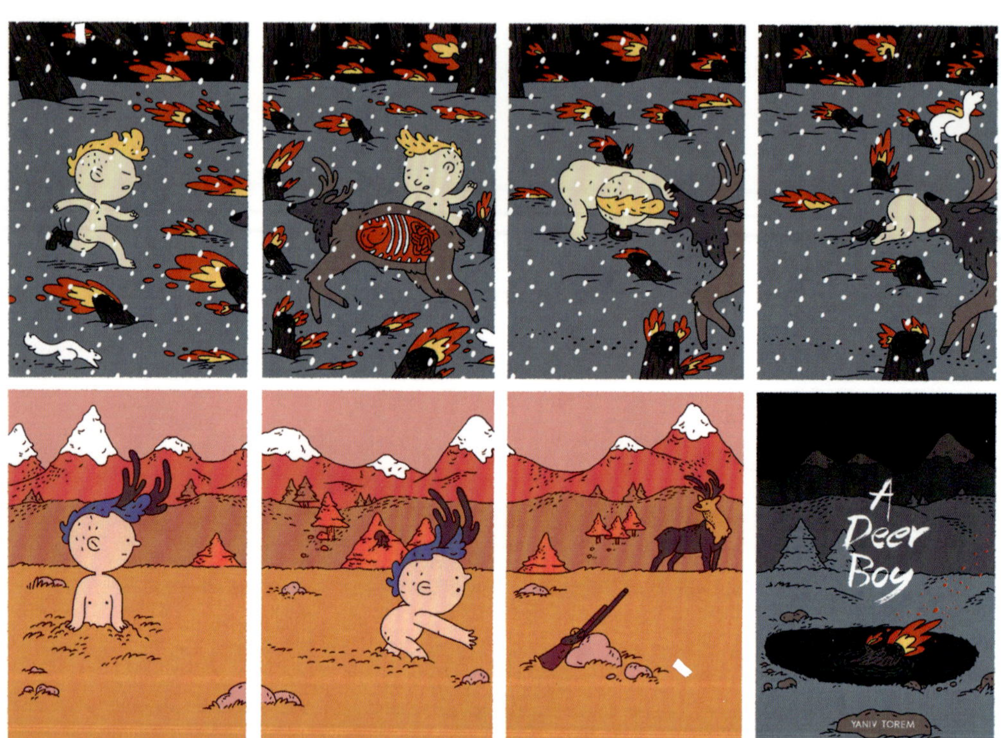


MERIT *Yaniv Torem*

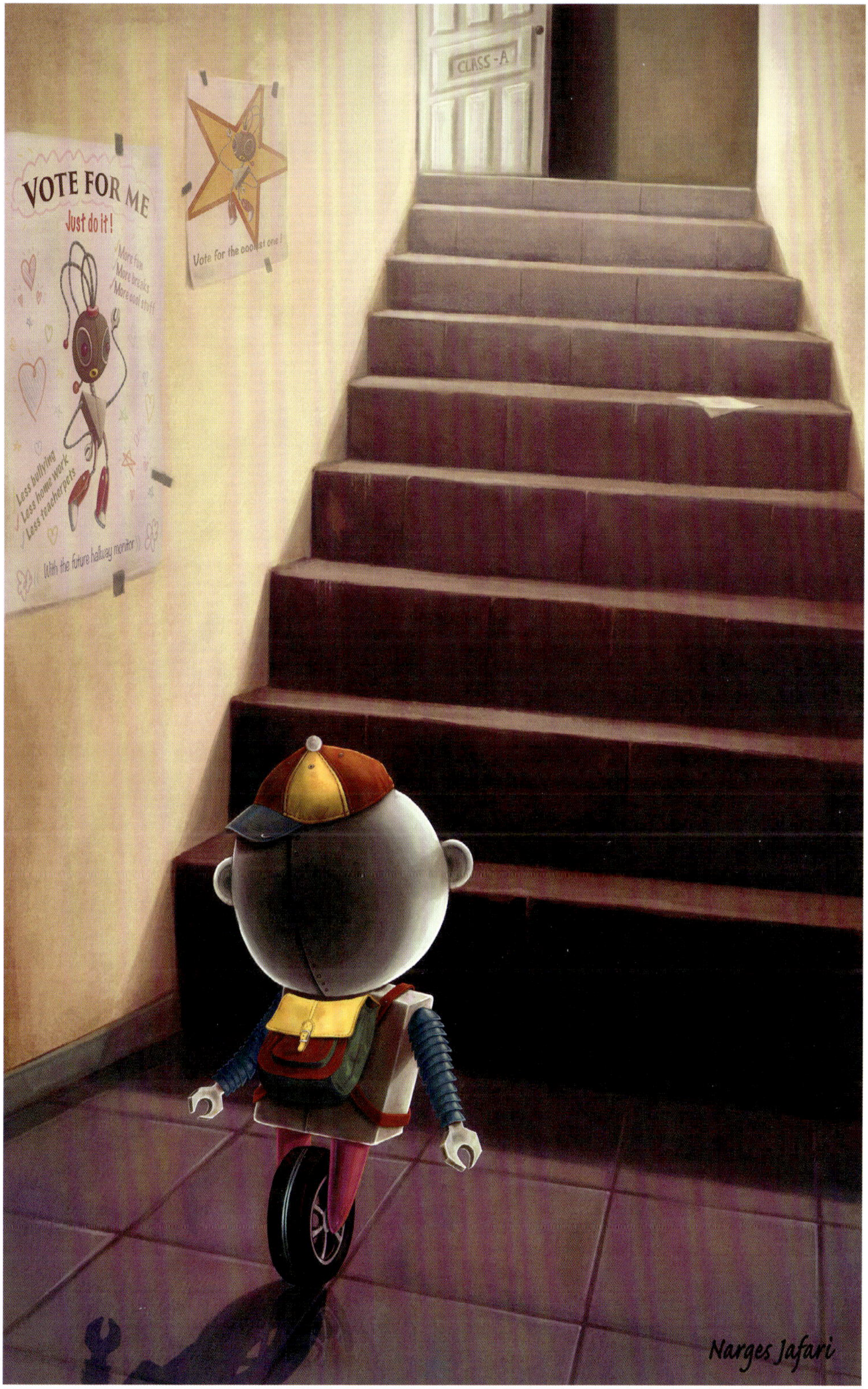

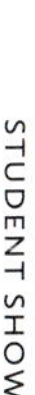

VOTE FOR ME
Just do it!
More fun
More breaks
More cool stuff
Less bullying
Less home work
Less teacherpets
With the future hallway monitor ))
Vote for the coolest one!
CLASS - A
Narges Jafari

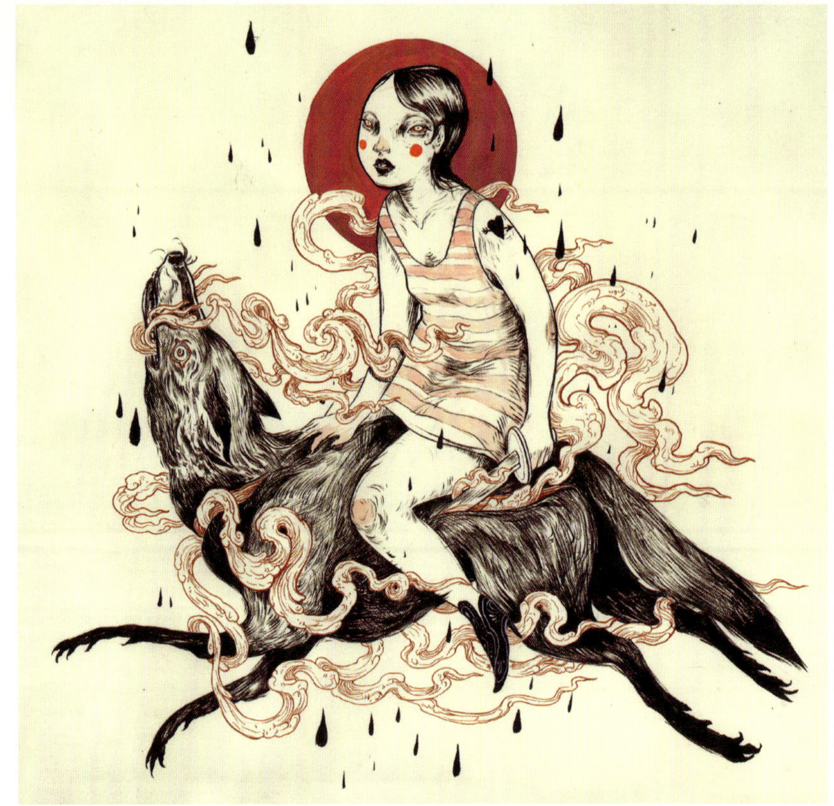

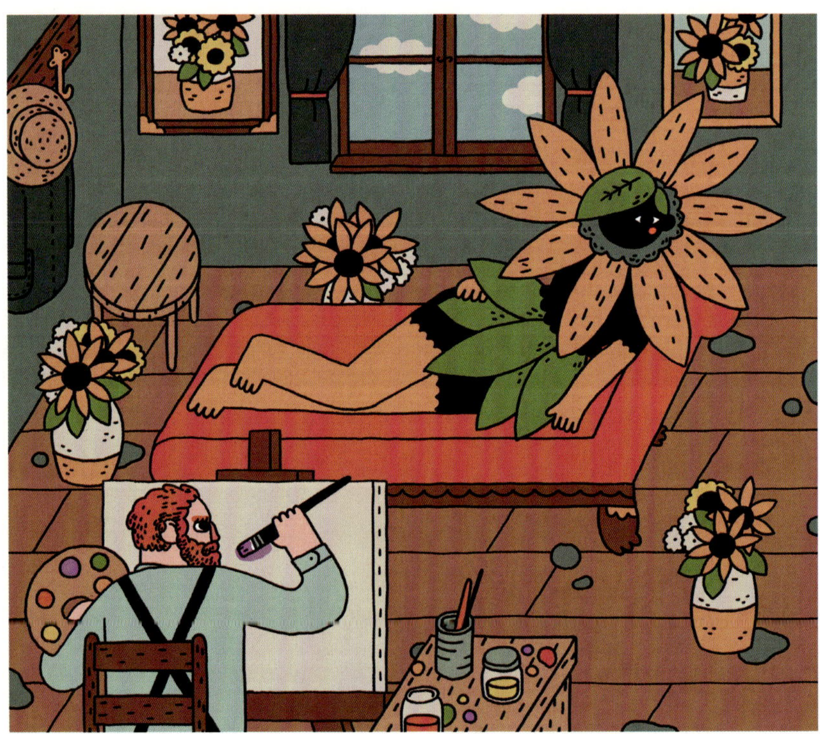

(TL) MERIT *Nomi Chi*   (BL) MERIT *Paige Clark*   (R) MERIT *Lynden Joudrey*

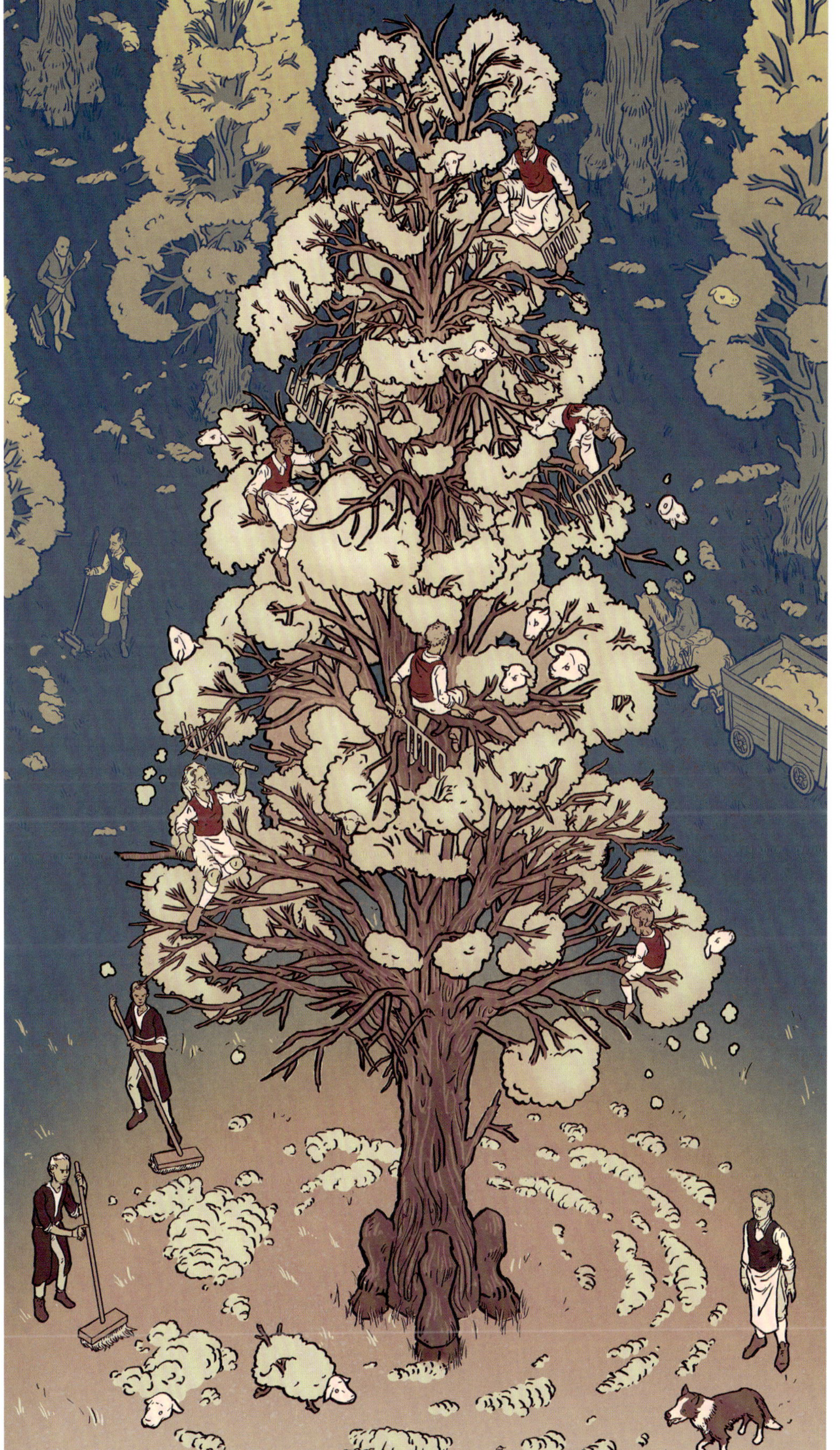
STUDENT SHOW

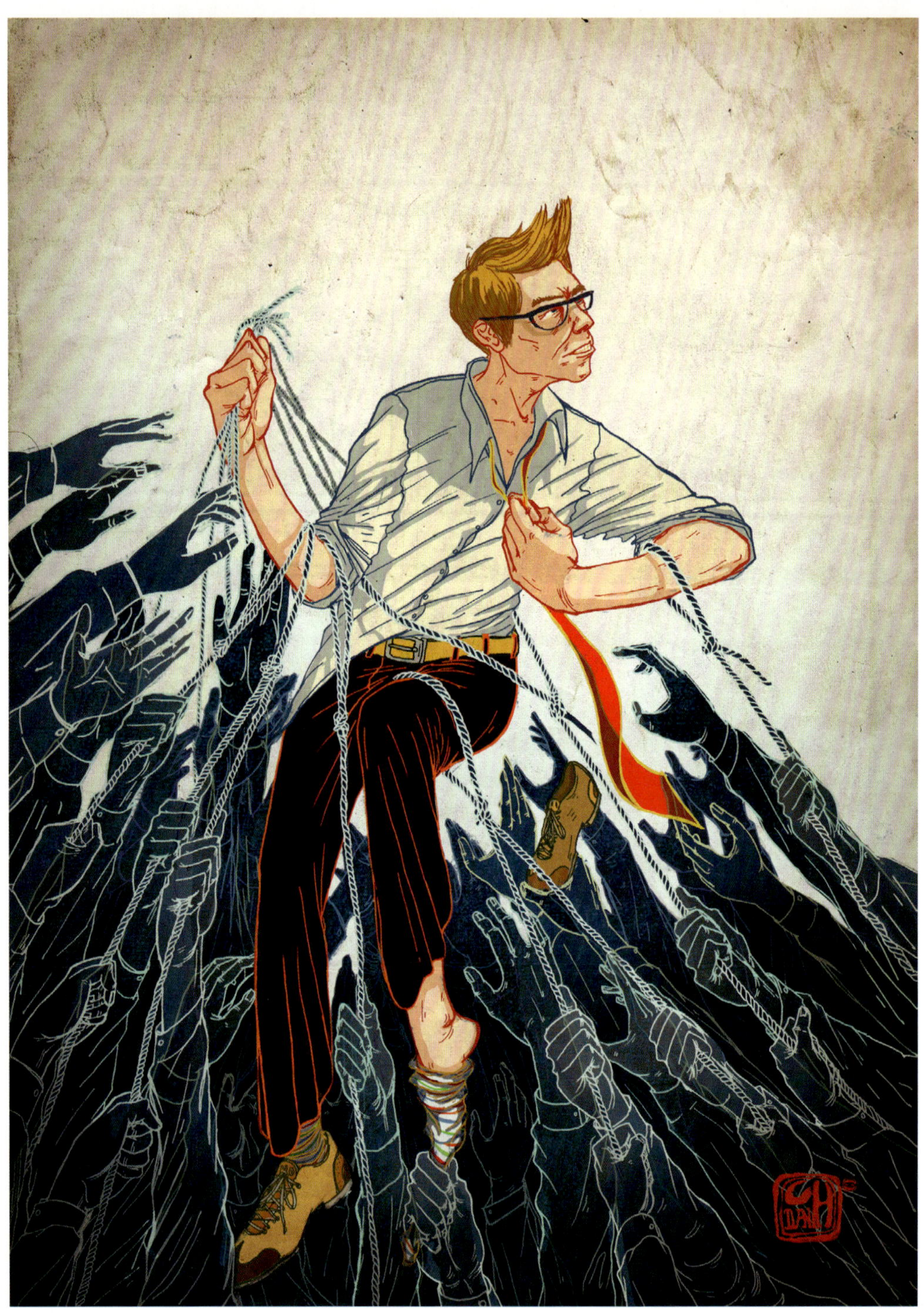



(L) MERIT *Hong Chen*   (R) BRONZE *Yohey Horishita*

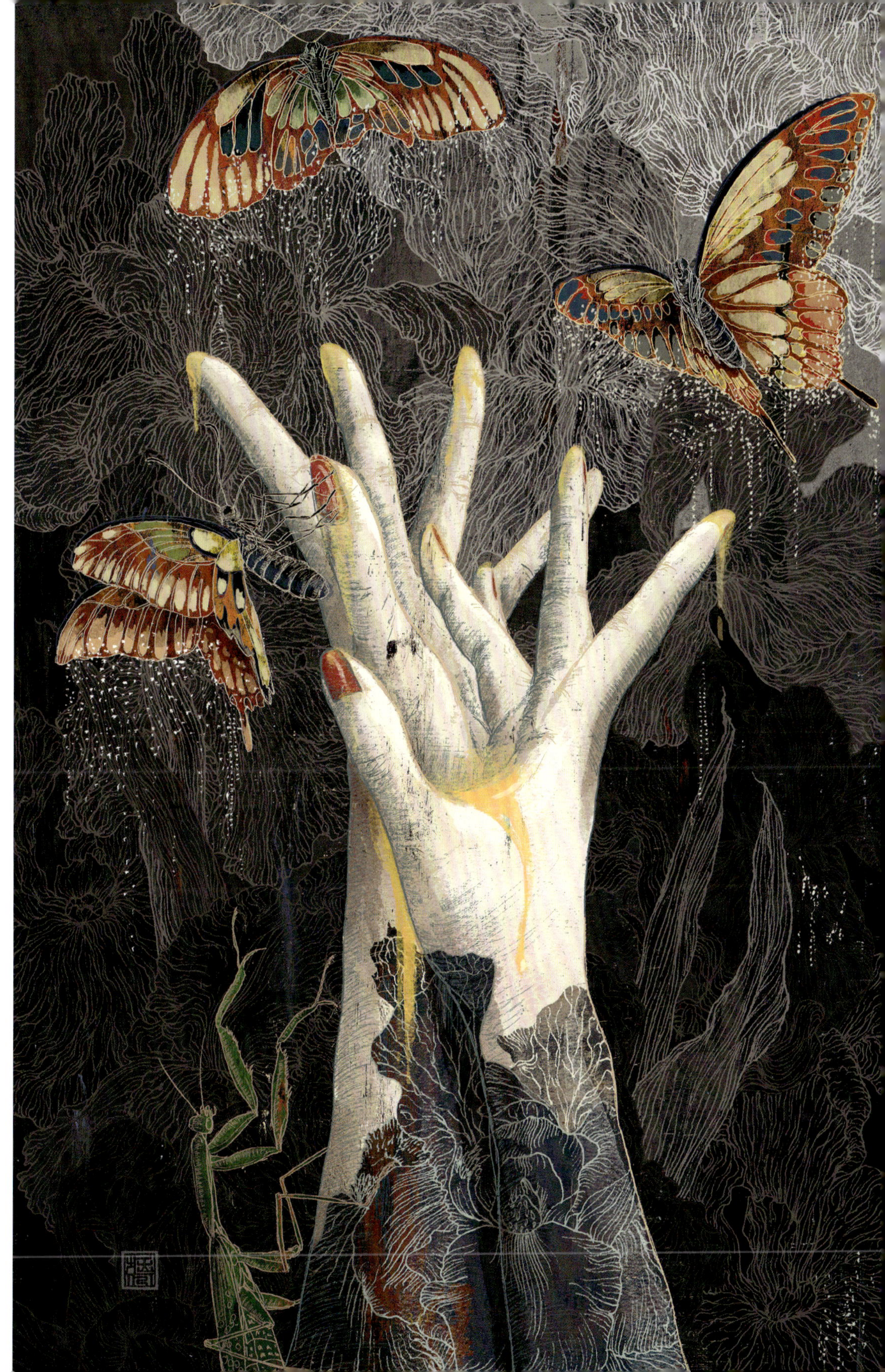

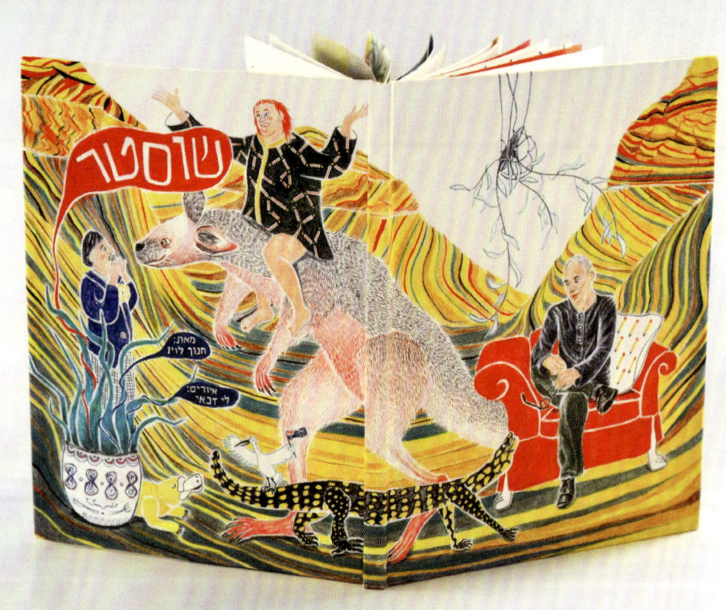

שוסטר
מאת: חנוך לוין
איורים: לי זבאי


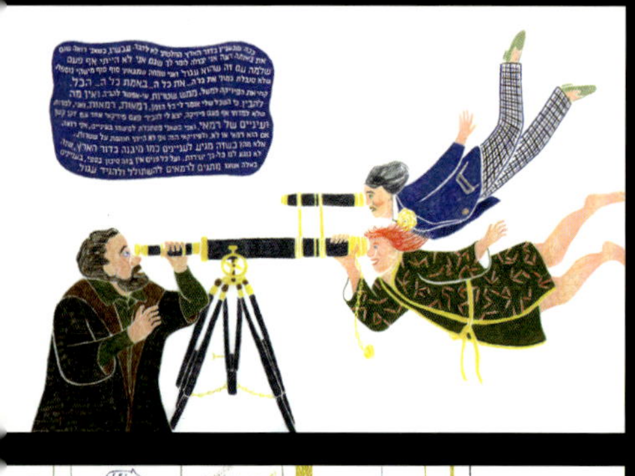

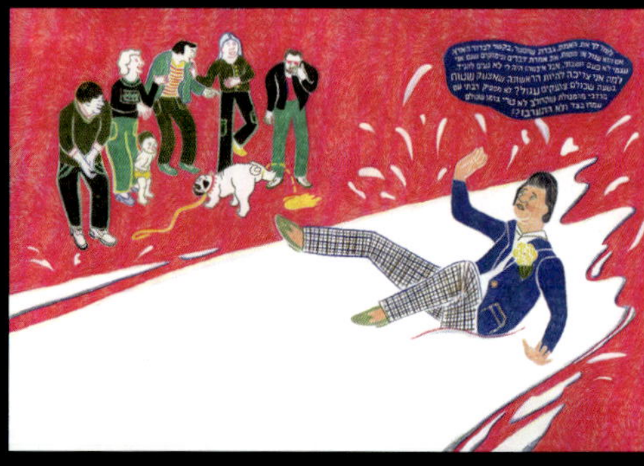

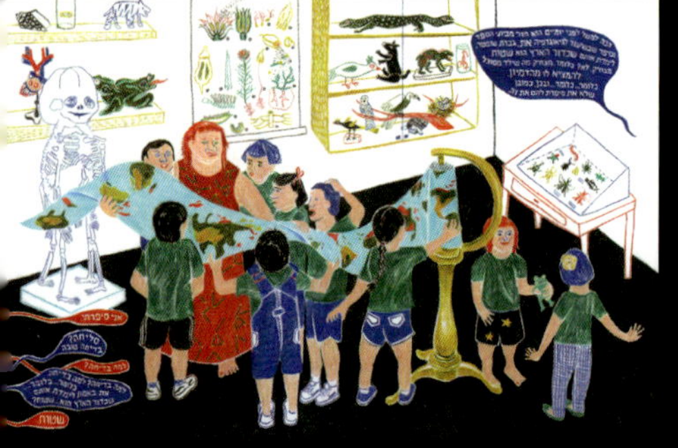

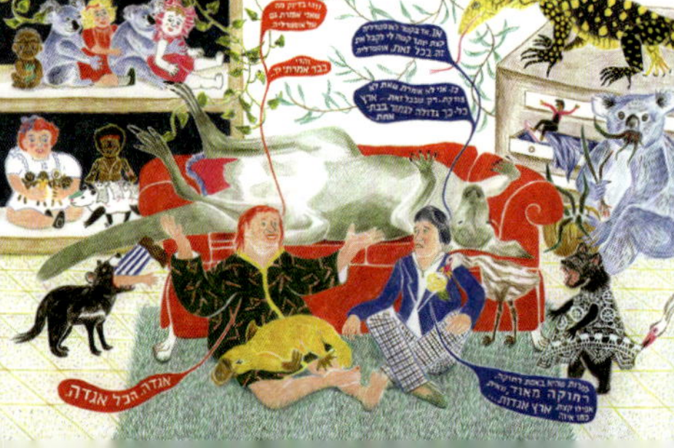

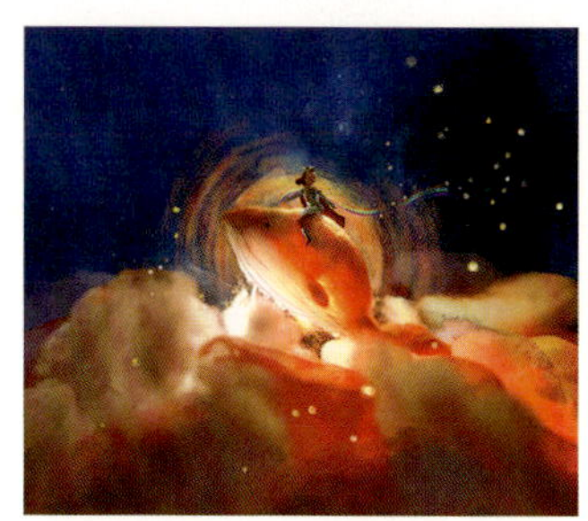
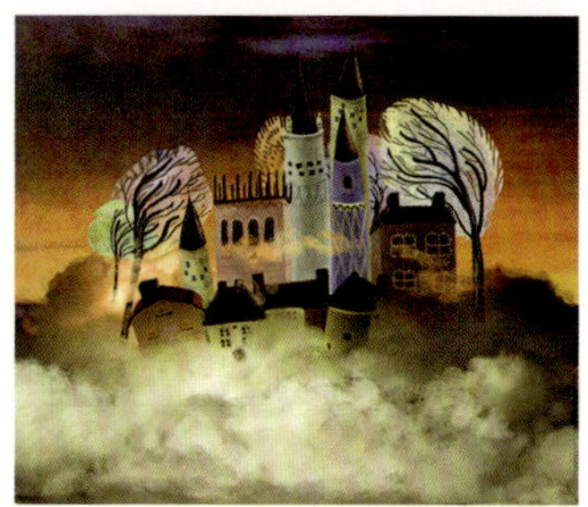
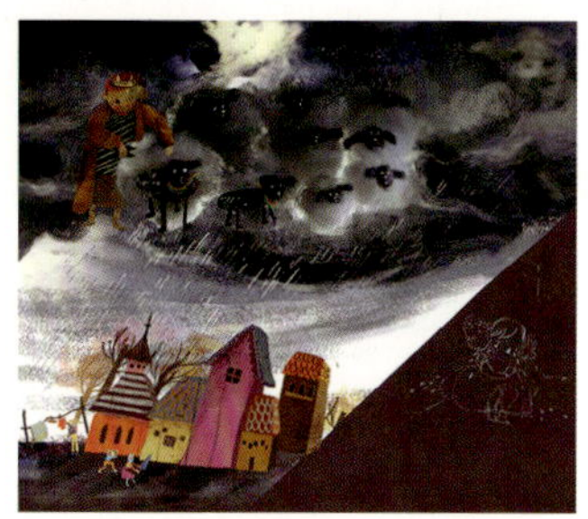
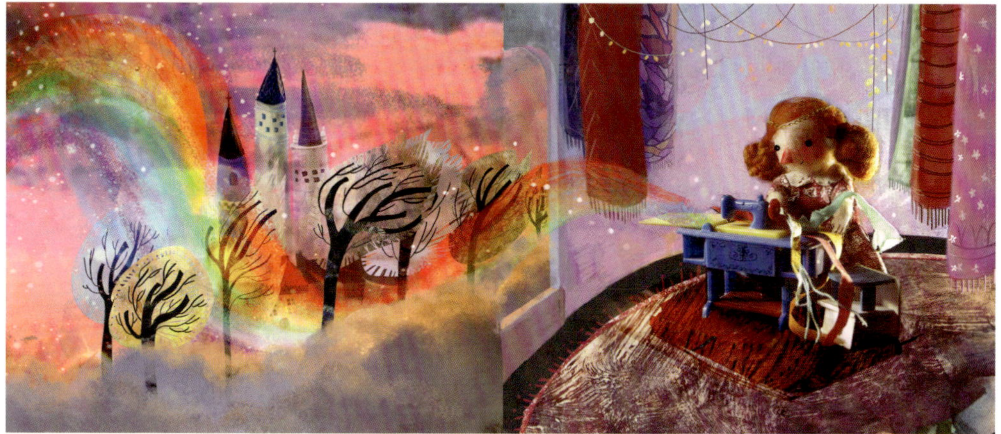
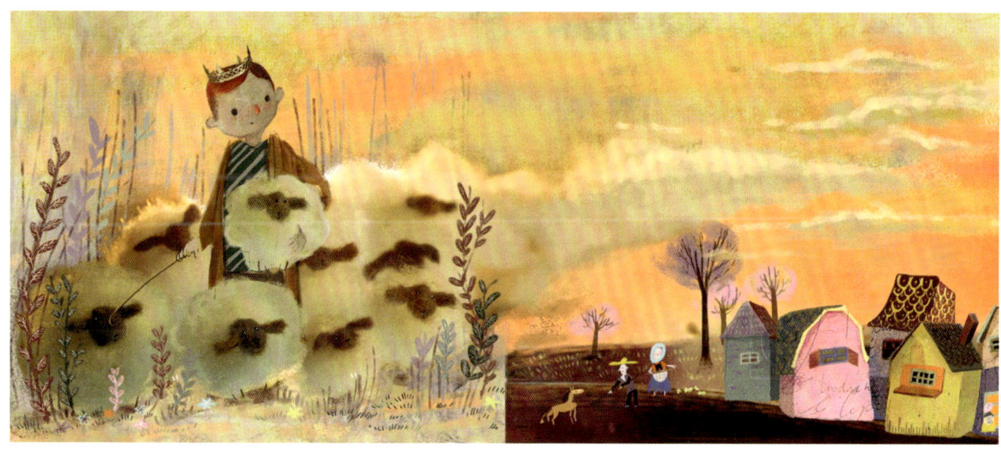

MERIT *Dream Chen*

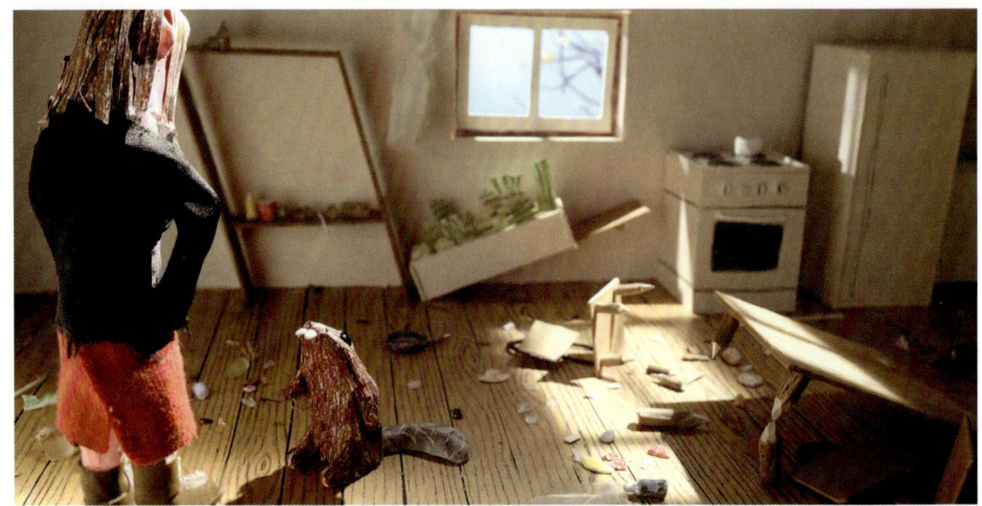

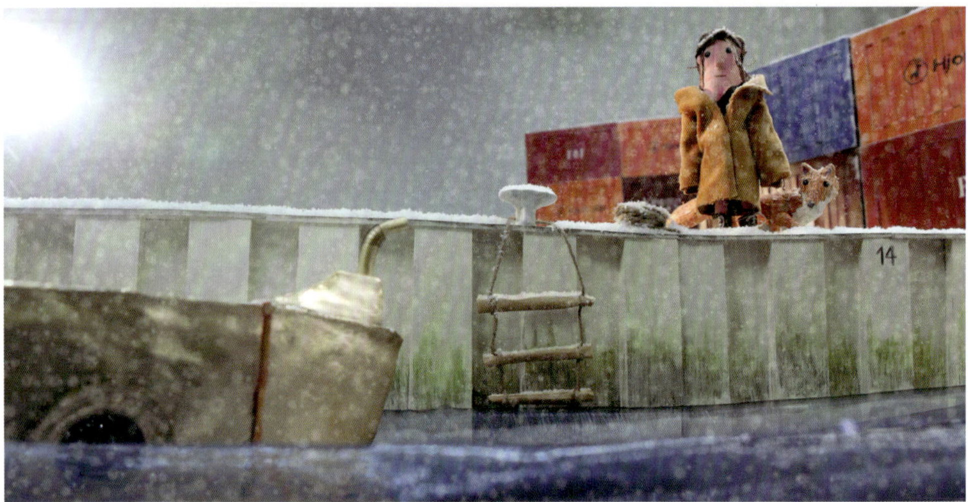

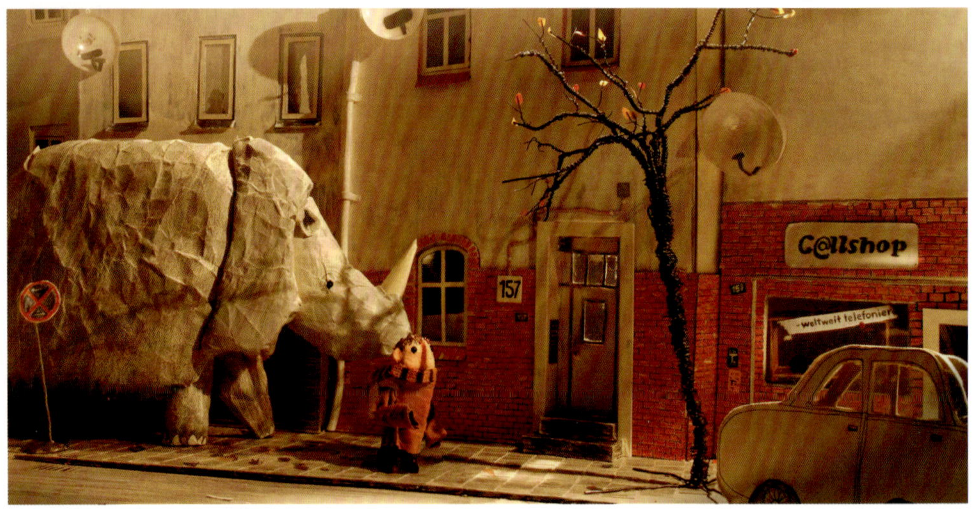


MERIT *Sarah Roloff*

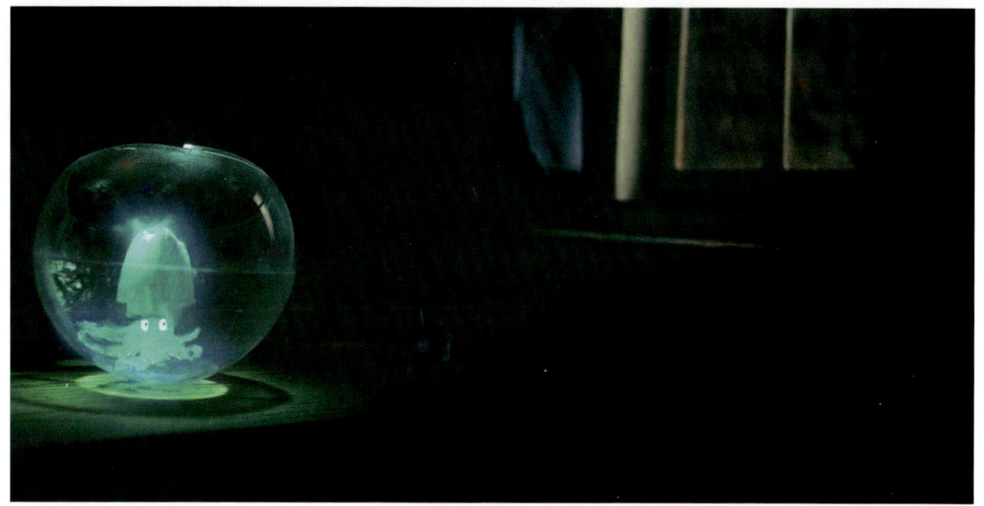

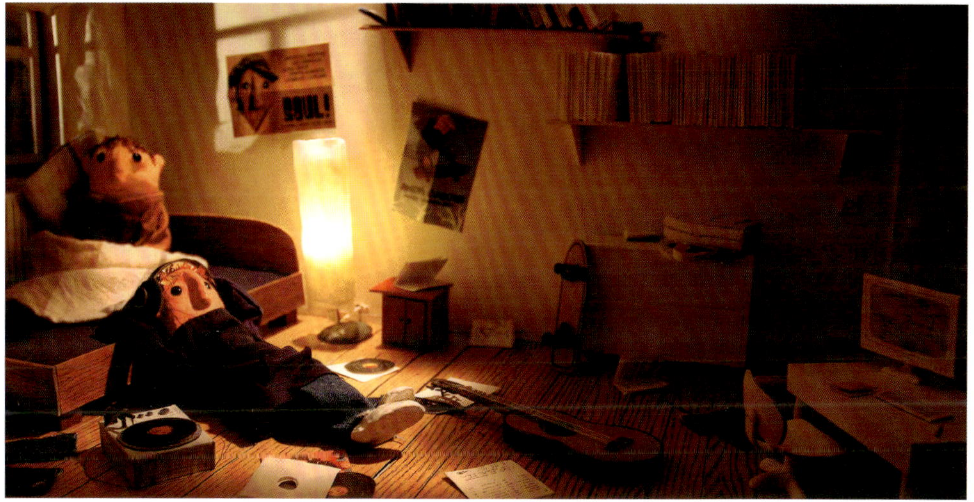

BOUL!

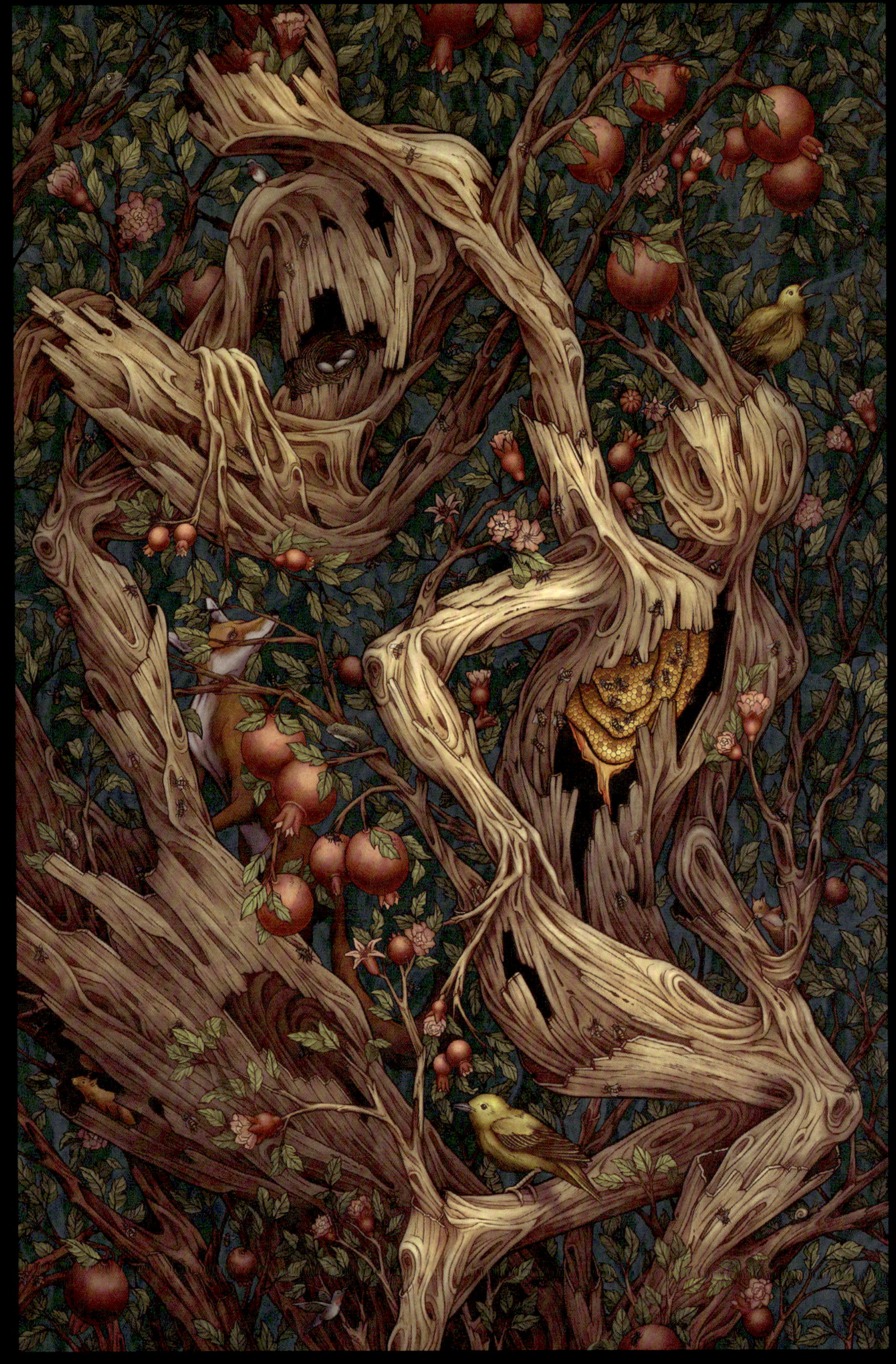

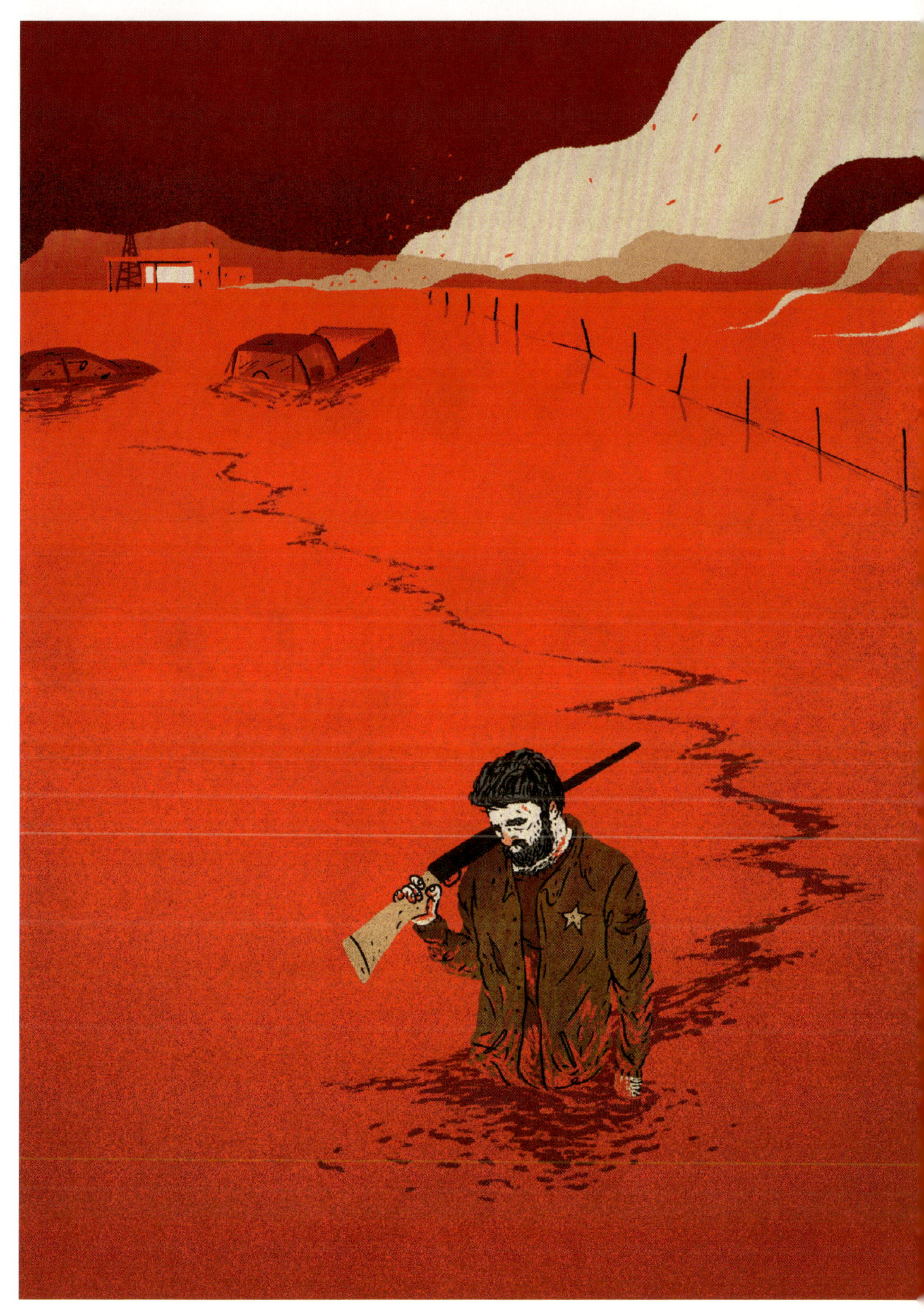

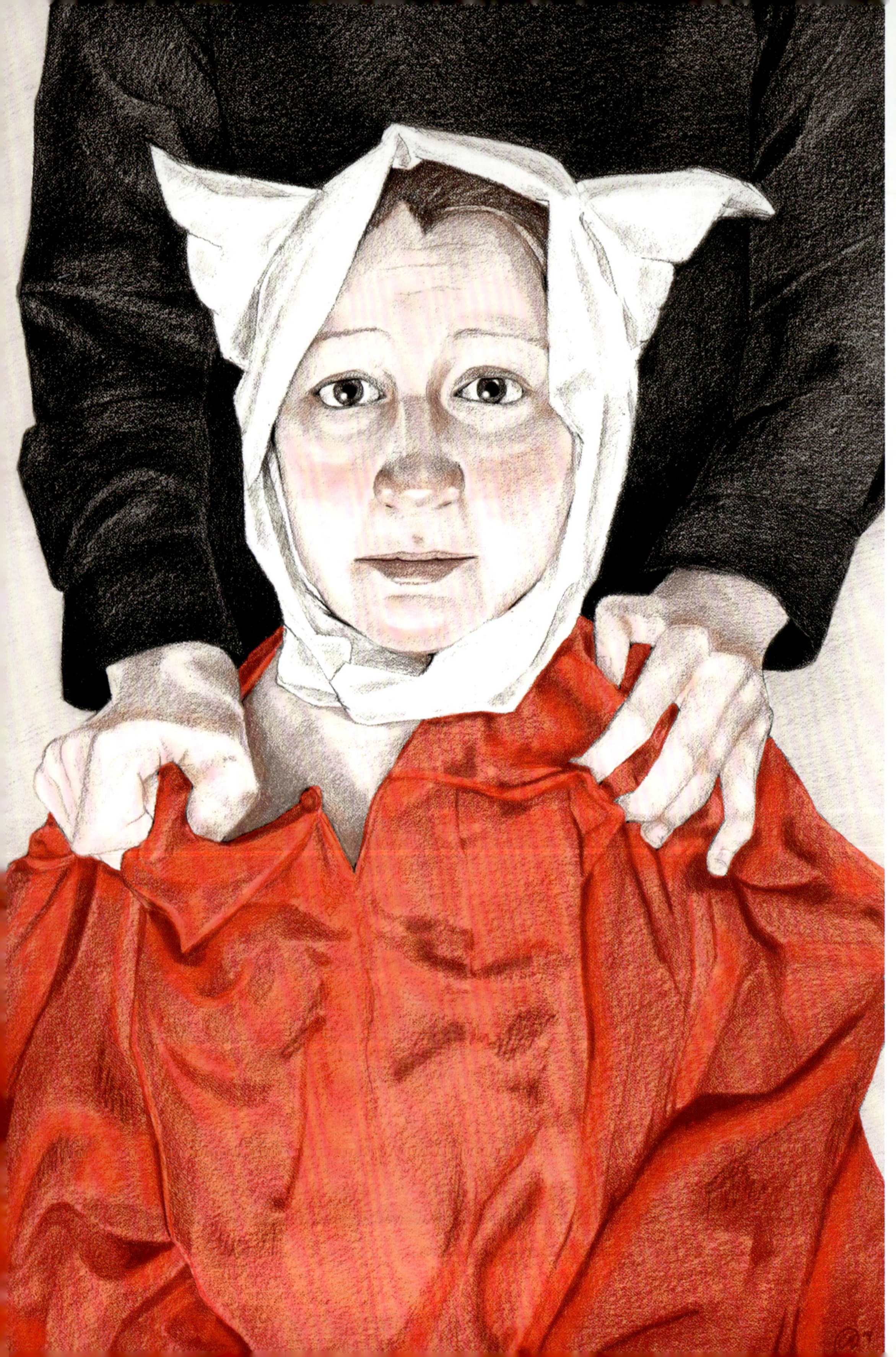

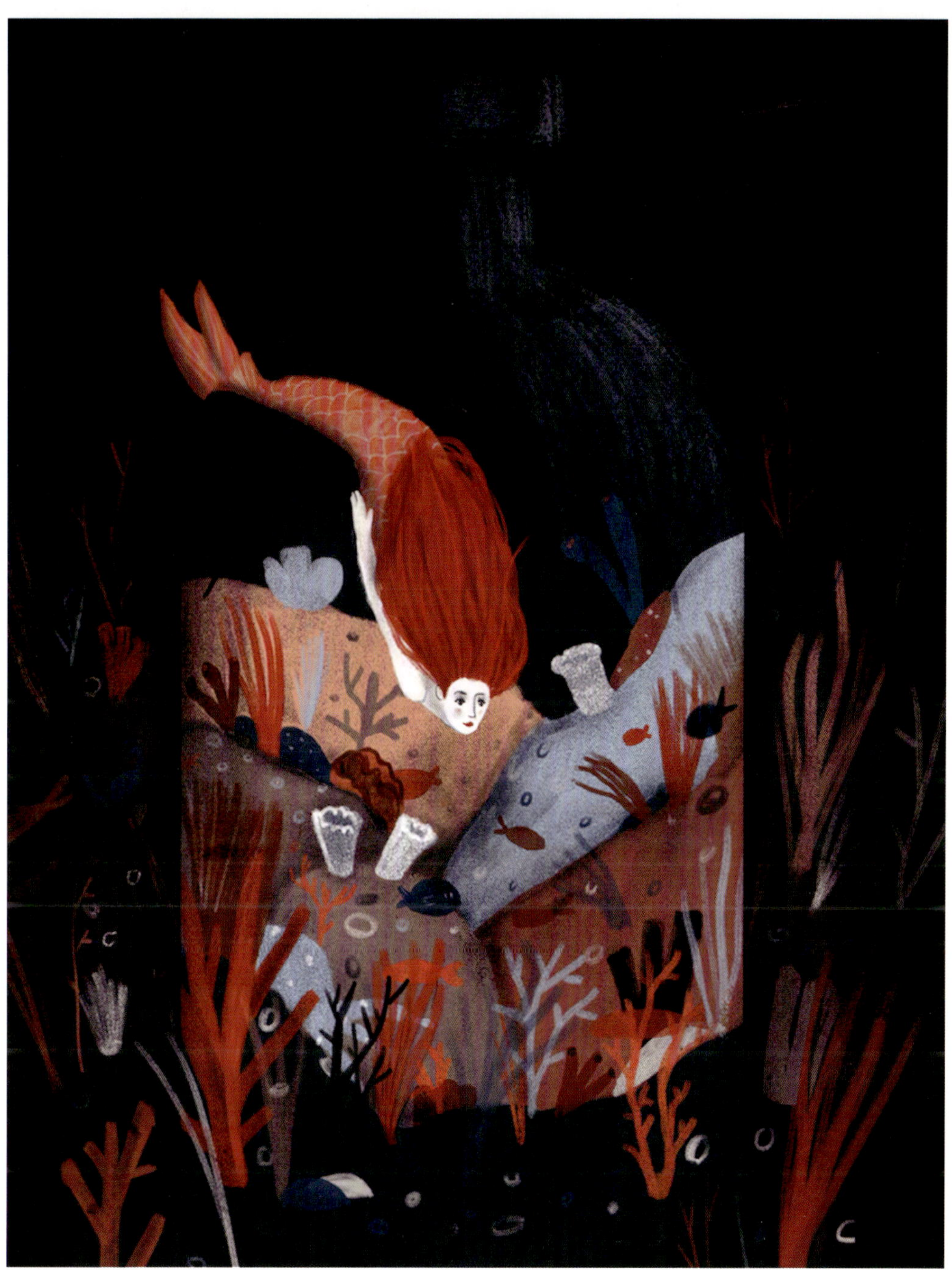



(L) MERIT *Christina Mastrull*    (R) MERIT *Sarah Green*

349

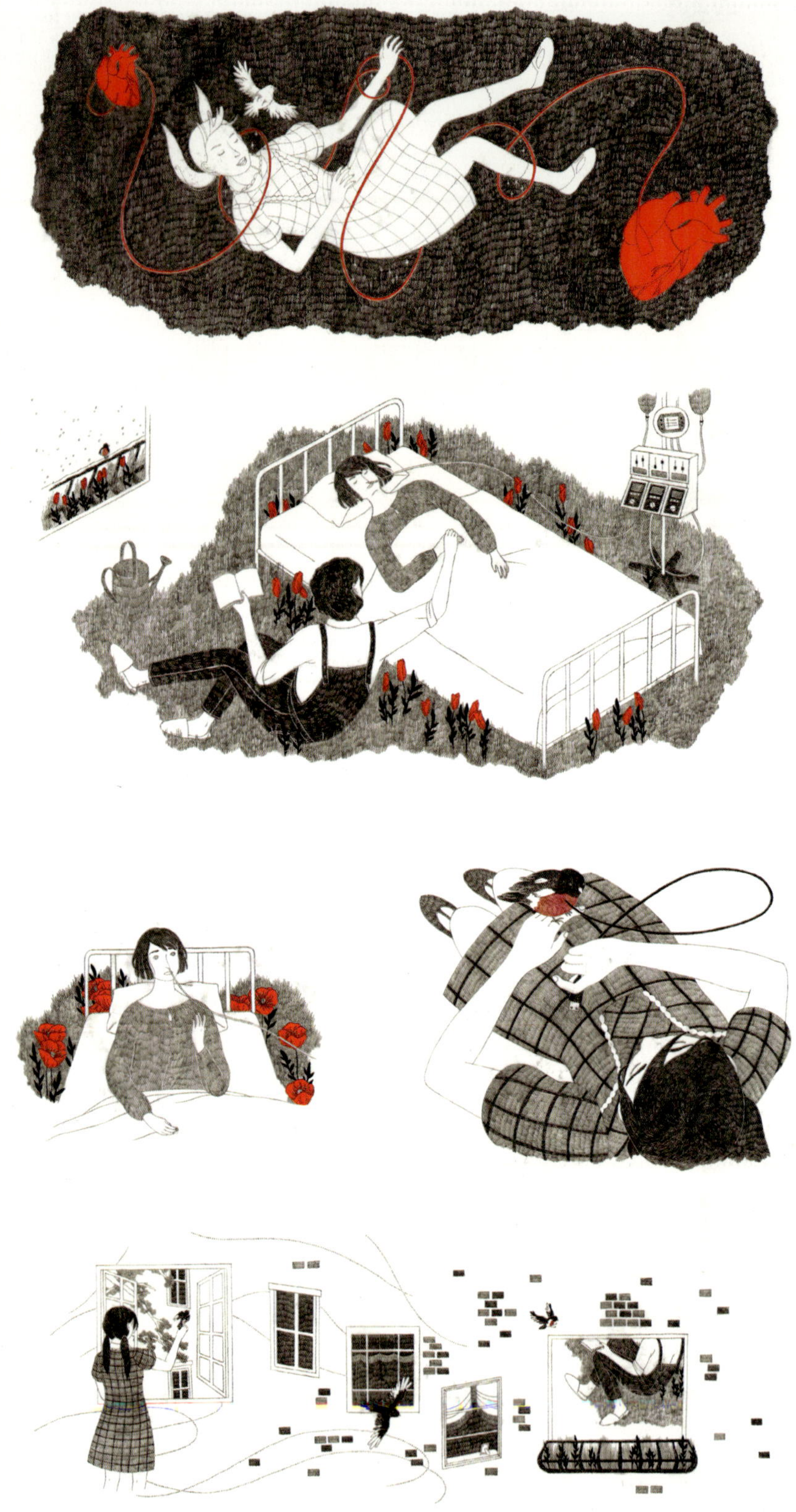

DISTINGUISHED MERIT *Jo Yeh*

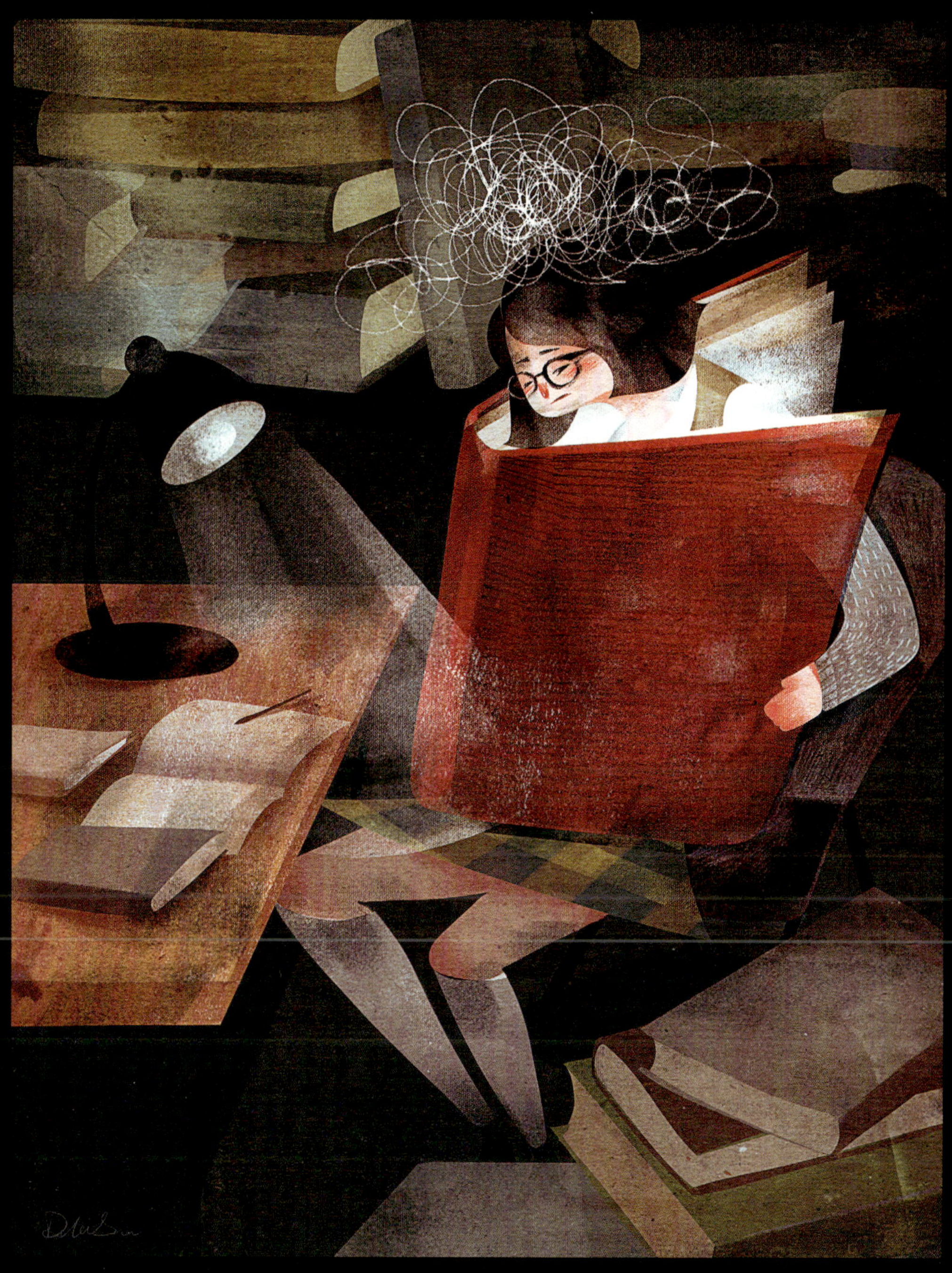

DISTINGUISHED MERIT *Dola Sun*

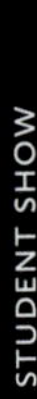

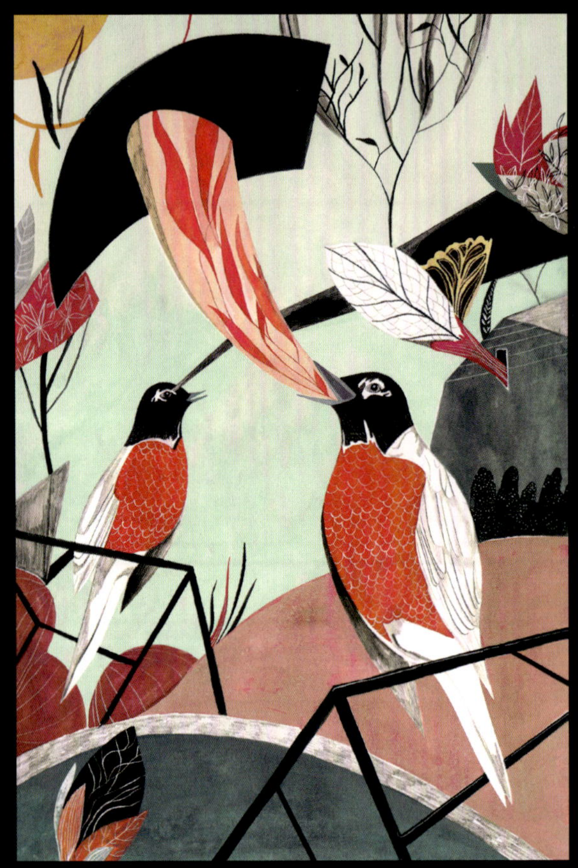

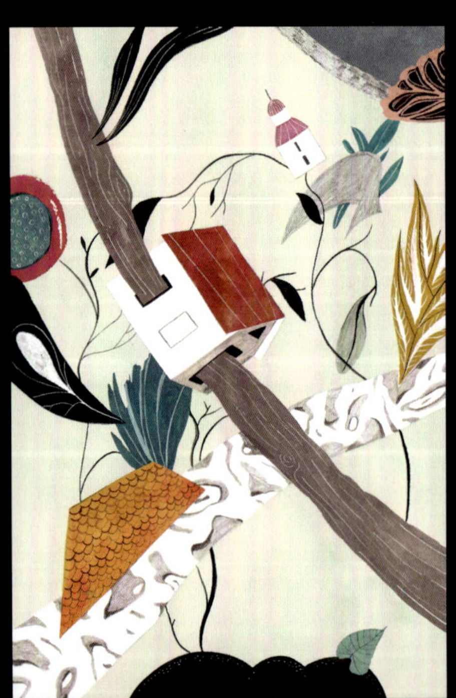

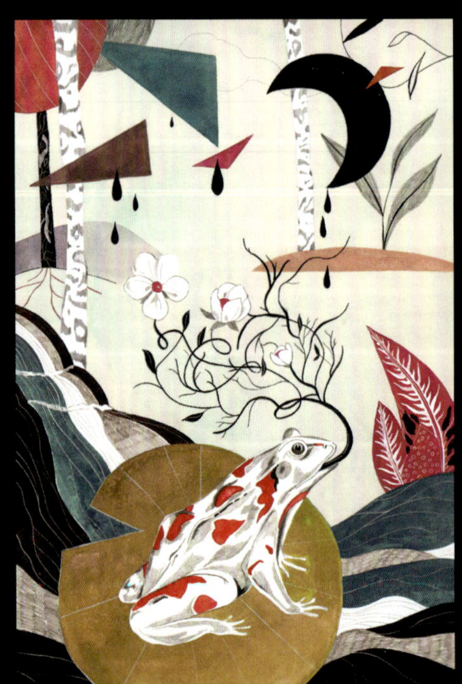

MERIT *Luisa Rivera*

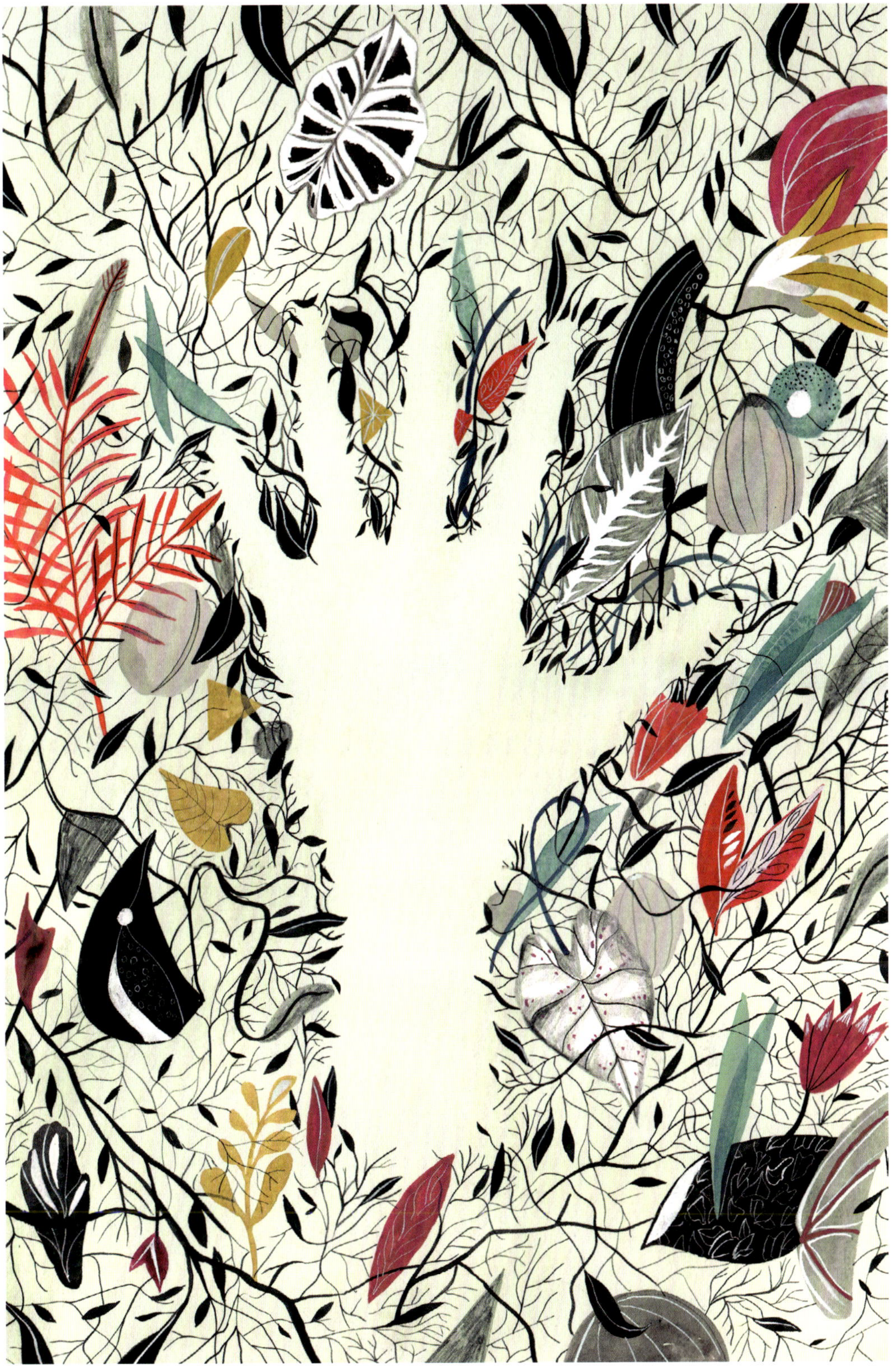

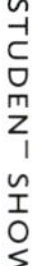


MERIT Luisa Rivera

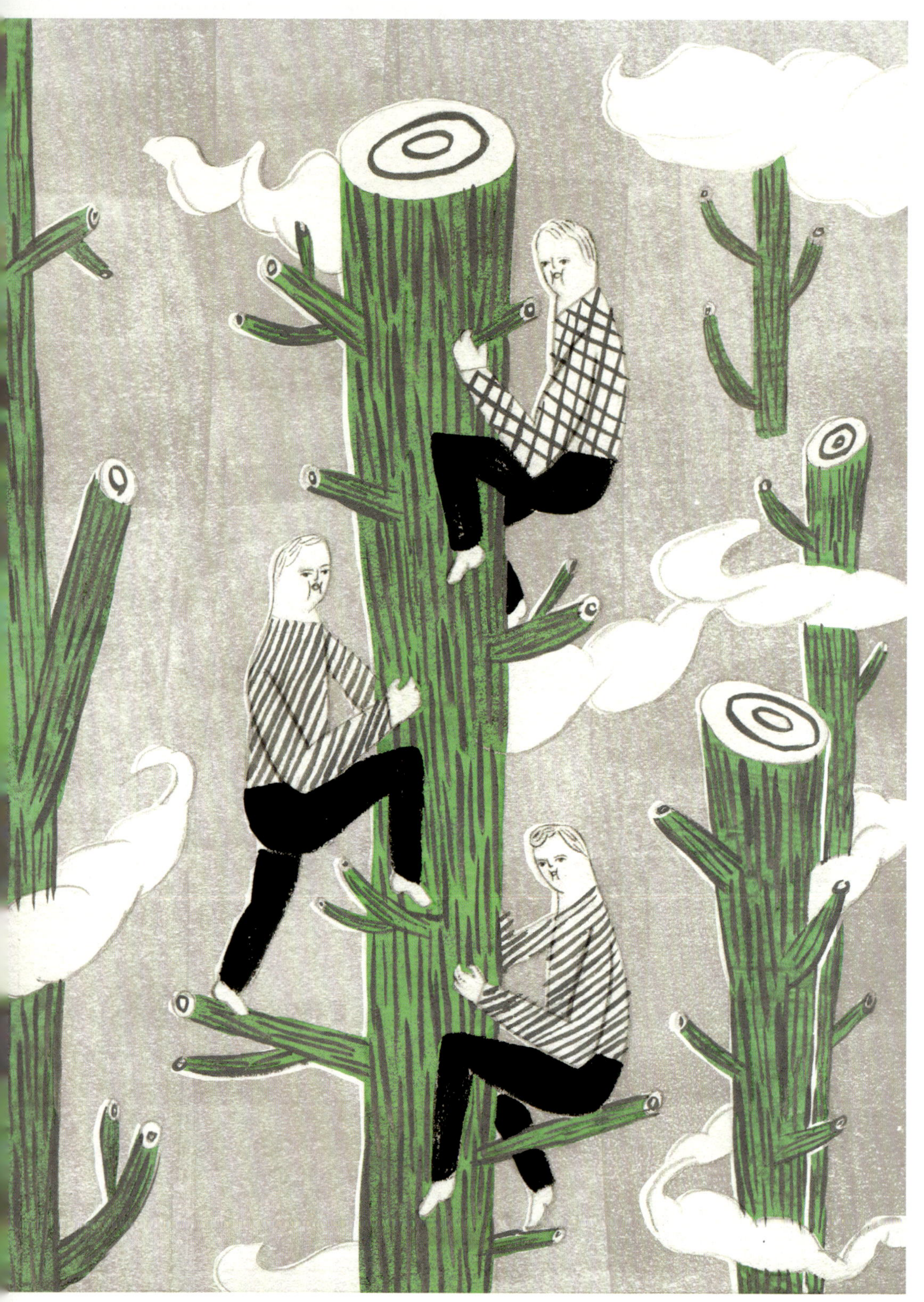

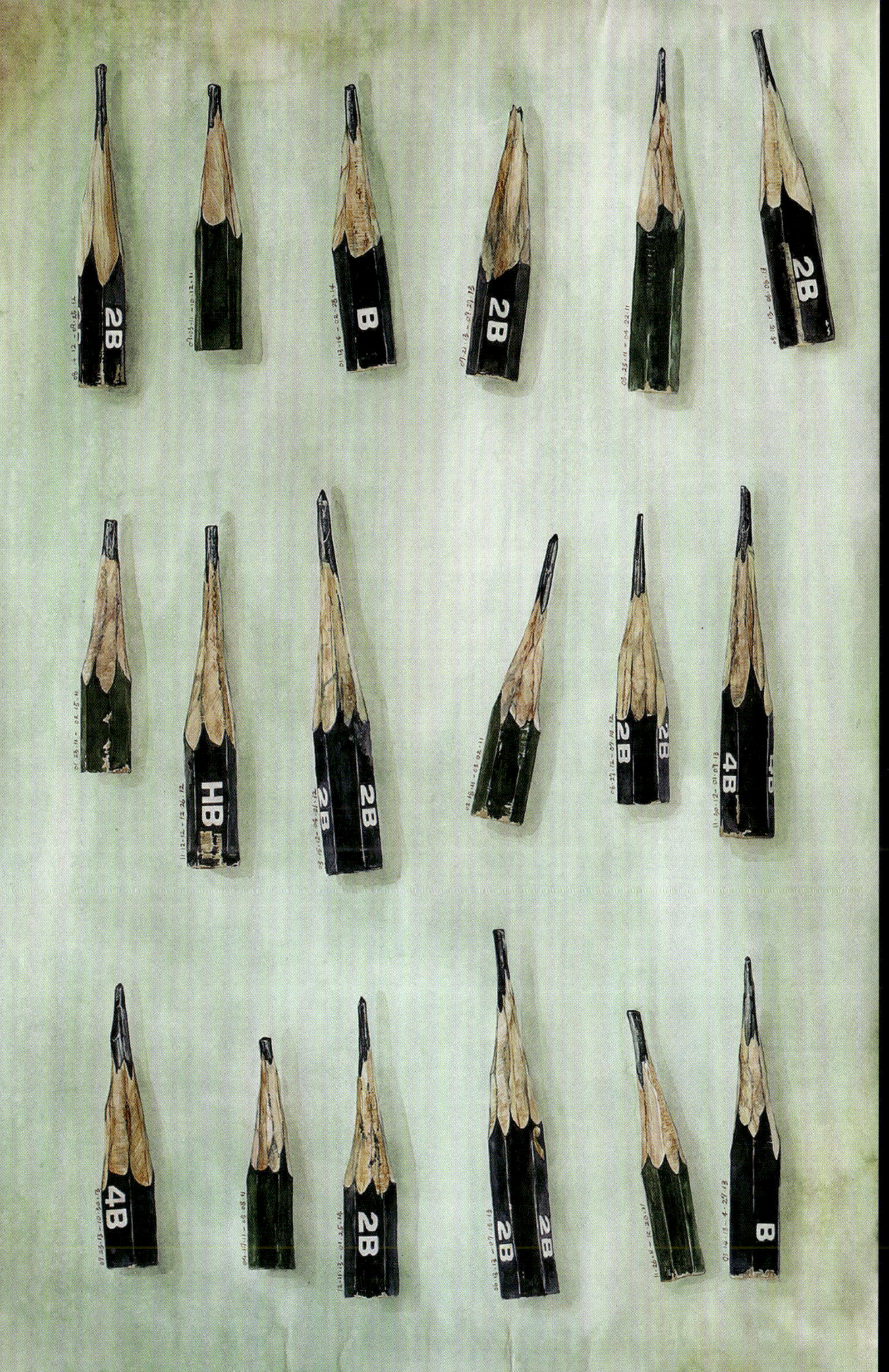

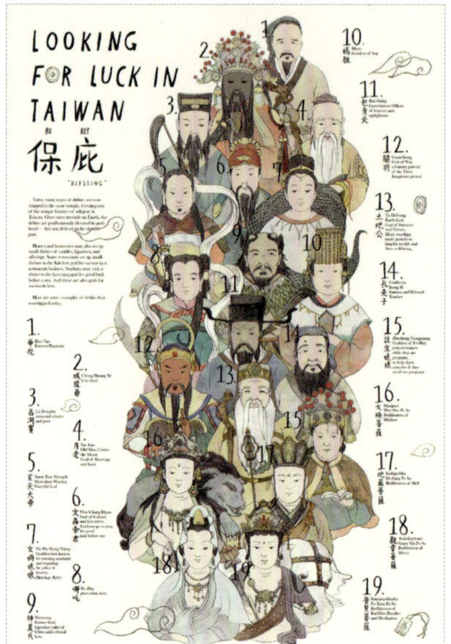

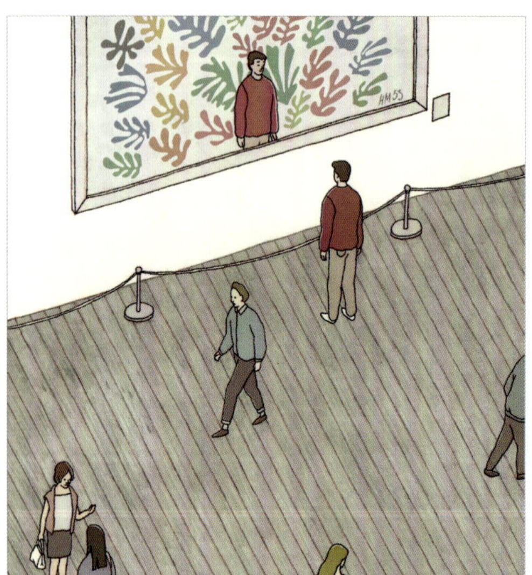

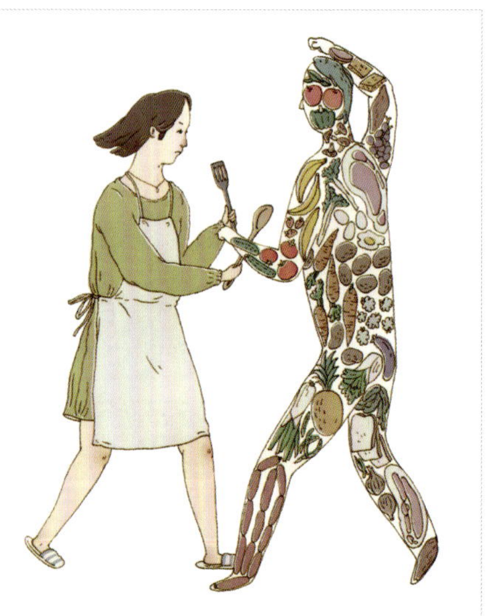

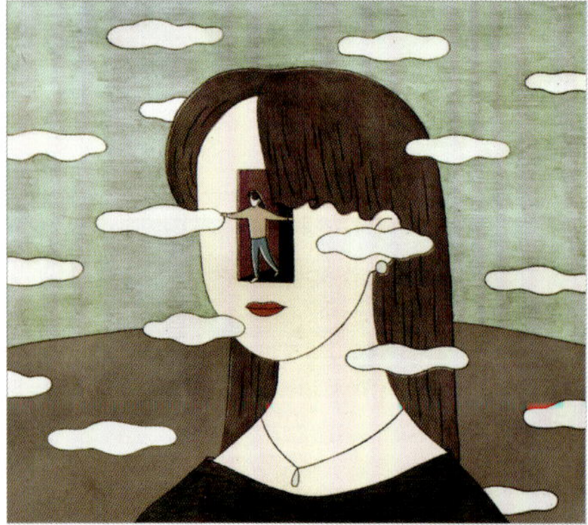

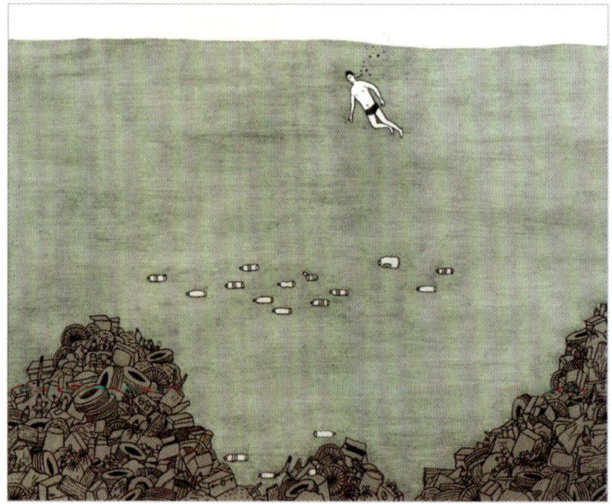

MERIT *Lily Liyi Chen*

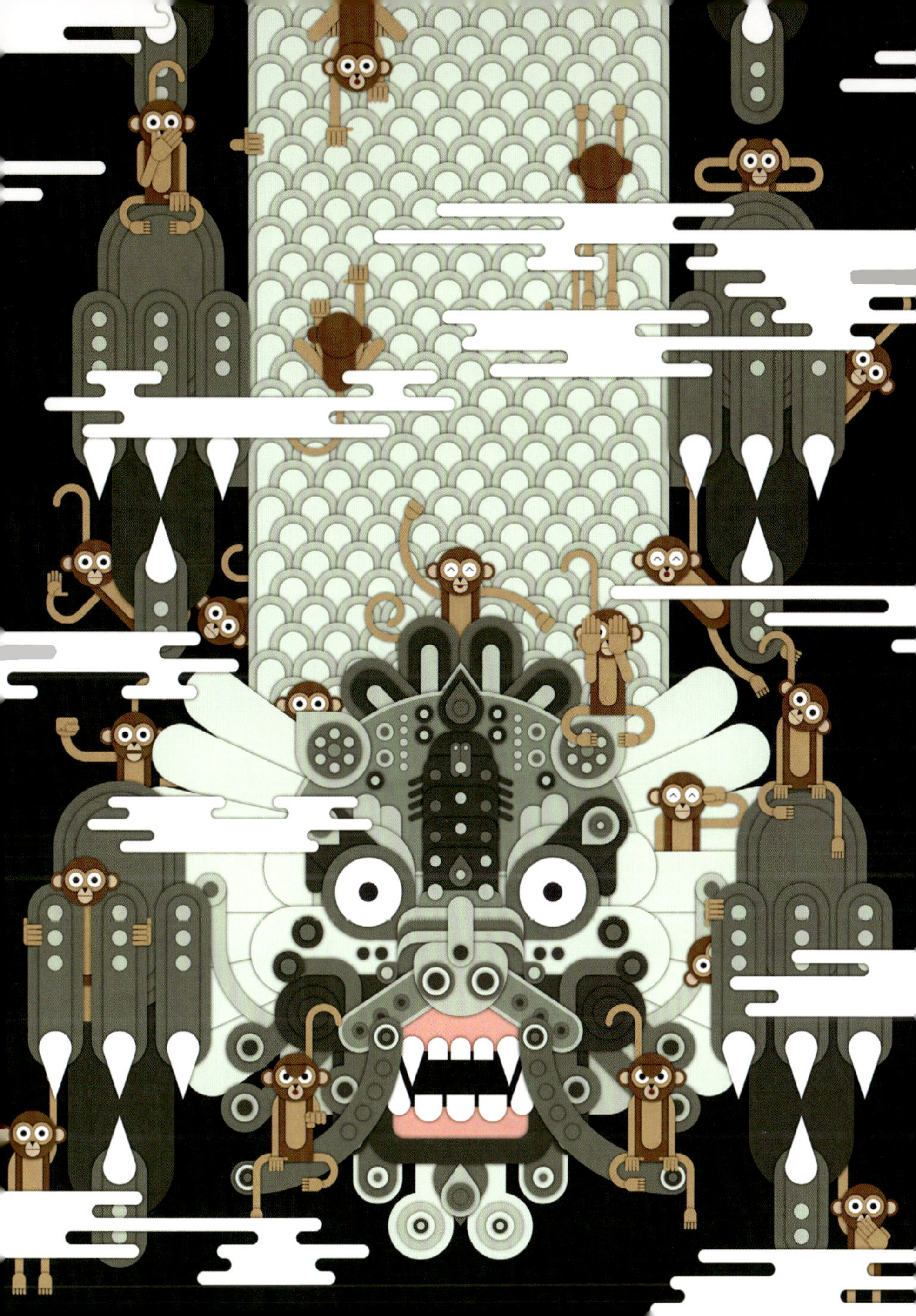

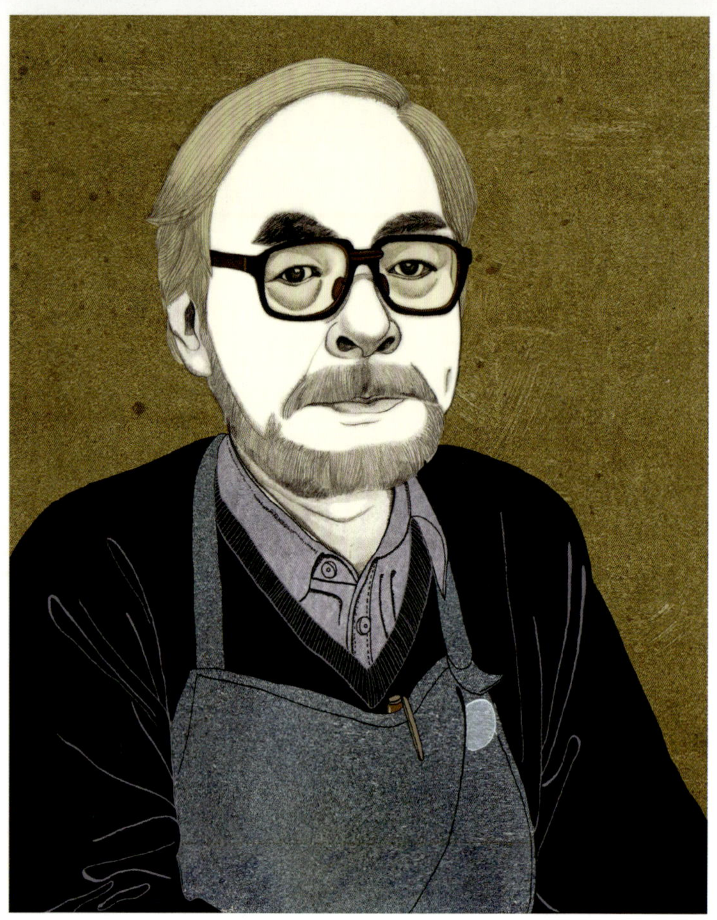

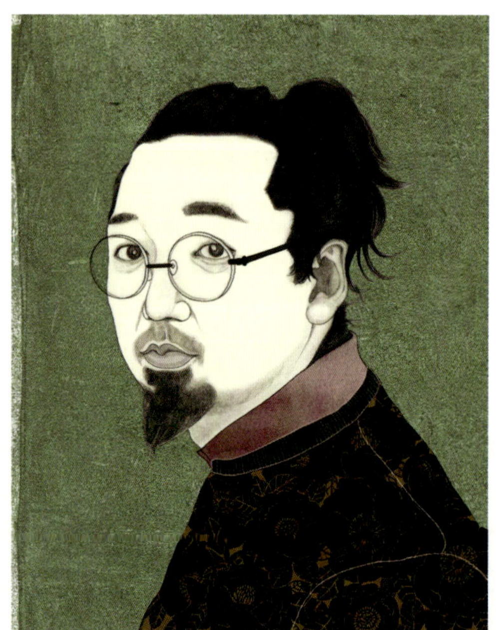

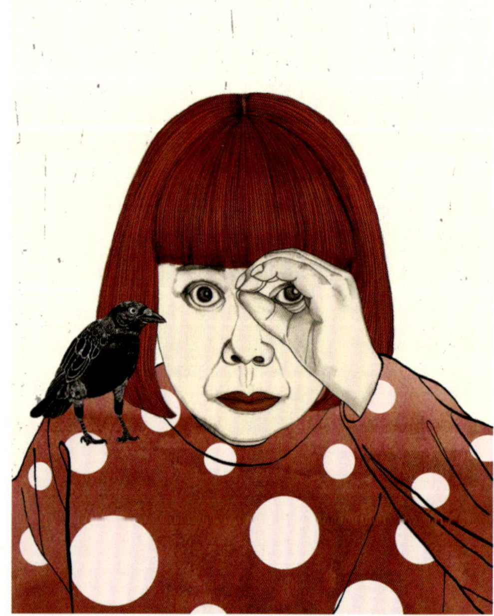

SILVER *Jing Li*

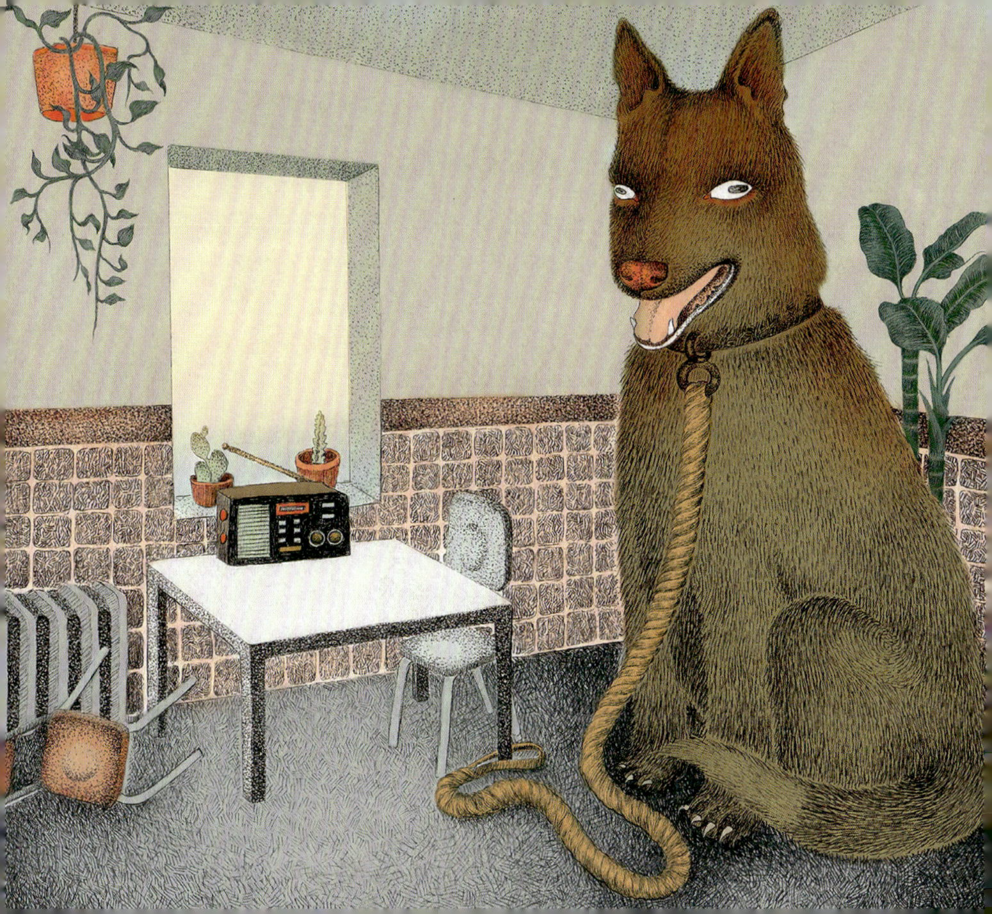

# THE LIFE OF MY FATHER

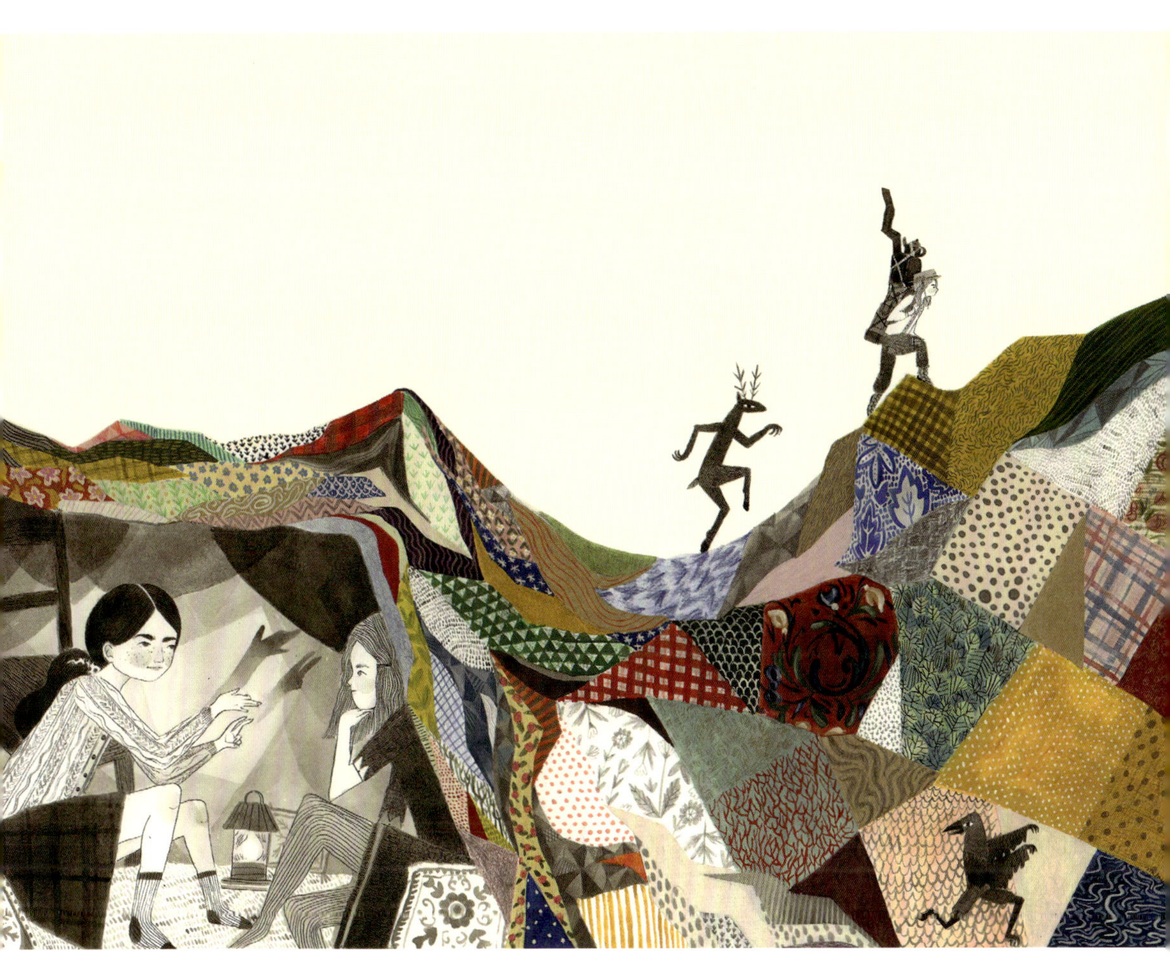





361

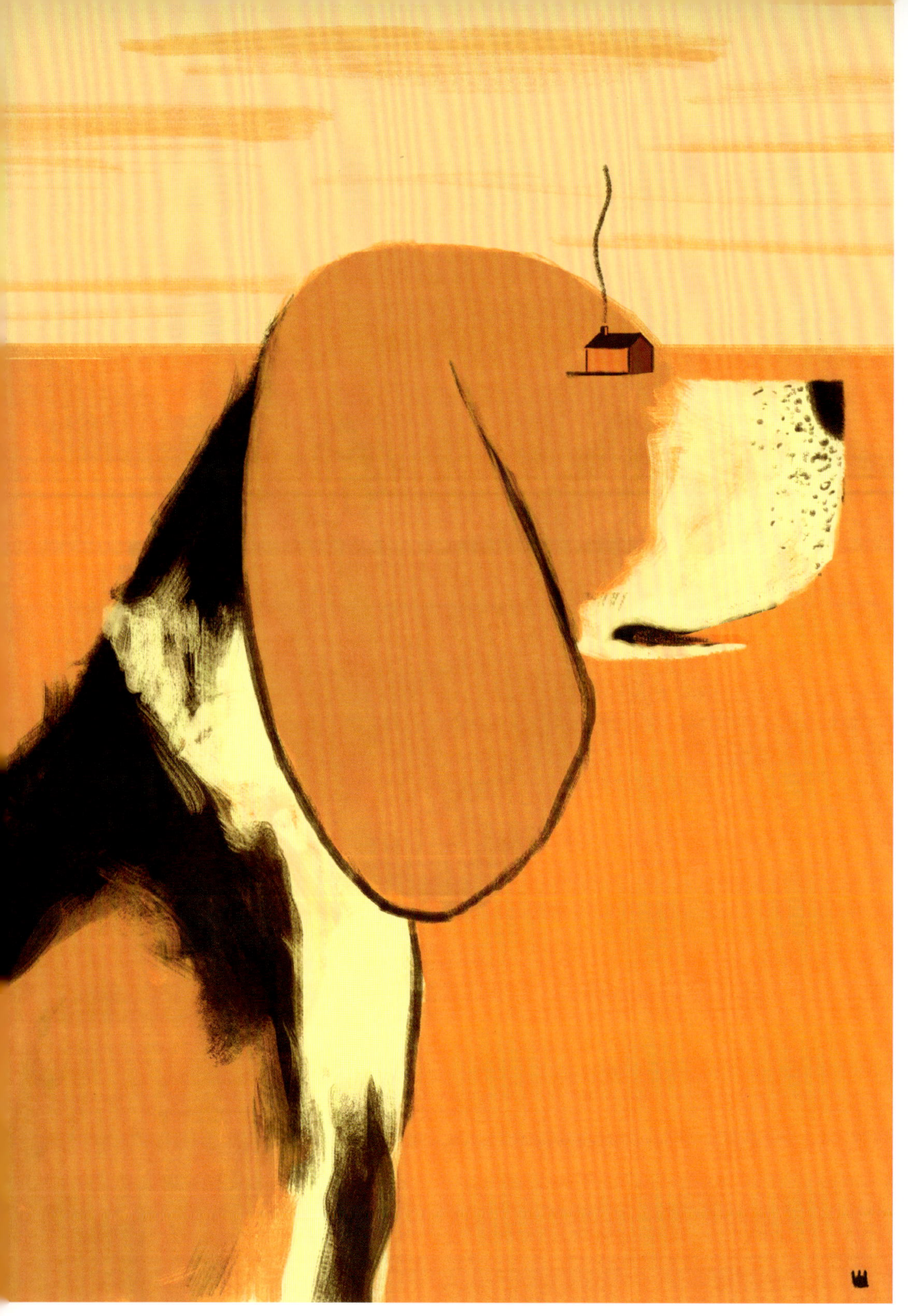

MERIT *Enzo Lo Re*

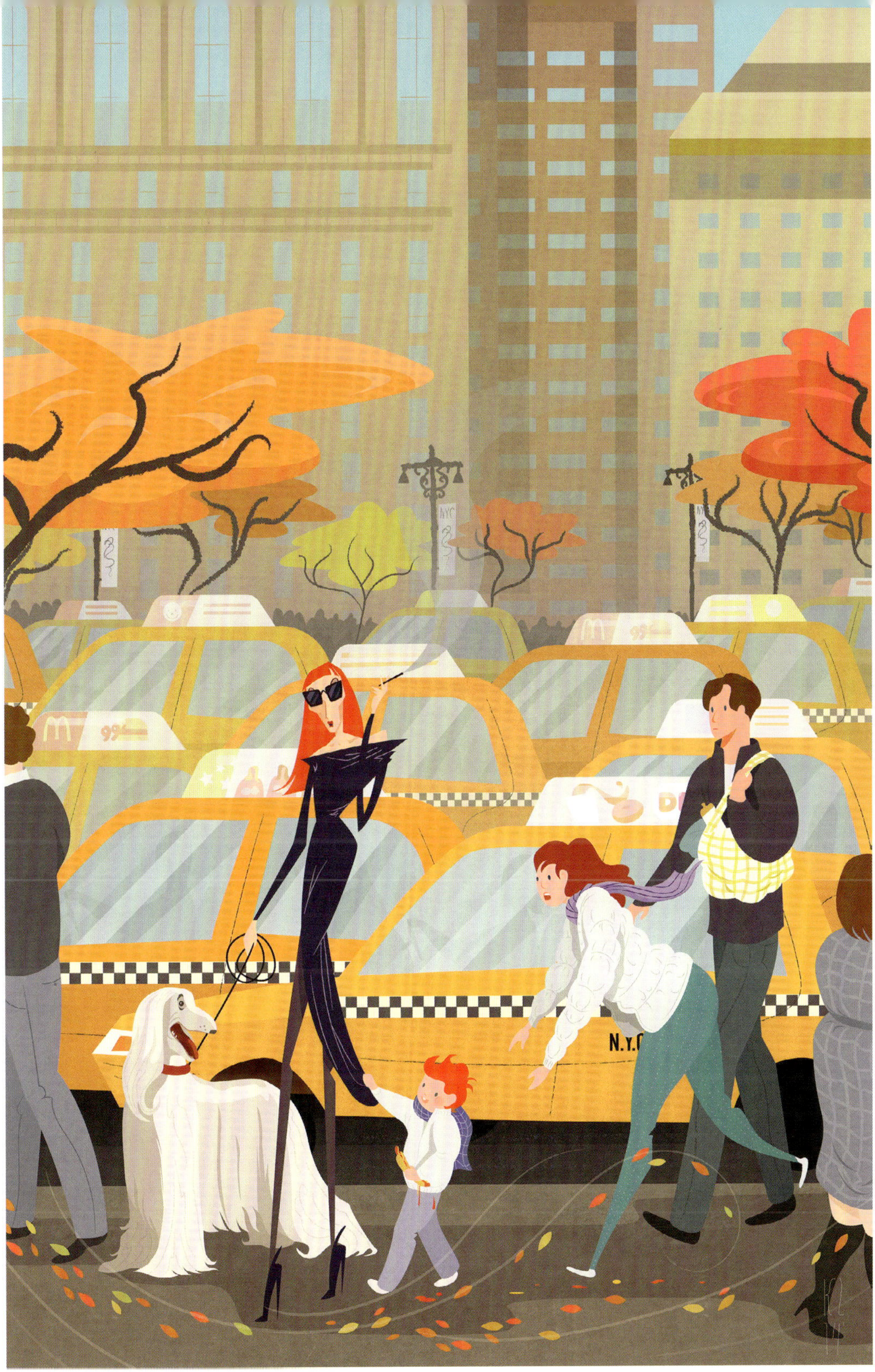

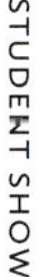

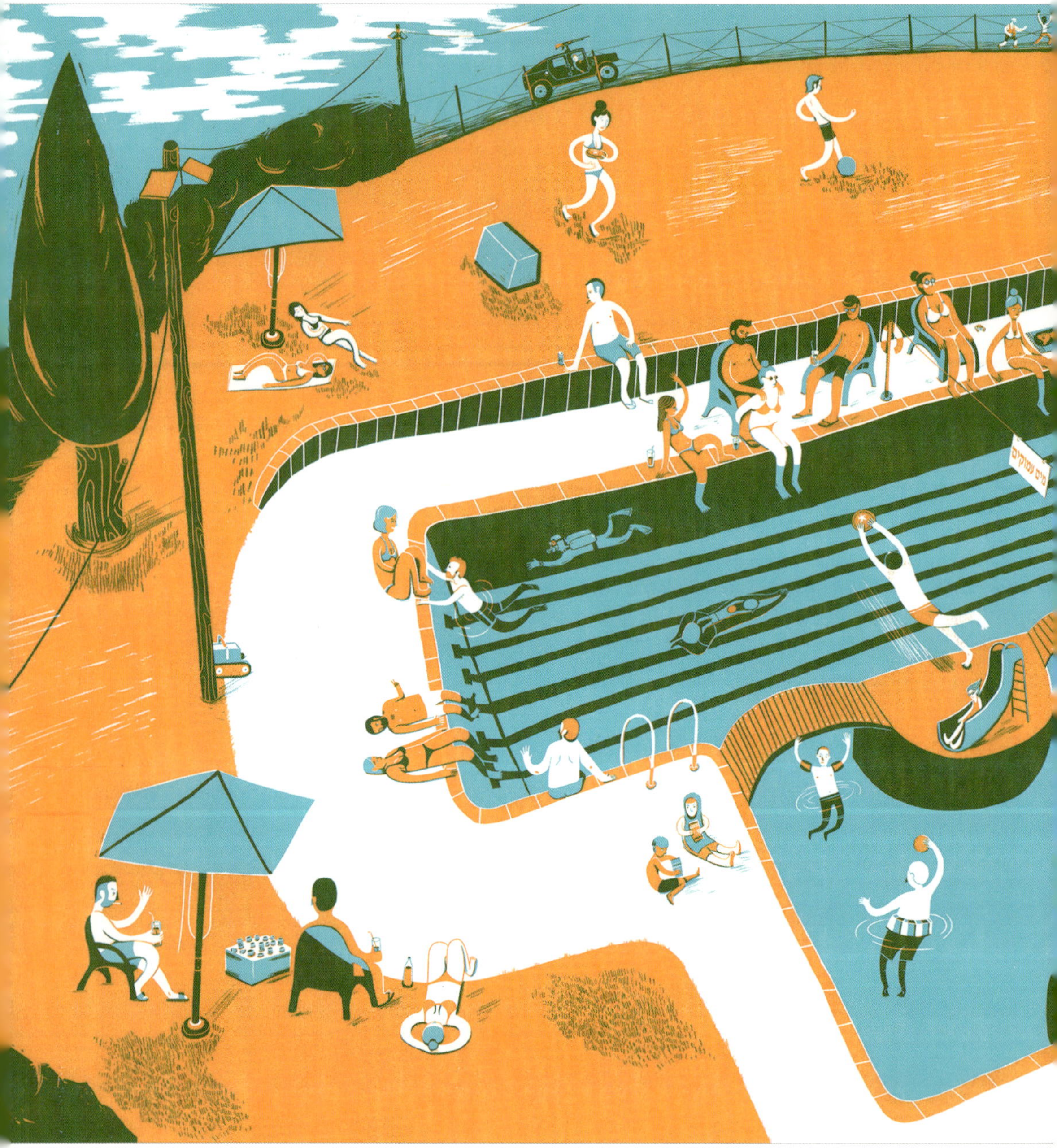

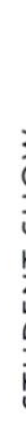


BRONZE *Or Yogev*

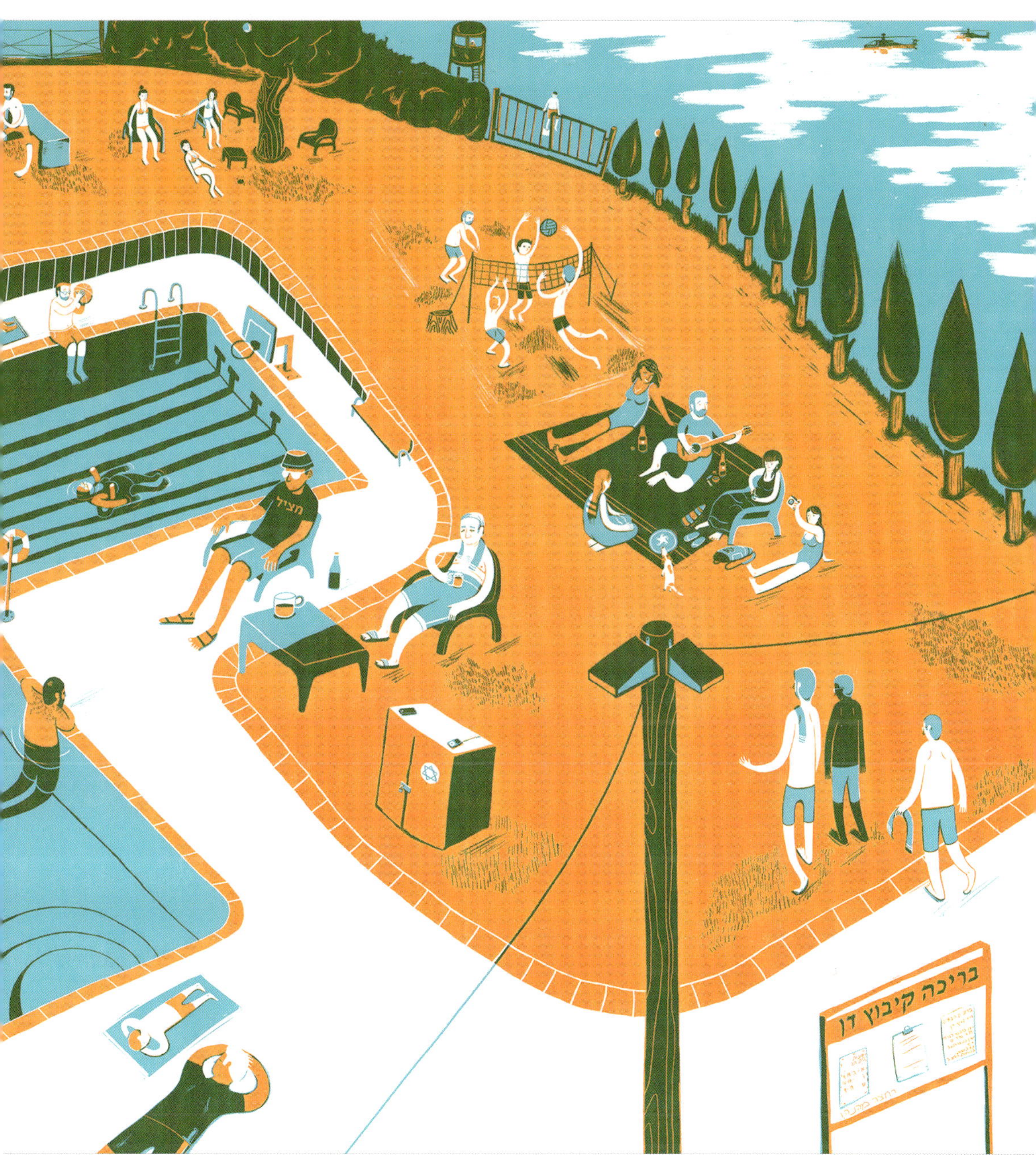

מציל
בריכה קיבוץ דן

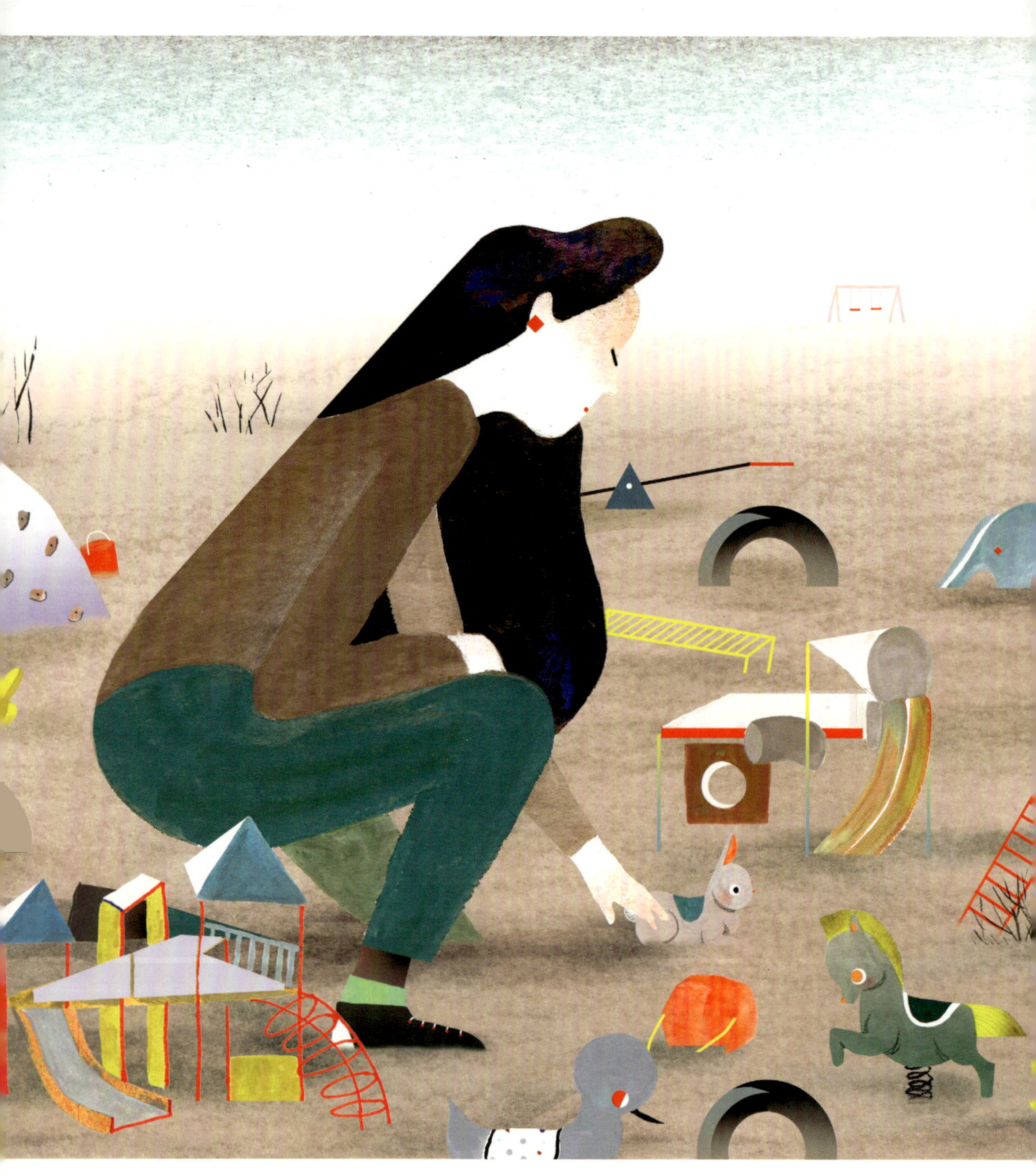



MERIT *Linda Yan*

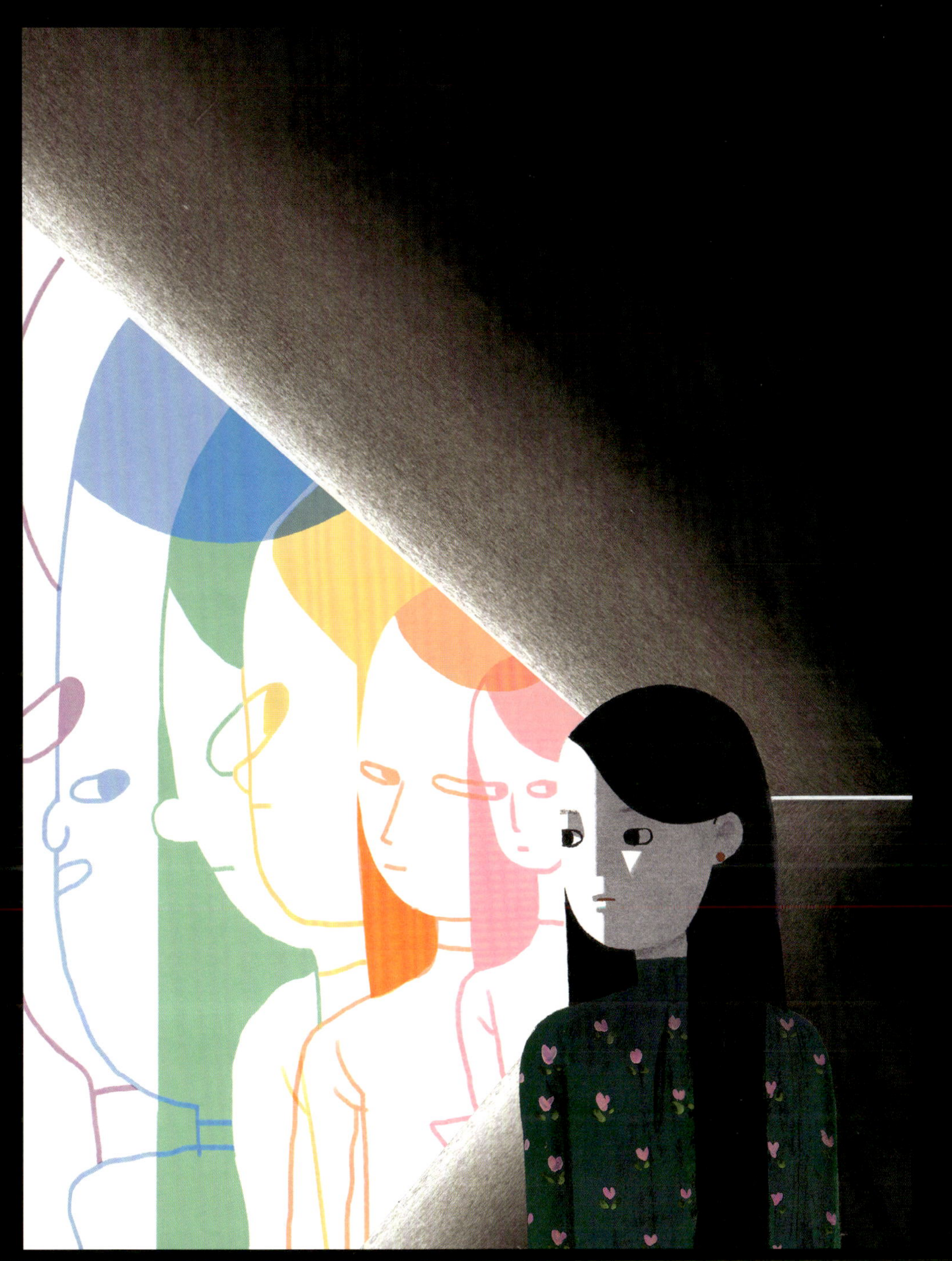



MERIT *Linda Yan*

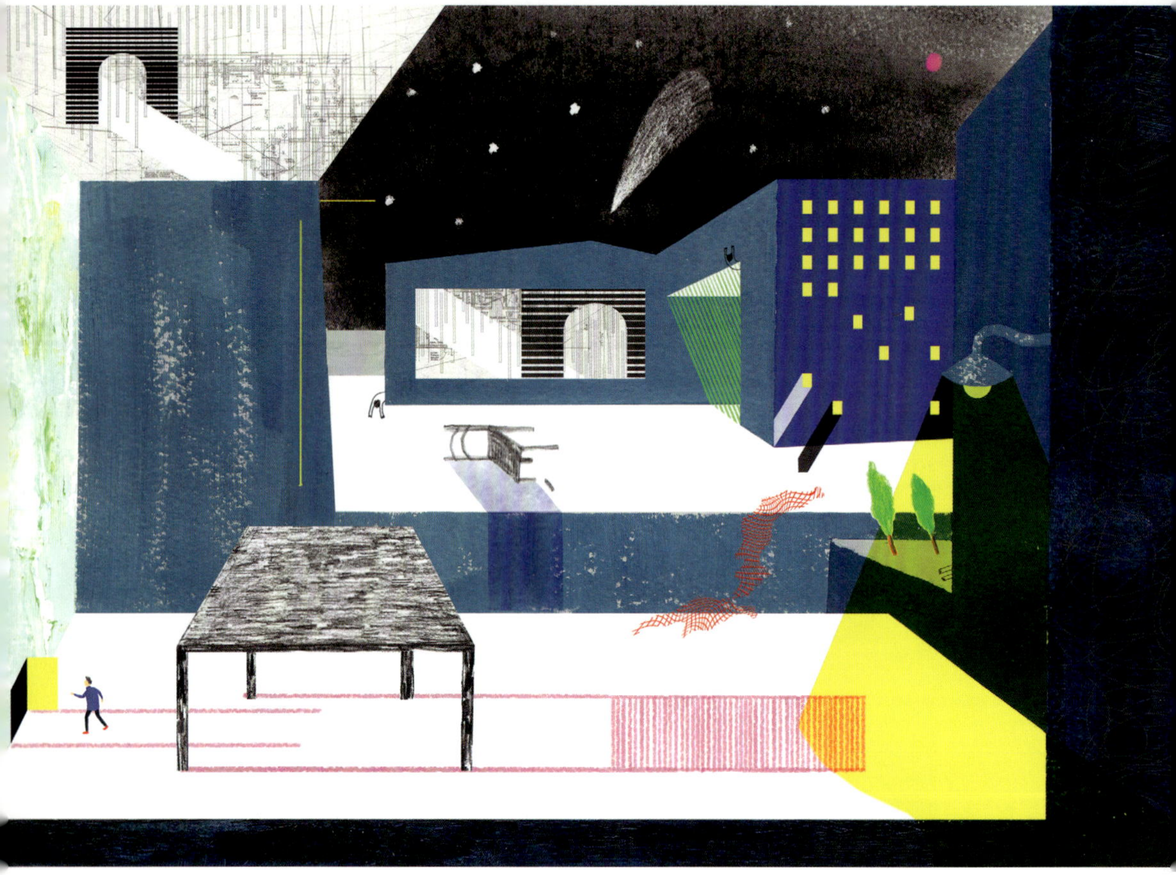

MERIT *Grace Heejung Kim*

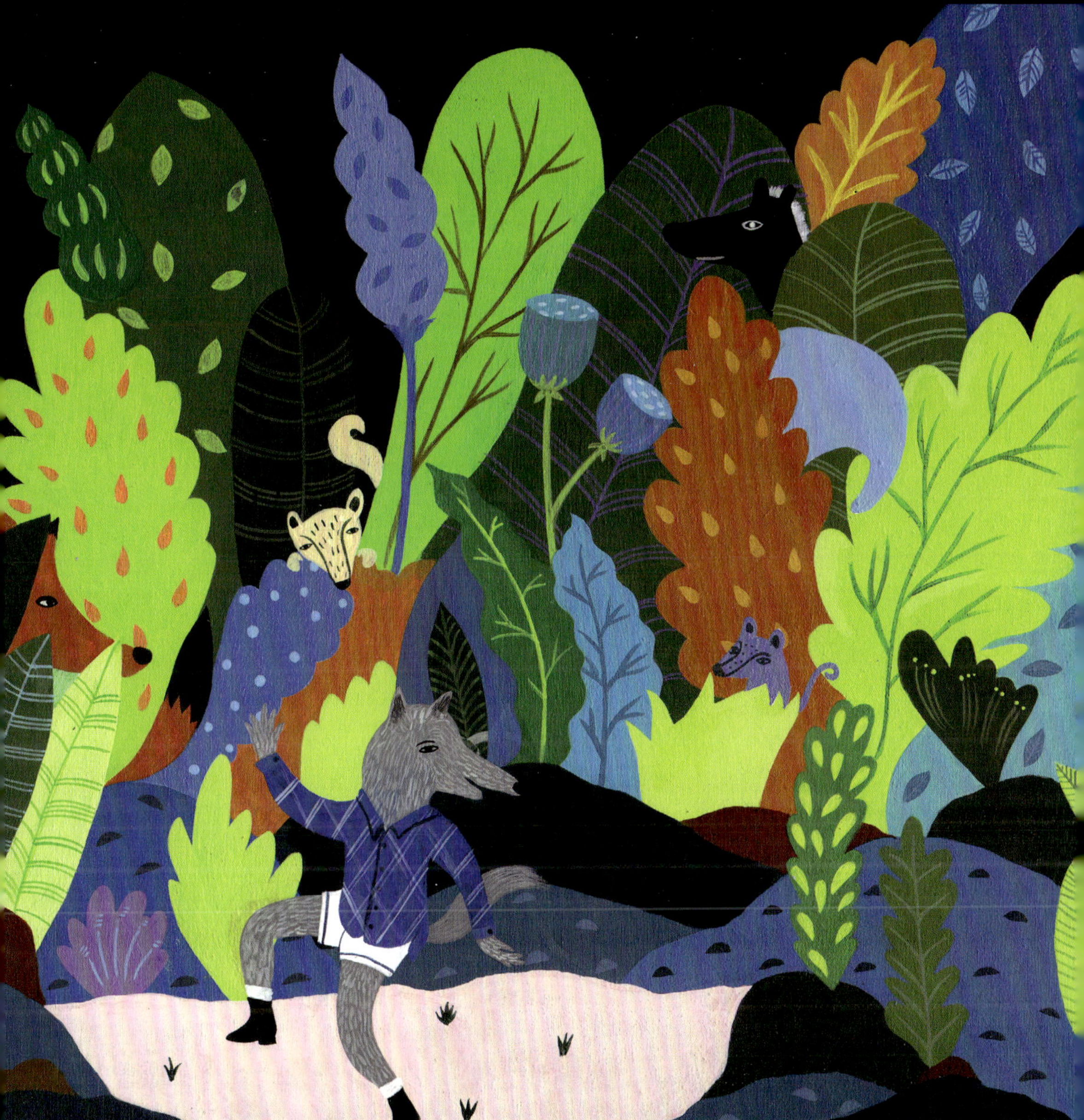

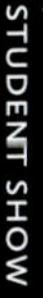


MERIT *Kristine Wang*

369

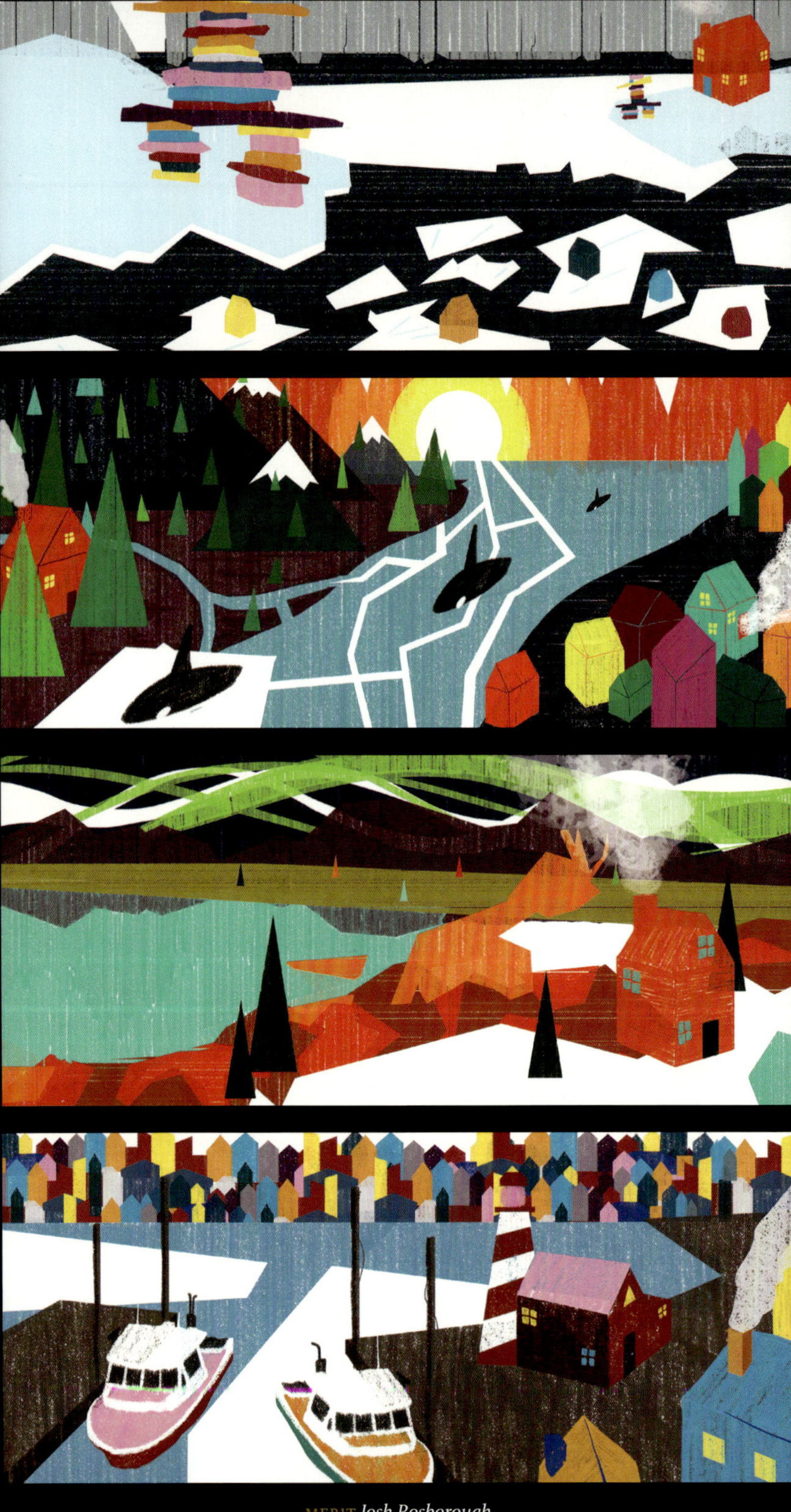

MERIT Josh Rosborough

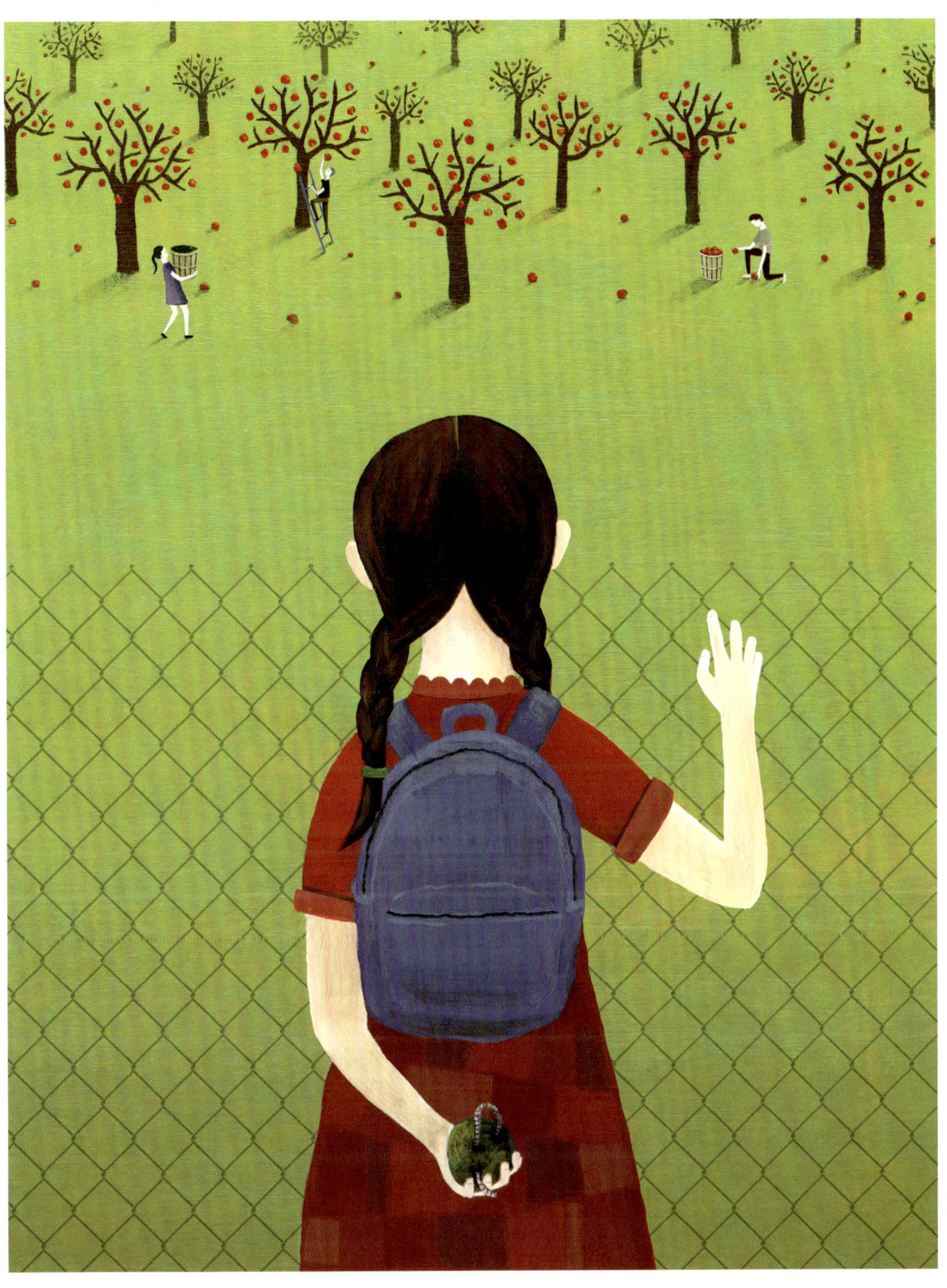



MERIT *Laura Weiszer*

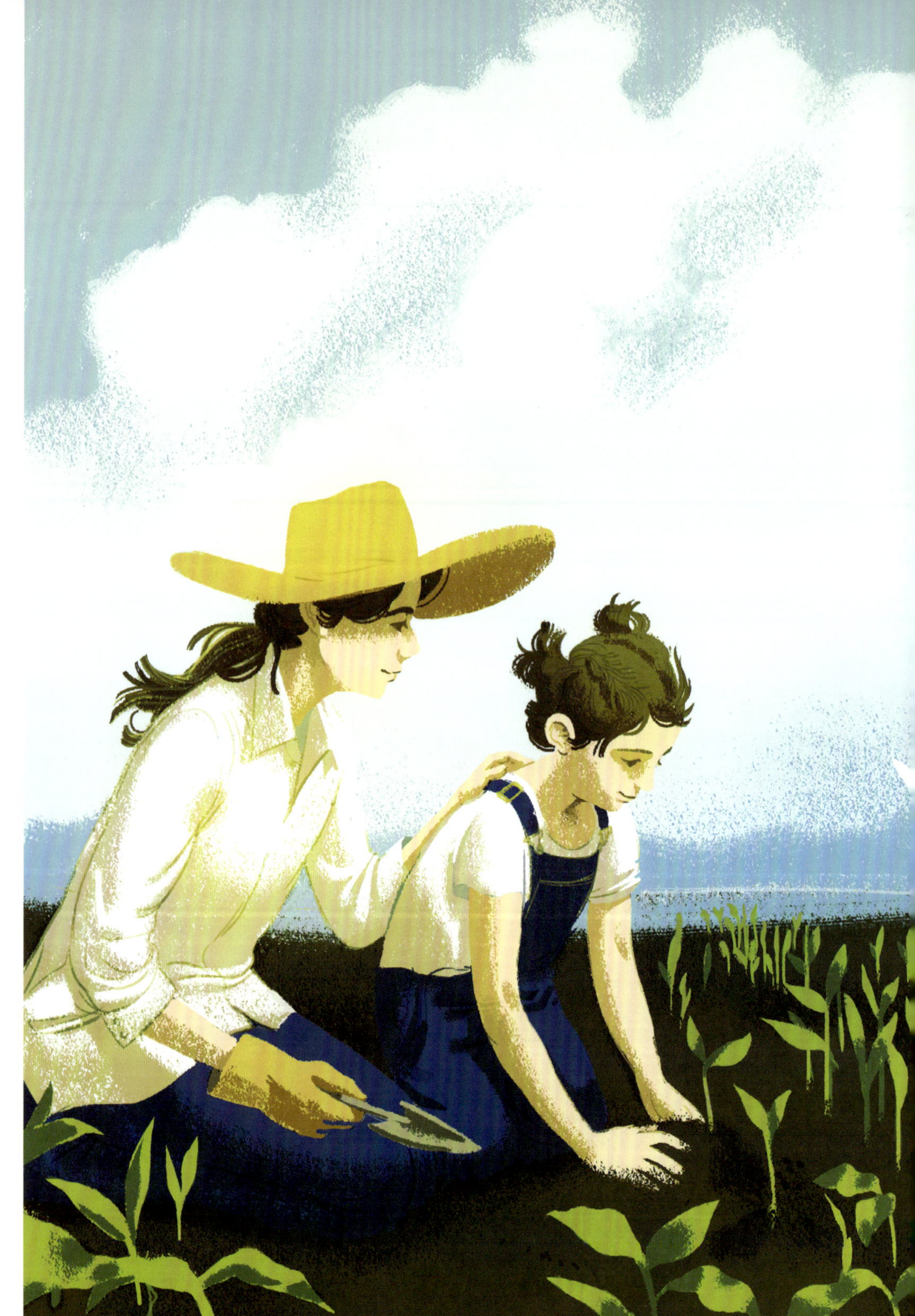

MERIT *Cristian Fowlie*

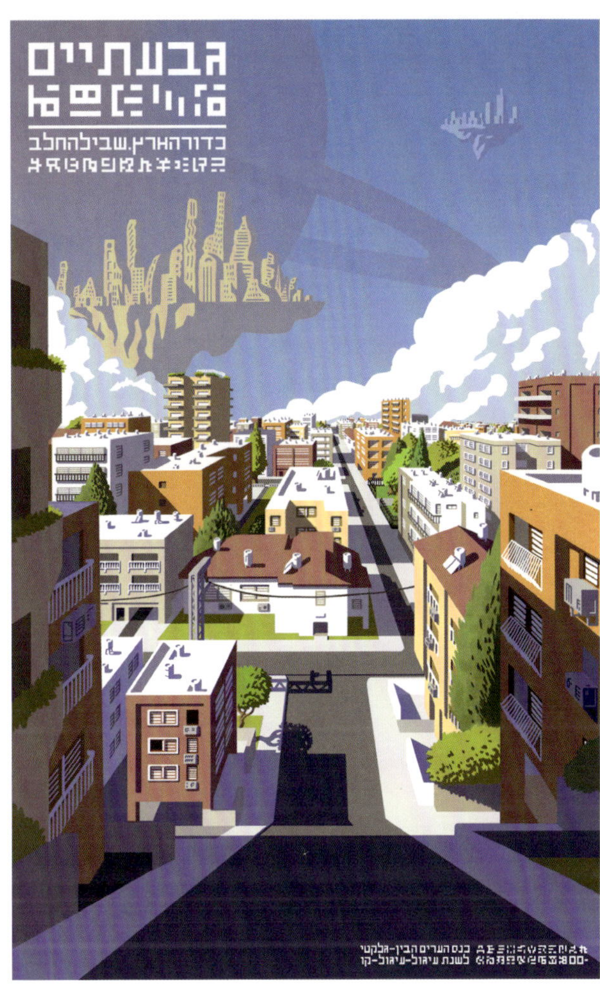




MERIT *Tom Engler*

373

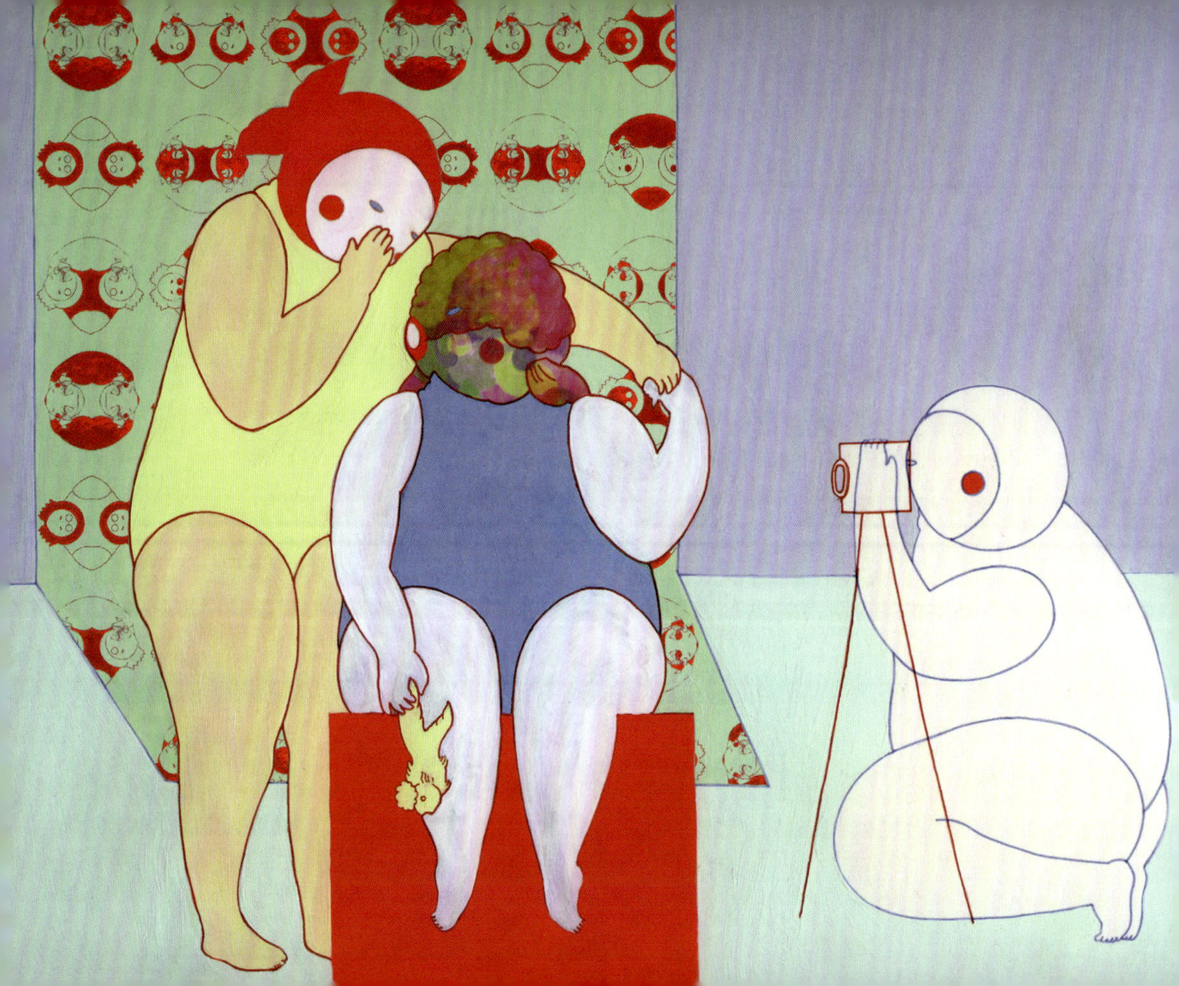

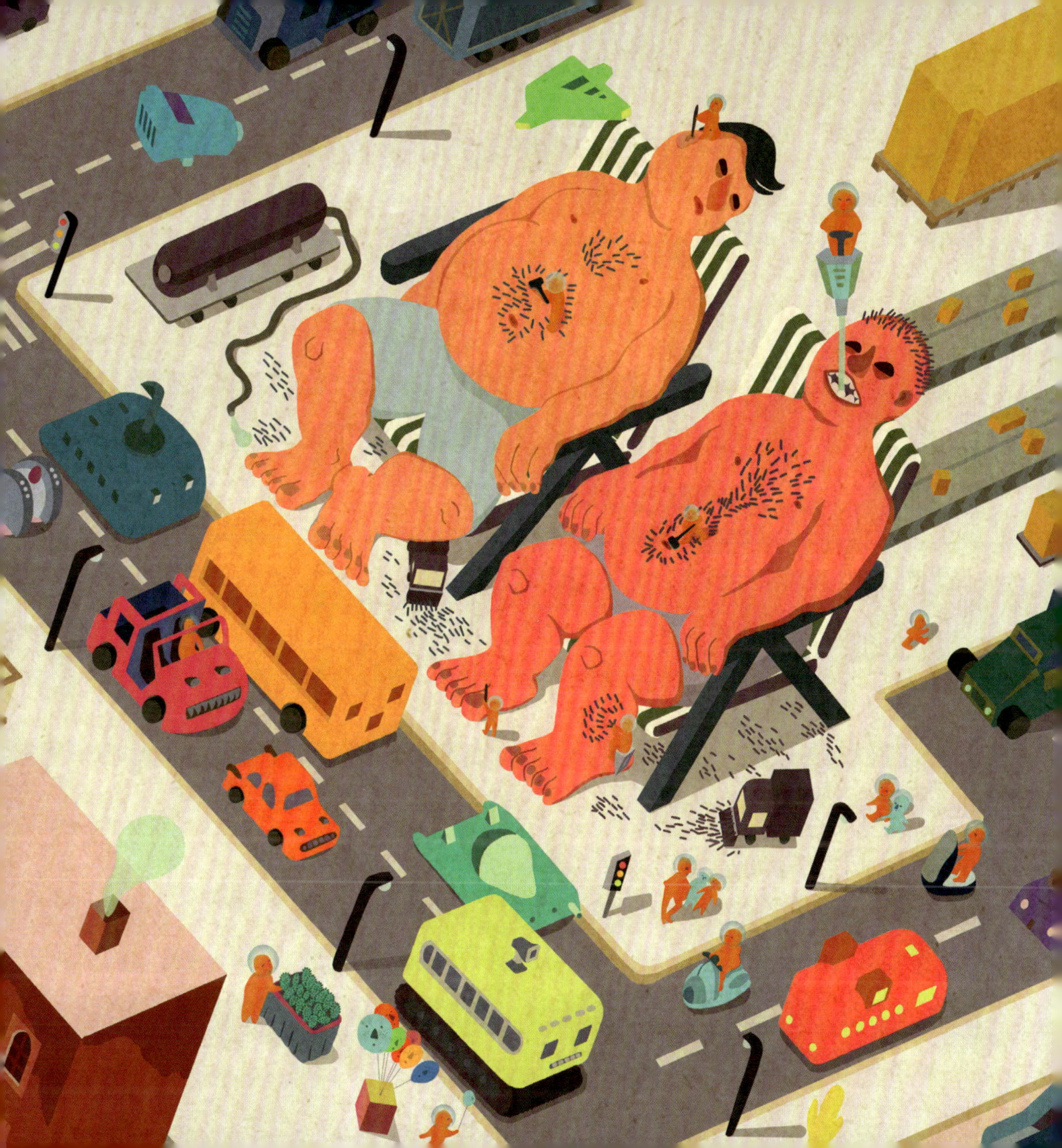

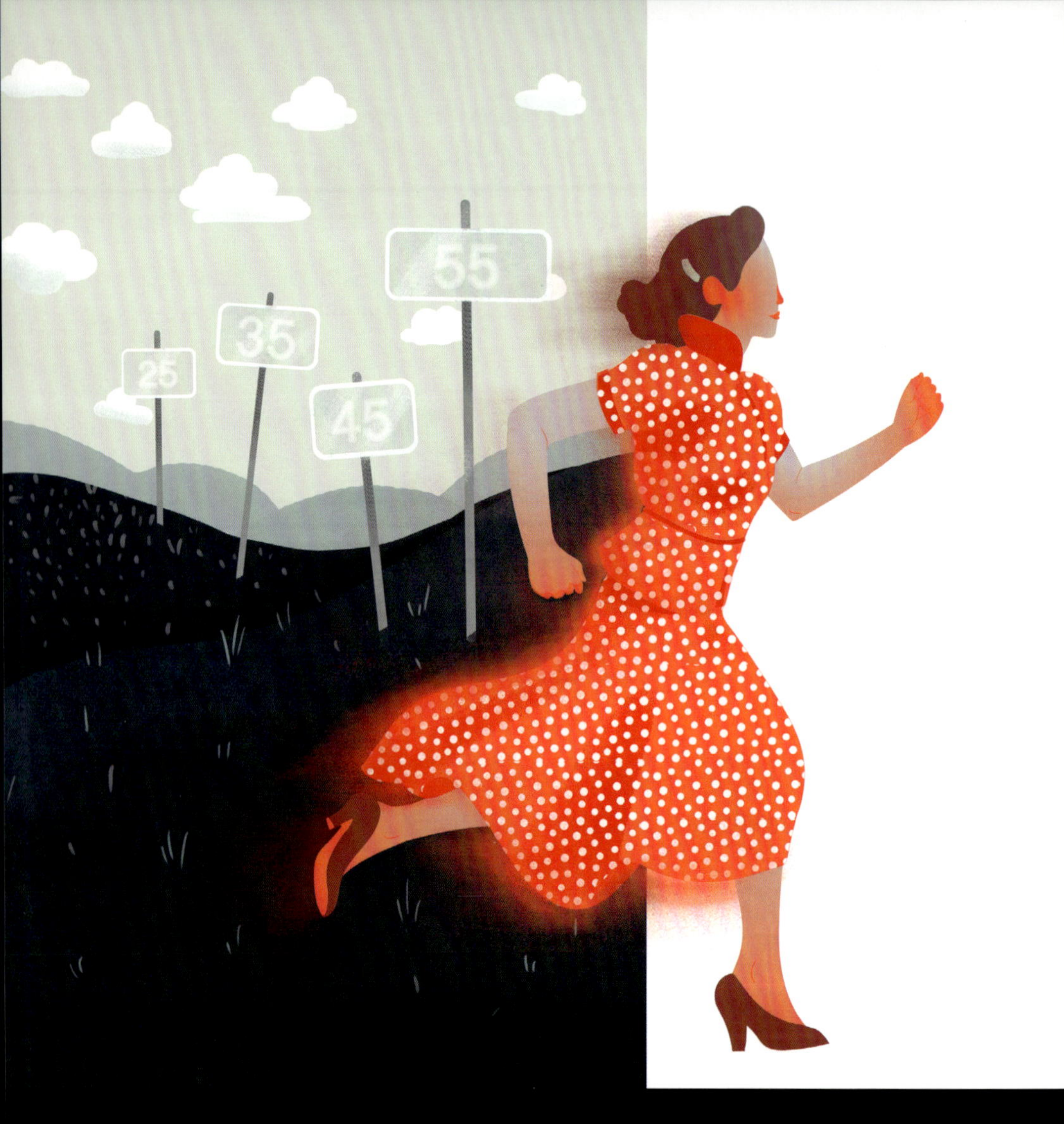





MERIT *Elyse Salazar*

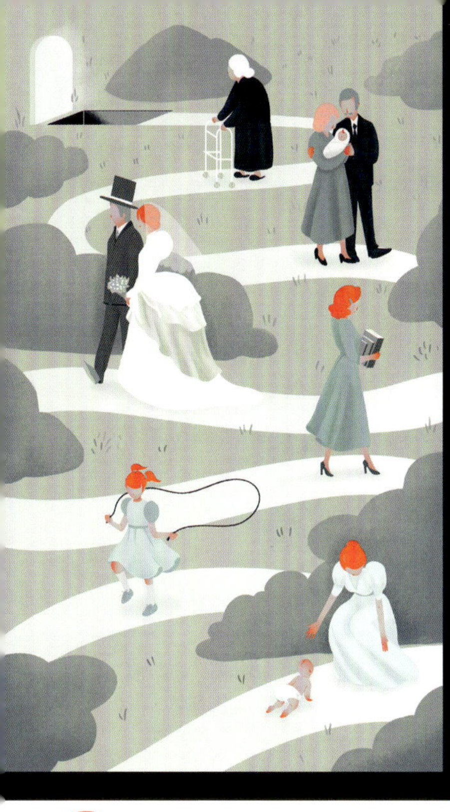
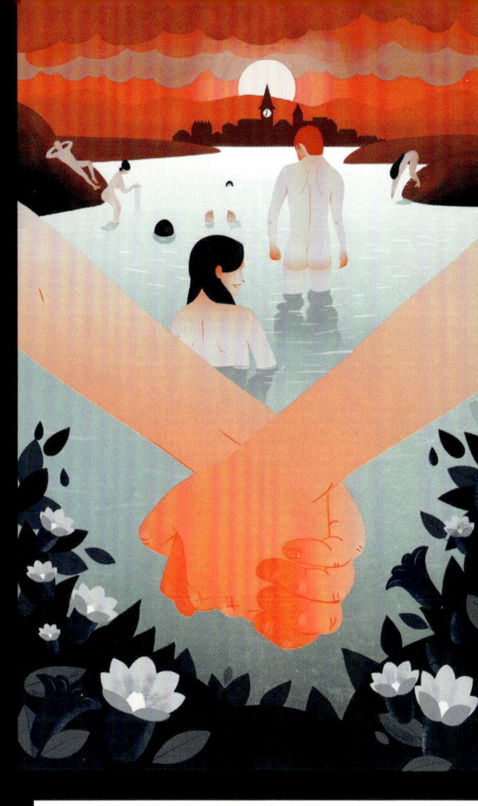
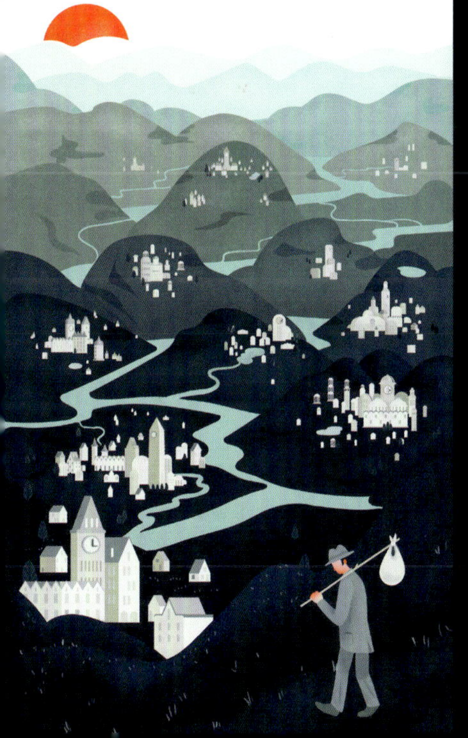
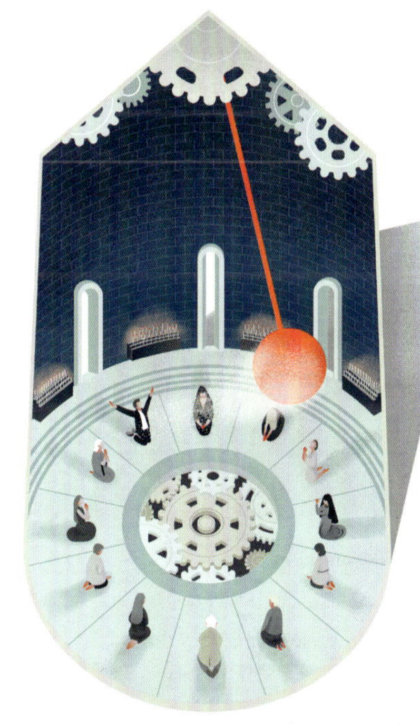

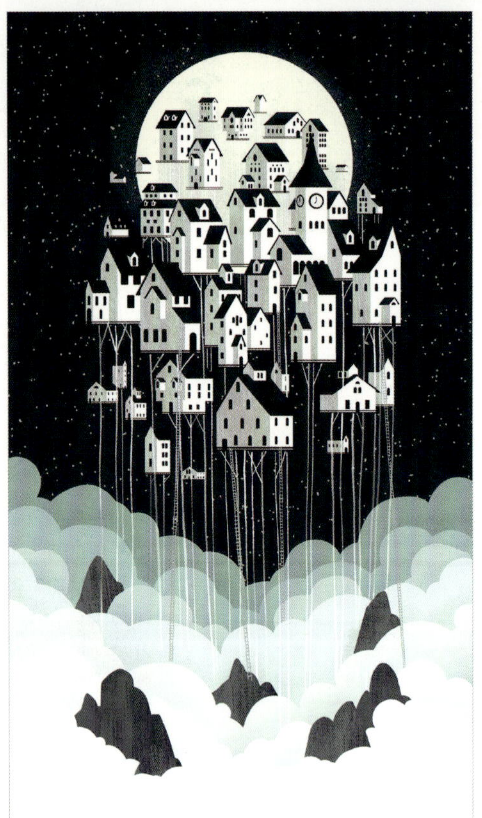
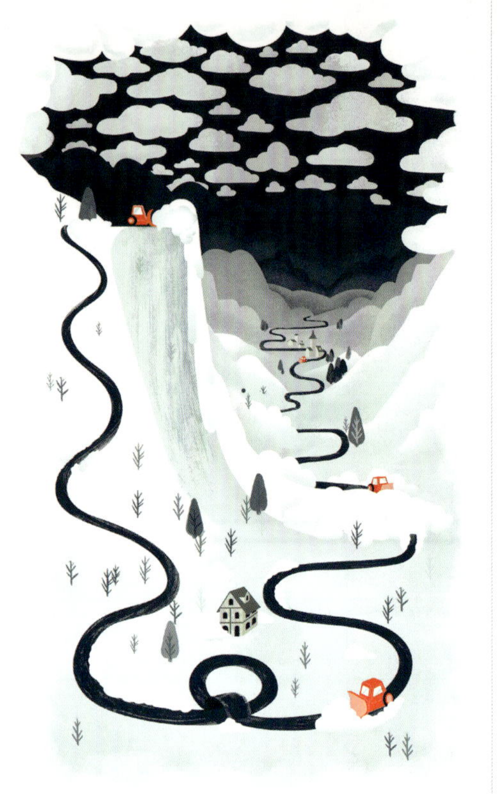
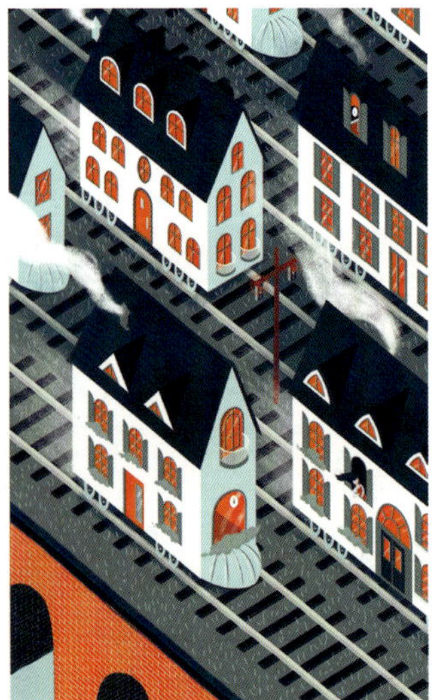
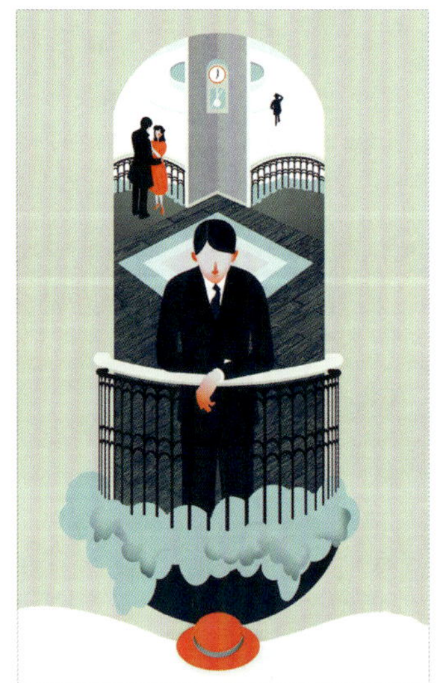
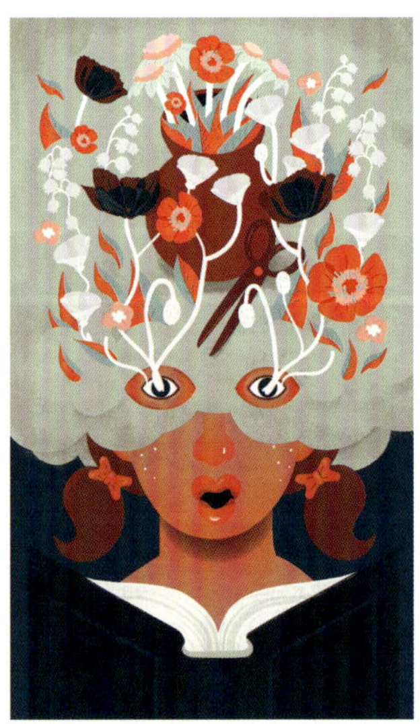

SILVER *Elyse Salazar*

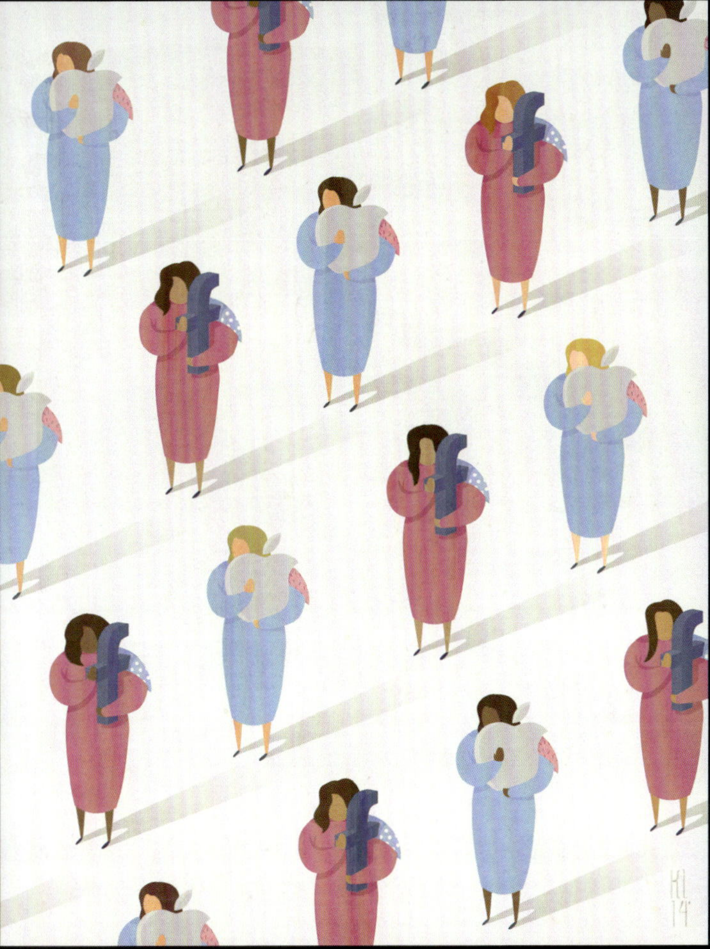

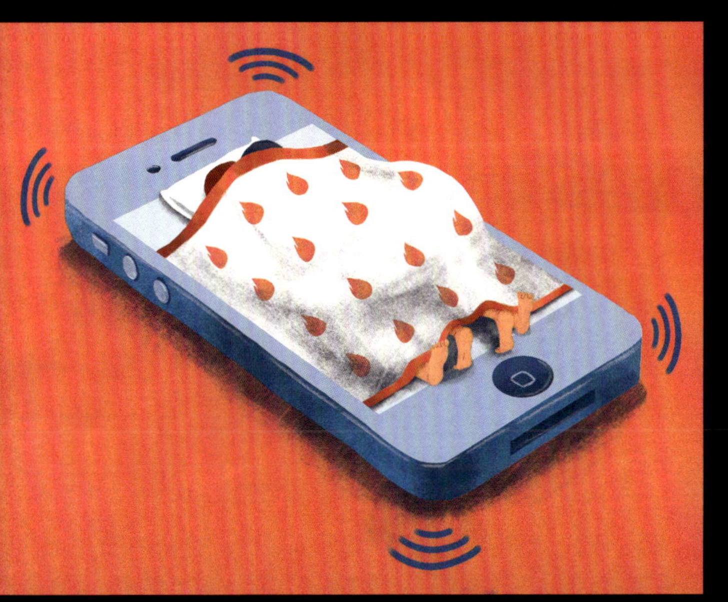

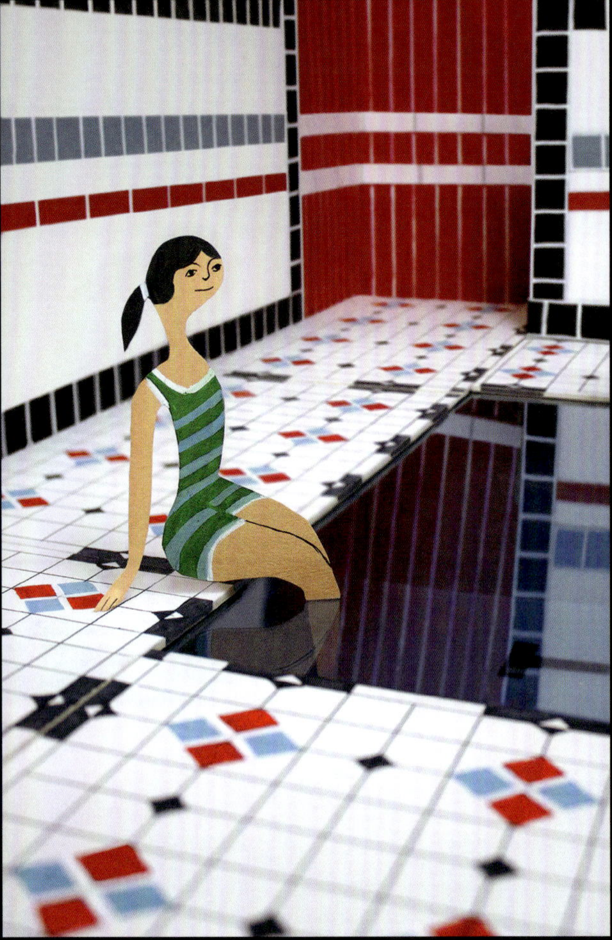

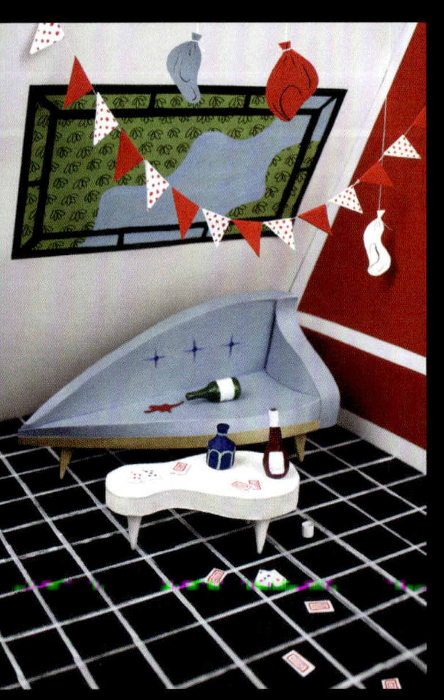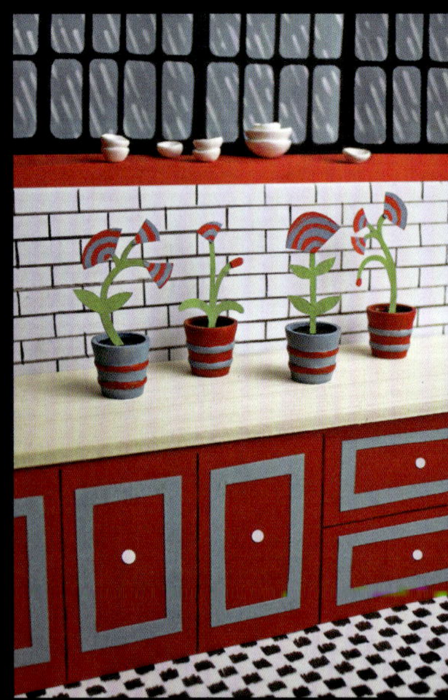

(L) MERIT Angela Rio     (R) MERIT Dola Sun

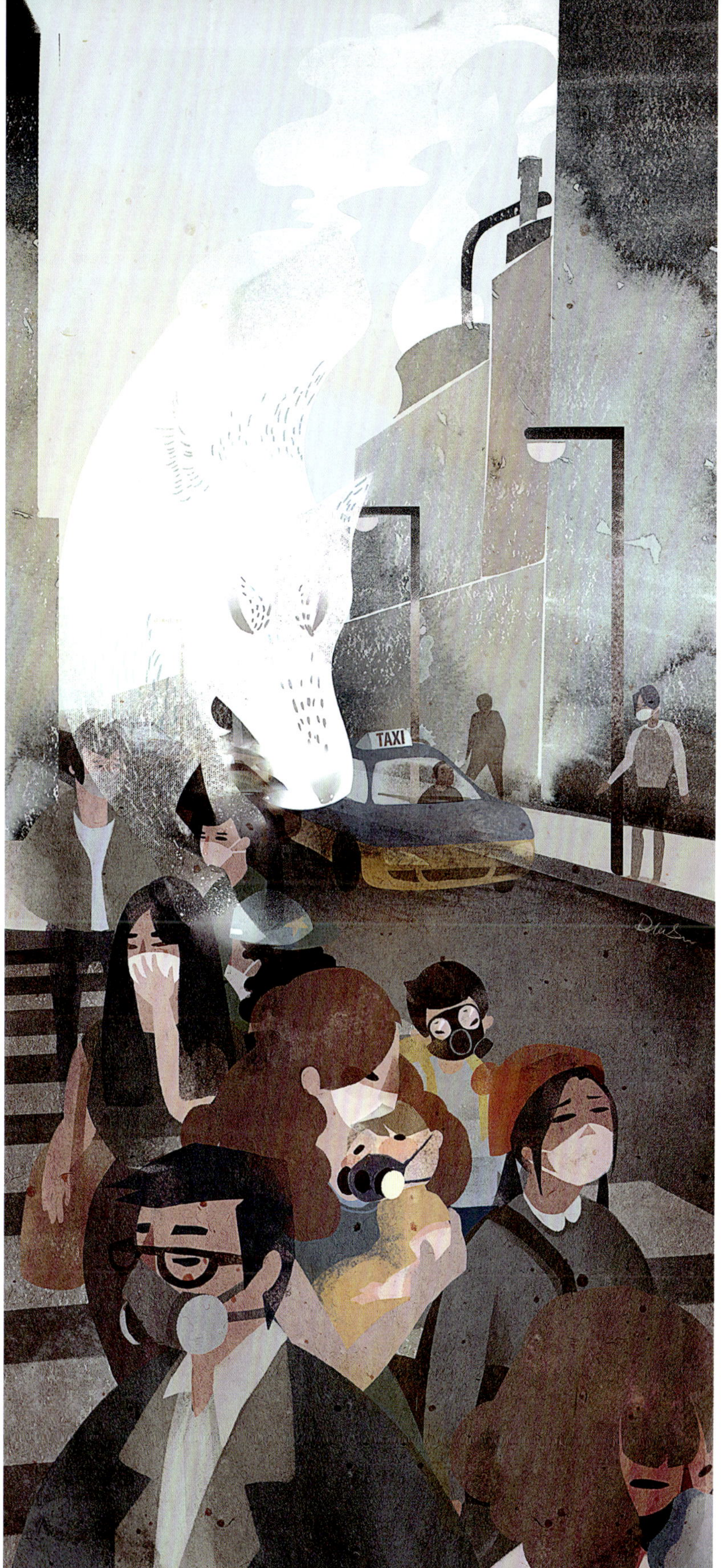
TAXI

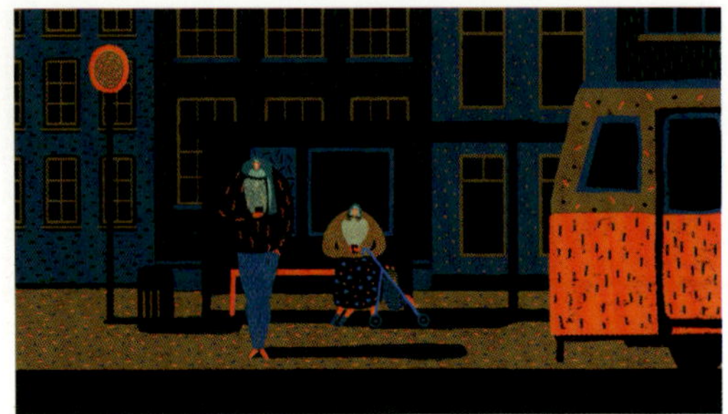

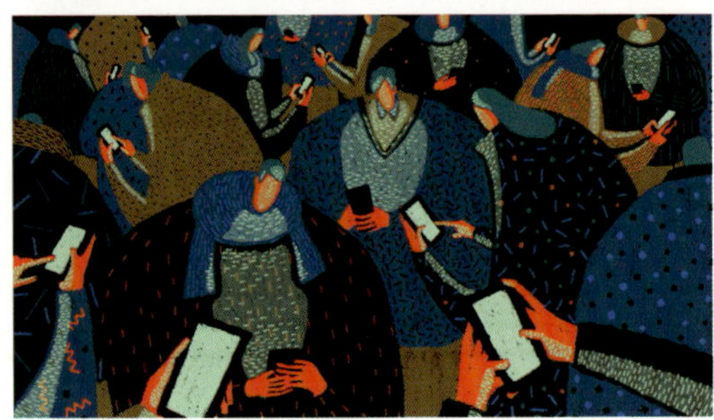

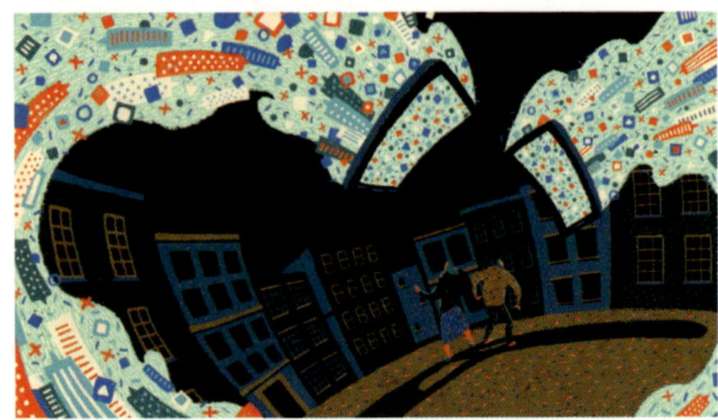

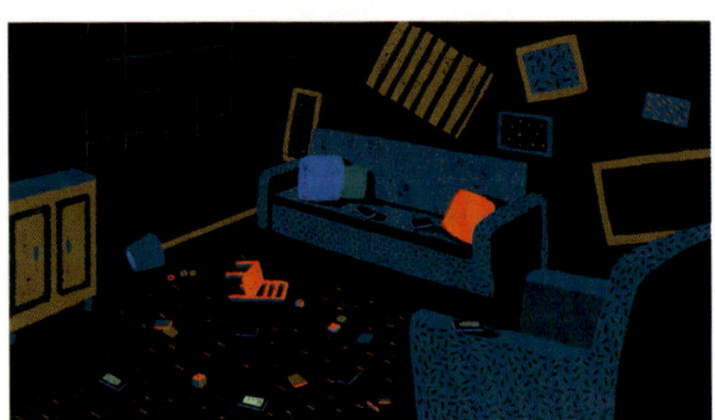

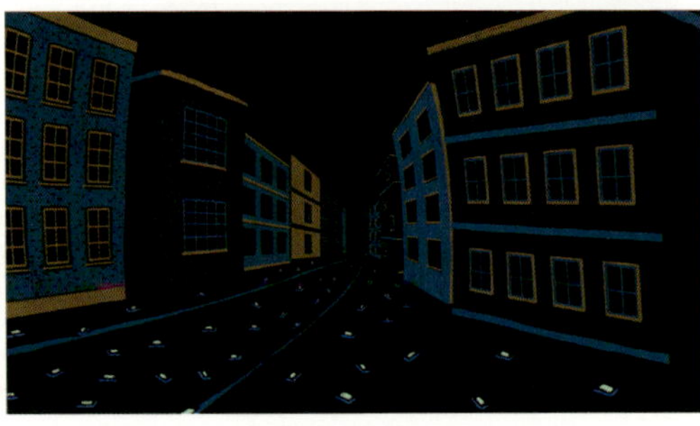

BEST OF SHOW *Yukai Du*

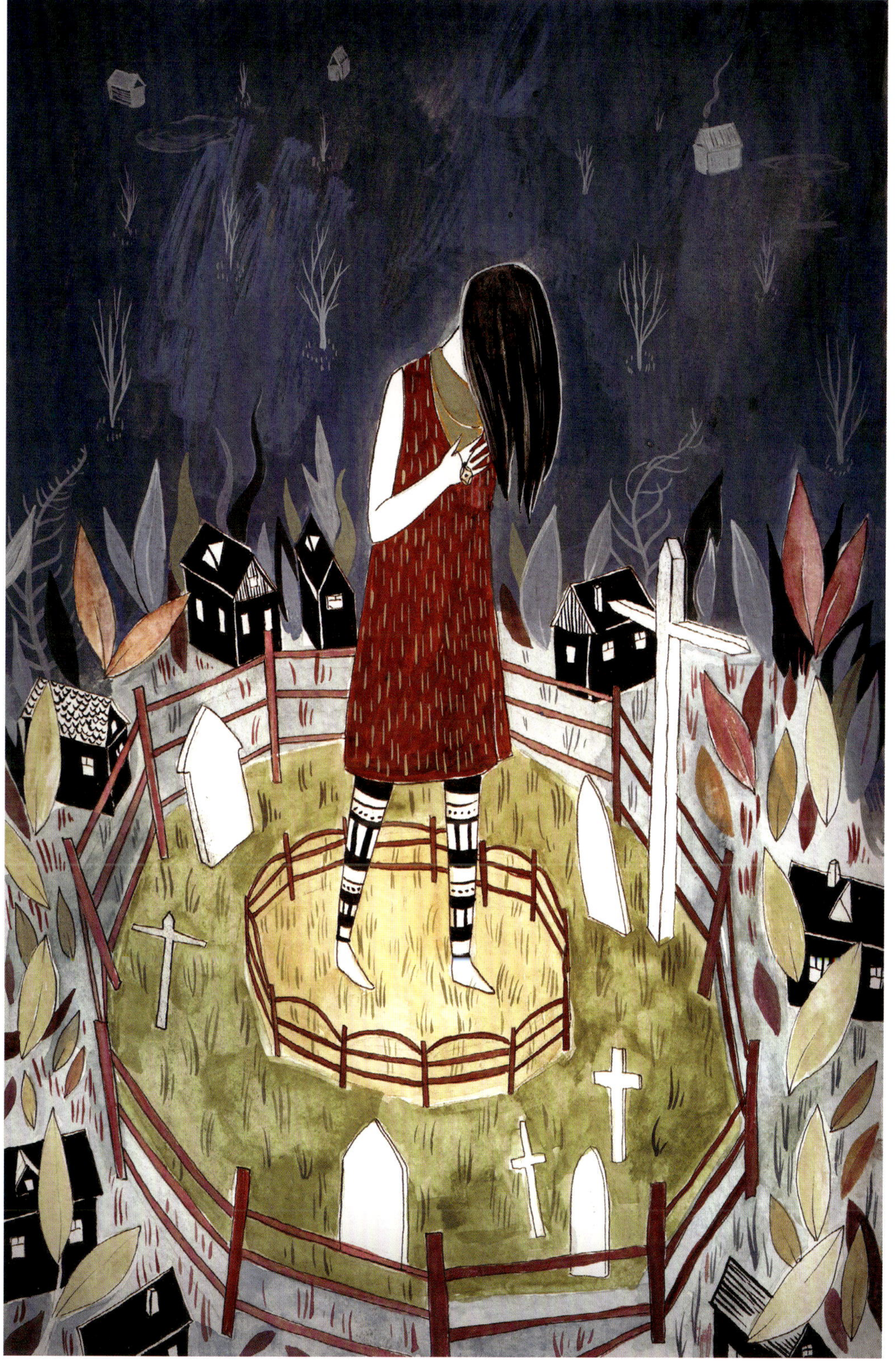



MERIT *Julia Iredale*

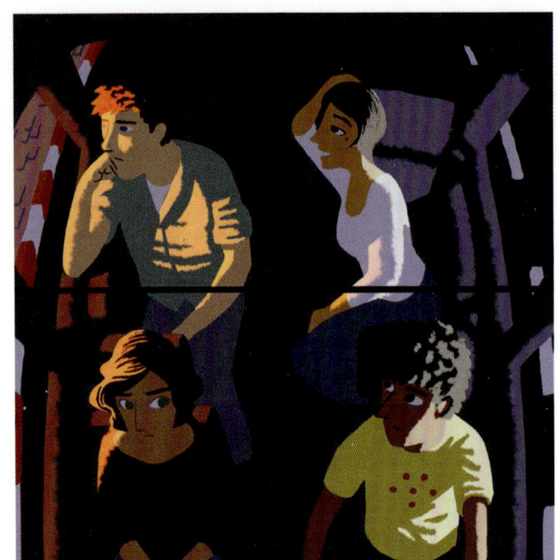

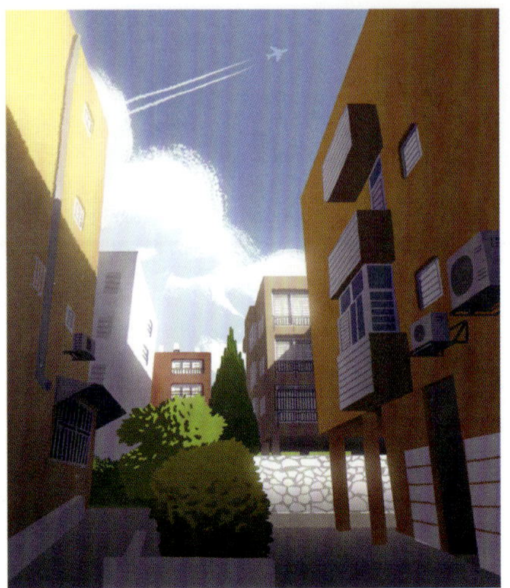

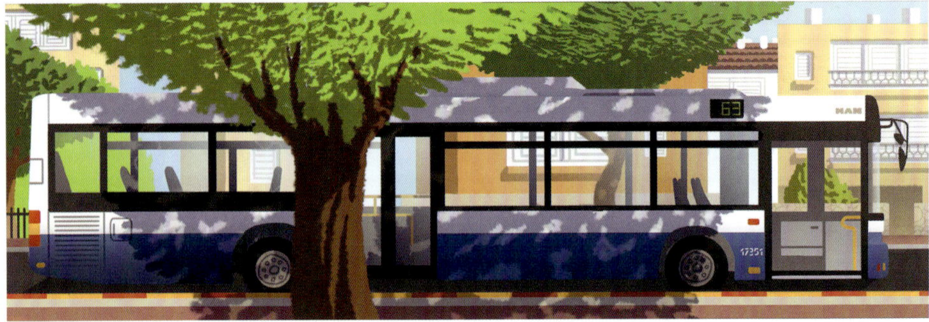

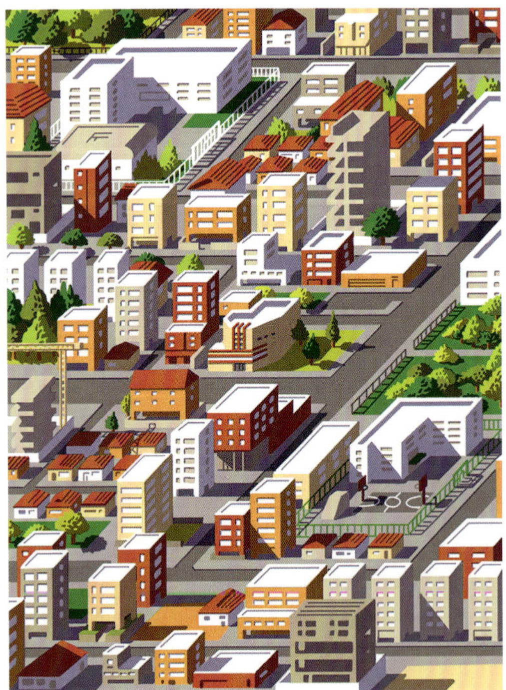

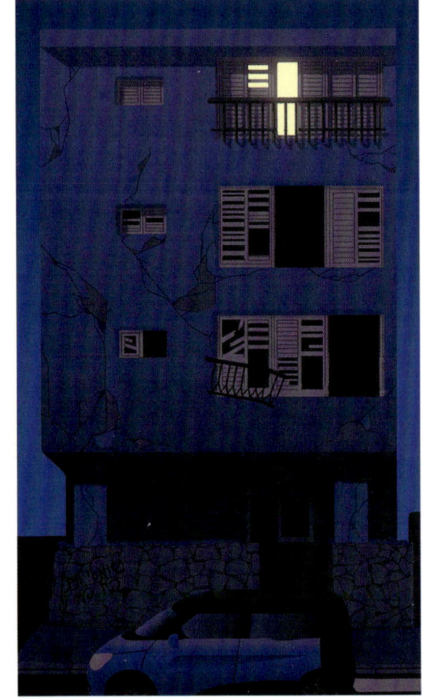

MERIT *Tom Engler*

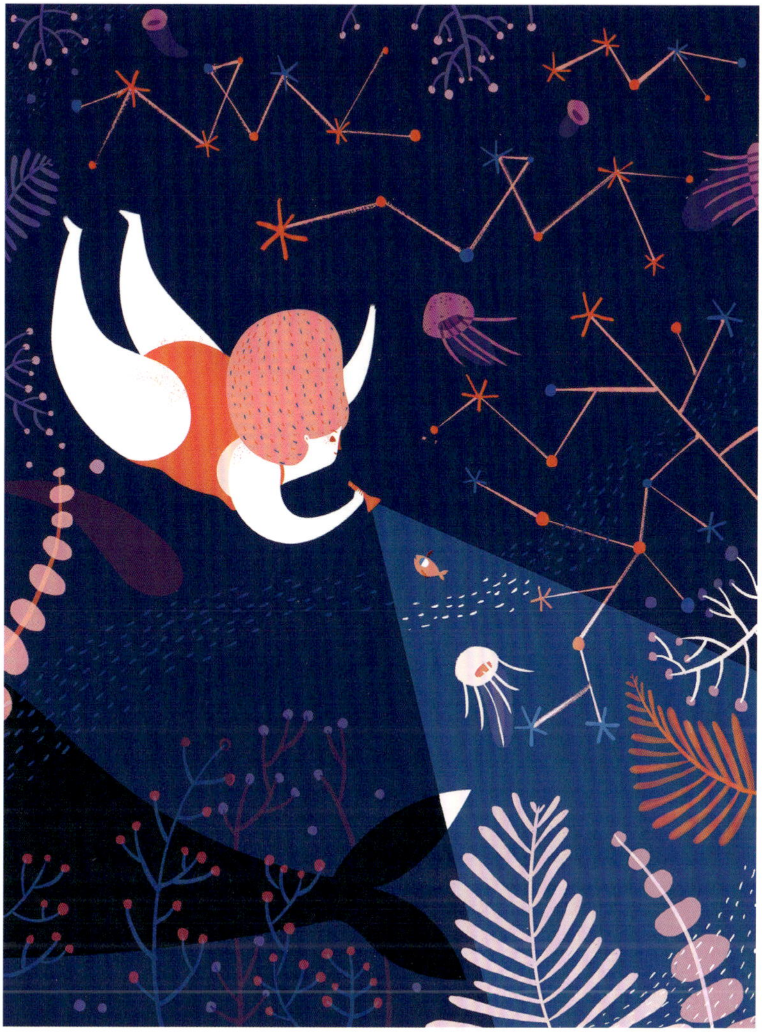

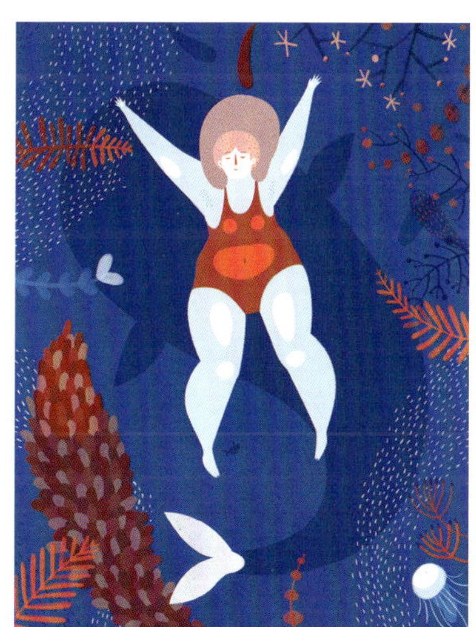

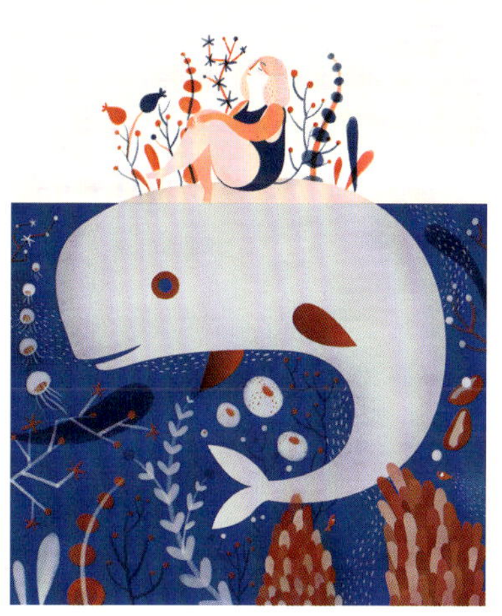

MERIT *Francesca Sanna*





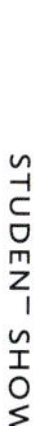

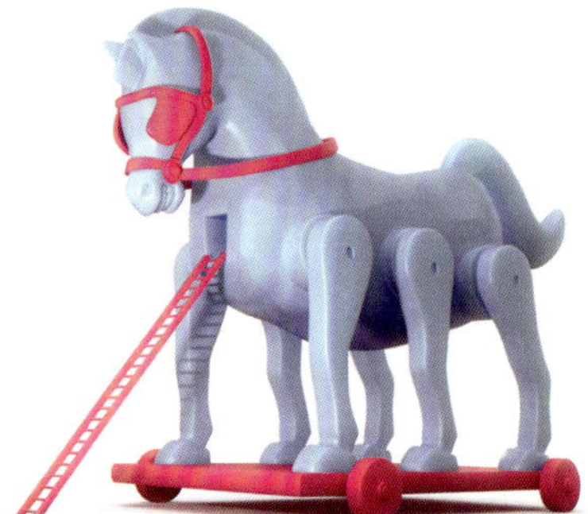

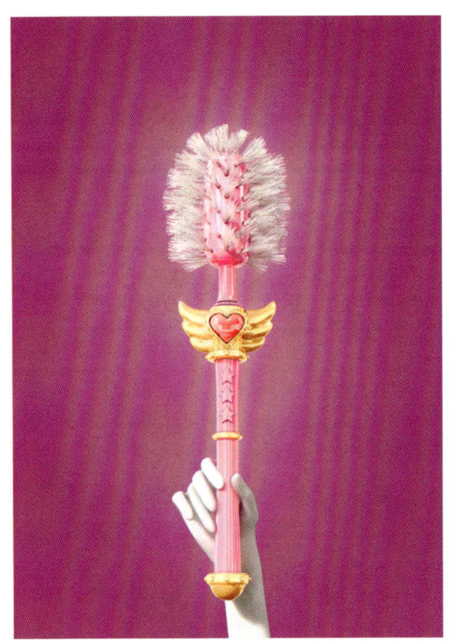

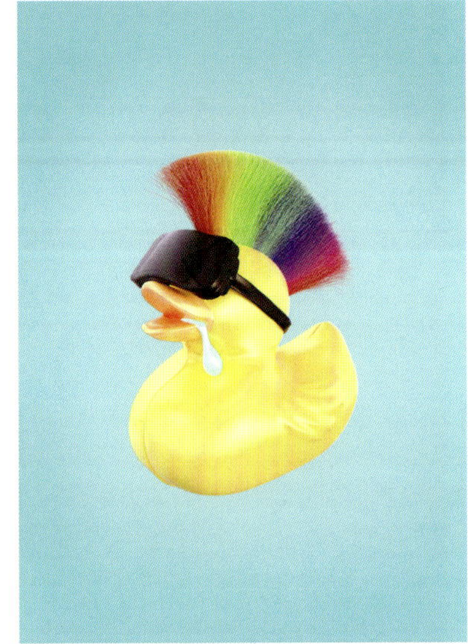

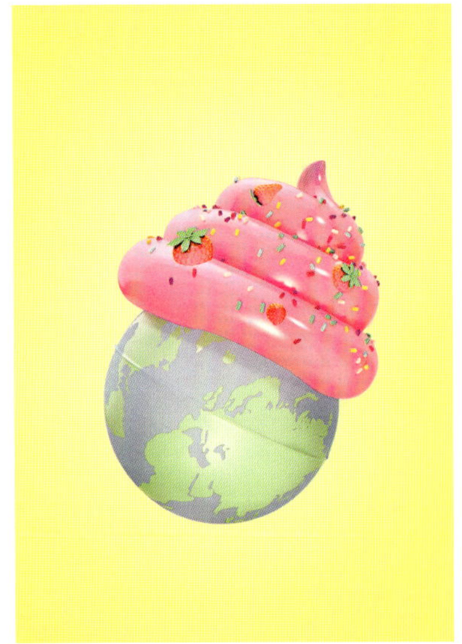

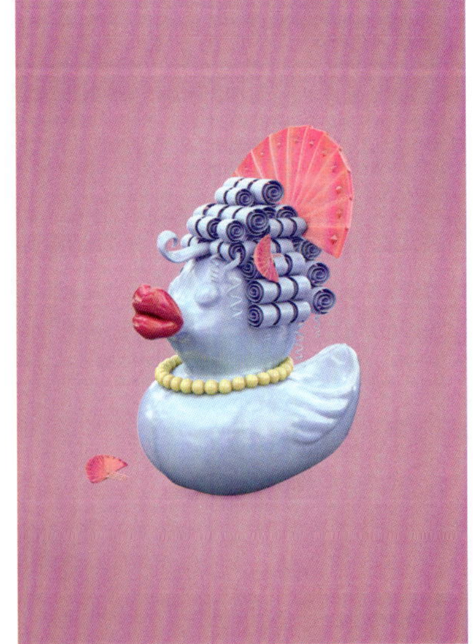

MERIT *Kathrin Rödl*

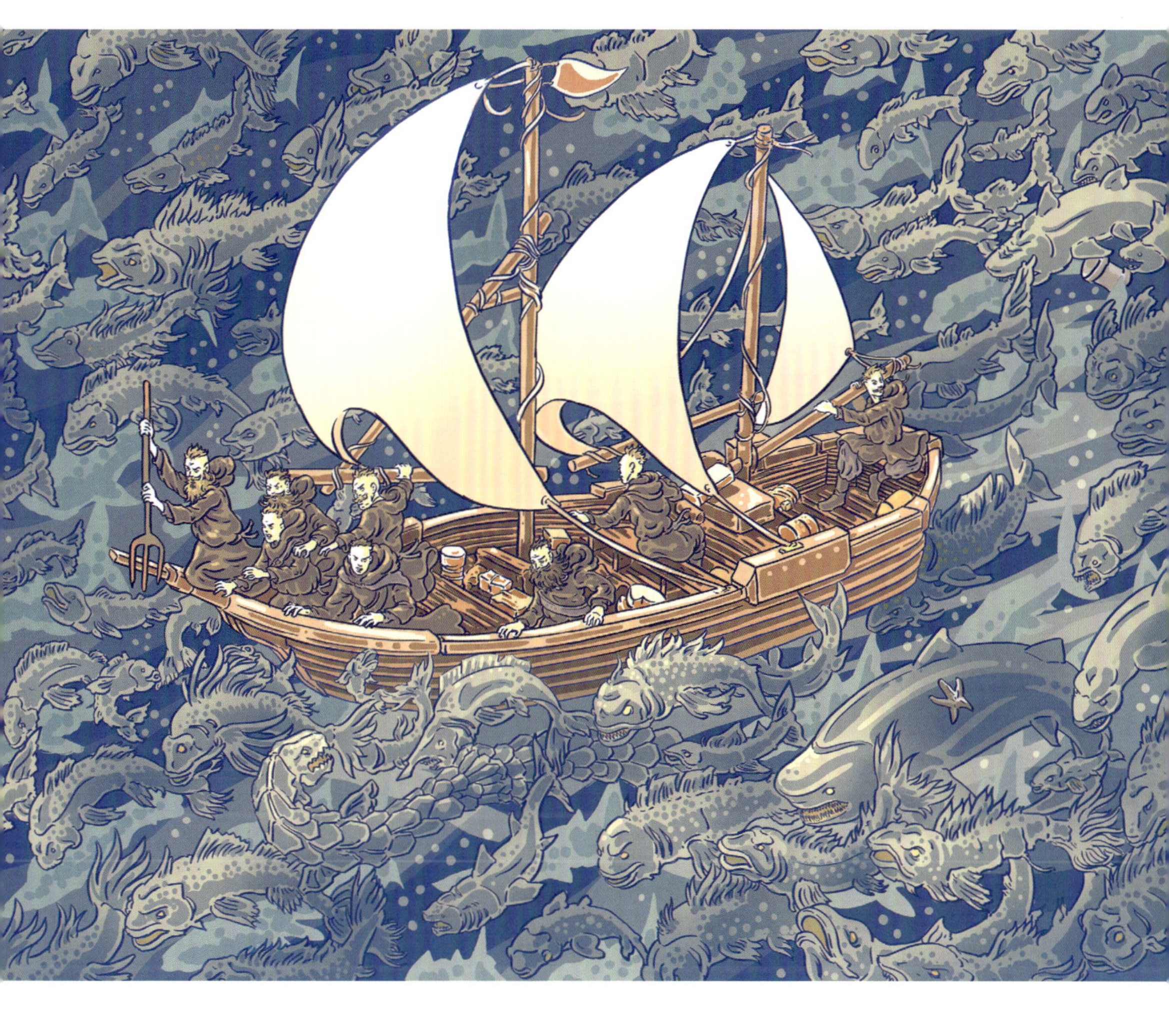



MERIT *Lynden Joudrey*

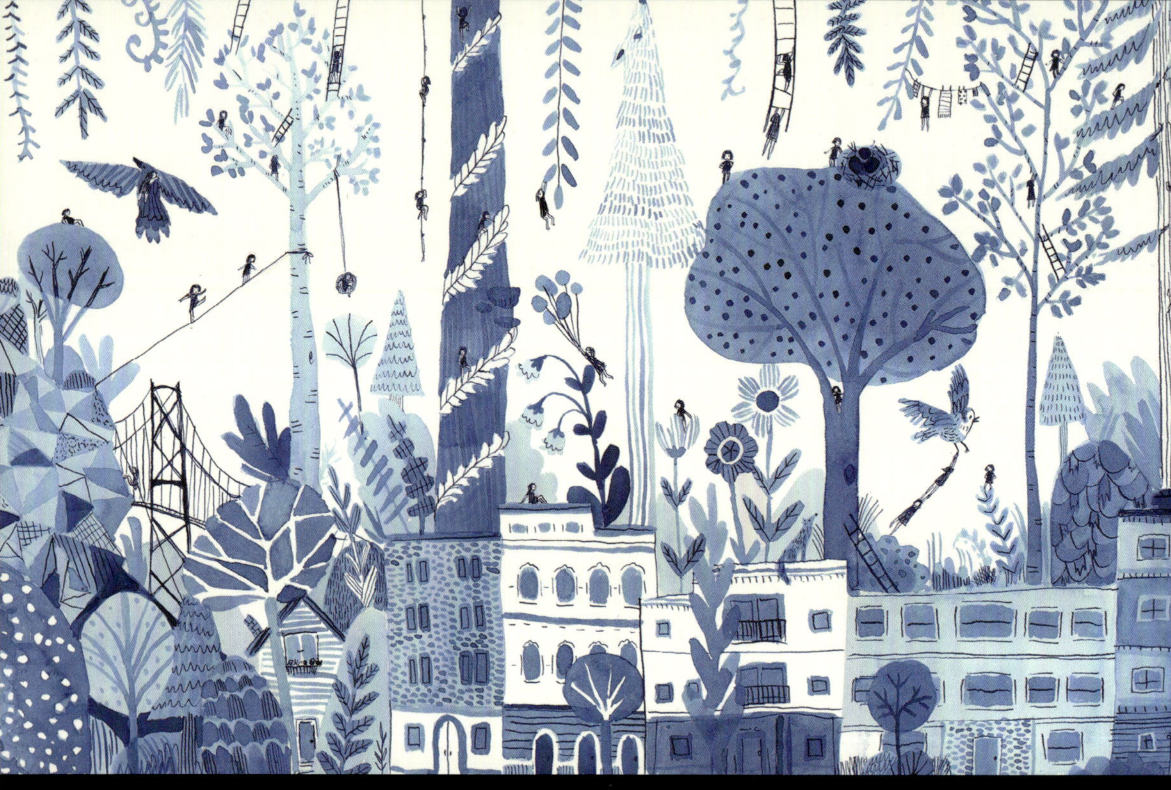

MERIT *Madeline Kloepper*

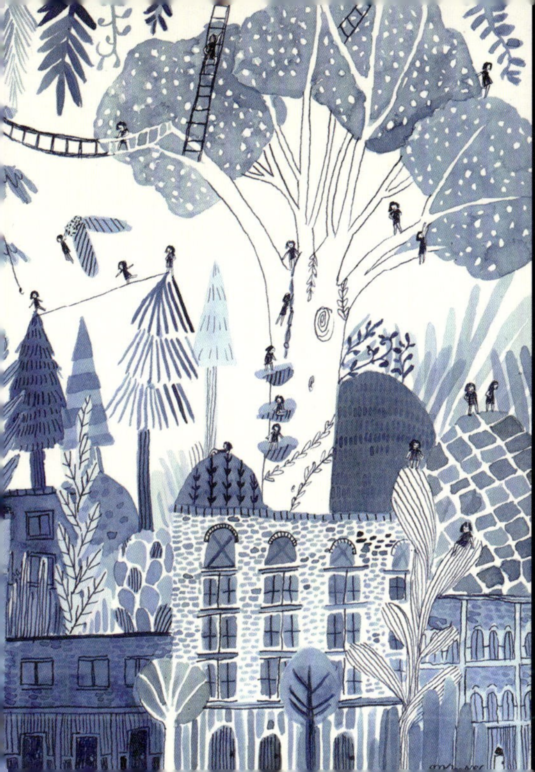

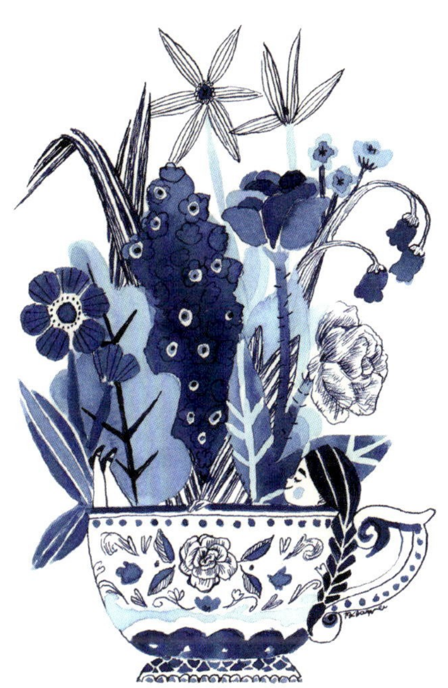

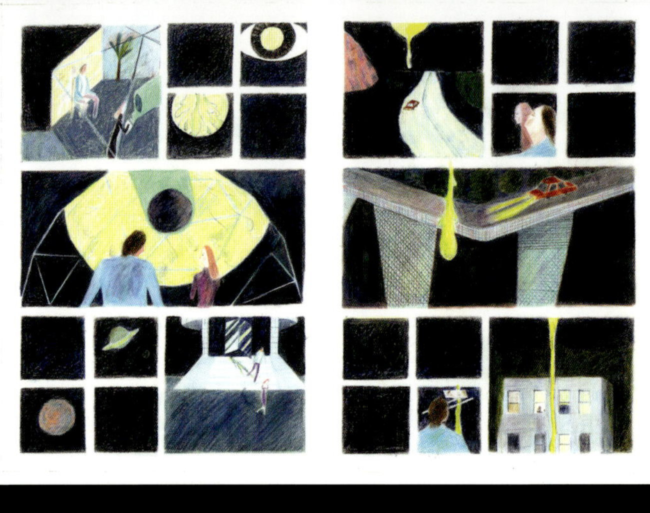

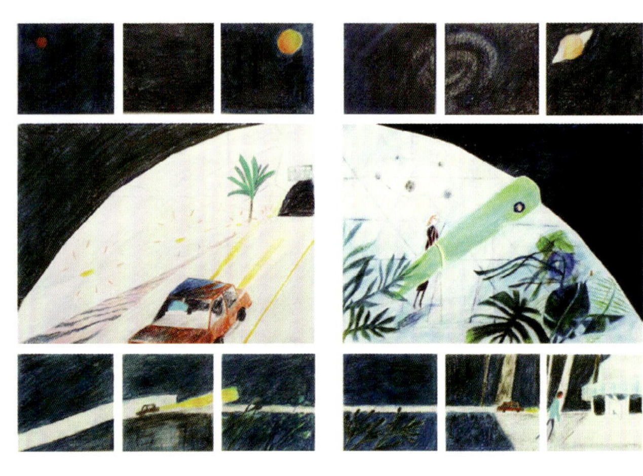

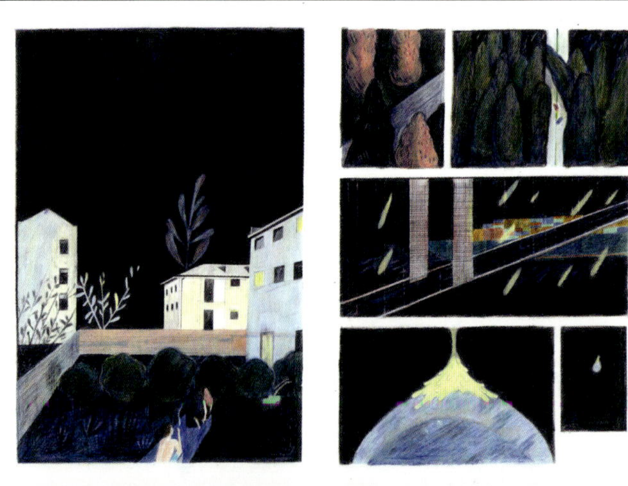

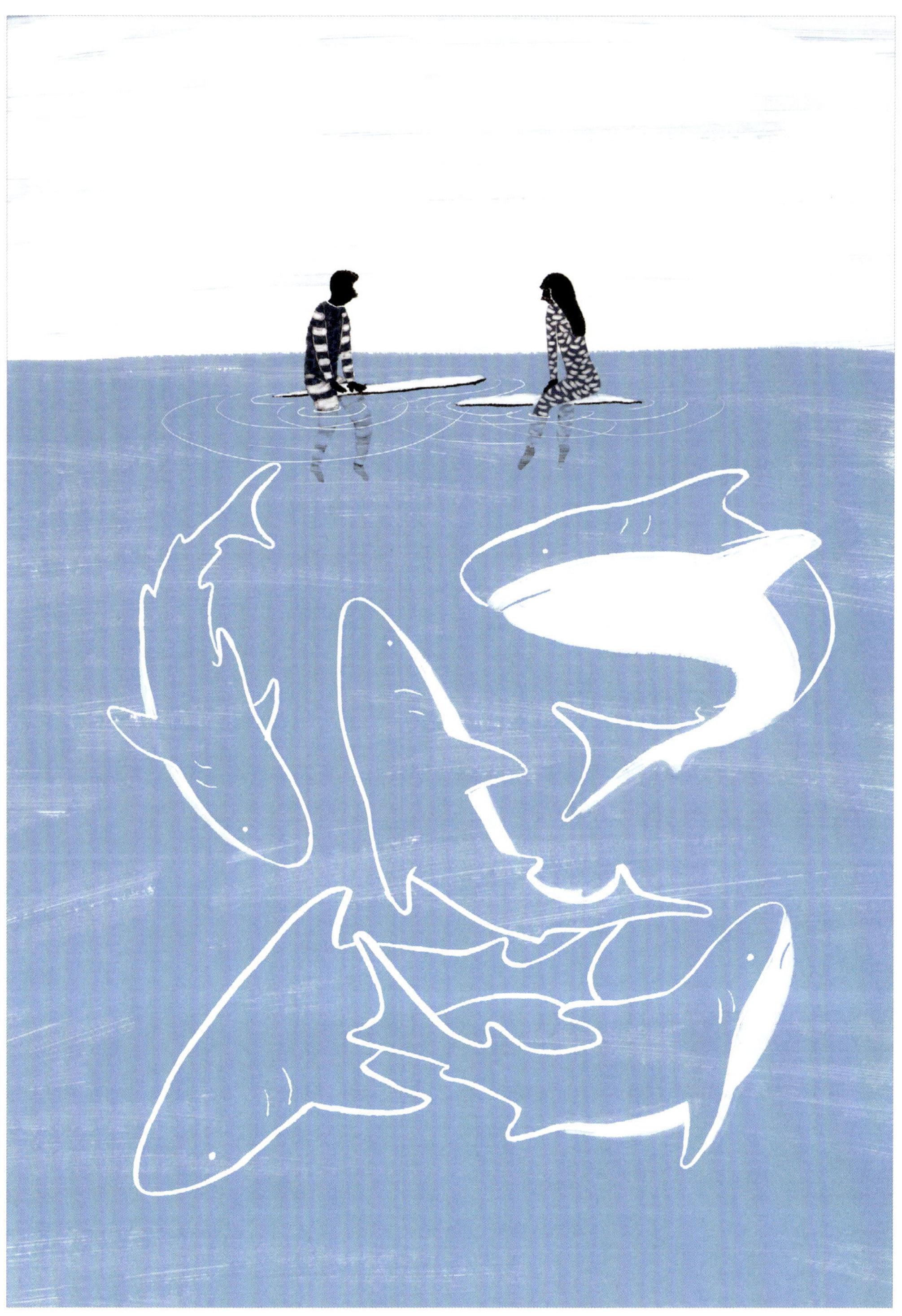

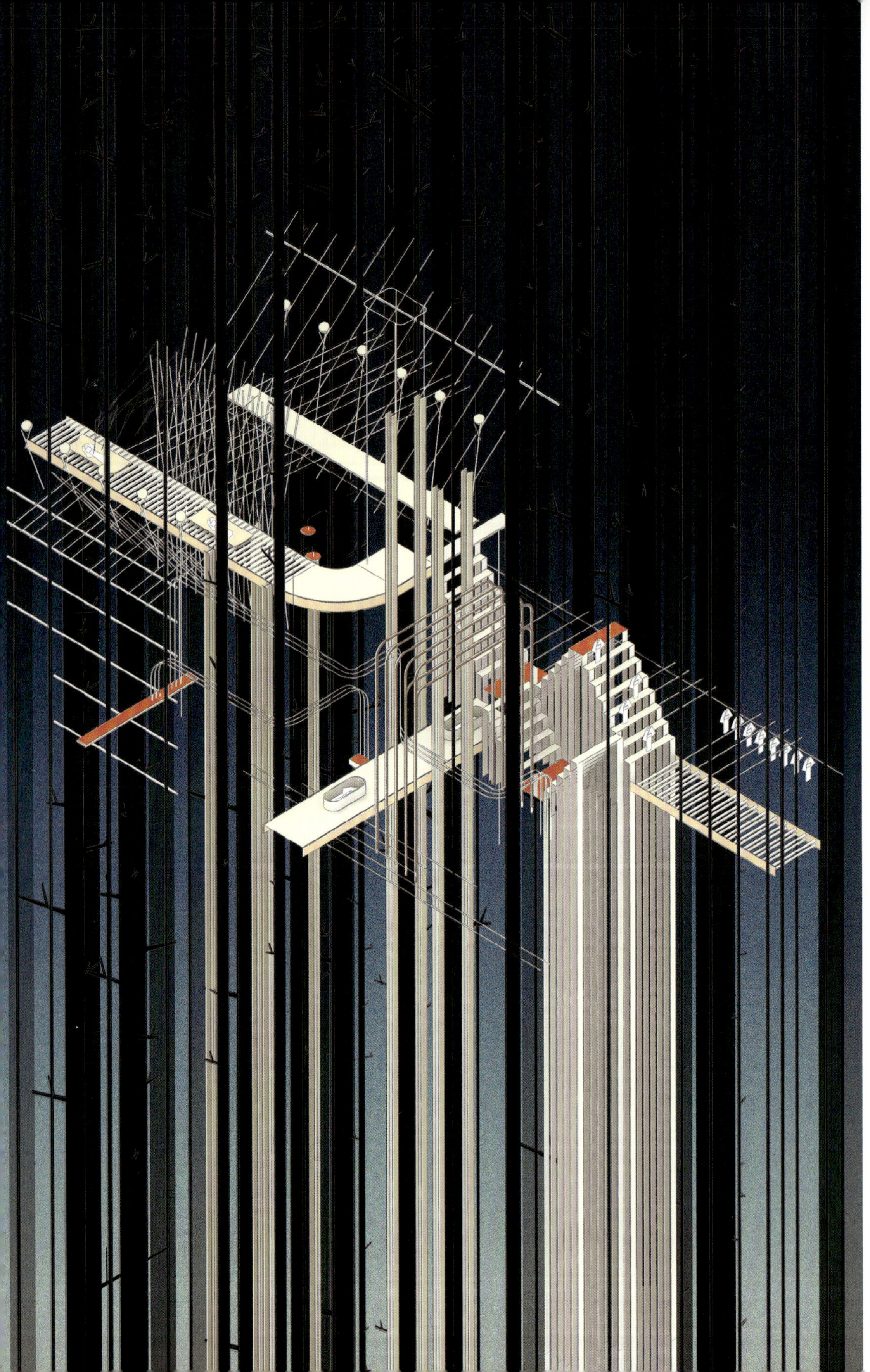

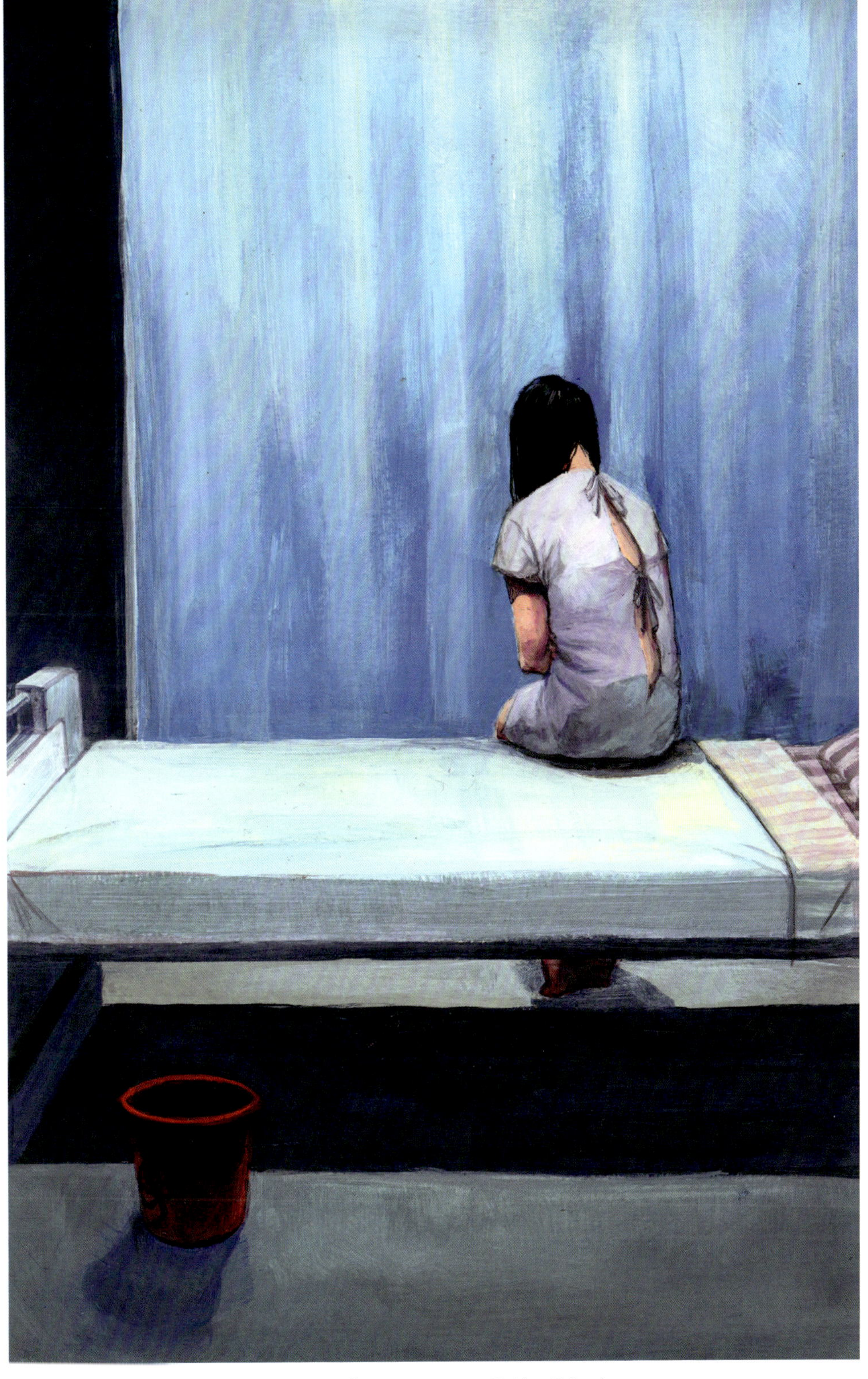



(L) MERIT *Carol Nung*   (R) MERIT *Kaitlyn Richardson*

393

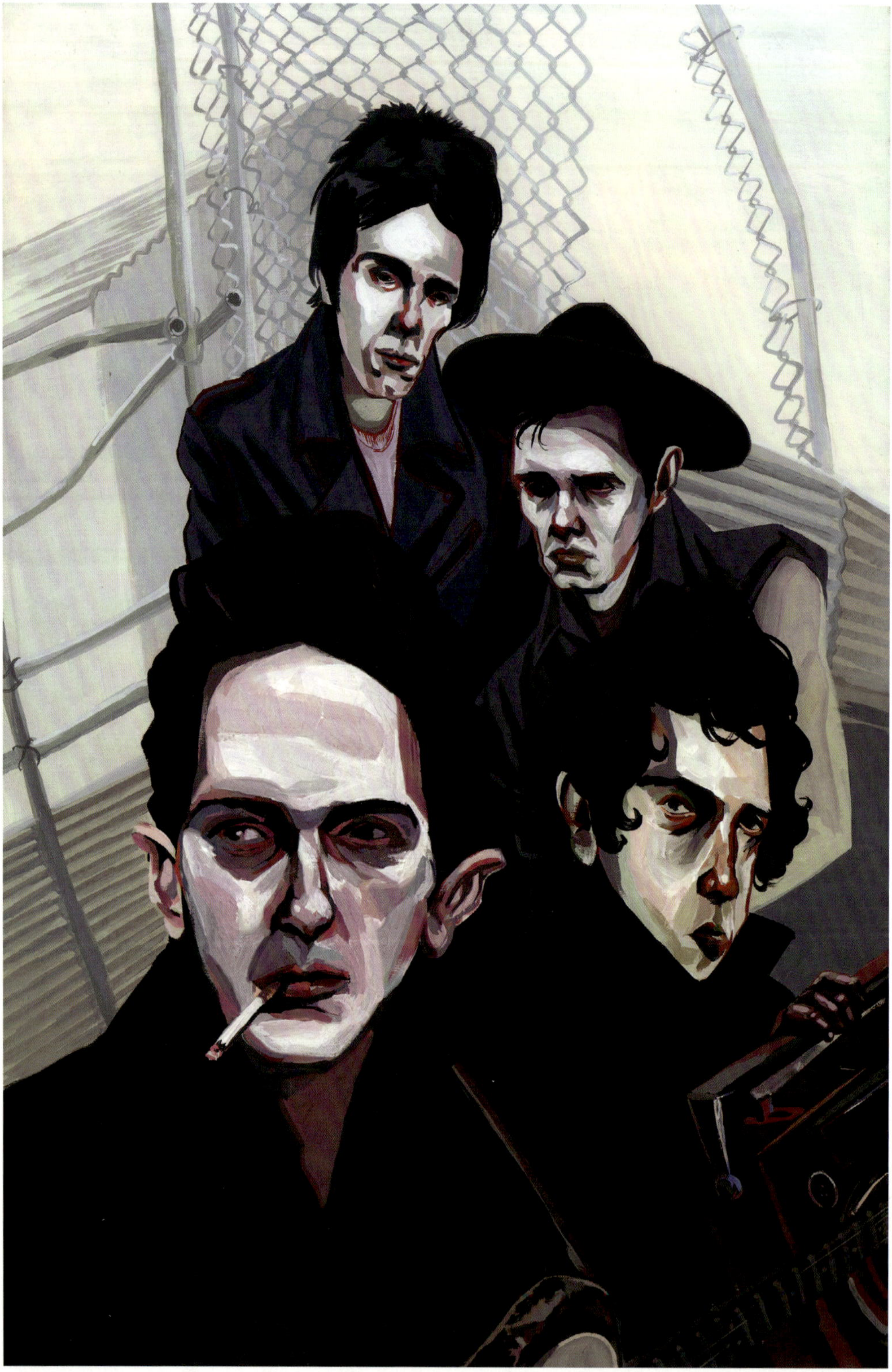

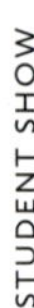

MERIT *Phil Robles*

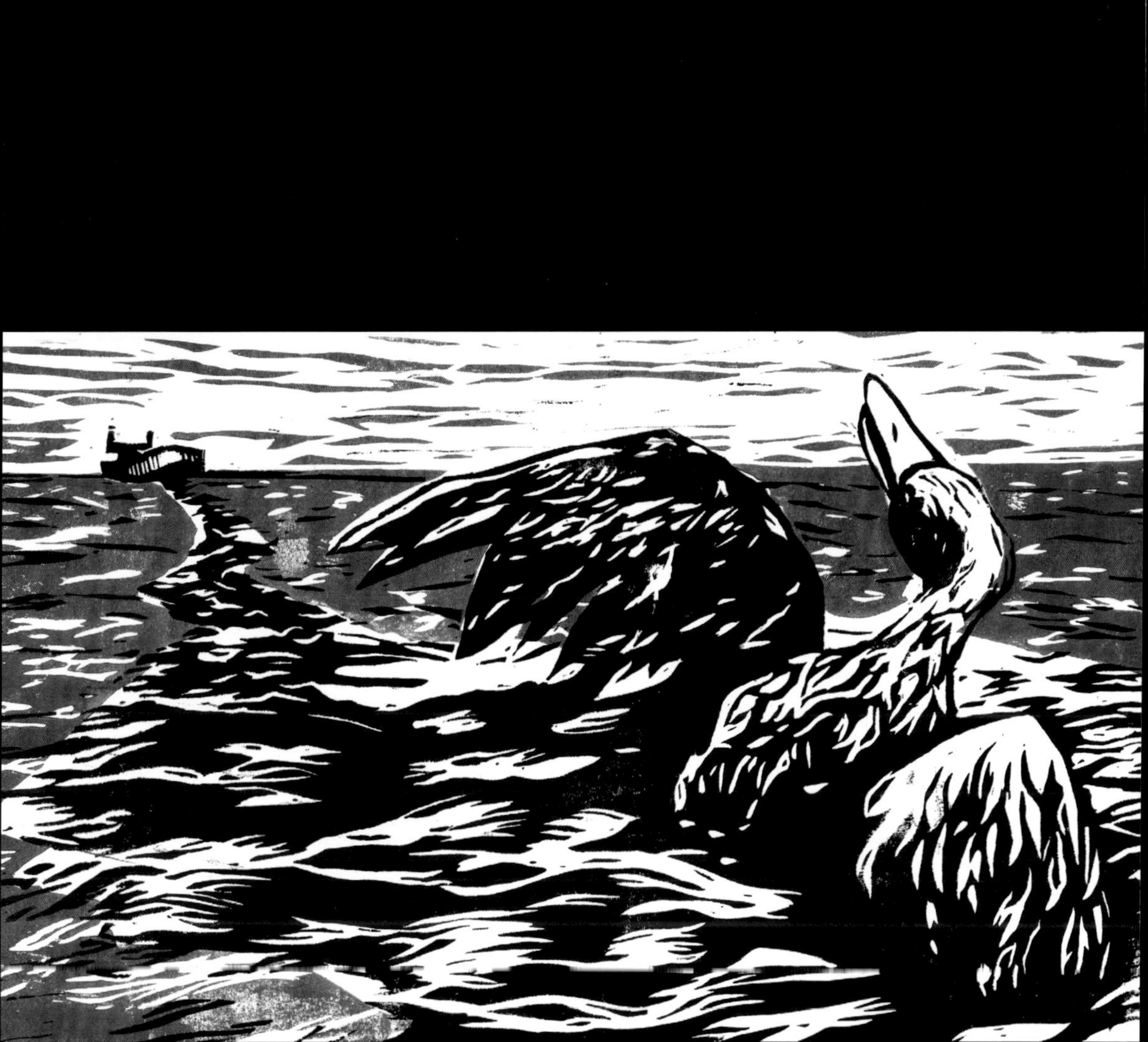

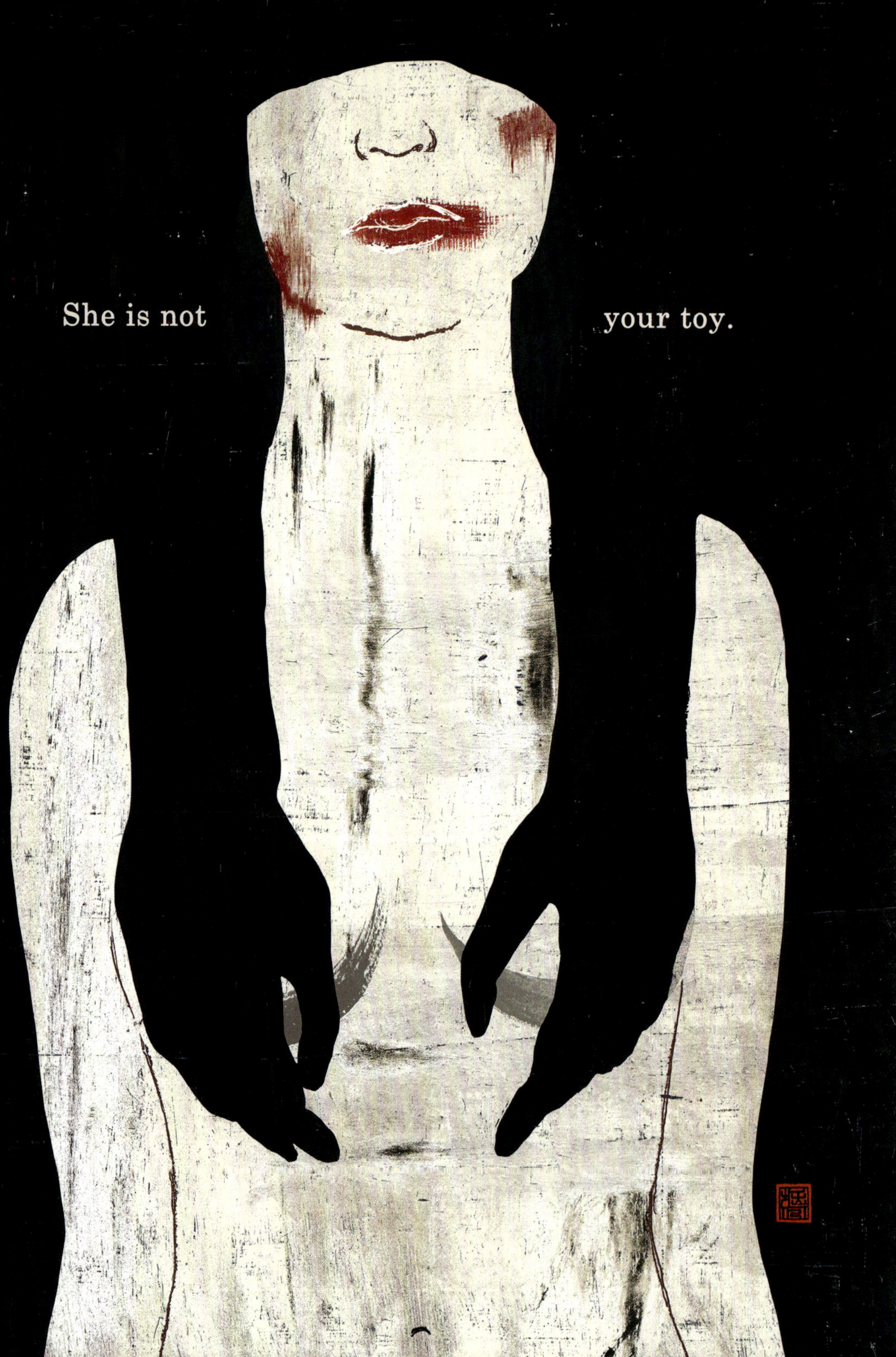

She is not
your toy.

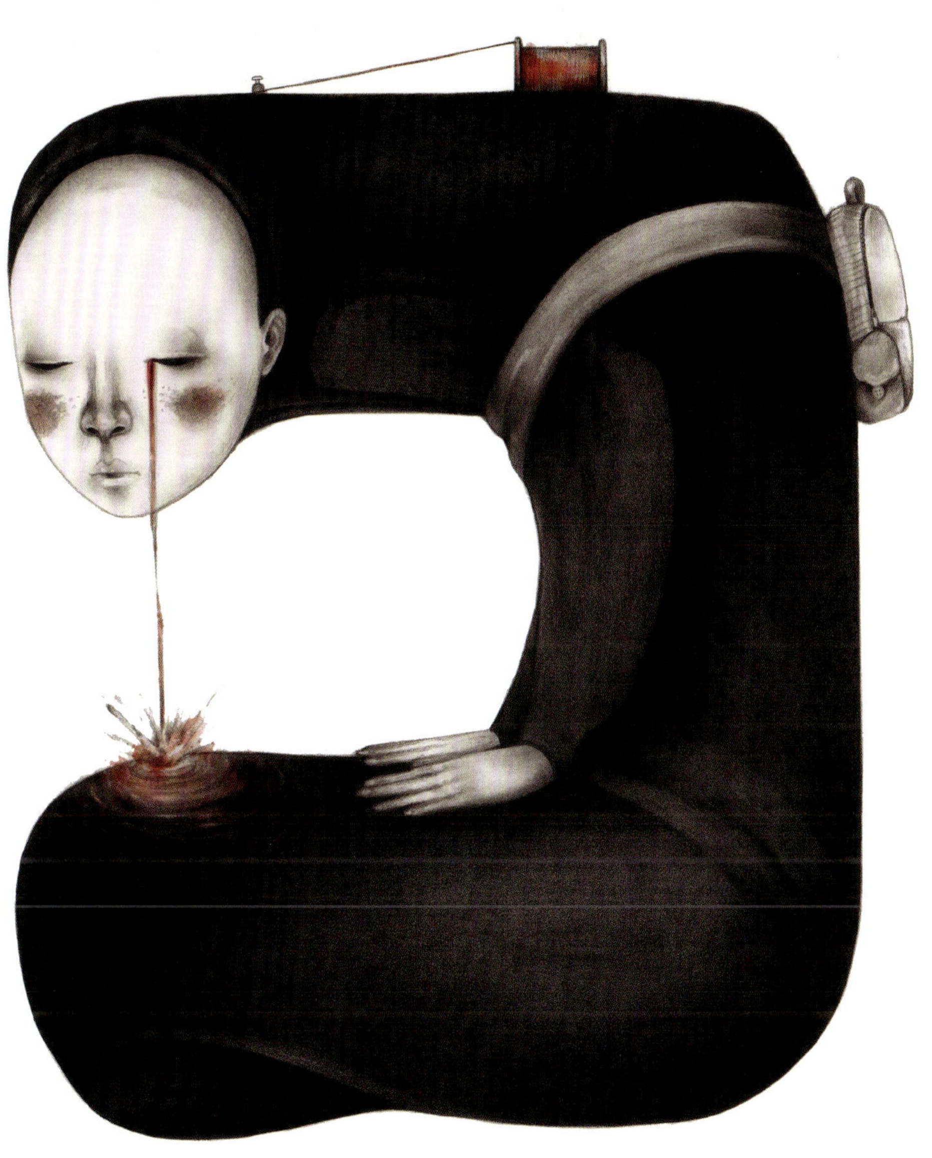

(L) MERIT *Yohey Horishita*   (R) MERIT *Phivi Spyridonos*

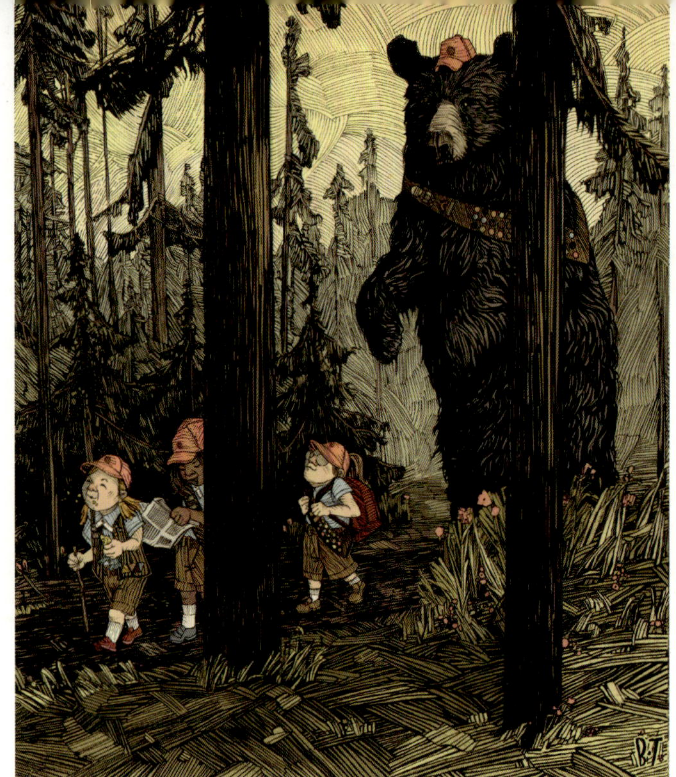

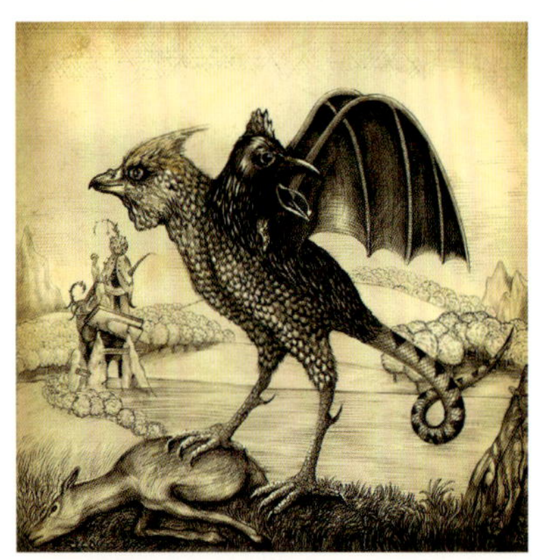

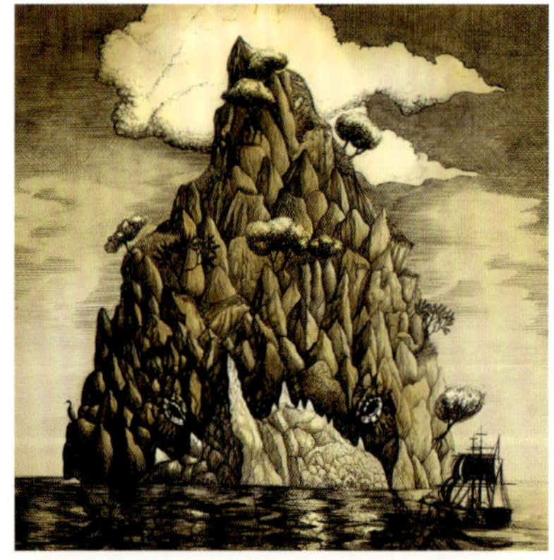

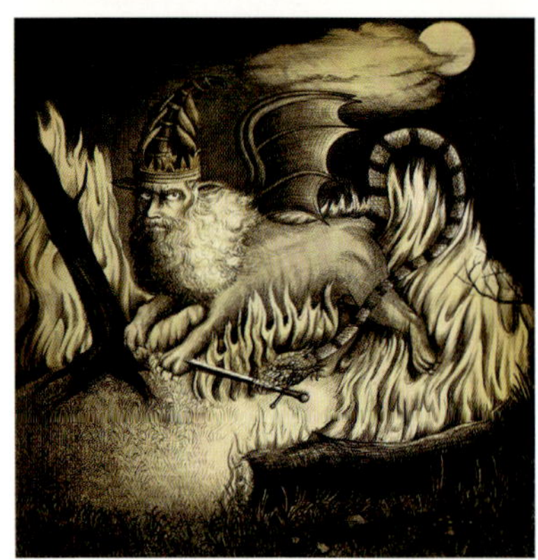

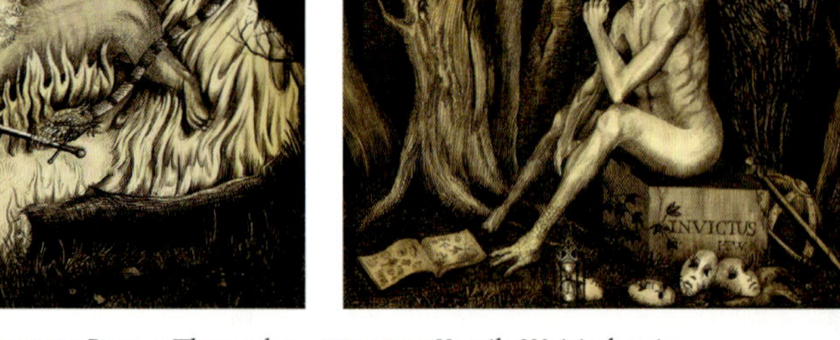

(T) MERIT *Brenna Thummler*   (B) MERIT *Kamila Wojciechowicz*

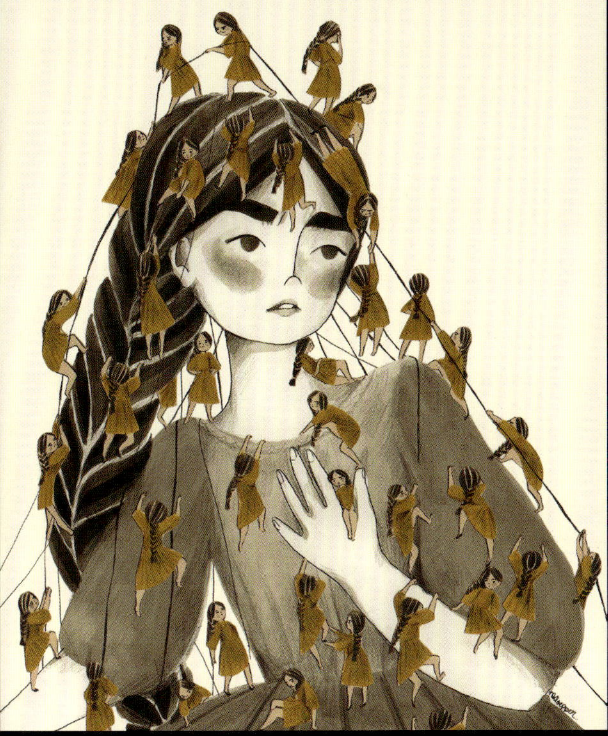

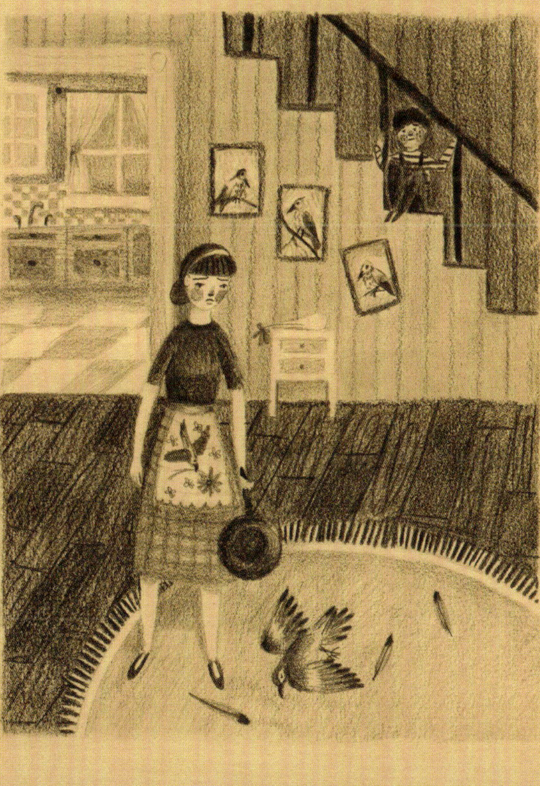

(T) MERIT *Madeline Kloepper*    (B) MERIT *Chelsea O'Byrne*

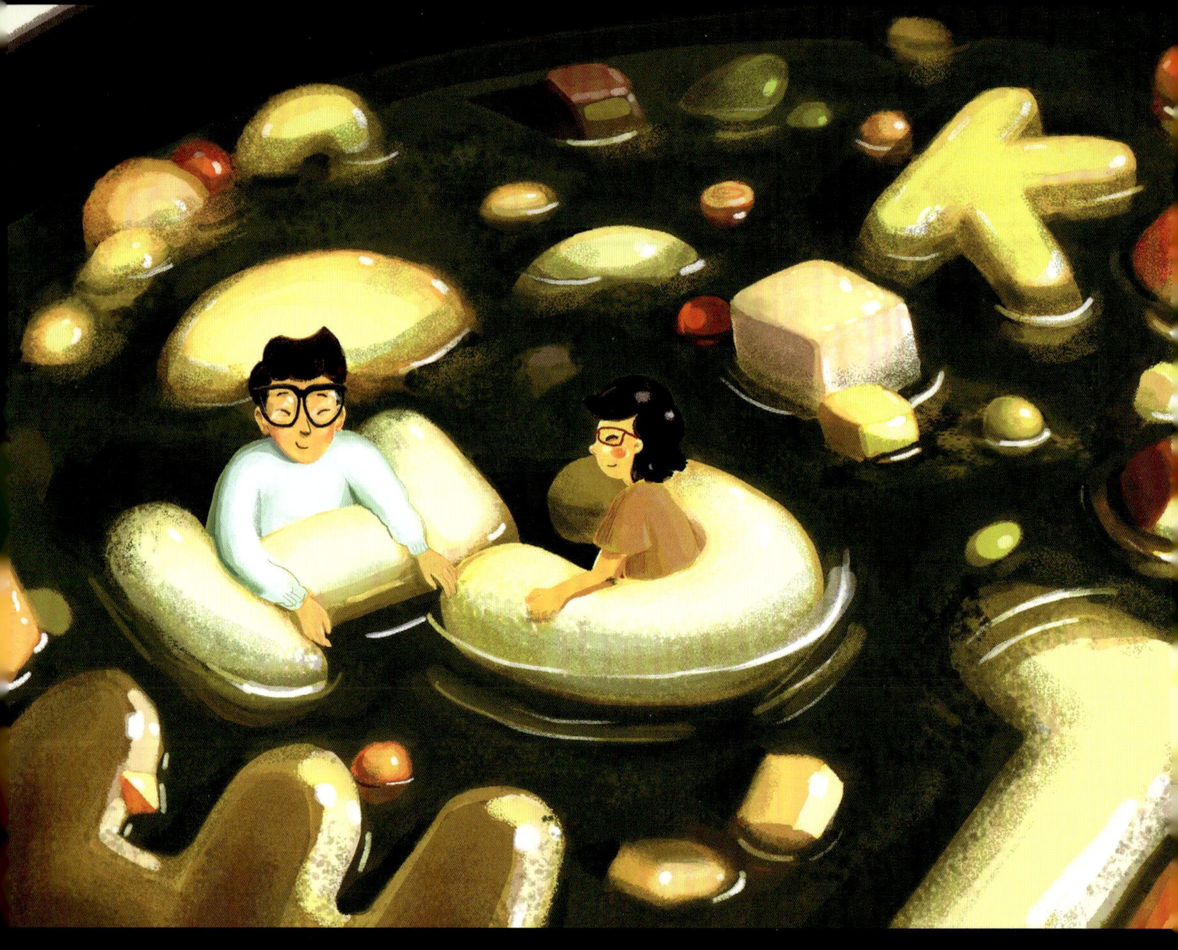

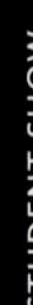

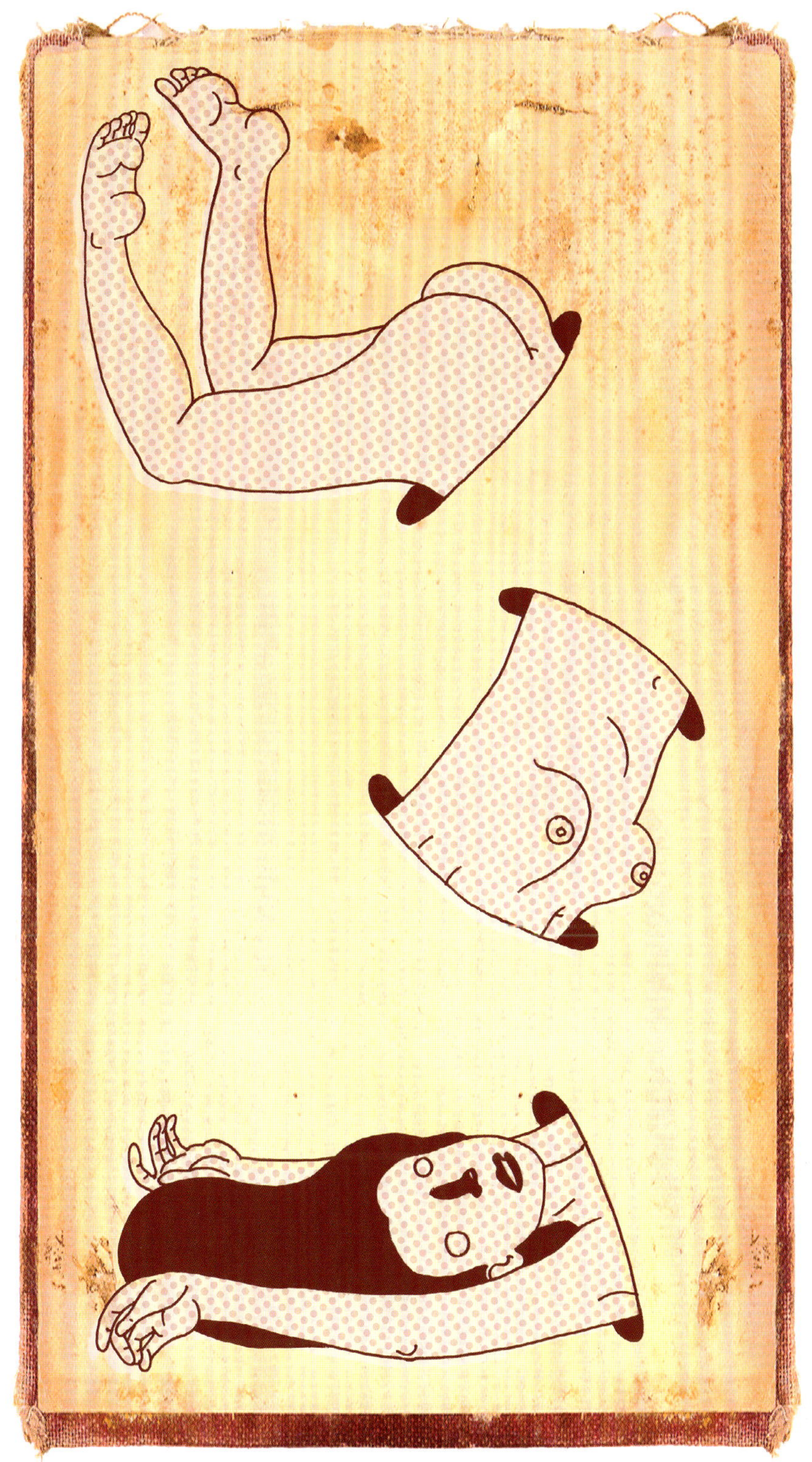

MERIT Elyse Salazar

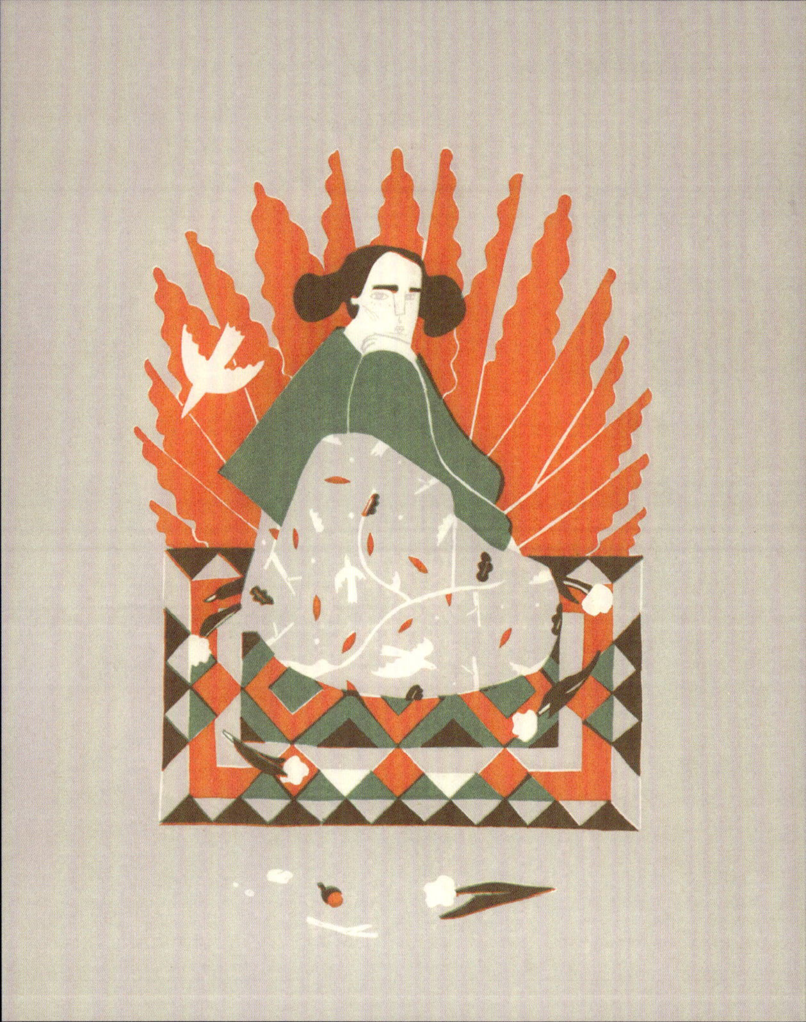

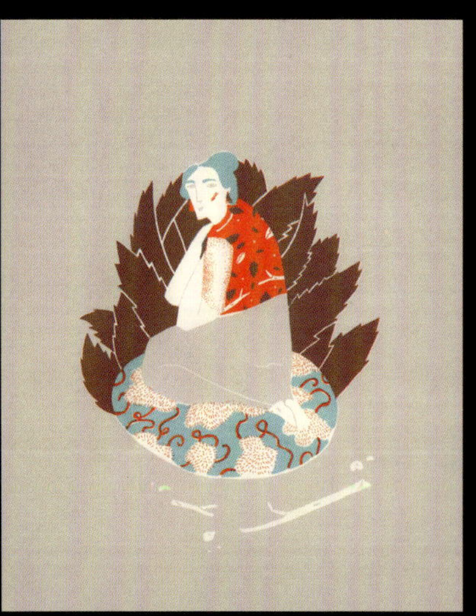
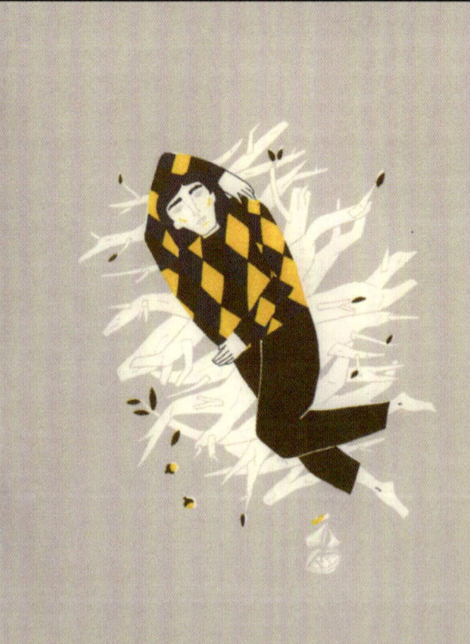

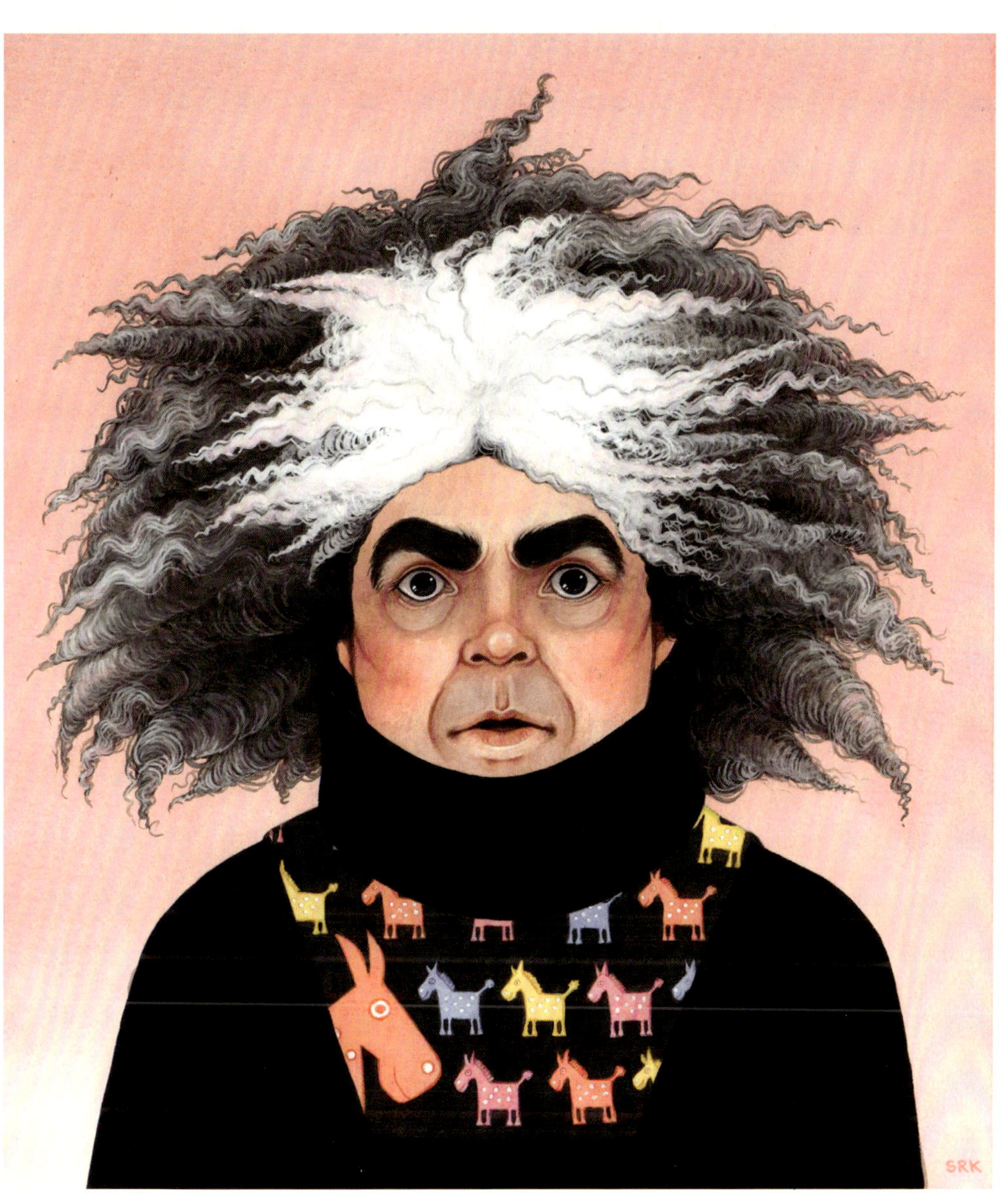



MERIT *Shannon Knight*

403

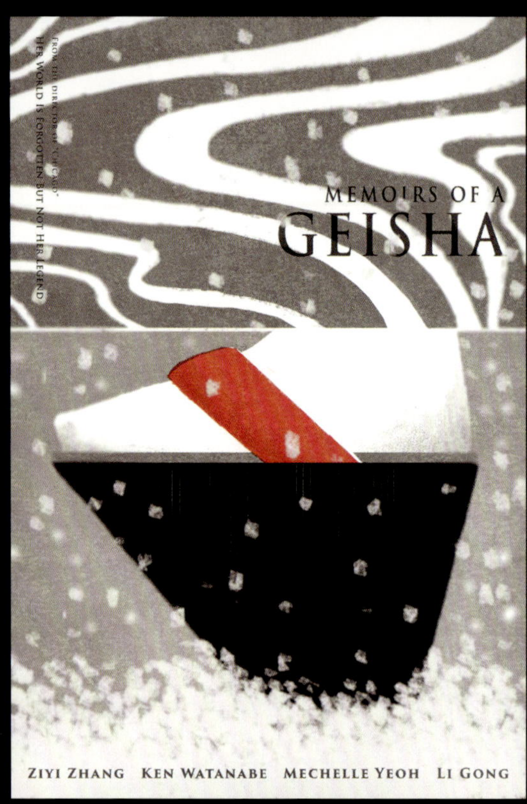


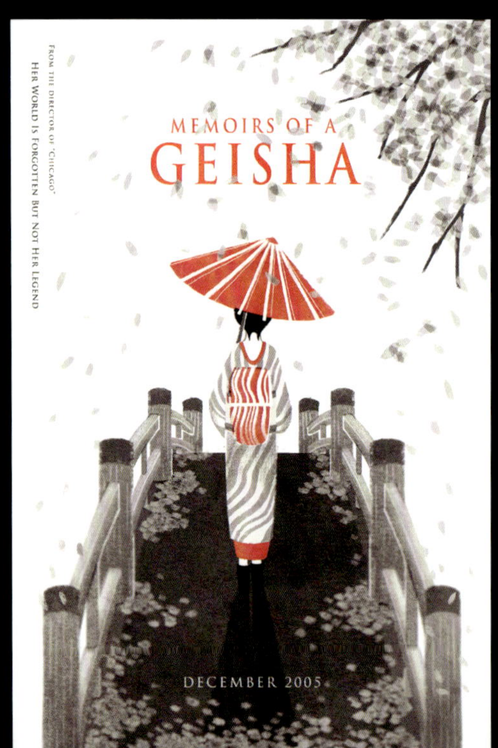


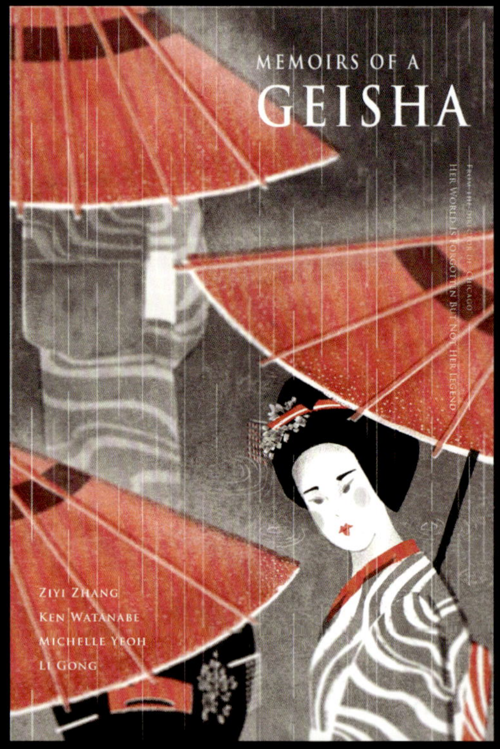


(L) MERIT *Wenjia Tang*    (R) MERIT *Chienya Kao*

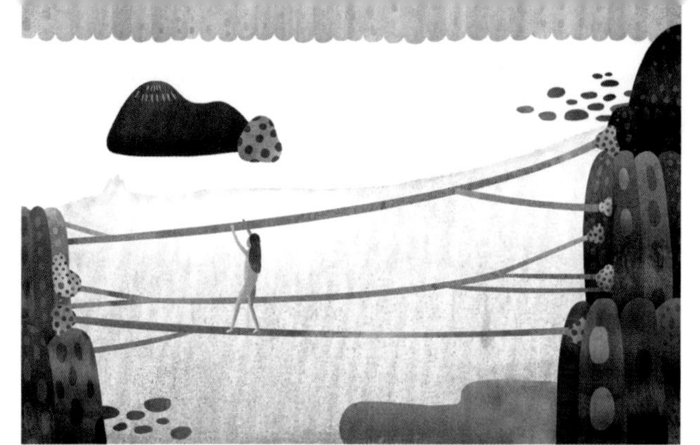

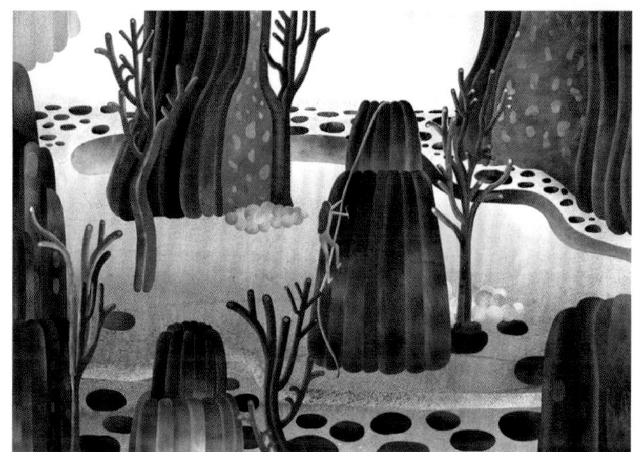

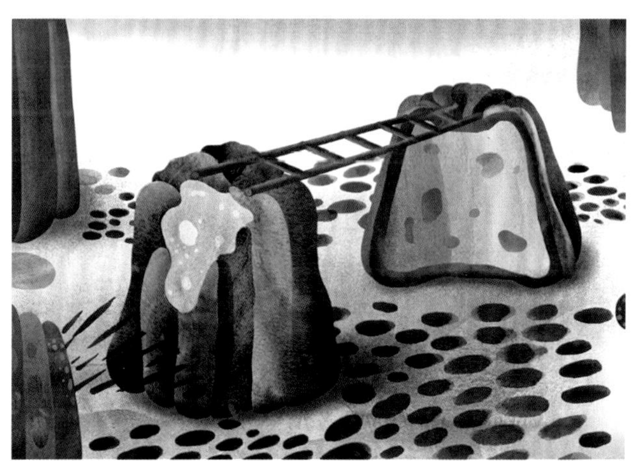

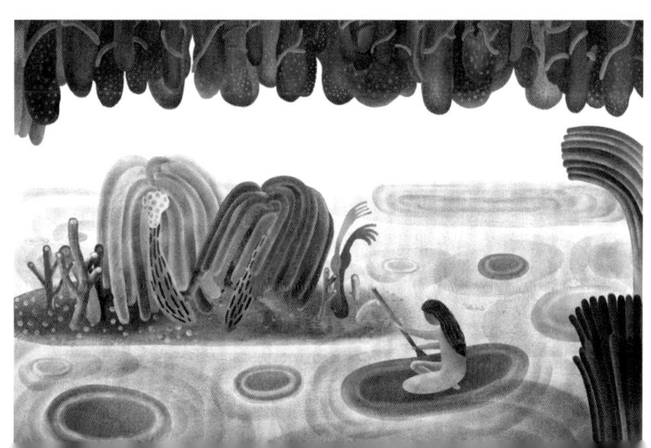

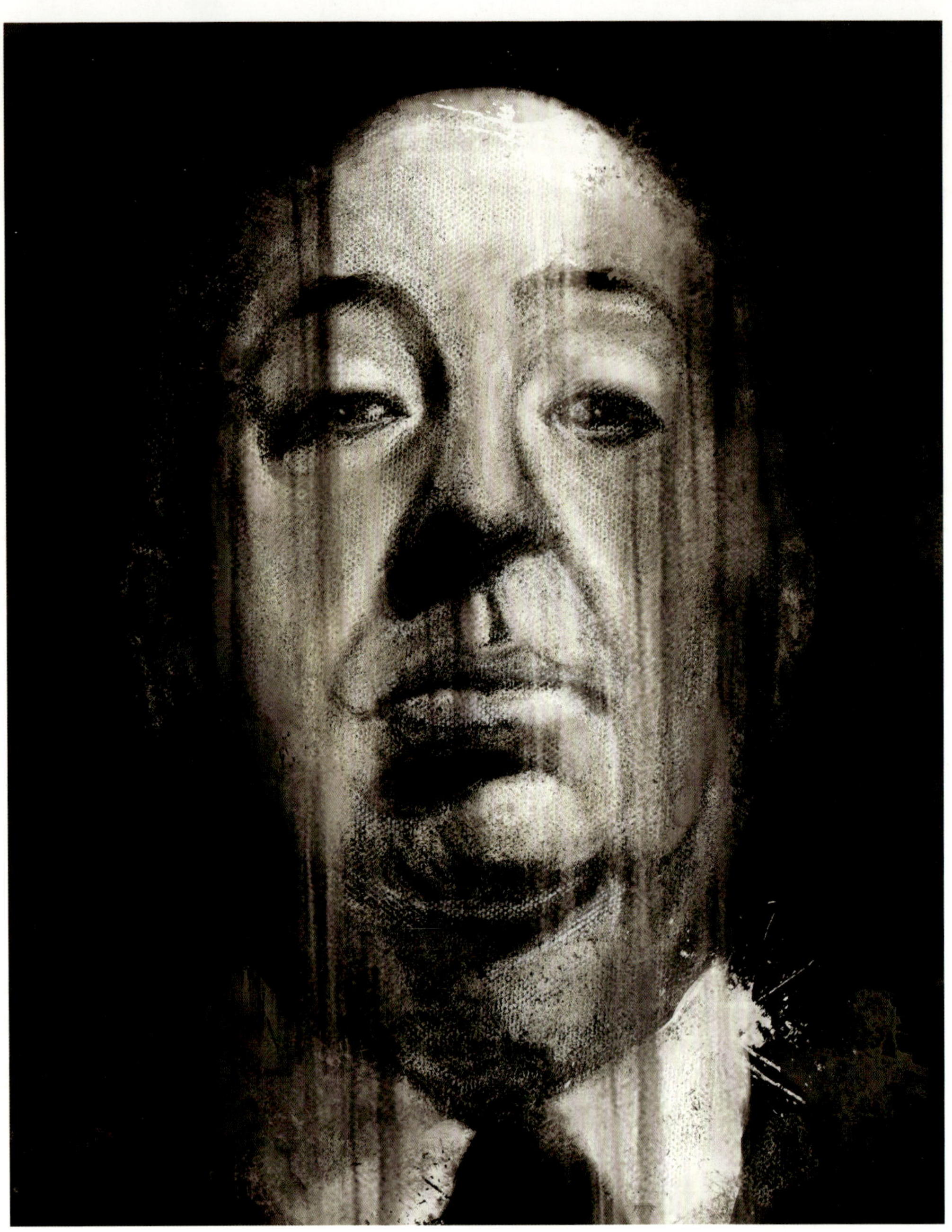



MERIT *Somya Raju*

406

# INDEX

**LIISA AALTIO**
info@liisaaaltio.com
www.liisaaaltio.com
p 214 MERIT
ART DIRECTOR: Liisa Aaltio

**MONIKA AICHELE**
mail@monikaaichele.com
www.monikaaichele.com
p 156 MERIT

**AILADI**
ailadi@me.com
www.ailadi.com
p 114 MERIT

**A.RICHARD ALLEN**
info@arichardallen.com
www.arichardallen.com
p 44 MERIT
ART DIRECTOR: Sheri Gee
PUBLISHER: The Folio Society

**OFRA AMIT**
ofraamit1@gmail.com
www.ofra-amit.com
p 63 GOLD
CLIENT: Israel Museum, Jerusalem

**VICTORIA ANTOLINI**
victoria@semykina.com
www.behance.net/viksa
p 250 MERIT

**MARION ARBONA**
marion.arbona@gmail.com
www.marionarbona.com
p 220 BRONZE
PUBLISHER: Isatis
p 229 MERIT
PUBLISHER: Mazurka
p 271 MERIT

**BJOERN ARTHURS**
ba@bjoernarthurs.com
www.brightlightsoldbones.com
p 55 MERIT
WRITER: Zachary Abram

**MARIA CECILIA AZZALI**
mariacecilia.azzali@gmail.com
www.mariaceciliaazzali.com
p 256 MERIT

**IDO BACK**
newstupi@gmail.com
www.behance.net/idoback
INSTITUTION: Bezalel Academy of Arts
and Design, Jerusalem
p 323 MERIT
INSTRUCTOR: Noam Shechter
ANIMATORS: Ido Back, Tal Klein

**SCOTT BAKAL**
info@scottbakal.com
www.scottbakal.com
p 37 MERIT
ART DIRECTOR: Irene Gallo
PUBLISHER: Tor Books/Tor.com
p 48 DISTINGUISHED MERIT
ART DIRECTOR: Irene Gallo
PUBLISHER: Tor Books/Tor.com
p 119 MERIT
CLIENT: Playboy Magazine
p 150 MERIT

**ANNA AND ELENA BALBUSSO**
apiue@balbusso.com
www.balbusso.com
p 34 MERIT
ART DIRECTOR: Sheri Gee
PUBLISHER: The Folio Society
p 81 MERIT
ART DIRECTOR: Maxine Davidowitz
CLIENT: Scrubs Magazine
p 193 MERIT
ART DIRECTORS: Anna and Elena
Balbusso

**GREGORY BALDWIN**
gregory@121illustration.com
www.121design.com.au
p 210 MERIT

**NATALYA BALNOVA**
natabalnova@gmail.com
www.natalyabalnova.com
p 178 BRONZE

**KAROL BANACH**
hello@karolbanach.com
www.karolbanach.com
INSTITUTION: Nicolaus Copernicus
University
p 316 GOLD
INSTRUCTOR: Edward Saliński

**KAREN BARBOUR**
karenbarbour@gmail.com
www.karenbarbour.com
p 94 MERIT
ART DIRECTOR: Catherine Gilmore-
Barnes
CLIENT: The New York Times
p 210 MERIT

**JONATHAN BARTLETT**
jb@bartlettstudio.com
www.bartlettstudio.com
p 14 MERIT
DESIGN DIRECTOR: Amir Mohammady
CLIENT: Ralph Lauren

**MELINDA BECK**
studio@melindabeck.com
www.melindabeck.com
p 59 MERIT
ART DIRECTOR: Melinda Beck
CLIENT: Coney Island Brighton Beach
Open Water Swimmers
p 70 MERIT
ART DIRECTOR: Laura Williams
p 84 MERIT
ART DIRECTOR: Frank Tagariello
CLIENT: Scholastic Administrator
Magazine
p 110 MERIT
ART DIRECTOR: Alyce Jones
CLIENT: Real Simple
p 128 MERIT
ART DIRECTOR: Matt Dorfman
CLIENT: The New York Times

**DAN BEJAR**
dabejar@gmail.com
www.bejarprints.com
p 138 MERIT
DESIGN DIRECTOR: Donald Partyka
ART DIRECTOR: Paula Daneze
CLIENT: Americas Quarterly

**JAN BIELECKI**
hello@janbielecki.com
www.janbielecki.com
p 251 MERIT
DESIGNERS: Isabel Eeles, Tom Howey

**GUY BILLOUT**
guy@guybillout.com
www.guybillout.com
p 61 MERIT
ART DIRECTOR: Marta Ibarrondo
CLIENT: Eastdil
p 186 MERIT
ART DIRECTOR: Guy Billout

**PAUL BLOW**
paul@paulblow.com
www.paulblow.com
p 113 MERIT
ART DIRECTOR: Pamela Fogg
CLIENT: Middlebury Magazine

**JUDGE BOCKMAN**
judgebockman@gmail.com
www.judgebockman.com
INSTITUTION: Missouri State University
p 309 MERIT
INSTRUCTOR: Eric Pervukhin

**ANNALISA BOLLINI**
annalisa_bollini@yahoo.it
www.annalisabollini.altervista.org
p 50 MERIT
DESIGN FIRM: Damir Jellici

CLIENT: Fondazione San Zeno,
Verona, Italy

**SILVIA BONANNI**
silvia@silviabonanni.it
www.silviabonanni.it
p 237 MERIT
PUBLISHER: Il Castoro Editore

**FRANCESCO BONGIORNI**
francesco.bongiorni@outlook.com
www.francescobongiorni.com
p 69 MERIT
ART DIRECTOR: Len Small
p 76 MERIT
DESIGN DIRECTOR: Blake Taylor
CLIENT: Inc Magazine
p 111 MERIT
ART DIRECTOR: Desiree Espada
CLIENT: Southwest Magazine
p 108 MERIT
CLIENT: Runner's World

**JENS BONNKE**
jb@jensbonnke.de
www.jensbonnke.de
p 122 MERIT
ART DIRECTOR: Viola Schmieskors
CLIENT: Cicero Magazine

**CALEF BROWN**
calef@calefbrown.com
www.calefbrown.com
p 151 MERIT
GALLERY: Flowerpepper Gallery

**NIGEL BUCHANAN**
nigel@nigelbuchanan.com
www.nigelbuchanan.com
p 60 MERIT
ART DIRECTOR: Ken Cato
CLIENT: IdeasonDesign
p 78 MERIT
ART DIRECTOR: Robert Preist
DESIGN FIRM: Preist and Grace
CLIENT: 8by8 Magazine
p 125 MERIT
ART DIRECTOR: Robert Preist
DESIGN FIRM: Preist and Grace
CLIENT: 8by8 Magazine

**DANIEL BUENO**
bu_eno@yahoo.com.br
www.buenozine.com.br
p 75 MERIT
DESIGN DIRECTOR: Craig Yoe
ART DIRECTOR: Clizia Gussoni
PUBLISHER: IDW + Yoe Comics
p 162 MERIT
DESIGN DIRECTOR: Larissa Ribeiro
CLIENT: Ilustração Voadora
p 248 BRONZE
DESIGN DIRECTOR: Guilherme Vieira

**JILL CALDER**
jill@jillcalder.com
www.jillcalder.com
p 225 MERIT
ART DIRECTOR: James Hutcheson
PUBLISHER: Birlinn Ltd

**MARIA CARLUCCIO**
mariacarluccio@verizon.net
www.mariacarluccio.com
p 281 MERIT
ART DIRECTOR: Karen Kohn
CLIENT: Cricket Magazine
p 285 MERIT

**ANDRÉ CARRILHO**
mail@andrecarrilho.com
www.andrecarrilho.com
p 56 BRONZE
ART DIRECTOR: Paulo Freitas
CLIENT: Diario de Noticias
p 96 MERIT
DESIGN DIRECTOR: Chris Dixon
CLIENT: Vanity Fair

**MATT CHASE**
matt@chasematt.com
www.chasematt.com

*p* 100  MERIT
ART DIRECTOR: Luke Shuman
CLIENT: The New York Times

**DREAM CHEN**
dreamchen.work@gmail.com
www.dreamchen.org
INSTITUTION: Minneapolis College
of Art & Design
*p* 343  MERIT
INSTRUCTOR: James O'Brian

**ESZTER CHEN**
eszterchen1989@gmail.com
www.eszterchen.com
*p* 176  MERIT

**HONG CHEN**
ivanhongchen@hotmail.com
www.hongillu.com
INSTITUTION: OCAD University
*p* 319  SILVER
*p* 321  MERIT
*p* 340  MERIT

**LILY LIYI CHEN**
lilyliyillus@gmail.com
www.lilyliyi.com
INSTITUTION: Art Center College
of Design
*p* 356  INSTRUCTORS: Paul Rogers, Brian Rea

**PEI-HSIU CHEN**
queereelegg@gmail.com
www.behance.net/peihsiu
*p* 288  MERIT

**RUNLIN CHEN**
opaltiad@gmail.com
chenrunlin.wordpress.com
INSTITUTION: Cambridge School of Art
*p* 390  MERIT

**NOMI CHI**
nomi@nomi-chi.com
www.nomi-chi.com
INSTITUTION: Emily Carr University Art
and Design
*p* 338  MERIT
INSTRUCTOR: Nick Conbere

**JULIEN CHUNG**
julienchung@hotmail.com
www.julienchung.com
*p* 240  MERIT
DESIGN DIRECTOR: Caroline Merola
DESIGNER: Mathilde Hébert
PUBLISHER: Bayard Canada
*p* 259  MERIT
ART DIRECTOR: Caroline Merola
DESIGNER: Mathilde Hébert
PUBLISHER: Bayard Canada
*p* 270  MERIT
ART DIRECTOR: Julien Chung

**PAIGE CLARK**
www.paigeclark.ca
paigeclarkillustration@gmail.com
INSTITUTION: OCAD University
*p* 338  MERIT
INSTRUCTOR: Paul Dallas

**ELLA COHEN**
Ellakookoo@gmail.com
www.ellakookoo.com
*p* 21  MERIT
ART DIRECTOR: Kevin Clarke
DESIGN FIRM: Adam and Eve DDB
AD AGENCY: Folio
CLIENT: Volkswagen UK
*p* 62  MERIT
DESIGN DIRECTOR: Alex Anderson
CLIENT: Airbnb

**ALAIN CORBEL**
ilhasnomato@gmail.com
www.alaincorbel-cos.blogspot.fr
*p* 129  MERIT
DESIGN DIRECTOR: Vera Tavares
ART DIRECTOR: Carlos Vaz Marques

DESIGNER: Vera Tavares
CLIENT: Tinta da China Publishing

**SARA CORBETT**
hi@saracorbett.com
www.saracorbett.com
*p* 187  MERIT
*p* 267  MERIT
*p* 267  MERIT

**CRISTIANA COUCEIRO**
7dias7@gmail.com
www.cristianacouceiro.com
*p* 133  MERIT
ART DIRECTOR: Nicholas Blechman
CLIENT: The New York Times

**PEDRO COVO**
illustration@colagene.com
www.colagene.com/en/illustration/
pedro-covo
*p* 198  MERIT
ART DIRECTOR: Pedro Covo

**ALLEN CRAWFORD**
allen@allencrawford.net
www.allencrawfordillustration.com
*p* 38  BEST OF SHOW
ART DIRECTOR: Diane Chonette
DESIGNER: Allen Crawford
DESIGN FIRM: Plankton Art Co.
PUBLISHER: Tin House

**BAILY CRAWFORD**
blycrawford@gmail.com
www.bailycrawford.com
INSTITUTION: Pratt Institute
*p* 308  MERIT
INSTRUCTOR: Chang Park

**NINA CUNEO**
ninacuneo@gmail.com
www.ninacuneo.com
*p* 274  MERIT

**SARA CUNHA**
sara@saracunha.net
www.saracunha.net
*p* 261  MERIT
ART DIRECTOR: Marianne Vilcoq
CLIENT: Tralalire Magazine
PUBLISHER: Bayard Jeunesse

**MIKE CURATO**
mikecurato@gmail.com
www.mikecurato.com
*p* 245  MERIT
ART DIRECTOR: April Ward
PUBLISHER: Macmillan
IMPRINT: Henry Holt Books for Young
Readers

**GIOVANNI DA RE**
info@giovannidare.com
www.giovannidare.com
*p* 291  MERIT
ART DIRECTOR: Marco Mercatali
PUBLISHER: Eli Publisher

**BRIAN DANAHER**
bdanaher25@comcast.net
www.briandanaher.com
*p* 165  MERIT
ART DIRECTOR: Brian Danaher
CLIENT: Courtney Barnett

**STEVEN DARDEN**
xstevendarden@gmail.com
www.stevendarden.com
*p* 196  MERIT

**JEFFREY DECOSTER**
misterjeff@charter.net
www.jeffreydecoster.com
*p* 131  MERIT
DESIGN DIRECTOR: Robert Priest
DESIGN FIRM: Priest and Grace
CLIENT: 8by8 Magazine

**MAI LY DEGNAN**
mailyillustration@gmail.com
www.mailydegnan.com
INSTITUTION: Maryland Institute
College of Art

*p* 194  MERIT
*p* 200  MERIT
*p* 265  MERIT
*p* 323  MERIT
INSTRUCTORS: Jaime Zollars, Sarah
McNeil
ANIMATOR: Mai Ly Degnan

**FEDERICA DEL PROPOSTO**
federica.delproposto@gmail.com
www.federicadelproposto.com
*p* 22  MERIT
ART DIRECTOR: Michel Lagarde
DESIGNER: Camille Pichon
CLIENT: Association of the Shops of
Paris's 10th District

**DEVOURS BACON**
vogueskyskull@gmail.com
www.behance.net/robomb-devours
INSTITUTION: Asia University
*p* 297  MERIT

**PETER DIAMOND**
peter@peterdiamond.ca
peter@peterdiamond.ca
*p* 39  BRONZE
ART DIRECTOR: Chris Stevens
PUBLISHER: Locust Moon
*p* 137  MERIT
ART DIRECTOR: Dirk Merbach
DESIGNER: Raphael Moser
CLIENT: Falter

**YUKAI DU**
yukaidu.doralice@gmail.com
yukaidu.com
INSTITUTION: Central Saint Martins
College of Art and Design
*p* 382  BEST OF SHOW
ANIMATOR: Yukai Du

**ROB DUNLAVEY**
rob@robd.com
www.robd.com
*p* 199  MERIT
*p* 231  MERIT
DESIGNER: Deb Sfetsios-Conover
PUBLISHER: Simon & Schuster
IMPRINT: Atheneum Books for Young
Readers

**JEAN-MANUEL DUVIVIER**
jmduvivier@skynet.be
www.jmduvivier.com
*p* 93  MERIT
ART DIRECTOR: Elisabeth Arata
CLIENT: The Wall Street Journal Europe
*p* 94  MERIT
ART DIRECTOR: Elisabeth Arata
CLIENT: The Wall Street Journal Europe
*p* 140  MERIT
ART DIRECTOR: Elisabeth Arata
CLIENT: The Wall Street Journal Europe

**JOHN S. DYKES**
john@jsdykes.com
www.jsdykes.com
*p* 52  MERIT
ART DIRECTOR: Jim Burke
CLIENT: The Illustration Department
*p* 112  MERIT
ART DIRECTOR: Maria Jackson
CLIENT: American University

**TOM ENGLER**
tom.engler1@gmail.com
www.flickr.com/tomengler
INSTITUTION: Bezalel Academy of Arts
and Design, Jerusalem
*p* 326  MERIT
INSTRUCTOR: Merav Salomon
*p* 373  MERIT
INSTRUCTOR: David Polonsky
*p* 384  MERIT
INSTRUCTOR: Eric Lerner

**EVAH FAN**
evah.fan@gmail.com
www.evahfan.com

*p* 157  MERIT
ART DIRECTOR: Evah Fan

**LISK FENG**
liskfeng@gmail.com
www.liskfeng.com
*p* 206  MERIT

**JOSHUA FETZER**
jfetzer.illustration@gmail.com
www.joshuafetzer.com
INSTITUTION: Maryland Institute
College of Art
*p* 305  MERIT
INSTRUCTOR: Rebecca Bradley

**SIVAN FITERMAN**
sivan.fiterman@gmail.com
www.sweetpotatocat.tumblr.com
INSTITUTION: Bezalel Academy of Arts
and Design, Jerusalem
*p* 322  MERIT
INSTRUCTOR: Orit Bergman

**BARRY FITZGERALD**
bfitz@ku.edu
www.barryfitzgeraldillustration.com
*p* 23  MERIT
ART DIRECTOR: Brad Allen
CLIENT: Lawrence Public Library
*p* 272  MERIT

**BRIAN FITZGERALD**
brian@brianfitzer.ie
www.brianfitzer.eu
*p* 238  MERIT
PUBLISHER: Blue Apple Books

**DILEYDI FLOREZ**
dileydiflorez@gmail.com
www.dileydiflorez.com
INSTITUTION: Ar.Co, Centro de Arte e
Comunicação
*p* 296  MERIT
INSTRUCTORS: Pedro Brito, Pedro
Moura

**CRISTIAN FOWLIE**
hello@cristianfowlie.com
www.cristianfowlie.com
INSTITUTION: The IDEA School of
Design, Capilano University
*p* 372  MERIT
INSTRUCTOR: Si Huyhn

**ANTHONY FREDA**
anthony@anthonyfreda.com
www.anthonyfreda.com
*p* 167  MERIT
DESIGN FIRM: HivelyDesigns
CLIENT: IH8War.com

**JUSTIN GABBARD**
jg@justingabbard.com
www.justingabbard.com
*p* 76  MERIT
ART DIRECTOR: Raffaella Bosurgi
CLIENT: The Lancet Journal
*p* 102  MERIT
ART DIRECTOR: Lisa Modica
CLIENT: The Scientist

**PAUL GARLAND**
paul@paul-garland.com
www.paul-garland.com
*p* 73  MERIT
ART DIRECTOR: Carrie Bremner
DESIGN FIRM: Redactive Publishing
Ltd
IMPRINT: Bulletin

**BEPPE GIACOBBE**
bgiacobbe@me.com
www.beppegiacobbe.com
*p* 123  MERIT
CLIENT: La Lettura, Corriere della Sera
*p* 134  MERIT

**CARLO GIAMBARRESI**
drawnus@gmail.com
www.carlogiambarresi.com
*p* 184  MERIT

**MICHAEL GLENWOOD GIBBS**
michael@mglenwood.com
www.mglenwood.com
*p* 205  MERIT
*p* 216  MERIT

**IGOR GNEDO**
igor@igorgnedo.com
www.igorgnedo.com
*p* 164  MERIT

**JOANNA GNIADY**
jo@joannagniady.com
www.joannagniady.com
*p* 166  MERIT
CLIENT: Shopiq

**AAD GOUDAPPEL**
aad@aadgoudappel.com
www.aadgoudappel.com
*p* 103  MERIT
CLIENT: Strategy & Business

**DANIEL GRAY**
dan@danielhgray.com
www.danielhgray.com
*p* 188  MERIT

**SARAH GREEN**
sarahgreenillustration@gmail.com
www.sarahgreenillustration.com
INSTITUTION: Rhode Island School of
Design
*p* 349  MERIT
INSTRUCTOR: Fred Lynch

**PETER GREENWOOD**
peter@brighton.co.uk
www.peter-mac.com
*p* 104  MERIT
DESIGN DIRECTOR: Tim Wan
DESIGN FIRM: Winkreative
CLIENT: Porter Airlines

**HALF DUTCH**
artist@halfdutchstudio.com
www.halfdutchstudio.com
*p* 192  MERIT

**GARRETT HAMON**
ghamon@outlook.com
www.ghamon.weebly.com
INSTITUTION: Brigham Young
University
*p* 301  MERIT
INSTRUCTOR: Boston Madsen

**SADIE SEUNGJIN HAN**
sadiehan.sj@gmail.com
www.sadiehan.com
INSTITUTION: Art Center College of
Design
*p* 315  MERIT
INSTRUCTOR: Steve Turk

**RUMI HARA**
contact@rumihara.com
www.rumihara.com
*p* 212  MERIT

**TAKAHISA HASHIMOTO**
contact@takahisahashimoto.com
www.takahisahashimoto.com
*p* 58  MERIT
ART DIRECTOR: Takahisa Hashimoto
DESIGN FIRM: Onde

**OREN HASKINS**
orenhaskins@gmail.com
www.oren.net
*p* 179  MERIT

**HEATHER HECKEL**
heather.heckel@gmail.com
www.heatherheckel.com
*p* 92  MERIT

**REBECCA HENDIN**
rebeccahendin@yahoo.com
www.rebeccahendin.com
*p* 54  MERIT
DESIGN DIRECTOR: John Glynn
PUBLISHER: Universal Uclick
IMPRINT: GoComics

**LARS HENKEL**
lars@reflektorium.de
www.larshenkel.com
*p* 35  MERIT
ART DIRECTOR: Igor Goldkind
DESIGNER: Rian Hughes
PUBLISHER: Chameleon Publishing

**JODY HEWGILL**
jody@jodyhewgill.com
www.jodyhewgill.com
*p* 89  DISTINGUISHED MERIT
DESIGN DIRECTOR: Joseph Hutchinson
ART DIRECTOR: Matthew Cooley
CLIENT: Rolling Stone

**KATE HINDLEY**
hindley.kate@googlemail.com
www.katehindley.com
*p* 239  SILVER
DESIGNER: Audrey Keri-Nagy
PUBLISHER: Walker Books UK

**JAKOB HINRICHS**
mail@jakobhinrichs.com
www.jakobhinrichs.com
*p* 31  MERIT
DESIGN DIRECTOR: Jan Köpper
ART DIRECTORS: Jan Köpper, Jakob
Hinrichs
CLIENT: Staatliche Schlösser, Burgen
und Gärten Sachsen gemeinnützige
GmbH
ANIMATORS: Jan Köpper, Nanna
De Jong
*p* 87  MERIT
DESIGN DIRECTOR: Andreas Wellnitz
ART DIRECTOR: Frauke Schnoor
CLIENT: Das Magazin des
Tagesanzeiger, CH
*p* 95  MERIT
ART DIRECTOR: Anne Mayeras
CLIENT: L' Express, Paris

**JAMIE HOGAN**
jamiehogan58@gmail.com
www.jamiehogan.com
*p* 227  MERIT
ART DIRECTOR: Whitney Leader-Picone
PUBLISHER: Charlesbridge

**DAVID HOHN**
david@davidhohn.com
www.davidhohn.com
*p* 264  MERIT
ART DIRECTOR: David Hohn

**PAUL HOPPE**
info@paulhoppe.com
www.paulhoppe.com
*p* 74  DISTINGUISHED MERIT
RISOGRAPH PRINTER: Kris Mukai

**YOHEY HORISHITA**
yohey@yoheyhorishita.com
www.yoheyhorishita.com
INSTITUTION: Savannah College of
Art & Design, Atlanta
*p* 71  MERIT
DESIGN DIRECTOR: Kelvin Lee
ART DIRECTOR: Thomas Burns
PUBLISHER: Oz Magazine
*p* 341  BRONZE
INSTRUCTOR: Thomas Burns
*p* 396  MERIT
INSTRUCTOR: Thomas Burns

**HUANG LING HSING**
hunter741015@gmail.com
www.behance.net/danmian
*p* 268  MERIT

**JASU HU**
jasuhuart@gmail.com
www.jasuhuart.com
INSTITUTION: Maryland Institute
College of Art
*p* 331  MERIT
INSTRUCTOR: Whitney Sherman

**ROD HUNT**
rod@rodhunt.com
www.rodhunt.com
*p 24*   MERIT
DESIGN DIRECTOR: Nikolay Fabrika
ART DIRECTOR: Nikolay Pere
AD AGENCY: Instinct BBDO
CLIENT: IKEA
*p 158*   MERIT
ART DIRECTOR: Camilla Parsons
DESIGN FIRM: Outline Editions
CLIENT: Transport for London

**IC4DESIGN**
info@ic4design.com
www.ic4design.com
*p 246*   MERIT
DESIGNER: IC4Design
PUBLISHER: Nagaoka Publishing

**STACY INNERST**
info@stacyinnerst.com
www.stacyinnerst.com
*p 235*   MERIT
ART DIRECTOR: Barbara Grzeslo
PUBLISHER: Boyd Mills Press
IMPRINT: Calkins Creek

**ANDREA INNOCENT**
innocentgirl@otoshimono.org
www.otoshimono.org
*p 283*   MERIT
ART DIRECTOR: Andrea Innocent

**JULIA IREDALE**
juliairedale@gmail.com
www.juliairedale.com
INSTITUTION: Emily Carr University Art
and Design
*p 383*   MERIT
INSTRUCTOR: Nick Conbere

**JORDIN ISIP**
jordin@jordinisip.com
www.jordinisip.com
*p 113*   MERIT
DESIGN DIRECTOR: Patrick Flynn
CLIENT: The Baffler

**NARGES JAFARI**
nargesjfr@gmail.com
www.nargesart.com
INSTITUTION: Savannah College of Art
and Design
*p 337*   MERIT
INSTRUCTOR: Benjamin Reid Phillips

**ANJA JAVELONA**
anja.javelona@gmail.com
www.anja-javelona.com
INSTITUTION: Sheridan College
*p 318*   MERIT
INSTRUCTOR: Michael Byers
*p 379*   MERIT
INSTRUCTOR: Marco Cibola

**TOM JELLETT**
tom@tomjellett.com
www.tomjellett.com
*p 224*   MERIT
DESIGNER: Megan Piggott
PUBLISHER: Allen & Unwin

**LYNDEN JOUDREY**
lyndenjoudrey@gmail.com
www.lyndenjoudrey.com
INSTITUTION: OCAD University
*p 339*   MERIT
INSTRUCTOR: Paul Dallas
*p 387*   MERIT
INSTRUCTOR: Paul Dallas

**JOHN JOVEN**
johnjoven@gmail.com
www.johnjoven.com
*p 293*   MERIT

**EDA KABAN**
edakaban@gmail.com
www.edakabanstudio.com
*p 29*   MERIT
ART DIRECTOR: Sebastian Kuhs

CLIENT: Lufthansa Airlines
*p 218*   MERIT
ART DIRECTOR: Maria Ines Mortes
PUBLISHER: 826 Valencia

**KATJA KAMM**
mail@katjakamm.de
www.katjakamm.de
*p 230*   MERIT
DESIGNER: Katja Kamm
PUBLISHER: Carlsen Verlag

**CHIENYA KAO**
chien-ya.kao@network.rca.ac.uk
www.cargocollective.com/chienya
INSTITUTION: Royal College of Art
*p 405*   MERIT
INSTRUCTORS: Peter Blegvad, Debbie
Cook

**CASSIE HART KELLY**
hartxart@gmail.com
www.cassiehart.com
*p 40*   MERIT

**ANGELA KEOGHAN**
angela@thepicturegarden.co.nz
www.thepicturegarden.co.nz
*p 286*   MERIT
DESIGN DIRECTORS: Astrid van der
Hulst, Irene Smit
ART DIRECTOR: Jocelyn De Kwant
CLIENT: Flow Weekly
*p 287*   MERIT
DESIGNER: Angela Keoghan
CLIENT: Jeremy Redmore

**GRACE HEEJUNG KIM**
heejung.gracekim@gmail.com
www.behance.net/graceheejungkim
INSTITUTION: Pratt Institute
*p 312*   MERIT
INSTRUCTOR: Jon Han
*p 368*   MERIT
INSTRUCTOR: Chang Park

**JAIME JIMYUNG KIM**
jaimeillustration@gmail.com
www.jaimekim.com
*p 266*   MERIT

**JEAN JI IN KIM**
jeankim0805@gmail.com
www.jeankim.me
*p 254*   MERIT

**MIN JEONG KIM**
mkim25@risd.edu
INSTITUTION: Rhode Island School
of Design
*p 354*   MERIT

**LUNA KIRSCHE**
lunakirsche@gmail.com
www.lunakirsche.com
*p 203*   MERIT

**TAL KLEIN**
franztal9@gmail.com
www.behance.net/4eyespretty
INSTITUTION: Bezalel Academy of
Arts and Design, Jerusalem
*p 323*   MERIT
INSTRUCTOR: Noam Shechter
ANIMATORS: Ido Back, Tal Klein

**MADELINE KLOEPPER**
madelinekloepper@gmail.com
www.madelinekloepper.com
INSTITUTION: Emily Carr
University Art & Design
*p 361*   MERIT
INSTRUCTOR: Nick Conbere
*p 388*   MERIT
*p 389*   MERIT
*p 399*   MERIT
INSTRUCTOR: Nick Conbere

**SHANNON KNIGHT**
info@shannonrknight.com
www.shannonrknight.com
INSTITUTION: Massachusetts College of
Art and Design

*p 403*   MERIT
INSTRUCTOR: Scott Bakal

**MIRA KO**
mira@mira-ko.com
www.mira-ko.com
INSTITUTION: Virginia Commonwealth
University, School of the Arts
*p 400*   MERIT
INSTRUCTOR: Sterling Hundley

**SHAHAR KOBER**
shaharkober@gmail.com
www.skober.com
*p 232*   MERIT
PUBLISHER: Matar Publishing House

**ALICE KOLB**
post@alicekolb.ch
www.alicekolb.ch
*p 26*   MERIT
DESIGN FIRM: Velvet Creative Office
CLIENT: Schauspielhaus Zürich

**JON KRAUSE**
jk@jonkrause.com
www.jonkrause.com
*p 116*   MERIT
CLIENT: NYU Physician
*p 142*   MERIT
ART DIRECTOR: Darrick Rainey
CLIENT: LA Weekly

**LOK KUANG**
kuangjiale@gmail.com
studentpages.scad.edu/~jkuang20
INSTITUTION: Savannah College of
Art & Design
*p 335*   MERIT
INSTRUCTOR: Julie Lieberman

**ANITA KUNZ**
akunz@anitakunz.com
www.anitakunzart.com
*p 79*   MERIT
ART DIRECTOR: Françoise Mouly
CLIENT: The New Yorker
*p 83*   MERIT
DESIGN DIRECTOR: Joe Hutchinson
CLIENT: Rolling Stone
*p 148*   MERIT
GALLERY: CFA gallery

**YENTING KUO**
skuoyenting@gmail.com
www.facebook.com/buddymake
*p 45*   MERIT
ART DIRECTORS: Yenting Kuo,
Yufeng Kuo
DESIGN FIRM: Buddymake Studio
PUBLISHER: Suncolor Publishing
Company

**YUFENG KUO**
skuoyenting@gmail.com
www.facebook.com/buddymake
*p 45*   MERIT
ART DIRECTORS: Yenting Kuo,
Yufeng Kuo
DESIGN FIRM: Buddymake Studio
PUBLISHER: Suncolor Publishing
Company

**MARIE LAFRANCE**
marie.lafrance@videotron.ca
marielafrance.carbonmade.com
*p 181*   MERIT

**MARIANNE LARVOL**
mamzelmarianne@yahoo.fr
www.mariannelarvol.sitew.fr
*p 223*   MERIT
PUBLISHER: Locus Solus
IMPRINT: Cloitre

**KRYSTAL LAUK**
krystal.lauk@gmail.com
www.krystallauk.com
INSTITUTION: Academy of Art
University
*p 320*   MERIT
INSTRUCTOR: Craig Nelson

p 363 MERIT
INSTRUCTOR: Craig Nelson
p 379 MERIT
INSTRUCTOR: David Ball

**GEE EUN LEE**
bambox@hanmail.net
www.tumblingfunnyl.com
p 234 MERIT
DESIGN DIRECTOR: Shin Hae Young
ART DIRECTOR: Yoon So Yoeun
PUBLISHER: Woongjin Junior

**HARRIET LEE-MERRION**
harriet@harrietleemerrion.com
www.harrietleemerrion.com
p 130 MERIT
CLIENT: Protein Journal: The Travel Report

**CORNELIA LI**
cornelia.illu@gmail.com
www.corneliali.com
INSTITUTION: OCAD University
p 304 MERIT
INSTRUCTOR: Paul Dallas

**HANNAH LI**
lihanrou@gmail.com
www.behance.net/hannahli
INSTITUTION: Savannah College of Art & Design, Atlanta
p 302 MERIT
INSTRUCTOR: Rick Lovell
p 302 MERIT
INSTRUCTOR: Rick Lovell

**JING LI**
jingli132@gmail.com
jingliwaa.tumblr.com
INSTITUTION: Savannah College of Art & Design, Atlanta
p 303 MERIT
INSTRUCTOR: Mike Lowery
p 358 SILVER
INSTRUCTOR: Rick Lovell

**MENGXIN LI**
xindoubleff@gmail.com
www.behance.net/MengxinLi
INSTITUTION: Savannah College of Art & Design
p 375 MERIT

**ELENA LLOYD**
elenalloyd17@yahoo.com
www.google.com
INSTITUTION: Parsons The New School for Design
p 359 DISTINGUISHED MERIT
INSTRUCTOR: Jordin Isip

**ENZO LO RE**
info@enzolore.net
www.enzolore.net
INSTITUTION: Accademia di Beller Arti di Brera, Milan
p 332 MERIT
INSTRUCTOR: Vinicio Bordin
p 362 MERIT
INSTRUCTOR: Vinicio Bordin

**MIKE LOWERY**
mike@mikelowery.com
www.mikelowery.com
p 115 MERIT

**RONGYUAN MA**
royaluc@gmail.com
www.lucroya.com
p 276 BRONZE

**MARTA MADUREIRA**
martamadureira@gmail.com
www.illustopia.com/portfolios/all-illustrators/marta-madureira
p 222 MERIT
DESIGN DIRECTOR: Pedro Amado
PUBLISHER: APCC, Associação para a Promoção Cultural da Criança
p 233 MERIT
ART DIRECTORS: João Paulo Cotrim, Inês Fonseca Santos

DESIGNER: Marta Madureira
PUBLISHER: Arranha-Céus

**JENS MAGNUSSON**
jens@jensjens.com
www.jensjens.com
p 28 MERIT
ART DIRECTOR: Jens Magnusson
AD AGENCY: Ventiocho Y Medio
CLIENT: The Canary Islands Tourism Board

**MAGOZ**
magoz@magoz.is
www.magoz.is
p 104 MERIT
ART DIRECTOR: Alessandro Zuffi
CLIENT: Causette
p 135 MERIT
CLIENT: Pacific Standard

**KATHLEEN MARCOTTE**
kathleen.t.marcotte@gmail.com
www.kathleenmarcotte.com
p 271 MERIT

**LAUREN MARRIOTT**
lauren.m.marriott@gmail.com
www.cargocollective.com/ralphiillustration
p 228 MERIT
ART DIRECTOR: Lauren Marriott
PUBLISHER: Beatnik Publishing

**SOPHIA MARTINECK**
sophia@martineck.com
www.martineck.com
p 163 MERIT
CLIENT: Alliance Graphique Internationale Congress Sao Paulo 2014
p 292 MERIT
DESIGN DIRECTOR: Regina Grenier
ART DIRECTOR: Emily Potts
DESIGNER: Henning Wagenbreth
PUBLISHER: Rockport Publishers

**CHRISTINA MASTRULL**
clmast0921@gmail.com
www.christinamastrull.com
INSTITUTION: Syracuse University
p 348 MERIT
INSTRUCTOR: John Thompson

**JESSICA MATTHEWS**
jess@jessmatthewsdesign.com
www.jessmatthewsdesign.com
p 226 MERIT
DESIGN DIRECTOR: Louise Coulthard
ART DIRECTOR: Pooja Desai
PUBLISHER: Hinkler
IMPRINT: Bonney Press

**YASMIN MATTICH**
yasmin.mattich@hotmail.com
yasminmattich.wix.com/portfolio
INSTITUTION: Hochschule der Künste Bern
p 402 MERIT
INSTRUCTOR: Patricia Schneider

**VICTORIA MAXFIELD**
maxfieldv@gmail.com
www.victoriamaxfield.com
INSTITUTION: Massachusetts College of Art and Design
p 300 MERIT
INSTRUCTOR: Polly Becker

**BILL MAYER**
bill@thebillmayer.com
www.thebillmayer.com
p 16 MERIT
DESIGN DIRECTOR: Rick Anwyl
ART DIRECTOR: Courtney Garvin
DESIGN FIRM: Son&Sons
CLIENT: Streamline
p 32 MERIT
ART DIRECTOR: Monte Beauchamp
PUBLISHER: Last Gasp/BLAB! World 3
p 33 MERIT
ART DIRECTOR: Monte Beauchamp

PUBLISHER: Last Gasp/BLAB! World 3
p 53 MERIT
ART DIRECTOR: Jim Burke
CLIENT: Frogfolio
p 82 MERIT
ART DIRECTOR: SooJin Buzelli
CLIENT: PlanSponsor
p 109 MERIT
ART DIRECTOR: SooJin Buzelli
CLIENT: PlanSponsor
p 208 MERIT
p 209 MERIT

**CURT MERLO**
art@curtmerlo.com
www.curtmerlo.com
p 191 MERIT

**AARON MESHON**
hello@aaronmeshon.com
www.aaronmeshon.com
p 176 MERIT

**MIGUEL MONTANER**
hello@miguelmontaner.com
www.miguelmontaner.com
p 144 MERIT
ART DIRECTOR: Jo Gulliver
CLIENT: Computer Arts

**MARTA MONTEIRO**
martamonteir@gmail.com
www.martamonteiro.com
p 290 DISTINGUISHED MERIT
PUBLISHER: Editorial Caminho

**JENNIFER E. MORRIS**
jemorris@jemorris.com
www.jemorris.com
p 273 MERIT

**KELLY MURPHY**
kelly@kelmurphy.com
www.kelmurphy.com
p 219 MERIT
ART DIRECTOR: Kristen Nobels
DESIGNER: Rachel Smith
PUBLISHER: Candlewick Press
p 257 DISTINGUISHED MERIT
ART DIRECTOR: Isabel Warren-Lynch
DESIGNER: Katrina Damkoehler
PUBLISHER: Knopf

**IAN MURRAY**
ian@mrmurray.co.uk
www.mrmurray.co.uk
p 51 MERIT
ART DIRECTOR: Helen Mair
CLIENT: The Design Solution, London
p 182 MERIT
ART DIRECTOR: Ian Murray

**MANICA K. MUSIL**
manica@manicamusil.com
www.manicamusil.com
p 249 MERIT
DESIGNER: Manica K. Musil

**IL SUNG NA**
ilsungna@hotmail.com
www.ilsungna.com
INSTITUTION: Maryland Institute College of Art
p 314 MERIT
INSTRUCTOR: Whitney Sherman
p 317 MERIT
INSTRUCTOR: Whitney Sherman

**ROBERT NEUBECKER**
robert@neubecker.com
www.neubecker.com
p 121 MERIT
ART DIRECTOR: Chris Barber
CLIENT: Washington Post Magazine
p 143 MERIT
ART DIRECTOR: Kathryn Finney
CLIENT: Live Happy Magazine
p 97 MERIT
ART DIRECTOR: Manuel Velez
CLIENT: The Wall Street Journal

**BEIBEI NIE**
beibei@beibeinie.com
www.beibeinie.com
p 90  MERIT
CLIENT: Art Bank Magazine

**NOMOCO**
nomoco@kazukonomoto.com
www.kazukonomoto.com
p 202  MERIT

**CAROL NUNG**
csnung@umich.edu
www.carolnung.wix.com/nung
INSTITUTION: University of Michigan
p 392  MERIT
INSTRUCTOR: Mireille Roddier

**CHELSEA O'BYRNE**
chelsea.obyrne@gmail.com
www.chelseaobyrne.com
INSTITUTION: Emily Carr University
Art and Design
p 311  MERIT
p 399  MERIT
INSTRUCTOR: Durwin Talon

**KATE O'HARA**
kateoharaillustration@gmail.com
www.kate-ohara.com
INSTITUTION: The University of
the Arts
p 298  DISTINGUISHED MERIT
INSTRUCTOR: Matt Curtius
p 346  MERIT

**JONGIK PARK**
bellow2498@naver.com
www.grafolio.com/bellow2498
p 36  MERIT

**JOHN PARRA**
john@johnparraart.com
www.johnparraart.com
p 59  MERIT
DESIGN DIRECTOR: Terry Hight
DESIGNER: Kathy King
CLIENT: Hitachi Data Systems
p 242  DISTINGUISHED MERIT
ART DIRECTOR: Amelia Mack
DESIGNER: Eloise Leigh
PUBLISHER: Chronicle Books
p 269  MERIT

**DARON PARTON**
daron@watermarkltd.com
www.watermarkltd.com
p 260  MERIT
DESIGN DIRECTOR: Jeanmarie Morosin
PUBLISHER: Random House Australia

**FILIP PERAIĆ**
filip@peraic.com
www.peraic.com
p 141  MERIT
ART DIRECTOR: Tyler Hoehne
CLIENT: Good Magazine

**VALERIA PETRONE**
valeria@valeriapetrone.com
www.valeriapetrone.com
p 79  MERIT
ART DIRECTOR: Maurizio Varotti
CLIENT: Io Donna Magazine
p 154  MERIT
GALLERY: CR Arte, Palazzo Taverna,
Rome
p 280  MERIT
ART DIRECTOR: Maurizio Varotti
CLIENT: Style Piccoli Magazine

**CHIARA PIERI**
chiara@chiarapieri.com
www.chiarapieri.com
INSTITUTION: Massachusetts College of
Art and Design
p 395  MERIT
INSTRUCTOR: Scott Bakal

**EMMANUEL POLANCO**
illustration@colagene.com
www.colagene.com/en/illustration/
emmanuel-polanco
p 120  MERIT
ART DIRECTOR: Laurent Barbarand
DESIGNER: Emmanuel Polanco
CLIENT: Les Inrocks
p 124  MERIT
ART DIRECTOR: Emmanuel Polanco
CLIENT: Institutional Investors

**GIORDANO POLONI**
giopa80@gmail.com
www.giordanopoloni.com
p 117  MERIT

**EMILIANO PONZI**
info@emilianoponzi.com
www.emilianoponzi.com
p 31  MERIT
DESIGN DIRECTOR: Alberto Baccari
ART DIRECTORS: Alberto Baccari,
Andrea Castelletti
CLIENT: Lavazza Coffee
ANIMATOR: Wearecaptive
p 43  MERIT
ART DIRECTOR: Paul Buckley
p 46  MERIT
ART DIRECTOR: Giacomo Callo
p 49  MERIT
DESIGN DIRECTOR: Charles Hively
DESIGN FIRM: HivelyDesigns
CLIENT: 3x3, The Magazine of
Contemporary Illustration
PUBLISHER: Artisanal Media LLC
p 66  SILVER
PUBLISHER: La Lettre P
p 86  MERIT
ART DIRECTOR: Nicole Dudka
CLIENT: Chicago Magazine
p 86  MERIT
ART DIRECTOR: Cathy Gontarek
CLIENT: Penn Gazette
p 98  MERIT
ART DIRECTOR: Yves Rospert
CLIENT: Le Monde
p 101  MERIT
DESIGN DIRECTOR: Alyce Jones
CLIENT: Real Simple
p 106  MERIT
ART DIRECTOR: Angelo Rinaldi
CLIENT: La Repubblica
p 155  MERIT
GALLERY: Nuages
p 172  MERIT
ART DIRECTORS: Rodd Whitney, Laura
Schairer
CLIENT: Arizona Opera

**MIGUEL PORLAN**
ella@purplerainillustrators.com
www.miguelporlan.com
p 139  MERIT
ART DIRECTOR: David Bamundo
CLIENT: The Wall Street Journal

**ANDY POTTS**
info@andy-potts.com
www.agoodson.com
p 174  MERIT

**CHARLIE POWELL**
cpowell@cruzio.com
www.charliepowell.net
p 177  MERIT

**NATALIE PUDALOV**
p2natalie@yahoo.com
www.nataliepudalov.com
p 253  MERIT

**PETER RA**
plexus6@iinet.net.au
www.true6.com
p 185  MERIT

**NETA RABINOVITCH**
neta.rabinovitch@gmail.com
www.cargocollective.com/neta
p 126  MERIT

**SOMYA RAJU**
somyaraju@gmail.com
www.somyaraju.com

INSTITUTION: Savannah College of
Art & Design
p 406  MERIT
INSTRUCTOR: Julie Lieberman

**FATINHA RAMOS**
hello@fatinha.com
www.fatinha.com
p 153  MERIT

**TOBY RAMPTON**
t_rampton@hotmail.co.uk
www.tobyrampton.com
p 197  MERIT

**KAITLYN RICHARDSON**
msmerkitten@gmail.com
www.kaitlynrichardson.com
INSTITUTION: OCAD University
p 393  MERIT
INSTRUCTOR: Lauchie Reid

**ANGELA RIO**
oh.angelario@gmail.com
www.angelario.com
INSTITUTION: The University of
the Arts
p 380  MERIT

**JELENA RISTIC**
jelena.risticeva@gmail.com
www.jelenaristic.com
p 191  MERIT

**LUISA RIVERA**
luisa@luisarivera.cl
www.luisarivera.cl
INSTITUTION: Minneapolis College
of Art & Design
p 352  MERIT
p 353  MERIT

**PHIL ROBLES**
phil@phillustrate.com
www.phillustrate.com
INSTITUTION: Art Center College
of Design
p 394  MERIT
INSTRUCTOR: Jim Salvati

**KATHRIN RÖDL**
kathrin@katenastudios.com
www.katenastudios.com
INSTITUTION: University of Applied
Sciences, Nuremberg, Germany
p 386  MERIT
INSTRUCTOR: Sybille Schenker

**SARAH ROLOFF**
sarah@ranokel.de
www.ranokel.de
INSTITUTION: HAW Hamburg
p 344  MERIT
INSTRUCTOR: Bernd Mölck-Tassel
LIGHTING: Sin Huh

**JOSH ROSBOROUGH**
joshrosborough@gmail.com
www.joshrosborough.com
INSTITUTION: Sheridan College
p 370  MERIT
INSTRUCTOR: Rick Sealock

**CHRISTINE RÖSCH**
hello@christineroesch.de
www.christineroesch.de
p 221  MERIT
DESIGN DIRECTOR: Doren Ritzau
ART DIRECTOR: Katja Klau
DESIGNER: Direb Ritzau
PUBLISHER: Bauhaus Foundation
Dessau & Seemann

**ISABEL ROXAS**
hello@studioroxas.com
www.studioroxas.com
p 262  MERIT
ART DIRECTOR: Suzanne Beck
CLIENT: Babybug Magazine

**SOL RYU**
sol7ryu@gmail.com
www.solryu.com
INSTITUTION: Pratt Institute

*p 355* MERIT
INSTRUCTOR: Kenichi Hoshine

**ELYSE SALAZAR**
elyse@elysesalazar.com
www.elysesalazar.com
INSTITUTION: Savannah College of
Art & Design, Atlanta
*p 378* SILVER
INSTRUCTOR: Mike Lowery
*p 376* MERIT
INSTRUCTOR: Mike Lowery
*p 401* MERIT
INSTRUCTOR: Rick Lovell

**FRANCESCA SANNA**
hello@francescasanna.com
www.francescasanna.com
INSTITUTION: Lucerne School of
Art and Design
*p 385* MERIT
INSTRUCTOR: Paolo Friz

**AMY SCHIMLER-SAFFORD**
amy@amyschimler.com
www.amyschimler.com
*p 284* MERIT
CLIENT: Oopsy Daisy

**STEPHAN SCHMITZ**
stephan.schmitz@gmx.ch
www.stephan-schmitz.ch
*p 180* MERIT
ART DIRECTOR: Stephan Schmitz

**ELLIE YEONHEE SEO**
yeonhee.illustration@gmail.com
www.instagram.com/yoni.illustration
INSTITUTION: Emily Carr University Art
and Design
*p 313* MERIT
INSTRUCTOR: Calef Brown

**QIAOYI SHI**
shiq0331@gmail.com
www.qy-shi.com
INSTITUTION: Parsons The New School
for Design
*p 333* MERIT
INSTRUCTOR: Paul Marcus
*p 374* MERIT
INSTRUCTOR: Chang Park

**RAY YEUNSU SHIN**
yeunsushin@alum.calarts.edu
www.behance.net/rayyshin
INSTITUTION: California Institute of the
Arts
*p 327* MERIT
INSTRUCTOR: Anther Kiley

**STEVE SIMPSON**
mail@stevesimpson.com
www.stevesimpson.com
*p 18* MERIT
DESIGN DIRECTOR: Cristina Rebolo
DESIGN FIRM: Veintiochoymedio
CLIENT: The Canary Islands Tourism
Board

**LASSE SKARBOVIK**
lasse@lasseskarbovik.com
www.lasseskarbovik
*p 19* DISTINGUISHED MERIT
DESIGN FIRM: HivelyDesigns
CLIENT: IH8War.com
*p 171* GOLD
DESIGN FIRM: HivelyDesigns
CLIENT: IH8War.com

**MARK SMITH**
marksmith7luk@gmail.com
www.marksmithillustration.com
*p 27* MERIT
DESIGN DIRECTOR: Larissa Thut-
Davidson
CLIENT: Savannah Music Festival
*p 42* MERIT
ART DIRECTOR: Sheri Gee
PUBLISHER: The Folio Society
*p 64* DISTINGUISHED MERIT
ART DIRECTOR: Sheri Gee

PUBLISHER: The Folio Society
*p 159* MERIT
CLIENT: Exeter Cavern Club

**OWEN SMITH**
owensmithart@att.net
www.owensmithart.com
*p 149* MERIT
GALLERY: Copro Nason

**CATARINA SOBRAL**
catarina@catarinasobral.com
www.catarinasobral.com
*p 236* BEST OF SHOW
ART DIRECTOR: André Letria
PUBLISHER: Pato Lógico
*p 282* SILVER
ART DIRECTOR: Jorge Silva
DESIGNER: Elisabete Gomes
DESIGN FIRM: Silvadesigners
CLIENT: TAP Air Portugal

**CRISTINA SPANÒ**
cristinaspano@gmail.com
www.cristinaspano.com
*p 146* MERIT
ART DIRECTOR: Alexandra Zsigmond
CLIENT: The New York Times
*p 294* MERIT
PUBLISHER: Eli Readers

**PHIVI SPYRIDONOS**
phivistudio@gmail.com
www.phivistudio.com
INSTITUTION: Savannah College of
Art & Design
*p 397* MERIT
INSTRUCTOR: Mohamed Danawi

**ANTONY SQUIZZATO**
anto@squizzato.com
www.mynameisanto.com
*p 168* MERIT
ART DIRECTOR: Antony Squizzato
CLIENT: Saveurs Jazz Festival, France

**OTTO STEININGER**
ottosteininger@gmail.com
www.ottosteininger.com
*p 72* SILVER
ART DIRECTOR: Françoise Mouly
CLIENT: The New Yorker
*p 170* MERIT
ART DIRECTOR: Otto Steininger
*p 215* MERIT

**KATHERINE STREETER**
ks@katherinestreeter.com
www.katherinestreeter.com
*p 85* MERIT
ART DIRECTOR: SooJin Buzelli
CLIENT: PlanSponsor

**STEPHANIE STRUSE**
sastruse86@gmail.com
www.stephaniestruse.com
*p 190* MERIT

**SUMMERISE**
summerise.com@gmail.com
www.behance.net/summerise
*p 197* MERIT
DESIGN DIRECTOR: Kay Tsai
CLIENT: Athena Chuang

**DOLA SUN**
dola@dolasun.com
www.dolasun.com
INSTITUTION: Savannah College of
Art & Design
*p 351* DISTINGUISHED MERIT
INSTRUCTOR: Ryan Sanchez
*p 381* MERIT
INSTRUCTOR: Mohamed Danawi

**RYO TAKEMASA**
mail@ryotakemasa.com
www.ryotakemasa.com
*p 65* MERIT
*p 67* MERIT

**BINNY TALIB**
binny@binny.com.au
www.binny.com.au
*p 275* MERIT

**WENJIA TANG**
wjtangart@gmail.com
www.wjtang.com
INSTITUTION: Maryland Institute
College of Art
*p 404* MERIT

**BENOIT TARDIF**
illustration@colagene.com
www.colagene.com/en/illustration/
benoit-tardif
*p 20* MERIT
DESIGNER: Marie-Love Petit
CLIENT: Théâtre de la Licorne
*p 47* MERIT
DESIGNER: Benoit Tardif
PUBLISHER: Les Éditions de Ta Mère
*p 118* MERIT
ART DIRECTOR: Benoit Dussault
CLIENT: Le Journal de Montréal
*p 130* MERIT
ART DIRECTOR: Catherine Gilmore-
Barnes
CLIENT: The New York Times
*p 136* MERIT
DESIGNER: Benoit Tardif
CLIENT: Aéroport de Paris Magazine
*p 145* MERIT
ART DIRECTOR: Benoit Dussault
CLIENT: Le Journal de Montréal

**JACOB THOMAS**
jthomasillustration@gmail.com
www.jthomasillustration.com
*p 204* MERIT

**BRENNA THUMMLER**
brennathummler@gmail.com
www.brennathummler.com
INSTITUTION: Ringling College of Art
and Design
*p 310* MERIT
INSTRUCTOR: Tom Casmer
*p 320* MERIT
INSTRUCTOR: Tom Casmer
*p 325* MERIT
INSTRUCTOR: Joe Thiel
*p 398* MERIT
INSTRUCTOR: Don Brandes

**SUE TODD**
sustodd@rogers.com
www.suetodd.com
*p 278* MERIT
ART DIRECTOR: Jeffrey Dinardo
DESIGN FIRM: Dinardo Design
PUBLISHER: Red Chair Press

**YANIV TOREM**
yaniv.torem@gmail.com
www.cargocollective.com/yanivtorem
INSTITUTION: Bezalel Academy of Arts
and Design, Jerusalem
*p 336* MERIT
INSTRUCTOR: Rotraut Susanne Berner
*p 347* MERIT
INSTRUCTOR: David Polonsky

**PAGE TSOU**
info@pagetsou.com
www.pagetsou.com
*p 244* GOLD
ART DIRECTOR: Page Tsou
DESIGNER: Paul Chiu
PUBLISHER: Department of Cultural
Affairs, Taipei

**POL TURGEON**
pol@polturgeon.com
www.polturgeon.com
*p 17* MERIT
DESIGN DIRECTOR: André Cellard
ART DIRECTOR: Pol Turgeon
CLIENT: Domaine des Météores

**JEAN TUTTLE**
jean@jeantuttle.com
www.jeantuttle.com
p 152 MERIT
GALLERY: Venue 222

**KIRSTEN ULVE**
kirsten@kirstenulve.com
www.kirstenulve.com
p 147 MERIT
DESIGN DIRECTOR: Steven Banks
ART DIRECTOR: Carly Hebert
CLIENT: Los Angeles Magazine

**EMMA VAKARELOVA**
besvo6@yahoo.com
www.youbook.fr/emmavakarelova
p 30 GOLD
DESIGN DIRECTOR: Emma Vakarelova
ANIMATORS: Emma Vakarelova,
Amandine Metton
PRODUCTION COMPANY: La Poudrière

**JOÃO VAZ DE CARVALHO**
contacto@jvazcarvalho.com
www.jvazcarvalho.com
p 255 MERIT

**AART-JAN VENEMA**
aartjan@aartjanvenema.com
www.aartjanvenema.com
p 98 MERIT
ART DIRECTOR: Michael Golan
CLIENT: Scrawl Magazine

**KLAAS VERPLANCKE**
mail@klaas.be
www.klaas.be
p 78 MERIT
p 243 MERIT
ART DIRECTOR: Klaas Verplancke
PUBLISHER: Lannoo Publishers
p 263 MERIT
ART DIRECTOR: Klaas Verplancke
PUBLISHER: Lannoo Publishers

**KRISTINE WANG**
ksetfreed@gmail.com
www.kristinewangillustration.com
INSTITUTION: Art Center College
of Design
p 369 MERIT

**LONGHUI (SPENCER) WANG**
spencer.wlh@iclould.com
spencerwang.format.com
INSTITUTION: OCAD University
p 330 SILVER
INSTRUCTOR: Gary Taxali

**MICHAEL WARAKSA**
michaelwaraksa@att.net
www.michaelwaraksa.com
p 211 MERIT

**LAURA WEISZER**
laweiszer@gmail.com
www.lauraweiszer.com
INSTITUTION: The University of
the Arts
p 329 MERIT
INSTRUCTOR: Jon Han
p 371 MERIT

**TAYLOR WESSLING**
taylor@taylorwessling.com
www.taylorwessling.com
p 15 MERIT
DESIGN DIRECTOR: Taylor Wessling
CLIENT: The Barbarians, Zack Hadley

**KAMILA WOJCIECHOWICZ**
kwojciechowicz@yahoo.com
www.szpilka91.wix.com/kama-arts
INSTITUTION: Camberwell College
of Arts
p 398 MERIT

**ARIEL WOLLEK**
arielwollek@gmail.com
www.cargocollective.com/arielwollek
INSTITUTION: Bezalel Academy of Arts
and Design, Jerusalem

p 306 DISTINGUISHED MERIT
INSTRUCTOR: Rutu Modan
p 357 MERIT
INSTRUCTOR: Rutu Modan
p 360 BRONZE
INSTRUCTOR: Henning Wagenbreth

**ALEX WUCHERER**
alex@wucherer.de
www.alexwucherer.com
INSTITUTION: Konstanz University of
Applied Sciences
p 334 MERIT
INSTRUCTOR: Thilo Rothacker

**STEPHANIE WUNDERLICH**
info@wunderlich-illustration.de
www.wunderlich-illustration.de
p 77 MERIT
CLIENT: Boneshaker Magazine

**LINDA YAN**
hilindayan@gmail.com
www.hilindayan.com
INSTITUTION: Sheridan College
p 366 MERIT
p 367 MERIT

**JAMES YANG**
james@jamesyang.com
www.jamesyang.com
p 30 MERIT
DESIGN DIRECTOR: John Ryan
CLIENT: James Yang
PRODUCERS: James Yang, David
Goldman
VOICES: Jason Porter and Jeffrey Rotter
ANIMATOR: Lucas Ryan
PRODUCTION COMPANY: Dagnabit!
Animation
p 57 MERIT
CREATIVE DIRECTOR: John Korpics
CREATIVE DIRECTOR, DIGITAL AND
PRINT MEDIA: Neil Jamieson
CREATIVE DIRECTOR: Chin Wang
CLIENT: ESPN
p 80 MERIT
ART DIRECTOR: SooJin Buzelli
CLIENT: PlanSponsor
p 88 MERIT
ART DIRECTOR: Patti Nemoto
CLIENT: Scientific American
p 105 MERIT
ART DIRECTOR: Fred Norgaard
CLIENT: The New York Times
p 160 MERIT
DESIGN FIRM: HivelyDesigns
CLIENT: IH8War.com
p 161 MERIT
ART DIRECTOR: Dario Paianesi
PRODUCER: Hélène Le Cannu
AD AGENCY: TITA (Milan)
CLIENT: Teatro alla Scala

**XIAOHUA YANG**
yangxiaohuaart@gmail.com
www.yangxiaohuaart.com
p 132 MERIT

**JO YEH**
jo.yehying@gmail.com
www.joyehillustration.com
INSTITUTION: Minneapolis College
of Art & Design
p 350 DISTINGUISHED MERIT

**CHEN YING-FAN**
catwiwi@gmail.com
www.childrensillustrators.com/yingfan
p 252 MERIT

**MORAN YOGEV**
yogevmoran@gmail.com
www.behance.net/moranyo
INSTITUTION: Bezalel Academy of Arts
and Design, Jerusalem
p 324 MERIT

**OR YOGEV**
oryogev6@gmail.com
www.flickr.com/photos/127968762@

N04
INSTITUTION: Bezalel Academy of Arts
and Design, Jerusalem
p 364 BRONZE
INSTRUCTOR: Amit Trainin

**YAO YU**
eileenyuyao@gmail.com
www.yaoyu.work
INSTITUTION: Savannah College of
Art & Design
p 312 MERIT
INSTRUCTOR: Linda Warner
Constantino
p 328 MERIT

**YEJI YUN**
seeouterspace@gmail.com
www.seeouterspace.com
p 258 MERIT
PUBLISHER: Humanist

**LEE ZAKAI**
leezakai1@gmail.com
www.cargocollective.com/leezakai
INSTITUTION: Bezalel Academy of Arts
and Design, Jerusalem
p 307 MERIT
INSTRUCTOR: Rutu Modan
p 342 MERIT
INSTRUCTOR: Rutu Modan

**CARLOS ZAMORA**
carloszamoradesign@gmail.com
www.carloszamora.com
p 169 MERIT
ART DIRECTOR: Carlos Zamora
DESIGN FIRM: Zamora Design &
Illustration

**NATALIA ZARATIEGUI**
nataliazaratiegui@gmail.com
www.nataliazaratiegui.com
p 68 MERIT
ART DIRECTOR: Darío Ochoa
DESIGNER: Álvaro Pérez D'ors
PUBLISHER: Automática Editorial
p 68 MERIT
ART DIRECTOR: Darío Ochoa
DESIGNER: Álvaro Pérez D'ors
PUBLISHER: Automática Editorial

**DANIEL ZENDER**
daniel@danielzender.com
www.danielzender.com
p 122 MERIT
ART DIRECTOR: Alexandra Zsigmond
CLIENT: The New York Times

**HILA ZWERGEL**
hilazwergel@gmail.com
www.zwergsworld.com
INSTITUTION: Kingston University
p 391 MERIT
INSTRUCTOR: Paul Postle

**PUBLISHER'S NOTE**

*Every effort has been made to ensure that the
credits and contact information comply with the
information provided us. 3x3 is not responsible for
missing information or credits.*
*We apologize for any omissions or spelling errors
that may have been carried through from the
original submission of materials.*

**SHOW CHAIRMAN**
Charles Hively

**DESIGN DIRECTOR**
Charles Hively

**SENIOR DESIGNER**
Sarah Munt

**SHOW COORDINATOR**
Jacob Berry

**COVER ILLUSTRATION**
Paul Garland

**HONOREE**
Ian Whadcock

ISBN 978-0-9896002-0-0

Printed in Canada by The Prolific Group

The text faces are Calluna and CallunaSans, designed by Jos Buivenga at the Exljbris Font Foundry, 2009.

The book was printed four-color process on 100lb uBrand Velvet Cover and 80lb uBrand Velvet text.

**SPECIAL THANKS**
To our judges for taking time out of their day to judge nearly 4,500 images. Judging was done digitally and independently over a two-week period. Judges were not given a quota nor any limits on how many pieces an entrant was allowed in the annual. Judging was done by image number, not by the name of the entrant; results were tabulated automatically once the judging process was complete. Winners were announced and promoted on our site, blog and social media.

And finally, thank you to all our entrants for entering our show. Without their engaging entries there wouldn't be a need to produce a volume dedicated to fostering interest in contemporary illustration.

If you are interested in our previous annuals they are available for purchase in our online shop at shop.3x3mag.com. We area also publishing a series of monographs of leading international illustrators, further information is available on our site.

If you are interest in entering next year's show please join our mailing list at 3x3mag.com/about/mailinglist and put shows@3x3mag.com in your address book to receive future announcements.

www.3x3mag.com